AF228414

The Shorter Writings of George Gillespie

Volume 2

Naphtali Press Special Editions

VIII

Series Editor
Chris Coldwell

Naphtali Press Special Editions
Volume VIII (2022). *The Shorter Writings of George Gillespie, Volume 2*
Produced for this series in a quantity of 750 ± 10%

2021–22 SERIES SPONSORS

1. Benjamin and Emily Albaugh, Kensington, Maryland.

2. Tom and Becky Albrecht, Downingtown, Pennsylvania.

3. The Anthony Family, Louisville, Kentucky

4. Paul J. Barth, Houston, Texas.

5. Christopher Bartkowski, Camp Hill, Pennsylvania.

6. Gavin Beers, Cornerstone Presbyterian Church, Free Church Cont., Burlington, North Carolina.

7. In memory of Lauren Bottomly. Vic Bottomly, Clarkston, Washington.

8. Brendon & Rose Branigin, Greenville, South Carolina.

9. In memory of Tim Broberg, Cheltenham, Pennsylvania.

10. Peter J. Butler, Jr., Maplewood, New Jersey.

11. Trent, Audrey, and Hannah Cannon, Blue Ridge, Georgia.

12. The Rev. David & Joelle Carnes, Covenant Reformed Presbyterian Church (OPC), Fort Pierce, Florida.

13. Mason Chase, Van Meter, Iowa.

14. Charles and Ann Coldwell, Tallahassee, Florida.

15. Drew and Eva Coldwell, West Palm Beach, Florida.

16. David and Barbara Coldwell, Lancaster, Pennsylvania.

17. Scott & Adria Cormier, Milford, Maine.

18. Matthew & Lindsey Cover, Richmond, Virginia.

19. Bradley S. Cupples, Eagle, Colorado.

20. Stephen P. D'Amato, Harrisville, Rhode Island.

21. Mr. & Mrs. Ken DeJong, Lansing, Illinois.

22. Zach and Wilma Dotson.

23. Reverend Mike and Mrs. Lynn Ericson, Trinity Presbyterian Reformed Church.

Naphtali Press Special Editions
Volume VIII (2022). *The Shorter Writings of George Gillespie, Volume 2*
Produced for this series in a quantity of 750 ± 10%

2021–22 Series Sponsors

24. Vin and Louisa Gebhart, Presbyterian Reformed Church of Rhode Island.

25. Greenville Presbyterian Theological Seminary, Greenville, South Carolina.

26. Zachary & Jocelyn Groff.

27. Vaughn R. Hamilton, Brainerd Hills Presbyterian Church, Chattanooga, Tennessee.

28. Chris and Christina Hansen, Salem, Virginia.

29. Rev. Dr. Martin L. & Shari R. Hawley, Hope Presbyterian Church (PCA) Marietta, Georgia.

30. Christian Herring, Radford, Virginia.

31. Anonymous, Apache Junction, Arizona.

32. James and Valorie Hoffman, Jr., Presbyterian Reformed Church, Corbin City, New Jersey.

33. Anonymous, Jasper, Indiana.

34. Stephen and Anna Huffman, Montgomery, Alabama.

35. Rev. Edgar & Mrs. Juana Ibarra, Las Vegas Reformed Presbyterian Church (RPCNA).

36. Mr. and Mrs. Andrew Imeson, Southfield, Michigan.

37. Anonymous, Cheshire, United Kingdom.

38. William Keyton, Charlotte, North Carolina.

39. Adam King, Topeka, Kansas.

40. Rev. & Mrs. Trevor Kirkland, Ballyclare & Doagh Free Church Continuing.

41. Ricky and Deborah Kortyna.

42. Michael Krueger, Centennial, Colorado.

43. Rev. Adam & Mrs. Maegan Kuehner, Southfield Reformed Presbyterian Church (RPCNA)

Naphtali Press Special Editions
Volume VIII (2022). *The Shorter Writings of George Gillespie, Volume 2*
Produced for this series in a quantity of 750 ± 10%

2021–22 SERIES SPONSORS

44. Dr. and Mrs. Ben Manring, Edinburgh, Indiana.

45. Campbell McBain, Scotland.

46. Donald John and Ruth MacLean, Cambridge, United Kingdom.

47. Ian Macleod, Tillsonburg, Ontario.

48. Mr. & Mrs. Delbert McGowan, Greeneville, Tennessee.

49. Matthew Messer, Reformed Presbyterian Church of North America.

50. Mr. & Mrs. Daniel Miller, Holly Springs, Mississippi.

51. The Mora Family, Modesto, California.

52. Brian & Debbie Myers, Trinity Presbyterian Reformed Church, Des Moines, Iowa.

53. Marty O'Connell, Sperry, Oklahoma.

54. Anonymous, Pewaukee, Wisconsin.

55. Alexander & Tiffany Paunovic, Newland, North Carolina.

56. Rev. & Mrs. Bryan Peters, Presbyterian Reformed Church, Columbus, Indiana.

57. The Phillips Family, Cape May Court House, New Jersey.

58. Pilgrim Covenant Church, Singapore.

59. Dr. & Mrs. Joseph A. Pipa, Jr., Greenville, South Carolina.

60. Thomas & Rebecca Powell, Mechanicsburg, Pennsylvania.

61. Lucas and Kayla Procee, La Center, Washington.

62. Arnie & Judy Robertstad, Lakewood Presbyterian Church, Dallas, Texas.

63. Anonymous, Essex, United Kingdom.

64. Paul Rowland, Charleston, Scotland.

65. David Sargent.

66. Mr. and Mrs. Nick Schoeneberger, Dallas, Texas.

67. R. Martin Snyder, Speedway, Indiana.

68. Wayne Sparkman, PCA Historical Center, St. Louis, Missouri.

Naphtali Press Special Editions

Volume VIII (2022). *The Shorter Writings of George Gillespie, Volume 2*
Produced for this series in a quantity of 750 ± 10%

2021–22 Series Sponsors

69. Rev. Dr. and Mrs. Justin B. Stodghill, Royse City, Texas.

70. Bob Suden, Lynden, Washington.

71. Sycamore Reformed Presbyterian Church, Kokomo, Indiana.

72. A. Taglieri, Reformed Presbyterian Church of North America.

73. Richard Tallach, Perth, United Kingdom.

74. David and Jeri Tanner, Trussville, Alabama.

75. The Teoh Family, Edmonton, Alberta, Canada.

76. Stephen Trigero, San Jose, California.

77. Thomas and Esther Walters, Allenspark, Colorado.

78. Steven Welch, Lawrenceville, Georgia.

79. The Logan West Family.

80. Kevin and Sarah White, Oakdale, Pennsylvania.

81. Dr. & Mrs. C. N. Willborn, Covenant Presbyterian Church, Oak Ridge, Tenn.

82. Jeremiah and Alison Wood, Denver, Colorado.

83. Yarashus Family, Annandale, Virgina.

The preceding sponsors of Naphtali Press Special Editions have made this series of books possible.

Thank you all very much.

Chris Coldwell

Naphtali Press Special Editions

The Shorter Writings

of

George Gillespie

Volume 2

Edited by Chris Coldwell

Be wise now therefore, O ye kings: be instructed, ye judges of the earth. Serve the LORD with fear, and rejoice with trembling. Kiss the Son, lest he be angry, and ye perish from the way, when his wrath is kindled but a little. Blessed are all they that put their trust in him. Psalm 2:10–12.

NAPHTALI PRESS &
REFORMATION HERITAGE BOOKS

Naphtali Press
P. O. Box 141084
Dallas, Texas, 75214
www.naphtali.com
naphtali@naphtali.com

Reformation Heritage Books
3070 29th St. SE
Grand Rapids, Michigan, 49512
616-977-0889 / Fax 616-285-3246
orders@heritagebooks.org
www.heritagebooks.org

ISBN 978-1-60178-999-0

The Fell Types used in the border designs in this publication are from the versions digitally reproduced by Igino Marini. www.iginomarini.com. The Naphtali Press Special Editions logo designs were created by Jean Withnell.

Contents

Abbreviations of Common References

Analecta	Robert Wodrow, *Analecta: or, Materials for a History of Remarkable Providences; mostly relating to Scotch Ministers and Christians*, 4 volumes. Edinburgh: for the Maitland Club, 1842–43.
ANF	*The Ante-Nicene Fathers.* Edited by James Donaldson et al. 10 volumes. Buffalo: The Christian Literature Company, 1885.
Letters & Journals	*The Letters and Journals of Robert Baillie, 1637–1662*, ed. David Laing. 3 volumes. Edinburgh: [Bannatyne Club], 1841–1842.
Bellarmine, *Opera*	Roberti Bellarmini, *Opera Omnia.* 12 volumes. Parisiis: Ludovicum Vivès, 1870–1874.
Calvin, *Commentaries*	Calvin's *Commentaries*, 45 volumes. Edinburgh: Calvin Translation Society, 1844–1856; repr. Grand Rapids: Baker Book House, 1983.
Confession of Faith, etc.	*Confession of Faith, Larger and Shorter Catechism*, etc. Edinburgh: Johnstone and Hunter, 1855; repr. Free Presbyterian Publications, 1990.
CO	*Ioannis Calvini Opera quæ supersunt omnia*, 59 volumes, in *Corpus Reformatorum*, volumes 29–87.
CR	*Corpus Reformatorum*, ed. G. Baum, Ed Cunitz, Eduard Reuss, and Alfred Erichson. 87 volumes. Brunsvigæ: C.A. Schwetschke, 1834–1900.
CSEL	*Corpus Scriptorum Ecclesiasticorum Latinorum.* Vienna, 1866–.
DSL	Dictionary of the Scottish Language, www.dsl.ac.uk.
Minutes	Chad Van Dixhoorn, *The Minutes and Papers of the Westminster Assembly 1643–1652.* 5 volumes. Oxford University Press, 2012.
NPNF1	*A Select Library of the Nicene and Post-Nicene Fathers, first series.* Edited by Philip Schaff. 14 volumes. Buffalo: The Christian Literature Company, 1886–1890.
NPNF2	*A Select Library of the Nicene and Post-Nicene Fathers, second series.* Edited by Philip Schaff and Henry Wace. 14 volumes. Buffalo: The Christian Literature Company, 1890–1900.
PG	*Patrologiæ cursus completus, series Græca.* Edited by J. P. Migne. 166 volumes. Petit-Montrouge, Apud J.-P. Migne, 1857–1866.
PL	*Patrologiæ cursus completus, series Latina.* Edited by J. P. Migne. 217 volumes. Petit-Montrouge: Apud J.-P. Migne, 1844–1855.
Scots Sermons	*Sermons Preached before the English Houses of Parliament by the Scottish Commissioners to the Westminster Assembly of Divines, 1643–1645.* Dallas, Texas: Naphtali Press, 2011.
Thomason	*Catalogue of the Pamphlets, Books, Newspapers, and Manuscripts Relating to the Civil War, the Commonwealth, and Restoration collected by George Thomason, 1640–1661.* 2 volumes. London: British Museum, 1908.
Works	*Works of Mr. George Gillespie*, The Presbyterian's Armoury. Edinburgh: Robert Ogle and Oliver and Boyd, 1844–46.

PREFACE

THE READER bears in their hand volume VIII of the Naphtali Press Special Editions series, which is the second of three volumes making up *The Shorter Writings of George Gillespie*. This volume contains two works transcribed from manuscript, which have not generally been seen before. The first contains brief notes from a sermon or lecture on *Why Christmas Day ought not to be Observed*, delivered not long after Gillespie's arrival in London for the Westminster Assembly, on December 24, 1643. The other is the sermon on Psalm 2 delivered before the meeting of the Scottish Parliament on March 2, 1648. These, with the two familiar sermons preached before each House of the English Parliament, make up the current known-to-exist sermonic material of George Gillespie. In addition, four significant subsections contain the remaining writings for this volume. The first, the *Anti-Erastian Tracts*, contains the polemical pieces written by Gillespie in his exchange with Thomas Coleman. It is said that Gillespie does some of his best writing in these tracts, *A Brotherly Examination*, *Nihil Respondes*, and *Malè Audis*.

Gillespie's standing in the Church of Scotland had only continued to rise after his selection to attend as a commissioner to the Westminster Assembly. When Gillespie took a brief trip back to Scotland for the General Assembly in February 1645, he was tasked with not only writing a solemn warning to the nation regarding the disastrous losses in battle on their native soil and spread of the plague, but he also was appointed to write the preface approving the Westminster Assembly's Directory for the Public Worship of God, which customarily appears with the directory in volumes containing the Westminster Standards. That Gillespie wrote both of these is not well known, and it is a pleasure to include them fully attributed in the second subsection, *Acts of the General Assembly, Edinburgh, February 1645*.

When Gillespie left the Westminster Assembly for good it was again to make a meeting of the General Assembly of the Church of Scotland. The third subsection, *Acts of the General Assembly, August 1647*, includes the speech Gillespie gave on the status of the work of the Westminster Assembly to that date. He was also tasked with writing *A Declaration and Brotherly Exhortation of The General Assembly of the Church of Scotland, Met at Edinburgh, August 20, 1647, To their Brethren of England*. The New Model Army (which some Scots would call the Army of Sectaries) had begun to take over in England and this letter exhorts the English to stay the course charted by the Solemn League & Covenant. It was also at this meeting that Gillespie lay before the General Assembly his *One Hundred and Eleven Propositions Concerning the Ministry and Government of the Church*, which he had written in London at the urging

II

of Gisbertus Voetius. After these propositions were published, Gillespie sent the Propositions to Voetius in Utrecht. A first time translation from Latin of Voetius's assessment of the propositions and of the text of the letter Gillespie wrote him is included in the preface for this section.

The fourth subsection is *Anti-Engagement Writings, 1648*. Gillespie was at the apex of his short career in the Church of Scotland. It was clear at this point that the Sectaries represented in the New Model Army were in control of England, in possession of the king, and the Presbyterians of England out of power. Alarmed, the royalist faction in the Scottish parliament persuaded a majority to approve a plan, known as The Engagement, to invade England and rescue the king, breaking the Solemn League and Covenant and setting the two nations at war. Gillespie and others vigorously opposed the plan. He was chosen to preach before the opening of parliament by the Commission of the Kirk. He chose for his text Psalm 2:10–12. That he so preached is a little known fact, and that a portion of the sermon survived in the notes of George Maxwell, even lesser known. As already noted, it is again a pleasure to include the text of this sermon in this volume. All the other pieces of the section relate to The Engagement—*The Humble Representation, Answer of the Commission to the Committee of Estates*, as well as the final pieces written as Gillespie was dying from the effects of tuberculosis, his letter to the Commission of the Kirk, his *Testimony Against Association and Compliance with Malignant Enemies of the Truth and Godliness, written two days before his death*, and portion of his will.

The texts in volume two of *The Shorter Writings of George Gillespie*, have been revised as far as possible without marring the author's work to reflect contemporary spelling, punctuation, and usage, including paragraph breaks and correction or addition of numbering where needed. Words and notes supplied by the editor are in [square brackets]. Bracketed words or phrases that are italicized define the preceding archaic or Scottish words or phrases. Greater bibliographical information has been provided in notes. Significant paraphrases of Scripture are put within single quotation marks. Generally, longer and significant quotations from sources such as Baillie's *Letters & Journals* and *Records of the Commissions of the General Assemblies of the Church of Scotland* are given with modernized spelling and usage. Any editing specific to the various writings of Gillespie are given in the separate introductions or in notes. The epigraphs on title pages have been provided for this edition, or are original to the first printing, which if so, will be noted on the Editions pages.

My thanks to Brandon Jones for accessing Early English Books for many of the titles referenced in this volume. This saved me from an untold number of trips to the local university.

Unless there are further discoveries, the third and final volume appearing in 2023, should contain the *Miscellany Questions, Notes on the Westminster Assembly*, and letters, which should complete *The Shorter Writings of George Gillespie*, D.V.

Sermons in London
1643–1645

Why Christmas Day ought not to be Observed:
Notes from a Sermon or Lecture
Given by George Gillespie,
on December 24, 1643

2 Kings 18:4

He removed the high places, and brake the images, and cut down the groves, and brake in pieces the brasen serpent that Moses had made: for unto those days the children of Israel did burn incense to it: and he called it Nehushtan.

Why Christmas Day ought not to be Observed: Notes from a Sermon or Lecture Given by George Gillespie on December 24, 1643.

EDITIONS

1. Revised from the text first published in "*Antiquary:* Why Christmas Day ought not to be Observed, A Transcription from Manuscript of Notes from a Sermon by George Gillespie, December 24, 1643," in *The Confessional Presbyterian* 15 (2019): 184–199.

The Epigraph on the prior title page has been added for this volume.

Why Christmas Day ought not to be Observed

THE DISCOVERY of any sermon by George Gillespie, fragmentary though it be, is significant because all the manuscript sermons preached while he was in London at the Westminster Assembly, were allowed to be destroyed by the printer in whose care he had left them to prepare for the press.[1] The notes presented here of a sermon or lecture given not long after Gillespie's arrival in London are so brief as would hardly merit much attention except for this fact. But as sparse as they are, these notes underscore what was a key point, often overlooked or not appreciated, in Gillespie's *Dispute Against the English Popish Ceremonies*,[2] which concerned the necessity of putting away monuments to idolatry. It is also of interest because it augments the details of the brief controversy the Westminster divines faced as far as what to do about preaching on Christmas day in 1643. Presented here is a transcription of these notes followed by a modernized text with commentary.

The notes from this address by George Gillespie are recorded in a commonplace book compiled by Walter Boothby.[3] The Gateway to Early Modern Manuscript Sermons Catalogue record for this manuscript provides the following detailed information:

> Content Note: A commonplace book entitled "A Nosegay of Everlasting Orifficall Flowers, gathered out of Heavens paradice" (p. 1). Contains Boothby's

---

1. "He had all his sermons in England, part polemical, part practical, prepared for the press; and but one copy of them, which he told the printer's wife he used to deal with, and bade her have a care of them. And she was prevailed on by some money from the sectaries, who were mauled by him, to suppress them." Memoir of the Rev. George Gillespie, in *The Presbyterians' Armoury*, ed. William M. Hetherington, volume 1 (Edinburgh: R. Ogle and Oliver & Boyd, 1846), xl; with revisions, see the Memoir in *The Shorter Writings of George Gillespie*, volume 1 (2021), p. 52. See also Robert Wodrow, *Analecta: or, Materials for a History of Remarkable Providences; mostly relating to Scotch Ministers and Christians*, volume 1, pages 159–160.

2. Upon its arrival in Scotland shortly after the start of the Second Reformation (having been printed most likely in the Netherlands), Gillespie's *Dispute* became the intellectual argument against the imposition of Laud's service book and the popish ceremonies. George Gillespie, *A Dispute Against the English Popish Ceremonies obtruded upon the Church of Scotland* (1637; critical edition, Naphtali Press, 2013).

3. "Why Christmas Day must not be obserued," auditor's notes, in Commonplace book of Walter Boothby of Tottenham (ca. 1631–1665). MS Eng. c. 2693. Bodleian Library. xxvii + 914 pages.

notes on about 150 sermons, mostly by Presbyterians (pp. vii–766). The manuscript is organized as a commonplace book but is divided by subjects rather than following a chronological order, with Boothby's notes on sermons he has heard under the subject headings (e.g. "Of Christ", "Of Sinne"). Includes an index of the sermons by subject (pp. iii–xiv). Also includes correspondence, mainly Boothby's letters to family members, dated 1640–1643 (pp. 768–913).

Material features: xxviii + 914 pages. Bound in vellum wrapper. Boothby has put subheadings in the margin, apparently to summarize the point of the sermon that he has cited under the general heading.

Aquisition: Purchased at auction from D. P. White (Occasional List 35 [1991], item 137).

Other Note: The cataloguer dates this manuscript c. 1632–1655, but some of the sermons are dated 1631. This volume contains notes on many sermons that Boothby attributes to 'Dr. Stawton' (occasionally spelled Staughton). The most likely identity of Stawton is John Stoughton (1593–1639),[4] whom the cataloguer identifies as a preacher mentioned in this volume. However, in some cases the name seems more like 'Stanton,' so it could be Edmund Staunton (1600–1671). Both of these preachers were Presbyterians, like Boothby and like most of the other preachers mentioned in this volume. It could also be one of two preachers named John Stawton in CCEd (Person IDs: 101994 and 108233).[5] Since Stoughton is the most likely attribution, these sermons have been attributed to him, but they remain uncertain. Among these sermons, those that are dated were all preached before Stoughton's death in 1639, except the sermon 'of feare [3]' (pp. 272–273), but in this case Boothby has clearly written 'Doc. Stanton' so this sermon is attributed to Edmund Staunton. For more information on this manuscript, see also John Spurr, *The Laity and Preaching in Post-Reformation England* (London: Dr Williams's Trust, 2013), pp. 18–19.[6]

---

4. As noted below, the baptism of Boothby's daughter at St. Mary Aldermanbury seems to confirm the identity as John Stoughton. This church was destroyed in the Great Fire of 1666. It was rebuilt and that structure was gutted in the Blitz in 1940. The stones of the structure were moved in 1966 to the campus of Westminster College, Fulton, Missouri, and a church reconstructed as a memorial to Winston Churchill, who gave his famous iron curtain speech at the college in 1946.

5. Clergy of the Church of England Database. https://theclergydatabase.org.uk/.

6. GEMMS-MANUSCRIPT-000541, Gateway to Early Modern Manuscript Sermons, Catalogue record. https://gemms.itercommunity.org/view_record.php?table=manuscript&id=541 Source of data: "Jeanne Shami; Bodleian Library Catalogue of manuscripts acquired singly: albums, commonplace books, notebooks and scrapbooks (online)."

The Transcription.

The following transcription is rendered in more reader friendly form in the commentary. Words in italics have some degree of doubt as to the transcription. A question mark means a letter was not decipherable. Text that reads ???? is intentionally crossed out text that is no longer legible. Crossed out text is legible text the writer crossed out. Interline text is surrounded by the caret symbol (^). Words in braces were originally in abbreviated form. Double underlining is in the original and seems to indicate titles. The fact that the first portion identified as from Gillespie takes up the middle of page 286 with almost enough room for the next portion on page 287, which is titled as a new topic, at least raises the question whether the second portion is a separate new topic in Boothby's commonplace book and not necessarily from the same source or occasion (and there is a case to make that it is by an Englishman). However, since it is a topic Gillespie addressed in his *Dispute*, the text is included and some ties to that work are noted in the comments.

Why Christmas Day must not be obserued.

By Mr Gelaspe
a Scot. Minister
Dec. 24, 1643.

1. If it had bin God's will that such a day as {this} should have bin observed, then certainly he would have mayd knowne the day, that soe the self same day wh. did appertaine unto his (its) commemoration, should have bin celebrated, and not another, but that day is consealed and so close as {that} all {the} witts in the world cannot pouynt it out, and I contend for {that} self same reason {that} Moses' body was,[7]

2. {That} worship wh. God *never* commanded must be unlawfull, as was the washing of the Pharasees [Mat. 15.9],[8] and therefore Christ accompted them but vayne inventions of man's brayne, if so, then though it did teach them holiness, yet it having his *entre* from men, and a human institution, it was a vayne thing, but so is this day merely instituted by man, and therefore but vayne,

3. Such things wh. have bin abused unto superstition must not bee allowed; but this day hath binn grossly abused to superstition, therefore unlawfull.

---

7. "Yee se then as God hid the body of Moses, so hath he hid this day and other dayes depending on the calculation of it, wherein he declared his wil concerning the other daies of his notable acts. David Calderwood, *Perth Assembly* (1619), p. 80. Cf. *Altare Damascenum* (1623), p. 651.

8. "Mat. 15.9" is in the left-hand margin.

Instance in the Brazen Serpent [a thing of *greate* use]9 wh. though appoynted by God, yet when once it was abused to idollatry, it was broken to powder, much more should {that} be abolished wh. hath only man's warrant for its institution.

4. In *regarde* of the late Sollem covenante, where{with} the State hath bound themselves to observe, wherein they, and wee have covenanted, to oppose and withstand all superstitious worshippe, and to furder a Reformation to our uttmost power, such as shall be most agreeable unto God's Sacred word, and will,

5. More particularly it is ????? now to be refused because of the unsutabellnes thereof unto our times, now God calls us not unto his Sollum feast in wh. we should joy, and make merry, attending to the aboundance wh. he hath given, but he callas us unto weepeing mourneing, and lamentation [Isa. 22:12]10 *as* now how unagreeable should our ~~condition~~ ^*carrage*^ be unto {*our*} condition, if upon God's call for weepeing mourneing and lamentation, behould feasting and mirth. this did much insense the Lord agaynst the Jews and So would it agaynst us.

Whether the observation of holy Dayes bee lawfull.11

[Whether it be in the power of a state, king *or* parliament to establish holy Dayes]12 For answer unto this question. I affirm {that} it is not in the power of any state or kingdome to establish an holy Day, and {that} it hath bin the Sinne of our State to ????? make holy dayes, and to rayse them up in *equepage* {with} the Lord's Day, my Reason is this.

The effect cannot rise higher than the cause, as a stream cannot assend above the fountaine, but for a civill state to establish holy rights is to assend above there prinsipell: therefore it's unlawfull. true it is, a state may establish Sivill dayes.

---

9. This text was in the left-hand margin next to this line of text and would seem to refer to the brazen serpent.

10. "22 Esa. 12" (Isa. 22:12) is in the right-hand margin. The subsequent "as" is very faint.

11. This new topic is on page 287 in the manuscript. It is unattributed and no occasion given, so it may be from the same occasion or not since the volume is arranged topically. The "our state" would seem to indicate the comment is by an Englishman, though Scotland also had recently with the Second Reformation once again thrown off the yoke of the pretended holy days, which had indeed been on a par with the Lord's Day as well. Stoughton may have been the speaker since he opposed the popish innovations and was punished by Laud. See below.

12. The first text in square braces was in the right-hand margin. The text runs into the binding and the presumed "or" is obscured.

Walter Boothby's Commonplace Book

The brief notes of this sermon are found in a commonplace book penned circa 1631–1665 by Walter Boothby of Tottenham (1600–1669).[13] Boothby was a merchant, a Haberdasher,[14] both in Tottenham and in London.[15] The Worshipful Company of Haberdashers via its leadership if not general membership, supported puritan lectureships for forty years prior to the time of the Westminster Assembly, including the successful St. Bartholomew lectureship of John Downame in London.[16] The most frequent preacher recorded by Boothby in this commonplace book is John Stoughton, "one of the most popular godly preachers in England" at the time.[17] For seven years Stoughton was the permanent curate and lecturer at St Mary Aldermanbury in London, where "he was a laborious, orthodox, and useful preacher; but having occasionally touched upon the popish and arminian innovations, he was, by the instigation of Laud, prosecuted in the high commission.[18] He died in the year 1639, when he was succeeded by Mr. Edmund Calamy...."[19] St Mary Aldermanbury appears to have been Walter Boothby's parish church. His daughter, Rebecca, was baptized there on March 13, 1633/34.[20] In his commonplace book Boothby recorded sermons or extracts and arranged them topically, apparently at least in part or in whole drawing on notes from sermons he had recorded previously between 1631 and 1655. The entries include material from Stoughton and Calamy. In another manuscript he records sermons by Calamy (1653, 1661–2) as well as by Thomas Watson (1661), Simeon Ashe (1661), and Stephen Marshall (1641).[21]

---

13. Frederick Arthur Crisp, ed., *Visitation of England and Wales, Notes Vol. 12* (Privately Printed, 1917), p. 149.

14. Haberdashers "sold, amongst other wares, French and Spanish gloves, and French cloth or frizarde (frieze), Flanders-dyed kersies, daggers, swords, knives, Spanish girdles, painted cruses, dials, tables, cards, balls, glasses, fine earthen pots, saltcellars, spoons, tin dishes, puppets, pennons, inkhorns, toothpicks, silk, and silver buttons." Dorothy Williams Whitney. "London Puritanism: The Haberdashers' Company," *Church History* 32, no. 3 (1963): 299.

15. *The History of Parliament: the House of Commons 1660–1690*, ed. B. D. Henning (London: Published for the History of Parliament Trust by Secker & Warburg, 1983), p. 657. The entry is for John Jolliffe (Jolley) who married Rebecca Boothby, Walter's daughter.

16. Whitney, pp. 298, 310.

17. *The Diary of Samuel Rogers, 1634–1638*, ed. Tom Webster and Kenneth Shipps (Trowbridge, Wiltshire: Cromwell Press, A Church of England Record Society publication published by The Boydell Press, an imprint of Boydell & Brewer Ltd, 2004), p. 130.

18. It may well be that Stoughton is the source for the second question in the MS, since nonconformists as well as Scots Presbyterians viewed the pretended holy days as popish innovations.

19. Benjamin Brook, *The Lives of the Puritans*, 3 vols. (1813), 3.527.

20. Crisp, p. 150.

21. "The Churches Cordiall in her fainting Fitts MS," MS I.f.18, Congregational Library Collection, Dr. Williams's Library, London. The first pieces are from 1661 with the Marshall

George Gillespie and Alexander Henderson were admitted by parliament and welcomed into the Westminster Assembly on September 14 and September 15 respectively,[22] and Samuel Rutherford and Robert Baillie arrived later and were admitted to the assembly on November 20.[23] It is not certain if Boothby heard Gillespie preach or obtained a manuscript from which he made these brief notes; but it is not improbable he heard Gillespie himself. Calamy might have invited the Scot to preach or lecture on the Lord's Day, December 24, 1643, though as will be seen there is reason to think he would not have done so. But if he did, Boothby certainly could have heard Gillespie in his own parish church. But if not, he also may have attended where Gillespie was preaching or lecturing that day. Laing writes that previously when Baillie and Henderson were in London in 1640–41 for the treaty ending the Second Bishops' War and later with others during the years of the Westminster Assembly, they resided at Worcester House (or Place), and were given nearby St. Antholins to hold services (at least in the earlier period).[24]

> At this time [1643], as well as during their former mission to London, the Scotish Commissioners resided in Worcester House, in the City, and St. Antholin's Church was set apart for their use, the ministers preaching in their turn, for a time, at least, to very crowded audiences. "The people throngs to our sermon (he [Baillie] says in January 1641), as ever you saw any to Irwin [Irvine] communion; their crowd daylie encreases." Lord Clarendon also refers to their great popularity at that time. The Treaty being now adjourned to London, the Scotish Commissioners, he states, "came thither in great state, and were received by the king with that countenance, which he could not choose but shew to them; and were then lodged in the heart of the city, near London-stone, in a house which used to be inhabited by the Lord Mayor or one of the Sheriffs, and was situated so near to the church of St. Antholins,

---

and an undated unattributed sermon in the middle followed by a sermon from 1653 by Calamy and others dating to 1661 and 1662. It is not clear why the earlier sermons are in the middle, but it may be Boothby was creating a new collection from previous and current notes sometime around 1661. See GEMMS record, https://gemms.itercommunity.org/view_record.php?table=manuscript&id=323.

22. *Journal of the House of Commons*, vol. 3, September 14, 1643 (H. M. Stationery Office, 1803), p. 241. *The Letters and Journals of Robert Baillie*, ed. David Laing, 3 vols. (Edinburgh: Alex. Lawrie & Co. for The Bannatyne Club, 1841–42), 1.xlix. *The Minutes and Papers of the Westminster Assembly 1643–1652*, 5 vols., ed. Chad Van Dixhoorn (Oxford University Press, 2012), 2.123, 124.

23. *Letters & Journals*, vol. 1, p. 1.

24. This may have been granted by the king. At least there is no record in the parliament journals for the time of the Treaty. Nor have I found confirmation of this for the later period, though it stands to reason if the Scots Commissioners were given a church in which to hold services of the Scottish Presbyterian form, a similar accommodation would have been extended or had been in continuance for the later period.

that there was a way out of it into a gallery of the church. This benefit was well foreseen on all sides in the accommodation, and this church assigned to them for their own devotions, where one of their own chaplains ſtill preached, (amongſt which Alexander Henderson was the chief, who was likewise joined with them in the treaty in all maters which had reference to religion;)….” [25]

This Worceſter House has been confused by another of the same name which later belonged to Edward Hyde (Earl of Clarendon),[26] but as he indicates in his hiſtory, the Scottish miniſters at the earlier time resided in a house next to St. Antholins, which had private access to it. This could not have been Worceſter House, which judging by current maps would have been about 0.3 miles south on the banks of the Thames. So either the commissioners moved at leaſt once or perhaps it was juſt the Scottish miniſters who lived in the adjacent house in 1641.

It is also not clear if the Scottish Commissioners, who arrived in September and November of 1643, were immediately accommodated again at Worceſter House, though parliament would have had to have made accomodations for those present to negotiate the Solemn League and Covenant in September. The earlieſt notice of Parliament providing for Worceſter House is an order dated January 30, 1644, which was either the order setting it aside for the Scots use again or to further provision the house.[27] While Baillie rarely signs his letters as at “Worceſter House,” and the earlieſt is dated in July 1645,[28] he seems to indicate Worceſter House was his residence for the entire time and both before and after the January provision refers to his accommodation as “our

---

25. *Letters & Journals*, 1.l–li.

26. “This was not the house of the Earls of Worcester, which Lord Clarendon afterwards inhabited, on the site of the present Beaufort-buildings in the Strand; but Worcester Place, the house of John Tiptoft, Earl of Worcester, Lord High Treasurer of England, also on the banks of the Thames, but nearer the Tower.” *Letters & Journals*, 1.l, n3.

27. January 30, 1643. “It is this Day Ordered, by the Lords and Commons in Parliament assembled, That Worcester House be forthwith fitted and prepared for the Receipt and Accommodation of the Commissioners and Committees sent from our Brethren of Scotland; and that all manner of Household Stuff, Linen, and other Necessaries for the same, be provided and supplied out of any of his Majesty’s Wardrobes, or other Stores, to make up what is wanting, at the present, in the said House….” House of Commons Journal, vol. 3, p. 383.

28. *Letters & Journals*, 2.281. Some of Gillespie’s letters from September 1644 are all signed “Worcester House.” *Letters & Journals*, 2.500. Other letters by all or some of the commissioners later in their stay are so signed as well. *Letters & Journals*, 3.541. Other such letters are noted in, Publications of the Scottish History Society, volume XI, General Assembly Commission Records. May 1892. *The Records of the Commissions of the General Assemblies of the Church of Scotland Holden in Edinburgh in the Years 1646 and 1647*, edited from the Original Manuscript by Alexander F. Mitchell, D.D., LL.D. and James Christie, D.D. with an Introduction by the former (Edinburgh: Printed at the University Press by T. and A. Constable for the Scottish History Society, 1892) pp. xxiv, 12, 99, 162, 182, 187, 189, 200, 210, 223, 233, 257, 274, 275, 310, 312, 326.

house" (Gillespie, Rutherford, Henderson and Maitland all residing there).[29] And as much preaching as the Scottish ministers did, the parliament may have continued the prior practice of giving them St. Antholins to use, though Baillie indicates he preached regularly at the Savoy, which may indicate they had places aplenty in which to preach.[30]

So though it remains in the realm of supposition, it may well be that on December 24, 1643, Gillespie's turn had come to preach at St. Antholins if that was the custom as in 1641, which was not half a mile south from St. Mary Aldermanbury, and so Walther Boothby could easily have attended.[31] Or it may be that Gillespie had been invited to speak at St. Mary Aldermanbury or some other nearby church, though as will be seen there may be some doubt if Calamy would have done so on this occasion.

The Subject of the Sermon Notes

The Church of Scotland had rejected the entire church calendar of holy days at the Reformation. These had been imposed again by the king at the 1618 Perth Assembly, and jettisoned again at the Second Reformation in 1638. The English church had retained much of the ceremonies and holy days which to varying degrees with little choice the Puritan movement tolerated. But with the signing of the Solemn League and Covenant, the two nations and

---

29. *Letters & Journals*, 2.107, 133, 145 and 206. Baillie writes, "from the 1643 to 1647, I lived at Worcester House, and preached in the Savoy...." *Letters & Journals*, 3.265.

30. Rutherford preached at least all the sermons making up *Trial and Triumph of Faith* while in London, and the lost volume of sermons Gillespie preached has already been noted. The Savoy Chapel was part of the Savoy Hospital built by Henry VIII replacing the Savoy Palace destroyed in the peasant revolt of 1381. The hospital was demolished in the 19TH century but the chapel, which dates to the 1490s, still survives. At the time Baillie was in London, the congregation of St. Mary le Strand held worship services there, which they did from 1549–1714. Thomas Fuller was appointed lecturer in 1642, but when the Solemn League and Covenant was drawn up he would not sign without reservation and left Savoy and attended upon the king at Oxford. He was reinstated at the Savoy at the Restoration (*The Collected Sermons of Thomas Fuller, D.D., 1631–1659*, Volume 1 [London: The Gresham Press, 1891] pp. xxiii; ccxcii).

31. See the discussion of Worcester House and the map of locations in "Appendix: Westminster Abbey Library: And Other Theological Resources of the Assembly of Divines (1643–1652)," *The Grand Debate* (Naphtali Press, 2014), pp. 393–396; or similarly in an earlier version of the same material in *The Confessional Presbyterian* 6 (2010): 274–276. The map has an error in that location 11 is St Mary Aldermary which was confused with St Mary Aldermanbury (Aldermanbury is location 1). This affects the accuracy of some of the statements regarding proximity in these prior articles dealing with Worcester House. Both St. Antholins and St. Mary Aldermanbury no longer stand, but based on their locations comparing with the Agas Map of London, it appears roughly 0.4 miles distance between them, and it would have been about a mile's distance from where Worcester House stood and St. Mary Aldermanbury.

churches had agreed to conform to the best doctrine and practice of the Reformed churches. Within weeks of arriving and becoming part of the Westminster Assembly, the Scottish ministers and their English counterparts faced the question of what to do about the English custom of holding services on Christmas Day, which was a Monday in 1643.[32]

Whether to Preach on Christmas in 1643?

George Gillespie did not just randomly pitch upon the subject of "Why Christmas Day should not be Observed" for his December 24, 1643 address. The minutes of the Westminster Assembly do not survive for December 21, 1643 to February 14, 1644, but John Lightfoot records the following for the session on Friday, December 22.

> After this vote, was a proposal made by some, 'That the Assembly would determine whether there should be any sermon upon Christmas-day': but it was waived to treat of it, because we are not yet come to it. Then was there some question how long we should adjourn, and some few would have had us to have sitten on Christmas-day; but it was more generally thought otherwise; and so we adjourned till after the fast, viz. till Thursday. In the afternoon, the city-ministers met together to consult whether they should preach on Christmas-day, or no. Among them there were only Mr. Calamy, Mr. Newcomen, and myself, of the Assembly. And when Mr. Calamy began to incline that there should be no sermon on that day, and was like to sway the company that way, I took him aside, and desired him to consider seriously upon these things. 1. That one sermon preached at the feast of the dedication, which had but a human original, John x. 2. That the thing in itself was not unlawful. 3. That letting the day utterly fall without a sermon, would most certainly breed a tumult. 4. That it is but this one day, for the next we hope will be resolved upon about it by authority. 5. That he, being an Assembly-man, and advising them, would bring an odium undeserved upon the Assembly. With these things I prevailed with him to change his mind; and so he also prevailed with the company; and it was put to the question, and voted affirmatively, only some four or five gainsaying, that they would preach, but withal resolving generally to cry down superstition of the day.[33]

---

32. The Presbyterians were not alone in struggling with the holy day issue. Initially, many of the Reformed desired to reduce or eliminate them, but they were retained or re-imposed due to political circumstances and by insistence of magistrates. See Rev. R. D. Anderson "Why are Ecclesiastical Feast Days in the Reformed Church Order?", *The Confessional Presbyterian* journal 15 (2019): 81–88 and Andrew J. Webb and Chris Coldwell, "American Presbyterianism and the Religious Observance of Christmas," *CPJ* 11 (2015): 142–187 and *"In Translatiōne:* John Calvin's Letters to the Ministers of Montbéliard (1543–1544): The Genevan Reformer's Advice and Views of the Liturgical Calendar," *CPJ* 13 (2017): 198–220.

33. John Lightfoot, "Journal of the Assembly of Divines," *The Whole Works of the Rev. John Lightfoot,* volume 13 (London: 1824), pp. 91–92.

The agreement which Lightfoot reasoned from Calamy would seem to caſt some doubt that Calamy would have immediately had Gilleſpie preach againſt observing the day at St. Mary Aldermanbury. However, it likely would have been arranged before the meeting on the 22ND and if so it would seem as unlikely the invitation would have been rescinded. So it remains a possibility that Boothby could have heard Gilleſpie at St. Mary Aldermanbury. As to the controversy, Baillie records this same matter brought up on Friday, December 22, giving the Scottish point of view. In an undated letter "For Scotland" but with a poſtscript dated January 1, 1644, he writes,

> On Friday [i.e. Dec. 22] I moved Mr. Henderson to go to the Assembly; for else he purposed to have ſtayed at home that day; that as all of us ſtoutly had preached againſt their Chriſtmass, so we might in private soliſt [*importune*] our acquaintance[s] of the Assembly, and ſpeak something of it in public; that for the discountenancing of that superſtition, it were good the Assembly should not adjourn, but sit on Monday, their Chriſtmas day. We found sundry willing to follow our advice, but the moſt resolved to preach that day, till the Parliament should reform it in an orderly way; so, to our small [*little*] contentment, the Assembly was adjourned from Friday till Thursday next: yet we prevailed with our friends of the Lower House to carry it so in Parliament, that both Houses did profane that holy day, by sitting on it, to our joy, and some of the Assembly's shame. On Wednesday we kept the solemn faſt. Mr. Henderson did preach to the House of Commons as moſt gracious, wise, and learned sermon, which you will see in print. Mr. Rutherford is desired by them to preach the next faſt day **34**

According to Baillie it appears that the Scots may well have been among those behind the raising of the queſtion in the assembly and that some discussion did take place in the assembly on the queſtion and not juſt in the afternoon meeting where the only assemblymen present were Newcomen, Calamy and Lightfoot, though he may have been drawing from knowledge he gained of that meeting in his report. While there was some "joy" that the parliament did not take Chriſtmas day off, the Scottish miniſters were clearly "little content" the assembly took a Chriſtmas break. It is in this context that two days later on the Lord's Day, December, 24, 1643, that Gilleſpie preached a sermon or lectured on the topic of "Why Chriſtmas should not be observed."

As Lightfoot suggeſted, the subject did come up again the next year and during the debates the assembly had concerning a Directory for the Public

---

34. *Letters & Journals*, 2.120. Spelling modernized. The sermons noted are Alexander Henderson, *Faſt Sermon to the House of Commons, December 27, 1643* (text: Ezra 7:23) and Samuel Rutherford, *Faſt Sermon to the House of Commons, January 31, 1643/44* (text: Daniel 6:26). See *Sermons Preached before the English Houses of Parliament by the Scottish Commissioners to the Weſtminſter Assembly of Divines, 1643–1645* (Naphtali Press, 2011).

Worship of God. Lightfoot notes the following: "Thursday, Dec. 19 [1644].], Then was there a motion made, and order accordingly, that some of our members should be sent to the Houses, to desire them to give an order, that the next fast-day might be solemnly kept, because the people will be ready to neglect it, being Christmas-day."[35] The minutes omit the actual concern that the fast would be neglected for the accustomed holiday.[36] Neal gives greater background,

> But that which occasioned the greatest disturbance over the whole nation, was an order of both houses relating to Christmas-day. Dr. Lightfoot says, the London ministers met together last year to consult whether they should preach on that day; and one of considerable name and authority opposed it, and was near prevailing with the rest, when the doctor convinced them so far of the lawfulness and expediency of it, that the question being put it was carried in the affirmative with only four or five dissenting voices. But this year it happening to fall on the monthly fast,[37] so that either the fast or the festival must be omitted, the parliament, after some debate, thought it most agreeable to the present circumstances of the nation to go on with fasting and prayer; and therefore published the following order:

> "Die Jovis 19 Dec. 1644. Whereas some doubts have been raised, whether the next fast shall be celebrated, because it falls on the day which heretofore was usually called the feast of the nativity of our Saviour; the lords and commons in parliament assembled do order and ordain, that public notice be given, that the fast appointed to be kept the last Wednesday in every month ought to be observed, till it be otherwise ordered by both houses; and that this day in particular is to be kept with the more solemn humiliation, because it may call to remembrance our sins, and the sins of our forefathers, who have turned this feast, pretending the memory of Christ, into an extreme forgetfulness of him, by giving liberty to carnal and sensual delights, being contrary to the life which Christ led here on earth, and to the spiritual life of Christ in our souls, for the sanctifying and saving whereof, Christ was pleased both to take a human life, and to lay it down again."

---

35. Lightfoot, 13.344.

36. Van Dixhoorn, 3.484.

37. Writing about an ordinance prohibiting public diversions and recreations during England's civil war, Neal explains, "The set times of humiliation mentioned in the ordinance refers to the monthly fast appointed by the king, at the request of the parliament [January 8, 1641], on account of the Irish insurrection and massacre, to be observed every last Wednesday in the month, as long as the calamities of that nation should require it. But when the king set up his standard at Nottingham, the two houses, apprehending that England was now to be the seat of war, published an ordinance for the more strict observation of this fast, in order to implore a divine blessing upon the consultations of parliament, and to deprecate the calamities that threatened this nation." Daniel Neal, *The History of the Puritans*, 3 vols. (1837), 2.155.

DIRECTORY FOR THE PUBLIC WORSHIP OF GOD

Around this same time in 1644, the assembly was working on the last portions of its directory for worship, and the topic of holy days came under discussion again in relation to their actual work. With their intended deliberations on the preface delayed because Dr. Burges had taken the text to meet with members of parliament, the assembly began to debate a portion of text to add to the section on the Sabbath day regarding abuses, which evolved into a separate section, and finally an "appendix touching days and places of public worship."[38]

> Sess. 324. (Novemb. 18, 1644). Munday morning. "Ordered to report the Preface to the directory, and that concerning the Sabbath day."[39]

> Sess. 325. Novemb. 19, 1644. Tuesday morning. "Ordered: That in the Directory for the sabbath day something be expressed <against parish feasts, commonly called by the name of Rushbearing[s], whitsunales,> wakes, as prophane and superstitious."

> "Some motions made about holy dayes, to expresse something against them."[40]

> "Ordered: [The Lord's Day][41] being the standing holy day under the New Testament to be kept by all the churches of Christ, consider of something concerning holy dayes <& holy places> & what course may be thought upon for the releife of servants. To meet tomorrow in the afternoone. Wakes & feasts Whitsunales, Rushbearings & garlands [and] all other <such like> superstitious customes."[42]

---

38. The appendix was sent up on December 30, approved in the House on January 1 by the Lords with changes on January 4, and after conference approved by both houses on the January 5, 1645. Van Dixhoorn, 3.491. See William A. Shaw, *A History of the English Church during the Civil Wars and under the Commonwealth*, 2 vols. (New York: Longmans, Green, and Co., 1900), 1.353. See the text in Document 54, Van Dixhoorn, 5.159.

39. Van Dixhoorn, 3.457. Text inserted interline in the manuscript minutes are noted by <braces>; [brackets] are editorial insertions.

40. Rushbearings: "The practice of covering the church floor with rushes through the winter developed as a rural festival with accompanying entertainment." Whittsunales: "The Whitsun ale was one of the main annual parish ales. Held at Whitsun (Pentacost), the event was a festive fundraiser for a local church." Wakes: "A wake could refer to funeral ceremonies prior to the burial of the body, a party on the eve of a festival, or an annual feast honouring the patron saint of a church." Van Dixhoorn, 3.458.

41. Van Dixhoorn (3.458) inserts "The Lord's Day." Struthers reads "the only standing holy day...." *Minutes of the Sessions of the Westminster Assembly of Divines*, ed. Rev. Alex F. Mitchell, D. D. and Rev. John Struthers LL.D. (Edinburgh: William Blackwood, 1874), 4. At this place, John Struthers has other minor variations in his rendering of the text.

42. Van Dixhoorn, 3.458. "Tuesday, Nov. 19.]—Then was there speech about Holydays, and

Sess. 329. Novemb. 25, 1644. Munday morning. "Mr. Coleman made report of the directory for Holy dayes and holy places; it was read."[43]

Sess. 338. Decemb. 10, 1644. <Tuesday> morning." Report 'of holy places' debated." "Ordered: To proceed in the debate tomorrow morning <upon a motion that the committee for the drawing up the directory or others that may be gotten.>"[44]

Sess. 339. <Decemb. 11, 1644.> Wensday morning. "Debate upon the Directory for dayes."[45]

Sess. 340. Decemb. 12. <Thursday> morning. "Neg: Resolved: the report concerning holy dayes shall not be waved."[46]

Sess. 348. Decemb. 27, 1644. Fryday Morning. "Report of the Appendix concerning dayes and places for publique worship." "Debate about holy dayes."[47]

Sess. 349. Decemb. 30, 1640 [*sic* 1644], Munday morning. "Ordered: That the Appendix be sent up tomorrow morning."[48]

The development of this appendix to the directory for worship again has George Gillespie coming to the foreground. From Gillespie's notes on the assembly for December 30, 1644, we learn:

> December 30. There were many abuses spoken of to be condemned in the Directory, as Wakes, etc. I said, if these be put in the Directory, the Church of Scotland must put in abuses among them in the Directory too, and it is not fit to make public in both kingdoms what is proper to either. So it was agreed to send up this in a paper by itself to the Parliament.[49]

---

some motion about declaring against them. This held us much canvassing; and it was well approved that the superstition of Holydays should be cried down, but yet some days allowed for relief of servants. The conclusion was, that the business was recommitted to the first committee to consider of it." Lightfoot, 13.332–333.

43. Van Dixhoorn, 3.468.

44. Van Dixhoorn, 3.477, 478. In this session an exchange takes place concerning "holy places" between Palmer, Rutherford, Gillespie, Burges, Seaman and Marshall. Lightfoot records some of this debate as well. Ibid., 341–342.

45. Van Dixhoorn, 3.479. "Next did we fall upon the debate about holy days; and had some debate about one proposition concerning the Sabbath..." Lightfoot, 342.

46. Van Dixhoorn, 3.480; Struthers, 19. Struthers: "waived. (?)"

47. Van Dixhoorn, 3.489.

48. Van Dixhoorn, 3.491.

49. George Gillespie, "Notes of Proceedings of the Assembly of Divines at Westminster,"

What is clear is that as the divines perceived many corruptions in the English worship, there was an idea suggested during the forming of the directory, to add a list of condemned abuses in worship to the directory's preface. As noted, Gillespie opposed this, as it would require enumerating practices in one kingdom not practiced in the other. Subsequently, it was determined to send a separate paper to parliament regarding the matter.[50] C. G. M'Crie writes:

> From Gillespie's "Notes of Debates and Proceedings," however, we learn that at a certain stage of the discussion as to what should find a place in the book, it was proposed to insert a statement of abuses "to be condemned, as Wakes, etc." The proposal was resisted by Gillespie on the ground that, if English abuses were to be specified, then the Church of Scotland would claim an enumeration of abuses peculiar to that kingdom, and he did not think it "fit to make public in both kingdoms what is proper to either." Ultimately, it was agreed to send up a separate paper to Parliament containing a list of such abuses.
>
> Interesting light would seem to be thrown upon this document by a loose paper in Gillespie's writing preserved by Wodrow, and printed among the "Notes" of the former. On the one side of the MS. is an incomplete list of eight practices or ceremonies, beginning with "Gloria Patri," and breaking off with "the people's responsals." On the other side is a statement "concerning other customs or rites in the worship of God formerly received in any of the kingdoms," to the effect that, "though not condemned in this Directory," yet if "they have been, or apparently will be, occasions of divisions and offences," it is judged "most expedient that the practice and use of them be not continued, as well for the nearer uniformity betwixt the Churches of both kingdoms, as for their greater peace and harmony within themselves, and their edifying one another in love."
>
> If, as it appears likely, the list on the one side of this paper consists of an unfinished enumeration of "customs or rites" spoken of on the other, then it is probable the latter was drafted as a proposed, but not accepted, addition to the preface as it now stands. In that case the Doxology, along with the Creed, standing up at the reading of the Gospel, preaching on Christmas, funeral sermons, churching of women, saying the three Creeds after reading of Scripture, and congregational responses, will rank among practices "not condemned in this Directory," but the observance of which Gillespie and his fellow-commissioners judged it expedient to be discontinued in the interests of uniformity, peace, harmony, and mutual edifying in love.[51]

Works: The Presbyterian's Armoury (Edinburgh: Robert Ogle and Oliver and Boyd, 1844–46), page 97.

50. Gillespie, "Notes," p. 108.

51. C. G. M'Crie, *Public Worship of Presbyterian Scotland* (Edinburgh and London: William

The English Puritans had their own strong feelings about the old pretended holy days such as Christmas, but it seems clear that the influence of the Scottish Commissioners and Gillespie in particular, is seen even in this small issue of what to do about preaching on Christmas day. The idea to add a list of abuses was dropped, but an appendix condemning the entire old calendar of holy days was crafted and added to one of the most approved and authorized of the documents produced by the Westminster Assembly, having been approved by both governments and churches in England and Scotland, whereas the confession of faith and larger catechism were not authorized by the English parliament.

The Content of Gillespie's Address
At first glance the contents of these notes seem so brief as to be relatively inconsequential to merit much comment. However, as noted in the opening, the content harks back to Gillespie's prior work, *A Dispute Against the English Popish Ceremonies*, and highlights one of the more crucial principles he spends a good amount of space explaining and defending in that work. Therefore, it is worthwhile to present some commentary along with a modernization of the text of the prior transcription.

1. If it had been God's will that such a day as this should have been observed, then certainly He would have made known the day, that so the selfsame day which did appertain unto its commemoration should have been celebrated, and not another; but that day is concealed and so close [*so completely*] as that all the wits in the world cannot point it out, and I contend for that selfsame reason that Moses' body was.

In his *Dispute*, Gillespie does not descend to particular or detailed arguments against each of the specific holy days that had been imposed at Perth Assembly, so it is interesting to see a specific argument here. The point is founded on often cited statements he makes regarding elemental versus circumstantial matters in the Worship of God. In his preface to "All the Reformed Churches," Gillespie writes,

> Besides all this, there is nothing which any way pertains to the worship of
> God left to the determination of human laws, beside the mere circumstances,
> which neither have any holiness in them, forasmuch as they have no other use
> and praise in sacred than they have in civil things, nor yet were particularly
> determinable in Scripture, because they are infinite; but sacred, significant
> ceremonies, such as cross, kneeling, surplice, holy days, bishopping, etc.,
> which have no use and praise except in religion only, and which, also, were

Blackwood and Sons, 1892), pp. 208–210. See Thomas Leishman, *The Westminster Directory, Edited, with an Introduction and Notes* (Edinburgh and London: William Blackwood and Sons, 1901), pp. 152–153.

most easily determinable (yet not determined) within those bounds which the wisdom of God did set to His written Word, are such things as God never left to the determination of any human law.[52]

He addresses the same subject again in part one of his *Dispute* against the necessity of the ceremonies.

> And as for particularities, all the particular causes, occasions, and times of fasting could not be determined in Scripture, because they are infinite, as Camero says.[53] But all the particular causes of set festivities, and the number of the same, might have been easily determined in Scripture, since they are not, nor may not be infinite; for the Bishop himself acknowledges that to appoint a festival day for every week cannot stand with charity, the inseparable companion of piety. And albeit so many were allowable, yet who sees not how easily the Scripture might have comprehended them, because they are set, constant, and anniversary times, observed for permanent and continuing causes, and not moveable or mutable, as fasts which are appointed for occurring causes, and therefore may be infinite.[54]

And again under part three concerning the unlawfulness of the ceremonies he writes,

> That which the church may lawfully prescribe by her laws and ordinances, as a thing left to her determination, must be one of such things as were not determinable by Scripture, on that reason which Camero has given us, namely, because *individua* are *infinita*. We mean not in any wise to circumscribe the infinite power and wisdom of God, only we speak upon supposition of the bounds and limits which God did set to His written Word, within which he would have it contained, and over which he thought fit that it should not exceed. The case being thus put, as it is, we say truly of those several and changeable circumstances which are left to the determination of the church, that, being almost infinite, they were not particularly determinable in Scripture; for the particular definition of those occurring circumstances which were to be rightly ordered in the works of God's service to the end of the world, and that ever according to the exigency of every present occasion and different case, should have filled the whole world with books. But as for other things pertaining to God's worship, which are not to be reckoned among the circumstances of it, they being in number neither many, nor in change various, were most easily and conveniently determinable in Scripture. Now, since God would have His Word (which is our rule in the works of his

<hr>

52. Gillespie, *Dispute* (2013), p. 16.

53. John Cameron, *Prælectiones*, tom. 1, de Potest. Eccl., contr. 2. See *Prælectiones Theologicæ in selectiora quædam loca N.T.*, 3 vols. (Saumur, 1626–1628), 1.369, 370.

54. Gillespie, *Dispute* (2013), p. 51.

service) not to be delivered by tradition, but to be written and sealed unto us, that by this means, for obviating Satanical subtilty, and succoring human imbecility, we might have a more certain way for conservation of true religion, and for the inſtauration [*reſtoration*] of it when it fails among men, how can we but assure ourselves that every such acceptable thing pertaining any way to religion, which was particularly and conveniently determinable in Scripture, is indeed determined in it; and consequently, that no such thing as is not a mere alterable circumſtance is left to the determination of the church?[55]

As for the analogy to Moses' body, Gilleſpie may be drawing for David Calderwood's *Perth Assembly* (1619), which work he twice references in his *Diſpute* (though not in this point).

> The diversity of the ancients observing some the 6th day of January, some the 19th of April, some the 19th of May, some the 25th day of December, argueth that the Apoſtles never ordained it. Bellarmine nor no other can produce a writer for 300 years to teſtify that the nativity day was kept.... Ye see then as God hid the body of Moses, so hath He hid this day and other days depending on the calculation of it, wherein He declared his will concerning the other days of his notable acts. To wit that not Chriſt's action, but Chriſt's inſtitution maketh a day holy.[56]

2. That worship which God never commanded muſt be unlawfull, as was the washing of the Pharasees (Matt. 15:9), and therefore Chriſt accounted them but vain inventions of man's brain. If so then, though it did teach them holiness, yet it having its entering from men, and a human inſtitution, it was a vain thing; but so is this day merely inſtituted by man, and therefore but vain.

This second point is a condensed version of the following section of Gilleſpie's *Diſpute*, which is found in part three againſt the lawfulness of the ceremonies, which also brings in material relevant to the firſt point.

> §10. 3. The church is forbidden to add anything to the commandments of God which He has given unto us, concerning His worship and service (Deut. 4:2; 12:32; Prov. 30:6); therefore she may not lawfully prescribe anything in the works of divine worship, if it be not a mere circumſtance belonging to that kind of things which were not determinable by Scripture.

> Our opposites have no other diſtinctions which they make any use of againſt this argument, but the very same which papiſts use in defense of their un-written dogmatical traditions, namely, that *additio corrumpens* [*deſtructive*

---

55. Gillespie, *Diſpute* (2013), pp. 261–262.

56. David Calderwood, *Perth Assembly* (1619), p. 80.

addition] is forbidden, but not *additio perficiens* [*perfecting addition*]: that there is not alike reason of the Christian church and of the Jewish; that the church may not add to the essential parts of God's worship, but to the accidentary she may add.

To the first of those distinctions, we answer (1) That the distinction itself is an addition to the Word, and so does but beg the question.

(2) It is blasphemous; for it argues that the commandments of God are imperfect, and that by addition they are made perfect.

(3) Since our opposites will speak in this dialect, let them resolve [*answer*] us whether the washings of the Pharisees, condemned by Christ, were corrupting or perfecting additions. They cannot say they were corrupting, for there was no commandment of God which those washings did corrupt or destroy, except that commandment which forbids men's additions. But for this respect our opposites dare not call them corrupting additions, for so they should condemn all additions whatsoever. Except, therefore, they can show us that those washings were not added by the Pharisees for perfecting, but for corrupting the Law of God, let them consider how they rank their own ceremonial additions with those of the Pharisees. We read of no other reason wherefore Christ condemned them but because they were doctrines which had no other warrant than the commandments of men (Matt. 15:9); for as the law ordained diverse washings, for teaching and signifying that true holiness and cleanness which ought to be among God's people, so the Pharisees would have perfected the law by adding other washings (and more than God had commanded) for the same end and purpose.

3. Such things which have been abused unto superstition must not be allowed; but this day has been grossly abused to superstition, therefore unlawful. Instance in the Brazen Serpent [a thing of great use],[57] which though appointed by God, yet when once it was abused to idolatry, it was broken to powder; much more should that be abolished which hath only man's warrant for its institution.

This third point brings in one of the important principles laid down by Gillespie in his *A Dispute against the English Popish Ceremonies obtruded on the Church of Scotland*, often found in other works.[58] It could be called the principle of the brazen serpent, or of the necessity of putting away monuments of or memorials to gross idolatry.

––––––––––––––

57. The phrase in square braces was in the margin in the manuscript text.

58. "The brazen serpent (having been God's own ordinance) was for Idolatrous abuse to be abolished. Therefore human inventions, for the like abuse, much more." William Ames, *A Fresh Suite Against Human Ceremonies in God's Worship* (1633), p. 395.

We see this illustrated in Calvin, who in his sermons presses the avoidance of evil and necessity to advance edification, and remove anything that would "foster superstition" and "divest ourselves of all silly superstitions and frivolous inventions, renounce all idolatry in order to worship God in spirit and in truth."[59] Along these same lines, Calvin articulates a principle against "monuments of idolatry" in one of his tracts, elaborated upon by later writers and which is also adduced in some of the Reformed Confessions.[60] In 1561 Calvin wrote a response to George Cassander's work arguing for a reunification of the Protestant churches with Rome.[61] In perhaps the standout portion of this tract, Calvin writes,

> Recognizing that God's law commands the form of his worship, and by this he expresses detestation of all false gods, of course it is a repugnant thing to say that in pleasing men something must be added to his Commandments. The vile buffoonery of the Papacy soils all religion. This also is not a thing suitable to good conscience. If some customs are useful and of good faith, I confess that the error that detains the spirits of some must not stop those who are well instructed to use only that which is good—provided that it would not become a common error confirmed by use. But because superstition is bindingly connected with many ceremonies which in themselves are good, anyone who would want to keep them shows in effect that he is of those who fall short. In this way, a false opinion, commonly received, will soil by abuse customs that otherwise are good. It becomes not only necessary to flee from

---

59. This material is drawn from the 2013 article, *In Translatiōne:* John Calvin's Letters to the Ministers of Montbéliard (1543–1544): The Genevan Reformer's Advice and Views of the Liturgical Calendar," *The Confessional Presbyterian* 13 (2017): 198–220.

60. The phrase or idea of "monuments of idolatry" can be found in The Debrecen Synod (1567), The Synod at Szikszo (1568), The Nassau Confession (1578) and Bremen Consensus (1595). Calvin does not use the term in his tract, and this may just as well be called the principle of the brazen serpent. The Westminster Assembly would appropriately state the duty from the principle: "The duties required in the second commandment are … the disapproving, detesting, opposing all false worship; and, according to each one's place and calling, removing it, and all monuments of idolatry" (WLC 108). Foxe compared Edward VI to Josiah in the destruction of "all monuments of idolatry." See also usage in Edward VI's injunctions for such destruction (1547), and in Hooper's injunctions (1551). Knox and Hooper likely picked up the language from the earlier use. See "American Presbyterianism and the Religious Observance of Christmas," *The Confessional Presbyterian* 11 (2015): 178–179; Andrew Lang, *John Knox and the Reformation* (1905), p. 113; John Foxe, *Acts and Monuments* (1570), book 9, pp. 1521–1522; *Visitation Articles and Injunctions*, volume 2, 1536–1557, ed. W. H. Frere et al. (London: Longmans Green & Company, 1910), p. 126; *Later Writings of Bishop Hooper together with his letters and other pieces,* ed. Charles Nevinson for The Parker Society (Cambridge: University Press, 1852), p. 135.

61. G. Cassandro, *De officio pii ac publicae tranquillitatis vere amantis viri in hoc religionis dissidio,* edited by F. Bauduin (Basel: 1561; repr. Lazari Zetzneri, 1612).

it in your personal observation, but also that the fault be liberally noted out of fear that simple people would be hardened by it more and more. For it is not proper for a zealous Christian to say, "To each his own," without also admonishing the others to be on their own guard.

Similarly, what is alleged of an Italian writer, that abuse does not take away good use, will not be true if one holds to it without exception: because it is clearly commanded to us to prudently watch that we would not offend the infirm brothers by our example, and that we should never undertake what would be illicit. For Saint Paul prohibits offending the brothers in eating flesh that was sacrificed to idols [1 Cor. 10:28], and speaking to this particular issue he shows a general rule that we are to keep ourselves from troubling the consciences of the weak by a bad or damaging example. One might speak better and more wholesomely if he were to say that what God himself ordains may not be abolished for wrong use or abuse that is committed against it. But even here, it is necessary to abstain from these things if, by later human ordinance, they have become corrupt with error, and if their use is harmful or scandalizes the brothers.

Here I marvel how this "Reformer," after granting that superstitions sometimes have such strong popularity that it is necessary to remove from the realm of man those things once ordained by public authority (as we read of Hezekiah doing with the bronze serpent), finally does not consider even a little that his shrewdness is a horror to the ways of good action: as if in defending supportable rituals, he would oblige that all superstitions should be considered as safe and whole because they are weighty. For what is there in the papacy now that would not resemble the bronze serpent, even if it did not begin that way? [Numbers 21:9.] Moses had it made and forged by the commandment of God: he had it kept for a sign of recognition. Among the virtues of Hezekiah told to us is that he had it broken and reduced to ash [2 Kings 18:4]. The superstitions for the most part, against which true servants of God battle today, are spreading from here to who knows where as covered pits in the ground. They are filled with detestable errors that can never be erased unless their use is taken away. Why, therefore, do we not confess simply what is true, that this remedy is necessary for taking away filth from the church?[62]

At a crucial point in his *Dispute*, George Gillespie elaborated upon this principle which Calvin articulated, in crafting his argument for the necessity

---

62. "Response a Un Certain Moyenneur Rusé" [French], *Recueil des Opuscules* (Geneva: Stoer, 1611) 2191–2192. Cf. *Responsio Ad Versipellem Quendam Mediatorem* [Latin], *CR* 37 (*CO* 9), col. 542. For a full translation of this tract into English from the French see, R. V. Bottomly, "Calvin's Response to a Certain Tricky Middler," *The Confessional Presbyterian* 8 (2012): 254–275. For this quotation see page 264.

of putting away monuments of idolatry.[63] Much like Cassander, the Anglo-Catholics, who had been arguing for the rites imposed by King James in the Articles of Perth (1618), including the re-imposition of some of the old pretended holy days which the Scottish Kirk had rejected completely at the Reformation, argued "that it is needless to abolish utterly things and rites which the papists have abused to idolatry and superstition, and that it is enough to purge them from the abuse, and to restore them again to their right use." Gillespie answered, citing Calvin's response to Cassander,

> Calvin, answering that which Cassander alleges out of an Italian writer, *abusu non tolli bonum usum* [abuse does not take away the good use], he admits it only to be true in things which are instituted by God Himself, not so in things ordained by men, for the very use of such things or rites as have no necessary use in God's worship, and which men have devised only at their own pleasure, is taken away by idolatrous abuse…. [*The safer part*] here, is to put them wholly away, and there is, by a great deal, more danger in retaining than in removing them.[64]

Gillespie shows in his argument against the popish ceremonies, that the old pretended holy days and other popish ceremonies "are thrice idolatrous: "because they are monuments of by-past idolatry"; 2. "because they are badges of present idolatry"; 3. "because they are idols themselves." Ceremonies such as the old holy days "are unlawful, because they are monuments of by-past idolatry, which not being necessary to be retained, should be utterly abolished."[65]

> By communicating with idolaters in their rites and ceremonies, we ourselves become guilty of idolatry; even as Ahaz, was an idolater, *eo ipso* [for that very reason], that he took the pattern of an altar from idolaters (2 Kings 16:10). Forasmuch, then, as kneeling before the consecrated bread, the sign of the cross, surplice, festival days, bishoping, bowing down to the altar, administration of the sacraments in private places, etc., are the wares of Rome, the baggage of Babylon, the trinkets of the whore, the badges of popery, the ensigns of Christ's enemies, and the very trophies of AntiChrist: we cannot

---

63. The ceremonies, including the pretended holy days, "are idolatrous, because having been notoriously abused to idolatry heretofore, they are the detestable and accursed monuments, which give no small honor to the memory of that by-past idolatry which should lie buried in hell." The principle which Gillespie draws from Calvin among others is "All things and rites which have been notoriously abused to idolatry, if they are not such as either God or nature has made to be of a necessary use, should be utterly abolished and purged away from divine worship, in such sort that they may not be accounted nor used by us as sacred things or rites pertaining to the same." Gillespie, *Dispute*, p. 149.

64. Gillespie, *Dispute*, pp. 156–157.

65. Gillespie, *Dispute*, pp. 149ff.

conform, communicate and symbolize with the idolatrous papists in the use of the same, without making ourselves idolaters by participation.[66]

Just prior to citing Calvin's answer to Cassander, Gillespie reinforced his argument for the necessity of removing monuments of idolatry with a twofold reason, drawing from Calvin again.

Fifthly, our proposition is backed with a twofold reason, for things which have been notoriously abused to idolatry should be abolished: (1) *Quia monent* [*because they remind*]. (2) *Quia movent* [*because they move*]. First, then, they are monitory [*admonitory; give a warning*], and preserve the memory of idols; *monumentum* [*a monument*] in good things is both *monimentum* [*a memorial*] and *munimentum* [*fortification*]; but *monumentum* in evil things (such as idolatry) is only *monimentum*, which *monet mentem* [*instructs the mind*], to remember upon such things as ought not to be once named among saints, but should lie buried in the eternal darkness of silent oblivion. Those relics therefore of idolatry, *by which succeeding generations, as though by a memorial, may be reminded* (as Wolphius rightly says),[67] are to be quite defaced and destroyed, because they serve to honor the memory of cursed idols.

God would not have so much as the name of an idol to be remembered among his people, but commanded to destroy their names as well as themselves (Exod. 23:13; Deut. 12:3; Joshua 23:7); whereby we are admonished, as Calvin says, how detestable idolatry is before God, *whose memory a repentant man wants to be erased so no trace of it may be seen afterward.*[68] Yea, he requires, *that the memory be erased [abolished; put away] of all those things which were at anytime consecrated to idols.*[69] If Mordecai would not give his countenance (Esther 3:2), nor do any reverence to a living monument of that nation whose name God had ordained to be blotted out from under heaven (Deut. 25:19), much less should we give connivance, and far less countenance, but least of all reverence, to the dead and dumb monuments of those idols which God has devoted to utter destruction, with all their naughty [*bad, wicked*] appurtenances, so that he will not have their names to be once mentioned or remembered again.

But, secondly, *movent* [*they move*] too; such idolotrous remainders move

---

66. Gillespie, *Dispute*, pp. 172ff.

67. "Com. in 2 Reg. 23:6. *quibus quasi monumentis posteritas admoneatur* [*Melachim; id est,* 1599 ed., ibid., p. 398r]."

68. "Com. in Isa. 27:9. *cujus memoriam vult penitus deleri, ne posthac ullum ejus vestigium appareat.* [Cf. *CR* 63 (*CO* 26), 456; *Commentaries*, vol. VIII, 2.261.]"

69. "Calv., Com. in Exod. 23:24. *eorum omnium memoriam deleri* [*sic* aboleri], *quæ semel dicata sunt idolis.* [*CR* 52 (*CO* 23), 546; *Commentaries*, vol. II, 2.387. The compositer of the 1637 text may have transposed the *deleri* from the citation from Isaiah just prior.]"

us to turn back to idolatry. For *by experience we have verified, that, even after superstitions have been cast out, if any monuments of them be left to remain, not only has the memory of those persisted, but in the end it has obtained that they might be revived*, says Wolphius;[70] who hereupon thinks it behoveful [*necessary*] to destroy *funditus* [*utterly*] such vestiges of superstition, for this cause, if there were no more: *so that both for those aspiring to resume idolatry, hope may be diminished, and for those attempting new things the opportunity and material may be forestalled.*[71]

God would have Israel to overthrow all idolatrous monuments, lest thereby they should be snared (Deut. 7:25; 12:30). And if the law command to cover a pit, lest an ox or an ass should fall therein (Exod. 21:33), shall we suffer a pit to be open wherein the precious souls of men and women, which all the world cannot ransom, are likely to fall? Did God command to make a battlement for the roof of a house, and that for the safety of men's bodies (Deut. 22:8), and shall we not only not put up a battlement, or object some bar for the safety of men's souls, but also leave the way slippery and full of snares? Read we not that the Lord, who knew what was in man, and saw how propense he was to idolatry, did not only remove out of His people's way all such things as might any way allure or induce them to idolatry (even to the cutting off the names of the idols out of the land (Zech. 13:2), but also hedge up their way with thorns that they might not find their paths, nor overtake their idol-gods, when they should seek after them (Hosea 2:6, 7)? And shall we by the very contrary course not only not hedge up the way of idolatry with thorns, which may stop and stay such as have an inclination aiming forward, but also lay before them the inciting and enticing occasions which add to their own propension, such delectation as spurs forward with a swift facility?[72]

4. In regard of the late Solemn covenant, wherewith the State hath bound themselves to observe, wherein they and we have covenanted to oppose and withstand all superstitious worship, and to further a Reformation to our utmost power, such as shall be most agreeable unto God's sacred Word and will.

Here Gillespie adduces the Solemn League and Covenant sworn by Scotland and England in its call to Reformation and to abandon all superstitious worship. "II. That we shall, in like manner, without respect of persons, endeavour the extirpation of popery, prelacy (that is, Church government

---

70. "Ubi Supra [2 Kings 23:6]. *usu compertum habemus, superstitiones etiam postquam explosæ essent, si qua relicta fuissent earum monumenta, cum memoriam sui ipsarum apud homines, tum id tandem ut revocarentur obtinuisse.* [*Melachim; id est,* 1599 ed., ibid., p. 398r.]"

71. "*ut et aspirantibus ad revocandam idololatriam spes frangatur, et res novas molientibus ansa pariter ac materia præripiatur.*"

72. Gillespie, *Dispute*, pp. 154–155.

by archbishops, bishops, their chancellors and commissioners, deans, deans and chapters, archdeacons, and all other ecclesiastical officers depending on that hierarchy), superstition, heresy, schism, profaneness, and whatsoever shall be found contrary to sound doctrine and the power of godliness; lest we partake in other men's sins, and thereby be in danger to receive of their plagues; and that the Lord may be one, and his name one, in the three kingdoms."[73]

5. More particularly it is now to be refused because of the unsuitableness thereof unto our times. Now God calls us not unto His solemn feast in which we should joy and make merry, attending to the abundance which He hath given, but He calls us unto weeping, mourning, and lamentation (Isa. 22:12), as now how un-agreeable should our [carriage] be unto [such a] condition, if upon God's call for weeping, mourning, and lamentation, behold feasting and mirth. This did much incense the Lord against the Jews and so would it against us.

Gillespie here is making the point of how inappropriate it is to set recurring feast (or fast) days, holy days commemorating Christ's acts in redeeming His people, because in God's providence our condition will change from one year to the next. Set anniversary feast or fast days (holy days) are not the same thing as God's providential calls for fasting or feasting. The Directory for the Public Worship of God and Confession of Faith which Gillespie helped to draft, recognize the latter but not the former. Gillespie writes in his *Dispute*:

> §6. The Bishop has yet a third dart to throw at us: *If the church* (he says) *has power, upon occasional motives, to appoint occasional fasts or festivities, may not she, for constant and eternal blessings, which do infinitely excel all occasional benefits, appoint ordinary times of commemoration or thanksgiving?* ANSWER. There are two reasons for which the church may and should appoint fasts or festivities upon occasional motives, and neither of them agrees with ordinary festivities. 1. Extraordinary fasts, either for obtaining some great blessing, or averting some great judgment, are necessary means to be used in such cases; likewise, extraordinary festivities are necessary testifications [*testimonies*] of our thankfulness for the benefits which we have impetrate [*procured*] by our extraordinary fasts; but ordinary festivities, for constant and eternal blessings, have no necessary use. The celebration of set anniversary days is no necessary mean for conserving the commemoration of the benefits of redemption, because we have occasion, not only every Sabbath day, but every other day, to call to mind these benefits, either in hearing, or reading, or meditating upon God's Word. *I esteem and judge that the days consecrated to Christ must*

---

73. The Solemn League & Covenant, in *The Confession of Faith*, etc. (Edinburgh: Johnstone and Hunter, 1855), p. 359.

be lifted, says Danæus: *Christ is born, is circumcised, dies, rises again for us every day in the preaching of the Gospel.*[74]

God has given his church a general precept for extraordinary fasts (Joel 1:14; 2:15), as likewise for extraordinary festivities to praise God, and to give him thanks in the public assembly of his people, upon the occasional motive of some great benefit which, by the means of our fasting and praying, we have obtained (Zech. 8:19 with 7:3). If it is said that there is a general command for set festivities, because there is a command for preaching and hearing the word, and for praising God for his benefits; and there is no precept for particular fasts more than for particular festivities, I answer: Albeit there is a command for preaching and hearing the word, and for praising God for his benefits, yet is there no command (no, not in the most general generality) for annexing these exercises of religion to set anniversary days more than to other days; whereas it is plain that there is a general command for fasting and humiliation at some times more than at other times.[75]

The Westminster Confession of Faith at chapter 21, paragraph 5 reads:

The reading of the Scriptures with godly fear; the sound preaching and conscionable hearing of the Word, in obedience unto God, with understanding, faith, and reverence; singing of psalms with grace in the heart; as also, the due administration and worthy receiving of the sacraments instituted by Christ; are all parts of the ordinary religious worship of God: beside religious oaths, vows, solemn fastings, and thanksgivings, upon special occasions, which are, in their several times and seasons, to be used in a holy and religious manner. WCF 21.[76]

The concluding appendix to The Westminster Directory for the Public Worship of God *Touching Days and Places for Publick Worship* has this to say about so called "holy days":

There is no day commanded in Scripture, to bee kept holy under the Gospel, but the Lords Day, which is the Christian Sabbath. Festival dayes vulgarly

---

74. Apud [cited *in*] Balduin, *de Cas. Consc.*, lib. 2, cap. 12, cas. 1. *Dies Christo dicatos tollendos existimo judicoque, quotidie nobis in evangelii prædicatione nascitur, circumciditur, moritur, resurgit Christus.* Cf. Balduin, *Tractatus Luculentus* (1654), p. 348. See the text in Lambertus Daneau, *Ad Roberti Bellarmini disputationes theologicas De Rebus in religione controversis Lamberti Danaei responsio* (Joannes le Preux, 1598), pp. 1519–1520.

75. Gillespie, *Dispute*, pp. 50–51.

76. The text is that as given in S. W. Carruthers, M.D., Ph.D, *The Westminster Confession of Faith, Being an account of the Preparation and Printing of its seven leading editions to which is appended a critical text of the Confession with notes thereon* (Manchester: R. Aikman & Son, [1937]), p. 130.

called Holy dayes, haveing no warrant in the word, are not to bee continued. Nevertheless, it is lawfull & necessary upon special emergent occasions, to separate a Day or dayes for publique Fasting, or Thanksgiveing, as the several eminent & extraordinary dispensations of Gods providence shall administer cause, & opportunity to his people.[77]

Whether the observation of holy Dayes bee lawfull.

Whether it be in the power of a state, king, [or] parliament to establish holy days. For answer unto this question, I affirm that it is not in the power of any state or kingdom to establish a holy day, and that it hath been the sin of our state to make holy days and to raise them up in equipage (i.e., equipace, equal establishment) with the Lord's Day. My Reason is this: The effect cannot rise higher than the cause, as a stream cannot ascend above the fountain, but for a civil state to establish holy rites is to ascend above their principle: therefore, it's unlawfull. True it is, a state may establish civil days.

In his *Dispute*, Gillespie deals extensively with what power the magistrate has and does not have with regard to the church. With regard to rites and ceremonies and the elemental aspects of worship, he writes,

§19. But in all the Scripture princes have neither a commendable example, nor any other warrant, for the making of any innovation in religion, or for the prescribing of sacred significant ceremonies of men's devising. Jeroboam caused a change to be made in the ceremonies and form of God's worship, whereas God ordained the ark of the covenant to be the sign of His presence, and that his glory should dwell between the cherubims. Jeroboam set up two calves to be the signs representative of that God who brought "Israel out of Egypt;" and this he means while he says, "Behold thy gods," etc. (1 Kings 12:28), giving to the signs the thing signified. Whereas God ordained Jerusalem to be the place of worship, and all the sacrifices to be brought to the temple of Solomon; Jeroboam made Dan and Bethel to be places of worship, and built there altars and high places for the sacrifices. Whereas God ordained the sons of Aaron only to be his priests, Jeroboam made priests of the lowest of the people, which were not of the sons of Levi. Whereas God ordained the feast of tabernacles to be kept on the fifteenth day of the seventh month, Jeroboam appointed it on the fifteenth day of the eighth month.

Now, if any prince in the world might have fair pretences [*claims*] for the making of such innovations in religion, Jeroboam much more. He might allege for his changing of the signs of God's presence, and of the place of worship, that since Rehoboam's wrath was incensed against him, and against

---

77. Van Dixhoorn, 5.159. See also the directories for fast and thanksgiving days, 5.154–157.

the ten tribes which adhered unto him (as appears by the accounting of them to be rebels, 2 Chronicles 13:6, and by the gathering of a huge army for bringing the kingdom again to Rehoboam, 2 Chron. 11:1), it was no longer safe for his subjects to go up to Jerusalem to worship, in which case God, who required mercy more than sacrifice, would bear with their changing of a few ceremonies for the safety of men's lives. For his putting down of the priests and Levites, and his ordaining of other priests which were not of the sons of Levi, he might pretend [*claim*] that they were rebellious to him, in that they would not assent unto his new ordinances,[78] which he had enacted for the safety and security of his subjects, and that they did not only simply refuse obedience to these his ordinances, but in their refusal show themselves so steadfastly minded, that they would refuse and withstand even to the suffering of deprivation and deposition; and not only so, but likewise drew after them many others of the rest of the tribes to be of their judgment (2 Chron. 11:16), and to adhere to that manner of worship which was retained in Jerusalem. Lastly, for the change which he made about the season of the feast of tabernacles, he might have this pretence [*claim*], that as it was expedient for the strengthening of his kingdom[79] to draw and allure as many as could be had to associate and join themselves with him in his form of worship (which could not be done if he should keep that feast at the same time when it was kept at Jerusalem); so there was no less (if not more) order and decency in keeping it in the eighth month, when the fruit of the ground were perfectly gathered in (for thankful remembrance whereof that feast was celebrated) than in the seventh, when they were not so fully collected.[80]

These pretences [*claims*] he might have made yet more plausible, by professing and avouching that he intended to worship no idols, but the Lord only; that he had not fallen from anything which was fundamental and essential in divine faith and religion; that the changes which he had made were only about some alterable ceremonies which were not essential to the worship of God, and that even in these ceremonies he had not made any change for his own will and pleasure, but for important reasons which concerned the good of his kingdom and safety of his subjects. Notwithstanding of all this, the innovations which he made about these ceremonies of sacred signs, sacred places, sacred persons, sacred times, are condemned for this very reason,

---

78. Martyr in 1 Reg. 8:31. [Cf. *Melachim, id est, Regum libri duo posteriores cum commentariis Petri Martyris Vermilii Florentini sacrarum literarum in schola Tigurina professoris, in primum totum & secundi priora XI. capita, et Ioannis Wolphii Tigurini in secundi quatuordecim vltima capita: accesserunt indices locupletissimi, cùm rerum & verborum insignium, tùm Sacræ Scripturæ tam veteris, videlicet, quàm Noui Testamenti, vnà cum nouo locorum communium, qui inter cœteros copiosiùs in his commentariis explicantur.* (Heidelberg: 1599), pp. 59v–61r.]

79. Ibid., 1 Reg. 8:32 [1599 ed., ibid.].

80. Ibid.

because he devised them of his own heart (1 Kings 12:33), which was enough to convince [*convict*] him of horrible impiety in making Israel to sin.

Moreover, when king Ahaz took a pattern of the altar of Damascus, and sent it to Urijah the priest, though we cannot gather from the text that he either intended or pretended any other respect beside the honoring and pleasuring of his patron and protector, the king of Assyria (for of his appointing that new altar for his own and all the people's sacrifices, there was nothing heard till after his return from Damascus, at which time he began to fall back from one degree of defection to a greater), yet this very innovation of taking the pattern of an altar from idolaters is marked as a sin and a snare (2 Kings 16:10, 18).

Last of all, whereas many of the kings of Judah and Israel did either themselves worship in the groves and the high places, or else, at least, suffer the people to do so, howsoever they might have alleged specious reasons for excusing themselves,[81] as namely, that they gave not this honor to any strange gods, but to the Lord only; that they chose these places only to worship in wherein God was of old seen and worshipped by the patriarchs; that the groves and the high places added a most amiable splendor and beauty to the worship of God, and that they did consecrate these places for divine worship in a good meaning, and with minds wholly devoted to God's honor; yet notwithstanding, because this thing was not commanded of God, neither came it into His heart, He would admit no excuses; but ever challenges it as a grievous fault in the government of those kings, that those high places were not taken away, and that the people still sacrificed in the high places. From all which examples we learn how highly God was and is displeased with men for adding any other sacred ceremonies to those which He himself has appointed.[82]

CONCLUSION

In 1644, when the subject of the holy day had come up again with the regular fast falling on December 25, Edmund Calamy preached the fast sermon for the House of Lords.[83] He concluded, paralleling some of what George Gillespie briefly noted the prior year,

This day is the day which is commonly called *The Feast of Christ's Nativity*, or *Christmas day:* A day that hath been heretofore much abused to *superstition* and *profaneness.* It is not easy to reckon whether the superstition hath been

---

81. Hospin., *De Orig. Templ.*, lib. 1, cap. 1 [Cf. "Rudolf Hospinian, De Templis hoc est, de Origine, Progressu, usu et abusu Templorum & Rerum ad Templa pertinentium," in *Opera omnia in septem tomos distributa*, volume 1 (Geneva: Samuel de Tournes, 1672) pp. 3–4.]; Wolph. in 2 Reg. 12:4 [Johann Wolf, 1599 ed., ibid., p. 270v ff].

82. Hospin., ibid., p. 3.

83. Edmund Calamy, *An indictment against England because of her selfe-murdering divisions* (London: Meredith, 1645), pp. 40–41.

greater, or the profaneness. I have known some that have preferred *Christmas day* before the *Lord's Day,* and have cried down the *Lord's Day,* and cried up *Christmas day.* I have known those that would be sure to receive the sacrament upon Christmas day, though they did not receive it all the year after. This and much more was the superstition of the day. And the profaneness was as great. Old Father Latimer saith in one of his sermons, That the Devil had more service in the twelve Christmas holy days (as they were called) then God had all the yeare after.[84] Seneca saith of his time, *Olim December mensis erat, nunc annus est.*[85] There are some that though they did not play at cards all the year long, yet they must play at Christmas; thereby, it seems, to keep in memory the birth of Christ. This and much more hath been the profanation of this feast. And truly I think that the superstition and profanation of this day is so rooted into it, as that there is no way to reform it but by dealing with it as Hezekiah did with the brazen serpent. This year God by a providence hath buried this *feast* in a *fast,* and I hope it will never rise again. You have set out (Right Honourable) a strict order for the keeping of it, and you are

---

84. Edmund Calamy is paraphrasing from Hugh Latimer's second sermon before a convocation of the clergy in 1536. Cotton Mather seems to have picked up this paraphrase in his denunciation of Christmas in 1712, and this seems to be the source in modern citations of the saying, which do not actually cite from Latimer (e.g. Stephen Nissenbaum, *The Battle for Christmas* [New York: A Division of Random House, Inc. Vintage Books, 1997], p. 7).

Hugh Latimer's words to the clergy in 1536 were: "Do ye see nothing in our holidays? of which very few were made at the first, and they to set forth goodness, virtue, and honesty: but sithens, in some places, there is neither mean nor measure in making new holidays, as who should say, this one thing is serving of God, to make this law, that no man may work. But what doth the people on these holidays? Do they give themselves to godliness, or else ungodliness? See ye nothing, brethren? If you see not, yet God seeth. God seeth all the whole holidays to be spent miserably in drunkenness, in glossing, in strife, in envy, in dancing, dicing, idlenes, and gluttony. He seeth all this, and threatenth punishment for it. He seeth it, which neither is deceived in seeing, nor deceiveth when he threateneth. Thus men serve the devil; for God is not thus served, albeit ye say ye serve God. *No, the devil hath more service done unto him on one holiday, than on many working days."* Emphasis added. *Sermons by Hugh Latimer,* edited for the Parker Society by George Elwes Corrie (Cambridge, 1844), pp. 52–53.

Cotton renders the saying as, "Yea, the zealous Martyr Latymer complained, That Men dishonour Christ more in the Twelve days of Christmas, than in all the twelve Months of the Year besides." Cotton Mather, *Grace defended. A censure on the ungodliness, by which the glorious grace of God, is too commonly abused. A sermon preached on the twenty fifth day of December, 1712. Containing some seasonable admonitions of piety. And concluded, with a brief dissertation on that case, whether the penitent thief on the cross, be an example of one repenting at the last hour, and on such a repentance received unto mercy?* (Boston: Printed by B. Green, for Samuel Gerrish, at his shop in Marlborough Street, 1712), p. 20.

85. "Once December was a month, now it is a year." "... qui dixit olim mensem Decembrem fuisse, nunc annum." *Seneca ad Lucilium Epistulae Morales,* trans. Richard M. Gummere, The Loeb Classical Library (London: William Heinemann, [1925]), pp. 116, 117.

here this day to observe your own order, and I hope you will do it strictly. The necessity of the times are great. Never more need of prayer and fasting. The Lord give us grace to be humbled in this day of humiliation for all our own, and England's sins; and especially for the old superstition, and profanation of this feast: always remembering upon such days as these, Isa. 22. 12, 13, 14. ["And in that day did the Lord God of hosts call to weeping, and to mourning, and to baldness, and to girding with sackcloth: And behold joy and gladness, slaying oxen, and killing sheep, eating flesh, and drinking wine: let us eat and drink; for to morrow we shall die. And it was revealed in mine ears by the Lord of hosts, Surely this iniquity shall not be purged from you till ye die, saith the Lord God of hosts."

*A Sermon Preached Before the Honorable House of Commons: At their late Solemn Fast,
Wednesday, March 27, 1644. By George Gillespie, Minister at Edinburgh.*

EDITIONS

1. *A Sermon Preached Before the Honorable House of Commons At their late Solemn
   Faſt, Wednesday, March 27, 1644* (London: printed for Robert Bostock, dwelling
   at the Kings head in Pauls Church-yard, Anno 1644). [4], 42, [2] p.; 4⁰. ESTC
   R12051 (Wing G757). This impression has several variants. Some have the
   errata at the end of the last quire (G). "Quire G is in three settings: (A) with
   errata at foot of the order to print, (B) with errata at foot of Grv, or (C) with
   no errata listed." Some examples have "solemn" and some "solemne." The two
   examples of the London and one of the Edinburgh all have "Psal. 102:6" in the
   epigraph instead of the correct "Psal. 102:16." The errata only note three errors
   and ask forgiveness for the other minor errors not worth their mentioning.
   These will be noted in the appropriate places in the text.
2. *A Sermon Preached Before the Honorable House of Commons At their late Solemne
   Faſt, Wednesday, March 27, 1644* (London: printed for Robert Bostock,
   dwelling at the Kings head in Pauls Church-yard, Anno 1644). ESTC R24966.
   This is called a second edition in Wing. It is paginated [4], 42. The order to
   print and errata are facing the title page.
3. *A Sermon Preached Before the Honorable House of Commons: At their late Solemne
   Faſt, Wednesday, March 27, 1644* (Edinburgh: printed by Evan Tyler, printer to
   the Kings most excellent Majestie, 1644). R20524. [6], 41, [1] p.; 4⁰ (but Wing
   describes this edition as octavo).
4. *A Sermon Preached Before the Honorable House of Commons at their late Solemn
   Faſt, Wednesday, March 27, 1644* (Edinburgh: Robert Ogle and Oliver and
   Boyd, 1844). In *Works* in *A Presbyterian's Armoury.* 26 pp.; royal octavo.
5. "A Sermon Preached Before the Honorable House of Commons at their
   late Solemn Fast, Wednesday, March 27, 1644" in *Sermons Preached Before the
   English Houses of Parliament by the Scottish Commissioners to the Weſtminſter
   Assembly of Dvines 1643–1645* (Dallas, Texas: Naphtali Press, 2011). Hard bound
   in dust jacket, 6x9.

The Epigraph on the prior page is from the first edition.

PREFACE

GEORGE GILLESPIE'S prospects for serving the church in 1637 were as dim as those for the revitalizing of Presbyterianism in general. However, with the bursting forth of the Second Reformation in Scotland, through the contacts he had made while an obscure tutor and through the impact of his first book *Against the English Popish Ceremonies* that gave the intellectual argument for that reformation, Gillespie rose quickly to greater use in the kirk. As noted in his biography,[1] Gillespie was ordained to the gospel ministry on April 26, 1638, to the church at Wemyss, wrote a tract against the prayer book for the kirk that summer, and preached at the historic Glasgow General Assembly on November 21, 1638. With the outbreak of the Second Bishop's War in 1640, Gillespie served as one of the chaplains who were empowered to act as their own presbytery. When peace negotiations begun at Ripon moved to London in 1641, Gillespie, with Alexander Henderson, Robert Blair, and Robert Baillie, travelled as chaplains with the Scottish peace delegation and resided there, where in their many opportunities to preach they astonished the crowds who came to hear them. With the agreement between the Scots and English in the Solemn League and Covenant, the Scottish Church appointed commissioners to join the already in progress Westminster Assembly of Divines to help settle the English church and form new doctrinal standards for the three kingdoms. Gillespie was chosen to attend along with Samuel Rutherford, Robert Baillie and Alexander Henderson. He and Alexander Henderson were admitted to the assembly by the House of Commons on September 14, 1643 and took their seats the next day in the assembly.[2]

Over the following months, the assembly, on orders from parliament,

---

1. *Shorter Writings*, volume 1, pp. 15–98.

2. *Minutes*, 2.124, n1. "Die Jovis, 14 Septembris, 1643. The Assembly. Resolved, That the Lord Maitland, Mr. Henderson, Mr. Gillaspie, and Mr. Robert Meldrum, shall be admitted into the Assembly, to be present there, and to debate upon Occasion." *Journals of the House of Commons*, [Volume 3] *From March the 15TH, 1642, In the Eighteenth Year of the Reign of King Charles the First, to December the 24TH, 1644, In the Twentieth Year of the Reign of King Charles the First* (Re-printed by Order of the House of Commons, 1803), p. 241. James King Hewison writes that "Meldrum, a political agent, was a member from the beginning," but Chad van Dixhoorn's brief bio of assemblymen states, "Robert Meldrum, fl. 1620–1647, Scottish parliamentary commissioner who did not attend the assembly." *Minutes*, 1.129; James King Hewison, *The Covenanters*, 2 vols (Glasgow: John Smith and Son, 1908; revised and corrected edition, 1913), 1.385. Baillie and Rutherford joined the assembly on November 20, 1643. *Minutes*, 2.343.

would turn from revising the Thirty-Nine Articles to debating and settling "church discipline and liturgy"—and the "particulars of church government … beginning with church officers and offices,"[3] determining the biblical offices of the church and whether the church was governed by the presbyterian system. Gillespie participated frequently in the debates and on February 20–21 gave a defense of the Presbyterian understanding of Matthew 18 in reply to both the Erastians (namely Selden), and Independents (namely Nye), which may be the occasion on which the fabled defeat Gillespie gave Selden is based.[4] In session 174 on March 11, the assembly passed the proposition "that the various congregations in Jerusalem were under one presbyterial government and that Acts 11 and 21 proved that elders met together for acts of government," and on March 13 "that the church of Jerusalem proves 'that many particular congregations may be under one presbyterial government.'"[5] On March 22, the last recorded attendance of Selden,[6] in the morning session, the assembly "voted that ordination is the act of a presbytery," and on March 25, that "the power of ordering the whole act of ordination is in the whole presbytery," before adjourning for the monthly fast[7] on March 27 at which Gillespie preached and referred to this progress by the assembly.[8] He was thanked for the sermon, allowed to have it published, and it was in print and available by April 16, 1644.[9]

---

3. *Minutes*, 2.190, 198.

4. See *Shorter Writings*, vol. 1, p. 89–98. Gillespie spoke at least 32 times prior to March 27.

5. *Minutes*, 2.600, 611.

6. Selden appears to have stopped debating or possibly even attending after the March 22 session 184 when ordination as an act of presbytery was affirmed. The minutes do not mention Selden for that date (*Minutes*, 2.637–642), but Lightfoot's account does. John Lightfoot, "The Journal of the Proceedings of The Assembly of Divines from January 1, 1643, to December 31, 1644," in *Works*, volume 13 (London: J. F. Dove, [1824]), p. 234. See also Ofir Haivry, *John Selden and the Western Political Tradition* (Cambridge University Press, 2017), p. 418.

7. "At the time of the Irish insurrection and massacre of 1641, the English Parliament requested King Charles I to appoint a monthly fast for the last Wednesday of every month "as long as the calamities of that nation should require it." The state of affairs went from bad to worse and the fast was more strictly pressed by the Parliament when King and Parliament became entangled in civil war. The sermons delivered before each house at these monthly occasions, as well as those preached on other occasions, were ordered published by the Parliament and they form an invaluable contribution to the literature of the time of the English Civil War and the Westminster Assembly." Preface, *Sermons Preached before the English Houses of Parliament by the Scottish Commissioners to the Westminster Assembly of Divines, 1643–1645* (Naphtali Press, 2011), p. ix. Hereafter *Scots Sermons*.

8. *Minutes*, 2.637, 643. See discussion of the subject of ordination in the assembly in Chad Van Dixhoorn, *God's Ambassadors: The Westminster Assembly and the Reformation of the English Pulpit, 1643–1653* (Reformation Heritage Books, 2017), pp. 44–50, 73–87, 114–119.

9. Die Mercurii, 27 Martii, 1644. Dies publicae Humiliationis. Preachers thanked. Ordered, That Mr. Bond and Mr. Nicoll do, from this House, give Thanks unto Mr. Bond and

The House of Commons had invited Gillespie to preach for the March fast day at the end of the prior monthly fast in February, which was a week after the exchanges between Gillespie and Nye and Selden.[10] With those debates and the votes by the majority and work trying to accommodate the Independents on his mind, it is not surprising that in his sermon Gillespie at points defends the Lord's prerogative to order His own worship and the government of His church. What may surprise is that he does so in preaching from a highly eschatological text from the Book of Ezekiel.

Gillespie states in his preface and in his sermon that his purpose was to remove obstructions to humiliation for past defections and to stir up reformation of the same on the part of his hearers (p. 87). He preached, "The symptoms are your high places not yet taken away, many of your old superstitious ceremonies to this day remaining" (p. 91); and more seriously, "the cause of this evil, in the very bowels and heart of the church": "The people of the land, great and small, have not as yet prepared their hearts unto the Lord their God. Mercy is prepared for the land, but the land is not prepared for mercy" (pp. 91–92).

Gillespie proposes a remedy to this condition and then removes an objection to his use of this prophetic passage for this purpose, wherein we get a glimpse into his eschatological views as he shows by eight reasons the vision does not concern the temple at Jerusalem (p. 92–93), but that the New Testament church is intended, which he proves by four reasons, before dividing the text (pp. 94–98). He divides his text into three particulars to address. I. That his hearers must not only seek reformation but be humbled for their past "evil ways." He proves this, removes an objection, and applies it four ways: to their enemies, to the Kingdom of England, to England's ministers, and to every Christian (pp. 99–113). II. He builds two doctrines from the command to "Show them the form of the house." For the first doctrine, we find Gillespie on familiar ground in defending that the church is tied to God's patterns prescribed in Scripture and maintaining the differences between mere circumstantial matters and sacred ceremonies (pp. 114–116).

Mr. Gillaspie, for the great Pains they took in the Sermons they preached this Day, at the Intreaty of this House, at St. Margaret's, Westminster, it being the Day of Publick Humiliation; and to desire them to print their Sermons: And they are to have the like Privilege in printing of them, as others in the like kind usually have had. *Journals of the House of Commons*, vol. 3, p. 439. Thomason dates his copy "Apr. 16" (ESTC R12051). However, it is listed in *Catalogue* under the date of the sermon, which seems to be the editor's practice for both Thomason's dated and undated fast sermons. *Catalogue of the Pamphlets, Books, Newspapers, and Manuscripts Relating to the Civil War, the Commonwealth, and Restoration Collected by George Thomason, 1640–1661, vol. I., Catalogue of the Collection, 1640–1652*, p. 317. See the similar problem with undated sermons noted in *Shorter Writings*, volume 1, page 31–32, n20.

10. Die Mercurii, 28 Februarii, 1643. Dies publicae Humiliationis. Ordered, That Mr. Rous do desire, from this House, Mr. Bond and Mr. Gillaspie to preach before the Commons the next Fast Day at Saint Margaret's, Westminster. Ibid., p. 410.

For the second doctrine, Gillespie addresses the Lord's purposes to build such a temple as described, for the accomplishment of which he says his hearers should look for it in the days of the gospel as he described previously. He first makes several observations about Ezekiel's temple that shall come to pass in Christ's church: her unity, increase, courts, strength, and her latter day glory, which he denies to have any "affinity with the opinion of an earthly or temporal kingdom of Christ, or of the Jews' building again of Jerusalem, and the material temple, and their obtaining a dominion above other nations, or the like." He then makes application to that time with six signs that God was going to build a new temple in England at that time, where we again get some idea of his eschatology (116–124). III. He then concludes briefly with the third division of his text, that "reformation ends not in contemplation but in action" (pp. 124–126). Here Gillespie mildly reproves his hearers for the slow pace and neglect of settling the church and presses for the quick establishment of presbyteries and means of ordination of ministers as the assembly of divines had "found in the Word of God a pattern for presbyterial government over many particular congregations, and have found also from the Word that ordination is an act belonging to such a presbytery."

Except for cursory notices and at least one nineteenth century dismissive citation of some of Gillespie's eschatological statements,[11] this sermon had received little scholarly attention. However, for these same statements, this sermon has received quite a bit of analysis in the last twenty years, though, just as with Gillespie's views of the Old Testament civil penalties,[12] the desire to draw parallels to fit modern theories has led to the need for correction as well.

In his 1999 dissertation, Crawford Gribben attempted to the place Gillespie

---

11. There is this very negative assessment from a mid 19TH century Anglican: "As a specimen of the degradation of the pulpit in those days of confusion, the following passages may be taken, in which the Parliament are filled with the hope of being the appointed instruments for the accomplishment of the prophecies respecting Christ's kingdom and the fall of Antichrist." The author then goes on to cite Gillespie's House sermon. Thomas Lathbury, "The Pulpit Under the Long Parliament," *The British Magazine and Monthly Register of Religious and Ecclesiastical Information*, etc. (London: Petheram, 1849): 368.

12. See *Shorter Writings*, 1.324, n7. Both Crawford Gribben and David Drinnon advocate against the usefulness of imposing the modern terms of amillennial, postmillennial, and premillennial onto the views of seventeenth century Scottish writers. This of course pertains to the millennium and the interpreting of Revelation 20. The generally accepted Protestant hermeneutic of interpreting the whole Book of Revelation at the time was historicist in nature rather than idealist, preterist, or futurist (again, to use the modern terms). On the anachronistic use of millennial terms, see Crawford Gribben, *The Puritan Millennium: Literature and Theology, 1550–1682* (Paternoster, repr. Wipf & Stock, 2008), preface to the revised edition, and David Andrew Drinnon, "The Apocalyptic Tradition in Scotland, 1588–1688," A Thesis Submitted for the Degree of PhD at the University of St. Andrews (2013). On the latter point and for a brief defense of Gillespie's sermon and historicism, see Steven Dilday,

into the English millenarian camp,[13] which is in the school of misguided studies that aimed to show that the Second Reformation was fueled by English millenarian-like fervor.[14] While Gribben subsequently modified his view on Gillespie, the idea has been put to rest by David Drinnon's study. Drinnon explains that the Scots had their own apocalyptic view made up of pessimistic and optimistic branches, that each rejected English millenarianism,[15] and these views remained fairly constant and consistent until the late seventeenth century.[16] The pessimistic camp was according to Drinnon founded by King James I in his *A Fruitefull Meditation … of the 7.8.9. and 10 verses of the 20. chap. of the Revelation* (Edinburgh, 1588).[17] The optimistic view was founded in John Napier's *A Plaine Discovery of the Whole Revelation of Saint John* (Edinburgh, 1593).[18] Drinnon writes,

---

The Eschatology of George Gillespie: An Introductory Analysis and Evaluation, ed. R. Andrew Myers (Culpeper, Virginia: Master Poole Publishing, 2008).

13. See Gribben, pp. 115–145. Gribben's *The Puritan Millennium* is a reissue of his PhD thesis for Department of English Studies at the University of Strathclyde, "Writing at the edge of the promises: negotiating the puritan apocalypse" (1999). He advises in the 2008 preface that the work retained the "interdisciplinary approaches" and this makes for impenetrable reading at times, and at points, Gribben is surely reading more into the text than the words support. See Gribben, pp. 140ff.

14. Drinnon, pp. 16, 63–64. "Sidney Burrell, Margaret Steele, and Crawford Gribben have each claimed that millenarian beliefs fueled the Scottish revolution of 1638, and influenced apocalyptic thought in Scotland well into the 1640s." See: Gribben, ibid.; Sidney Burrell, "The Apocalyptic Vision of the Early Covenanters," *Scottish Historical Review* 43 (1964); Margaret Steele, "The 'Politick Christian': The Theological Background to the National Covenant," in *The Scottish National Covenant in its British Context*, ed. John Morrill (Edinburgh, 1990).

15. "Supporters of both strands of apocalyptic belief were united by their aversion to millenarianism." Drinnon, p. 104.

16. Drinnon identifies Robert Fleming, who wrote *The Fulfilling of the Scriptures* (1669; 1671), as a rare but clear Scottish proponent of millenarianism.

17. "Several historians have pointed out that James based his interpretation of biblical prophecy largely upon preexisting Protestant apocalyptic commentaries and offered little that was original or exceptional. However, as Bernard Capp reminds us, during the early modern period, 'it was a major step for a reigning monarch to give public endorsement to Protestant apocalyptic teaching.'" Drinnon, p. 20, citing Bernard Capp, "The Political Dimension of Apocalyptic Thought," in *The Apocalypse in English Renaissance Thought and Literature: Patterns, Antecedents and Repercussions*, ed. C. A. Patrides and Joseph Wittreich (Manchester, 1984), p. 102.

18. "In accordance with mainstream Protestant eschatology, Napier largely conducted his exegesis in order to prove to a wider European audience that the pope was Antichrist and that Rome had served as the seat of his power for centuries." "Napier broke with mainstream apocalypticism by utilizing his strength in mathematics to incorporate chronological calculations into his exegesis. He completed his study of Revelation using the highly systematic Ramist method which he possibly encountered while travelling abroad after leaving

beginning in the late-1580s and early-1590s, two distinct patterns of apocalyptic belief were established in the exegetical commentaries on Revelation published by James VI and John Napier which influenced Scottish apocalyptic thinking over the next century. James, as a reigning monarch, gave credibility to the view espoused by the majority of Protestant apocalyptic thinkers in the sixteenth century who believed that the forces of Satan would persecute the Church militant until Christ returned on Judgment Day to punish the wicked and gather the elect for the kingdom of heaven. This rather pessimistic understanding of the latter-days was shared by subsequent Scottish apocalyptic thinkers such as William Cowper, Robert Baillie, David Dickson, William Guild, and John Welsh. Conversely, notable Scots such as Patrick Forbes, George Gillespie, James Durham, John Welwood, and Richard Cameron followed Napier by anticipating a period of latter-day glory for the Church before the Last Judgment. Typically, these Scots believed this period would witness the destruction of Antichrist, a greater spread of the Gospel throughout the world, and the conversion of the Jews to Christianity.[19]

Gillespie is classed as falling into the optimistic Scottish school of eschatological thought, which is based upon this sermon preached before the House of Commons. "Gillespie anticipated that a 'greater spread of the Gospel' throughout the world and the 'conversion of the Jewes' would accompany the fall of Antichrist [p. 96].... that the destruction of the beast in Rome would usher in a period of latter-day glory for the Church militant. During the 'last times,' [p. 96] ... the Lord would repair the 'breaches and ruines of the Christian Church,' and 'build a more excellent and glorious Temple' than former generations had seen" [p. 96]. Drinnon points out that in his sermon "Gillespie avoided projecting dates for the future apocalyptic events" and that just because he "may have looked forward to the glorification of the Church after the defeat of Antichrist, we should be careful [to] not confuse this belief with the millennial dreams of English puritans in the 1640s."[20] While the optimist camp generally avoided chronology and date setting that was a feature of Napier's work, Gillespie does

---

St Andrews. Napier combined his mathematical skills with his knowledge of Ramism to produce a series of propositions, or conjectures, based on the numbers and symbols he encountered in the Scriptures. Using these propositions, he developed a detailed chronological framework through which he attempted to demonstrate exactly when and how many of the prophecies of Revelation had been fulfilled over the course of history." Robert Rollock and others objected to Napier's date conjecturing. No other commentator would make such "extensive use of chronological calculations" until James Durham. As to the minor use of date calculation by Gillespie, his "calculations for 1260 days and the 42 months prove to be an anomaly within Scottish eschatological works published during the reign of Charles I." Drinnon, pp. 30–31, 32, 99, 142.

19. Drinnon, p. 197.

20. Drinnon, p. 91.

borrow from that camp's founder a little bit of this, "[t]o give his sermon a sense of apocalyptic urgency," modifying "Napier's chronological calculations for the 42 months described in Rev. 11:3 and 12:6, along with his positioning of the 1260 days noted in Rev. 13:5" and positing "that the 'likelier time' for the 1260 years fell between 383 and 1643 … to demonstrate that the 'year of Israels Jubilee, and the day of vengeance upon Antichrist' was not 'farre off'" [p. 122–123].[21] As far as Gillespie's goal, Drinnon writes,

> Through apocalyptic imagery, Gillespie tried to prove the eschatological importance of reforming the Church of England along Presbyterian lines. The Lord had already "put Antichrist from his utterworks in Scotland" [p. 121], Gillespie noted, and now he had "come to put him from his innerworks in England." He then proclaimed that Christ was presently working to "make a new face of a Church" in the kingdom, and emphasised that this new "house of God" should be built upon the pattern of "Presbyteriall Government" [p. 126].[22]

On this last point, Drinnon states emphatically that in his sermon "Gillespie most certainly did not suggest that the Lord was building a 'new Temple in England' which would last a millennium…." "Thus, it is misleading to claim that millenarian ecclesiology lay behind the Covenanter's desire to see the establishment of a Britannic, or international Protestant church framed upon Presbyterian principles."[23] Therefore, while it is clear Scottish apocalyptic thought of the optimistic variety is displayed in Gillespie's preaching in this instance, which makes it striking and unusual, and while it is a part of the history and adds to what we know of the Westminster Assembly and its work, this sermon is not some "key to understanding some of the most important events of mid-seventeenth century history,"[24] as pertaining to English millenarianism of that time. While the sermon is certainly historically important, assigning it such a "key" place is a bit overinflating its importance and to a wrong end.

George Gillespie's Sermon before the House of Commons did not have his desired effect of hastening the settling of the English church upon a Presbyterian form. Indeed, things had not been going well in the Westminster Assembly for all the success of the Presbyterian majority. Problems to come were clearly portended in late December when the Independents bypassed the assembly and took their appeal for independent churches free of a national

---

21. Drinnon, pp. 90–91.

22. Drinnon, p. 92.

23. Drinnon, p. 92, n114. Gillespie clearly rejected "chiliastic notion[s]" in his sermon. What Gillespie was saying "had 'no affinity with the opinion of an earthly or temporall kingdome of Christ.' Nor did he believe, upon the return of Christ, the Jews would rebuild Jerusalem and obtain 'dominion above all other Nations' before Judgement Day." Ibid., pp. 91–92.

24. Gribben, p. 127.

establishment to the parliament and public with the publication of their *Apologetical Narration*.[25] While there were hopes of bringing the Independents along in agreeing to a whole unfractured reformed church in England, which hope Gillespie expressed on a number of occasions, the evidence was clear that the dissenting brethren would play the obstructionists after the debates of January 23, 1644. Gillespie had proposed rules on ordination and censuring of clergy and the Erastian John Selden deftly used his speeches to roil the assembly and raise alarm amongst the Independents, in an effort to impede the efforts of the presbyterian majority. The day's end marked the end of the "Presbyterian-Independent alliance."[26] Weeks of debates that followed cemented the divide.[27] A committee of accommodation between the Scots Commissioners, English Presbyterians, and Independents was appointed on March 8, 1644, but on April 10, after Gillespie's sermon but before it was in print, the Independents were threatening a minority report if the assembly reported votes in favor of presbyteries to the Parliament, and another committee for accommodation was appointed. The papers of these failed attempts to bring the Independents along in establishing a unified national English church are contained in *The Reasons Presented by the Dissenting Brethren Against Certain Propositions Concerning Presbyteriall Government* (1648).[28] The Independents of the Westminster Assembly were effectively playing the role of spoiler. Likewise, while John Selden ceased actively debating in the assembly and possibly even attending, he simply took his advocacy over to the House of Commons of which he was a member and joined the friendlier Erastian majority there in advancing that party's views and agendas. But damage was done. Debates stretched into March to the time of Gillespie's sermon, in which "Selden and his allies had scored some significant tactical successes, and it was clear the Assembly would not produce a swift and near-unanimous Presbyterian-inspired settlement, as was initially hoped by the latter."[29]

---

25. The Stationers record the publication for December 30, 1643, but it likely had come out a few days before that because Thomas Edwards writes that he was sure it was available in late December. See Ethan H. Shagan, "Rethinking Moderation in the English Revolution: The Case of An Apologeticall Narration," in *The Nature of the English Revolution Revisited: Essays in Honour of John Morrill*, ed. Stephen Taylor, Grant Tapsell (The Boydell Press, 2013), pp. 36-37. See *A transcript of the registers of the Worshipful Company of Stationers from 1640–1708*, ed. G. E. Briscoe Eyre, volume 1 (Privately printed, 1913-14), p. 92.

26. Haivry, *John Selden*, p. 412.

27. See the description of these sessions of the assembly in Haivry, *John Selden*, pp. 412–419.

28. *Minutes*, 2.593, 600, 617, 636, 678, 3.709. The papers were reissued with a new title four years later as *The Grand Debate* (1652). See *The Grand Debate* (Naphtali Press, 2014).

29. Haivry, *John Selden*, p. 418, 419.

Bibliography for George Gillespie's
House of Commons Sermons

Those Westminster divines who did not live in London clearly missed their personal libraries. John Lightfoot raised this early in their proceedings in August 1643, and in October the divines made a request for remedy to the House of Commons to be supplied with books needed for their debates.

> Munday. Aug. 31 [sic 21]. "The first Committee reported the aspersions upon the 3 first Articles [of the 39 Articles] & this forenoone was taken up in concluding which way to take about aspersions, whether to name the errors in the Authors owne words & under their name, which thing I vehemently opposed for this would be a worke long & tedious, & we should be sure to misse of many Authors that were enemies to these truths of our Articles, because of the distance of us all from our libraries, and the exunpectednesse [unexpectedness] of this taske layd upon us; & so should we be censured either of incogetency or connivence: therefore I desired that we might onely name erronious opinions, but let names & their owne words alone, for opinions I knew we could not misse, but Authors we should be sure to misse of. But it was carried the other waie & voted that every Committee should bring in aspersions under the aspersers name & wordes & the bookes also quoted for the thing, for the Assemblies ocular & full satisfaction."

> [Minutes, Oct. 17] 76 Sess. 17th 1643: Tuesday Morning. "Mr Ley: A motion to disperse the bookes of a church government to the severall members of the Assembly.

> Mr Goodwin: Many ministers severed from their bookes; that ther may be a provision of all those bookes in some publique place.

> Mr Seaman: A request to have liberty to have some designed together out of those libraryes that are sequestered [in order to have] bookes for this purpose.

> Mr White: I will move the house in this."[30]

The Commons granted authority to obtain volumes from the sequestered libraries, and evidence survives indicating the divines took advantage of

---

30. Chad B. Van Dixhoorn, "Reforming the Reformation: Theological Debate at the Westminster Assembly 1643–1652," Ph.D. dissertation, University of Cambridge, 2004; Lightfoot's first journal, August 21, 1643, vol. 2, p. 37; Minutes, October 17, 1643, vol. 3, pp. 183–184; *Minutes* (Oxford, 2012), 2.206.

this grant, in a manuscript list of books taken out of Archbishop Laud's personal library.[31] However, this hardly was sufficient to meet the need of a full research library. Happily, there was a remarkable library on the premises. As may be verified by the surviving *Benefactors' book*, many of the works cited in the Scottish Commissioners' fast sermons could have been found in the Westminster Abbey Library. Other works not in the *Benefactors' book* but presently in the library, may have come into the library before 1623. There was also a significant library at Sion College, and while it likely was not available and open to their use, there was a large collection of books at the Lambeth Palace Library. Various assemblymen also had extensive private collections. Two known libraries were those of Lazarus Seaman and William Greenhill. See the Bibliography in *Scots Sermons* (p. 539) for works cited in their sermons which Gillespie and the other Scottish Commissioners might have been able to find in the Abbey Library, or possibly in other libraries to which they had access at the time. Those works cited by Gillespie in his House of Commons, which are located in various collections of the time, are below. See a similar listing prefacing the House of Lords sermon.

Some of George Gillespie's Potential Sources for Books[32]
Laud: Collection of 98 books taken from Laud's study by the assembly.[33]
MS 46: Westminster Abbey Library Benefactors' Book.
Abbey Library: Westminster Abbey Library, present in collection.
Sion: Sion College Library 1650 Catalogue:
Lambeth: Lambeth Palace Library, MS Catalogue.
LS: Lazarus Seaman Library.
WG: William Greenhill Library.

---

31. For more detail on the resources available to the Westminster assembly, see Chris Coldwell, "Westminster Abbey Library: and other theological resources of the Assembly of Divines 1643–1652," *The Confessional Presbyterian* 6 (2010): 263–282. See also with some revision in *The Grand Debate* (Dallas, Texas: Naphtali Press, 2014), Appendix: Westminster Abbey Library: and other theological resources of the Assembly of Divines 1643–1652, pp. 379–403; and with yet further revision and correction in the Scottish Reformation Society's *Historical Journal* 10 (2020): 27–50.]

32. The following bibliography has been updated with collations against the auction lists for the libraries of Seaman and Greenhill from that presented in *Scots Sermons*.

33. Laud: see *The Grand Debate*, pp. 382–388. MS 46: see Benefactors' book, Westminster Abbey Library MS 46. Abbey Library: See the Card catalogue. Sion: See John Spencer, *Catalogus universalis libroum omnium in bibliotheca Collegii Sionii apud Londinenses* (Londini: Ex officina typographica Rob. Leybourni, 1650). Lambeth: see Cambridge University Library, MS Oo.7.51. LS: See *Catalogus Variorum & Insignium Librorum Instructissimæ Bibliothecæ … Lazari Seaman* (London: Ed Brewster & Guil. Cooper, 1676). WG: See *Zacharias Bourne, Catalogus variorum & insignium liborum selectissimæ bibliothecæ reverendi viri Gulielmi Greenhill … Per Zachariam Bourne. Catalogi gratis distribuentur ad insigne Unicornu in vico dicto Breadstreat* (London: Tho. Hodgkins, [1678]).

Bibliography for the Sermon Preached Before
The House of Commons

Ambrose. Epiſtola XVIII. *PL* 16; *NPNF2* v. 10. [**MS 46**: *Opera*, 2v.a9. **Sion**: *Opera* (Paris: 1614; Basil: 1538), *Epiſtolæ cam alias* Med. 1596 (cf. Mediolani, 1490), p. 7. **Lambeth**: *Opera* (1603; 1506), 1r, 27r. **LS**: *Opera* (1614), p. 2, #4.]

Andrews, Lancelot. *XCVI Sermons*. Printed by Richard Badger, 1635. [**Abbey Library**: 4th edition (1641), X.4.48, acquisition date unknown. **Sion**: (1631), p. 8. **Lambeth**: (1629), 4v.]

Anonymous. *Eruditi Commentarii in Evangelium Matthæi, Incerto Auĉtore* [*Opus Imperfeĉtum*]. Chrysoſtom, *PG* 56. English: *Incomplete Commentary on Matthew (Opus imperfeĉtum)*. Translated by James A. Kellerman. 2 vols. IVP, 2010. [**MS 46**: Chrysoſtom, *Opera*, 2r.a21; *Chrysoſtomi Florus*, Grk. & Lat., 6r.a34; Grk., 6v.b5. **Sion**: *Opera* (Paris: 1621; Basil: 1525; Etonæ: 1613), *Homiliæ Græce* MS, *Homil. in Mattheum* (n.d.), p. 38–39. **Lambeth**: Chrysoſtom, *Opera* (Venice: 1548–49; Paris: 1536; Basil: 1539; 1558), iv, 27r, 42r. **LS**: Chrysoſtom, *Opera* (1636), p. 1, #1.]

Anselm. *Orationes*. *PL* 158. [**MS 46**: *Opera*, 4r.a10. **Sion**: *Opera* (1612), p. 10. **Lambeth**: *Opera*, multiple eds., 1r, 27r, 42r.]

Arias Montanus (Benito Arias Montano). [*Antwerp Polyglot Bible*] *Biblia Sacra Hebraice, Chaldaice, Græce, & Latine: Philippi II. Reg. Cathol. pietate, et ſtudio ad Sacrosanĉtæ Ecclesiæ usum Chriſtoph. Plantinus excud. Antuerpiæ. Excud.* Antuerpiæ: Chriſtoph. Plantinus, 1569–1572. [**MS 46**: *Biblia ... Interlinearis. Plantin.: 1584*, 2r.a3. **Sion**: p. 20. Lambeth: 125r.]

______. *Libanus*. Cf. *Antiquitatum Iudaicarum libri IX., in quîs, præter Iudeæ, Hierosolymorum, & Templi Salomonis accuratam delineationem, præcipui sacri ac profani gentis ritus describuntur....* Apud F. Raphelengium: Lugduni Batavorum, 1593. This work is also in the polyglot. [**MS 46**: *Antiquitat. Judaicis*, 6r.a29; Chr. Curlitors, Oct. 20, 1623, 20r.a4. **Lambeth**: *Antiq. Judaic.*, 31r. **WG**: *Antiquitatibus Judaicis* (1593), p. 9, #1. **LS**: *Antiquitatibus Judaicarum* (1593), p. 32, #5.]

Arnobius of Sicca. *Adversus Gentes* (Againſt the Nations). *PL* 5; *ANF* 6. [**MS 46**: *contra Gentes*, 2v.b27, 14r.a11. **Sion**: *contra Gentes*, n.d., p. 12. **Lambeth**: (1560 and 1582), 42r. **LS**: *Diſputationum adversus Gentes* (1631) p. 96, #429. *Adversus Gentes* (1560; 1582) p. 99, #539, 540.]

Auguſtine. *Ad Inquisitiones Januarii*. Cf. *PL* 33; *NPNF1* v. 1 [**Abbey Library**: *Omnia opera D. Aurelii Auguſtini*, 10 vols. in 9 (Basil: 1543) inscription, "Omptus Capero[?] 27 Maie 1567," G.1.21; *Omnium operum D. Aurelii Auguſtini*, 10 vols. in 5 (Paris: 1555), G.3.33. Acquisition dates unknown. **Sion**: *Opera* (Basil: 1543; Paris: 1637), p. 14. **Lambeth**: *Opera* (1556; 1563), 1r, 42r; *Sermons* (Antwerp: 1576–77), 1r. **LS**: *Opera* (1569), p. 2, #1.]

______. *Confessions*. Cf. *PL* 32; *NPNF1* v. 1. [**MS 46**: *Auguſtini Confessio*, 15v.a6. **Lambeth**: 153r. Also, see entry for *Ad Inquisitiones Januarii*.]

Auguſtine (pseudo). *Meditationes*. See "Appendix: Meditationum Liber Unus," *PL* 40. [**Sion**: *Meditationes varie* MS 4°, p. 14. **Lambeth**: in MS, 74v. **LS**: *Divi Aurelii Au-*

gustini … Meditationes, Soliloquia et Manuale. Meditationes B. Anselmi cum tractatu de humani generis redemptione, D. Bernardi, Idiotæ (1631), #110, p. 133. See also above for *Ad Inquisitiones Januarii.*]

Barclay, William. *De Regno et regali potestate.* Paris, 1600. [**ABBEY LIBRARY:** Gal.H.3.23, acquisition date unknown. **LAMBETH:** (1610 *sic* 1600?), 33v.]

Beza, Theodore. *Jesu Christi Domini Nostri Novum Testamentum… Euisdem Theod. Bezæ Annotationes.* Cambridge: Rogeri Danielis, [1642]. [**MS 46:** *Theod: Bezæ Testamentum Novum cum. Annotat: Fol:* (no date), 4v.a8. **ABBEY LIBRARY:** Vignon (1598), E.5.28, acquisition date unknown. Sion: (1598; 1642), p. 2. **LAMBETH:** multiple eds., 6(2)r; 126r. **WG:** (1638), p. 1, #7. **LS:** *Testamentum Novum* (1589), p. 11, #30.]

Bilson, Thomas. *The True Difference between Christian Subjection and un-Christian Rebellion.* 1585; 2ND ed., 1586. There is an extract in *A Discourse upon Questions in debate between the King and Parliament With certaine observations collected out of a treatise called, The diffrence between Christian subjection, and unchristian rebellion* (1643).[1] [**MS 46:** *of Christian subjection,* 15r.b5. **SION:** (1625), p. 22. **LAMBETH:** *True Difference* (1585), 17r. **LS:** *True Difference between Christian Subjection and un-Christian Rebellion* (1585), p. 54, #93.]

Brightman, Thomas. *A revelation of the Apocalyps, that is, the Apocalyps of S. Iohn illustrated with an analysis & scolions.* Amsterdam: Printed by Iudocus Hondius & Hendrick Laurenss, 1611; repr. Amsterdam: Printed by Thomas Stafford, 1644. [**MS 46:** *Brightman: in Apocalypsim,* IIr.a32. Sion: (1609), p. 25. Lambeth: (1609), and English (1611), 28v. **LS:** *in Apocalypsim* (1618), p. 110 (2ND pagination), #243.]

Brown, K. M., et al. *The Records of the Parliaments of Scotland to 1707.* St. Andrews, 2007–2022. Date accessed: 22 March 2022. http://www.rps.ac.uk/trans/1644/6/247.

Cappel, Louis. *Historia apostolica illustrata, ex Actis apostolorum et epistolis Paulinis … in compendium contracta … Una cum veræ epistolarum Paulinarum … seriei historica demonstratione. His additum est historiæ Judaice, ab Asamonæorum, sive Machabæorum tempore, ad Hierosolymorum & templi pe Titum Vespasianum ultimum excidium, breve ex Josepho compendium … Omnia studio & opera Lud. Cappelli….* Genevæ: Sumptibus Ioan. de Tournes & Iac. de la Pierre., [1634]. [**WG:** p. 20, #43.]

Casaubon, Isaac. *Novi Testamenti…* [Notes by Casaubon]. London: Ioannem Billium. 1622. [**MS 46:** IIr.b1. **LAMBETH:** 126r.]

Caspensis, Ludovicus. *Cursus theologicus, amplectens præcipuas materias, quæ in scholis tradi, & legi solent, secundùm ordinem D. Thomæ.* Lugduni: Boissat & Anisson, 1641, 1643. [Not found.]

Chaldee Paraphrase. See Arias Montanus, [*Antwerp Polyglot Bible*] *Biblia Sacra Hebraice, Chaldaice, Græce, & Latine.* [**MS 46:** *Biblia … Interlinearis. Plantin.: 1584,* 2r.a3. **SION:** p. 20. Lambeth: 125r.]

Dickson, David. *Sermons on Jeremiah's Lamentations.* NPSE, volume III. Naphtali Press and Reformation Heritage Books, 2020.

Du Plessis-Mornay (Philippe de Mornay). *Le Mystére d'Iniquité, c'est à dire, l'histoire de la Papauté … Ou sont … defendus les droicts des Empereurs, Rois & Princes Chrestiens, contre les assertions des Cardinaux Bellarmin & Baronius.* Saumur:

---

1. In *Scots Sermons* this was misdated as published in 1641.

T. Portau, 1611. See also, Philippe de Mornay, *The Mysterie of Iniquitie: that is to say, The historie of the papacie … Englished by Samson Lennard.* London: Printed by Adam Islip, 1612. [Sion: (1611), p. 99. Lambeth: (1611), Engl., (1612), 5v. LS: Latin (1601), p. 105, #92.]

Funck, Johann. *Chronologia.* Witebergæ: Excudebat Johannes Schwertel, 1570. [MS 46: *Funccij Chronologiæ,* 6v.b29. Sion: Funccius (1601), p. 59. Lambeth: (1552; 1578), 130r.]

Gellius, Aulus. *Noctes Atticæ (Attic Nights).* See, *The Attic nights of Aulus Gellius, with an English translation by John C. Rolfe.* London, W. Heinemann; New York: Putnam's Sons, 1927–1928. [MS 46: *Aulus Gellius,* 11r.a31, 15v.a14. Sion: *Opera* (1581), p. 14. Lambeth: 118v]

Gillespie, George. *Wholesome Severity.* See *Anonymous Writings of George Gillespie.* Dallas, Texas: Naphtali Press, 2008.

______. *A Dispute Against the English Popish Ceremonies.* Edited by Christopher Coldwell. Dallas, Texas: Naphtali Press, 1993; second critical edition, 2013.

______. *The Works of Mr. George Gillespie.* The Presbyterian's Armory, vols. 1–2. Edited by W. M. Hetherington. Edinburgh: Ogle and Oliver and Boyd, 1846.

Gregory (the Great). *Homiliæ XL in Ezechielem.* See *PL* 76. [MS 46: *Opera,* 2v.a14. Sion: *In Ezechielem,* MS, p. 65. Lambeth: *Opera,* multiple eds., 2v. WG: *Opera* (1628), p. 1, #3.]

______. *Moralia in Job.* See *PL* 75. [Ibid.]

Gregory Nazianzens. *Orationes.* See "Opera omnia," *Collectio selecta SS. ecclesiæ patrum,* vol. 50. Paris: Apud Parent-Desbarres, 1835–1840. *Orationes,* 25–45. 1835. [MS 46: *Opera,* 2r.b10. Sion: *Opera.* n.d., p. 101. Lambeth: *Opera,* multiple eds., 3r, 43v.]

Grotius, Hugo. *De iure belli ac pacis libri tres. Editio nova.* Amsterdami: Apud Ioh. & Cornelium Blæu., 1642. [Sion: (1631), p. 68. Lambeth: 101v. Laud: *Grand Debate,* p. 382. WG: (1626), p. 17, #18. LS: (1646), p. 83, #336.[2]]

Hall, Joseph. *Contemplations vpon the Histoire of the Old Testament. The seventh volume.* London: J. Haviland, 1623. [Sion: *Works* (1634), p. 67; *Catalogus Interpretum S. S. Scripturæ,* p. 2, *Contemplations.*]

Innocentius. Epistle 2 *ad Victricium episcopum Rothomagensem.* Cited from Philippe de Mornay, *Le Mystére d'Iniquité.* See *PL* 20.

Irenæus. *Against Heresies.* Cf. *ANF* 1. [Sion: *Opera* (Paris: 1570; Col.: 1625), Contra Hæreses (Bas.: 1571), p. 78. Lambeth: *Opera,* multiple eds., 2v.]

James I. The Book of Sports. *The Kings Majesties declaration to his subjects, concerning lawfull sports to be used.* London: Printed by Bonham Norton, and John Bill, deputie printers for the Kings most excellent Majestie, M.D.C.XVIII. [1618]. See also, Charles I, *The Kings Majesties,* etc. London: By Robert Barker, printer to the Kings most excellent Majestie and by the assignes of John Bill, M.DC.XXXIII [1633].

Jerome. *In Epitaphio Fabiola.* Cf. *PL* 22. "Letters and Select Works." *NPNF2* v. 6. [MS 46: *Opera,* 2v.a10. Sion: *Opera* (1546, 1456, 1533), p. 70. Lambeth: *Opera* (1553; 1579), 2v.]

---

2. This was acquired by Seaman after the preaching of Gillespie's sermon. It is noted for interest since Greenhill owned a copy of an earlier edition. Note, since there are no acquisition dates for either Seaman or Greenhill, it cannot be certain that even earlier dated volumes where in their possession at the time Gillespie was preparing his sermon.

_______. *In Ezechielem*. Cf. *PL* 25. [Ibid.]

Jerusalem Targum. Cf. Daniel Bomberg, *Biblia Hebraica*. Venice: 1517; Johann Buxtorf, *Biblia Sacra Hebraica*. Basilæ: 1618; 1619; 1620. [**ABBEY LIBRARY**: Bomberg (1517), with an owner signature of John Pimme, but not dated or in the Benefactors' Book. A.6.10. **SION**: Buxtorf (1620), p. 20; Bomberg (1121 {*sic* 1521}), p. 21. Lambeth: *Biblia Hebraica*, Venet., 2 vols., 126v.]

Josephus. Cf. *The Complete Works of Flavius Josephus*. Translated by William Whiston. Chicago: Thompson & Thomas, 1901. [**MS 46**: *Opera*, 2r.a22; anr. ed., 3v.b5; anr. ed., 9r.a26. **SION**: *Opera* (Geneva, 1611; MS), p. 77. **LAMBETH**: *Opera*, 131r.]

Lange, John Peter. *A Commentary on the Holy Scriptures …*, translated by Philip Schaff. Volume IV of the New Testament: Containing the Acts of the Apostles. New York: Charles Scribner, & Co., 1867.

Lapide, Cornelius à. *Commentaria in qvatvor Prophetas Maiores*. Antverpiæ: apud Martinum Nutium & Fratres, 1622. Also, *Commentaria in Sacram Scripturam*, 10 vols. Antwerp, 1681; Neapoli: I. Nagar, 1854–1859. [**MS 46**: Julius Cralor, Oct. 20, 1623, *in Prophetas Majoros*, 18r.a10. **SION**: *in 4 Prophetas Majores* (1625), p. 81. **LAMBETH**: *in 4 Prophetas maiores* (1622), 13v. **WG**: *Opera* (Paris), p. 3, #1. **LS**: Seaman owned a later edition of the Old Testament and New Testament commentaries of à Lapide, which would not have been available to Gillespie. *Commentaria in Vetus et Novum Testamentum* (Antverpiæ: Nutium, 1648), p. 11, #1.]

Lavater, Ludwig. *Ezras. Liber primus Ezræ, homiliis xxxviii. Ludovici Lauateri Tigurinæ ecclesiæ ministri opera & labore expositus: Accessit index rerum & verborum, locorum item S. Scripturæ*. Tiguri: [1586]. [**ABBEY LIBRARY**: *Ezras* (Tiguri: 1586), Gal.G.5.30(2). Signed, difficult hand, acquisition date unknown. **LAMBETH**: (1586), 30v.]

L'Empereur, Constantine. *Masekhet Midot me-Talmud Bavli: hoc est Talmudis Babylonici codex Middoth, sive de mensuris templi, unà cum versione Latina*. Lugduni Batavorum [Leiden]: Bonaventuræ & Abrahami Elzevir, 1630. [**LAMBETH**: 127r.]

Leslie, Henry (Bishop of Down). *A Treatise of the Authority of the Church*. Printed by the Society of Stationers, 1637; reissued 1639. [Not found.]

Livy. *History of Rome*. Cf. *Livy*. Cf. *The History of Rome*. Everyman's Library. Edited by Ernest Rhys. London: J. M. Dent & Sons, 1921. [**MS 46**: *Titi Liviis, Historia Romæ*, 2v.b25; anr. ed., 3r.a3; Dr. Harry King, *Opera græce*, 49r, line 2; English trans. by Holland, Richard Juston, July 4, 1624, 63r.a1. **SION**: *Historia* (1568; vol. 3: 1470), p. 87. **LAMBETH**: 131r; 149v.]

Meyer, Heinrich August Wilhelm, *Critical and Exegetical Handbook to the Acts of the Apostles*, trans. Paton J. Gloag, rev. William P. Dickson. New York: Funk & Wagnalls, 1883.

Pareus, David. *Ad Romanos S. Pauli apostoli epistolam commentarius*. Frankfurt, Rhodes, 1608. Cf. *Operum theologicorum partes quatuor*. Edited by Philipp Pareus. 3 vols. Frankfurt: Jonas Rose, 1647. [**MS 46**: Richard Burrel, Nov. 12, 1623, *Ad Romanos* (1620), 47r.a9. **SION**: *Opera Theologica comment*. 2 vols. (Geneva: 1616), p. 107. Though there is no Romans commentary listed in the section *Catalogus Interpretum S. S. Scripturæ*, this entry is probably referencing a collection of various commentaries from different dates. There is a 1617 edition of the Romans volume published in Geneva by Paul Marceau. **LAMBETH**: *Opera* (1642), 5v; *ad Romanos* (1618), 31v.]

LS: David. Parei, *Opera omnia Theologica*, 3 vols (1628). The 1628 edition is said to be two volumes. Either Seaman's set was 2 volumes in 3 or it includes a volume from later editions from 1642 through 1650.]

Plato. *Apology of Socrates*. Cf. D. F. Nevill, *The Apology of Socrates*. London: F.E. Robinson & Co, 1901. [MS 46: *Opera*, 2v.a31. Sion: *Opera* (Ven.: 1513; Franc.: 1602), p. 115. Lambeth: Opera (1556; 1578), iiiv.]

Polanus, Amandus. *In librum Prophetiarum Ezechielis commentarii*. Basileæ: Conradus Waldkirchius, 1608. [MS 46: Chr. Curlitors, Oct. 20, 1623, 20v.813. Lambeth: (1619), 31v. WG: (1610), p. 11, #9.]

Ribera, Francisco de. *De templo et de ijs quæ ad templum pertinent, libri qvinqve*. Antverpiæ: Apud Petrum & Ioannem Belleros, 1623. [MS 46: Ribera in Apocalyps., 10r.a19. Cf. Abbey Library: *Francisci Riberæ in sacram beati Joannia Apocalypsin commentarii. His adjuncti sunt, quinque libri de Templo, & de iis quæ ad Templum pertinent* (Antverpiæ: 1603), M.2.20. Lambeth: *Apocalypsin*, 32r, 60r.]

Rivet, Andrew. *Andreæ Riveti Pictavi, S.S. Theol. Doctoris, et Sacrarum Literarum in Academia Batavorum Professoris, Prælectiones in cap. xx. Exodi: In quibus ita explicatur Decalogus, ut casus conscientiæ, quos vocant, ex eo suborientes, ac pleraque controversiæ magni momeni, quæ circa legem moralem solent agitari, fusè & accuratè discutiantur*. Lugduni Batavorum: Apud Franciscum Hegerum, 1632; anr. ed. 1637. [Not found.]

Robinson, Henry. *Liberty of Conscience*. London, 1643/44.

Rogers, John. *The Doctrine of Faith. …* Printed by E. G[riffin] for Henry Ouerton, and Samuell Endirby, 1640. [Not found.]

Rolfe, John Carew. *Suetonius*. London: W. Heinemann, 1920.

Sànchez, Gaspar. *Gasparis Sanctii Centumputeolani, e Societate Iesu Theologi, in Collegio Complutensi sacrarum literarum interpretis, In Ezechielem & Danielem Prophetas commentarij cum paraphrasi*. Lugduni: Sumptibus Horatij Cardon, [1619]. [MS 46: Julius Cralor, Oct. 20, 1623, *in Ezechielem*, 18v.b10. Sion: p. 128. Lambeth: (1619), 13r. WG: (1619), p. 4, #21.]

Solemn League and Covenant. Cf. *The Confession of Faith, the Larger and Shorter Catechism … Covenants, National and Solemn League*. Edinburgh: Johnstone and Hunter, 1855; repr. Free Presbyterian Publications, 1990.

Spalding, John. *The History of the Troubles and Memorable Transactions in Scotland from 1624 to 1645*. Aberdeen: George King, 1829.

Suarez, Francisco. *Tractatus de legibus, ac Deo legislatore in decem libros distributus*. Conimbricæ: 1612. Also, *Opera Omnia*. Paris, 1860. [Abbey Library: *Tractatus de legibus* (1619); however the inscription would seem to put the acquisition date after 1677 (George Monck signed, and then Thomas Sandys for 1677). Lambeth: 1613, 91v. WG: *Opera* (1630), p. 6, #9.]

Tostado, Alonso. Commentary on 1 Kings. In *Alphonsi Tostati Hispani episcopi Abulensis, Opera omnia, quotquot in Scripturæ Sacræ expositionem et alia, adhuc extare inuenta sunt*. 28 vols. Venetiis: apud Io. Baptistam, et Io. Bernardum Sessam, 1596. Vols. 11–12. [MS 46: *Opera*, 3v.a16. Sion: *Opera* (1613), p. 143; *Catalogus Interpretum S. S. Scripturæ*, p. 7. Lambeth: *Opera* (1613), 15r. WG: *Opera* (1613), p. 3, #2.]

Ussher, James. *The Soveraignes Power, and the Subjects Duty*. Oxford: 1644.

Vermigli, Peter Martyr. *Most learned and fruitfull commentaries of D. Peter Martir Ver-*

milius Florentine, Professor of divinitie in the Schole of Tigure, vpon the Epistle of S. Paul to the Romanes. London: By Iohn Daye, 1568. [**ABBEY LIBRARY:** *In epistolam S. Pauli Apostoli ad Romanos* (1570), acquisition date unknown, S.4.44. **SION:** *In Romanos* (1613), p. 94. **LAMBETH:** *ad Romanos* (1570) 7r. **WG:** *ad Romanos* (1568), p. 3, #4. LS: In Latin in *Opera Omnia*, 7 vols (1562). The date must represent one of the dates of the volumes. *In epistolam S. Pauli Apostoli ad Romanos* was first published in 1558 (Basileæ: apud Petrum Pernam). By *Opera Omnia* must be meant a collection of volumes of various dates making up the whole works.]

Villalpando, Juan Bautista. *In Ezechielem explanationes, et apparatus urbis, ac templi Hierosolymitani, commentariis et imaginibus illustratus.* 3 vols. Romæ, 1596–1604. [**MS 46:** *Jo: Bapt: Villalpandi Apparat: in Ezechielem, 3 vol: Fol: Romæ. 1604,* 3r.b9–10. **SION:** (1606), p. 148. **LAMBETH:** 15v. **WG:** p. 3, #5.]

Walæus, Antonius. Concerning the opinion of the Millenialists. Cf. *De Opinione Chiliastærum.* In *Opera omnia.* Lvgdvni Batavorvm: Ex officina Francisci Hackii, 1643. [Not found.]

Wolf, Johann. *Lectionum Memorabilium et Reconditarum Centenarii XVI.* 2 vols. Lauingæ: Leonhardus Rheinmichel, 1600; vol. 3 Index, 1608. [Sion: (1600), p. 152. **LAMBETH:** 1600, 135r.]

THE PREACHING OF THE SCOTTISH COMMISSIONERS TO THE WESTMINSTER ASSEMBLY

IT HAS BEEN pointed out that there are two inherent dangers for the person who seeks to write on the subject of preaching. On the one hand, such an individual runs the risk of being perceived as an expert on the subject by his readers. But, on the other hand, he may actually be tempted to believe that he really is an expert and that the opportunity to write on the subject is proof positive of that fact. While many readers who know me well may suggest that I have no reason to fear the first danger (!), I feel compelled, nonetheless, to assure all who read this introduction, at the very beginning of it, that I most emphatically do not consider myself to be an expert on the subject of preaching. I, like most preachers, am all too aware of my own inadequacies as a preacher, all of which make me quite unwilling to write anything that could give the slightest impression that I have this "art of prophesying"—to borrow the familiar words of William Perkins—all figured out.[1]

My purpose in writing this introduction, therefore, is not to show that I am an expert on the subject of preaching but to do what I can to make reading the following sermons more enjoyable and beneficial by sharing some of what I have learned about these men as preachers in one of the most important periods in the history of the church. In a very real sense, I consider myself to be, as the saying goes, one beggar showing other beggars where I have found bread. My hope is that in reading the sermons in this volume and in studying seventeenth-century preaching more generally, the church in the twenty-first century might be strengthened by the sustenance provided by the examples of these men and the times in which they lived.

That being said, I do not think that it is overstating the matter to say that the Scottish Commissioners to the Westminster Assembly are among the best preachers the church has ever produced. These men knew their Bibles extensively—long before the advent of computers and search engines! They possessed a deep wisdom and a profound insight that came from spending long hours in their studies and closets. Even reading their sermons for the third and fourth times I still find myself challenged, encouraged, motivated, humbled, and deeply impressed with the breadth and depth of their

---

1. This was the title of Perkins' massively important sixteenth-century treatise on preaching. It can be found in *The Workes of the Famous and Worthie Minister of Christ, in the Universitie of Cambridge, Mr. William Perkins*, 3 vols. (Cambridge, 1616–18), 2.644–73, or, in the more recent edition, *The Art of Prophesying* (Edinburgh: Banner of Truth, 1996).

knowledge, the boldness of their application, the warmth of their piety, and the strength of their faith. There is no doubt that these men were leading lights in the church of their day.

But to be leading lights in their day means even more than it would mean today, because their day is widely known for producing great preachers and great preaching. Thus, Robert Gilmour, in his early twentieth-century biography of Samuel Rutherford, argues that the "age of the Covenant" in Scotland—i.e., that period running roughly from the signing of the National Covenant in 1638 to the Toleration Act in 1689—is "pre-eminently an age of great preachers."[2] Hughes Old, in his important work on the history of the preaching and reading of Scripture, corroborates Gilmour's claims by distinguishing the seventeenth century above all others as that which "produced profound preaching" and "engendered a popular revival of preaching, especially of biblical preaching."[3] And historian Robert Wodrow refers to at least one of the Scottish Commissioners, Samuel Rutherford, as "one of the most moving and affectionate preachers in his time, or perhaps in any age of the church."[4] It is no great exaggeration, therefore, to say that these fast sermons really are among the best examples of great preaching that the church has to offer, and, for this reason, there is much in them that we can learn from today.

Before moving on, however, let me be quick to say that in referring to these men as great preachers and their sermons as some of the best examples of great preaching that we have, I am in no way suggesting that these men did everything right; nor am I advocating that we look to them or to the seventeenth century as a whole for the definitive example of what our preaching ought to look like. I realize that the seventeenth century is not the twenty-first century. Each period has its own peculiar situations and urgencies, to be sure. But what I am advocating is that we look to these men and to the seventeenth century as a whole as *one* example (among many) to learn from—both in what they did right and in what they did not do right—so that, by standing on their shoulders, we might gain a better vantage point to discern how it is that we should move forward in our own day.

And while it is true that the seventeenth century is not the twenty-first century, this should not be taken to imply that there is no similarity at all

---

2. Robert Gilmour, *Samuel Rutherford: A Study Biographical and Somewhat Critical, in the History of the Scottish Covenant* (Edinburgh and London: Oliphant Anderson & Ferrier, 1904), p. 40.

3. Hughes Oliphant Old, *The Reading and Preaching of the Scriptures in the Worship of the Christian Church*, vol. 4, The Age of the Reformation (Grand Rapids, Mich.: Eerdmans, 2002), p. 251.

4. Robert Wodrow, *Analecta: or, Materials for a History of Remarkable Providences; Mostly Relating to Scotch Ministers and Christians*, 1.205. Not only do accounts of Rutherford's preaching given by his contemporaries support Wodrow's conclusions but a quick perusal of Rutherford's *Letters* do as well.

between these two eras. There are, in fact, very clear and important links between the seventeenth century and the twenty-first century that make our studying the one all the more relevant for our thinking about the other. Two links are worth mentioning here. First, those of us who follow in the Calvinistic tradition of the Scottish Commissioners share a common conviction with them, namely, that the Bible is the primary means of grace in the Christian life. More of what this means for these Scottish ministers will be seen in short measure. But, for now, suffice it to say that this common bond serves to build a closer connection between the seventeenth century and our own. Second, the people of the seventeenth century and the people of the twenty-first century share a common trait: by and large, both groups are characterized by a lack of biblical knowledge. Although the reasons for this are different in each time period—i.e., the people of the seventeenth century did not know their Bibles, because they *could not* read them;[5] and the people of the twenty-first century do not know their Bibles, because they *do not* read them[6]—nevertheless, the link is there and, because it is there, we in the twenty-first century have a great deal that we can learn from such seventeenth-century preachers as Alexander Henderson, Robert Baillie, George Gillespie, and Samuel Rutherford.

But these men were not only the best of the best in terms of their preaching abilities. These men were national leaders in what is arguably the most important era of all time. Remember first that in seventeenth century Britain there was an extremely close relationship between church and state. As Samuel Logan reminds us,

---

5. The illiteracy problem in early-modern Scotland was significant, according to Margo Todd. She estimates, based on an individual's ability to sign his or her name, that "urban literacy as late as the 1630s hovered around 50 per cent" and that rural literacy was "closer to 10–20 per cent for men" and "less than 10 per cent" for women (Margo Todd, *The Culture of Protestantism in Early Modern Scotland* [New Haven and London: Yale University, 2002], p. 25). This means that between 50 and 90 percent of the population in the seventeenth century would not have been able to read their Bibles. For them, the only exposure that they would have gotten to biblical teaching would be on Sundays in the minister's sermons.

6. Neil Postman gives an interesting and insightful critique of twentieth (and twenty-first) century apathy towards reading in his book, *Amusing Ourselves to Death: Public Discourse in the Age of Show Business* (New York: Penguin, 1986). In his book, he argues that Aldous Huxley—and not George Orwell—was right in his anti-utopian predictions for the future of society. Whereas Orwell feared that no one would *be able* to read because books would be banned by Big Brother, Huxley feared that no one would *want* to read because society would be wholly built upon pleasure and amusement rather than upon thinking. In such a "Brave New World," even though everyone would *be able* to read their Bibles, very few in fact ever would. It follows, therefore, that for those living in this world too, the only exposure that they would get to biblical teaching would be on Sundays in the minister's sermons.

> *All* of society, for most British Protestants in the early 1640s, was essentially one. The church and the state might have different activities and responsibilities; but the notion of separation between them was thus far held by only a tiny minority of extreme radicals.[7]

The close ties between church and state in the seventeenth century ensure that the Scottish Commissioners would not only have been seen as leaders within the church but as leaders within the nation as well, at least to some degree. And the sermons that they preached were not just aimed at setting the course for a church that was functioning *within* the society but for a church that was *at one with* the society.[8] For this reason alone, the fast sermons preached by the Scottish Commissioners to the members of Parliament are extremely important. They give us valuable insight into the historical context of not just the church in the seventeenth century but the nation as a whole.

But when we remember that the seventeenth century is perhaps the most important century of all time, the value of these sermons increases even more. The English early-modern scholar, Christopher Hill, has called the seventeenth century "the decisive century in English history" and the particular decades of the 1640s, 50s, and 60s "the decisive decades."[9] If he is correct in his analysis, and if we remember the influence that England has had upon so many other nations in the history of the world—perhaps especially upon the United States—it would seem nearly impossible to overstate the importance of this collection of fast sermons.

Perhaps the greatest reason why this collection of sermons is important, however, is because most of them are not readily available today. Even though many have been reprinted since their original publication in the seventeenth century, most, if not all, are still not readily available. Cornmarket Press did recently attempt to republish the entire collection of *Fast Sermons to Parliament* in 1970–71. But apparently the high price and limited availability combined to ensure that these books would remain quite rare. A modern, cost-effective, readily available edition of these sermons is long overdue.

In the space that remains, I would like to examine these sermons in more detail and, in doing so, to answer several questions about them—questions like: What do these sermons look like? What do they have in common? What are some of their main differences? And what can we in the twenty-first century learn from them? I hope to demonstrate that these sermons are expositional, scholastic, and specific to their audience.

---

7. Samuel T. Logan, Jr., "The Context and Work of the Assembly," in *To Glorify and Enjoy God: A Commemoration of the 350th Anniversary of the Westminster Assembly,* ed. John L. Carson and David W. Hall (Edinburgh: Banner of Truth, 1994), pp. 31–2, emphasis original.

8. The Scottish Commissioners all went so far as to select their sermon texts from Scripture with an eye to applying them to the current events of the day.

9. Christopher Hill, *God's Englishman: Oliver Cromwell and the English Revolution* (Harmondsworth, Middlesex: Penguin, 1972), pp. 13–14.

EXPOSITIONAL

All of the sermons in this volume are expositional sermons, that is, they seek to explain, unfold, make clear, or open up the original meaning of a text of Scripture and then to apply that meaning. The Scottish Commissioners' desire to preach in this way reveals their conviction that Scripture is a perfect "rule of faith and life" (WCF §1.2). In other words, it is because the Scottish Commissioners believed that the Bible is the primary means by which God brings His people to a saving knowledge of Himself and then grows and matures them in their faith and instructs them in how they are to live, that they were led to preach expositionally from the Bible. This may be an obvious point, but I think it bears mentioning simply because they understood something that may not be so readily understood today. They understood that the minister's chief responsibility is not so much to look for new techniques, methods, or tools to expand the kingdom of Christ, and not so much to win political alliances or friendships, but to declare faithfully the Word of God, which is the primary tool that He has given us for "faith and life."

But while it is true that the Scottish Commissioners' sermons are expositional, they are not all expositional in the same way, nor are they always consistent with the historical-grammatical method of exegesis that was so typical of the reformers. An obvious example of what I mean can be found in Alexander Henderson's second sermon, the thanksgiving sermon he preached July 18, 1644, to the House of Lords and the House of Commons together. In this sermon, Henderson begins by taking an allegorical approach to Matthew 14:31, applying the specific situation of Jesus saving Peter from drowning while walking on the water to the specific situation of the army's July 2 victory at Marston Moor.

To be fair to Henderson, this practice of going beyond the historical-grammatical method of exegesis was fairly typical among the Puritans in general. Samuel Rutherford, for instance, also frequently followed an allegorical approach to understanding Scripture, even historical narrative. In one sermon on John 20, Rutherford spiritualizes the event of the disciples at Christ's tomb, taking the specific details of the story and the race between Peter and John to the empty tomb as indicative of the Christian's experience:

> Now, to say nothing of the race that Peter and John had in going to Christ's grave, it is said the other disciple he outran Peter, and came first to the sepulchre. John is he who is called the other disciple, and he outran Peter. As it is among the children of God, all of them have not a like speed. Some of them get a sight of Christ before others ever get a sight of Him.[10]

---

10. See Samuel Rutherford, *Quaint Sermons of Samuel Rutherford Hitherto Unpublished with a preface by the Rev. Andrew A. Bonar, D. D.* (London: Hodder & Stoughton, MDCCCLXXV [1885]), pp. 66–83.

A SERMON BEFORE THE HOUSE OF COMMONS   69

Likewise, Thomas Shepard and, later, Jonathan Edwards, take virtually every detail in the parable of the ten virgins in Matthew 25, and apply it directly to the Christian life.[11]

According to Hughes Old, the Puritans as a whole were less "objective" in their exegesis than was Calvin, and they "saw a legitimate place for introspection in the interpretation of the Scriptures."[12] Though they were generally committed to the historical-grammatical method, they demonstrated a greater propensity than Calvin did to read each verse of Scripture in the light of other verses, thereby expanding the truths taught in any given passage. Most probably this was an attempt on the part of the Puritans to make the Bible practical by applying it to daily Christian life. The Bible taught that in the Christian life salvation was experiential, and the concept of experiential salvation was used, in turn, to explain what Scripture taught about the Christian life.

While this idea may sound cyclical and, therefore, unhelpful, it is actually neither in Puritan thinking. It is simply an application of the Reformation principle, *sacra Scriptura sui interpres*, or, Scripture interprets Scripture. One of the many things that this principle signifies for the practice of exegesis is that the general teaching of Scripture helps the reader to understand the meaning of specific passages. In other words, for Henderson and Rutherford, and the Puritans in general, this principle signifies that specific passages ought to be understood experientially, because the general teaching of Scripture is that the Christian life is profoundly experiential.

Such an interpretation of Scripture is helpful for our own twenty-first century context, because, in our day and time, the most common knock against Scripture is that it is neither practical nor relevant to contemporary life. But the Scottish Commissioners and their post-Reformation peers give us an example of preaching that aims at showing the auditor that the Bible is patently practical and unmistakably relevant to everyday life. At the same time, however, a word of caution is needed, because this Puritan practice can

---

11. See Thomas Shepard, *The Parable of the Ten Virgins* (1660; Morgan, Pa.: Soli Deo Gloria, 1990). Several articles have been written examining Shepard's sermon series, including among them, O. R. Johnston, "Thomas Shepard's 'Parable of the Ten Virgins,'" in *Puritan Papers*, vol. 1, ed. J.I. Packer (Phillipsburg, N.J.: P&R, 2000), pp. 115–27; and Randall C. Gleason, "The Parable of the Ten Virgins by Thomas Shepard (1605–1649)," in *The Devoted Life: An Invitation to the Puritan Classics*, ed. Kelly M. Kapic and Randall C. Gleason (Downers Grove, Ill.: InterVarsity, 2004), pp. 123–37. Edwards's sermons on the parable have never been published but have been examined in the secondary literature. See, e.g., Ava Chamberlain, "Brides of Christ and Signs of Grace: Edwards's Sermon Series on the Parable of the Wise and Foolish Virgins," in *Jonathan Edwards's Writings: Text, Context, Interpretation*, ed. Stephen J. Stein (Bloomington and Indianapolis: Indiana University, 1996), pp. 3–18; and William K. B. Stoever, "The Godly Will's Discerning: Shepard, Edwards, and the Identification of True Godliness," in ibid., pp. 85–99.

12. Old, *Reading and Preaching of the Scriptures*, 4.276.

easily be abused. We need to be careful in the application of this exegetical technique, lest we lose the objectivity in our interpretation completely and fall into the same trap that ensnared men like Karl Barth. In defending the Word of God from the whims of liberal historical critics, Barth destroyed the Bible's objectivity in favor of a subjective event in which the written word became the Word of God for the individual.[13] The Puritans clearly did not go as far as Barth did. But they did on occasion go beyond the bounds of the historical-grammatical method of exegesis. Henderson's sermon on Matthew 14, mentioned above, is proof of this.

There is a lesson here for us as well. Although our experiential reading of a given passage may be scriptural, it may not be taught in the specific text of Scripture that is under examination. We need to be careful in our approach to Scripture to ensure that our experiential reading of it is always held subject to the intent of the original author of the passage under review. We may be teaching a scriptural truth; but if it is not a scriptural truth taught in the specific passage in front of us, then we are skating on thin exegetical ice. Whatever we may think Scripture is saying, it cannot be saying anything other than what was intended by the author when it was originally written.

One of the ways these exegetical differences between the Scottish Commissioners and Calvin manifested themselves is in the pericope sizes of the texts they selected from which to preach. Whereas Calvin typically preached on more than four or five verses in each sermon,[14] the Scottish Commissioners followed the Puritan tendency and frequently preached on only one or two verses. The result is that Calvin tended to preach through entire books of the Bible sequentially verse by verse, following the *lectio continua* approach—and apparently he did so on a regular basis.[15] But the Scottish Commissioners, like the Puritans in general, tended to preach through select *chapters* sequentially and rarely if ever made it through a complete book.[16]

------

13. See, e.g., Karl Barth, *Church Dogmatics,* I/1, trans. G. T. Thomson (Edinburgh: T&T Clark, 1936), §4.

14. James Montgomery Boice, Foreward to John Calvin, *Sermons on Psalm 119 by John Calvin* (1580; Audubon, N.J.: Old Paths, 1996), p. viii. Boice states that Calvin averaged four to five verses per sermon and often selected many more than that when preaching on narrative sections of Scripture.

15. "Publisher's Introduction: John Calvin and his Sermons on Ephesians," in Calvin, *Sermons on The Epistle to the Ephesians* (Edinburgh: Banner of Truth, 1998 reprint) ix. The introduction states that the "books of Scripture [Calvin] is known to have preached through are: Genesis, Deuteronomy, Job, Judges, I and II Samuel, I and II Kings, the Major and Minor Prophets, the Gospels, Acts, I and II Corinthians, Galatians, Ephesians, I and II Thessalonians, I and II Timothy, Titus, and Hebrews."

16. In the collection of fast sermons of the Scottish Commissioners, six of the nine sermons are drawn from only one verse of Scripture. Two of the remaining three sermons are

Sometimes the Puritan tendency to preach through chapters of the Bible one verse at a time was carried out in excruciating detail, as the examples of Thomas Manton, Arthur Hildersam, and Joseph Caryl conclusively demonstrate. Manton preached 190 sermons on the 176 verses of Psalm 119, which is more than one sermon per verse. The scope of the content of Manton's work on this psalm is so comprehensive that the entire collection has been referred to as "an encyclopedia of practical Christian living."[17] Hildersam went one better than Manton and preached 108 sermons on the 54 verses of John 4, and 152 sermons on Psalm 51, which only has nineteen verses! And, not to be outdone by his peers, Joseph Caryl preached on the book of Job for his entire ministry, compiling enough sermons to fill twelve volumes totaling over 8,600 pages! Granted, Caryl did preach through *a book* of the Bible and not just chapters. But it was only *one book*, and it took his entire ministry. It is no big surprise that the congregation of 800 strong dwindled to a meager eight by the end of his tenure.

To be sure, Manton, Hildersam, and Caryl are extreme examples of the Puritan tendency to preach *lectio continua* at a much slower pace than did Calvin and the Continental Reformers.[18] The Scottish Commissioners may have been a less extreme example, but they still support Hughes Old's claims about Puritan preaching in general:

> Given [the scholastic] form [of their sermons, the Puritans] tried to make the best they could of the *lectio continua*. The scholastic sermon form slowed down the *lectio continua*. Rarely could one cover in one sermon more than a single verse of Scripture using this form; in fact, it often took several sermons to treat but one verse, if the method was used to its full rigor. Consequently, the Puritans got to the place where they preached through chapters rather than whole books.[19]

Old's comments introduce the second indisputable feature of these fast sermons: they are quite obviously scholastic productions through and through. Over the last few decades, there has been much misinformation regarding what scholasticism is and how, if at all, it affects the content of

---

based upon two verses. Only one of the nine sermons is drawn from more than two verses of Scripture.

17. See Thomas Manton, *Psalm 119*, 3 vols. (Banner of Truth, 1990), inside cover.

18. Zwingli is known to have preached through Matthew, John, Acts, Romans, 1 and 2 Corinthians, Galatians, Ephesians, Philippians, Colossians, 1 and 2 Thessalonians, 1 and 2 Timothy, Titus, Philemon, Hebrews, 1 and 2 Peter, and through the Old Testament at least as far as the Prophets. Capito, Oecolampadius, and Bucer also were in favor of preaching *lectio continua* through books of the Bible. Luther, on the other hand, seems to have used both the *lectio continua* and the lectionary of the liturgical calendar. See the discussion in Old, *Reading and Preaching of the Scriptures*, 4.27, 36–7, 46–7.

19. Old, *Reading and Preaching of the Scriptures*, 4.327.

theology. In the following section, we will examine this unmistakable aspect of these sermons and determine what kind of affect it had upon them.

SCHOLASTIC

The Scottish Commissioners were all children of their times. They lived and ministered in the century after the inauguration of the great Protestant Reformation. And as Richard Muller has gone to great lengths to prove, this fact, more than any other, affected the writing, teaching, and preaching of the men of their generation.[20] In the seventeenth century, there was little need to establish the basic truths recovered by the Reformation. That had already been done. Expansion and systematization was now the main order of the day. Leonard Trinterud reminds us that in rejecting the authority of the Roman Catholic Church, the reformers and post-reformers had to re-establish "a new basis ... for personal and public religious life and morals, educations, civil governments, family life, and even international relations."[21] The Reformation required more than expounding one or two isolated doctrines; it required constructing a comprehensive and cohesive system of faith. Thus, as Muller says, we should expect to find evidence of a movement towards systematization within Calvin himself, which would then be carried over into the post-Reformation period and into the thinking of men like the Scottish Commissioners. And this is precisely what we do find.[22]

In order to carry out this required systematization of Reformation theology, the Scottish Commissioners and their Reformed Orthodox contemporaries turned for help to the methods of the medieval scholastics—men such as Thomas Aquinas, John Duns Scotus, William of Ockham, and Gabriel Biel. According to Richard Muller, the primary technique that distinguishes the

---

20. Richard Muller has written extensively on the link between the Reformation and post-Reformation periods. See, e.g., Muller, *Christ and the Decree: Christology and Predestination in Reformed Theology from Calvin to Perkins* (Durham, N.C.: Labyrinth Press, 1986); idem, "Calvin and the 'Calvinists': Assessing the Continuities and Discontinuities between the Reformation and Orthodoxy," *Calvin Theological Journal* 30 (1995): 345–75, and 31 (1996): 125–60; idem, "The Problem of Protestant Scholasticism—A Review and Definition," in *Reformation and Scholasticism: An Ecumenical Enterprise*, ed. Willem J. Van Asselt and Eef Dekker (Grand Rapids, Mich.: Baker, 2001) pp. 45–64; idem, *Post-Reformation Reformed Dogmatics: The Rise and Development of Reformed Orthodoxy, ca. 1520 to ca. 1725*, 4 vols. (Grand Rapids, Mich.: Baker Academic, 2003).

21. Trinterud, "Origins of Puritanism," *Church History* 20 (March 1951): 38.

22. Muller shows the movement towards systematization in Calvin by pointing to the early versions of the *Institutes*, which he says contained a "simple and catechetical structure," and then to the final edition of 1559, which he says contained a "more formal, more systematic presentation" of theology (*Christ and the Decree*, 17). Muller then goes on to trace the continuation of this trend towards systematization into the succeeding generations after Calvin (in part two of *Christ and the Decree*).

scholastic method is the technique of the *quaestio*, involving the following four main components:

> 1. The presentation of a thesis or *quaestio*, a thematic question;
>
> 2. The indication of the subjects that stand to be discussed in the *quaestio*, the so-called *status quaestionis*;
>
> 3. The treatment of a series of arguments or objections against the adopted positions, the so-called *objectiones*;
>
> 4. The formulation of an answer (*responsio*), in which account is taken of all available sources of information, and all rules of rational discourse are upheld, followed by an answer to the objections, which is as comprehensive as possible.[23]

The theological writings of the Scottish Commissioners fit the pattern thus outlined by Muller and would, therefore, seem to be products of the scholastic method. A quick perusal of just about any of their works will reveal many of the abovementioned categories.

Samuel Rutherford's *Examen Arminianismi* offers a clear example of this.[24] Rutherford's *Examen* is a collection of the divinity lectures he gave at St. Mary's College in St. Andrews, which were retained in manuscript form until his death and published in the Netherlands in 1668. Each chapter of the *Examen* is explicitly organized around a series of questions (*quaestiones*), readily identifiable from the recurring introductory Latin verb *Quaeritur*, "It is asked."[25] Rutherford then uses the *status quaestionis* to further define the *quaestio* by offering clarification and expansion from other sources.[26] After this, relevant *objectiones* are offered and rebutted by appropriate *responsiones* from Rutherford.[27] As Muller warns, these responses can sometimes be quite comprehensive. At one point in the *Examen*, Rutherford offers no less than twenty responses to a particular objection, and, quite frequently, he amasses sixteen or more.[28] Only rarely is the number of responses from Rutherford less than four.

---

23. Muller, "Scholasticism and Orthodoxy in the Reformed Tradition: An Attempt at Definition" (Inaugural Address, Grand Rapids, Mich., 1995), pp. 4–5.

24. Samuel Rutherford, *Examen Arminianismi* (Utrecht, 1668).

25. See, e.g., *Examen*, "Index Capitum & Quaestionum," which begins immediately after the main body of the text, for a complete listing of every *quaestio* in each chapter.

26. See, e.g., *Examen*, pp. 453, 463, 464, 498, 520, 551.

27. See, e.g., *Examen*, pp. 28–9, 56, 100–103, 108–21.

28. *Examen*, 171–4 (shows 16 responses), pp. 185–91 (16 responses), pp. 206–10 (18 responses),

This same scholastic emphasis can be seen clearly in the fast sermons of the Scottish Commissioners. Each of their sermons is organized around the same basic skeletal framework of "introduction," "division of the text," "doctrines," "reasons," and "uses." We will briefly discuss each in turn.

Introduction

Each sermon begins with an introduction. But the lengths and uses of these introductions vary greatly. Rutherford, for instance, has the shortest introductions. In his first sermon in this collection, the introduction consists of three short sentences; in the second, it is only one sentence. For whatever reason, this is typical for Rutherford. He did not use long or elaborate introductions. Instead, he preferred to get right into the text of Scripture as quickly as he could. It is quite possible that there is a link between the length of Rutherford's introductions and the length of his sermons. Although Rutherford had the shortest introductions, he also had the longest sermons by far.[29] Maybe he realized this going in and, in good conscience, could not bring himself to give a longer introduction than just a few short sentences. Or, it may be that Rutherford was the least gifted orator among the Scottish Commissioners. We do know, for instance, that his voice was "rather shrill" and that one of his friends—a *friend*, mind you, and not an enemy!—said that he had a "strange utterance" in the pulpit, "a kind of *skreigh* [i.e., a screech], that I never heard the like." And, as if this were not enough, we also know that he is described as having poor elocution.[30] So, it is distinctly possible that Rutherford, realizing his weaknesses in the area of public speaking and realizing that his trust was not in his own strength but in the God who speaks through His Word, opted to jump right into the text of Scripture without wasting any time on preliminaries.

Gillespie and Baillie, on the other hand, tended to have the longest and most elaborate introductions. This is because they used them to establish the context for the verse or verses that they would be examining in the course of their sermons. One of the most interesting introductions is also Gillespie's longest. It appears in his first sermon on Ezekiel 43:11. From the beginning of this sermon, Gillespie attempts to lay out to his hearers why and how the text that he has selected is applicable to them. He also devotes a great deal of time in the introduction to discussing the nature of the temple in the latter chapters of Ezekiel.

Before moving on, let me briefly say that there are at least two good lessons for us here. First, whatever the real reasons are behind Rutherford's

---

pp. 241–4 (16 responses), pp. 249–52 (16 responses), pp. 458–65 (19 responses), pp. 553–63 (20 responses).

29. Rutherford's sermons are more than twice as long as Henderson's. And Baillie's and Gillespie's longest sermons are still not quite three quarters of Rutherford's.

30. A. A. Bonar, "Sketch of Samuel Rutherford," in *Letters of Samuel Rutherford*, ed. A. A. Bonar (Edinburgh and London: Oliphant Anderson & Ferrier, 1891), p. 5.

short introductions, it is nevertheless true that we need to be aware of our own gifts and limitations. We need to have a sober understanding of where our weaknesses are and be content to build upon our strengths rather than plowing ahead oblivious to whether we are gifted in a certain area or not. Second, there is great wisdom in demonstrating to our hearers, as Gillespie did, at the beginning of the sermon the reasons why the forthcoming sermon will be relevant to them. The congregation will be more apt to listen carefully if they know from the beginning that this sermon will speak to a particular situation that they are currently experiencing or have experienced in the past.

DIVISION OF THE TEXT

After the introduction, the text is divided into parts. These parts—or points, as we know them—will then form the basic outline for the rest of the sermon. Rarely are the number of points less than three. And in four of the nine sermons, there are as many as four, five, or even six points. This is in spite of the fact that these sermons are typically drawn from only one or two verses of Scripture![31]

Once the preacher divides the text into parts, he typically explains the portion of Scripture contained in that part and then draws out any relevant doctrines and seeks to apply them to his hearers. The interesting thing is that the Puritans did not attempt to force the text of Scripture into three carefully crafted points (no doubt all arranged according to alliteration!). With the aid of their more expansive exegesis, they adapted the outline to fit the points that they saw coming out of the text naturally, even if it took five or six points or more to do it.

DOCTRINES

After explaining a given part of the text of Scripture, the Scottish Commissioners then draw out the appropriate doctrines or principles that they see as being taught in the portion of the text that is under examination. This process of "unfolding … the passage into its various doctrines" is what William Perkins in his textbook on preaching refers to as "resolution."[32] It involves breaking a passage down into the relevant theses or main ideas that that passage teaches. These main ideas are the homiletical equivalents of the *quaestiones* in the abovementioned description of scholastic methodology. Just as the *quaestio* is essential to the scholastic method, so the process of

---

31. One of my professors in Edinburgh once commented on this tendency in the Puritans and stated that he did not understand how they could glean enough to preach on from just one verse. But not only did these men glean *enough* to preach on, they gleaned *more than enough*. They routinely got four, five, or six points out of the one verse they were preaching on and preached sermons which were typically much longer than ours are today.

32. Perkins, *Art of Prophesying* (Banner of Truth, 1996), p. 48.

resolution is essential to preaching, because, as Perkins also says, the preacher who fails to draw out the appropriate doctrines from a given passage fails to fulfill his duty of "rightly dividing the word of truth."[33]

By beginning with an explanation of what a portion of the text means and then drawing appropriate doctrines from it, the Scottish Commissioners show that they are beginning with Biblical Theology and then moving into Systematic Theology. In other words, they begin by discerning what the text means in its redemptive-historical context and then move to discerning what the text teaches about things like God, ourselves, Christ, salvation, the church, etc. Granted sometimes their exegesis is a little more broad than we might prefer. But much of the time, especially so with Baillie and Gillespie, the Scottish Commissioners are extremely careful to anchor their exegesis within the context of the overall passage, on the one hand, and all of redemptive history, on the other.

One thing that is overwhelmingly obvious is that the Scottish Commissioners do not balk at presenting even particularly challenging doctrines to their listeners when they are warranted by the text of Scripture at hand. Henderson, for instance, takes up a discussion of the nature of faith near the end of his second sermon and an intricate discussion of the relationship between the church and state in his third sermon. Baillie frequently doles out polemical punches to erroneous and heretical groups like the antinomians, papists, prelatists, Arminians, Brownists, and Socinians, which he deals with in his first sermon. And he enters into a complex and helpful examination of God's relationship to sin in his second sermon, taking up the following weighty topics: how God wills sin but is not the author of it, how He permits sin, how He punishes sin, and how He hardens men's hearts. Rutherford's sermons are replete with discourses of all sizes on particular doctrinal issues like general revelation, the place of the affections in the Christian life and their relationship to the mind and the will, the nature of faith, the assurance of salvation, the nature and character of God, and the question of suffering in the Christian life.

Reasons

After delineating the doctrines that flow from the exposition of the biblical text, the Scottish Commissioners oftentimes add a number of reasons to support and develop the true meaning and relevance of each doctrine. Frequently the reasons are drawn from other passages of Scripture that amplify the text in question or some aspect of it. Most of the time Henderson, Baillie, Gillespie, and Rutherford use these reasons to prove that the text really does teach what they claim it does and to clarify and unfold the full meaning of each doctrine. In the terminology of the scholastic method, this is the *status quaestionis*. It is here that these men seek to clarify the essence of the *quaestio*, the main idea propounded in the doctrine.

---

33. *Art of Prophesying*, chapter 6.

USES

Only after explaining the point raised from the text, selecting the relevant doctrines that arise from it, and giving any necessary support for those doctrines, do the Scottish Commissioners turn to application. But if we think this means that application is simply an afterthought for the Scottish Commissioners, we need to think again. As a whole, they place incredible emphasis on application in their fast sermons. Many of the sermons are almost half application. See especially Henderson's and Gillespie's second sermons and Rutherford's first in this regard.[34] Henderson's third sermon has an even greater emphasis on practical uses, with perhaps as much as two-thirds of it is devoted to application!

Sometimes these applications take the form of practical exhortations, encouragements, or warnings. Sometimes they are geared toward eliminating error and protecting against heresy. And sometimes they raise potential objections and then answer them in detail—which is another sign of the scholastic method being carried over into sermon construction.[35] For the Scottish Commissioners, there is no blanket approach to application or one-size-fits-all understanding of practical uses but instead a particular devotion to applying the scalpel of God's Word to the specific cancers of their hearers' souls.

What a lesson there is here for us! Our tendency in the twenty-first century—at least in those traditions that place greater emphasis on expository preaching—is to spend most of our time on exegesis and relatively little on application. The example of the Scottish Commissioners speaks against this. They devoted a vast amount of time and effort to making their sermons practical to their hearers. Granted they did preach for longer periods of time than most preachers have available to them today. But the point is still valid. These men did not simply explain a passage of Scripture and leave their hearers to apply it to their own hearts and lives. They drove their points home with great specificity and with great boldness.

By organizing the sermon into "introduction," "division of the text," "doctrines," "reasons," and "uses," the Scottish Commissioners reveal the influence of the scholastic method upon their preaching. As we mentioned before, the Puritans were, as a whole, much more scholastic in the organization of their sermons and in their treatment of specific doctrines than were sixteenth-century Reformers like Luther and Calvin. Whereas the preaching of Luther, Oecolampadius, and Calvin tended to focus upon a "verse-by-verse commentary of a longer portion of Scripture" and to produce a "simple and straightforward enthusiasm to dig out of the text what is to be found," the preaching of the post-Reformation orthodox—like Henderson, Baillie, Gillespie, and Rutherford—tended to concentrate on one or two verses only,

---

34. This does not even take into account the large teaching portions of these sermons (especially Rutherford's).

35. Rutherford has an eight-page section in his first sermon in which he deals with five different objections and answers them in great detail (see *Scots Sermons*, pp. 422–429).

drawing from them one or two themes that would be examined in intricate detail.[36] And the scholastic method outlined above was just what they needed to help them do this.

It is important to say that in calling these sermons scholastic, we are not at all suggesting that they are academic sermons. To be sure, they are not insignificant sermons; i.e., they are not homiletical appetizers. Rather, they are quite weighty and insightful; they display an eloquence and an erudition that is both broad and deep; and they are decidedly didactic in content. But they are not classroom lectures. They are not intended simply to communicate information but to warm the heart and to motivate the members of Parliament to be fervent in their pursuit of God. "When we are lukewarm in the matters of God," Henderson says, "then the wrath of God waxes hot, and when we are fervent and zealous, then his anger ceases and the fire of his wrath is extinguished."[37] The term "scholastic" has more to do with the organization and structure of the sermon than it does with its content. The Scottish Commissioners' sermons are clearly scholastic, but they are not academic treatises designed only to stimulate the mind. They are consistently and overtly concerned with reaching beyond the mind into the affections and will.

Perhaps the best example of this is seen in Rutherford's sermons. His sermons (along with Baillie's) are probably the most scholastic. And, yet, they are also arguably the most "affectionate." Rutherford ascribes a central place to the affections in the Christian life, even going so far as to say that "faith is a work of the heart and affection[s], rather than of the mind."[38] Even if someone were to perform great acts of piety seemingly in obedience to God's commands and yet not have his or her affections full of love for Christ in doing them, it would all be in vain:

> [I]f you had ten tongues to speak for God, a hundred hands to fight for him, many lives to lose for him, Ahithophel's wisdom to employ in his service, except you engage the heart and affections in his service, you do nothing to him.[39]

Whereas our "[d]uties to prince, parents, husband, wife, children, [and] parliament," require only "half" our affections, "reformation, God, [and] religion calls for *all* the heart, *all* the soul, *all* the strength."[40] Rutherford understands that the heart condition (or the condition of the affections) of each member of Parliament and their continuing the work of the Reformation are really two sides to the same coin. If the members of Parliament are fervent

---

36. Old, *Reading and Preaching of the Scriptures*, 4:284.

37. *Scots Sermons*, p. 80.

38. *Scots Sermons*, p. 417.

39. *Scots Sermons*, p. 415.

40. *Scots Sermons*, p. 414, emphasis added.

in their faith toward Christ, then they will want to do all that they can to complete the work of the Reformation by doing all that is written in His Word. And, so, Rutherford warns the members of Parliament to do more than give assent to the truth. He appeals to them to put their trust in God and to "cleave" to the truth with all their "heart … with a heat and warmness of soul resting upon the grace" of Christ.[41] If they do not do so, he says, they will incur God's wrath, because "God detests lukewarmness, and coldness in his matters."[42]

SPECIFIC TO THEIR AUDIENCE

Besides being expositional and scholastic, however, all the sermons in this collection are also specific to their audience. They are not general sermons that could be preached anywhere at any time. They are specifically crafted and aimed with particular audiences in mind. Beginning with the selection of the text of Scripture from which the Commissioners determined to preach, which are predominantly from the Old Testament (six out of nine of them are), these sermons are targeted at addressing the current events and chief concerns of the day. To a man, the Scottish Commissioners are principally concerned with the same thing—to encourage Parliament to see the work of the Reformation through to completion. Gillespie openly acknowledges that this is his primary purpose in preaching before the House of Commons:

> It is far from my meaning to cool your affections to the laws, liberties, peace and safety of the kingdom. I desire only to warm your hearts with the zeal of reformation, as that which, all along, you must carry on in the first place.[43]

Then he continued by overtly stating what he thought completing the Reformation would look like—it would look like Presbyterianism.

> But since now, by the blessing of God, they [i.e., the Westminster Assembly] are thus far advanced that they have found in the word of God a pattern for presbyterial government over many particular congregations; and have found also from the word that ordination is an act belonging to such a presbytery; I beseech you improve that, *whereto we have already attained* (Phil. 3:16), till other acts of a presbytery be agreed on afterward. Yourselves know better than I do, that much people is perishing (Prov. 29:18), because there is no vision: *the harvest is great and the laborers are few* (Luke 10:2). Give me leave, therefore, to quicken you to this work, that, with all diligence and without delay, some presbyteries be associated and erected (in such places as yourselves in your wisdom shall judge fittest), with power to ordain ministers with the consent of the congregations, and after trial of the gifts, soundness and conversation

---

41. *Scots Sermons*, p. 418.

42. *Scots Sermons*, p. 409.

43. See page 125.

of the men. In so doing you shall both please God and bring upon yourselves the blessing of many poor souls that are ready to perish (Job 29:13); and you shall likewise greatly strengthen the hearts and hands of your brethren in Scotland, joined in covenant and in arms with you.[44]

It is certain that the Scottish Commissioners' pleading with Parliament was not always received well, especially in light of the longstanding tensions that have existed between Scotland and England down through the centuries. Such no doubt was the case with Henderson's comments in his first sermon to Parliament, when he encouraged the English to be more like their Scots brethren:

> We have also cause to rejoice that in the one kingdom [i.e, Scotland] a course has been taken for doing everything in the house of God according to his commandment, and that in this kingdom [i.e., England] it is ordered that a wise and holy assembly of divines shall search diligently into the Word of God, *That whatsoever is commanded by the word of* [the] *God of heaven* [be diligently done for the house of the God of heaven].[45]

But regardless of how these sermons were perceived by Parliament, all nine of them share a common theme. They are all designed to encourage the members of Parliament to devote themselves to completing the work of reformation in Britain.

We also see the specificity of the fast sermons in the use they make of the original languages and Latin. The Scottish Commissioners are somewhat freer in their use of Greek, Hebrew, and Latin in their sermons before the Parliament than they are in their sermons to their own congregations. Rutherford's sermons in Anwoth and St. Andrews, for instance, are ordinarily very simple. They contain almost no trace of the original languages or of Latin. If someone did not know that he was once Regent of Humanities at the University of Edinburgh and that he was offered the chair of Divinity and Hebrew at the University of Harderwyck in the Netherlands, he or she would never have guessed it by reading or hearing the majority of his sermons. Only here in his sermons before Parliament do we see his evident mastery of Hebrew, Greek, and Latin.[46] Obviously, Rutherford believed that there was a difference in the education or ability levels of the members of Parliament as compared with the members of his congregations, and he tailored his use of language in his sermons to the specific audience to which he was speaking.

Rutherford's sermons before Parliament are unique in another way as well.

---

44. See page 126.

45. *Scots Sermons*, p. 90.

46. In his sermon before the House of Commons, Rutherford cites Hebrew, Latin, or Greek 47 times (with a majority being Latin); and in his sermon before the House of Lords, he cites them 53 times (with the majority being Hebrew and Greek).

They do not contain anywhere near as much of the "quaint" speech that so defines his other sermons. There is a common manner of speaking in Rutherford's other sermons that is in keeping with a more "common" audience, who would ordinarily probably not have had the educational opportunities or exposure to logic and rhetoric that the members of Parliament would have had. One of the reasons why Rutherford's sermons are so difficult for many to read today is actually the very reason why they were so popular in his own day: they are full of words, phrases, and colloquialisms that were familiar to common folk in his own day and time but that are virtually unknown today. A couple of examples will suffice to demonstrate this:

> Christ aye blows at the coal ere it wear out: Christ would win a friend, yea a foe, to be kind to Him. He is aye threaping [i.e., insisting on] and claiming kindness of us, as if He were the beggar and the poor man, and we the king.... Would ye ken [i.e., know] for whom Christ died, and prayed? even for dyvours [i.e., debtors], such as swore themselves bare [i.e., declared on oath that they kept nothing], and came out of prison upon caution, or a *cessio bonorum* [i.e., a giving up of all they had]. Poor men that have been upon the dyvours-stone, and are far from payment by the dyvour bill, when there is not a finger in all your hand fastened upon yourself, then ye are meet for Christ.[47]

And:

> Christ loves not professors that never wan to love to pray [i.e., go the length of loving to pray], and such as hate not the world.... The word of God is seed sown that brings forth thirty, sixty, and an hundred fold. Ilk [i.e., each] boll brings out thirty; ilk sermon, ilk Communion should bring out an hundred good works.... Bring forth fruit, or else ye will make God say, My curse and God's malison be upon thy heart, thou hearest much, and bringest forth no fruit. Therefore beware; a tree that once gets a dadd [i.e., knock] with God's axe, it will never do well again.... For there be some that come never in God's sight, they are God's dyvours [i.e., debtors]: they are aughting [i.e., owing] so much that they dare not come to God, and compt [i.e., reckon] and pay....[48]

As John Coffey has pointed out, Rutherford's language is so "tailored to the understanding of [his] hearers" that the Oxford English Dictionary quotes from select of his writings nearly seven hundred times in order to illustrate what a colloquial or contextualized manner of speaking looks like.[49]

---

47. Samuel Rutherford, *Fourteen Communion Sermons*, ed. A. A. Bonar (Glasgow: Glass & Co., 1877), p. 256. This is one of the few times that Rutherford makes use of Latin in his "congregational" sermons.

48. Rutherford, *Communion Sermons*, p. 257.

49. Coffey, *Politics, Religion and the British Revolutions*, p. 102, citing from the second edition on CD-Rom. Coffey notes that "only the most famous of seventeenth-century English

In comparison, Rutherford's sermons before the English Parliament contain very little of this kind of common language and much more of Hebrew, Greek, and Latin. They are aimed at a different audience. If John Brown is correct in stating that, "The only language which will reach men is that to which they are accustomed,"[50] then Rutherford's preaching—both his sermons before Parliament and his sermons before local congregations—certainly would seem to be perfectly pitched to reach the men and women of his day.

But what about the other Scottish Commissioners? Can the same thing be said of their preaching? Those who are familiar with the preaching of Alexander Henderson may conclude that the same thing cannot be said of his sermons that was said of Rutherford's—namely, that their language is specifically tailored to the capacities of their hearers. The reason for this is probably because R. Thomson Martin, the editor of a collection of sermons preached by Henderson in 1638, argues that all of Henderson's sermons were virtually identical, regardless of the audience before whom they were given. Martin says:

> Though addressed to plain country people, and to people of whose ignorance Henderson himself more than once complains, they [i.e., Henderson's sermons to his congregation in Leuchars] are characterized throughout by *the same weight of matter and dignity of style* as those preached on more public occasions, and to more refined and learned auditories.[51]

While it is no doubt true that Henderson's sermons to his congregation in Leuchars contain "the same weight of matter" as the sermons that he preached to "more refined and learned auditories," it is not at all clear that both types of sermons contain the same "dignity of style." The Puritans rarely, if ever, skimped on content; that much is obvious. It did not matter to the Puritans how "ignorant" or "refined and learned" their audiences were, they still presented particularly challenging doctrines regularly in the course of their preaching. Thus, we see Henderson treating weighty topics like union with Christ, assurance of salvation, the necessity of prayer, the nature of faith, and the relationship of faith to good works in his sermons to his congregation in Leuchars.[52] Surely Martin is right about Henderson's sermons containing "the same weight of matter" regardless of the intellectual capacities of his hearers.

---

writers are referred to more often [than Rutherford]: Baxter (1,526), Locke (1,529), Hobbes (2,283), and Milton (12,845)."

50. John Brown, *Puritan Preaching in England: A Study of Past and Present* (1900; Eugene, Oreg.: Wipf & Stock, 2001), p. 113.

51. "Preface," in Alexander Henderson, *Sermons, Prayers, and Pulpit Addresses*, ed. R. Thomson Martin (Edinburgh: John Maclaren, 1867) ix, emphasis added.

52. Henderson, *Sermons, Prayers, and Pulpit Addresses*, pp. 284–300 and 124–34.

A Sermon Before the House of Commons

But it is not true that Henderson's sermons all exhibit the same use of language. Like Rutherford, Henderson uses the original languages and Latin much more frequently in his sermons to Parliament than he does in his sermons to his more "ignorant" congregation.[53] He also cites Josephus, Eusebius, Augustine, and several other scholars or philosophers in his sermons to Parliament and does not do so in his sermons to his congregation in Leuchars. And although Henderson is nowhere near as colloquial or contextual as is Rutherford in his manner of speaking, he does still adopt the same kind of common speech in his sermons to the "plain country people" of his congregation and does not do so when speaking to Parliament. In just one of his sermons to his Scottish congregation, for example, Henderson uses common words like "mickle," "kythes," "hose-net," "artailzie," "assaying," "midses," "sickerer," "whilk," "pedmented," "speir," and "lippen"—none of which occur in his sermons before the English Parliament.[54] Thus, it would seem safe to conclude that Martin's comments about Henderson's "dignity of style" being the same regardless of the capacity of the audience to whom he was preaching require further clarification. Whatever else is intended in Martin's phrase "dignity of style," it is not Henderson's use of language. For, Henderson plainly adapts his use of language to the audience before whom he is speaking, albeit not to the degree that others like Rutherford do. To a man, the Scottish Commissioners, like the Puritans in general, show an ability to evaluate their audiences and to craft their sermons with each one specifically in mind.[55]

CONCLUSION

We live in a day and time—at least in the U.S.—in which Christianity appears to be on the increase. A majority of what we see and read today suggests that the evangelical church is experiencing something akin to revival. But if we scratch below the surface, we can see right through such superficial

---

53. The current author did find several instances where Henderson uses Latin words and phrases in his sermons to his congregation, but the frequency was much less than in his sermons to parliament. Every one of Henderson's fast sermons contained not only Latin but also the original languages, whereas only two or three of his sermons to his congregation in Leuchars contained any Latin and none of them contained the original languages.

54. Henderson, *Sermons, Prayers, and Pulpit Addresses*, pp. 124–134.

55. Unfortunately, the two sermons by Gillespie are the only surviving full examples that we have of his preaching, which means that we have nothing to compare them to in this regard. Two MS volumes of sermon and lecture notes by Baillie were said by David Laing to have survived, but even at that point (in 1841), they were in poor condition ("much injured by damp"). See Robert Baillie, *The Letters and Journals of Robert Baillie*, ed. David Laing (Edinburgh, 1841), pp. cvi–cix. Most likely, both Baillie and Gillespie would mirror the trend we see in Rutherford, Henderson, and the Puritans in general. Two partial examples from manuscript are presented in this present volume, a portion of a sermon preached before the Scottish Parliament on Psalm 2, and brief notes of another on observing Christmas.]

evaluations. Listen to one such attempt at scratching below the surface by Michael Horton:

> Countless articles in Christian magazines and books and numerous features on Christian radio and television tell us how evangelicalism is booming, brimming with enthusiasm and excitement. We have our own networks, publishing companies, advertising agencies, amusement parks, and cruises!
>
> … The successes of evangelical marketing have even been characterized as a revival. Nevertheless, according to pollsters George Barna and William P. McKay, "Despite the millions of dollars spent on media ministry and evangelistic publishing, there has been no real growth in the size of the Christian population in the last five years."
>
> … According to a prestigious research group, Oxford Analytica, the presumed religious revival lacks substance: "Despite impressive statistics and the appearance of surprising vitality, there is evidence that the state of religion in America is not quite what it appears. Almost all the statistical indicators on religion are up," the group reports. "But indicators of the social influence of religion are down."
>
> The myths of power, popularity, and growth have led to an unhealthy preoccupation with superficial success, methods over message, technique over truth, quantity over quality.[56]

Horton ends his evaluation by looking forward to a day when things will be different both in the church and in the culture around us:

> Let us hope for a day in the not-too-distant future when the world sees a humble church that no longer shelters hypocrisy, that no longer offers stones of legalism when the world needs the bread of life; a church that bids the world, "Come now, let us reason together" (Isa. 1:18) instead of expecting national awakening on the basis of slogans, shallow assertions, and unfounded myths. Let us hope that the time has run out for being "at ease in Zion." Let us pray for the day when the Christian community will no longer patronize the supermarket of pop religion, when there will be a recovery of passionate, warm-hearted orthodoxy and historic continuity, not with American legends, but with Christian truths.[57]

But how will this happen? When will this hoped-for day come? If John Brown is correct that "the preacher's message and the Church's spiritual condition

---

56. Michael Scott Horton, *Made in America: The Shaping of Modern American Evangelicalism* (1991; Eugene, Oreg: Wipf & Stock, 2006), pp. 11–12.

57. Horton, *Made in America*, p. 13.

have [historically] risen or fallen together" and that "[w]hen life has gone out of the preacher it is not long before it has gone out of the Church also," then it would seem that this hoped-for day will only come when there is a recovery of passionate, warm-hearted, bold, orthodox, biblical preaching.[58] The seventeenth century had this kind of preaching. The sermons contained in this volume are testament enough to that. What remains to be seen is whether or not our day will have this kind of preaching. Will our day be one of small things (humanly speaking)? Or will our day be one in which the church sees a modern reformation?

We need a new generation of preachers like Alexander Henderson, Robert Baillie, George Gillespie, and Samuel Rutherford—not those who mimic them at every point but those who preach to a twenty-first century audience with their passion, their uncompromising boldness, and their deep, warm-hearted orthodoxy, those who preach sermons that are expositional, systematic (if not scholastic), and specific to their audience. Then and only then will we see any impact in the church. Then and only then will we see the church exerting real influence on culture. Then and only then will we see a modern-day reformation.

Amen. Even so, may it be.
Guy M. Richard

---

58. Brown, *Puritan Preaching in England*, p. 7.

DIVINE PROVIDENCE has made it my lot and a calling has induced me (who am less than the least of all the servants of Christ) to appear among others in this cloud of public witnesses. The scope of the sermon is to endeavor the removal of the obstructions both of *humiliation* and *reformation,* two things which ought to lie very much in our thoughts at this time. Concerning both I shall preface but little. *Reformation* has many unfriends, some upon the right-hand, and some upon the left; while others cry up that *detestable indifferency* or *neutrality,* abjured in our solemn covenant, in so much that Gamaliel (Acts 5:38, 39) and Gallio (Acts 18:14–17), men who regarded alike the Jewish and the Christian religion, are highly commended as examples "for all Christians," and as men walking by the rules not only of policy, but of "reason and religion."[1] Now, let all those that are either against us, or not with us, do what they can, the right-hand of the most High shall perfect the glorious begun reformation. Can all the world keep down the *Sun of Righteousness* from rising? Or being risen, can they spread a veil over it? And though they dig deep to hide their counsels, is not this a time of God's overreaching and befooling all plotting wits? They have conceived iniquity, and they shall bring forth vanity [Job 15:35]. "They have sown the wind, and they shall reap the whirlwind" (Hos. 8:7).

Wherefore, we "will wait upon the Lord that hideth his face from the house of Jacob, and will look for him" (Isa. 8:17). And "though he slay us, yet will we trust in him" (Job 13:15). The Lord has commanded to proclaim and to say "to the daughter of Zion, Behold thy salvation commeth" (Isa. 62:11). "Rejoice with Jerusalem all you that mourn for her" (Isa. 66:10); for "behold now is the accepted time; behold now is the day of salvation" (2 Cor. 6:2).

But I have more to say. Mourn, O mourn with Jerusalem all you that rejoice for her. "This day is a day of trouble, and of rebuke, and of blasphemy; for the children are come to the birth, and there is not strength to bring forth" (Isa. 37:3). It is an interwoven time, warped with mercies and woofted with judgments. Say not thou in thine heart, the days of my mourning are at an end [cf. Isa. 60:20]. Oh, we are to this day an unhumbled and an unprepared people, and there are among us both many cursed Achans and many sleeping Jonahs, but few wrestling Jacobs, even the wise virgins are

---

1. *Liberty of Conscience,* page 34, 35. [Henry Robinson, *Liberty of Conscience* (London, 1643/44). Gillespie is referring to the Solemn League and Covenant. Cf. The Solemn League & Covenant, in *The Confession of Faith,* etc. (Edinburgh: Johnstone and Hunter, 1855), pp. 358–360.

slumbering with the foolish (Matt. 25:5). Surely, unless we are timely awakened and more deeply humbled, God will punish us yet *seven times* more for our sins (Lev. 26:18, 21, 24, 28); and if He has chastised us with *whips*, He will chastise us with *scorpions,* and He will yet give a further charge to the sword to "avenge the quarrel of" His "covenant" (Lev. 26:25). In such a case I cannot say according to the now Oxford Divinity, that *preces et lachrymae,* prayers and tears, must be our only one shelter and fortress, and that we must cast away defensive arms as unlawful, in any case whatsoever, against the supreme magistrate (that is, by interpretation, they would have us do no more than *pray,* to the end [they] themselves may do no less than *prey*). Wherein they are contradicted not only by Pareus, and by others that are *eager for a Presbytery* (as a prelate of chief note has lately taken, I should say *mistaken,* his mark), [2] but even by those that are *eager royalists.*[3] (Pardon me that I give them not their right name; I am sure when all is well reckoned we are better friends to royal authority than they). Yet herein I do agree with them, that *prayers and tears* will prove our strongest weapons, and the

---

2. Armagh, Sermon at Oxford, March 3, p. 17, 19, 27. [James Ussher (1581–1656), *The Soveraignes Power, and the Subjects Duty* (Oxford, 1644). Just prior, Gillespie is referring to Pareus on Romans, wherein he earned the ire of James I in advocating that it was lawful for subjects at the direction of lesser magistrates to take up defensive arms to defend themselves and the true religion. See David Pareus, *Operum theologicorum partes quatuor,* 3 vols. (Frankfurt: Jonas Rose, 1647) 2.246–263.]

3. Grotius, *de jure Belli ac Pacis,* lib. 1. cap. 4. sect. 7. *Hæc autem lex de qua agimus (de non resistendo supremis potestatibus) pendere videtur a voluntate eorum qui se primum in societatem civilem consociant, a quibus jus porro ad imperantes manat. Hi vero si interrogarentur an velint omnibus hoc onus imponere, ut mori præoptent, quam ullo casu vim superiorum armis arcere, nescio an velle se sint responsuri. Ibid, sect 13. Si rex partem habeat summi imperii, partem alteram populus aut senatus, regi in partem non suam involanti, vis justa opponi poterit.* [Hugo Grotius (1583–1645), *De iure belli ac pacis libri tres. Editio nova* (Amsterdami: Apud Ioh. & Cornelium Blaeu., 1642). Grotius, *Concerning the Law of War and of Peace,* bk. 1, ch. 4, sec. 7. "This law, moreover, about which we are deliberating (concerning non-resistance to the supreme powers) seems to hang upon the will of those who, in the first place, join together in a civil association, from whom, furthermore, the right extends to those who command. If these people, indeed, were asked whether they wished to place this burden on everyone, that they should choose to die rather than hold off a superior force with weapons, I am inclined to think they would respond that they do wish it. Ibid., sec. 13. If the king has a part of the highest command, and the people or senate another part, a just force can then be set against the king if he seizes a part not his own."] I might add the testimonies of Bilson, Barclaius, and others. [See Thomas Bilson, *The True Difference between Christian Subjection and un-Christian Rebellion* (1585; 2ND ed., 1586); extract in "A Discourse upon Questions in debate between the King and Parliament" (1641); and William Barclay, *De Regno et regali potestate* (Paris, 1600). Rutherford cites Barclay to this effect (book 3, chapter 8), "It is lawful for the people, in case of tyranny, to defend themselves, *adversus immanem sævetiam,* against extreme cruelty." *Lex Rex* (1644; Edinburgh: Ogle and Oliver & Boyd, 1843) ch. 29, p. 147.]

only *tela divina*, the weapons that fight for us from above. O then "fear the Lord ye his saints" (Ps. 34:9). O ſtir up yourselves to lay hold on him (Isa. 64:7). "Keep not silence and give him no reſt, till he eſtablish, and till he make Jerusalem a praise in the earth" (Isa. 62:6, 7). O that we could all *make wells* in our dry and desert like hearts (Ps. 84:6), that we may draw out water (1 Sam. 7:6), even buckets full, to quench the wrath of a sin revenging God, the fire which ſtill burns againſt the Lord's inheritance. God grant that this sermon be not as water ſpilt on the ground, but may drop as the rain and "diſtill as the dew" of heaven upon thy soul (Deut. 32:2).

Die Mercurii 27. Martii, 1644.

It is this day ordered by the Commons assembled in Parliament, That Mr. Nicoll do from this House give thanks unto Mr. Gillespie for the great pains he took in the sermon he preached this day at the entreaty of the said Commons, at St. Margaret's Westminster (it being the day of public humiliation), and to desire him to print his sermon. And it is ordered that no man shall presume to print his sermon, but whom he shall authorize under his hand writing.

H. Elsynge Cler. Parl. D. Com.

I appoint *Robert Bostock* to print this sermon.

George Gillespie

A Sermon Preached

Before the Honorable House of Commons at their late Solemn Fast, Wednesday, March 27, 1644

Ezekiel 43:11. *And if they be ashamed of all that they have done, show them the form of the house, and the fashion thereof, and the goings out thereof, and the comings in thereof, and all the forms thereof, and all the ordinances thereof, and all the forms thereof, and all the laws thereof: and write it in their sight, that they may keep the whole form thereof, and all the ordinances thereof, and do them.*

It is not long since I did upon another day of humiliation, lay open England's disease from that text, 2 Chronicles 20:33,[1] "Howbeit the high places were not taken away; for as yet the people had not prepared their hearts unto the God of their fathers." Though the Sun of Righteousness be risen "with healing in his wings" (Mal. 4:2), yet the land is not healed, no, not of its worst disease, which is corruption in religion and the iniquity of your holy things. I did then show the symptoms and the cause of this evil disease. The symptoms are your high places not yet taken away, many of your old superstitious ceremonies to this day remaining, which though not so evil as the high places of idolatry in which idols were worshiped, yet are parallel to the high places of will worship, of which we read that the people, thinking it too hard to be tied to go up to Jerusalem with every sacrifice, "did sacrifice still in the high places, yet unto the Lord their God only" (2 Chron. 33:17), pleading for their doing so, antiquity, custom, and other defenses of that kind, which have been alleged for your ceremonies. But albeit these are foul spots in the church's face, which offend the eyes of her glorious Bridegroom, Jesus Christ, yet that which does less appear is more dangerous, and that is

England's Disease

---

1. [The occasion of this earlier sermon is uncertain and there is no record indicating that Gillespie preached before Parliament prior to this date. He may be referring to an occasion that he had to preach at a church in London observing the monthly fast. That he had preached on more than one occasion around London is clear, because upon Gillespie's return to Scotland, he left a collection of sermons in manuscript with a printer, who for money allowed them to be destroyed (*Works*, "Memoir" {1846}, p. xl; *The Shorter Writings of George Gillespie*, volume 1, p. 52). Gillespie took his seat at the Assembly on September 14, 1643, and he may have preached the earlier sermon on one of the fasts of September 27, October 15, November 29 or December 27, 1643, or January 31 or February 28, 1643/44. For similar comments on 2 Chronicles 33:17, see "Wholesome Severity Reconciled with Christian Liberty," in *The Shorter Writings of George Gillespie*, volume 1, p. 337.]

the cause of this evil, in the very bowels and heart of the church. The people of the land, great and small, have not as yet prepared their hearts unto the Lord their God. Mercy is prepared for the land, but the land is not prepared for mercy. I shall say no more of the disease at this instant.

But I have now chosen a text which holds forth a remedy for this malady; a cure for this case. That is, that if we will "humble our uncircumcised hearts, and accept of the punishment of our iniquity" (Lev. 26:41); if we be "ashamed and confounded" (Ezek. 36:32) before the Lord this day for our evil ways; if we judge ourselves as guilty, and put our mouth in the dust, and clothe ourselves with shame, as with a garment; if we repent and abhor ourselves in dust and ashes; then the Lord will not abhor us, but take pleasure in us, to dwell amongst us, to reveal Himself unto us, to set before us the right pattern of His own house, that the Tabernacle of God may be with men (Rev. 21:3), and pure ordinances, where before[2] they were defiled and mixed. He "will cut off the names of the idols out of the land" (Zech. 13:2), and cause the false "prophet, and the unclean spirit to pass out of the land" and the glory of the Lord shall dwell in the land (Ps. 85:9). But withal we must take heed, that we "turn not again to folly" (Ps. 85:8) that our hearts start not aside, "like a deceitful bow" (Ps. 78:57), that we "keep the ways of the Lord" (Ps. 18:21), and do not wickedly depart from our God. Thus you have briefly the occasion and the sum of what I am to deliver from this text, the particulars whereof I shall not touch till I have in the first place resolved a difficult, yet profitable question.

A Remedy for It

You may ASK, "What house or what temple does the prophet here speak of, and how can it be made to appear that this Scripture is applicable to this time?"

I ANSWER, some have taken great pains to demonstrate that this temple which the prophet saw in this vision, was no other than the temple of Solomon, and that the accomplishment of this vision of the temple, city, and division of the land, was the building of the temple and city again, after the captivity, and the restoring of the Levitical worship and Jewish republic, which came to pass in the days of Nehemiah and Zerubbabel.[3] This sense is also most obvious to everyone that reads this prophecy. But there are very strong reasons against it, which make other learned expositors not to embrace it.

Another Temple Meant in this Vision than that of Jerusalem

---

2. [The word "before" was omitted from the text in *Scots Sermons* (p. 296).]

3. J. Bapista Villalpandus, *Explan. Ezek.*, tom. 2, part. 2, lib. 1, *Isag.*, cap. 9, 12, 13. Corn. à Lapide in Ezek. 40. [Juan Bautista Villalpando (1552–1608), *In Ezechielem explanationes, et apparatus urbis, ac templi Hierosolymitani, commentariis et imaginibus illustratus*, 3 vols. (Romæ, 1596–1604); the first volume is by Jerónimo de Prado. Book 2, part 2: *Templvm Salomonis ab Ezechiele defcriptum imaginibus exprimendum effe. Liber Primvs Isagogicvs*; chapter nine, *Hierofolymitanum Templum Ezechieli fuiffe in vifione oftenfum*, pp. 21–25, chapter 12, pp. 32–35, chapter 13, pp. 35–37. Cornelius à Lapide (1567–1637), *Commentaria in qvatvor Prophetas Maiores* (1622); also *Commentaria in Sacram Scripturam*, 10 vols. (Antwerp, 1681; Neapoli: I. Nagar, 1854–1859), volume 6, pp. 977ff.]

For 1. The temple of Solomon was 120 cubits high. The temple built by Zerubbabel was but 60 cubits high (Ezra 6:3).   Proved by Eight Reasons

2. The temple of Zerubbabel was built in the same place where the temple of Solomon was, that is in Jerusalem upon mount Moriah (Ezra 3:1, 8; 6:3, 5, 7). But this temple of Ezekiel was without the city, and a great way distant from it (Ezek. 48:10 compared with 48:15).[4] The whole portion of the Levites and a part of the portion of the priests was between the temple and the city.

3. Moses' greatest altar, the altar of burnt offerings, was not half so big as Ezekiel's altar (compare Ezekiel 43:16 with Exodus 27:1).[5] So is Moses' altar of incense much less than Ezekiel's altar of incense (Exodus 30:2 compared with Ezekiel 41:22).

4. There are many new ceremonial laws (different from the Mosaical) delivered in the following part of this vision, as interpreters have particularly observed upon these places (Ezek. 45 & 46).[6]

5. The temple and city were not of that greatness which is described in this vision; for the measuring reed containing six cubits of the sanctuary (not common cubits, 40:5), which amount to more than ten feet, the outer wall of the temple being 2,000 reeds in compass (42:20), was by estimation four miles, and the city, six and thirty miles in compass (48:16, 35).

6. The vision of the holy waters issuing from the temple (Ezek. 47), and after the space of 4,000 reeds growing to a river which could not be passed over, and healing the waters and the fishes, cannot be literally understood of the temple at Jerusalem.

7. The land is divided among the twelve tribes (Ezek. 48), and that in a way and order different from the division made by Joshua, which cannot be understood of the restitution after the captivity, because the twelve tribes did not return.

8. This new temple has with it a new covenant, and that an everlasting one (Ezek. 37:26, 27). But at the return of the people from Babylon there was no new covenant, says Irenaeus,[7] only the same that was before continued till Christ's coming.

---

4. C. à Lapide himself reckons the city to be 27 miles distant from the temple [*Commentaria in Sacram Scripturam* (1876), 6.979, §IV.]

5. See also *Codex Middoth*, cap. 3, sect. 1. [Constantine L'Empereur, *Masekhet Midot me-Talmud Bavli: hoc est Talmudis Babylonici codex Middoth, sive de mensuris templi, unà cum versione Latina* (Lugduni Batavorum {Leiden}: Bonaventuræ & Abrahami Elzevir, 1630).]

6. Polanus and Sanctius. [Amandus Polanus (1561–1610), *In librum Prophetiarum Ezechielis commentarii* (Basileæ: Conradus Waldkirchius, 1608). Gaspar Sànchez (1554–1628), *Gasparis Sanctii Centumputeolani, e Societate Iesu Theologi, in Collegio Complutensi sacrarum literarum interpretis, In Ezechielem & Danielem Prophetas commentarij cum paraphrasi* (Lugduni: Sumptibus Horatij Cardon, {1619}).]

7. [Irenaeus,] Lib. 4, cap. 67. [Cf. *Against Heresies*, 4, c. 34. See *The Ante-Nicene Fathers*, vol. 1 (Edinburgh: T. & T. Clark, 1873), p. 512.]

A Sermon Preached Before the House of Commons   93

The Church of
Christ Intended

Wherefore, we must needs [*necessarily*] hold with Jerome, and Gregory,[8] and other later interpreters, that this vision of Ezekiel is to be expounded of the spiritual temple and church of Christ made up of Jews and Gentiles, and that not by way of allegories only, which is the sense of those whose opinion I have now confuted, but according to the proper and direct intendment of the vision, which in many material points cannot agree to Zerubbabel's temple.

I am herein very much strengthened while I observe many parallel passages between the vision of Ezekiel and the Revelation of John;[9] and while I remember withal that the prophets do in many places foretell the institution of the ordinances, government, and worship of the New Testament, under the terms of temple, priests, sacrifices, etc., and do set forth the deliverance and stability of the church of Christ under the notions of Canaan, of bringing back the captivity, etc., God speaking to His people at that time so as they might best understand Him.

Now, if you ASK, "how the several particulars in the vision may be particularly expounded and applied to the church of Christ"? I ANSWER: the Word of God, the "river that makes glad the city of God," though it has many easy and known fords, where any of Christ's lambs may pass through, yet in this vision and other places of this kind, it is a *great deep*, where the greatest elephant (as he said)[10] may swim. I shall not say with the Jews that one should not read the last nine chapters of Ezekiel before he is thirty years old.[11] Surely a man may be twice thirty years old, and a good divine too, and yet not able to understand this vision.[12] Some tell us that no man can understand it without skill in geometry, which cannot be denied; but there is greater need of ecclesiometry, if I may so speak, to measure the church in her length, or continuance through many generations; in her breadth, or spreading through many nations; her depth of humiliation, sorrows, and sufferings; her height of faith, hope, joy, and comfort, and to measure each part according to this pattern here set before us.

Wherein, for my part, I must profess (as Socrates in another case)[13]

---

8. [Jerome,] Lib. 13 in Ezek. [Gregory,] Hom. 13. in Ezek. [Cf. *PL* 25 and *PL* 76 respectively. In English see Jerome, *Commentary on Ezekiel*, translated by Thomas P. Scheck (New York; Mahwad, NJ: The Newman Press, 2017) and Gregory, *Homilies on the book of the Prophet Ezekiel*, translated by Theodosia Tomkinson, second ed. (Etna, Calif: Center for Traditionalist Orthodox Studies, 2008).]

9. Compare Ezekiel 37:27 with Revelation 21:3; Ezek. 40:2 with Rev. 21:10; Ezek. 40:3–5 with Rev. 11:1 and Rev. 21:15. Ezek. 43:2 with Rev. 14:2. Ezek. 45:8–9 with Rev. 17:16, 17 and 21:24. Ezek. 38:2 and 39:1 with Rev. 20:8. Ezek. 47:12 with Rev. 22:2. Ezek. 48:1–8 with Rev. 7:4–9. Ezek. 48:31–34 with Rev. 21:12, 13, 16. Ezek. 40:4 with Rev. 1:11 and 4:1.

10. [Unidentified "he": Cf. Gregory, *Moralia in Job*, Epistola Leandro 4, *PL* 75.515a.]

11. [Cf. Jerome, Letter 53 to Paulinus, *NPNF2*, vol. 6, page 101.]

12. [Gillespie was Thirty-one years old when he delivered this sermon.]

13. [Plato, *Apology of Socrates* (21 d). "I know that I do not know."]

Scio quod nescio. I know that there is a great mystery here which I cannot reach. Only I shall set forth unto you that little light which the Father of lights has given me.

I conceive that the Holy Ghost in this vision has pointed at four several times and conditions of the church, that we may take with us the full meaning without addition or diminution.

Four Things Held Forth in the Vision

Observing this rule, that what agrees not to the type must be meant of the thing typified, and what is not fulfilled at one time must be fulfilled of the church at another time.

First of all, it cannot be denied that he points in some sort at the restitution of the temple, worship of God, and city of Jerusalem after the captivity, as a type of the church of Christ. For though many things in the vision do not agree to that time, as has been proved, yet some things do agree: this, as it is least intended in the vision, so it is not fit for me at this time to insist upon it. But he that would understand the form of the temple of Jerusalem, the several parts and excellent structure thereof, will find enough written of that subject.[14]

1. The Material Temple as a Type

Secondly, this and other prophecies of building again the temple may well be applied to the building of the Christian church by the master-builders, the apostles, and by the ministers of the gospel since their days. Let us hear but two witnesses of the apostles themselves applying those prophecies to the calling of the Gentiles. The one is Paul. "For ye are the temple of the living God, as God hath said, I will dwell in them and walk in them, and I will be their God, and they shall be my people" (2 Cor. 6:16). The other is James, who applies to the converted Gentiles that prophecy of Amos, "After this I will return and build again the tabernacle of David, which is fallen down; and I will build again the ruins thereof, and I will set it up" (Acts 15:16).

2. The Church of the Gentiles

But there is a third thing aimed at in this prophecy, and that more principally than any of the other two, which is the repairing of the breaches and ruins of the Christian church and the building up of Zion in her glory, about

3. A More Glorious Church in the Latter Days

---

14. *Codex Middoth cum Commentariis Const. L'Empereur.* Arias Montanus, in his *Libanus.* J. Baptista Villalpandus, *Explan. Ezek.*, tom. 2, part 2; tom. 3. Tostatus, in 1 Reg. 6. Lud. Cappellus, in *Compendio Hist. Judaicæ.* Ribera, *de Templo*, lib. 1; and many others. [Constantine L'Empereur, *Masekhet Midot me-Talmud Bavli: hoc est Talmudis Babylonici codex Middoth.* Benito Arias Montano, *Libanus.* First published in *Biblia Sacra Hebraice, Chaldaice, Græce, & Latinæ* (Antwerp: Plantinus, 1569–1572); cf. *Antiquitatum Iudaicarum libri IX., in quîs, praeter Iudeae, Hierosolymorum, & Templi Salomonis accuratam delineationem ...* (Lugduni Batavorum: F Raphelengium: 1593). Juan Bautista Villalpando, *In Ezechielem explanationes.* Alonso Tostado (1400–1455), *Alphonsi Tostati Hispani episcopi Abulensis, Opera omnia, quotquot in Scripturae Sacrae expositionem et alia, adhuc extare inuenta sunt,* 28 vols. (Venetiis: apud Io. Baptistam, et Io. Bernardum Sessam, 1596) vol. 11–12, Commentary on 1 Kings. Louis Cappel (1585–1658), *Historia apostolica illustrata ... additum est historiae Iudaicae ...* (Genevae: Sumptibus Ioan. de Tournes & Iac. de la Pierre., [1634]). Francisco de Ribera, *De templo et de ijs quae ad templum pertinent, libri qvinqve* (Antverpiae: Apud Petrum & Ioannem Belleros, 1623).]

---

the time of the destruction of Antichrist and the conversion of the Jews; and this happiness has the Lord reserved to the last times to build a more excellent and glorious temple than former generations have seen. I mean not of the building of the material temple at Jerusalem, which the Jews do fancy and look for, but I speak of the church and people of God; and that I may not seem to expound an obscure prophecy too conjecturally, which many in these days do, I have these evidences following, for what I say:

Proved by Five
Reasons

(1) If Paul and James, in those places which I last cited, do apply the prophecies of building a new temple to the firstfruits of the Gentiles, and to their first conversion, then they are much more to be applied to the fullness of the Gentiles, and most of all to the fullness both of Jews and Gentiles, which we wait for. "Now if the fall of them" (says the apostle, speaking of the Jews) "be the riches of the world, and the diminishing of them the riches of the Gentiles; how much more their fullness?" (Rom. 11:12). And again, "If the casting away of them be the reconciling of the world, what shall the receiving of them be, but life from the dead?" (Rom. 11:15). Plainly insinuating a greater increase of the church and a larger spread of the gospel at the conversion of the Jews, and so a fairer temple, yea, another world in a manner to be looked for.

(2) The Lord himself in this same chapter ([Ezek. 43:]7), speaking of the temple here prophesied of, says, "The place of my throne, and the place of the soles of my feet, where I will dwell in the midst of the children of Israel forever, and my holy name shall the house of Israel no more defile, neither they nor their kings," etc; which as it cannot be understood of the Jews after the captivity, who did again forsake the Lord, and were forsaken of Him, as Jerome notes upon the place,[15] so it can as ill be said to be already fulfilled upon the Christian church, but rather that such a church is yet to be expected in which the Lord shall take up His dwelling forever, and shall not be provoked by their defilements and whoredoms again to take away His kingdom and to remove the candlestick.

(3) This last temple is also prophesied of by Isaiah (Isa. 2:2). "And it shall come to pass in the last days, that the mountain of the Lord's house shall be established in the top of the mountains" (even as here Ezekiel did see this temple "upon a very high mountain," Ezek. 40:2) "and shall be exalted above the hills, and all the nations shall flow unto it," etc. "And they shall beat their swords into plough shares, and their spears into pruning hooks: nation shall not lift up sword against nation, neither shall they learn war any more" (Isa. 2:4). Here is the building of such a temple as shall bring peaceable and quiet times to the church, of which that evangelical prophet speaks in other places also (Isa. 11:9; 60:17, 18). And if we shall read that which follows, as the Chaldee paraphrase[16] does (Isa. 2:5), "And the men of the house of Jacob shall say, Come ye," etc., then the building of

---

15. [Cf. Jerome, *In Ezechielem*, *PL* 25.414d–418d.]

16. [The Chaldee paraphrase is in the Antwerp Polyglot.]

the temple there ſpoken of shall appear to be joined with the Jews' conversion; but, howsoever, it is joined with a great peace and calm, such as
yet the church has not seen.

(4) We find in this vision, that when Ezekiel's temple is built, princes shall
no more oppress the people of God, nor defile the name of God (Ezek. 45:8;
43:7),[17] which are in like manner joined (Ps. 102:15, 16), "The heathen shall
fear the name of the Lord and all the kings of the earth thy glory, when the
Lord shall build up Zion, he shall appear in his glory," (v. 22), "when the people are gathered together, and the kingdoms" (underſtand here also kings
as the Septuagint does) "to serve the Lord"; which psalm is acknowledged
to be a prophecy of the kingdom of Chriſt, though under the type of bringing back the captivity of the Jews, and of the building again of Zion at that
time. The like prophecy of Chriſt we have in Psalm 72:11: "All kings shall fall
down before him, all nations shall serve him." But I ask, have not the kings
of the earth hitherto for the moſt part set themselves "againſt the Lord, and
againſt his Chriſt"[18] (Ps. 2:2)? And how then shall all those prophecies hold
true, except they be coincident with Revelation 17:16, 17, and that time is yet to
come,[19] when God shall put it in the hearts of kings to "hate the whore" (of
Rome) "and they shall make her desolate and naked, and shall eat her flesh,
and burn her with fire." It is foretold that God shall do this great and good
work, even by those kings, who have before subjeĉted themselves to Antichriſt.

(5) That which I now draw from Ezekiel's vision is no other but the same
which was showed to John (Rev. 11:1, 2), a place so like to this of Ezekiel, that
we muſt take ſpecial notice of it, and make that serve for a commentary to
this. "And there was given me (says John) a reed like unto a rod: and the angel ſtood, saying, Rise, and measure the temple of God, and the altar, and
them that worship therein. But the court which is without the temple leave
out, and measure it not; for it is given unto the Gentiles; and the holy city
shall they tread under foot forty and two months." This time of two and forty
months muſt be expounded by Revelation 13:5, where it is said of the beaſt,

---

17. Polanus, in Ezek. 45. *De Reformatione Status Civilis agitur, v. 8–10* [*sic* 9, 10, 11 &12]. *In
quibus prædiĉtio eſt, etiam principes et magiſtratus politcos, adducendos ad obedientiam fidei in
Chriſtum, aut saltem coercendos et in officio continendos, ne amplius opprimant populum Dei.*
[Polanus, *In librum prophetiarum Ezechielis commentarii* (Basileae: typis Conradi Waldkirchii,
1608), p. 822. "Dispute over the Reformation of the Civil State, v. 8–10. In these matters the
admonition is that even princes and political magistrates must be brought to the obedience
of faith in Christ, or at least restrained and repressed in their office, lest they oppress the
people of God more severely."]

18. [The text in *Works* (p. 8) and in *Scots Sermons* (p. 303) was set as "against his Anointed"
as in the Authorized Version.]

19. ["that time yet [to] come." The "to" is missing from the early impressions. This was
corrected by the brief errata that appears in some London impressions, and was corrected in
the Edinburgh edition. The text in *Works* (p.8) is correct, but the "to" was omitted from the
text in *Scots Sermons*.]

"power was given unto him to continue forty and two months"; which, according to the computation of Egyptian years (reckoning thirty days to each month) makes three years and a half, or 1,260 days, and that is the time of the witnesses' prophesying in sackcloth, and of the woman's abode in the wilderness (Rev. 11:3; 12:6).

Now, lest it should be thought that the treading down of the holy city by the Gentiles (that is, the treading under foot of the true church, the city of God, by the tyranny of Antichrist and the power of his complices) should never have an end in this world, the angel gives John to understand that the church, the house of the living God, shall not lie desolate forever, but shall be built again (for the measuring is in reference to building), that the kingdom of Antichrist shall come to an end, and that after 1,260 years, counting days for years, as the prophets do. It is not my purpose now to search when this time of the power of the beast and of the church's desolation did begin, and when it ends, and so to find out the time of building this new temple. Only this much I trust I may say, that if we reckon from the time that the power of the beast did begin, and withal consider the great revolution and turning of things upside down in these our days, certainly the work is upon the wheel. The Lord has plucked His hand out of His bosom, He has "whet his sword; he hath bent his bow, … he hath also prepared [for him] the instruments of death," against Antichrist. So says the Psalmist of all persecutors in Psalm 7:12–13, but it will fall most upon that capital enemy. Whereof there will be occasion to say more afterward.

[4.] Let me here only add a word concerning a fourth thing which the Holy Ghost may seem to intend in this prophecy, and that is the church triumphant, the new Jerusalem which is above,[20] unto which respect is to be had (as interpreters judge) in some parts of the vision, which happily cannot be so well applied to the church in this world. Even as the new Jerusalem is so described in the Revelation (Rev. 21), that it may appear to be[21] the church of Christ, reformed, beautified, and enlarged in this world, and fully perfected and glorified in the world to come, and as many things which are said of it can very hardly be made to agree to the church in this world, so other things which are said of it can as hardly be applied to the church glorified in heaven; as where it is said, "Behold the tabernacle of God is with men (having "come down from God out of heaven"), "and he will dwell with them, and they shall be his people, and God himself shall be with them, and be their God" (v. 3). Again, "And the nations of them that are saved shall walk in the light of it: and the kings of the earth do bring their glory and honor into it" (v. 24).

But now I make haste to the several particulars contained in my text: "I pray God," says the apostle, "your whole spirit and soul and body be preserved blameless" (1 Thessalonians 5:23; so Philippians 1:9, 11). And what he

[Marginal notes: 4. Some Respect had to the Church Triumphant]

[Marginal note: The Text Divided]

---

20. [Cf. Galatians 4:26; Revelation 3:12; 21:2.]

21. [The word "be" was omitted from the text in *Scots Sermons* (p. 305). The "So" at Philippians 1:9, 11 in the next paragraph was also omitted.]

there prays for this text rightly understood and applied may work in us, that is, gracious affections, gracious minds, gracious actions. I. In the first place, a change upon our corrupt and wicked affections. *If they be ashamed of all that they have done*, saith the Lord. II. A change upon our blind minds, *Show them the form of the house, and the fashion thereof,* etc. III. A change also upon our actions, *That they may keep the whole form thereof, and all the ordinances thereof, and do them.*

I. For the first, the word here used is not that which signifies blushing through modesty, but it signifies shame for that which is indeed shameful, filthy, and abominable,[22] so that it were impenitency and an aggravation of the fault not to be ashamed for it.

I shall here build only one doctrine, which will be of exceeding great use for such a day as this. *If either we would have mercy to ourselves, or would do acceptable service in the public reformation, we must not only cease to do evil and learn to do well, but also be ashamed, confounded, and humbled for our former evil ways.* Here is a twofold necessity, which presses upon us this day, to loathe and abhor ourselves for all our abominations, to be greatly abashed and confounded before our God. First, without this we shall not find grace and favor to our own souls. Secondly, we shall else miscarry in the work of reformation.

1. I say, let us do all the good we can, God is not pleased with us unless we are ashamed and humbled for former guiltiness. "Be zealous" "and repent" says Christ to the Laodiceans. Be zealous in the time coming, and repent of your former lukewarmness (Rev. 3:19). "What fruit had ye then in those things whereof now ye are ashamed," says the apostle to the saints at Rome (Rom. 6:21), of whom he says plainly that they[23] were "servants to righteousness," and had their "fruit unto holiness" (Rom. 6:19, 22).[24] But that is not all. They were also ashamed while they looked back upon their old faults, which is the rather to be observed because it makes against the antinomian error now afoot.[25] It has a clear reason for it, for without this God is still

Reformation not Enough without Humiliation, Proved Two Ways

---

22. It is not בּוֹשׁ, *bosch* [buwsh], but כּלם, *calam* [kalam]. Which two, some Hebricians distinguish by referring the former to the Greek αἰδὼσ [*aidos*], and the Latin *verecundia* [*bashfulness*]; the latter to the Greek αἰσχύνη [*aischune*], and the Latin *pudor* [*dishonor*]. [The London errata instructed as the second of four corrections to make, the relatively minor change to put a missing comma before *bosch*, but for some reason not before *calam*, which was also missing. The Edinburgh edition omits the renderings in Hebrew and puts a comma after *bosch* and a colon after *calam*. *Works* (p. 9) puts a comma after both Hebrew words. *Scots Sermons* did not punctuate satisfactorily and omitted the correction (*Sermons Preached before the English Houses of Parliament by the Scottish Commissioners*, p. 328).]

23. [The word "they" was omitted from the text in *Scots Sermons* (p. 306).]

24. [The "22" was omitted from the text in *Scots Sermons* (p. 306) and *Works* (p. 10).]

25. Vid. Martyr in Rom. 6:21. [Peter Martyr Vermigli (1499–1562), *In epistolam S. Pauli Apostoli Ad Romanos*, third ed. (Basel, 1568), p. 236; *Most learned and fruitfull commentaries of D. Peter Martir Vermilius Florentine, Professor of divinitie in the Schole of Tigure, vpon the Epistle of S. Paul to the Romanes* (London: By Iohn Daye, 1568), p. 156v.]

dishonored and not restored to His glory. "O Lord," says Daniel, "righteousness belongeth unto thee, but unto us confusion of faces" (Dan. 9:7).

Those two go together. We must be confounded that God may be glorified. We must be judged that God may be justified. Our mouths must be stopped and laid in the dust that the Lord may be just when He speaketh and clear when he judgeth (Ps. 51:4). And as the apostle teaches us (1 Cor. 11:31), that "if we judge ourselves, we shall not be judged of God"; and by the rule of contraries, if we judge not ourselves, we shall be judged of God; so say I now, if we give glory to God and take shame and confusion of faces to ourselves, God shall not confound us nor put us to shame. But if we will not be confounded and ashamed of ourselves, God shall confound us and poor shame upon us. If we do not loath ourselves, God shall loath us.

Nay, let me argue from the manner of men, as the prophet does (Mal. 1:8): "offer it now unto the [*sic*] governor; will he be pleased with thee, or accept thy person?" Will your governor, nay, your neighbor who is as you are, after an injury done to him, be pleased with you, if you do but leave off to do him any more such injuries? Will he not expect an acknowledgement of the wrong done? Is it not Christ's rule (Luke 17:4), that he who seven times trespasses against his brother, "seven times … turn again, … saying, I repent?" David would hardly trust Ittai to go up and down with him, who was but a stranger (2 Sam. 15:19). How much more if he had done him some great wrong and then refused to confess it? And how shall we think that it can stand with the honor of the most high God, that we seem to draw near unto Him and to walk in His ways, while, in the meantime, we do not acknowledge our iniquity and even accuse, shame, judge, and condemn ourselves? Nay, "be not deceived, God is not mocked" (Gal. 6:7).

This is the first necessity of the duty which this text holds forth. The Lord requires of us not only to do His will for the future, but to be ashamed for what we have done amiss before.

2. The other necessity of it (which is also in the text) is this: that except we are thus ashamed and humbled, God has not promised to show us the pattern of His house, nor to reveal His will unto us; which agrees well with that in Psalm 25:9: "The meek will he teach his way," and (v. 12), "What man is he that feareth the Lord? Him shall he teach in the way that he shall choose," and (v. 14), "The secret of the Lord is with them that fear him, and he will show them his covenant." There is sanctification in the affections, and here is humiliation in the affections, spoken of as necessary means of attaining the knowledge of the will of God. Let the affections be ordered aright, then light which is offered shall be seen and received; but let light be offered when disordered affections do overcloud the eye of the mind, then is all in vain.

As the Affections
are, so is the
Judgment

In this case, a man shall be like "the deaf adder" (Ps. 58:4, 5), which will not be taken by the voice of the charmers, "charming never so wisely." Let the helm of reason be stirred as well as you can imagine, if there is a contrary wind in the sails of the affections, the ship will not answer to the helm. It is a good argument: he is a wicked man, a covetous man, a proud man, a carnal man, an unhumbled man; *Ergo* [*therefore*], he will readily miscarry in his judgment. So divines have argued against the Pope's infallibility! The Pope has been and may be a profane man; *Ergo*, he may err in his judgment and decrees. And what wonder that they who receive not the love of the truth are given over to "strong delusion, that they should believe a lie" (2 Thess. 2:9, 10[, 11])? It is as good an argument: he is a humbled man and a man that fears God; *Ergo* (insofar as he acts and exercises those graces), the Lord shall teach him in the way that He shall choose [Ps. 25:12]. I say, insofar as he acts those graces, because when he grieves the Spirit and cherishes the flesh, when the child of God is more swayed by his corruptions than by his graces, then he is in great danger to be given up to the counsel of his own heart, and to be deserted by the Holy Ghost, which should lead him "into all truth" (John 16:13).

But we must take notice of a seeming contradiction here in the text. God says to the prophet in the former verse [Ezek. 43:10], *Show the house to the house of Israel, that they may be ashamed of their iniquities*; and in Jeremiah 31:19, Ephraim is first instructed, then ashamed. And here it is quite turned over in my text; if they are ashamed show them the house.

I shall not here make any digression unto the debates and distinctions of schoolmen, what influence and power the affections have upon the understanding and the will. I will content myself with this plain answer. Those two might very well stand together: light is a help to humiliation, and humiliation a help to light. As there must be some work of faith and some apprehension of the love of God in order before true evangelical repentance, yet this repentance helps us to believe more firmly that our sins are forgiven. The soul in the pains of the new birth is like Tamar travailing of her twins, Pharez and Zarah (Gen. 38:28–30): faith, like Zarah, first putting out his hand, but has no strength to come forth, therefore draws back the hand again till repentance, like Pharez, has broken forth; then can faith come more easily—which appears in that woman in Luke 7:47, 48. She wept much because she loved much; she loved much because she believed and by faith had her heart enlarged with apprehending the rich grace and free love of Christ to poor sinners. This faith moves her bowels, melts her heart, stirs her sorrow, kindles her affection. Then, and not till then, she gets a prop to her faith and a sure ground to build upon. It is not till she has wept much that Christ intimates mercy and faith: "Thy sins are forgiven thee." Just so is the case in this text. Show them the house, says the Lord, that they may be ashamed. Give them a view of it that they may think the worse of themselves that they want [*lack*] it, that they may be ashamed for all their iniquities whereby they have separated between their God and themselves, so that they cannot "behold the beauty of the Lord," nor "inquire in his temple" (Ps. 27:4); and if, when they begin to see it, they have such thoughts as these and humble themselves and acknowledge their iniquities, then go to and show them the whole fabric, and structure, and all the gates thereof, and all the parts thereof, and all things pertaining thereto.

I suppose I have said enough for confirmation and clearing of the doctrine concerning the necessity of our being ashamed and confounded before the Lord. I have now a fourfold application to draw from it.

1. The first application shall be to the malignant enemies of the cause and people of God at this time, who deserve Jeremiah's black mark to be put upon them. "Were they ashamed when they had committed abomination? Nay, they were not at all ashamed, neither could they blush" (Jer. 6:15; 8:12). When he would say the worst of them, this is it: "Thou hadst a whore's forehead, thou refusedst to be ashamed" (Jer. 3:3). There are some sons of Belial risen against us, who have done some things whereof, I dare say, many heathens would have been ashamed; yet they are as far from being ashamed of their outrages as Caligula was, who said of himself that he loved nothing better in his own nature than that he could not be ashamed.[26] Nay, "their glory is their shame" (Phil. 3:19), and if the Lord does not open their eyes to see their shame, their end will be destruction. Is it a light matter to swear and blaspheme, to coin and spread lies, to devise calumnies, to break treaties, to contrive treacherous plots, to exercise so many barbarous cruelties, to shed so much blood, and, as if that were too little, to bury men quick [*alive*]?[27] Is all this no matter of shame? And when they have so often professed to be for the true Protestant religion, shall they not be ashamed to thirst so much after Protestant blood, and in that cause desire to associate themselves with all the papists at home and abroad whose assistance they can have, and particularly with those matchless monsters (they call them subjects) of Ireland, who, if the computation fails not, have shed the blood of some hundred thousands in that kingdom? For our part, it seems they are resolved to give the worst name to the best thing which we can do, and therefore they have not been ashamed to call a religious and loyal covenant a traitorous and damnable covenant.[28] I have no pleasure to take up these and other dunghills, the text has put this in my mouth which I have said. O that they could recover themselves out of the "gall of bitterness, and bond of iniquity" (Acts 8:23). O that we could hear that they begin to be ashamed of their abominations. "Lord when thy hand is lifted up, they will not see; but they shall see and be ashamed, for their envy at thy people" (Isa. 26:11). "The Lord shall appear to your joy, and they shall be ashamed" (Isa. 66:5).

26. [Cf. John Carew Rolfe. *Suetonius* (London: W. Heinemann, 1920), pp. 450–451.]

27. [The text in *Scots Sermons* (p. 310) incorrectly rendered this "quick[ly.]"]

28. ["and particularly especially that act concerning that traitorous and damnable covenant drawn up and taken between them and the rebels here…." Called a "declaration at Oxford and rebellion in the north and south" by the Scottish Parliament and referred to as a remonstrance by the authors. "Act anent the declaration at Oxford and rebellion in the north and south," in *The Records of the Parliaments of Scotland to 1707*, ed. K.M. Brown et al. (St. Andrews, 2007–2022), 1644/6/247. Date accessed: 22 March 2022. http://www.rps.ac.uk/trans/1644/6/247. Cf. John Spalding, *The History of the Troubles and Memorable Transactions in Scotland from 1624 to 1645* (Aberdeen: George King, 1829), p. 386.]

2. But now in the second place let me speak to the kingdom, and to you whom it concerns this day[29] to be humbled, both for your own sins, and for the sins of the kingdom which you represent. Although yourselves, whom God has placed in this honorable station, and the kingdom which God has blessed with many choice blessings, are much and worthily honored among the children of men, yet when you have to do with God, and with that wherein His great name and His glory is concerned, you must not think of honoring, but rather [of] abashing yourselves, and creeping low in the dust. Livy tells us when M. Claudius Marcellus would have dedicated a temple to *Honor* and *Virtue*, the priests hindered it, *quod utri Deo res divina fi eret, sciri non posset*, because so it could not be known to which of the two gods he should offer sacrifice (*Decad.*, 3. l. 7).[30] Far be it from any of you to suffer the will of God and your own credit to come in competition together, or to put back any point of truth because it may seem, peradventure, some way to wound your reputation, though, when all is well examined, it shall be found your glory.

2. [Second] Application to the Kingdom

You are now about the casting out of many corruptions in the government of the church and worship of God. Remember, therefore, it is not enough to cleanse the house of the Lord, but you must be humbled for your former defilements wherewith it was polluted. It is not enough that England says with Ephraim in one place, "What have I to do any more with Idols?" (Hos. 14:8). England must say also with Ephraim in another place, "Surely after that I was turned, I repented; and after that I was instructed, I smote upon my thigh: I was ashamed and even confounded because I did bear the reproach of my youth" (Jer. 31:19). Let England sit down in the dust and wallow itself in ashes and cry out as the lepers did (Lev. 13:45), "Unclean, unclean," and then rise up and cast away the least superstitious ceremony, "as a menstruous cloth, and say unto it, Get thee hence" (Isa. 30:22).

In Regard of Former Defilements

I know that those who are not convinced of the intrinsical evil and unlawfulness of former corruptions, may, upon other considerations, go along and join in this reformation; for according to Augustine's rule,[31] men are to let go those ecclesiastical customs which neither Scriptures nor councils

---

29. [The word "day" was omitted from *Scots Sermons* (p. 311).]

30. [Cf. *Livy*, trans. George Baker, 7 volumes (London: Valpy, 1833–34), volume 5, History of Rome, book xxvii, page. 45.]

31. Augustine, Epistle 119, c. 19. [See "Ad Inquisitiones Januarii, Libri Secundus, seu, Epistola LV, Caput XIX. *PL* 33.221; *NPNF1* 1.315.] *Omnia itaque talia quæ neque sacrarum Scripturarum auctoritatibus continentur nec Episcoporom Conciliis statuta inveniuntur, nec consuetudine universæ ecclesiæ roborata sunt, sed diversorum locorum diversis moribus innumerabiliter variantur, ita ut vix aut omnino nunquam inveniri possint causæ, quas in eis instituendis homines secuti sunt, ubi facultas tribuetur, sine ulla dubitatione, resecanda existimo. *[And so I judge that all such things that are neither contained in the authority of the Holy Scripture nor found set forth in the Councils of the Bishops, and not confirmed by the usage of the whole church, but vary innumerably because of the different customs of different places, so that hardly, or

bind upon us, nor yet are universally received by all churches. And according to Ambrose's rule to Valentinian,[32] epistle 31, *Nullus pudor est ad meliora transive*, it is no shame to change that which is not so good for that which is better. So does Arnobius answer the pagans who objected the novelty of the Christian religion. You should not look so much, says he, *quid reliquerimus*, as *quid secuti simus*—be rather satisfied with the good which we follow, than to quarrel why we have changed our former practice.[33] He gives instance that when men found the art of weaving clothes, they did no longer clothe themselves in skins, and when they learned to build houses, they left off to dwell in rocks and caves. All this carries reason with it, for *Optimum est eligendum*.[34] If all this does not satisfy, it may be Nazianzen's rule will move some man.[35] When there was a great stir about his archbishopric of Constantinople, he yielded for peace; because this storm was raised for his sake, he wished to be cast into the sea. He often professes that he did not affect riches nor dignities, but rather to be freed of his bishopric. We are like

---

indeed never, could the causes be found which men were following in establishing them, must without any doubt, when the possibility is allowed, be cut off.]

32. [Ambrose, Epistola XVIII, Migne, *PL* 16.1015; *NPNF1* 10.418. *PL* reads *transire* for *transive*.]

33. Arnob., *adversus Gentes*, lib. 2. *Cum igitur et vos ipso modo illos mores, modo alias leges, fueritis secuti, multaque vel erroribus cognitis, vel animadversione meliorum sint a vobis repudiata: quid est a nobis factum, contra sensum judiciumque commune, si majora et certiora delegimus?* [Arnobius, of Sicca (died c. 330 AD). See Migne, *Patrologiæ Latinæ*, 5.921. "Arnob., *against the Nations*, bk. 2. Therefore, since you had been following at one particular time those customs, then other laws, and many things have been repudiated by you, either by having recognized errors or by paying attention to better things: what has been done by us against common sense and judgment, if we have chosen greater and more certain things?" See also, *The Ante-Nicene Fathers (ANF)*, vol. 6, ¶68, page 460.]

34. [The best must be chosen.]

35. Gregory Nazianzens, Orat. 28. *Primariæ sedis dignitatem nobis eripient? quam prudentum etiam quispiam aliquando admiratus est: nunc autem eam fugere ut mihi quidem videtur prinæ et singularis est prudentiæ: propter hanc enim res omnes nostræ jactantur ac concutiuntur propter hanc fines orbis terræ suspicione et bello flagrant, &c. Utinam autem ne ullus quidem sedis principatus esset, nec ulla loci prælatio, et tyrannica prærogativa, ut ex sola virtute cognosceremur. Vile etiam Orat. 27, 32; Carm. 12, ad Constantinop.* [*Opera omnia*, 2 vols. (Paris: 1583), 1.683, 693, 720 and 2.1315. See Orat. 26 (alias 28), 36 (alias 27), and 42 (alias 32), in *PG* 35.1247, 36.266, 457. See Carmina X, Ad Constantinopolitanos sacerdotes, et ipsam urbem, Liber II, Poemata Historica, PG 37.1028. Carmina X is numbered XII in *Opera nunc primum Graece et Latine* Tomus 2 (Paris, 1611), p. 85. "Will they snatch from us the dignity of the primary position? which indeed, anyone among the prudent has, at some time, regarded with admiration: now, however, to flee that position seems to me to be of the most obvious and particular prudence, for on account of it all our business is tossed about and agitated. On account of it the ends of the earth are ablaze with suspicion and war, and so on. But of [*sic* if] only, indeed, there were not any preeminence of position, nor any preference of place and tyrannical privilege, that we might be recognized on the basis of our virtue alone." *Scots Sermons* read "of."]

to listen long before we hear such expressions either from Archbishop or Bishop in England, who seem not to care much who sink, so that they themselves swim above. Yet I shall name one rule more, which I shall take from the confessions of two English prelates. One of them has this contemplation upon Hezekiah's taking away the brazen serpent, when he perceived it to be superstitiously abused. "Superstitious use," says he, "can mar the very institutions of God; how much more the most wise and well grounded devices of men?"[36] Another of them acknowledges that whatsoever is taken up at the injunction of men and is not of God's own prescribing when it is drawn to superstition, comes under the case of the brazen serpent.[37] You may easily make the assumption and then the conclusion concerning those ceremonies which are not God's institutions but men's devices, and have been grossly and notoriously abused by many to superstition.

Now, to return to the point in hand, if upon all or any of these or the like principles, any of this kingdom shall join in the removal of corruptions out of the church, which yet they do not conceive to be in themselves and intrinsically corruptions in religion, in this case I say (as the apostle in another place) "I therein do rejoice and will rejoice" (Phil. 1:18), because *every way* reformation is set forward. But let such a one look to himself how the doctrine drawn from this text falls upon him, that he who only ceases to do evil, but repents not of the evil, he who applies himself to reformation, but is not ashamed of former defilements, is in danger both of God's displeasure, and of miscarrying in his judgment about reformation. It is far from my meaning to discourage any who are with humble and upright hearts seeking after more light than yet they have. I say it only for their sake who through the presumption and unhumbledness of their spirits will acknowledge no fault in anything they have formerly done in church matters.

I cannot leave this application to the kingdom till I enlarge it a little further. There are four considerations which may make England ashamed and confounded before the Lord.

(1) Because of the great blessings which it has so long wanted. Your flourishing estate in the world could not have countervailed the want [*lack*] of the purity and liberty of the ordinances of Christ. That was a heavy word of the prophet, "Now for a long season Israel has been without the true God, and without a teaching priest, and without law" (2 Chron. 15:3). It has not been altogether so with this land, where the Lord has had not only a true church, but many burning and shining lights, many gracious preachers and professors, many notable defenders of the Protestant cause against papists, many

---

36. Bp. Hall, lib. 7., *Contemplations*. [Joseph Hall (1574–1656), *Contemplations vpon the Histoire of the Old Testament. 7th volume* (1623). Cf. *Works* (1863), 1.167.]

37. Bp. Andrewes, Sermon on Phil. 2:10. [Lancelot Andrewes (1555–1626), *XCVI Sermons* (1635). Cf. *Ninety-Six Sermons* (Oxford: Parker, 1841), 2.336–337. Gillespie cites Hall and Andrewes similarly in *English Popish Ceremonies*. See respectively 4.9.7 and 3.2.5, or pages 417 and 153 in the 2013 Naphtali Press edition.]

who have preached and written worthily of practical divinity, and of those things which most concern a man's salvation. Nay, I am persuaded that all this time past there have been in this kingdom many thousands of His secret and sealed ones, who have been groaning under that burden and bondage which they could not help, and have been "waiting for the consolation of Israel" (Luke 2:25). Nevertheless, the reformation of the Church of England has been exceedingly deficient in government, discipline, and worship. Yea, and many places of the kingdom have been "without a teaching priest" and other places poisoned with false teachers. It is said in 1 Samuel 7:2 that all the house of Israel lamented after the Lord when they wanted [*did not have*] the ark twenty years. O let England lament after the Lord until the Ark is brought into the own place of it [*its own place*].

2. For its Great Sins Engraven in the Present Judgments   (2) There is another cause of this great humiliation, and that is the point in the text, to be ashamed *of all that you have done.* Sin, sin is that which blacks our faces and covers us with confusion as with a mantle; and then most of all when we may read our sin in some judgment of God which lies upon us. Therefore, the Septuagint here instead of being "ashamed of all that they have done," reads "accept their punishment for all that they have done,"[38] which agrees to that word in the Law, "If then their uncircumcised hearts be humbled" (the Greek reads there "ashamed") "and they then accept of the punishment of their iniquity" (Lev. 26:41). This is now England's case, whose sin is written in the present judgment and graven in your calamity as "with a pen of iron, and with a point of a diamond" (Jer. 17:1), to make you say, "The Lord our God is righteous in all his works, which he doeth: for we obeyed not his voice" (Dan. 9:14).

Did not the land make idol gods of the court, and of the prelatical clergy, and feared them, and followed them more than God, and obeyed them rather than God, so that their threshold was set by God's threshold and their posts by God's posts (as it is said, v. 7 [8])? (I speak not now of lawful obedience to authority.) Is it not a righteous thing with the Lord to make these your idols His rods to correct you? Has not England harbored and entertained papists, priests, and Jesuits in its bosom? Is it not just that now you feel the sting and poison of these vipers? Has there not been a great compliance with the prelates for peace sake, even to the prejudice of truth? Does not the Lord now justly punish that episcopal peace with an episcopal war? Was not that prelatical government first devised and since continued to preserve peace and to prevent schism in the church? And was it not God's just judgment that such a remedy of man's invention should rather increase than cure the

---

38. καὶ αὐτοὶ λήμψονται τὴν κόλασιν αὐτων περὶ πάντων ὧν ἐποίησαν. [The brief London errata instructed for its third correction to change κόλαβιν to κόλασιν. However, this was correct in all the examples of the London edition examined (including the two examples with the errata in the front and in the back) and in the Edinburgh edition. Presumably, some early examples in the print run retain the error. It is correct in *Works* (p. 13) and in *Scots Sermons* (p. 316).]

evil? So that sects have most multiplied under that government, which now you know by sad experience. Has not this nation for a long time taken the name of the Lord in vain by a formal worship and empty profession? Is it not a just requital upon God's part that your enemies have all this while taken God's name in vain and taken the Almighty to witness of the integrity of their intentions for religion, law, and liberty, thus persuading the world to believe a lie?

What shall I say of the Book of Sports, and other profanations of the Lord's Day?[39] This licentiousness was most acceptable to the greatest part, and they "loved to have it so" (Jer. 5:31). Does not the great famine of the Word almost everywhere in the kingdom except in this city, make the land mourn on the Sabbath and say, "I do remember my faults this day" (Gen. 41:9)? Yea, does not the land now enjoy her Sabbaths, while men are constrained not only to cease from sports on that day but from laboring the ground and from other works of their calling upon other days? What should I speak of the lusts and uncleanness, gluttony and drunkenness, chambering and wantonness, prodigality and lavishness, excess of riot, masking, and balling, and sporting, when Germany and the Palatinate and other places were wallowing in blood, yea, when there was so much sin and wrath upon this same kingdom? Will you not say now, that for this the Lord God has caused "your sun to go down at noon," and has turned "your feasts into mourning, and all your songs into lamentation" (Amos 8:9, 10)? Or what should I say of the oppressions, injustice, cozenage in trading and in merchandise, which yourselves know better than I can do how much they have abounded in the kingdom? Does not God now punish the secret injustice of His people by the open injustice of their enemies? Do you not remember that mischief was framed by a law [Ps. 94:20]? And now, when your enemies execute mischief against law, will you not say, righteous art thou O Lord, and just are thy judgments [cf. Ps. 119:137]?

One thing I may not forget, and that is that the Lord is punishing blood with blood, the blood of the oppressed, the blood of the persecuted, the blood of those who have died in prisons, or in strange countries, suffering for righteousness' sake. He that departed from evil did even make himself a prey (Isa. 59:15). There was not so much as one drop of blood spilt upon the pillory for the testimony of the truth but it cries to heaven, for precious is the blood of the saints (Ps. 72:14). Does not all the blood shed in Queen Mary's days cry? And does not the blood of the Palatinate and Rochel[40] cry? And does not

---

39. [James I, *The Kings Majesties declaration … concerning lawfull sports* (1618; 1633).]

40. [La Rochelle. The accounts heard in Scotland and England of the sufferings of Protestants during the Thirty Years War (1618–1648) were fresh and the war had yet five more years to run. David Dickson was likely not unique in bringing current events as illustrations into his sermons on Jeremiah preached in 1628 from news received. Throughout his sermons unfolds the siege and final fall of La Rochelle, a Huguenot stronghold, drawn from news arriving each week. See Dickson, *Sermons on Jeremiah's Lamentations,* NPSE vol. III (Naphtali Press and Reformation Heritage Books, 2020), pp. 53, 58, 59, 83-84, 120, 235, 246, 272, 278.]

the blood of souls cry, which is the loudeſt cry of all? God said to Cain, "The voice of thy brother's blood cries unto me from the ground" (Gen. 4:10). The Hebrew has it, "thy brother's bloods," which is well expounded both by the Chaldee paraphrase and the Jerusalem Targum,[41] "the voice of the blood of all the generations and the righteous people which thy brother should have begotten crieth unto me." I may apply it to the thing in hand: the silencing, deposing, persecuting, imprisoning, and banishing of so many of the Lord's witnesses, of the moſt painful and powerful preachers, and the preferring of so many either dumb dogs or false teachers makes "the voice of bloods" to cry to heaven, even the blood of many thousands, yea, thousands of thousand souls, which have been loſt by the one or might have been saved by the other. God will require the blood of the children which those righteous Abels might have begotten unto Him. There is beside all this more blood-guiltiness which is secret but shall sometime be brought to light. O blood! blood! O let the land tremble while the righteous Judge makes "inquisition for blood" (Ps. 9:12). O let England cry, "Deliver me from blood guiltiness O God" (Ps. 51:14).

But you will say, peradventure, many of these things whereof I have ſpoken ought not to be charged upon the kingdom; they were only the acts of a prevalent faction for the time.

An Objection
Answered

[1] I answer: God will impute them to the kingdom unless the kingdom mourns for them. God gives not a charge to the deſtroying angel (Ezek. 9:4), to ſpare those who have not been actors in the public sins and abominations, but to ſpare those only who cry and sigh for those abominations.

[2] Secondly, when the miniſters of ſtate or others having authority in church or commonwealth, take the boldness to do such acts, the kingdom is not blameless; for they durſt not have done as they did had the land but disclaimed, discountenanced, and cried out againſt them. It is marked both of John Baptiſt (Matt. 14:5), and of Chriſt (Matt. 21:46), and of the apoſtles (Acts 4:21), that so long as the people did magnify them and eſteemed them highly, their enemies durſt not do unto them what else they would have done.

3. For Its
Presumption

(3) A third consideration concerning the kingdom is this: Notwithſtanding of all the happiness and goſpel blessings which it has wanted [*lacked*] in so great a measure, and notwithſtanding of all the sins which have so much abounded in it, yet the servants of God have charged it with great presumption,[42] that the Church of England has said with the Church of Laodicea, "I am rich and increased with goods, and have need of nothing" (Rev. 3:17). It has been proud of its clergy, learning, great revenues, peace, plenty, wealth, and abundance of all things, and as the apoſtle charges the Corinthians, "Ye are puffed up, and have not rather mourned," that the wicked

---

41. [The Jerusalem Targum (fragmentary targum) was published in the rabbinic bibles printed by Bomberg and Buxtorf. The Chaldee paraphrase is in the Antwerp Polyglot.]

42. Brightman on Rev. 3:17. Rogers, of faith, ch. 10. [Thomas Brightman (1562–1607), *A Revelation of the Apocalyps* (1611; 1644); John Rogers (1572?–1636), *The Doctrine of Faith …* (1640).]

ones "might be taken away from among you" (1 Cor. 5:2). And would God this presumption had taken an end when God did begin to afflict the land. It did even make an idol of this parliament, and trusted to its own strength and armies, which has provoked God so much that He has sometimes almost blasted your hopes that way, and has made you to feel your weakness even where you thought yourselves strongest. God would not have England say "Mine own hand hath saved me" (Judges 7:2); neither will he have Scotland to say, "My hand hath done it." But He will have both to say, "His hand hath done it, when we were lost in our own eyes." God grant that your leaning so much upon the arm of flesh be not the cause of more blows. God must be seen in the work, and He will have us to give Him all the glory, and to say, "Thou hast wrought all our works for us" (Isa. 26:12). O that all our presumption may be repented of and that the land may be yet more deeply humbled! Assuredly God will arise and subdue our enemies, and command deliverances for Jacob [Ps. 68:1; 44:4]; but it is certain God will not do this till we are more humbled, and (as the text says) ashamed of all that we have done.

(4) There is another motive more evangelical. Let England be humbled even for the mercy, the most admirable mercy which God has shown upon so undeserving and evil-deserving a kingdom. See it in this same prophecy: "I will establish my covenant with thee; and thou shalt know that I am the Lord: that thou maist remember, and be confounded, and never open thy mouth any more because of thy shame, when I am pacified toward thee for all that thou hast done, saith the Lord God" (Ezek. 16:62, 63). And again: "Not for your sakes do I this, saith the Lord God, be it known unto you: be ashamed and confounded for your own ways O house of Israel" (Ezek. 36:32). "O my God," says Ezra, "I am ashamed and blush to lift up my face to thee" (Ezra 9:6).

4. Because of God's Goodness

And what was it that did so confound him? You may find it in that which follows: God had shown them mercy, and had left them a remnant to escape, and had given them a nail in His holy place, and had lightened their eyes. "And now," says he, "O our God, what shall we say after this? For we have forsaken thy commandments" (Ezra 9:10). Let us this day compare (as he did) God's goodness and our own guiltiness. England deserved nothing but to get a bill of divorce and that God should have said in His wrath, "away from me, I have no pleasure in you" [Mal. 1:10]; but now He has received you into the bond of His covenant; He rejoices over you to do you good, and to dwell among you; His banner over you is love [Song of Sol. 2:4]. O let our hard hearts be overcome and be confounded with so much mercy, and let us be ashamed of ourselves that after so much mercy we should be yet in our sins and trespasses.

3. There is a third application, which I intend for the ministry, who ought to go before the people of God in the example of repentance and humiliation. You know the old observation, *Raro vidi clericum poenitentem:* "I have seldom seen a clergyman penitent."[43] As Christ says of rich men (Mark 10:24, 25),

[Third] Application to the Ministry—Their Repentance Rare

---

43. This is an oft cited saying as Gillespie noted and more fully and accurately quoted:

I may say of learned men, it is easier for a camel to go through the eye of a needle than for a man that trusts in his learning to enter into the kingdom of heaven. He will needs maintain the lawfulness of all which he has done, and will not be (as this text would have him) ashamed of all that he has done.

Yet Examples There be of It

Yet, it is not impossible with God to make such a one deny himself, and that whatsoever in him exalts itself against Christ should be brought in captivity to the obedience of Christ (2 Cor. 10:5). Among all that were converted by the ministry of the apostles, I wonder most at the conversion of a great company of priests (Acts 6:7). I do not suspect, as two learned men have done,[44] that the text is corrupted in that place, and that it should be otherwise read. I am rather satisfied because there is nothing there mentioned of the conversion of the high priest, or of the chief priests, the heads of the four and twenty orders, which were upon the council and had condemned Christ. The place cannot be understood but of a multitude of common or inferior priests, even as by proportion in Hezekiah's reformation, "the Levites were more upright in heart than the priests" (2 Chron. 29:34).

And now many of inferior clergy (as they were abusively called) are more upright in heart unto this present reformation than any of those who had assumed to themselves high degrees in the church. The hardest point of all, is so to embrace and follow reformation as to be ashamed of former prevarications and pollutions. But in this also the Holy Ghost has set examples before the ministers of the gospel. I read in 2 Chronicles 30:15: "The priests and the Levites were ashamed, and sanctified themselves, and brought in the burnt offerings into the house of the Lord." They thought it not enough to be sanctified, but they were ashamed that they had been before defiled. A great prophet is not content to have his judgment rectified which had

---

"Quis aliquando vidit clericum cito poenitentiam agentem?" It comes from the *Opus Imperfectum In Matthaeum*, long attributed to Chrysostom, but now considered to have been penned by some "uncertain" fifth century author with a few Arian tendencies. Migne includes it in Chrysostom's works, *incerto auctore*. Cf. *Eruditi Commentarii in Evangelium Matthaei, Incerto Auctore* [Opus Imperfectum], *PG* 56.852. An English translation has been published which renders the phrase: "Who ever sees a cleric quickly repenting?" *Incomplete Commentary on Matthew (Opus imperfectum)*, trans. James A. Kellerman, 2 vols. (IVP, 2010), 2.315.]

44. Beza and Casaubon. [Cf. Theodore Beza's annotation on Acts 6:7 in *Jesu Christi Domini Nostri Novum Testamentum* ... (Cantabrigiae: Rogeri Danielis, [1642]), p. 313. In *Scots Sermons* it was noted to see Casaubon's note appended at the end of *Novi Testamenti* ... (London: Ioannem Billium. 1622) Ff (no pagination). However, there is no comment on that verse there and it is likely Gillespie is just referring to Beza's note which mentions Casaubon and the latter's similar handling of Acts 21:16, for which see *Novum Testamentum* ... (Cantabrigiae: Rogeri Danielis, [1642]), pp. 114–115. On this question, see *A Commentary on the Holy Scriptures* ... by John Peter Lange, trans. Philip Schaff, vol. IV of the New Testament: Containing the Acts of the Apostles (New York: Charles Scribner, & Co., 1867). p. 102, fn 3; and Heinrich August Wilhelm Meyer, *Critical and Exegetical Handbook to the Acts of the Apostles*, trans. Paton J. Gloag, rev. William P. Dickson (New York: Funk & Wagnalls, 1883), p. 127.]

been in an error, but he is ashamed of the error he had been in. "So foolish was I," says he, "and ignorant: I was as a beast before thee" (Ps. 73:22). A great apostle must glorify God and humbly acknowledge his own shame. "For I am the least of the apostles," says he, "that am not meet to be called an apostle, because I persecuted the church of God" (1 Cor. 15:9). And shall I add the example of a great father? Augustine confesses honestly that for the space of nine years he both was deceived and did deceive others.[45] Nature will whisper to a man to look to his credit; but the text here calls for another thing, to look to the honor of God and to your own shame, and yet in so doing you shall be more highly esteemed both by God and by His children. Now, without this, let a man seem to turn and reform never so well, all is unsure work and built upon a sandy foundation. And whosoever will not acknowledge their iniquity and be ashamed for it, God shall make them bear their shame, according to that which is pronounced in the next chapter against the Levites, who had gone astray when Israel went astray after their idols ([Ezek. 44:]10–15), and according to that in Malachi 2:8, 9, "Ye have corrupted the covenant of Levi, saith the Lord of Hosts; therefore have I also made you contemptible and base before all the people."

4. The fourth and last application of this doctrine is for every Christian. The text teaches us a difference between a presumptuous and a truly humbled sinner. The one is ashamed of his sins, the other not. By this mark let every one of us try himself this day. It is a saving grace to be truly and really ashamed of sin. It is one of the promises of the covenant of grace. "Then shall ye remember your own evil ways, and your doings that were not good, and shall loath yourselves in your own sight, for your iniquities, and for your abominations" (Ezek. 36:31). Try then, if you have but thus [*this*] much of the work of grace in your soul, and if you have been assured of your interest in Christ and in the New Covenant. A reprobate may have somewhat which is very like this grace, but I shall lay open the difference between the one and the other, in these particulars:

(1) To be truly ashamed of sin is to be ashamed of it as an act of filthiness and uncleanness. The child of God, when he comes to the throne of grace, is ashamed of an unclean heart, though the world cannot see it. A natural man at his best looks upon sin as it damns and destroys the soul, but he cannot look upon it as it defiles the soul. Shame arises properly from a filthy act, though no other evil is to follow upon it.

(2) As we are ashamed of acts of filthiness, so of acts of folly. A natural man may judge himself a fool in regard of the circumstances or consequences of his sin, but he is not convinced that sin in itself is an act of madness and folly. When the child of God is humbled he becomes a fool in his own eyes;

[margin: [Fourth] Application to Every Christian]

[margin: Five marks of Difference between the Humiliation of the Child of God and that of the Hypocrite]

---

45. [Augustine,] *Confessions*, lib 4. *Per idem tempus annorum novem, etc., seducebamur et seducebamus, falsi atque fallentes in variis cupiditatibus, etc. Irrideant me arrogantes, et nondum salubriter prostrati et elisi a te Deus meus: ego tamen confiteor tibi dedecora mea, in laude tua.* [Cf. *PL* 32.693; *NPNF1* 1.68.]

he perceives he has done like a mad fool (1 Cor. 3:18); therefore, he is said then to come to himself (Luke 15:17).

(3) The child of God is ashamed of sin as an act of unkindness and unthankfulness to a sweet, merciful Lord (Ps. 130:4; Rom. 2:4). Though there were no other evil in sin, the conscience of so much mercy and love so far abused and so unkindly recompensed is that which confounds a penitent sinner. As the wife of a kind husband, if she plays the whore (though the world know it not), and if her husband, when he might divorce her, shall still love her and receive her into his bosom; such a one, if she has at all any sense or any bowels of sorrow, must needs be swallowed up of shame and confusion for her undutifullness and treachery to such a husband. But now, the hypocrite is not at all troubled or afflicted in spirit for sin as it is an act of unkindness to God.

(4) Shame, as philosophers have defined it,[46] is "the fear of a just reproof"; not simply the fear of a reproof, but the fear of a just reproof. That is servile, this filial. The child of God is ashamed of the very guiltiness and of that which may be justly laid to his charge; the hypocrite not so. Saul was not ashamed of his sin, but he was ashamed that Samuel should reprove him before the elders of the people (1 Sam. 15:15, 30). Christ's adversaries were ashamed (Luke 13:17), not of their error, but because their mouths were stopped before the people, and they could not answer Him. A hypocrite is ashamed, "as a thief is ashamed when he is found" (Jer. 2:26); mark that, "when he is found." A thief is not ashamed of his sin, but because he is found in it, and so brought to a shameful end.

(5) When the cause of God is in hand, a true penitent is so ashamed of himself that he fears the people of God shall be put to shame for his sake, and that it shall go the worse with them because of his vileness and guiltiness. This made David pray, "O God, thou knowest my foolishness; and my sins are not hid from thee. Let not them that wait on thee, O Lord God of hosts, be ashamed for my sake; let not those that seek thee be confounded for my sake, O God of Israel" (Ps. 69:5, 6). The sorrow and shame of a hypocrite (as all his other seeming graces) are rooted in self-love, not in the love of God. He has not this in all his thoughts, that he is a spot or blemish in the body or church of Christ, and therefore to be humbled, lest for his sake God be displeased with His people; lest such a vile and abominable sinner as he brings wrath and confusion upon others, and make Israel turn their back before the enemy. O happy soul that has such thoughts as these!

---

46. Gellius, lib. 19, cap. 6. *Pudor est timor justæ reprehensionis. Ita enim philosophi definiunt,* ἀισχύνη [εστι] φόβος δικαίου ψόγου [*aischynê estin phobos dikaiou psogou*]. [Aulus Gellius (c. 125–after 180), *Noctes Atticae (Attic Nights),* book 19, chapter 6. "Shame is the fear of deserved blame, for so the philosophers define it." [The fourth and last correction the London errata instructed to make was to change φύβος to φόβος. Unlike the prior correction, this was not corrected in any of the London editions examined, including those with the errata. It is correct in *Works* (p. 17), *Scots Sermons* (p. 325) and in the Edinburgh 1644 edition (p. 25).]

I have now done with the first part of the text, wherein I have been the larger, because it most fit the work of the day. II. The second follows: *Show them the form of the house,* etc.

Before I come to the doctrines which do here arise, I shall first explain the particulars mentioned in this part of the text, so as they may agree to the spiritual temple or church of Christ, which in the beginning I proved to be here intended.

1. First, we find here the form and fashion of a house, in which the parts are very much diversified one from another. There are in a formed and fashioned house, doors, windows, posts, lintels, etc.; there is also a multitude of common stones in the walls of the house. Such a house is the visible ministerial church of Christ, the parts whereof are *partes dissimilares,* some ministers and rulers, some eminent lights, others of the ordinary rank of Christians, that make up the walls. If God has made one but a small pinning in the wall, he has reason to be content and must not say, "why am not I a post, or a cornerstone, or a beam?" Neither yet may any cornerstone despise the stones in the wall, and say, "I have no need of you" [1 Cor. 12:15–21].

2. Secondly, the prophet was here to show them "the goings out of the house, and the comings in thereof." These are not the same, but different gates, it is plain. "When the people of the land shall come before the Lord in the solemn feasts, he that entereth in by the way of the north gate to worship, shall go out by the way of the south gate," etc., "he shall not return by the way of the gate whereby he came in" (Ezek. 46:9). And that not only to teach us order and the avoiding of confusion (occasioned by the contrary tides of a multitude), but to tell us further that "no man having put his hand to the plough, and looking back, is fit for the kingdom of God" (Luke 9:62). We must not go out of the church the way that we came in (that were a door of defection), but hold our faces forward till we go out by the door of death.

3. Thirdly, the text has twice *all the forms thereof,* which I understand of the outward forms and of the inward forms, which two I find very much distinguished by those who have written of the form and structure of the temple. The church is exceedingly beautified, even outwardly, with the ordinances of Christ, but the inward forms are the more glorious. "For behold the kingdom of God is within you," and it "commeth not with observation" (Luke 17:20, 21). "The king's daughter is all glorious within"; yet even "her clothing is of wrought gold" (Ps. 45:13). When the angel had made an end of measuring the inner house (Ezek. 42:15), then he brought forth Ezekiel by the east gate (which was the chief gate by which the people commonly entered) and measured the outer wall in the last place. God's method is first to try the heart and reins, then to give to a man according to his works (Jer. 17:10). So should we measure by the reed of the sanctuary, first the inner house of our hearts and minds, and then to measure our outer walls, and to judge of our profession and external performances.

4. Lastly, the prophet is commanded to write in their sight *all the ordinances thereof, and all the laws thereof*; for the church is a house not only in

an architectonic but in an economic sense. It is Christ's family governed by His own laws, and a temple which has in it "them that worship" (Rev. 11:1). It has its own proper laws by which it is ordered. *Aliae sunt leges Caesarum, aliae Christi*, says Jerome.[47] Ceasar's laws and Christ's laws are not the same, but diverse one from another. Schoolmen say[48] that a law properly so called is both illuminative and impulsive: illuminative to inform and direct the judgment; impulsive to move and apply the will to action. And accordingly there are two names in this text given to Christ's laws and instructions: one which imports the instruction and information of our minds;[49] another which signifies a deep imprinting or engraving (and that is made upon our hearts and affections), such as a pen of iron and other instruments could make upon a stone.[50] It is not well when either of the two is wanting; for the light of truth without the engraving of truth may be extinguished; and the engraving of truth without the light of truth may be obliterated.

All these I shall pass and only pitch upon two doctrines which I shall draw from this second part of the text: one concerning the will of God's commandment, what God requires of Israel to do; another concerning the will of God's decree, what He has purposed Himself to do.

The Church Tied to God's Own Pattern

1. The first is this: *God will have Israel to build and order His temple, not as shall seem good in their eyes, but according to His own pattern only which He sets before them*, which does so evidently appear from this very text, that it needs no other proof. For what else means the showing of such a pattern to be kept and followed by His people? Other passages of this kind there are which do more abundantly confirm it.

The Lord did prescribe to Noah both the matter, and fashion, and measures of the ark (Gen. 6:14–16). To Moses He gave a pattern of the tabernacle, of the ark, of the mercy seat, of the veil, of the curtains, of the two altars, of the table and all the furniture thereof, of the candlesticks and all the instruments thereof, etc. And though Moses was the greatest prophet that ever arose in Israel, yet God would not leave any part of the work to Moses's arbitrance, but straitly commands him, "look that thou make them after their pattern which was showed thee in the mount" (Exod. 25:40). When it came to the building of the first temple, Solomon was not in that left to his own wisdom, as great as it was, but David, the man of God, gave him a perfect

---

47. In Epitaphio Fabiola. [Migne, *PL*, 22.691; Jerome, "Letters and Select Works," in *NPNF2*, vol. 6, Letter LXXVII, To Oceanus, pp. 157–163.]

48. Suarez. *de Leg.*, lib. 1, cap. 5. Caspensis, *Curs. Theol.*, tract. 13, disp. 1, sect. 1. [Francisco Suarez, *Tractatus de legibus, ac Deo legislatore in decem libros distributus* (Lyon: Horace Cardon, 1613), pp. 15–19; also *Opera Omnia*, vol. 5 (Paris: Vives, 1856), pp. 17–23; Ludovicus Caspensis, *Cursus theologicus, amplectens præcipuas materias, quæ in scholis tradi, & legi solent, secundùm ordinem D. Thomæ* (Lugduni: Boissat & Anisson, 1641, 1643), 1.456, 1.456–458.].

49. תורה, *torah* [towrah], from ידה, *jarah* [yarah], *demostravit, docuit* [showed, taught].

50. חק, *Chok* [Choq], from [ה]חקק, *Chakak* [Chuqqah], which is *insculpere lapidi vel ligno* ["to carve in stone or wood"].

"pattern of all that he had by the Spirit" (1 Chron. 28:11–13). The second temple was also built "according to the commandment of the God of Israel" (Ezra 6:14), by Haggai and Zechariah. And for the New Testament, Christ our great Prophet and only King and Lawgiver of the church, has revealed His will to the apostles, and they to us, concerning all His holy things. And we must hold ourselves at these unleavened and unmixed ordinances, which the apostles from the Lord delivered to the churches. "I will put upon you," says He Himself, "none other burden; but that which ye have already, hold fast till I come" (Rev. 2:24, 25).

I know the church must observe rules of order and conveniency in the common circumstances of times, places, and persons; but these circumstances are none of our holy things. They are only prudential accommodations, which are alike common to all human societies, both civil and ecclesiastical, wherein both are directed by the same light of nature, the common rule to both in all things of that kind; providing always that the general rule of the Word is observed: "Do all to the glory of God" (1 Cor. 10:31); "Let all things be done to edifying" (1 Cor. 14:26); "It is good neither to eat flesh, nor to drink wine, nor anything whereby thy brother stumbleth, or is offended, or made weak" (Rom. 14:21); "Let every man be fully persuaded in his own mind. To him that esteemeth anything to be unclean, to him it is unclean" (Rom. 14:5, 14).[51]

Common Circumstances & Sacred Ceremonies Distinguished

The text gives some clearing to this point. There is here shown to the house of Israel a pattern of the whole structure, and of the least part thereof, and all the measures thereof; yet no pattern is given of the kind, or quantity, or magnificence of the several stones, or of the instruments of the building. The reason is because the former is essential to a house, the latter accidental.[52] The former, if altered, makes another building; the latter, though altered, the building is the same; therefore, where we have in the text, *the forms thereof*, the Septuagint reads, ὑπόστασιν αὐτου [*hupostasin autou*], "the substance thereof."

But to clear it a little further, I put two characters upon those circumstances which are not determined by the Word of God, but left to be ordered by the

---

51. [Cf. George Gillespie, *A Dispute Against the English Popish Ceremonies*, ed. Christopher Coldwell (Dallas, Texas: Naphtali Press, 1993) xli; 281–284; critical edition (Naphtali Press, 2013), pp. 16, 259–261.]

52. *Illa quasi naturam ædificii substantiamque denotant, hæc accidentia. Illa si tollas deerit fabrica: hæc quamvis desiderentur, manet tamen ædificium. Illa si invertas aut muties, non idem ædificium manebit, sed aliud: hæc quamvis tollas, idem manere potest ædificium: haud secus quam de homine quoquam, deque ejus vestimentis philosopheris.* Villalpandas, tom. 2, part. 2, lib. 1; *Isag.*, cap.12. [Villalpando, *In Ezechielem explanationes, et apparatus urbis, ac templi Hierosolymitani, commentariis et imaginibus illustratus*, 3 vols. (Romæ, 1596–1604); chapter 12, pp. 32–35. "Those things mean, as it were, the nature and material of the building; these the qualities. If you take those away, the fabric will suffer; these might be somehow lost, but the building remains. If you turn or change those, the building will not remain itself, but will be different: take away these however you wish, the building can remain the very same. Hardly otherwise than what is said about a certain man and his philosopher's clothing."]

---

church as shall be found moſt convenient. (1) Firſt, they are not things sacred, nor proper to the church, as has been said. They are of the same nature, they serve for the same end and use, both in sacred and civil things; for order and decency, the avoiding of confusion and the like, are alike common to church and commonwealth.

(2) Secondly, I shall describe them as one of the prelates has done, who tells us,[53] that the things which the Scripture has left to the discretion of the church, are those things "which neither needed, nor could be particularly expressed. They needed not, because they are so obvious; and they could not, both because they are so numerous, and because so changeable."

The Application to England

I will not insiſt upon queſtions of this kind, but will make a short application of the doctrine unto you, honorable and beloved. You may plainly see from what has been said, that neither kings, nor parliaments, nor synods, nor any power on earth, may impose or continue the leaſt ceremony upon the consciences of God's people, which Chriſt has not imposed. Therefore, let neither antiquity, nor cuſtom, nor conveniency, nor prudential considerations, nor show of holiness, nor any pretext whatsoever, plead for the reservation of any of your old ceremonies, which have no ground nor warrant from the Word of God. Much might have been said for the high places among the Jews, as I hinted in the beginning; and much might have been said by the Pharisees for their frequent washings (Mark 7:2–4, 7), which as they were ancient and received by the traditions of the elders, so they were used to teach men purity and to put them in mind of holiness; neither was their washing contrary to any commandment of God, except you underſtand that commandment of not adding to the Word (Deut. 4:2; 12:32; Prov. 30:6), which does equally ſtrike againſt all ceremonies devised by man.

"A little leaven leaveneth the whole lump" (Gal. 5:9); and a little leak will endanger the ship. Thieves will readily dig through a house, how much more will they enter if any poſtern is left open to them? The wild beaſts and boars of the foreſt will attempt to break down the hedges of the Lord's vineyard (Ps. 80:13); how much more if any breach is left in the hedges? If, therefore, you would make a sure reformation, make a perfect reformation, leſt Chriſt have this controversy with England: "Nevertheless I have somewhat againſt thee" (Rev. 2:4). And so much of our duty.

God's Purpose to Build Such a Temple

2. The second doctrine concerns God's decree, and it is this: *It is concluded in the council of heaven, and God has it in the thoughts of His heart, to repair the breaches of His house, and to build such a temple to Himself, as is shadowed forth in this vision of Ezekiel.* For the comparing of this verse with verse 7, in this same chapter, and with 37:26, 27, will easily make it appear that this showing of the pattern and all this measuring was not only in reference to Israel's duty,

---

53. The Bishop of Down, *Of the Authority of the Church*, page 29. [Henry Leslie, *A Treatise of the Authority of the Church. The summe whereof was delivered in a sermon preached at Belfaſt, at the visitation of the Diocese of Downe and Conner* (Printed by the Society of Stationers, printers to the Kings most Excellent Majesty, 1637; reissued 1639).]

but to God's gracious purpose towards Israel, according to that in Zechariah 1:16: "Therefore thus saith the Lord, I am returned to Jerusalem with mercies: my house shall be built in it, saith the Lord of Hosts, and a line shall be stretched forth upon Jerusalem." Now, this vision cannot be said to be fulfilled in Zerubbabel's temple, as I proved before. Only here take notice, that the second destruction of the temple by the Romans was worse than the first by the Babylonians. That desolation was repaired, but this could never be repaired, though the Jews did attempt the building again of the temple,[54] first under Adrian the Emperor, and afterward under Julian the Apostate. The hand of God was seen against them most terribly by fire from heaven, and other signs of that kind; and about the same time (observe that by the way) the famous Delphic temple was without man's hand by fire and earthquake utterly destroyed and never built again, to tell the world that neither Judaism nor paganism should prevail, but the kingdom of Jesus Christ.

Where, then, must we seek for the accomplishment of Ezekiel's vision— I mean for the new temple in which the Lord will dwell forever, and where His holy name shall be no more polluted? Surely, we must seek for it in the days of the gospel, as has been before abundantly proved. But that the thing may be the better understood, let us take with us, at least, some few general observations concerning this temple of Ezekiel, as it represents what should come to pass in the church of Christ.

(1) First of all, there is but one temple, not many, shown to him, which is in part, and shall be yet more fulfilled in the church of the New Testament; according to that in Zechariah [14:]8–9, "And it shall be in that day, that living waters shall go out of Jerusalem"; which is the same that we have in Ezekiel 47:1. Then follows: "And the Lord shall be king over all the earth: in that day shall there be one Lord, and his name one." The like promise we find elsewhere: "I will give them one heart, and one way" (Jer. 32:39; Ezek. 11:19). It is observed that for this very end of uniformity, the heathens also did erect temples that they might all worship the same idol god in the same manner. The plague of the Christian church hitherto has been temple against temple and altar against altar. "But thou O Lord, how long" (Ps. 6:3)?

The Church's Unity

(2) Secondly, Ezekiel's temple and city are very large and capacious, as I showed in the beginning, and the city had three gates looking toward each of the four quarters of the world (48:31–34): all this to signify the spreading of the gospel into all the earth; which is also signified by the holy waters issuing from the threshold of the temple and rising so high that they were waters to swim in (47:1, 5). God has said to his church: "Enlarge the place of thy tent, and let them stretch forth the curtains of thine habitations: spare not, lengthen thy cords, and strengthen thy stakes; for thou shalt break forth on the right hand and on the left" (Isa. 54:2, 3). A great increase of the church

Her Increase

---

54. Wolph., *Lection. Memor.*, Cent. 16, page 692. [Johann Wolf (1537–1600), *Lectionum Memorabilium et Reconditarum Centenarii XVI*, 2 vols. (Lauingæ: Sumtibus autoris impressit Leonhardus Rheinmichel, 1600; vol. 3 Index, 1608).]

there was in the apostles' times (Col. 1:6); but a far greater is to be yet looked for (Rom. 11:12). Though "the enemy" did come "in like a flood, the spirit of the Lord lifted up a standard against him" (Isa. 59:19). "The sea saw it and fled, Jordan was driven back" (Ps. 114:3). But when the gospel comes, "like a noise of many waters" (as the prophet calls it in verse 2, signifying an irresistible increase), it is in vain to build bulwarks against it. God will even break open "the fountains of the great deep," and open "the windows of heaven" (Gen. 7:11), and the gospel will prove a second flood which will overflow the whole earth, though not to destroy it (as Noah's did) but to make it glad; for "the earth shall be filled with the knowledge of the glory of the Lord, as the waters cover the sea" (Hab. 2:14; Isa. 11:9).

(3) In this temple, beside the holy of holies, were three courts;[55] the court of the priests, the court of the people, commonly called *Atrium Israelis*, and without [*outside*] both these, *Atrium Gentium*, the court of the heathen, so called because the heathen, as also many of those who were legally unclean, might not only come unto the mountain of the house of the Lord, but also enter within the utter [*outer*] wall (mentioned in Ezekiel 42:20), and so worship in the utter court, or *intramural*; unto which did belong (as we learn from Josephus)[56] the great east porch, which kept the name of *Solomon's porch*, in which both Christ Himself did preach (John 10:23), and the apostles after Him (Acts 5:12); by which means the free grace of the gospel was held forth even to heathens, and publicans, and unclean persons, who were not admitted into the court of Israel, there to communicate in all the holy things; "For the son of man came to seek and to save that which was lost" (Luke 19:10). This utter [*outer*] court of the temple is meant when it is said that the Pharisees brought a woman taken in adultery into the temple and set her before Christ (John 8:2, 3). Now, all this will hold true answerably of the spiritual temple. For [1] first, as the uncircumcised and the unclean were not admitted into the temple among the children of Israel (Ezek. 44:9), so all that

Her Different
Courts

---

55. Vid. Joseph. *Antiq.*, lib. 15, cap. 14; Tostat., in 1 Reg. 6., quest. 21; A. Montan., *de Sacri. Fabric.*, p. 15; L'Empereur *Ann. in Cod. Middoth.*, cap. 2, sect. 3. [Flavius Josephus, *Antiquities of the Jews*, in *Works* (1901), b. 15, c. 11, p. 391; Tostado, *Opera omnia, quotquot in Scripturae Sacrae expositionem et alia, adhuc extare inuenta sunt*, 28 vols. (Venetiis: apud Io. Baptistam, et Io. Bernardum Sessam, 1596) vol. 11–12 (Commentary on 1 Kings), pp. 72v–73v; Arias Montanus, "Exemplar, sive de sacris fabricis," in *Biblia sacra Hebraice, Chaldaice, Graece, & Latine*, Liber Joseph, tomus 8 (Antwerp: Plantinus, 1571), p. 15; Constantine L'Empereur, *Masekhet Midot me-Talmud Bavli: hoc est Talmudis Babylonici codex Middoth, sive de mensuris templi, unà cum versione Latina* (Lugduni Batavorum {Leiden}: Bonaventuræ & Abrahami Elzevir, 1630), annotations, pp. 42ff.]

56. *Antiq.*, lib. 20, cap. 8. *Suasit (populus) regi ut orientalem instauraret portiocum. Ea Templi extima claudebat, profundæ valli et angustæ imminens, etc. Opus Solomonis regis qui primus integrum templum condidit.* Compare this with lib. 15, cap. 14. [*Antiquities*, book 20, chapter "9"). "They (the people) persuaded the king to restore the east portico. This portico enclosed the outermost parts of the temple, projecting over a deep and narrow, etc. It was the work of Solomon the King, who first built the whole temple." Cf. *Works* (1901), p. 495.]

live in the church of Christ are not to be admitted promiscuously to every ordinance of God, especially to the Lord's Table, but only those whose profession, knowledge, and conversation, after trial, shall be found such as may make them capable thereof. Yet, as heathens and unclean persons did enter into the utter [*outer*] court, and there hear Christ and His apostles, so there shall ever be in the church a door of grace and hope open to the greatest and vilest sinners who shall seek after Christ and "ask the way to Zion, with their faces hitherward" (Jer. 50:5). [2] Secondly, there shall be also somewhat answerable to the court of the children of Israel: God can raise up even of the stones, children to Abraham (Matt. 3:9); He will not want [*lack*] a people to trade in the courts of His house and to inquire in His temple. [3] Thirdly, and as in the typical temple there was a court for the priests, so has the Lord promised to the church: "thy teachers shall not be removed into a corner anymore, but thine eyes shall see thy teachers (Isa. 30:20); and again, I will give you pastors according to my heart, which shall feed you with knowledge and understanding" (Jer. 3:15). [4] Fourthly, and as there was a secret and most holy place, where the ark was, and the mercy seat, and where the glory of God dwelt, so Christ has His own "hidden ones" (Ps. 83:3), "the children of the marriage chamber" (Matt. 9:15), who, "with open faces beholding as in a glass the glory of the Lord, are changed into the same image, from glory, to glory, even as by the Spirit of the Lord" (2 Cor. 3:18). There is also a time coming when God will open the secrets of His temple, and make the ark of His testament to be seen otherwise than yet it has been, which shall be at the sounding of the seventh trumpet (Rev. 11:15, 19).

(4) The fourth thing wherein Ezekiel's temple represents the church of Christ, is in regard of the great strength thereof. It stood "upon a very high mountain" (Ezek. 40:2). The material temple also in Jerusalem, as it is described by Josephus, was a very strong and impregnable place. Interpreters think that Cyrus was jealous of the strength of the temple, and for that cause gave order that it should not be built above threescore cubits high, whereas Solomon had built it six score cubits high (Ezra 6:3). The Romans afterwards, when they had subdued Judea, had a watchful eye upon the temple, and placed a strong garrison in the castle Antonia (which was beside the temple), the Commander whereof was called, "the captain of the temple" (Acts 4:1); and all this for fear of sedition and rebellion among the Jews when they came to the temple. Now, the invisible strength of the spiritual temple is clearly held forth unto us by Him that cannot deceive us: "Upon this rock," says He (meaning Himself), "will I build my church, and the gates of hell shall not prevail against it" (Matt. 16:18). The princes and powers of the world are more jealous than they need of the church's strength; and yet (which is a secret judgment of God) they have not been afraid to suffer Babylon to be built in her full strength. "There were they in great fear where no fear was" (Ps. 53:5), for when all shall come to all, it shall be found that the gospel and true religion is the strongest bulwark, and chief strength for the safety and stability of kings and states.

Her Glory

(5) Lastly, the glory of this temple was very great, insomuch that some have undertaken to demonstrate that it was a more glorious piece than any of the seven miracles of the world, which were so much spoken of among the ancients.[57] But the greatest glory of this temple was that "the glory of the God of Israel" came into it, and "the earth shined with his glory" (Ezek. 43:2); Christ "the brightness of his Father's glory" (Heb. 1:3), walking in the midst of the seven golden candlesticks (Rev. 1:13), is and shall be more and more the church's glory; therefore, it is said to her, "Arise, shine, for thy light is come, and the glory of the Lord is risen upon thee" (Isa. 60:1). Surely, as it was said of the new material temple in reference to Christ, so it may be said of the new spiritual temple, which yet we look for, "The glory of this latter house shall be greater than of the former, saith the Lord of hosts, and in this place will I give peace, saith the Lord of hosts" (Hag. 2:9). Christ will keep the best wine till the end of the feast (John 2:10), and He will bless our latter end more than our beginning (Ezek. 36:11).

That which I have said from grounds of Scripture concerning a more glorious, yea, more peaceable condition of the church to be yet looked for, is acknowledged by some of our sound and learned writers[58] who have had

---

57. Villalpandus, tom. 2, part. 2, lib. 5, cap. 61–63. [*In Ezechielem explanationes, et apparatus urbis, ac templi Hierosolymitani, commentariis et imaginibus illustratus*, 3 vols. (Romæ, 1596–1604), vol. 2. part 2, pp. 364–368.]

58. Walæus *de Opinione Chiliastærum*, tom. 1, page 558. *Hæc quidem (ruina Babylonis & deletio hostium) a nobis expectari, et fortassis non longe absunt succedetque lætior aliquis ecclesiæ status, et amplior.* Vide ibid., p. 541; Rivetus, *Explic. Decal.*, page 229. *Posset etiam dici, et fortasse non misnus apte vaticiniæ de regno Christi suam habere latitudinem nec semper intelligi debere de eo quod vel continuo vel omni tempore fieri debet, sed de aliqua periodo temporis, quæ et si nondum advenerit, adveniet nihilominus. Fieri enim potest, ut quemadmodum expectatur adhuc Judæorum generalis conversio, ita etiam ecclesia sua tempore ea pace fruitura sit, in qua ad literam implebuntur, quæ hujus vaticinii verbis [Isa. 2:4] significantur.* Others of this kind might be cited. [Antonius Walaeus (1573–1639), *Opera omnia* (Lvgdvni Batavorvm: Ex officina Francisci Hackii, 1643). Walaeus, *concerning the Opinion of the Millenialists*, tom. 1, p. 558. "These things indeed (the ruins of Babylon and destruction of enemies) are to be expected by us, and perhaps are not far away, and some happier and fuller set of circumstances for the church will follow. See the same work, p. 541"—Andrew Rivet (1572–1651), *Andreæ Riveti Pictavi, S.S. Theol. Doctoris, et Sacrarum Literarum in Academia Batavorum Professoris, Praelectiones in cap. xx. Exodi: In quibus ita explicatur Decalogus, ut casus conscientiæ, quos vocant, ex eo suborientes, ac pleraque controversiæ magni momeni, quæ circa legem moralem solent agitari, fusè & accuratè discutiantur* (Lugduni Batavorum: Apud Franciscum Hegerum, 1632; also 1637, the edition cited). Rivetus, *Explic. Decal.*, p. 229. "It could even be said, and perhaps no less aptly, of the prophecy of the reign of Christ, that it has its own breadth and ought not always to be taken to mean something which has to happen in continuous or all time, but to mean some period which, even if it has not yet occurred, will occur nevertheless. For it can happen that just as the general conversion of the Jews is as yet expected, so also the church may be about to enjoy that peace in her time, in which the things meant by the words of this prophecy will be discharged to the letter."]

occasion to express their judgment about it. And it has no affinity with the opinion of an earthly or temporal kingdom of Christ, or of the Jews' building again of Jerusalem, and the material temple, and their obtaining a dominion above other nations, or the like.

I shall now bring home the point. There are very good grounds of hope to make us think that this new temple is not far off. And (for your part) that Christ is to make a new face of a church in this kingdom, a fair and beautiful temple for His glory to dwell in. And He is even now about the work.

1. For first, "the set time" to build Zion is come, when the people of God "take pleasure in her stones, and favor the dust thereof" (Ps. 102:13, 14, 16). The stones which the builders of Babel refused, are now chosen for cornerstones; and the stones which they chose, do the builders of Zion now refuse. "They shall not take of thee a stone for a corner, nor a stone for foundation" (Jer. 51:26). Those that have anything of Christ and of the image of God in them begin to creep out of the dust of contempt, and to appear like stars of the morning. Nay, to go further than that, the old stones, the Jews, who have been for so many ages lying forgotten in the dust, those poor "outcasts of Israel" (Ps. 147:2), have of late come more into remembrance, and have been more thought of, and more prayed for, than they were in former generations.

2. Secondly, are there not great preparations and instruments fitted for the work? Has not God called together for such a time as this the present parliament, and the assembly of divines, His Zerubbabels, and Jehoshuas, and Haggaies, and Zechariahs? Are there not also hewers of stones and bearers of burdens; much wholesome preaching, much praying and fasting, many petitions put up to God and man? The covenant also going through the kingdom as the chief preparation of materials for the work? Is not the old rubbish of ceremonies daily more and more shoveled away, that there may be a clean ground? And is not the Lord by all this affliction humbling you, that there may be a deep and a sure foundation laid?

3. Thirdly, the work is begun and shall it not be finished? God has laid the foundation, and shall He "not bring forth the headstone" (Zech. 4:7–9)? Christ has put Antichrist from his utterworks [*outer works*] in Scotland, and He is now come to put him from his inner works in England. "His work is perfect" (Deut. 32:4), says Moses. "I am Alpha and Omega" (Rev. 1:8), says Christ, "the beginning and the ending. Shall I bring to the birth, and not cause to bring forth, saith the Lord? Shall I cause to bring forth, and shut the womb, saith thy God" (Isa. 66:9)?

I may add three other signs whereby to discern the time, from Revelation 11:1, the place before cited.

1. First, is there not now a measuring of the temple, ordinances, and worshipers, by "a reed like unto a rod"? [Rev. 11:1]. The reed of the sanctuary in the Assembly's hand, and the rod of power and law in your hand, are well met together.

2. Secondly, there is a court which before seemed to belong to the temple, left out and not measured: "from him that hath not shall be taken away even

that which he has" (Matt. 25:29). The Samaritans of this time, who serve the Lord and serve their own gods too (2 Kings 17:33, 34), and do after the manners of idolaters, have professed (as they of old to the Jews, Ezra 4:2) that they would build with you; that they will be for the true Protestant religion as you are; that they will also consent to the reformation of abuses, for the ease of tender consciences. But God does so alienate and separate between you and them, by His overruling providence, discovering their designs against you, and their deep engagements to the popish party, as if He would say unto them, "you have no portion, nor right, nor memorial in Jerusalem" (Neh. 2:20); or as it is in the parable concerning those who had refused to come when they were invited, yea, had taken the servants of Christ and entreated them spitefully, and killed them; the great king has said in his[59] wrath that they shall not taste of his supper, and he sends forth his armies to destroy those murderers, and to burn up their city (Matt. 22:6, 7; Luke 14:24). Surely, what they have professed[60] concerning reformation is scarce so much as the Pope did acknowledge when reformation did begin in Germany. However, as it is our hearts' desire and prayer to God for them that they may be saved, so we are not out of hopes that God has many of His own among them, unto whom He will give "repentance to the acknowledging of the truth" (2 Tim. 2:25).

3. Lastly, the time seems to answer fitly: The new temple is built when the 42 months of the beast's reign and of the treading down the holy city (that is by the best interpretation 1,260 years), come to an end. This computation, I conceive, should begin rather before the four hundredth year of Christ than after it; both because the Roman Emperor (whose falling was the Pope's rising) was brought very low before that time by the wars of the Goths and other barbarous nations, and otherwise, which will appear from history. And further because Pope Innocentius[61] (who succeeded about the

---

59. [The word "his" was omitted from *Scots Sermons* (p. 339).]

60. *In exortu Evangelicæ doctrinæ, legatus Hadriani pontificis in comitiis Nerobergæ habitis, publice confessus est, in doctrina et vita spiritualium, recessum esse a regula verbi divini: reformationem ecclesiæ in capitibus et membris esse necessariam: ut hac confessione cursum Evangelii impediret.* Lavater, hom. 9, *in lib. Ezræ.* [Ludwig Lavater (1527–1586), *Ezras. Liber primus Ezræ, homiliis xxxviii. Ludovici Lauateri Tigurinæ ecclesiæ ministri opera & labore expositus Accessit index rerum & verborum, locorum item S. Scripturæ* (Tiguri: In officina Froshoviana, {1586}), p. 24v. "On the preaching of evangelical doctrine, the legate of Pope Hadrian in the assemblies held at Neroberga publicly confessed that he had departed from the rule of the divine word in the doctrine and life of spiritual men: that reformation of the church is necessary in its heads and in its limbs: even if, by confessing this, he were hindering the course of the gospel. Lavater, homily 9, on the book of Ezra."]

61. Innoc., Epist. 2, *ad Victricium Rothomag. Majores causæ in medium devolutæ, ad sedem apostolicam, sicut synodus statuit, et beata consuetudo exigit post judicium episcopale, referantur.* Vide *Myster. Iniq.*, edit. Salmur., 1611, page 51. [Innocentius, Epist. 2, *ad Victricium Rothomag.* "The more important cases, fallen down into the middle level, should be referred back to the apostolic seat, just as the synod has established and the blessed custom has enforced after the

year 401) was raised so high that he drew all appeals from other bishops to the apostolical see, according to former statutes and customs, as he says. I cannot pitch upon a likelier time than the year 383, at which time (according to the common calculation) a general Council at Constantinople (though Baronius and some others reckon that Council in the year 381) did acknowledge the primacy of the Bishop of Rome (Can. 5. [*sic* Canon 3]), only reserving to the Bishop of Constantinople the second place among the Bishops. Did not then the beast receive much power when this much was acknowledged by a council of 150 bishops, though sitting in the East, and moderated by Nectarius, archbishop of Constantinople. Immediately after this council, it is acknowledged by one of our great antiquaries,[62] that the bishop of Rome did labor mightily to draw all causes to his own consistory, and that he does scarce read of any heretic or schismatic condemned in the province where he lived, but straight he had his recourse to the bishop of Rome. Another of our antiquaries[63] notes not long before that council, that Antichrist did then begin to appear at Rome, and to exalt himself over all the other bishops.

Now, if we should reckon the beginning of the beast's reign about the time of that council, the end of it will fall in at this very time of ours. But I dare not determine so high a point. God's work will, ere it be long, make a clearer commentary upon His Word. Only let this be remembered, we must not think it strange if after the end of the 1,260 years, Antichrist is not immediately and utterly abolished; for when that time is ended he makes war against the witnesses, yea, overcomes and kills them. But that victory of his lasts only three days and a half, and then God makes as it were a resurrection from the dead, and a tenth part of the great city falls before the whole fall (see Rev. 11:3, 7, 11, 13). Whether this killing of the witnesses (which seems to be the last act of Antichrist's power) is past, or to come, I cannot say. God knows. But assuredly, the acceptable year of Israel's jubilee, and the day of vengeance upon Antichrist is coming and is not far off.

But now, is there no other application to be made of this point? Is all this said to satisfy curious wits or at the best to comfort the people of God? Nay, there is more than so: it must be brought home to a practical use. As the assurance of salvation does not make the child of God the more presumptuous,

The Practical
Use Hereof

---

episcopal decision." See *Myster. Iniq.*, edit. Salmur., 1611, p. 51. Philippe de Mornay, seigneur du Plessis-Marly, *Le Mystére d'Iniquité, c'est à dire, l'histoire de la Papauté … Ou sont … defendus les droicts des Empereurs, Rois & Princes Chrestiens, contre les assertions des Cardinaux Bellarmin & Baronius* (Saumur: T. Portau, 1611). See also: Philippe de Mornay, *The Mysterie of Iniquitie: that is to say, The historie of the papacie … Englished by Samson Lennard* (London: Printed by Adam Islip, 1612)].

62. Mornay, *Myster. Iniq.*, page 46.

63. Wolphius, *Lection. Memorab.*, tom. 1, page 113. *Hoc scilicet tempore jam gliscebat Antichristus Romæ.* [*Lectionum Memorabilium et Reconditarum Centenarii XVI*, 2 vols. (Lauingæ: Sumtibus autoris impressit Leonhardus Rheinmichel, 1600; vol. 3 Index, 1608). "At this time, of course, Antichrist appeared at Rome."]

but the more humble (Ezek. 16:63), neither does it make him negligent, but diligent in the way of holiness and in all the acts of his spiritual warfare (Phil. 3:13, 14; 2 Peter 1:10); so that "every man that hath this hope in him, purifieth himself" (1 John 3:3): so answerably, the assurance of the new temple, and of the sweet days to come, serves for the twofold practical use; even as David also applies God's promise of Solomon's building the temple in 1 Chronicles 22:10; for thus he speaks to the princes of Israel [in] 1 Chronicles 22:19: "Now set your heart and your soul to seek the Lord your God, arise therefore and build ye the sanctuary of the Lord God." And this is beside the charge which he gives to Solomon.

1. First, then, you must set your heart and your soul to seek God, forasmuch as you know it is not in vain to seek Him for this thing (Dan. 9:2, 3). When Daniel understood by books that the 70 years of Jerusalem's desolation were at an end, and that the time of the building the temple again was at hand, then he says, "I set my face unto the Lord God to seek by prayer and supplications, with fasting, and sackcloth and ashes." O let us do as he did! O let us "cry mightily unto God" (Jonah 3:8); and let us with all our soul and all our might, give ourselves to fasting and prayer. Now if ever, "the effectual fervent prayer of a righteous man availeth much" (James 5:16).

2. Secondly, and the more actively you must go about the business. "Be ye steadfast, immovable, always abounding in the work of the Lord, forasmuch as ye know that your labor is not in vain in the Lord" (1 Cor. 15:58). What greater motive to action than to know that you shall prosper in it? "Arise therefore and be doing" (1 Chron. 22:16).

III. And so I am led upon the third and last part of the text, of which I shall speak but very little.

The doctrine is this: *Reformation ends not in contemplation, but in action.* The pattern of the house of God is set before us to the end it may be followed, and the ordinances thereof to the end they may be obeyed. "Give me understanding," says David, "and I shall keep thy law, yea, I shall observe it with my whole heart" (Ps. 119:34); "If ye know these things," says Christ, "happy are ye if ye do them" (John 13:17). The point is plain and needs no proof but application.

Let me therefore, honorable worthies, leave in your bosoms this one point more. Many of the servants of God who have stood in this place (and could do it better than I can) have been calling upon you to go on in the work of reformation. "O be not slothful in business" (Rom. 12:11), and forget not to do as you have been taught. Had you begun at this work and gone about the building of the house of God as your first and chief business, I dare say you should have prospered better. It was one cause, among others, why the children of Israel (Judges 20:21, 25) though the greater number, and having the better cause too, did twice fall before Benjamin, because, while they made so great a business, for the villainy committed upon the Levite's concubine, they had taken no course with the graven image of the children of Dan (Judges 18:30, 31), a thing which did more immediately touch God in His honor.

We Must Put in Practice what is Revealed Concerning the Pattern

But I am confident errors of this kind will now be amended, and that you will by double diligence redeem the time. I know your trouble is great, and your cares many, in managing the war, and looking to the safety of the kingdom; yet mark what David did in such a case. "Behold, in my trouble I have prepared for the house of the Lord an hundred thousand talents of gold, and a thousand thousand talents of silver, and of brass and iron without weight" (1 Chron. 22:14). David did manage great wars with mighty enemies (2 Sam. 5, 8, 10, 11), the Philistines, Moabites, Ammonites, and Syrians, beside the intestine war made first by Abner (2 Sam. 2:8), and afterward by Absalom (2 Sam. 15:10), and after that by Sheba (2 Sam. 20:1). Notwithstanding of all this, in his trouble and poverty (the word signifies both) he made this great preparation for the house of God, and if God had given him leave he had in his trouble built it too; for you well know he was not hindered from building the temple by the wars or any other business, but only because God would not permit him.

Set before you also the example of the Jews when the prophets of God did stir them up to the building of the temple (Ezra 5:1, 2). They say not, we must first build the walls of Jerusalem to hold out the enemy, but the text says, "they began to build the house of God." They were not full four years in building the temple, and finished it in the sixth year of Darius (Ezra 4:24 with 6:15). Now, all the rest of his reign did pass and all Xerxes' reign and much of Artaxerxes Longimanus's reign, before the walls of Jerusalem were built, for about that work was Nehemiah from the twentieth year of Artaxerxes to the two and thirtieth year (Neh. 5:14). And if great chronologers are not very far mistaken, the temple was finished fourscore and three years before the walls of Jerusalem were finished.[64]

It is far from my meaning to cool your affection to the laws, liberties, peace, and safety of the kingdom. I desire only to warm your hearts with the zeal of reformation, as that which, all along, you must carry on in the first place.

One thing I cannot but mention; the reverend Assembly of Divines may lament (as Augustine in another case) *Heu heu, quam tardè festino*! Alas, alas, how slowly do I make speed![65]

Civil Affairs Must not Hinder Reformation

---

64. Vide Funcc. *Chron.*, fol. 51–53. [Johann Funck (1518–1566), *Chronologia Hoc Est: Omnivm Temporvm Et Annorvm Ab Initio Mvndi Vsqve Ad Resvrrectionem Domini Nostri Iesv Christi, compvtatio: In qua methodicè enumerantur omniu[m] populorum, Regnorumq[ue] memorabiliu[m] origines ac successiones* (Norimberga: Wachter, 1545), pp. 51r–53r.]

65. [Gillespie may be citing Augustine's *Meditationes*, wherein are the words, "Heu mihi quam sero venio! Heu quam tarde festino!" ("Appendix: Meditationum Liber Unus," Caput III, Migne, *Patrologiæ Latinæ*, 40.903). This work is now classed as pseudo-Augustine. Migne himself suggests Anselm and references Anselm's tenth oration (or prayer) to God (*PL* 40.902, note a). Interestingly, it seems as well that Gillespie has conflated the words of Anselm from his tenth oration, who doubles the "heu," as in the quotation given, "Heu mihi! quam sero venio, heu, heu! quam tarde festino, heu me!" ("Oratio X Ad Deum," *Patrologiæ Latinæ*, 158:880C). It may also be the case that Gillespie had Anselm in mind, and misspoke.]

But since now, by the blessing of God, they are thus far advanced that they have found in the Word of God a pattern for presbyterial government over many particular congregations, and have found also from the Word that ordination is an act belonging to such a presbytery, I beseech you improve that, "whereto we have already attained" (Phil. 3:16), till other acts of a presbytery be agreed on afterward. Yourselves know better than I do, that much people is perishing (Prov. 29:18), because there is no vision: "the harvest is great and the laborers are few" (Luke 10:2). Give me leave, therefore, to quicken you to this work, that with all diligence and without delay some presbyteries be associated and erected (in such places as yourselves in your wisdom shall judge fittest), with power to ordain ministers with the consent of the congregations, and after trial of the gifts, soundness and conversation of the men. In so doing you shall both please God and bring upon yourselves the blessing of many poor souls that are ready to perish (Job 29:13); and you shall likewise greatly strengthen the hearts and hands of your brethren in Scotland, joined in covenant and in arms with you. I say, therefore, again, "arise and be doing, and the Lord be with thee" (1 Chron. 22:16); yea, the Lord is with you (Hag. 2:4, 5), according to the word that He has covenanted with you, so his Spirit remains among you. Fear ye not, but "be strong in the Lord, and in the power of his might" (Eph. 6:10).

A Sermon Preached

Before the Right Honorable the House of Lords,

in the Abbey Church at Westminster,

upon the 27th of August, 1645

Being the day appointed for

solemn and public Humiliation

Hieronymus in Epitaphio Fabiolae.
Aliae sunt leges Caesarum, aliae Christi:
aliud Papinianus, aliud Paulus noster praecipit.

A Sermon Preached Before the Right Honorable the House of Lords, in the Abbey Church at Westminster, upon the 27th of August, 1645. Being the day appointed for solemn and public Humiliation. Whereunto is added A Brotherly Examination of some Passages of Mr. Coleman's late Printed Sermon upon Job 11:20. In which he hath endeavoured to strike at the root of all Church-Government.

EDITIONS

1. *A sermon preached before the Right Honourable the House of Lords, in the Abbey Church at Westminster, upon the 27th. of August. 1645. Being the day appointed for solemne and publique humiliation. Whereunto is added a brotherly examination of some passages of Mr Colemans late printed sermon upon Iob 11.20. in which hee hath endeavoured to strike at the root of all church-government. By George Gillespie minister at Edinburgh* (London: printed for Robert Bostock dwelling in Pauls Church-yard at the sign of the Kingshead, 1645). [8], 48 p.; 4⁰. ESTC R200235 (Wing G758). "Wing has 'by F. Neile for Robert Bostock' in imprint. No copy seen has Neile's name in imprint." This appeared in before or around October 13. *A Transcript of the Registers of the Worshipful Company of Stationers from 1640–1708 A.D.*, ed. G.E. Briscoe Eyre, 3 vols. (London, 1913-14), p. 197 Brief errata at the end of the Epistle to the Reader. These are corrected without notice unless the error is of some interest.

2. *A sermon preached before the Right Honourable the House of Lords, in the Abbey Church at Westminster, upon the 27th. of August. 1645. Being the day appointed for solemne and publique humiliation. Whereunto is added a brotherly examination of some passages of Mr. Colemans late printed sermon upon Job 11.20. In which he hath endeavoured to strike at the root of all church-government. By George Gillespie minister at Edenburgh* (London: printed by F. Neile for Robert Bostock dwelling in Pauls Church-yard at the sign of the Kings Head, 1646). [4], 44 p.; 4⁰. ESTC R30413 (Wing G759).

3. *A sermon preached before the Right Honourable the House of Lords, in the Abbey Church at Westminster, upon the 27th. of August. 1645. Being the day appointed for solemne and publique humiliation* (Edinburgh: Robert Ogle and Oliver and Boyd, 1844). In *Works* in *A Presbyterian's Armoury*. 26 pp.; royal octavo.

4. "A Sermon Preached Before the Right Honourable the House of Lords in the Abbey Church at Westminster, August 27, 1645. The Day Appointed for Solemn and Public Humiliation," in *Sermons Preached Before the English Houses of Parliament by the Scottish Commissioners to the Westminster Assembly of Dvines 1643–1645* (Dallas, Texas: Naphtali Press, 2011). Hard bound in dust jacket, 6x9.

The Epigraph on the prior page is from the first edition. Jerome, *The Eulogy of Fabiola*. "The laws of Cæsar are different, it is true, from the laws of Christ: Papinianus commands one thing; our own Paul another." "Letters and Select Works," in *NPNF2*, v. 6, Letter LXXVII to Oceanus, p. 151, §7.

PREFACE

ON JULY 31, 1645, the House of Lord's ordered that George Gillespie be one of the preachers for the fast for August 27, 1645 in the abbey church in Westminster cathedral.[1] When he stepped into the pulpit to preach on that day, it had been exactly seventeen months to the day from when he preached before the House of Commons on March 27, 1644. Gillespie had expressed optimism at the end of that sermon because the presbyterian majority in the assembly had "found in the Word of God a pattern for presbyterial government over many particular congregations, and have found also from the Word that ordination is an act belonging to such a presbytery...." As indicated in the introduction to the Commons sermon, the Independents (congregationalists), or dissenting brethren, had begun playing obstructionists to the designs of the presbyterian majority of the assembly. They had published their *Apologeticall Narration* at the end of 1643, which had and would continue to have disastrous effects on the objective of settling a reformed national church in England.[2] On the other hand, while it seems clear it was not understood in time, the strength of Erastian views in parliament were the more imminent threat to a *jure divino* presbyterian establishment.

GILLESPIE'S WORK IN THE ASSEMBLY AFTER MARCH 27, 1644

George Gillespie had only been in London six and a half months when he preached before the House of Commons. The most significant debates or exchanges he had in the assembly at that time were with John Selden, who appears to have stopped attending after the March 22 session when the assembly approved ordination as an act of presbytery.[3] After his Commons

---

1. The other was Anthony Burges. *Journal of the House of Lords*, volume 7 (London, 1767–1830), p. 518. Both were thanked afterward and desired to have their sermons printed, a usual courtesy. *Journal of the House of Lords*, ibid., 7.555.

2. As one writer has noted, "The destructiveness of this one publication cannot be overstated. This little book set off one of the most violent and protracted printed debates in an era replete with them, definitively splitting the godly community into presbyterian and independent factions." Shagan, "Rethinking Moderation in the English Revolution: The Case of An Apologeticall Narration," pp. 36–37. The assembly protested to parliament against the *Apologeticall Narration*, disclaiming any responsibility for it on March 6, 1644. See *Minutes*, document 17, pp. 49–50.

3. Lightfoot and Gillespie record Selden speaking at the March 22, 1644, Session 184, in the morning (the minutes record no debate for that morning session). Lightfoot, p. 234; Gillespie, Notes, p. 45. Elliot Vernon suggests Selden departed after Session 159 on February 21, 1644,

sermon, in the seventeen months leading up to his sermon before the House of Lords (or Peers), Gillespie spoke at least seventy-nine times in the assembly,[4] and at least a dozen times afterward. His speeches ranged from brief points of order, or to better frame the question, to more significant speeches. On many topics related to church polity, Gillespie spoke on ordination, presbyteries, synods, membership of such synods, church censures, suspension from the sacrament and excommunication, and the divine right of church government. With regard to the directory for worship, Gillespie spoke to allow expectants to the ministry to preach and read the scriptures aloud, and against the use of foreign languages in preaching. He spoke on the signification of baptism, against the necessity of dipping, and against restricting that sacrament to the public worship service. On the Lord's Supper, he spoke against dismissing from the service those not receiving it and against two blessings which that practice would necessitate, and joined with his fellow Scottish Commissioners in defending the use of a table with the communicants sitting around it, and the practice of successive tables, which carried over many sessions and was finally assigned to a committee for accommodation. He spoke on marriage, against holy places, against the warrant for feasts at fast days, and defended the necessity of the preface to the directory for worship to explain the setting aside of old ceremonies and the Book of Common Prayer. He spoke in favor of censuring those who separated from the established church, noting the problem of an erring conscience, which he also had discussed in his

---

which was the last debate where Independents and Erastians objected to the Presbyterians' proof from Matthew 18. He surmises that at the same time when an exasperated Lord Saye said the presbyterians do not agree among themselves, Selden, maybe figuring "his work was done," stopped attending (Elliot Vernon, "They agree not in opinion among themselves': two-kingdoms theory, 'Erastianism' and the Westminster assembly debate on church and state, c. 1641–48," in *Church Polity and Politics in the British Atlantic World, c. 1635–66* [Manchester University Press, 2020], ebook, location 4102.). However, Selden attended the very next session on February 22. As indicated, it rather appears that Selden left a month later at the least, to focus his attention on defeating the acceptance of presbyterianism in the Commons, leaving Coleman and Lightfoot to do what they could against the clear presbyterian majority in the assembly. It is true that this majority were divided over "finer ecclesiological points" such as "theories of church power." However, the presbyterians were willing to establish a system based on "straightforward" "exegetical principles," and craft documents of "homogenous practical" advice on biblical church government, rather than suspend such a system on hashing out and agreeing to finer theological points, as frustrating as that may have been to the Erastians and congregationalists. On this, see the conclusion in Chad Van Dixhoorn, "Presbyterian ecclesiologies at the Westminster assembly," in *Church Polity*.

4. Gillespie likely spoke more times because the minutes are sadly far from comprehensive and at points the scribes ceased taking extensive notes; nor were they complete when they did make longer notations. Both Lightfoot's and Gillespie's notes are helpful in giving more detail at times. A collated listing of the times Gillespie spoke in the assembly will be given in the third and final volume of *Shorter Writings*, D.V.

English Popish Ceremonies.[5] In a topic for the confession of faith, he joined the discussion of whether there was a divine decree of reprobation in which he urged wording that all might understand their own sense.[6] He was also given opportunity by a direct query from an MP member, to speak to if "Christ be in the New Testament named the king and head of a visible, political, ministerial church."[7] As far as a direct impact on the wording of the Westminster Confession of Faith, Gillespie made a motion to alter three uses of the word "Christ" to "God" in chapter 23.3. The assembly approved a memorandum in the minutes stating that this change "was not intended to determine the controversy about the subordination of the civill magistrate to Christ as mediatour."[8]

However, while the Independents continued to be obstructionists for part of this seventeen months of time and the Erastianism of the House of Commons was a wall to erecting a *jure divino* presbyterian church for England, the parliament still required the assembly's work as ordered and a lot was accomplished despite the obstacles. Also, a self exile of the dissenting brethren for several months before Gillespie's House of Lords sermon and seven weeks after it, improved the workflow significantly.

As to how this self imposed hiatus of the Independents came about, the assembly had clearly become exasperated with the intransigence of the dissenting brethren in always opposing but never bringing in their own plan for church government so that it could be formally debated. In Session 402 on March 21, 1645, the assembly asked but did not order the brethren to bring in their model of church government.[9] In Session 404 on March 27, the brethren

---

5. *A Dispute Against the English Popish Ceremonies* (1637; Naphtali Press, 2013), pp. 42–43. See John R. Bower, *The Confession of Faith: A Critical Text* (RHB, 2020), p. 115n73.

6. See Bower, *The Confession of Faith*, pp. 60–62.

7. "This was a query after the young Scot's own heart. 'That is a question worthy of debate,' he replied, and then went on to suggest that the kingly office of Christ is proved both in the Old and New Testaments; Christ is called the king of the house of Jacob, and head of the church. In what relation Jesus Christ is a prophet in the church, in that same relation he is a king; his kingly office serves to add efficacy to his prophetical office. Christ is a prophet not only to the elect, but to the visible, political, and ministerial church. There is a place in the Gospel, said Gillespie, which held out this business: 'there be some of them that stand here, which shall not taste of death, till they have seen the kingdom of God come with power.' Some interpret the passage as of the government of the church, and the sending forth of the apostles and other ministers to rule the church; 'and some of them did not see death till an order and policy in the churches were settled.' Other members of the Assembly associated themselves with this point of view, and adduced Scriptures in support of it." John R. de Witt, *Jus Divinum: The Westminster Assembly and the Divine Right of Church Government* (Kampen: J. H. Kok N.V., 1969), p. 201. See Session 606 (original), March 18, 1646, *Minutes*, 419, 21.

8. *Minutes*, Session 752, 4.756–757. See Bower, ibid., pp. 118, 160.

9. The dissenting brethren apparently sent up to parliament a dissent on this request, but the text is missing and it is not certain that was the subject matter. *Minutes*, doc. 65, p. 185.

read a dissent and a paper of seven propositions which then they would not submit formally afterward.[10] Then there was published John Cotton's *The Way of the Churches of Christ in New England*. This title had been entered by the Stationers for February 27, 1644/5,[11] and had appeared in print by April 4, 1645, which is the date Thomason records buying a copy.[12] The preface to Cotton's book chastised the "presbyterians for not producing their own platform for church government, for not engaging with the seven propositions" the congregationalists presented and withdrew in Session 404, as well as "for *not providing the congregationalists an opportunity to produce their own statement on church government*" (emphasis added)![13] This audacious chastising of the assembly clearly backfired on the dissenting brethren. Having seen this preface, on that same date of April 4, in session 410, the majority of the assembly, against the will of the dissenting brethren despite the complaint of that preface, ordered them to be a committee charged with bringing to the assembly their plan for church government. That it was really not their desire can be seen the next day, when Nye moved that the order be changed and "that the dissenting brethren be required to refute a proposition rather than provide a positive statement of church government." This fooled no one and the motion failed. Aside from at least one appearance, the dissenting brethren generally absented themselves to supposedly work on their plan for church government. Six months later in September, a month after Gillespie had preached his sermon to the House of Lords, the assembly ordered the congregationalists to bring in their report on October 13, 1645.[14] The report they made was a refusal to bring in a plan at all and in terms that Baillie labeled as libelous. Then, contrary to assembly rules but in keeping with their behavior, the brethren had it published the next month, the printer

---

10. Dr. Van Dixhoorn catalogs this paper as missing. See *Minutes*, vol. 5, doc. 66, p. 186.

11. *A transcript of the registers of the Worshipful Company of Stationers from 1640–1708* ed. G. E. Briscoe Eyre, volume 1 (Privately printed, 1913–14), p. 151.

12. Thomason, *Catalogue of the Pamphlets*, etc., 1.371, ESTC R209858.

13. *Minutes*, 3.571. See document 98 dated December 11, 1645, in which the assembly asked permission from the parliament to answer this preface to Cotton's book as well as the Remonstrance the brethren brought in after six months in which they refused to give in their plan (document 92), where the preface is referenced and seems to be the reason for them ordering the brethren to be a committee. One may speculate how the brethren managed to get into the preface of a book available on April 4 these charges based on the March 27 session 404 (which of course in itself broke the confidentiality oath taken by members of the assembly). Cotton's work was likely complete since it had been entered in the Stationers' record with a date of February 27, and either lacked only a preface or it was changed. It is possible that plans had been laid to do something in the preface as far back as session 402 on March 21, or that it was a plan always to say something contra the assembly with the preface. Since Cotton's work was "Published according to order," the assembly may have had advance notice of the preface.

14. *Minutes*, Session 506, 3.667.

saying he had discovered the text "by a divine providence.[15] The assembly responded by seeking permission from parliament to answer,[16] which the House of Lords approved but the Commons halted for two months.[17] The end result of all this drama for the brethren, at the very least, was that they had removed themselves for six months for nothing and allowed the presbyterian majority to work unimpeded.[18]

There was a significant amount of work done by the assembly both before, during, and after the six month leave of the dissenting brethren. Documents, reports, petitions, etc., approved by the assembly to send up to the Houses of Parliament after Gillespie's sermon to the Commons may be grouped under, 1. Papers related to church government; 2. Ordination; 3. Directory for Public Worship; 4. Church censures; and 5. Papers related to the *Grand Debate*.

1. Regarding a directory for church government, here the brethren of course were at their most obstructionist, forcing committees of accommodation and eventually following through with their threats to produce minority reports submitted directly to parliament.[19] The assembly still passed a draft directory on March 25, 1644,[20] a paper concerning a part of church government on November 8,[21] an explanation to parliament of the term elder on November 14,[22] and another draft directory for church government

---

15. *Minutes*, Session 518, 3.687. See Baillie's account in *Letters & Journals*, 2.318. See the dissenting brethrens' report in *Minutes*, volume 5, document 92, pp. 252–256.

16. *Minutes*, Session 552, 3.720. Notably, this was after the brethren's remonstrance had appeared in print. See the assembly's report in *Minutes*, volume 5, document 98 and 99, pp. 263–296. This paper by the assembly "is important, among other reasons, for providing chronologies of events and for preserving responses and position papers of the assembly as well as papers of individual congregationalists and a congregational committee." Ibid., p. 264.

17. "Instead of their long expected model, they presented a libel of invectives as reasons why they would present no model to the Assembly. This, understand, they caused print; and when the assembly had drawn up a sober and true answer, and gotten an order from the House of Lords to print it, they make their friends in the House of Commons as yet to keep it in." Baillie, *Letters & Journals*, 2.344 and n2.

18. One may speculate that this refusal was not just about differences of polity but over the extent of the toleration the Independents could demand without alienating both moderate and extremist supporters. Haivry, *John Selden and the Western Political Tradition*, p. 420.

19. The papers of these committees for accommodation and the dissenting brethren's answers, or 'minority reports,' and the assembly's replies make up the book known as *The Grand Debate*. These were first published in 1648, and reissued with the title for which they are known in 1652. A Scottish version of the 1648 text revised with Scottish efforts "to correct the alleged congregationalist bias" was published by Evan Tyler in 1648. *Minutes*, 5.iii.

20. See *Minutes*, volume 5, document 19, p. 52ff.

21. *Minutes*, volume 5, document 35, p.90ff. This is the famous third proposition concerning church government about which much of the *Grand Debate* revolved.

22. *Minutes*, volume 5, document 39, p. 113ff.

on December 11, 1644.[23] While the dissenting brethren were absent, the assembly sent up advice on presbytery boundaries and selection of elders on May 30, 1645,[24] a paper on congregational elders and membership in various ecclesiastical assemblies on June 4,[25] a petition for the divine right of church government on June 16,[26] and the assembly passed the final form of a directory for church government on July 3,[27] with votes in favor of the subordination of synods and power to discipline by broader synods on July 4, 1645.[28]

2. The work on ordination was all passed before the hiatus from the assembly of the dissenting brethren. Regarding ordination, the assembly presented to parliament the doctrine of and directory for ordination on April 19, 1644, a paper of amendments on August 26, 1644, the revised directory for ordination for *the time being* on August 26, 1644 (both the day before Gillespie's sermon to the Commons), and a paper on September 4, 1644 defending ordination "as an 'ordinance of Christ' and ministers ruling."[29]

3. There were few differences between the assembly and the dissenting brethren in areas of worship, and the directory was completed before the absenting of the latter for half a year. The assembly was rushing to have the full directory in time for the Scottish General Assembly. On November 12, 1644, the parts were passed for "assembling the congregation, public reading of scripture, public prayer before the sermon, preaching, prayer after the sermon, baptism, and the Lord's supper."[30] In fairly rapid order, the assembly passed the part on the Lord's Day on November 20, marriage on December 3, partial draft for visiting the sick on December 11, burying the dead on December 13, final draft on visiting the sick on December 16, fasting, thanksgiving, and psalm singing on December 30, and later a formal title on March 6, 1645.[31]

Once the directory was completed except for the belated title, Gillespie's presence at the assembly had an interruption. He and Baillie had the task of giving a progress report in Scotland. Robert Baillie and George Gillespie left the assembly on January 6 for Edinburgh to present the directory and other work before the General Assembly of the Church of Scotland, which was meeting on January 22, 1645.[32]

---

23. *Minutes*, ibid., document 45, p. 127ff.

24. *Minutes*, ibid., document 71, pp. 193–194.

25. *Minutes*, ibid., document 72, pp. 195ff.

26. *Minutes*, ibid., document 73, pp. 198–199.

27. *Minutes*, ibid., document 77, pp. 204ff.

28. *Minutes*, ibid., document 78, pp. 222ff.

29. See *Minutes*, volume 5, documents 20, p. 63ff, and 28, 29 and 30, pp. 75–86.

30. *Minutes*, ibid., document 36, pp. 93–110.

31. *Minutes*, ibid., documents 42, 44, 46, 50, 51, 53, 54 and 62, pp. 118–158, 178.

32. See the letter from the assembly to the General Assembly of the Church of Scotland, *Minutes*, 5.160–161, document #55; Baillie, 2.248, 250; and Shaw, *A History of the English Church During the Civil Wars*, 1.184n3.

Gillespie's speech to the Westminster assembly upon departing is recorded in Session 353 on January 3, 1645.[33]

> I acknowledge it to be one of the greatest mercies that I ever received in this world to have liberty … that I might contribute … and be edified … and now when I am called away, I thank God for it. I go away more confirmed in my own conscience that the government is most agreeable to the word of God … And what I say for myself, Mr. Bayly is of the same mind … I must return humble thanks … I am assured that my infirmities have appeared too much in this Assembly, that at some times I have offended some, and that at some times I have taken up time in speaking, to hinder others that would have spoken better … and … I am confident that He that hath begun the good work will finish it… Your difficulties have been many … The greatest difficulties sometimes was the prelacy and Book of Common Prayer … but other impediments are fallen in, which I pray God may…. You have here some dissenting brethren to whom I owe great respect … a word of love and affection … I wish they prove to be as unwilling to divide from us, as we have been unwilling to divide from them. I wish that instead of toleration, there may be a mutual endeavour for a happy accommodation … There is a certain measure of forbearance, but it is not so seasonable now to be talking of forbearance, but mutual endeavours for accommodation … It is true two are better than one, but it is not true of parties … since God hath promised to give His people one heart and one way … Now, if you have any other commands for us that are going home, we shall be careful of them; though we go from you, we shall [be] present with you in spirit.[34]

Dr. Burges spoke and addressed the prolocutor to give the departing men thanks.

> It hath pleased the commissioner to acknowledge it a great happynesse that he had opportunity to be amongst us soe long. I thinke the assembly will acknowledge it a happynesse to have injoyed their helpe. For his modest expression of speaking in the assembly, the assembly acknowledgeth with all thankefullnesse. It's a pious & Christian close [conclusion]. What he hath desired is the desire of us all. I hope you will be pleased to let them knowe how much we doe value their paines.

The prolocutor, William Twisse, replied addressing Gillespie: "All of us have had great experience of your learned paines; for myselfe, I have taken great comfort in your learned discourses."[35]

---

33. *Minutes*, pp. 497–98.

34. Mitchell & Struthers, *Minutes of the Sessions of the Westminster Assembly of Divines*, pp. 28–29.

35. *Minutes*, 3.498.

There were some mishaps and dangers slowing the Scotsmen's party in their journey. Evading capture by royalists forces and places with outbreaks of plague, Gillespie and Baillie arrived in Edinburgh on January 23 in time to speak and present a report on the progress of the Westminster assembly and the materials which had been passed.[36] Both men spoke but only Baillie's speech survives in his *Letters & Journals*. He reported to his cousin more succinctly that they read in the General Assembly, "the letters of the English Assembly, our commissioners' letters, the Directory [for worship] from end to end,[37] the Directory for Ordination, the votes of Government so far as had passed the [Westminster] assembly, and some other papers." He opined that "It was one of the fairest Assemblies I had seen."[38] However, things had not been going well in Scotland. Plague was raging and James Graham, Marquis of Montrose had gone over to the king's side at the end of August, 1644, and had beaten Covenanter forces in Scotland at Tippermuir on September 1, 1644 and Aberdeen on September 13. So, there were causes for a fast to be called and according to Baillie, "the Assembly sent out a printed Warning to the country, very well penned by Mr. Gillespie."[39]

---

36. Baillie wrote from Newcastle to Archibald Johnson, who was already in Edinburgh apparently, "God be thanked, Mr. Gillespie and I came hither yesternight, without one fall or any miss-accident to any of our company. It's a pity the officers should not be with the army; the mutiny here was dangerous and great. You must look to your army in England above all things. God helped me to speak my mind freely this day in Nicolas church, and I trust shall help Mr. Gillespie to do the same presently, in the same place. We are very weary and fashed with a long evil way; we will not be able to be in Edinburgh before Thursday at noon. You must be doing your best to entertain the Assembly till then, and a day or two more, with private business. It is necessar[y] Mr. Robert Douglas be moderator, and that you have set your committees of well-affected wise men." They made better progress and arrived Wednesday night as he wrote his cousin William Spang, "This is the first I wrote to you since I come from London. It pleased God to give us a very prosperous journey: however, the ways were very deep, and the excursions of the enemy from Newark hazardous; yea, much more than we knew; for we learned thereafter that we were pursued, and escaped scarcely one hour. The pest also was in many places of our way; yet God brought us both to Edinburgh safe, without a fall or great weariness, on the Wednesday at night, the first day of the Assembly. *Letters & Journals*, 2.254–55, 258. Spelling has been modernized in citations from Baillie, while citations from the *Minutes* are as in the published text.

37. The English Parliament ordered the directory printed on March 13, 1644/45. It had been issued and approved on January 4, 1644/45 (not January 3 as in the printed order; cf. William A. Shaw, *A History of the English Church during the Civil Wars and under the Commonwealth* [New York: Longmans, Green, and Co., 1900], 1.353). The Scottish Parliament approved it on February 6, 1645 and the General Assembly of the Church of Scotland on February 3, 1645.

38. Baillie's speech is dated January 23, 1645 and the letter to Spang dates to after he had returned to London, April 25, 1645. *Letters & Journals*, 2.255–57, 258–266.

39. *Letters & Journals*, 2.263. This warning follows in this volume after the sermon to the House of Lords and the three Anti-Erastian tracts.

While in Scotland a truce called under the Treaty of Uxbridge in January and February apparently did not hold for Montrose, who was victorious a third time in a battle with Covenanter forces at Inverlochy on February 2, On the commissioners return to the assembly in Session 413 on April 9, 1645,[40] Gillespie spoke, presenting the letter from and giving the respects of the General Assembly of the Scottish Church, and an account of the receiving of the directory for worship, government, ordination and the psalter.[41] He also opened with an apology for being a month late because their ship was carried away by weather to Holland. Baillie at least did some book buying and had at least one pamphlet mailed on to London which he complains about the cost of the postage (which Gillespie had to pay).[42] Baillie and Gillespie spent time in Rotterdam and Middelburg and on April 5 advised Alexander Petrie on some need for discipline of unruly Scots in the country.[43] Gillespie's speech as recorded in the *Minutes* reads:

> If the relation that we are to make of the letter we bring seem too late … desire you to take notice of the first excuse…. We did intend to be here a month ago, but were carried away to Holland…. We are comforted to see this. Present the great respects of the General Assembly of the Church of Scotland, and to assure you their hearts are much with you…. Mentioned in their prayers both publicly and privately…. For the account…. The Directory accepted with great joy and contentment, both to the General Assembly and Parliament, approved in both without one contrary vote in either…. So much comforted by those first-fruits, that it makes them long for the full harvest…. They pray, and are confident the Lord will not desert the work in your hand…. The propositions of government and ordination are also approved…. The Psalms sent down with us they have put it in the hands of a select Committee. In the general the[y] like very well the correcting and amending of the Psaltery, and they wish the work may be carried on…. It is desired that we may be as quickly at home as possible.[44]

---

40. *Minutes*, 3.574.

41. The assembly had sent the draft of the revisions to that date which they had made to the psalter, which was submitted to the assembly by MP Francis Rous. The assembly, tired of waiting for Scottish input, approved their final version on November 12, 1645. *Minutes*, document 94, 5.259. The Scots continued to work on the psalter and produced it in 1650. It is substantially different from both Rous's original and the assembly's final text. The 1650 Psalter has had long continuous use in churches, but Rous's and the assembly's productions never caught on for ecclesiastical use.

42. Baillie, 2.266.

43. See William Steven, *The History of the Scottish Church, Rotterdam* (Edinburgh: Waugh and Innes, 1833), p. 15. "As is apparent from the minutes of the Consistory of the Scots Kirk in Rotterdam, both ministers attended the session of 5 April." Willem Nijenhuis, *Ecclesia Reformata: Studies on the Reformation*, Volume 2 (Brill, 1994), p. 293.

44. Mitchell & Struthers, *Minutes of the … Assembly*, pp. 77. See *Minutes*, 3.574; 5.160–161.

4. While the Scots had been gone, the assembly began churning out papers regarding church censures and keeping the ordinances pure. On February 3, 1645, they sent up advice on excommunication, a directory on admonition, excommunication, and absolution, to which the brethren submitted a dissent, after which followed an answer from the assembly on February 6.[45] On March 5, the assembly made a petition for "settling a preaching ministry and for keeping the sacraments pure." Twenty days later, they sent up a paper answering the House of Commons on "the duty and feasibility of elders examining persons prior to their attending the supper, a point the majority of the assembly maintain, and a majority in the house dispute." On March 29, the assembly produced "its first theological paper" in response to "persistent questions" from the House of Commons, which was a paper on the doctrine of the Trinity under the heading of "Particulars of the knowledge" needed to be able to partake of the Lord's Supper.[46] Once Baillie and Gillespie had returned but after the exodus for a time of the dissenting brethren, the assembly continued to send up papers, petitions, and advice on censures and sacraments. They completed more articles of belief required to take communion on April 10, a paper on scandalous sins on June 16, a petition for permitting ministers and elders to perform church discipline on July 31, another petition on the same topic on August 7, advice on "discipline and the sacrament" on August 13, a second such paper on the same date, and on August 18, a paper concerning "the right of elderships to suspend persons from the Lord's Supper" and a paper giving "examples of discipline" used in churches in other countries.[47]

5. The final group of assembly documents to note that were created during this seventeen month period, are those relating the *Grand Debate*. These are the debate papers over church government exchanged between the Westminster assembly and the dissenting brethren, when in committees of accommodation and over the papers the brethren submitted directly to parliament. Most of these papers were created before the brethren took their hiatus from the assembly and before the trip to Scotland by Baillie and Gillespie.

On November 7, 1644, there appeared at the Session 317 meeting of the assembly a delegation from both houses of parliament, who "insisted again that the assembly produce a directory for the church government."[48] The assembly, unwilling to send up its directory in progress, decided to send up its votes about presbyterian church government" from the April 11, 1644 Session 197,[49] which they had not sent due to the threat of the dissenting brethren to draft a minority report, and a committee for accommodation

---

45. *Minutes*, volume 5, documents 57–60, pp. 167–175.

46. *Minutes*, ibid., documents 61, 64, 65, 67, pp. 176–189.

47. *Minutes*, volume 5, documents, 68, 74, 81–88, pp. 190–192, 200–248. The texts are missing for documents 82, 84, and 85.

48. *Minutes*, 3.439.

49. *Minutes*, 2.678.

had been appointed. The brethren had their votes against this registered. The next day, November 8, in session 318, the assembly voted to send up the prior mentioned document 35 on its third proposition of church government defending presbyterianism. The congregationalists voted against this and then outside the assembly asked permission from the Commons to submit a minority report responding to the assembly's paper, which they submitted on November 14. This paper is document 38 in Van Dixhoorn's *Minutes*, "The Reasons of the dissenting brethren against the third proposition concerning presbyterial government."[50] The assembly complained in a November 19 message to the Commons and Lords that they were aware of this paper and that it contained arguments not debated yet and would delay their work.[51] Undaunted, the dissenting brethren sent three more papers to the Commons on December 12. These were their answers to the proofs for presbyterianism from the church at Ephesus, against subordination of synods, and against the assembly's proposition that "no single congregation that can conveniently associate" with other churches "should 'assume to itself all and sole power in ordination.'"[52] On December 20, 1644, the assembly sent up to parliament a lengthy reply defending presbyterianism as understood by the assembly in "Answer to the reasons of the dissenting brethren against the third proposition concerning presbyterian government."[53] The assembly would wait a year to answer the brethren's objections to the proofs of presbyterianism from the example of the church at Ephesus, which they did on October 13, 1645.[54] After Gillespie had left the assembly, they would answer the brethren's objections to "the subordination of congregational, classical, provincial and national assemblies," on August 19, 1646.[55] And considerably later on April 19, 1648, the assembly turned in a reply to the brethren's objections to the assembly's findings on ordination.[56]

Gillespie's Work Outside the Assembly

When not in the assembly, Gillespie filled his time researching and drafting papers on various ecclesiastical subjects (some of which were published as *Miscellany Question*),[57] preaching around London or to the army, and writing for publication.

---

50. *Minutes*, volume 5, p. 111. Due to their length, the text of this and the other *Grand Debate* papers are not given in *Minutes* volume 5. The Commons ordered the papers published and the volume appeared about February 5, 1645. Ibid.

51. *Minutes*, volume 5, document 41, pp. 116–117.

52. Ibid., document 47, 48, 49, pp. 141–144.

53. Ibid., document 52, pp. 152–153.

54. Ibid., document 91, pp. 250–251.

55. Ibid., document 111, p. 307.

56. Ibid., document 134, p. 340.

57. Gillespie had many resources available to consult for such research (see p. 57).

In addition to working on books such as *Aaron's Rod Blossoming*,[58] Gillespie engaged in two pamphlet campaigns, not surprisingly each addressed to the extremes of the two groups impeding presbyterianism in and outside the assembly of divines: the independents and the Erastians. The latter are the tracts written against Thomas Coleman's brazen attack launched in his sermon before the Commons which continued in the assembly until he suddenly died. The other tracts form a set written against granting a broad toleration of all sects and heresies. These are *Faces About, or, A recrimination charged upon Mr. John Goodwin* (October 21, 1644), *A Late Dialogue betwixt a civilian and a divine* (October 30, 1644), and *Wholesome Severity reconciled with Christian Liberty* (January 8, 1645).[59] These do not relate directly to debates in the assembly at the time, but derived from the concern that many in the city were in favor of a broad toleration of all sorts of sects and heresies. Gillespie was not inactive in the assembly in September through December, particularly with the rush to get the Directory for Worship and other things ready for the trip to Scotland around January 6, but he found time to write these three tracts. With their departure to have been around January 6, and the fact that *Wholesome Severity* appeared by January 8 when Thomason purchased a copy, it is not surprising and interesting to see that a similar plea to the dissenting brethren for accommodation that was in his departing speech ends that anonymously published tract.

Also, outside the assembly, as already noted, besides the two official sermons before parliament, Gillespie did spend enough time in London preaching to fill a volume of practical and polemical sermons, which he left to be published when he departed London for the final time. According to Wodrow, the printer for money allowed these to be destroyed by some sectaries who were "mauled by him" in the aforementioned tracts against a toleration of sects and heresies. Their loss is certainly to be lamented. Gillespie on at least one occasion went to the Scottish forces with the Earl of Cassilis, presumably to preach.[60]

OUTLINE OF GILLESPIE'S SERMON BEFORE THE HOUSE OF LORDS.
Gillespie begins his sermon on Malachi 3:2 by giving the meaning of the text, that it is about Christ and the day of His coming. Mainly "intended is Christ's coming and appearing in a spiritual, but yet most powerful and glorious manner, to erect His kingdom, and to gather and govern His churches by the ministry of His apostles and other ministers, whom He sent forth after His ascension." Christ has come many times in this way and "manifested Himself to His churches" and there will be "a more glorious coming of Jesus Christ

---

58. *Aarons Rod Blossoming, or, the divine ordinance of church government vindicated* (1646).

59. See the texts of these three tracts in *The Shorter Writings of George Gillespie*, volume I, NPSE volume V (2021).

60. Baillie, *Letters & Journals*, 2.273, 279. For more information on Gillespie's relationship to John Kennedy, Earl of Cassilis, see *The Shorter Writings of George Gillespie*, vol. I, pp. 70ff.

before the end" when He "shall turn away ungodliness from Jacob," "destroy Antichrist," and there is "the church's tranquility, the filling of the earth with the knowledge of the Lord, and the restoring of the dispersed Jews" (157–158).[61] Christ comes "to save the spirit, but to destroy the flesh" and "He will have the heart-blood of sin, that the soul may live forever," which "is set forth by a double metaphor, one taken from the refiner's fire, which purifies the metals from the dross; the other, from the fuller's soap" (159). Gillespie then derives and gives a general and first doctrine: *The way of Christ, and fellowship with Him, is very difficult and displeasing to our sinful nature, and is not so easy a matter as most men imagine.* He proves the doctrine four ways: 1. From the text itself. 2. From other Scriptures. 3. From Christ's excellence. And 4. From the nature of the covenant of grace. He makes one use about the narrowness of the way for the Christian and answers an objection to this from Matthew 11:30, "For my yoke is easy, and my burden is light" (160–162). After this general doctrine, Gillespie pursues the specific observation that Christ is a refiner's fire and fuller's soap with respect to: 1. Reformation (163–173). 2. Tribulation (173–178). 3. Mortification (178–180).

The first of these denoted as the second doctrine reads: *The right reformation of the church, which is according to the mind of Jesus Christ, is not without much molestation and displeasure to men's corrupt nature. It is a very purgatory upon earth. It is like the fire to drossy silver, and like fuller's soap to slovenly persons, who would rather keep the spots in their garments than take pains to wash them out.* He then applies this "manner of reformation": "1. To magistrates and statesmen. 2. To ministers. 3. To a people reformed. 4. To a people not reformed" (163–166). For uses he first applies the doctrine "to the opposers of Reformation" (166–167). His second and longest application is to the House of Lords themselves, which he pursues with regard to: 1. Connivance at or correspondence with malignants (i.e., hinderers of reformation who fought for the king). 2. Liberty of conscience. 3. Restraint of scandalous persons from the Lord's Supper (167–171). His third application to ministers he applies "actively" and "passively" (171–173). In this section he adds an application of eight lines of text against ministers who "will neither be active nor passive in the establishing of the church-refining and sin-censuring government of Jesus Christ, but will needs appear upon the stage against it." He then notes that "this was done in a late sermon now come abroad,[62] which has given no small scandal and offence." This is the only reference, and an oblique one at that, to Thomas Coleman's sermon preached at the prior monthly fast before the Commons, *Hopes Deferred and Dashed* (172).

The second (or third) doctrine is *Tribulation does either accompany or follow after the work of reformation or purging of the house of God* (173), which he explains and draws with "haste" to three uses. First, to give to God the

---

61. On the eschatology of Gillespie see the preface to the House of Commons sermon.

62. Thomas Coleman, *Hopes Deferred and Dashed, observed in a sermon to the Honourable House of Commons, in Margarets Westminster, July 30, 1645* (1645).

glory of His truth, in that "the sword of the Lord has gotten a charge against these three covenanting and reforming kingdoms," in which he mainly addresses the charge against the righteousness of Scotland's involvement in England in that they had suffered difficulties contrary to Exodus 34:23, 24. Second, the use is to give God glory for "His just and righteous dealings," where he presses the point to "take heed you conceive not an ill opinion of the covenant and cause of God, or the reformation of religion, because of the tribulation which follows thereupon" (175). Third, Gillespie answers the complaint of "how long," concluding "We have need of all the sore strokes which we mourn under, and if one less could do the turn, it would be spared, for the Lord does not afflict willingly" (176–177). In a fourth and final use, Gillespie urges to "give God the glory of His mercy," which he presses two ways for comfort, in that a remnant shall be delivered and purified, and that "as the promises of spiritual and eternal blessings" are "not legal but evangelical," so are the "promises of peace and temporal deliverances" (177). "We must improve the office of the Mediator, and the promise of free grace, in the behalf of God's people, as well as of our own souls, which, if it be indeed done, will not hinder, but further a great mourning and deep humiliation in the land" (178).

Gillespie had now run out of time and so he pursued the third division with a fourth doctrine briefly with regard to mortification (178–180). *It is not enough to join in public reformation, yea, to suffer tribulation for the name of Christ, except we also endeavor mortification.* "This mortification is a third step distinct from the other two, and without this the other two can make us but *almost Christians*, or, 'not far from the kingdom of God.'"

After "enlarging" briefly upon this fourth doctrine, George Gillespie applies three brief uses from it. 1. "Let all and everyone of us be convinced of the necessity of our further endeavoring after mortification." 2. He tells the Lords that they must be "willing and contented, yea, desirous to be thoroughly mortified." 3. With regard to the difficulty of this, Gillespie closes by urging,

> Put yourself in the hands of Jesus Christ. Trust Him with the work. If you mark the text here, and the verse that follows, Christ is both the refiner and the refiner's fire. You shall be refined by Him and you shall be refined in Him. You deceive yourself if you think to be refined any other way but by this refiner and in this refiner's fire. The blood of Christ does not only wash us from guilt, but purges our consciences "from dead works, to serve the living God" (Heb. 9:14); "And they that are Christ's, have crucified the flesh, with the affections and lusts" (Gal. 5:24). Here you may see the thing is feasible and attainable, and not only by an apostle or some extraordinary man, but by all that are Christ's. Being His, and in Him, they are enabled, through His strength, to crucify the flesh, with the affections and lusts thereof.

Mistaken Scholarship Redux

As with his sermon before the House of Commons, writers have made mistakes regarding the causes, role, and background of not only Gillespie's sermon before the Lords, but Thomas Coleman's sermon to which it was in part a response as well. The fault lies in relatively brief comments made fifty years ago by Lawrence Kaplan. [63]

Mistakes Regarding Coleman's Sermon

With regard to Coleman, Kaplan deduced from comments made by Baillie almost a year apart on April 25, 1645 and March 17, 1646, from both before and after the sermon, that "Coleman had been selected at this time, as the Scots believed, to air the religious beliefs of a majority of the members" of the Commons.

On April 25, 1645 Baillie wrote "The most of the House of Commons are downright Erastians: they are like to create us much more woe than all the sectaries of England."[64] And on March 17, 1646, he wrote a long lamentation on English Erastianism in which he said,

> In the Assembly we are fallen on a fashious proposition, that has kept us diverse days, and will do so diverse more, coming upon the article of the church and the church-notes to oppose the Erastian heresy, which in this land is very strong, especially among the lawyers, unhappy members of this parliament. We find it necessary to say, "That Christ in the New Testament had instituted a church government distinct from the civil, to be exercised by the officers of the church, without commission from the magistrate." None in the Assembly has any doubt of this truth but one Mr. Coleman, a professed Erastian; a man reasonably learned, but stupid and inconsiderate, half a pleasant [*fool; clown*], and of small estimation. But the lawyers in the parliament, making it their work to spoil our presbytery, not so much upon conscience, as upon fear that the presbytery spoil their mercat [market], and take up the most of the country-pleas without law, did blow up the poor man with much vanity; so he is become their champion to bring out, in the best way he can, Erastus's arguments against the proposition, for the contentment of the parliament. We give him a free and fair hearing; albeit we fear when we have answered all he can bring, and have confirmed with undeniable proofs our position, the Houses, when it comes to them, shall scrape it out of the Confession; for this point is their idol. The most

---

63. Lawrence Kaplan, "English Civil War Politics and the Religious Settlement," *Church History* 41, no. 3 (1972): 313–14. The same material is also published in *Politics and Religion during the English Revolution: the Scots and the Long Parliament, 1643–1645* (New York: New York University Press, 1976), p. 126–128.

64. Baillie, *Letters & Journals*, 2.265. Baillie repeated this again in a letter to his cousin. "The Erastian party in the parliament is stronger than the Independent, and is like to work us much woe. Selden is their head." Baillie to Spang, about June 1645. Ibid., 2.277.

of them are incredibly zealous for it: The pope and the king were never more earnest for the headship of the church than the plurality of this parliament.[65]

While he may have been put up to it, there is nothing in Baillie's comments to imply the Scots or anyone suspected that Coleman was deliberately chosen to do what he did. It would be very improper to use the occasion of a fast to openly criticize the assembly which he served.[66] Nevertheless, he did breach this etiquette, betrayed the rules of the Westminster assembly, and directly undermined its authority in devoting a part of his sermon to deprecating,

> equally the Presbyterians[67] and the Independents, finding fault especially with their claims of *jure divino*, "the one with a national determination, the other with a congregational engagement." His advice to the Commons: ignore the pretensions of both and "establish as few things *jure divino* as can well be." To his responsive audience, Coleman went on to warn against giving clerics control over church administration. "Lay no more burden of government upon the shoulders of ministers, than Christ plainly laid upon them," he advised. And using a comparison which later drew fire from the Presbyterians, he maintained that those clerics who desired governing authority for themselves followed the same path as the Antichrist, the pope. To ward off creeping papism, Parliament should endeavor to keep the government of the English church in its own hands....[68]

---

65. Baillie, *Letters & Journals*, 2.360

66. Sadly, Kaplan's statement has been picked up and repeated even more emphatically. "The Scottish Commissioners believed that the House of Commons arranged to have Coleman deliver the monthly fast sermon to express their own religious convictions regarding church government and the relation to the magistracy. According to Lawrence Kaplan, Coleman was selected by Parliament at this time 'to air the religious beliefs of the majority of the members ... [he] was a well-known Erastian and had been encouraged to come forward as a religious spokesman for Parliament.'" Jaretha Joy Jimena-Palmer, *Church and Politics During the English Reformation: Ecclesiology and Politics in the Writings of Stephen Marshall* (1595–1655), ebook, location 2503. Haivry, also relying on Kaplan, goes so far as to postulate that perhaps John Selden engineered the sermon. *John Selden and the Western Political Tradition*, p. 422.

67. Trevor-Roper contended that Coleman was an English Presbyterian, just not Scottish, which simply does not withstand scrutiny if we are to understand any meaningful divisions within the Westminster assembly. The Scottish and English Presbyterians believed in the divine right of church government, and that the Scriptures give a form of that government. Hence the passing of all their petitions contending so! Some of the English Presbyterians may have compromised later and accepted out of necessity a "lame Erastian Presbytery," but Coleman was an Erastian pure and simple in denying this fundamental tenet. Hugh R. Trevor-Roper, "The Fast Sermons of the Long Parliament," in *The Crisis of the Seventeenth Century* (1956; repr., New York, 1968), pp. 322–323.

68. Kaplan, *Politics and Religion*, p. 127.

What Coleman had done was not just give his own advice, or cast insults, as when he compared to Antichrist's, the desire to have church censures in the church's hands rather than the state's. He actively prejudiced the work of the assembly on a petition drafted to send to both houses of parliament just the day prior before it had even been delivered to the House of Commons, one of the bodies to whom the petition was addressed.[69] On June 16, 1645, the assembly had approved and sent a petition to the Commons "regarding the divine right of church discipline," presenting "four arguments for permitting congregational elderships to discern a person's fitness for the Lord's supper on a case-by-case basis."[70] The assembly hearing nothing from the Commons, determined to vote on a second petition, which it began refining and approving in Session 476 on July 28, 1645, and because of the monthly fast on July 30, it did not finish the work until July 31.[71] In between those two sessions, Coleman preached against the intent of the petition in his sermon before the Commons. In Session 477 on July 31, someone, apparently Coleman, wanted it made clear that "Mr. Coleman hath not given a negative to any vote in this Assembly this day [on the petition], but only to that of Erastus, his learning."[72] At the end of the session, a complaint was brought against his sermon. In session 478, the assembly found itself debating about what to do with one if its own members, and resolved to query the Commons and at that point another report about the sermon came in to the assembly. It was moved that Coleman would speak and recant and he rose and said: "For much of what is reported, I deny. What I have acknowledged, it is my judgement. I am sorry I have given offence both to this Assembly & the commissioners of the church of Scotland, and for the printing of the Sermon, I shall not do it."[73] The assembly still sent up a complaint to the Commons, that the "sermon undermined the gathering's authority."[74] On the

---

69. Essentially, both the dissenting brethren with the *Apologeticall Narration* and Coleman in his sermon to the House of Commons betrayed the rules and purpose of the Westminster assembly in taking their cases to the public and directly to parliament. The ordinance calling the assembly had proscribed any such circumvention by stating that the assembly should only communicate with parliament and any dissent to any matter they had been ordered to take up should be sent to them via the assembly (see *Minutes*, 1.168). To put it in perspective, it was the same sort of undercutting of collegial trust and integrity and authority as was done this week at this writing, to the United States Supreme court by the leaking of the draft majority decision to overturn Roe v. Wade.

70. *Minutes*, document 73, 5.198.

71. See *Minutes*, 3.639–640, and the petition in document 81, 5.228–231.

72. The assembly had included a dig at Erastus, noting he was only a physician, not a theologian. "... Erastus, a Phisitian (who by his profession may be supposed to have had better skill in curing of the diseases of the natural, then the scandalls of the Ecclesiasticall body)...." *Minutes*, document 81, 5.230.

73. Session 478, August 1, 1645, *Minutes*, 3.641.

74. *Minutes*, document 82 (missing), 5.231. The assembly determined to ask that "the house

following Monday in Session 479 on August 4, Coleman asked to be released from his promise; but if the assembly did not do so, he still considered it null and void.[75]

The House of Commons had approved the usual boiler plate thanks and permission to print for Coleman's sermon on July 30. In response to the assembly's complaint, the Commons passed an unusual second motion with regard to the sermon on August 9, "That Mr. Coleman be enjoined to print his Sermon he preached before the Commons House the last Fast, as near as he can, as he preached it."[76] This is the wording of the authorization on the verso of the title page of the sermon. The result seems to have been twofold. First, it clearly sparked what became a tract war with George Gillespie. Second, as Mitchell notes, it added fuel to the assembly's continuing to oppose the pending Erastian order placing church censures in the government's hands. "A committee of ten of the members, assisted by the Scotch Commissioners, drew up a still more resolute, yet more importunate petition, which was duly adopted and presented by a large deputation on 8TH August to the House of Commons and on the 12TH to the House of Lords…." This petition stated matters even more emphatically, and Mitchell states that "No nobler paper proceeded from the Assembly…."[77] Coleman's provocation can be seen as one of the steps that led the assembly to go beyond petitions and file an actual protest with parliament on the passing of "an additional ordinance on church government, much relating to suspensions from the Lord's supper."[78] The assembly told the Commons on March 20, 1646, that what it proposed was "so contrary to that Way of Government which Christ hath appointed in His Church, in that it giveth a Power to judge of the Fitness of Persons to come to the Sacrament unto such as our Lord Christ hath not given that Power unto."[79] This resulted in the House of Commons charging the assembly with breach of privilege[80] and led to the drafting of nine queries about the divine right of church government, which they ordered the assembly to answer, while also publishing the queries "to discredit the claim that presbyterian discipline was

---

[of Commons] inable us or require him [Coleman] to give an account of the notes he preached." *Minutes*, 3.641.]

75. One imagines at this point one could deduce from Baillie's statement months later that Coleman's friends in the House of Commons persuaded him to change his mind over the weekend of August 2–3. This was before the August 9 renewed order enjoining him to publish. Likewise, the August 9 order could be seen as some sort of negative reaction to the assembly's August 8 petition, though Gillespie puts an honest cast to it (see p. 251).

76. House of Commons, *Journal*, volume 4, pp. 224, 235–36.

77. A. F. Mitchell, *The Westminster Assembly: Its History and Standards* (1883), p. 296–97.

78. *Minutes*, March 20, 1646, Session 608, 4.24–27.

79. *Minutes*, ibid., and document 104, 5.301.

80. "Seldom has the House of Commons put itself into a less dignified position than it did on this occasion." Mitchell, ibid., p. 306.

required by Scripture".[81] This ultimately resulted in the famous book by the London Provincial Assembly, *Jus Divinum Regiminis Ecclesiastici, or, the Divine Right of Church Government asserted and evidenced by the Holy Scriptures by Sundry Ministers of Christ within the City of London* (1646).[82]

Mistakes about Gillespie's House of Lords sermon

Kaplan and others are also to be faulted for spinning some narratives about Gillespie's sermon to the House of Lords that cannot withstand the facts. Kaplan writes that Gillespie "devoted almost his entire sermon lecture to what he euphemistically termed 'a brotherly examination of some passages of Mr. Coleman's late printed sermon.' Needless to say, his treatment of his fellow cleric was anything but brotherly. The Lords heard Coleman accused of being an Erastian (which he most certainly was), of working against the reformation of religion and of violating the Solemn League and Covenant. In a particularly sharp passage, Gillespie returned his antagonist's insult by likening Coleman, and all Erastians for that matter, to the hated Papists."[83] Kaplan then links the obvious offence the Lords would have taken to the fact that almost no Scot was ever asked to preach again before either House of Parliament.

On the first matter, Kaplan must not have read Gillespie's sermon carefully, nor his *Brotherly Examination*. Gillespie's reference to Coleman in his sermon was oblique and came with the appropriate hesitancy to fully engage Coleman in the context of a fast sermon. As published, the title adds a clear "whereunto is added" before the title of *Brotherly Examination,* and the order to print mentions only the sermon. And it is hard to miss that Gillespie makes it clear himself in the opening of the examination that it was not a part of his sermon (emphasis added),

> I have before touched this purpose in the third branch of the third application
> of my second doctrine: and did in my sermon in the Abbey church, express
> my thoughts of it at some length. But as I was then unwilling to fall upon
> such a controversy so publicly, and especially in a fast sermon, if that which

---

81. *Minutes,* 1.78. This was the greatest crisis that faced the assembly, and is detailed in John R. de Witt, *Jus Divinum: The Westminster Assembly and the Divine Right of Church Government,* pp. 169–208. For a study of the city of London Presbyterians' activities, see Elliot Vernon, *London Presbyterians and the British Revolution, 1638–64* (Manchester University Press, 2021), pp. 118–137. The London Presbyterian ministers through the city government petitioned against putting church discipline in the hands of county commissioners on March 9, before the assembly's bold protest on March 20, 1646, and it received a similar breach of privilege response from Parliament. Indeed, it apparently became a "predictable response," from the Commons at least. Vernon, ibid., p. 143.

82. See *Jus Divinum Regiminis Ecclesiastici, or, the Divine Right of Church Government,* NPSE volume ii (Naphtali Press and RHB, 2019).

83. Kaplan, *Politics and religion,* p. 128.

I intend to examine had not been as publicly and upon the like occasion delivered: So now in the publishing, I have thought good to open my mind concerning this thing diſtinctly and by itself. *That which had been too late to be preached after Sermon, is not too late to be Printed after Sermon.* Others (upon occasion offered) have given their teſtimony againſt his doctrine; and I should think my self unfaithful in the truſt put upon me, if upon such an occasion I should be silent in this business. And I believe no man will think it ſtrange, that a piece of this nature and ſtrain get an answer, and I go about it without any disreſpect either to the person or parts of my reverend brother. Only I muſt give a teſtimony to the truth when I hear it ſpoken againſt, and I hope his objections have made no such impression in any man's mind, as to make him unwilling to hear an answer.

As to the Scots not receiving another invitation to preach because Gilleſpie offended with all the things he said, that he had not 'preached' the *Brotherly Examination* to the Lords, completely undermines that ſpeculation.[84] Gilleſpie's sermon, which is all the House of Lords heard, is relatively mild by comparison to the appended tract.[85] If there was any reason for the lack

---

84. Kaplan himself qualifies this as almost never again, since a Scot was invited to preach at a fast for the miseries of Scotland in September just weeks after his August sermon. That he notes that it was Gillespie himself, should have been a clue that something was amiss in his speculation that Gillespie had offended the House of Lords. Coleman states that Gillespie addressed his sermon on two occasions, in the latter's published sermon before the House of Lords and again before the Commons at St. Margaret's on presumably this fast for the miseries in Scotland appointed by them for Friday, September 5, 1645 in their August 30 session. House of Commons Journal, 4.258. The Commons asked Gillespie, Ward, and Calamy to preach. It is unclear why the Commons did not thank any of the three in the September 6 session, though it may be because it was not the usual monthly fast. This seems to be borne out by the similar omission by the House of Peers. The Lords had appointed Henderson and Seaman to preach on the Friday fast, and there is no mention in their September 6 session of an extension of thanks either. House of Lords Journal, 7.563. Coleman complains about the two occasions in his *Brotherly Examination Re-examined.* Gillespie addresses this in his *Nihil Reſpondes.* See page 254. There is no evidence Gillespie handled the matter any less moderately in September and it is unlikely his Lords sermon was in print before that occasion.

85. "George Gillespie mentioned this disagreement very moderately when he preached to the Lords on the same day [*sic* a month later]. In the printed version, however, Gillespie added a 'Brotherly examination' over half the length of the sermon, where he set forth his position, claiming that 'I was then unwilling to fall upon such a Controversie so publickly, and especially in a Fast Sermon' (1645:31). The disagreement spilled over into a more hot-tempered exchange in the press, but, unsurprisingly, Coleman's stance was more appealing to the magistrates in parliament." Tom Webster, "Preaching and Parliament, 1640–1659, in *The Oxford Handbook of the Early Modern Sermon,* ed. Peter Mccullough, et al. (Oxford University Press, 2011), pp. 407–408. Trevor-Roper, whose animus is clear enough when the facts are known, criticized Gillespie rather than Coleman for misusing a fast sermon and

of any more invitations, it likely was due to the falling estimation of the
Scots in the eyes of the English, who at this point wanted the Scottish forces
gone, who had not been doing that well for them, and were not even doing
well for themselves against Montrose, and were costing England a fortune.
And in conjunction with the falling favor of the Scots in England, it may
also be the case that both Houses figured that they had done the appropriate
courtesy to the foreign preachers.

This brings up another narrative offered by Ofir Haivry, again influenced
by Kaplan.

> The Scottish Presbyterians and their English allies sensed Coleman's sermon
> had crucially damaged the chances of a Presbyterian settlement passing in
> Parliament, and attempted a counter move. Calculating that they enjoyed
> more support among the Puritan peers of the upper house, the Presbyterians
> enlisted the assistance of their supporters there, to secure an invitation to
> deliver the Fast Sermon to the House of Lords on August 27, for the most
> articulate and learned of the Scottish clerics, George Gillespie, who had
> preached a year earlier to the Commons…. In a make-or-break performance,
> Gillespie devoted almost his entire lecture to an examination of passages from
> Coleman's sermon of a month earlier, in which he accused the English cleric
> of being an 'Erastian' and of working against the reformation of religion.
> It appears that in this case, Gillespie incorrectly appraised the ideas and
> inclinations of his audience, since his sermon certainly did not achieve the
> hopes invested in it. Far from overturning the opinions of the MPs on church
> government, it seems to have been the last sermon invited by Parliament
> from a Scottish cleric.[86]

Again, this is all rather fanciful. The prior mistake that the *Brotherly
Examination* was part of the sermon has already been addressed. As to the
rest, while, certainly, Gillespie took advantage of his fast sermon to address
an ill done the assembly and more importantly the crown rights of Christ
to order His church, the invitation for the Scots to preach was set months
before when "beginning with the May fast the Scottish Commissioners

---

not lamenting his own country's sins instead. Gillespie merely a page later than the passage noted by Trevor-Roper (*Crisis of the Seventeenth Century*, pp. 322–323), in defending
his homeland from some baseless charges, said that he meant not to diminish the sins and
shame of Scotland that had brought the late miseries of the plague and the defeat at that
time in five battles with Montrose's forces. Montrose had continued success in Scotland,
beating the Scottish Covenanter forces at Auldearn (May 9, 1645), at Alford (July 2, 1645),
and again in the largest battle of the Civil War in Scotland at the Battle of Kylsyth (August
15, 1645). Finally, the Scottish Parliament recalled David Leslie and his troops from England
and at Philipbaugh the forces of Montrose were crushed (September 13, 1645). At the same
time as these losses there were severe outbreaks of the plague in Scotland.

86. Haivry, pp. 422–423.

A Sermon Before the House of Lords

appeared before the Lords in the same order which they had taken before the Commons one and a half years previously." [87] Or as Trevor-Roper put it, "The House of Lords, commiserating with the military disasters of the Scots, had invited the four dominies to preach at four successive fasts…."[88]

CONCLUSION

A brief allusion and condemnation of Thomas Coleman's July 30, 1645 fast sermon in George Gillespie's fast sermon before the House of Lords, led to a subsequent *Brotherly Examination* paired with that sermon in print. Two more tracts followed in reply to two responses from the Erastian divine. These "Anti-Erastian tracts" are said to be some of Gillespie's very best and powerful writing[89] and they and the Erastian controversy will be the subject of the introduction to those writings following in this same volume.

---

87. John F. Wilson, *Pulpit in Parliament; Puritanism during the English civil wars, 1640–1648* (Princeton, NJ: Princeton University Press 1969), pp. 83–84, 85.

88. Trevor-Roper, p. 322.

89. "In London, Gillespie came into collision with the English Erastians. This led to his Nihil Respondes and his Malè Audis, to be reckoned among his best productions." James Walker, *The Theology and Theologians of Scotland: Chiefly of the Seventeenth and Eighteenth Centuries,* second edition (Edinburgh: T&T Clark, 1888), p. 14. See Hetherington's Memoir, Shorter Writings of George Gillespie, volume 1, pp. 32–33.

Bibliography for the Sermon Preached Before
The House of Lords

Some of George Gillespie's Potential Sources for Books[1]
Laud: Collection of 98 books taken from Laud's study by the assembly.
MS 46: Westminster Abbey Library Benefactors' Book.
Abbey Library: Westminster Abbey Library, present in collection.
Sion: Sion College Library 1650 Catalogue:
Lambeth: Lambeth Palace Library, MS Catalogue.
LS: Lazarus Seaman Library.
WG: William Greenhill Library.

Alsted, Johann Heinrich. *Diatribe de Mille Annis Apocalypticis, non illis Chiliastarum &*
Phantastarum, sed B.B. Danielis & Iohannis. Francofurti: Conradi Eifridi, 1627. Also,
The beloved city or, The saints reign on earth a thousand yeares. Translated by William
Burton. London, 1643. [LS: possibly Jo. Hen. Alstedii Trisolium Propheticum in
Cant. Cant. Daniel, & Apocalipsin, H. 1640." p. 48, #74; but certainly, "Diatribe de
Mille Annis Apocalypticis" (1630), p. 128, #12.]

Aquinas. Commentary on Romans. Cf. "Super Epistolam ad Romanos lectura." In
S. Thomae Aquinatis Super Epistolas S. Pauli lectura. Edited by Raphael Cai. Mari-
etti, Taurini-Romae, 1953. [MS 46: *Tho: Aquinas in Epistolas; contra Gentes: Fol:, in*
Evang. vol: Fol:, 4r.a22, 23. Sion: *Opera* (Venice: 1594), p. 11; Paul's Epistles, *Cata-*
logus Interpretum S. S. Scripturae, p. 12. Lambeth: *Evang. et Epist.* (Paris: 1566), 12r;
Opera (1594), 88r.]

Arcularius, Daniel. *Commentarius in Esaiam prophetam.* Francofurti, 1607. [Abbey
Library: E.2.7, aquisition date unknown.]

Augustine. *Enarrationes in Psalmos.* Cf. *PL* 37. [Abbey Library: *Omnia opera D. Au-*
relii Augustini, 10 vols. in 9 (Basil: 1543) inscription, "Omptus Capero[?] 27 Maie
1567," G.1.21; *Omnium operum D. Aurelii Augustini,* 10 vols. in 5 (Paris: 1555), G.3.33.
Acquisition dates unknown. Sion: *Opera* (Basil: 1543; Paris: 1637), p. 14. Lambeth:
Opera (1556; 1563), 1r, 42r; *Sermons* (Antwerp: 1576–77), 1r. LS: *Opera* (1569), p. 2.]

Brightman, Thomas. *A Most Comfortable Exposition of the last and most difficult part*
of the prophecie of Daniel. Amsterdam: Successors of G. Thorp, 1635; London: 1644.
[MS 46: *Brightmannus in Cantica,* 13v.b29. Sion: *Commentarius in cantica cantico-*
rum et in ultima partem Danielis, p. 25. LS: "Commentaria in Cantica Canticorum"
(1514 *sic*), p. 112, #320.]

Broughton, Hugh. *A Reuelation of the Holy Apocalyps.* [Middelburg]: Printed [by
Richard Schilders], 1610. [Sion: p. 27. LS: p. 57, #46. MS 46: Thomas Hayne, Sept.
28, 1640 (will, 1645), 56r, line 1. A later appended note referencing Cecil Deed et al.,

---

1. See page 57. The following entries have been updated with collations against the auction lists for the libraries of Lazarus Seaman and William Greenhill from those presented in
Scots Sermons.

Old Town Hall Library of Leicester [Oxford: 1919], xvi) cites a 1645 will giving similar language to the entry. Hayne died July 27, 1645. The 1640 date may be an error or it is possible his books (works by Broughton) were given in 1640. The will was executed in 1640. The estate was settled on August 11, 1645. Gillespie would have needed the commentary sometime prior to August 17. It does not appear likely that this is the copy he could have used. The will does not indicate a bequeathal prior to Hayne's death.]

Bullinger, Heinrich. *Isaias excellentissimus Dei propheta, cuius testimoniis Christus ipse Dominus et eius apostoli creberrimè usi leguntur, expositus homilijs CXC.* Tiguri: Excudebat Christophorus Froschouerus, mense Februario, [1567]. [**MS 46:** John Walthem, Sept. 24, 1624, *in Esaiam.* fol., 25r.a20.]

Cajetan, Tommaso de Vio. *Commentarii illustres in quinque Mosaicos libros.* Paris: 1539. *Opera omnia quotquot in sacrae scripture.* Lugduni: Iacobi and Petri Prost, 1639. [**MS 46:** *in Mosom*, Paris, 1539, 3v.a11. **SION:** *Catalogus Interpretum S. S. Scripturae*, p. 3. **LAMBETH:** (1639), 12r.]

Chaldee Paraphrase. Cf. Benito Arias Montano, [*Antwerp Polyglot Bible*] *Biblia Sacra Hebraice, Chaldaice, Graece, & Latine.* [**MS 46:** *Biblia … Interlinearis. Plantin.: 1584,* 2r.a3. **SION:** *p. 20.* **LAMBETH:** *125r.*]

Chamier, Daniel. *Danielis Chamieri Delphinatis Panstratiae Catholicae: siue, controversiarum de religione aduersus Pontificios corpus.* Genevae: Typ. Roverianis, 1626. [**SION:** *Controversiae contra Pontificios* (Geneva: 1624), p. 37. **LAMBETH:** 4 vols. (1626), 4v. **LS:** (1626), p. 7, #2. **WG:** Ibid. (1626), p. 6, #16.. **MS 46:** Thomas Merill (Merrill), chief butler Westminster College, undated, 66r, last line. Merrill bequeathed money to purchase books for the library. Merrill's nephew of the same name also served as chief butler. The uncle died in 1631, and the nephew in 1664. Location in the Benefactors' book and handwriting indicate this was the elder Merrill. See Joseph Lemuel Chester, *The Marriage, Baptismal, and Burial Registers of the Collegiate Church or Abbey of St. Peter* (London: {Privately Published Edition}, 1876), p. 163, n4.]

Cicero. *De Oratore.* Loeb, *Cicero III, De Oratore I*, trans. E. W. Sutton (1942). [**LS:** "de Oratore Dialogi tres" (1525), p. 80, #172.

Coleman, Thomas. *Hopes Deferred and Dashed, observed in a sermon to the Honourable House of Commons, in Margarets Westminster, July 30, 1645.* London: Printed for Christopher Meredith, 1645.

Dickson, David. *Sermons on Jeremiah's Lamentations.* NPSE volume III. Naphtali Press and Reformation Heritage Books, 2020.

Gillespie, George. *A Brotherly Examination.* Cf. *The Works of Mr. George Gillespie.* The Presbyterian's Armory, vols 1–2. Edinburgh: Ogle and Oliver and Boyd, 1846.

______. *Aaron's Rod Blossoming.* Cf. *Works.*

______. *Malè Audis.* Cf. *Works.*

______. *Nihil Respondes.* Cf. *Works.*

______. *Wholesome Severity Reconciled with Christian Liberty.* Cf. *Anonymous Writings of George Gillespie.* Dallas, Texas: Naphtali Press, 2008.

Grotius, Hugo. *Grotii Annotata ad Vetus Testamentvm.* Lutetiae Parisiorum: Sumptibus S. Cramoisy, 1644. Halæ: 1775–1776. [Not found.]

Gwalther, Rudolf. *In Divi Pauli Apostoli Epistolas Omnes.* Frosch.: 1589. [Sion: "Homiliæ in Corinthios" (1585), p. 66. Lambeth: *Opera* (1582), 6(1)v. LS: "Opera omnia, 8 vols.," p. 11, #6. WG: (1578), p. 4, #17.]

__________. *In Prophetas duodecim, quos uocant minores.* Tiguri: 1577. [Lambeth/LS: Ibid. WG: *12 Minores Prophetas* (1582), ibid.]

__________. *Isaias: in Isaiam prophetam Rodolphi Gualtheri Tigurini homiliae CCCXXVII.* Tiguri: 1583. Lambeth/LS: Ibid.]

Kelly, James. *A Complete Collection of Scottish Proverbs: Explained and Made Intelligible to the English Reader.* London, 1818.

Jerome. *Commentariorum in Jeremiam Prophetam.* Cf. *PL* 24. [MS 46: *Opera,* 2v.a10. Lambeth: *Opera* (1553; 1579), 2v. Sion: *Opera* (1546, 1456, 1533), p. 70; cf. *in Matthaeum, Catalogus Interpretum S. S. Scripturae,* p. 91 (*sic* 19). Sion: *in Jeremiam, Catalogus Interpretum S. S. Scripturae,* p. 13. LS: *Opera* (1616), p. 2, #2.]

__________. *Commentariorum in Malachiam.* Cf. *PL* 25. [Ibid.]

Livy. *History of Rome.* Cf. D. Spillan and Cyrus Edmonds. *The History of Rome, by Titus Livius, Books Nine to Twenty-Six. Literally Translated, with Notes and Illustrations.* London: George Bell & Sons, 1887. [MS 46: *Titi Liviis, Historia Romae,* 2v.b25; anr. ed., 3r.a3; Dr. Harry King, *Opera graece,* 49r, line 2; English trans. by Holland, Richard Juston, July 4, 1624, 63r.a1. Sion: *Historia* (1568; vol. 3: 1470), p. 87. Lambeth: 131r; 149v. LS: "Titi Livii Histroria Romana" (1588), p. 76, #1.]

Plutarch. *Lives.* Cf. Charles W. Eliot, *Plutarch's Lives of Themistocles, Pericles, Aristides, Alcibiades and Coriolanus, Demosthenes and Cicero, Caesar and Antony, in the translation called Dryden's, corrected and revised by Arthur Hugh Clough with Introductions, Notes and Illustrations.* New York: P. F. Collier & Son, Copyright 1909. [MS 46: *Vitae,* 3r.b12, 11r.b7. Sion: *Opera* (1624), *Vitae illustrium* (Basil: 1533), p. 115. Lambeth: 133r (Engl.); 140r. WG: Page 25, #2. Greenhill owned an abstract of the *Lives. Vitarum Plutarchi Epitome per D. Tibertum* (1597).]

Ribera, Francisco. *In Librum Duodecim Prophetarum commentarii.* Duaci: ex Officina typographica Baltazaris Belleri, 1611. [MS 46: 6r.a9, 11v.b6. Sion: *Catalogus Interpretum S. S. Scripturae,* p. 14. Lambeth: (1600), 60r. LS: *In Librvm Dvodecim Prophetarum commentarij* (1599), p. 12, #87. WG: *In Librvm Dvodecim Prophetarum commentarij* (1599), p. 5, #35.]

Rivet, Andrew. *Commentarii, in librum secundum Mosis, qui Exodus apud Græcos inscribitur....* Lugduni Batavorum: 1632; 1633; 1634; 1642. [WG: Ibid. (1633), p. 11, #10.]

Robinson, Henry (attrib.). *An answer to Mr. William Prynn's twelve questions concerning church government at the end whereof, are mentioned severall grosse absurdities, and dangerous consequences of highest nature, which do necessarily follow the tenets of Presbyteriall, or any other besides a perfect independent government; together with certaine queries.* London, 1644. [Not found.]

Robinson, John. *Apologia iusta, et necessaria quorundam Christianorum, æque contumeliose ac Communiter dictorum Brownistarum sive Barrowistarum.* [Amsterdam?]: Giles Thorp? 1619. *A Just and Necessarie Apologie of Certain Christians, no lesse contumeliously then commonly called Brownists or Barrowists.* Amsterdam: Successors of G. Thorp, 1625. [Not found.]

Shaw, William A. *A History of the English Church during the Civil Wars and under the Commonwealth.* New York: Longmans, Green, and Co., 1900.

Socinus, Faustus. *De officio hominis Christiani in hodiernis istis de religione controversiis….* In Polish, 1599. In Latin, Irenopoli: Typis Theophili Adamidis, 1610. [Gillespie only alludes to this work and does not give the title. No copy was located in the source collections.]

Spillan, D. and Cyrus Edmonds. *The History of Rome, by Titus Livius, Books Nine to Twenty-Six. Literally Translated, with Notes and Illustrations.* London: George Bell & Sons, 1887.

Szlichting, Jonasz. *Quæstiones duæ: vna num in Euangelicorum religione dogmata habeantur, quæ vix ullo modo permittant, ut qui ea amplectatur, nullo in peccato perseueret? Altera num in eadem religione quædem co[n] cedantur Christi legibus incontesti? contra Balthasarem Meisnerum S. Theologiæ Doctorem & in Academia Wittebergensi Profess. publicum à Iona Schlichtingio à Bukowiec disputæ.* [Kraków]: Typis Pauli Sternacii, [1636]. [**LS:** "Quæstiones contra Meisner" (1636), p. 109, #19.]

Tossanus, Daniel. *Operum theologicorum.* Hanouiæ: Typis Wechelianis, apud Claudium Marnium & hæredes Iohannis Aubrii., 1604. [**MS 46:** Julius Cralor, Oct. 20, 1623, *Opera* {3 vols. 4to}, 3v.a14.]

Toulmin, Joshua. *Memoirs of the Life, Character, Sentiments, and Writings of Faustus Socinus.* London: Printed for the Author by J. Brown, 1777.

Vermigli, Peter Martyr. *In selectissimam S. Pauli Priorem ad Corinth.* Tiguri: Ex officina Christ. Froschoueri: [1551]. [**ABBEY LIBRARY:** *In D. Pauli Apostoli priorem ad Corinthios Epistolam Petri Martyris Vermilii commentarii.* Editio tertia. (Apud C. Froschoverum. Tiguri: 1579), V.4.44, acquisition date unknown. **SION:** *Catalogus Interpretum S. S. Scripturae,* p. 22. **LAMBETH:** *priorem ad Corinthios* (1570), 7r. **LS:** "Opera omnia, 7 vols.," p. 11, #4. **WG:** *Priorem Epist. ad Corinthios* (1567), p. 3, #4.]

Westminster Assembly. *The Directory for the Publick Worship of God.* 1645. See *The Confession of Faith,* etc. (Edinburgh: Johnstone and Hunter, 1855), pp. 373–394.]

I HAVE IN THIS sermon applied my thoughts toward these three things: 1. The soul-ensnaring error of the greatest part of men, who choose to themselves such a way to the kingdom of heaven as is broad, and smooth, and easy, and but little or nothing at all displeasing to flesh and blood; like him [*Marcus Lepidus*] that tumbled down upon the grass and said, *Utinam hoc esset laborare*.[1] 2. The grumbling and unwillingness which appears in very many, when they should submit to that reformation of the church which is according to the mind of Jesus Christ, like them that said to the seers, "See not; and to the prophets, prophesy not unto us right things, speak unto us smooth things" (Isa. 30:10); and again, "Let us break their bands asunder, and cast away their cords from us" (Ps. 2:3). 3. The sad and desolate condition of the Kingdom of Scotland, then calling for our prayers and tears, and saying, "Call me not Naomi (pleasant), call me Mara (bitter): for the Almighty hath dealt very bitterly with me" (Ruth 1:20). We were "pressed out of measure, above strength," and "had the sentence of death in ourselves, that we should not trust in ourselves, but in God which raiseth the dead; who delivered us from so great a death, and doth deliver; in whom we trust that he will yet deliver us" (2 Cor. 1:8–11). Our brethren also "helping together by prayer for us," that for the mercy bestowed on us by means of the prayers of many, thanks may be given by many on our behalf. "The Lord liveth, and blessed be my rock: and let the God of my salvation be exalted" (Ps. 18:46); "He is our God; and we will prepare for him an habitation; our fathers' God, and we will exalt him" (Exod. 15:2); "Blessed be the Lord God, the God of Israel, who only doeth wondrous things. And blessed be his glorious name forever: and let the whole earth be filled with his glory" (Ps. 72:18, 19). Scotland shall yet be "a crown of glory in the hand of the Lord, and a royal diadem in the hand of thy God" (Isa. 62:3, 4); and shall be called "Hephzi-bah" and "Beulah." Only let us remember our evil ways, and be confounded, and never open our mouth any more because of our shame, when the Lord our God is pacified towards us. Now are both kingdoms put to a trial, whether their humiliations are filial, and whether they can mourn for sin more than for judgment. And let us now hear what the Spirit speaketh to the churches, and not turn again to folly. New provocations, or the old unrepented, will create new ones; therefore, "sin no more, lest a worse thing come unto us" [John 5:14].

---

1. [If only this were exertion! "Vellem hoc esset laborare." Cicero, *De Oratione*, II, lxxi, 286–287. Loeb, *Cicero III, De Oratore I*, trans. E. W. Sutton (1942), pp. 416–417.]

Die Jovis 28. Aug. 1645.

It is this day ordered by the Lords in Parliament assembled, That Mr. Gillespie who preached yesterday before their Lordships in the Abbey Church Westminster, it being the day of the public fast, is hereby thanked for his great pains he took in the said sermon: And desired to print and publish the same, which is only to be done by authority under his hand.

Jo. Brown Cleric., Parliament.

I appoint *Robert Bostock* to print this sermon.

Geo. Gillespie

A Sermon Preached

Before the Right Honourable the House of Peers,

at a late Solemn Fast

Malachi 3:2. *But who may abide the day of his coming? And who shall stand when he appeareth? For he is like a refiner's fire, and like fuller's soap.*

IF YOU ASK, "Of whom speaketh the prophet this, of himself, or of some other man?" (Acts 8:34), it is answered, both by Christian and Jewish interpreters: the prophet speaks this of Christ, the Messenger of the covenant, then much longed and looked for by the people of God, as is manifest by the preceding verse. And as it was fit that Malachi, the last of the prophets, should shut up the Old Testament with clear promises of the coming of Christ (which you find in this and in the following chapter), so he takes the rather occasion from the corrupt and degenerate estate of the priests at that time (which he had mentioned in the former chapter), to hold forth unto the church the promised Messiah, who was to come unto them to purify the sons of Levi.

But if you ask again, of what coming or appearing of Christ does the prophet speak this, whether of the first, or of the last, or of any other? the answer of expositors is not so unanimous. Some understand the last coming of Christ, in the glory of His Father, and holy angels, to judge the quick and the dead. This cannot stand with verse 34, "He shall purify the sons of Levi, and purge them," etc.; but at the last judgment it will be too late for the sons of Levi to be purified and purged, or for Judah and Jerusalem to bring offerings unto the Lord, as in the days of old.

The Meaning of the Text Searched

Others understand the first coming of Christ. And of these some understand His incarnation, or appearing in the flesh; others take the meaning to be of His coming into the temple of Jerusalem to drive out the buyers and sellers (Matt. 21:10–12), at which time all the city was moved at His coming. This exposition has better grounds than the other, because the coming of Christ (here spoken of) did not precede, but soon followed after the ministry of John Baptist, and therefore cannot be meant of our Savior's incarnation, but rather of His appearing with power and authority in the temple. But this also falls short, and neither expresses the whole nor the principal part of what is meant in this text; for how can it be said that the prophecy which follows in verses 3 and 4 (which is all of a piece with verse 2), was fulfilled during Christ's appearing and sitting in the temple of Jerusalem? Or how can it be conceived that the offerings of Judah and Jerusalem were pleasant to the Lord at that time, when the Gentiles were not, and the Jews would not be brought in to offer unto the Lord an offering in righteousness? So that whether we understand by Judah and Jerusalem the Jewish church or the Christian, this thing could not be said to be accomplished while Christ was yet upon earth. And in like manner, whether we understand by the sons of Levi the priests and Levites of the Jews, or the ministers of the gospel, it cannot be said that Christ did, in the days of His flesh, purify the sons of Levi as gold and silver.

I deny not but the Lord Jesus did then begin to set about this work. But that which is more principally here intended is Christ's coming and appearing in a spiritual, but yet most powerful and glorious manner, to erect His kingdom, and to gather and govern His churches by the ministry of His apostles and other ministers, whom He sent forth after His ascension.

Of this coming He Himself speaks (Matt. 16:28), "Verily I say unto you, There be some standing here which shall not taste of death till they see the Son of Man coming in his kingdom." Mark adds "with power" (Mark 9:1). Neither was that all. He did not so come at that time as to put forth all His power, or to do His whole work. He has at divers times come and manifested Himself to His churches; and this present time is a time of the revelation of the Son of God, and a day of His coming. We look also for a more glorious coming of Jesus Christ before the end; for "the Redeemer shall come to Zion" (Isa. 59:20), "and shall turn away ungodliness from Jacob" (Rom. 11:26); and He shall destroy Antichrist "with the brightness of his coming" (2 Thess. 2:8); in which place the apostle has respect to Isaiah 11:4, where it is said of Christ, the rod of Jesse, "with the breath of his lips shall he slay the wicked." There, withal, you have the church's tranquility, the filling of the earth with the knowledge of the Lord, and the restoring of the dispersed Jews, as you may read in that chapter. Some have observed[1] (which ought not to pass without observation) that the Chaldee Paraphrase had there added the word *Romilus*: "He shall slay the wicked Romilus," whereupon they challenge Arias Montanus for leaving out that word to wipe off the reproach from the Pope.[2] However, the Scriptures teach us that the Lord Jesus will be revealed mightily, and will make bare His arm, as well in the confusion of Antichrist, as in the conversion of the Jews, before the last judgment and the end of all things.

By this time you may understand what is meant in the text by the day of Christ's coming, or *coming in* (Εἰσόδου), as the Septuagints read, meaning His coming, or entering into His temple, mentioned in the first verse; by which temple Jerome upon the place rightly understands the church, or spiritual temple.[3]

When this temple is built, Christ comes into it to fill the house with the cloud of His glory and to walk in the midst of the seven golden candlesticks.

---

1. [Hugh] Broughton on Rev. 9. [*A Revelation of the holy Apocalyps* (1610), p. 95. The 1645 has Brightman; the 1646 text corrected to Broughton. Compare with "Positions about the Hebrew Tongue," in *Works* (1662), p. 666.]

2. [See the text of the Chaldee Paraphrase in the Antwerp Polyglot, t. 4, pp. 36, 37.]

3. [Jerome, *Commentariorum in Malachiam, PL* 25.1565.]

The same thing is meant by His appearing: "When he appeareth," saith our translation; "When he shall be revealed," says the Chaldee (רְאָה). Others read: "When he shall be seen," or "in seeing of him." The original word I find used to express more remarkable, divine, and glorious sights, as Genesis 16:13–14, "Have I also here looked after him that seeth me? In the mount of the Lord it shall be seen." From this word had the prophets the name of seers (1 Sam. 9:9), and from the same word came the name of visions (2 Chron. 26:5), "Zechariah, who had understanding in the visions of God."

Now, "But what of all this?" might some think. "If Christ come, it is well; He is the desire of all nations." O but when Christ thus comes into His kingdom among men with power, and is seen appearing with some beams of His glory, *Who may abide, and who shall stand?* says the text. How shall sinners stand before the Holy One? How shall dust and ashes have any fellowship with the God of glory? How shall our weak eyes behold the Sun of Righteousness coming forth like a bridegroom out of his chamber? Did not Ezekiel fall upon his face at "the appearance of the likeness of the glory of the Lord" (Ezek. 1:28)? Did not Isaiah cry out, "Woe is me, for I am undone, for mine eyes have seen the King, the Lord of hosts" (Isa. 6:5)?

But why is it so hard a thing to abide the day of Christ's coming, or to stand before Him when He appears in His temple? If you ask of Him, as Joshua did, "Art thou for us, or for our adversaries?" (Josh. 5:13), He will answer you, "Nay; but as a [*sic*] captain of the host of the Lord am I now come" (v. 14). If you ask of Him, as the elders of Bethlehem asked of Samuel (while they were trembling at his coming), "Comest thou peaceably?" He will answer you as Samuel did, "Peaceably" [1 Sam. 16:4–5]. What is there here then to trouble us? Does He not come to save, and not to destroy? Yes, to save the spirit, but to destroy the flesh; He will have the heart-blood of sin, that the soul may live forever. This is set forth by a double metaphor, one taken from the refiner's fire, which purifies the metals from the dross; the other, from the fuller's soap. Others read the fuller's grass, or the fuller's herb. Some have thought it so hard to determine, that they have kept into the translation the very Hebrew word *borith*. Jerome tells us (in Jeremiah 2:2 [*sic* 2:22]),[4] that the fuller's herb which grew in the marsh places of Palestina, had the same virtue for washing and making white which nitre has. Yet, I suppose the fuller's soap has more of that virtue in it than the herb could have. However, it is certain that *borith* comes from a word which signifies to make clean ([barar,] בָּרַר), according to that in Mark 9:3, "His raiment became shining, exceeding white as snow; so as no fuller on earth can white them."

But to whom will Christ thus reveal Himself? And who are they whom He will refine from their dross, and wash from their filthiness? That we may know from the two following verses: He is not a refiner's fire to those that are "reprobate silver" (Jer. 6:30), and can never be refined; neither is He as fuller's soap to those whose spot "is not the spot of his children" (Deut. 32:5). Nay, Christ does not thus lose His labor, but He refines and makes clean the

---

4. [Jerome, *Commentariorum in Jeremiam Prophetam, PL* 24.693.]

sons of Levi, also Judah and Jerusalem. This, I doubt not to aver, principally belongs to the Jews, for to them pertain the promises (Rom. 9:4), says the apostle, and the natural branches shall be grafted into their own olive tree (11:24); but it belongs also to us Gentiles, who are cut out of the wild olive tree and are grafted into the good olive tree. God has persuaded Japhet to dwell in the tents of Shem [Gen. 9:27]; and so we are now the Judah and Jerusalem, and our ministers the sons of Levi. God's own church and people, even the best of them, have need of this refiner's fire and of this fuller's soap.

And so much for the scope, sense, and coherence of the text. The general

Doctrine 1 doctrine which offers itself to us from the words is this: *The way of Christ, and fellowship with Him, is very difficult and displeasing to our sinful nature, and is not so easy a matter as most men imagine.*

1. First of all, this clearly arises out of the text. As when the people said

Proved First
from the Text to Joshua, "God forbid that we should forsake the Lord, to serve other gods" (Josh. 24:16), Joshua answered, "Ye cannot serve the Lord, for he is an holy God; he is a jealous God" (v. 19). Just so does the prophet here answer the Jews, when they were very much desiring and longing for the Messiah, promising to themselves comfort, and peace, and prosperity, and the restoring of all things according to their heart's desire, if Christ were once come. Nay, says the prophet, not so. *Who may abide the day of his coming, and who shall stand when he appeareth?*

2. Other Scriptures do abundantly confirm it. The doctrine of Jesus Christ

Secondly, From
Other Places was such as made many of His disciples say, "This is an hard saying; who can hear it?" (John 6:60). And from that time many of them "went back, and walked no more with him". A young man, a ruler, who came to Him with great affection, was so cooled and discouraged at hearing of the cross, and selling of all he had, that he went away sad and sorrowful (Mark 10:21, 22). The apostles themselves having heard him say that "it is easier for a camel to go through the eye of a needle, than for a rich man to enter into the kingdom of God; They were exceedingly amazed" at His doctrine, "saying, who can be saved" (Matt. 19:24, 25)? As for His life and actions, they were such that not only did the Gadarenes beseech Him to depart out of their coasts (Matt. 8:34), but His own friends and kinsfolks were about "to lay hold on him, for they said, He is beside himself" (Mark 3:21). His sufferings were such that all His disciples did forsake Him, and went away every man to his own home again. And what shall be the condition of those that will follow Him? If we will indeed be His disciples, He has forewarned us to sit down first and count our cost (Luke 14:28). He has told us it will cost us no less than the bearing of the cross, the forsaking of all, yea, which is hardest of all, the denying of ourselves ([Luke 14:26; 9:23; 14:33]).[5] We must even cease to be ourselves, and cannot be His, except we leave off to be our own (Matt. 16:24). And what shall the world think of us all this while? "Know ye not," says James, "that the friendship of the world is enmity with God? Whosoever therefore will be a friend of the world is the

---

5. [In the original text in the margin "Ioh. v. 26, 2, 33" was beneath "Luke 14:28."]

enemy of God" (James 4:4). "Let no man deceive himself," says Paul. "If any man among you seems to be wise in this world, let him become a fool, that he may be wise" (1 Cor. 3:18). What do you think now? Are not all these hard sayings for flesh and blood to hear? I might add much more of this kind. But[6]

3. Thus it must be to set the higher value upon Christ and upon the lot of God's children: "Will I offer burnt offerings to the Lord my God," says David, "of that which doth cost me nothing?" (2 Sam. 24:24). And shall our "lines" fall to us in "pleasant places" [Ps. 16:6], or shall we have a "goodly heritage," which costs us nothing? How should the preciousness of the saint's portion be known, if we lose nothing that is dear to us to come by it? "What things were gain to me, those I counted loss for Christ" (Phil. 3:7). "The kingdom of heaven is like unto treasure hid in a field; the which when a man hath found, he hideth, and for joy thereof goeth and selleth all that he hath, and buyeth that field. Again, the kingdom of heaven is like unto a merchant man seeking goodly pearls; who, when he had found one pearl of great price, went and sold all that he had, and bought it" (Matt. 13:44–46). Jacob's family must give away all the strange gods, and all their earrings also (Gen. 35:4), before they get leave to build an altar unto the Lord at Bethel. Abraham must get himself out of his country, and from his kindred, if he will come unto the land which the Lord will show him. Moses must forsake the court of Egypt if he will take him to the heritage of Jacob his father. The disciples must leave ships, nets, fathers, and all, if they will follow Christ. And as they who come in sight of the south pole lose sight of the north pole, so when we follow Christ, we must resolve to forsake something else, yea, even that which is dearest to us. *(Thirdly, From the Excellency of Christ)*

4. If it were not so, there should be no sure evidence of our closing in covenant with Christ; for then, and never till then, does the soul give itself up to Christ to be His and closes with Him in a covenant, when it renounces all other lovers, that it may be His only. Shall a woman be married to a husband with the reservation of another lover, or upon condition that she shall ever stay in her father's house? So the soul cannot be married to Christ, except it not only renounce its bosom sins, lusts, and idols, but be content also to part with the most lawful creature comforts for His sake. "Forget also thine own people, and thy father's house" (Ps. 45:10). The repudiating of creature comforts, and a covenant with Christ, go hand in hand together (Isa. 55:2, 3). Nahash would not make a covenant with the men of Jabesh-Gilead, unless they would pluck out their right eyes, intending (as Josephus gives reason, [*Antiquities*, 6.5]) to disable them from fighting or making war; for the buckler or shield did cover their left eye when they fought, so that they had been hard put to it to fight without the right eye. This was a cruel mercy in him; but it is a merciful severity in Christ that He will make no covenant with us, except the right eye of the old man of sin in us be put out. *(Fourthly, From the Nature of the Covenant)*

The Use. O then, let us learn from all this how miserably many a poor soul is deluded, imagining, as the Jews did, that Christ shall even satisfy their carnal

---

6. [*Works* and *Scots Sermons* omit the "But."]

and earthly desires, and that the way of salvation is broad and easy enough. If the way of Christ is such as you have now heard, then surely they are far from it who give loose reins to the flesh, as David did to Adonijah (1 Kings 1:6); who have not displeased their flesh at any time, nor said, "Why hast thou done so?" Who do not withhold their heart from any joy, and whatsoever their eyes desire, they keep it not from them (Eccles. 2:10); who are like the "wild ass used to the wilderness, that snuffeth up the wind at her pleasure" (Jer. 2:24), and like "the swift dromedary, traversing her ways" (v. 23), who cannot endure to be enclosed into so narrow a lane as ministers describe the way to heaven to be. These are like fed oxen, which have room enough in the meadows, but they are appointed for slaughter, when the laboring oxen, which are kept under the yoke, shall be brought home to the stall and fed there. Was it not so with the rich man and Lazarus (Luke 16:25)? Nay, and many of the children of God fall into this same error of making the way of Christ broader and easier than ever Christ made it, and taking more liberty than ever He allowed; therefore, mark you well our Savior's words: "Enter ye in at the strait gate: for wide is the gate, and broad is the way, that leadeth to destruction, and many there be which go in thereat: because strait is the gate, and narrow is the way, which leadeth unto life, and few there be that find it" (Matt. 7:13, 14). There are but few that seek it, and yet fewer that find it, but fewest of all that enter in at it.

But how does all this agree with Matthew 11:30, "For my yoke is easy, and my burden is light;" and 1 John 5:3, "His commandments are not grievous"?

An Objection
Answered Four
Ways

I answer, (1) That is spoken to poor souls that are laboring and heavy laden; a metaphor taken from beasts drawing a full cart, which both labor in drawing and are weary in bearing. But my text speaks to those that are like undaunted heifers and like bullocks unaccustomed to the yoke. The same Christ is a sweet and meek Christ to some, but a sour and severe Christ to others.

(2) Christ's yoke is easy in comparison of the yoke of the law, which neither we nor our fathers were able to bear [Acts 15:10].

(3) As wisdom is easy to him that understands, so is Christ's yoke easy, and His burden light, to those that are well acquainted with it and have good experience of it: "When thou goest, thy steps shall not be straitened; and when thou runnest, thou shall not stumble" (Prov. 4:12). This is spoken of wisdom. But he says, "When thou goest," not "when thou beginnest," or "when thou enterest." If you are but once upon your progress, going and running, you shall find the way still the easier and still the sweeter.

(4) Mark Christ's own words. It is a yoke, though an easy one, and a burden, though a light one. A yoke to the flesh, but easy to the spirit. A burden to the old man, but light to the new man. He pours in wine and oil into our wounds; oil to cherish them, and wine to cleanse them. He can both plant us as trees of righteousness, and at the same time lay the axe to the root of the old tree. He will have mercy upon the sinner, but no mercy upon the sin. He will save the soul, but yet so as by fire [1 Cor. 3:15].

And this much, in general, of the difficulty and hardship of the way of Christ, the great point held forth in this text; which I have the rather insisted upon as a necessary foundation for those particulars which I am to speak of. Were this principle but rightly apprehended, it were easy to persuade you when we come to particulars.

Some papists have alleged this text for their purgatory. Here is indeed a purgatory, and a fire of purgatory, and such a purgatory that we must needs go through it before we can come to heaven. But this purgatory is in this world, not in the world to come. The flesh must go through it, and not the soul separated. And it must purge us from mortal, not from venial sins, and by a spiritual, not a material fire.

I will now come to the particulars. Christ is to us as a refiner's fire, and as fuller's soap, three ways: in respect of—I. Reformation, II. Tribulation, III. Mortification—which make not three different senses, but three harmonious parts of one and the same sense.

I. I begin with *Reformation*; concerning which I draw this doctrine from the text: *The right reformation of the church, which is according to the mind of Jesus Christ, is not without much molestation and displeasure to men's corrupt nature. It is a very purgatory upon earth. It is like the fire to drossy silver, and like fuller's soap to slovenly persons, who would rather keep the spots in their garments than take pains to wash them out.*[7]

Doctrine 2

Look but upon one piece of the accomplishment of this prophecy, and by it judge of the rest. When Christ comes to Jerusalem, "meek, and sitting upon an ass," as the prophet said, all the city is troubled at His coming (Matt. 21:5, 10); when He had but cast out the buyers and sellers out of the temple, the priests and scribes begin to plot His death (Luke 19:45, 47); nay, where Christ and the gospel come, there is a shaking of heaven and earth (Hag. 2:6). The less wonder if I call *reformation* like a refiner's fire. The dross of a church is not purged away without this violence of fire.

This is the manner of *reformation* held forth in Scripture, and that in reference: 1. To magistrates and statesmen. 2. To ministers. 3. To a people reformed. 4. To a people not reformed.

1. In reference to magistrates and statesmen,[8] reformation is a fire that purges away the dross: "And I will turn my hand upon thee, and purely purge away thy dross, and take away all thy tin" (Isa. 1:25). Here is the refiner's fire; and the Chaldee Paraphrase adds the fuller's *borith*. Then follows, "And I will restore thy judges as at the first, and thy counselors as at the beginning: afterward thou shalt be called, The city of righteousness, The faithful city" (v. 26). Interpreters note upon that place, that no effectual reformation can be looked for till rulers and magistrates are reformed, and that therefore the Lord promises to purge away the dross and tin of corrupt rulers and judges,

Second Doc-
trine, Cleared in
Four Branches
Thereof

---

7. Gault., hom. 8, in Malach.: *Vult enim docere propheta, venturum quidem Christum, sed reformatorem fore, et acerrimum divini cultum [cultus] vindicem.* [Gwalther, *In Prophetas duodecim, quos uocant minores* (1577), p. 401. "For the prophet wishes to teach that Christ will indeed come, but that he will be a reformer and a very fierce defender of the divine honor."]

8. [The marginal heading was originally next to the doctrine above.]

and to give His people such judges and rulers as they had of old, Moses, Joshua, the Judges, David, Solomon, and the like.

2. In reference to ministers the doctrine is most clear. The next words after my text tell you that this refining fire is specially intended for purifying the sons of Levi. The same thing we have more largely, though more obscurely, in 1 Corinthians 3:12–15. I do not say that the apostle there means only of times of reformation, but this I say, that it holds true, and most manifestly too, of times of reformation, and that this is not to be excluded, but to be taken in as a principal part of the Holy Ghost's intendment in that Scripture.[9] He is speaking of the ministers of the gospel and their ministry, supposing always that they build upon Christ and hold to that true foundation. Upon this foundation some build gold, silver, precious stones [1 Cor. 3:12, 13]; that is, such preaching of the Word, such administration of the sacraments, such a church discipline, and such a life as is according to the Word and savours of Christ. Others build wood, hay, stubble, whereby is meant whatsoever in their ministry is unprofitable, unedifying, vain, curious, unbeseeming the gospel; for the ministers of Christ must be purified, not only from heresy, idolatry, profaneness, and the like, but even from that which is frothy and unedifying, which savours not of God's Spirit, but of man's. Now, says the apostle, "Every man's work shall be made manifest, for the day shall declare it, because it shall try every man's work of what sort it is." The church shall not always be deluded and abused with vanities that cannot profit. A time of light and reformation discovers the unprofitableness of those things wherewith men did formerly please and satisfy themselves. There is a fire which will prove every man's work, even an accurate trial and strict examination thereof, according to the rule of Christ; a narrow inquiry into and exact discovery of every man's work (for so do our divines[10] understand the fire there spoken of), whether this fiery trial be made by the searching and discovering light of the Word in a time of reformation, or by afflictions, or in a man's own conscience at the hour of death. If by some or all of these trials, a minister's work is found to be what it ought

---

9. Gwalther on the place [1 Cor. 3:12–15]. Martyr on the place. [… *A*]*ccessione temporis declarantur. Experimur hodie retegi cõplura quae à multis annis latuerunt.* Gaulther. *Orietur dies, id est clarior lux veritatis, quae omnia protrahet.* Tossanus. [… *M*]*undus tande agnoscet vanitatem traditionum humanarum.* [Gwalther, "Ad Corinthios Priorem," in *In Divi Pauli Apostoli Epistolas Omnes* (Zurich: Frosch., 1589), p. 14v. "The day will rise, that is the clearer light of truth, which shall bring to light all things." Peter Martyr Vermigli, *In selectissimam S. Pauli Priorem ad Corinth* (Tiguri: Ex officina Christ. Froschoueri, [1551]), p. 74v. "With the passage of time they are revealed. We attempt to discover many things today which, for many years, lay hidden." Daniel Tossanus, *Operum theologicorum*, 2 vols. (Hanouiæ: Typis Wechelianis, apud Claudium Marnium & hæredes Iohannis Aubrii., 1604), 2.36. "The world will realize how great is the vanity of the traditions of men."]

10. Chamier *Panst.* Tom. 3. lib. 26. cap. 13, 14. [Daniel Chamier, *Danielis Chamieri Delphinatis Panstratiae Catholicae: siue, controversiarum de religione aduersus Pontificios corpus* (Genevae: Typ. Roverianis, 1626).]

to be, he shall receive a special reward and praise. But if he has built wood, hay, and stubble, he shall be like a man whose house is set on fire about his ears. That is, he shall suffer loss, and his work shall be burnt, yet himself shall escape, and get his life for a prey, "*so as by fire* [1 Cor. 3:15]. That is, so that he can abide that trial and examination whereby God distinguishes between sincere ones and hypocrites; or, so that he is found to have been otherwise a faithful minister, and to have built upon a right foundation.

3. In the third place, you shall find reformation to be a refining fire in reference to a people or church reformed. "He that is left in Zion, and he that remaineth in Jerusalem, shall be called holy," says the prophet, "when the Lord shall have washed away the filth of the daughters of Zion, and shall have purged the blood of Jerusalem from the midst thereof, by the spirit of judgment, and by the spirit of burning" (Isa. 4:3, 4). Where you may understand by the filth of the daughters of Zion, their former idolatries and such like abominations against the first table (which the prophets call often by the name of filth and pollution), and by the blood of Jerusalem, the sins against the second table.[11] These the Lord promises to purge away by the spirit of judgment; that is, by a spirit of reformation (according to that, John 12:31, "Now is the judgment of this world: now shall the prince of this world be cast out"). Which spirit of reformation is also a spirit of burning, even as the Holy Ghost is elsewhere called fire (Matt. 3:11), and did come down upon the apostles in the likeness of cloven tongues of fire (Acts 2:3). The spirit of reformation may be the rather called the spirit of burning, because ordinarily reformation is not without tribulation (as we shall hear), and by the voice of the rod does the Spirit speak to men's consciences. When the Lord has thus washed away the filthy spots, and burnt away the filthy dross of His church, then she becomes a glory or a praise in the earth; and the promise is that "upon all the glory shall be a defense" (Isa. 4:5). But you see, she is not brought to that condition till she goes through the refiner's fire. It is no easy matter to cast Satan out of a person, how much less to cast his kingdom out of a land? Another place for the same purpose we find [in] Zechariah 13:9. When two parts of the land are cut off, the remnant which escape, the third part which is *written to life in Jerusalem* [cf. Isa. 4:3], even they must be brought through the fire. "I will bring the third part through the fire, saith the Lord, and will refine them as silver is refined, and will try them as gold is tried." This is the fiery trial of affliction, but the fruit of it is a blessed reformation to make the church as most pure refined gold. "They shall call on my name, and I will hear them;" that is, they shall no longer worship idols, but Me only, and they shall offer to the Lord an offering in righteousness, which shall be accepted.[12] And what more? "I will say it is my

---

11. Bullinger on the place [Isa. 4:3, 4]. [Heinrich Bullinger (1504–1575), *Isaias excellentissimus Dei propheta, cuius testimoniis Christus ipse Dominus et eius apostoli creberrimè usi leguntur, expositus homilijs CXC* (Tiguri: Christophorus Froschouerus {1567}), pp. 21v–22v.]

12. Ribera upon the place [Zech. 13:9]. [Francisco de Ribera, *In Librum Duodecim Prophetarum commentarii* (Duaci: ex Officina typographica Baltazaris Belleri, 1611), pp. 751–752.]

people; and they shall say, the Lord is my God." Behold, a reforming people and a covenanting people. But He that "hath his fire in Zion, and his furnace in Jerusalem" (Isa. 31:9), does first refine them and purify them. We are not reformed in God's account till the refining fire has purged away our dross, till we are refined as silver is refined, and tried as gold is tried.

4. Lastly, in reference to a people not reformed, hear what the prophet says: (Jer. 6:28–30): "They are brass and iron; they are all corrupters. The bellows are burnt, the lead is consumed of the fire, the founder melteth in vain; for the wicked are not plucked away. Reprobate silver shall men call them, because the Lord hath rejected them." The Chaldee Paraphrase expounds it of the prophets who labored in vain, and spent their strength for nought, speaking to the people in the name of the Lord, to turn to the law and to the testimony; but they would not turn.

I might draw many USES from this doctrine; but I shall content myself with these few:

First of all, it reproves that contrary principle which carnal reason suggests: Reformation must not grieve, but please; it must not break nor bruise, but heal and bind up; it must be an acceptable thing, not displeasing; it must be "as the voice of harpers harping with their harps," but not "as the voice of many waters," or "as the voice of great thunders" [Rev. 1:15; 14:2]. Thus would many heal the wound of the daughter of Zion slightly, and daub the wall with untempered mortar [Jer. 6:14; Ezek. 13:11], and so far comply with the sinful humors and inclinations of men, as in effect, to harden them in evil, and to strengthen their hands in their wickedness; or at least, if men be moralised, then to trouble them no farther. Saith not the apostle, "If I yet pleased men, I should not be the servant of Christ" (Gal. 1:10)? And again, "The carnal mind is enmity against God; for it is not subject to the law of God, neither indeed can be" (Rom. 8:7). So that either we must have a reformation displeasing to God, or displeasing to men. It is not the right reformation which is not displeasing to a Tobiah, to a Sanballat, to a Demetrius, to the earthly minded, to the self-seeking politicians, to the carnal and profane; it is but the old enmity between the seed of the woman and the seed of the serpent (Gen. 3:15). Nay, what if reformation is displeasing to good men, insofar as they are unregenerate, carnal, earthly, proud, unmortified; for "who can say, I have made my heart clean, I am pure from my sin" (Prov. 20:9)? What if a Joshua envies Eldad and Medad (Num. 11:27–29)? What if an Aaron and a Miriam speak against Moses (Num. 12:1, 2)? What if a religious Asa is wroth with the seer (2 Chron. 16:10)? What if a David will not altar his former judgment, though very erroneous, and will not (no, not after better information) have it thought that he was in an error (2 Sam. 19:29)? What if a Jonah refuses to go to Nineveh when he is called (Jonah 1:3)? What if the disciples of Christ must be taught to be more humble (Mark 9:33–35)? What if Peter must be reproved by Paul for his dissimulation (Gal. 2:11)? What if Archippus must be admonished to attend better upon his ministry (Col. 4:17)? What if Christ must tell the angels of the churches that He has somewhat against

First, Application to the Opposers of Reformation

them (Rev. 2, 3)? If reformation displeases both evil men, and, in some respect, good men, this makes it no worse than *a refiner's fire*; and so it must be, if it is according to the mind of Christ.

My second and chief application shall be unto you, my noble lords. If you are willing to admit such a reformation as is according to the mind of Christ, as is like the *refiner's fire* and *fuller's soap*, then in the name of the Lord Jesus Christ (who will say, ere long, to everyone of you, "Give an account of thy stewardship; for thou mayest be no longer steward," Luke 16:2), I recommend these three things unto you. I mean, that you should make use of this *refiner's fire* in reference to three sorts of dross: 1. The dross of *malignancy*. 2. The dross of *heresy and corruption in religion*. 3. The dross of *profaneness*.

1. Touching the first of these, take the wise counsel of the wise man (Prov. 25:4, 5), "Take away the dross from the silver, and there shall come forth a vessel for the finer. Take away the wicked from before the king, and his throne shall be established in righteousness." Remember also, the fourth article of your *Solemn League and Covenant*,[13] by which you have obliged yourselves, with your hands lifted up to the most high God, to "endeavor the discovery," trial, and "condign punishment" "of all such as have been, or shall be incendiaries, malignants, or evil instruments, by hindering the reformation of religion, dividing the king from his people, or one of the kingdoms from another, or making any faction or parties among the people contrary to this covenant." There was once a compliance between the nobles of Judah and the Samaritans, which I hope you do not read of without abominating the thing. You find it in Nehemiah 6:17, 19. "In those days the nobles of Judah sent many letters unto Tobiah, and the letters of Tobiah came unto them." "Also," says Nehemiah, "they reported his good deeds before me, and uttered my words to him." But you have also the error of a godly man set before you as a rock to be avoided (2 Chron. 19:2), "Shouldest thou help the ungodly, and love them that hate the Lord? Therefore is wrath upon thee from before the Lord." I am not to dwell upon this point; "I speak as to wise men, judge ye what I say" [1 Cor. 10:15].

2. In the second place, think of the extirpation of heresy and of unsound dangerous doctrine, such as now springs up apace, and subverts the faith of many. There is no heretic nor false teacher which has not some one fair pretext or another; but bring him once to be tried by this refining fire, he is found to be "like a potsherd covered with silver dross" (Prov. 26:23). "What is the chaff to the wheat," saith the Lord (Jer. 23:28), and what is the dross to the silver? If this is the way of Christ which my text speaks of, then surely that which now passes under the name of *liberty of conscience* is not the way of Christ. Much has been written of this question.[14] For my part I shall, for

---

13. [Cf. The Solemn League & Covenant, in *The Confession of Faith*, etc. (Edinburgh: Johnstone and Hunter, 1855), pp. 359.]

14. ["Under these fair colors and handsome pretexts do sectaries infuse their poison, I mean their pernicious, God provoking, truth defacing, Church ruinating, and State shaking

the present, only offer this one argument. If *liberty of conscience* ought to be granted in matters of religion, it ought also to be granted in matters civil or military. But *liberty of conscience* ought not to be granted in matters civil or military, as is acknowledged, therefore, neither ought it to be granted in matters of religion. Put the case: Now there are some well-meaning men, otherwise void of offence, who from the erroneous persuasion of their consciences, think it utterly sinful, and contrary to the Word of God, to take arms in the Parliament's service, or to contribute to this present war, or to obey any ordinance of the Lords and Commons, which tends to the resisting of the king's forces. Now compare this case with the case of a Socinian, Arminian, antinomian, or the like. They both plead for *liberty of conscience*; they both say our conscience ought not to be compelled, and if we do against our conscience, we sin. I beseech you, how can you give liberty of conscience to the heretic, and yet refuse *liberty of conscience* to him that is the conscientious recusant in point of war? I am sure there can be no answer given to this argument which will not be resolved into this principle: Men's consciences may be compelled for the good of the state, but not for the glory of God. We must not suffer the state to sink, but if religion sinks we cannot help it. This is the plain English of it.

When I speak against liberty of conscience, it is far from my meaning to advise any rigorous or violent course against such as being sound in the faith and holy in life and not of a turbulent or factious carriage, do differ in smaller matters from the common rule. "Let that day[15] be darkness; let not God regard it from above, neither let the light shine upon it" (Job 3:4), in which it shall be said that the children of God in Britain are enemies and persecutors of each other. He is no good Christian who will not say *Amen* to the prayer of Jesus Christ (John 17:21), that all who are His may be one in Him. If this is heartily wished, let it be effectually endeavored, and let those who will choose a dividing way rather than a uniting way bear the blame.

Third, Touching Restraint of Scandalous Persons from the Sacrament

3. The third part of my application shall be to stir you up, right honorable, to a willing condescending to the settling of church government in such a manner as that neither ignorant nor scandalous persons may be admitted to the holy table of the Lord. Let there be in the house of God, fuller's soap, to take off those who are "spots in your feasts" [Jude v. 12], and a refining fire

---

toleration. The plain english of the question is this: whether the Christian Magistrate is keeper of both tables: whether he ought to suppress his own enemies, but not God's enemies, and preserve his own ordinances, but not Christ's ordinances from violation…. Whether not only pious and peaceable men (whom I shall never consent to persecute), but those also who are as a pestilence or a gangrene in the body of Christ, men of corrupt minds and turbulent spirits, who draw factions after them, make a breach and rent in Israel, resist the truth and reformation of religion, spread abroad all the ways they can their pernicious errors, and by no other means can be reduced; whether those also ought to be spared and let alone." *Wholesome Severity Reconciled with Christian Liberty*, in *Shorter Writings*, 1.334.]

15. [*Scots Sermons* omits "day."]

to take away the dross from the silver. "Thou puttest away all the wicked of the earth like dross" (Ps. 119:119), says David. Take away, therefore, the wicked from before the King of glory, for they shall not stand before Him who hates "all workers of iniquity" (Ps. 5:5). You see, God puts all profane ones in one category, and so should you. There is a like reason against seven and against seventy scandals; or, if you please to make a catalogue of seven, you may, provided it is such as God Himself makes in the fifth verse of this chapter, where seven sorts are reckoned forth, as some interpreters compute, but the last of the seven is general and comprehensive: Καί τοὺσ μη φοβουμένουσ με, as the Septuagints have it; "and those that fear not me";[16] those, says one, who are called in the New Testament, ἀσεβεὶσ [Jude 1:4,] *ungodly*. Jerome notes upon the place,[17] that though men shall not be guilty of the aforementioned particulars, yet God makes this crime enough, that they are ungodly. Nay, I dare undertake to draw out of Erastus himself, the great adversary, a catalogue of seven sorts of persons to be kept off from the Lord's table, and such a catalogue as godly ministers can be content with. But of this elsewhere.[18]

Most horribly has the Lord's table been profaned formerly in this kingdom, by the admission of scandalous persons. God will wink at it no longer. Now is the opportunity of reformation. The Parliament of England, if any state in the world, owes much to Jesus Christ, and He will take it very ill at your hands if you do Him not right in this. I say do Him right; for, alas! What is it to ministers? It were more for their ease, and for pleasing of the people, to admit all; but a necessity is laid upon us that we dare not do it, and woe unto us if we do it. And for your part, should you not establish such a rule as may put a difference between the precious and the vile, the clean and the unclean, you shall insofar make the churches of Christ in a worse condition and more disabled to keep themselves pure, than either they were of old under pagan emperors, or now are under popish princes. You shall also strengthen, instead of silencing, the objections both of Separatists[19] and Socinians,[20] who have, with more than a color of advantage, opened their

---

16. Grotius, Annot. in Mal. 3. [Hugo Grotius, *Hugonis Grotii Annotata ad Vetus Testamentvm* (1644; cf Halae: 1775–1776), p. 559.]

17. [Jerome, *Commentariorum in Malachiam, PL* 25.1568.]

18. [Cf. *Aaron's Rod Blossoming*," in *Works*, p. 77; "Nihil Respondes," herein p. 263]

19. See Mr. Robinson's *Apology*, cap. 12. [John Robinson, *Apologia iusta, et necessaria quorundam Christianorum, æque contumeliose ac Communiter dictorum Brownistarum sive Barrowistarum* (Amsterdam?: Giles Thorp? 1619); *A Just and Necessarie Apologie of Certain Christians, no lesse contumeliously then commonly called Brownists or Barrowists* (Amsterdam: Thorp, 1625).]

20. Faustus Socinus wrote a book to prove that all those in the Reformed churches of Poland, who desire to be truly godly, ought to separate themselves, and join with the assemblies, who (he says) are falsely called Arians and Ebionites. One of his arguments is this, because, in those Reformed churches, there is a great neglect of church discipline, whereby it comes to pass that scandalous persons are admitted to the Lord's table. The same argument is pressed against some Lutheran churches by Schlichtingius, *disput. pro Socino Contra*

mouths wide against some Reformed churches, for their not exercising of discipline against scandalous and profane persons, and particularly for not suspending them from the sacrament of the Lord's supper. Nay, which is yet more, if you should refuse that which I speak of, you shall come short of that which heathens themselves, in their way, did make conscience of; for they did interdict and keep off from their holy things all such as they esteemed profane and scandalous, whom therefore they called ἐναγεῖσ, that is, accused or delated persons. In this manner was Alchibades excommunicate at Athens,[21] and Virginia at Rome; the former recorded by Plutarch, the latter by Livy.[22] I trust God shall never so far desert this parliament as that in this

---

Mesnerum, p. 484: *Licet vero dolendum sit talia promiscue passimque fieri, et abiisse in morem: pejus tamen adhuc est quod malis istis, præter conciones interdum aliquas, quibusdam in locis, nulla adhibeatur medicina, nec rectores ecclesiarum hæc cura taugat, ut vitia tam late grassantia, disciplina et censura ecclesiastica, ab ipso Christo et apostolis instituta coerceantur. Unde factum est ut non solum ista peccata, qua leviora videntur, sed etiam alia graviora, puta comessationes, compotationes, chrietates, scortationes, libidines, iræ, inimicitæ, rimæ, obtrectationes, ædes ac bella, diluvio quodam ecclesiastico inundarint.* [Faustus Socinus, *De officio hominis Christiani in hodiernis istis de religione controversiis* … (1599; Latin, Irenopoli: Typis Theophili Adamidis, 1610). "The Duty of a Christian Man amidst the modern Controversies about Religion: i.e. To what Assembly, amongst all those who differ in Religion, he ought to join himself." Cf. Joshua Toulmin, *Memoirs of the Life, Character, Sentiments, and Writings of Faustus Socinus* (London: Printed for the Author by J. Brown, 1777), p. 337.—Jonasz Szlichting, *Quæstiones duæ: vna num in Euangelicorum religione dogmata habeantur, quæ vix ullo modo permittant, ut qui ea amplectatur, nullo in peccato perseueret? Altera num in eadem religione quædem co[n] cedantur Christi legibus incontesti? contra Balthasarem Meisnerum S. Theologiæ Doctorem & in Academia Wittebergensi Profess. publicum à Iona Schlichtingio à Bukowiec disputæ* ({Kraków}: Typis Pauli Sternacii, {1636}). "From Licet: Certainly it is allowed that it ought to be deplored that such things happen commonly and everywhere, and have passed into custom: but it is worse that thus far, in whatever places, except for some occasional assemblies, no medicine is applied to such injuries, nor does this concern touch the rectors of the churches, that offenses running riot so widely should be repressed by the ecclesiastical discipline and censure established by Christ himself and the apostles. From this it has come about that not only those sins which seem lighter, but even other weightier ones, namely greediness, drunkenness, fornication, whoring, lust, anger, hostility, divisions, gossip, destruction and war, have overflowed in a kind of ecclesiastical deluge." This list of sins are Latinized Greek verbs.]

21. ["He was condemned as contumacious upon his not appearing, his property confiscated, and it was decreed that all the priests and priestesses should curse him." *The Harvard Classics* edited by Charles W. Eliot, LL. D., *Plutarch's Lives of Themistocles, Pericles* etc. (New York: P. F. Collier & Son, Copyright 1909), p. 131.]

22. ["Virginia, daughter of Aulus, a patrician, but married to Volumnius the consul, a plebeian, was, because she had married out of the patricians, excluded by the matrons from sharing in the sacred rites…." *The History of Rome, by Titus Livius, Books Nine to Twenty-Six. Literally Translated, with Notes and Illustrations,* by D. Spillan and Cyrus Edmonds (London: George Bell & Sons, 1887), Book X, §23, 657.]

particular, pagan and popish princes, Separatists, Socinians and heathens shall rise up in judgment against you. I am persuaded better things of you, and things that accompany salvation; and, namely, that you will not suffer the name and truth of God to be, through you, blasphemed and reproached [cf. Heb. 6:9; 1 Tim. 6:1].

Do you not remember the sad sentence against Eli and his house, "Because his sons made themselves vile, and he restrained them not" (1 Sam. 3:13). The apostle tells us that the judgment of God abides not only [on] those that commit sin, but those also who consent with them (Rom. 1:32). Aquinas upon that place says,[23] we may consent to the sins of others two ways: One, directly, by counseling, approving, etc. Two, indirectly, by not hindering when we can. And so did Eli consent to the vileness of his sons, because, though he reproved them, he did not restrain them.

There is a law (Exod. 21:29), "[But] if the ox were wont to push with his horn in time past, and it hath been testified to his owner, and he hath not kept him in, but that he hath killed a man or woman; the ox shall be stoned, and his owner also shall be put to death." It could be no excuse to say, I intended no such thing, and it is a grief of heart to me that such mischief is done. That which I aim at is this: The Directory which you have lately established says, "The ignorant and the scandalous are not fit to receive this sacrament of the Lord's supper;" and therefore ministers are appointed to warn all such in the name of Christ, that they presume not to come to that holy table.[24] It is now desired that this, which you have already acknowledged to be according to the Word of God and nature of that holy ordinance, may be made effectual, and, for that end, that the power of discipline be added to the power of doctrine, otherwise you are guilty, in God's sight, of not restraining those that make themselves vile.

In the third and last place, I shall apply my doctrine to the sons of Levi, and that in a twofold consideration: 1. Actively; 2. Passively.

Third, Application to Ministers

1. Actively, because if we be like our Master, even followers of Jesus Christ, or partakers of His unction, then our ministry will have not only light, but fire in it. We must be burning as well as shining lights (John 5:35), not only shining with the light of knowledge, and of the doctrine which is according to godliness, but burning also with zeal for reforming abuses, and purging of

---

23. [Cf. Commentary on Romans 1, lecture 8, at the end, in *S. Thomae Aquinatis Super Epistolas S. Pauli lectura*, ed. Raphael Cai (Marietti, Taurini-Romae, 1953).]

24. [See "Of the Celebration of the Communion, or Sacrament of the Lord's Supper," *The Directory for the Publick Worship of God* (1645). The English Parliament ordered the Directory printed, March 13, 1644/45. It had been issued and approved on January 4, 1644/45 (not January 3 as in the printed order; cf. William A. Shaw, *A History of the English Church during the Civil Wars and under the Commonwealth* {New York: Longmans, Green, and Co., 1900} 1.353). Robert Baillie and George Gillespie presented it before the General Assembly of the Church of Scotland on January 23, and it was approved on February 3, 1644/45. The Scottish Government approved it three days later.]

the church from the dross thereof. Which made Augustine to apply propological to ministers,[25] that which is said of the angels of heaven (Ps. 104:4), "Who maketh his angels spirits," and "his ministers a flaming fire." Satan has many incendiaries against the kingdom of Christ. O that we were Christ's incendiaries against the kingdom of Satan! If we will indeed appear zealous for the Lord, let it not seem strange if the adversaries of reformation say of us, as they said of the apostles themselves, "Those that have turned the world upside down are come hither also" (Acts 17:6). Yet it shall be no grief of heart to us afterward, but peace and joy unspeakable, that we have endeavored to do our duty faithfully.

2. Passively also the application must be made, because the sons of Levi must, in the first place, go through this refining fire themselves, and they, most of all other men, have need to be, and must be, refined from their dross. I find in Scripture that these three things had a beginning among the priests and prophets: One, sin, error, and scandal, begins at them (Jer. 50:6), "Their shepherds have caused them to go astray; From the prophets of Jerusalem is profaneness gone out [forth] into all the land" (23:15). Two, judgment begins at them (Ezek. 9:6), "Slay utterly old and young, and begin at my sanctuary." Three, the refining work of reformation begins, or ought to begin, at the purging and refining of the sons of Levi; so you have it in the next words after my text, and where Hezekiah begins his reformation at the sanctifying of the priests and Levites (2 Chron. 29:4, 5), etc. But as it was then in Judah, it is now in England, some of the sons of Levi are more upright to sanctify themselves than others. The fire that I spake of before will prove every man and his work.

3. I am sorry I have occasion to add a third application. But come on, and I will show you greater things than these [cf. John 1:50; Ezek. 8:15]. What will you say, if any are found among the sons of Levi, that will neither be active nor passive in the establishing of the church-refining and sin-censuring government of Jesus Christ, but will needs appear upon the stage against it. This was done in a late sermon now come abroad,[26] which has given no small scandal and offence. I am confident every other godly minister will say, Let my tongue cleave to the roof of my mouth before I do the like [Ps. 137:6].

---

25. [Augustine,] Enar. in Ps. 104: *Cum audis, ignis est minister Dei, incensurum illum putas? incendat licet sed foennm* [Migne—*senum*] *tuum, id est, carnalia omnia tua desidera.* [When you hear 'fire is the minister of God,' do you think he will be the one to burn? But certainly let your foulness burn, that is, your fleshly desires. Cf. *Enarrationes in Psalmos, PL* 37.1649 ¶16.]

26. [This was Thomas Coleman's *Hopes Deferred and Dashed, observed in a sermon to the Honourable House of Commons, in Margarets Westminster, July 30, 1645*, in which he expressed firm Erastian views. Gillespie replied to it in *A Brotherly Examination*, which was published with this sermon to the House of Lords, but there is no reason to believe it was part of the sermon given at the fast. The *Examination* makes up a triad of pamphlets Gillespie wrote against Coleman, the other two being *Nihil Respondes* and *Malè Audis*. These follow in their place after this sermon.]

II. I have done with that which the text holds forth concerning reformation. The second way how Christ is like a refiner's fire,[27] and like fuller's soap, is in respect of tribulation, which either follows or accompanies His coming into His temple. Affliction is indeed a refining fire, "For thou, O God, hast proved us: thou hast tried us, as silver is tried" (Ps. 66:10); "We went through fire and through water" (v. 12); "Ye are in heaviness through manifold temptations; that the trial of your faith, being much more precious than of gold that perisheth, though it be tried with fire, might be found unto praise," etc. (1 Pet. 1:6, 7). Affliction is also the fuller's soap to purify and make white: "Many shall be purified, and made white, and tried" (Dan. 11:35; 12:10); where the same word is used from which I said before the fuller's soap has its name.

The doctrine shall be this: *Tribulation does either accompany or follow after*   Doctrine 3.
the work of reformation or purging of the house of God. So it was when Christ Himself came into His temple: "I am come to send fire on the earth. Suppose ye that I am come to send [*give*] peace on earth? I tell you, Nay; but rather division" (Luke 12:49, 51). So it was when the apostles were sent forth into the world. Peter applies to that time the words of Joel, "And I will show wonders in heaven above, and signs in [the] earth beneath; blood, and fire, and vapor of smoke: the sun shall be turned into darkness, and the moon into blood" (Acts 2:19, 20). The meaning is, such tribulation shall follow the gospel, which shall be like the darkening of the great lights of the world, and, as it were, a putting of heaven and earth out of their course, so great a change and calamity shall come. The experience both of the ancient and now Reformed churches does also abundantly confirm this doctrine. Neither must we think that all the calamities of the church are now overpast. Who can be assured that that hour of greatest darkness, the killing of the witnesses, is past, and all that sad prophecy fulfilled (Rev. 11)? And if some are not much mistaken,[28] it is told that there shall be greater tribulation about the time of the Jews' conversion than any we have yet seen: "At that time," says the angel to Daniel, "there shall be a time of trouble, such as never was since there was a nation even to that same time: and at that time thy people shall be delivered, everyone that shall be found written in the book" (Dan. 12:1).

Use One. I make haste to the uses; and, 1. Let me give unto God the glory of His truth. If we have been deceived, surely He has not deceived us; for He has given us plain warning in His Word, and has not kept up from us the worst things which ever have or ever shall come upon His church. And now when the sword of the Lord has gotten a charge against these three covenanting and reforming kingdoms, is this any other than the word of the

---

27. [*Scots Sermons* omits the "a."]

28. Brightman and Alsted in Dan. 12:1. [Thomas Brightman (1562–1607), *The Revelation … with A Most Comfortable Exposition of the last and most difficult part of the prophecie of Daniel …* (1644), p. 315. Johann Heinrich Alsted, *Diatribe de Mille Annis Apocalypticis, non illis Chiliastarum & Phantastarum, sed B.B. Danielis & Iohannis* (Francofurti: Eifridi, 1627), pp. 203–204; trans. William Burton, *The beloved city or, The saints reign on earth a thousand yeares* (1643), p. 49.]

Lord that when Christ comes into His temple, *Who may abide the day of his coming, and who shall stand when he appeareth? So he* [For he] *is like a refiner's fire, and like fuller's soap.*

And for the invasion of Scotland by such an enemy after a reformation, is it any new thing? May we not say, that which is, has been? Did not Senacherib invade Judah after Hezekiah's reformation (2 Chron. 32:1)? And though, after the reformation of Asa, and after the reformation of Jehoshaphat also (2 Chron. 14:9; 20:1), the land had a short rest and a breathing time, yet not long after a foreign invasion followed both upon the one reformation and the other. Nay, look what is the worst thing which has befallen to Scotland as yet; as much, yea, worse, has formerly befallen to the church and people of God toward whom the Lord had thoughts of peace, and not of evil, to give them an expected end. I say it not for diminishing anything either from the sin or shame of Scotland; the Lord forbid: we will bear the indignation of the Lord because we have sinned against Him; we will lay our hand upon our mouth and accept the punishment of our iniquity; we will bear our shame forever because our Father has spit in our face, our rock has sold us, and our strength has departed from us.[29] But I say it by way of answering him that reproaches in the gates, and by way of pleading for the truth of God. Some have objected to our reproach, that when the Lord required the Israelites to appear before Him in Jerusalem thrice a year, He promised that no man should invade their habitations in their absence (Exod. 34:23, 24); "which gracious providence of His, no doubt," says one,[30] "continues still protecting all such as are employed by His command;" yet it has not been so with Scotland during the time of their armies being in England. I answer, besides that which has been said already, even in this the word and work of God do well agree; and that Scripture ought not to be so applied to us, except the Cannaanites, and the Ammorites, and the Jebusites of our time had been all cast out of our borders (we find this day too many of them lurking there, and waiting their opportunity); for the Septuagints,[31] and many of the interpreters read that text thus:[32] "For when I shall cast out the nations before

---

29. [Cf. Micah 7:9; Job 40:4; Leviticus 26:43; Numbers 12:14(?); 14:9(?); Deuteronomy 32:30.]

30. Answer to Mr. Prynne's Twelve Questions. [*An answer to Mr. William Prynn's twelve questions concerning church government at the end whereof, are mentioned severall grosse absurdities, and dangerous consequences of highest nature, which do necessarily follow the tenets of Presbyteriall, or any other besides a perfect independent government; together with certaine queries* (London, 1644). Attributed to Henry Robinson (1605?–1664?).]

31. [Gillespie uses the term Septuagints (i.e., the Seventy), rather than Septuagint as in *Scots Sermons* and *Works*.]

32. Cajetan in Exod. 34:24: *Non obligabat (præceptum apparendi ter in annot.) usque ad dilatatos terminos terræ promissæ, quando secura universa regio futura erat.* D. River. *comment in illum loc., Tum quia Deus ejecturus erat hostes ex eorum terminis: tum quia dilataturus erint fines populi sui, ut vicinos non tam haberent hostes, quam subditos et tributarios.* [Tommaso de Vio Cajetan (1469–1534), *Opera omnia quotquot in sacrae scripture* (Lugduni: Iacobi and Petri Prost,

thee, and enlarge thy borders, no man shall desire thy land when thou shalt go up to appear before the Lord thy God thrice in the year." And this is the true sense, read it as you will; for the promise is limited to the time of casting out the nations and enlarging their borders (which came not to pass till the days of Solomon). It is certain that, from the time of making that promise, the people had not ever liberty and protection for keeping the three solemn feasts in the place of the sanctuary, as might be proved from divers foreign invasions and spoilings of that land for some years together, whereof we read in the book of the Judges. But I go on.

Use Two. In the second place, let God have the glory of His just and righteous dealings. Let us say with Job, "I will leave my complaint upon myself," and say unto God, "Show me wherefore thou contendest with me" (Job 10:1, 2). But, by all means, take heed you conceive not an ill opinion of the covenant and cause of God, or the reformation of religion, because of the tribulation which follows thereupon. Say not it was a good old world when we burnt incense to the queen of heaven, "for then we were well and saw no evil." "But," said the people to Jeremiah, "since we left off to burn incense to the queen of heaven, and to pour out drink-offerings unto her, we [have wanted all things, and] have been consumed by the sword and by the famine" (Jer. 44:18). To such I answer, in the words of Solomon, "Say not thou, what is the cause that the former times [*days*] were better than these? For thou dost not inquire wisely concerning this" (Eccles. 7:10). Was the people's coming out of Egypt the cause why their carcasses did fall in the wilderness? Or was it their murmuring and rebelling against the Lord which brought that wrath upon them? If you would inquire wisely concerning this thing, read Zephaniah chapter one. In the days of Isaiah, even in the days of Judah's best reformation, the Lord sent this message by the prophet: "I will utterly consume all things from off the land" (Zeph. 1:2); "And I will bring distress upon men, that they shall walk like blind men, [because they have sinned against the Lord:] and their blood shall be poured out as dust, and their flesh as [the][33] dung" (v. 17). What was the reason of it? It is plainly told them (and let us take it all home to ourselves), because, notwithstanding of that public reformation, there was a remnant of Baal in the land, and the Chemarims,

---

1639). "Cajetan on Exodus 34:24: It did not engage (the rule of obligatory appearance three times a year) until the borders of the promised land were enlarged, when the whole region was to be secure." Andrew Rivet, *Commentarii, in librum secundum Mosis, qui Exodus apud Græcos inscribitur: in quibus præter scholia, analysim, explicationem, & observationes doctrinarum in usum concionatirum, variæ quæstiones theoreticæ & practicæ discutiuntur, & solvuntur* (Lugduni Batavorum: {1634}). "D. Rivet., Comment. on the same place. Then, because God was about to drive out the enemies from their boundaries: then, because the borders of his own people were going to be enlarged, so that they would not have enemies for neighbors, but instead subjects and tributaries."]

33. [Many of these insertions or additions of words that were omitted from the Scripture citations were added "silently" in *Works*, which *Scots Sermons* followed.]

and those who halt between two opinions, who swear by the Lord (or to the Lord, which is expounded of the taking of the covenant in Josiah's time), but they swear by Malcham also (vs. 4, 5). There are others who do not seek the Lord, nor inquire after him and many that turn back from the Lord in a course of backsliding (v. 6); others clothed with strange apparel (v. 8); others, exercising violence and deceit (v. 9); a number of atheists also, living among God's people (v. 12). For these and the like causes does the land mourn. It is not the covenant, but the broken covenant; it is not the reformation, but the want of a real and personal reformation, that has drawn on the judgment. Blessed are they who shall keep their garments clean, and shall be able to say, "All this is come upon us; yet have we not forgotten thee, nor [*neither have we*] dealt falsely in thy covenant" (Ps. 44:17).

Use Three. Give God the glory of His wisdom. Many are now crying, "How long, Lord? Wilt thy hide thyself forever? Shall thy wrath burn like fire" (Ps. 89:46)? Your answer from God is that the rod shall be indeed removed and even cast into the fire in your stead. But when? It shall be "when the Lord has performed his whole work upon mount Zion, and on Jerusalem" (Isa. 10:12). If the judgment has not yet done all the work it was sent for, then "they shall go out from one fire, and another fire shall devour them" (Ezek. 15:7), saith the Lord. God is a wise refiner, and will not take the silver out of the fire till the dross is purged away from it. He is a wise father who will not cast the rod of correction till it has driven away all that folly which is bound up in the hearts of his children. "Behold, therefore," saith the Lord, "I will gather {you into the midst of Jerusalem, as they gather}34 silver, and brass, and iron, and lead, and tin, into the midst of the furnace, to blow the fire upon it, to melt it; so will I gather you in mine anger and in my fury, and I will leave you there, and melt you" (Ezek. 22:19, 20). He speaks it to those who had escaped the captivity of Jehoiakim, and also the captivity of Jehoiachin, and thought they should be safe and secure in Jerusalem when their brethren were in Babylon. 'I will gather you,' saith the Lord, 'even in the midst of Jerusalem, and when you think you are out of one furnace, you shall fall into another; and, if you will not be refined from your dross, you shall never come out of that furnace, but I will melt you there, and leave you there.' Which did come to pass; for the residue that escaped to Egypt, and thought to shelter themselves there, as likewise those that remained in Jerusalem, and held out that siege with Zedekiah, even all these did fall under the sword, and the famine, and the pestilence, till they were consumed (Jer. 24:8, 10). Let those that are longest spared take heed they be not sorest smitten. Say not with Agag, "The bitterness of death is past" [1 Sam. 15:32]. The child chastised in the afternoon weeps as sore as the child chastised in the forenoon.35 Remember the Lord will not take away

---

34. [The text between braces was omitted in *Scots Sermons*.]

35. ["As sair greets (sore cries) the bairn that is dung (beaten) after noon, as he that is dung afore noon." "He that is now in prosperity, when I am in adversity, may find as severe a change of fortune afterwards." James Kelly, *A Complete Collection of Scottish Proverbs:*

the judgment till He has performed His work, yea, His whole work, and that upon Mount Zion and Jerusalem itself. It is no light matter; the rod must be very heavy before our uncircumcised hearts can be humbled, and the furnace very hot before our dross departs from us. We have need of all the sore strokes which we mourn under, and if one less could do the turn, it would be spared, for the Lord does not afflict willingly. We ourselves rive [*tear; wrench*] every stroke out of his hand.

Use Four. But, in the fourth and last place, let us give God the glory of His mercy also; He means to do us good in our latter end. It is the hand of a father, not of an enemy: it is a refining, not a consuming fire. The poor mourners in Zion are ready to say, "Our bones are dried, and our hope is lost: we are cut off for our parts" (Ezek. 37:11); we are likely to lie in this fire and furnace forever, because our dross is not departed from us; we are still an unhumbled, an unbroken, an unmortified generation; yea, many like Ahaz, in the time of affliction, trespassing yet more against the Lord, many thinking of going back again to Egypt. To such I have these two things to say for their comfort:

(1) There is a remnant which shall not only be delivered, but purified, and shall come forth as gold out of the fire. The third part shall be refined, and the Lord shall say, "It is my people" (Zech. 13:9). And a most sweet promise there is after the saddest denunciation of judgment: "Yet, behold, therein shall be left a remnant that shall be brought [forth], both sons and daughters; behold, they shall come forth unto you, and ye shall see their ways and their doings: and ye shall be comforted concerning the evil that I have brought upon Jerusalem, even concerning all the evil that I have brought upon it. And they shall comfort you, {when ye see their ways and their doings: and}[36] ye shall know that I have not done without cause all that I have done in it, saith the Lord God" (Ezek. 14:22, 23). "Many shall be purified, and made white, and tried; but the wicked shall do wickedly: and none of the wicked shall understand; but the wise shall understand" (Dan. 12:10). After the promise of delivering those that were carried away to Babylon, there is another promise added of that which was much better: "I will give them an heart to know me, that I am the Lord; and they shall be my people, and I will be their God; for they shall return unto me with their whole heart" (Jer. 24:7); "He shall redeem Israel from all his iniquities" (Ps. 130:8); "I will also leave in the midst of thee an afflicted and poor people, and they shall trust in the name of the Lord. The remnant of Israel shall not do iniquity, nor speak lies; neither shall a deceitful tongue be found in their mouth" (Zeph. 3:12, 13). Let your souls now apply these and the like promises, and cry, "Lord, remember thy promises, and let not a jot of thy good Word fall to the ground."

(2) As the promises of spiritual and eternal blessings, so the promises of peace and temporal deliverances are not legal, but even evangelical. If we

---

Explained and Made Intelligible to the English Reader (London, 1818), #69, p. 8. Dickson also used this proverb. See *Sermons on Jeremiah's Lamentations* (2020), p. 279.]

36. [The text between braces was omitted in *Scots Sermons*.]

are not refined and purged as we ought to be, that is a matter of humiliation to us, but it is also a matter of magnifying the riches of free mercy. "For my name's sake will I defer mine anger, and for my praise will I refrain for thee, [that I cut thee not off]. Behold, I have refined thee, but not with silver; I have chosen thee in the furnace of affliction. For mine own sake,[37] yea, [even] for mine own sake, will I do it" (Isa. 48:9–11). The Lord is there arguing with His people, to humble them, to convince them, and to cut off all matter of glorying from them; and among other things, lest they should glory in this, that whatever they were before, they became afterward as silver refined seven times in the furnace:[38] 'Nay,' saith the Lord, 'I have refined you in some sort, but not as silver, not so as that you are clean from your dross; but I have chosen you, and set my love upon you, even while you are in the furnace not yet refined; and I will deliver you, even for my own name's sake, that you may owe your deliverance forever to free mercy, and not to your own repentance and amendment.' A land is accepted, and a people's peace made with God, not by their repentance and humiliation, but by Christ believed on: "This man shall be the peace, when the Assyrian shall come into our land" (Mic. 5:5). There were sin-offerings and burnt-offerings appointed in the law for a national atonement (Lev. 4:13, 21; Num. 15:25, 26), which did typify pardoning of national sins through the merit of Jesus Christ. We must improve the office of the Mediator, and the promise of free grace, in the behalf of God's people, as well as of our own souls, which, if it be indeed done, will not hinder, but further a great mourning and deep humiliation in the land. And so much of tribulation.

III. The third thing held forth in this text (of which I must be very short) is *mortification*. This also is a refining fire. "He shall baptize you with the Holy Ghost, and with fire" (Matt. 3:11); "For everyone shall be salted with fire, and every sacrifice shall be salted with salt" (Mark 9:49). He has been before speaking of mortification, of the plucking out of the right eye, the cutting off of the right hand, or the right foot, and now He presses the same thing by a double allusion to the law. There was a necessity both of fire and salt. The sacrifice was seasoned with salt (Lev. 2:13), and the fire upon the altar was not to be put out, but every morning the wood was burnt upon it, and the burnt-offering laid upon it (Lev. 6:12, 13). So if we will present ourselves as a holy and acceptable sacrifice to God, we must be seasoned with the salt [*with salt*], and our corruptions burnt up with the fire of mortification.

The doctrine shall be this: *It is not enough to join in public reformation, yea, to suffer tribulation for the name of Christ, except we also endeavor mortification*. This

Doctrine 4.

---

37. [In changing the "yea" to "even," *Works* inserted another "name's" in "For mine own sake." This was followed by *Scots Sermons*.]

38. Bulling., Gualt., and Aricularius on the place [Isa. 48:9–11]. [Bullinger, *Isaias excellentissimus Dei propheta*, p. 238v. Gwalther, *Isaias: in Isaiam prophetam Rodolphi Gualtheri Tigurini homiliae CCCXXVII* (Tiguri, 1583), p. 302. Daniel Arcularius (d. 1596), *Commentarius in Esaiam prophetam* (Francofurti, 1607), p. 637.]

mortification is a third step distinct from the other two, and without this the other two can make us but *almost Christians*, or, "not far from the kingdom of God" [Acts 26:28; Mark 12:34]. In the parable of the sower and the seed (as we find it both in Matthew 13, Mark 4, and Luke 8), this method may be observed, that of the four sorts of ground, the second is better than the first, the third better than the second, but the fourth only is the good ground, which is fruitful and gets a blessing. Some men's hearts are like the highway, and the hard-beaten road, where every foul spirit and every lust has walked and conversed. Their consciences, through the custom of sin, are as it were, "seared with a hot iron" [1 Tim. 4:2]. In these the Word takes no place, but all that they hear does presently slip from them. Others receive the Word with a present good affection and delight, but have no depth of earth; that is, neither having had a work of the law upon their consciences for deep humiliation, nor being rooted and grounded in love to the gospel, nor, peradventure, so much as grounded in the knowledge of the truth, nor having counted the cost and solidly resolved for suffering; thereupon it comes to pass, when suffering times come, these wither away, and come to nothing. There is a third sort, who go a step farther. They have some root and some more solid ground than the former, so that they can suffer many things and not fall away because of persecution, yet they perish through want of mortification. One may suffer persecution for Christ, not being sore tried in that which is his idol lust, yet enduring great losses and crosses in other things. Of such it is said that "the cares of this world, and the deceitfulness of riches, and the lusts of other things entering in, choke the word, and it becometh unfruitful" (Mark 4:19). Mark that, *the lusts of other things*; that is, whether it is the lust of the eyes, or the lust of the flesh, or the pride of life [1 John 2:16]; and he speaks of the *entering in*, meaning of some strong temptation coming upon a man to catch him in that which is the great idol of his heart, and his beloved lust, whatever it is. Such a temptation he never found before, and therefore thought the lust had been mortified, which was but lurking. Did not Judas suffer many things with Christ during the time of His public ministry? Did not Ananias and Sapphira suffer, for a season, with the apostles and church at Jerusalem? What was it then that lost them? They neither made defection from the profession of the truth, nor did they fall away because of persecution; but having sinned in the light of a sound profession, having also taken up the cross, and borne the reproach of Christ, they made shipwreck at last upon an unmortified lust.

I shall enlarge the doctrine no further, but touch upon some few uses, and so an end.

Use One. Let all and everyone of us be convinced of the necessity of our further endeavoring after mortification. The best silver which comes out of the earth has dross in it, and therefore needs the refiner's fire; and the whitest garment that is worn will touch some unclean thing or other, and therefore will need the fuller's soap. The best of God's children have the dross of their inherent corruptions to purge away; which made Paul say, "I keep under my body, and bring it unto subjection; lest that by any means, when I have preached to others, I myself should be cast away" (1 Cor. 9:27). It is a speech borrowed from reprobate silver which is not refined from dross, and so is the word used by the Septuagints (Isa. 1:22), τὸ ἀργύριον ἱμῶν ἀδόκιμον, "Thy silver is become dross." The apostle, therefore, sets himself to the study of mortification, 'lest,' says he, 'when I have been refining and purifying others, I myself be found to be drossy silver.' And as there is *inherent* dross, so there is *adherent* uncleanness in the best; and who can say that he has kept his garments so clean that he is "unspotted of the world" (Isa. 1:27 [*sic* James 1:27]), or that he has so separated himself from the pollutions of the world as that he has touched no unclean thing. So that there is a universal necessity of making use both of the refiner's fire and of the fuller's soap.

Use Two. Let us once become willing and contented, yea, desirous to be thoroughly mortified. A man's lusts and corruptions are indeed so strongly interested in himself, {that sin is himself,}[39] and his corruptions are his members; therefore, when we leave off sin, we are said to live no more "to ourselves" (2 Cor. 5:15). And mortification is the greatest violence that can be done to nature; therefore, it is called a cutting off of the chief members of the body (Mark 9:43, 45, 47), a salting with salt, and a burning with fire (v. 49), a circumcision (Col. 2:11), a crucifying (Rom. 6:6): so that nothing can be more difficult or displeasing, yea, a greater torment to flesh and blood. Yet now are you willing, notwithstanding of all this, to take Christ on His own terms? To take Him not only for righteousness and life, but to take Him as a refiner's fire and as fuller's soap? O that there were such a heart in you! When Christ bids you pluck out your right eye and cut off your right hand, say not in your heart, "How shall I do without my right eye, and my right hand?" Nay, you shall do well enough, you shall even enter into life without them. You shall be a gainer, and no loser. Say not, "How shall I go through this refining fire?" Fear not; you shall lose nothing but your dross. Thus get your heart wrought to a willingness, and a condescending in the point of mortification.

Use Three. Lastly, if you say, "but after all this, how shall I attain unto it?" Put yourself in the hands of Jesus Christ. Trust Him with the work. If you mark the text here, and the verse that follows, Christ is both the refiner and the refiner's fire. You shall be refined by Him and you shall be refined in Him. You deceive yourself if you think to be refined any other way but by this refiner and in this refiner's fire. The blood of Christ does not only wash us from guilt, but purges our consciences "from dead works, to serve the living God" (Heb. 9:14); "And they that are Christ's, have crucified the flesh, with the affections and lusts" (Gal. 5:24). Here you may see the thing is feasible and attainable, and not only by an apostle or some extraordinary man, but by all that are Christ's. Being His, and in Him, they are enabled, through His strength, to crucify the flesh, with the affections and lusts thereof.

---

39. [The text between braces was omitted in *Works* and in *Scots Sermons*.]

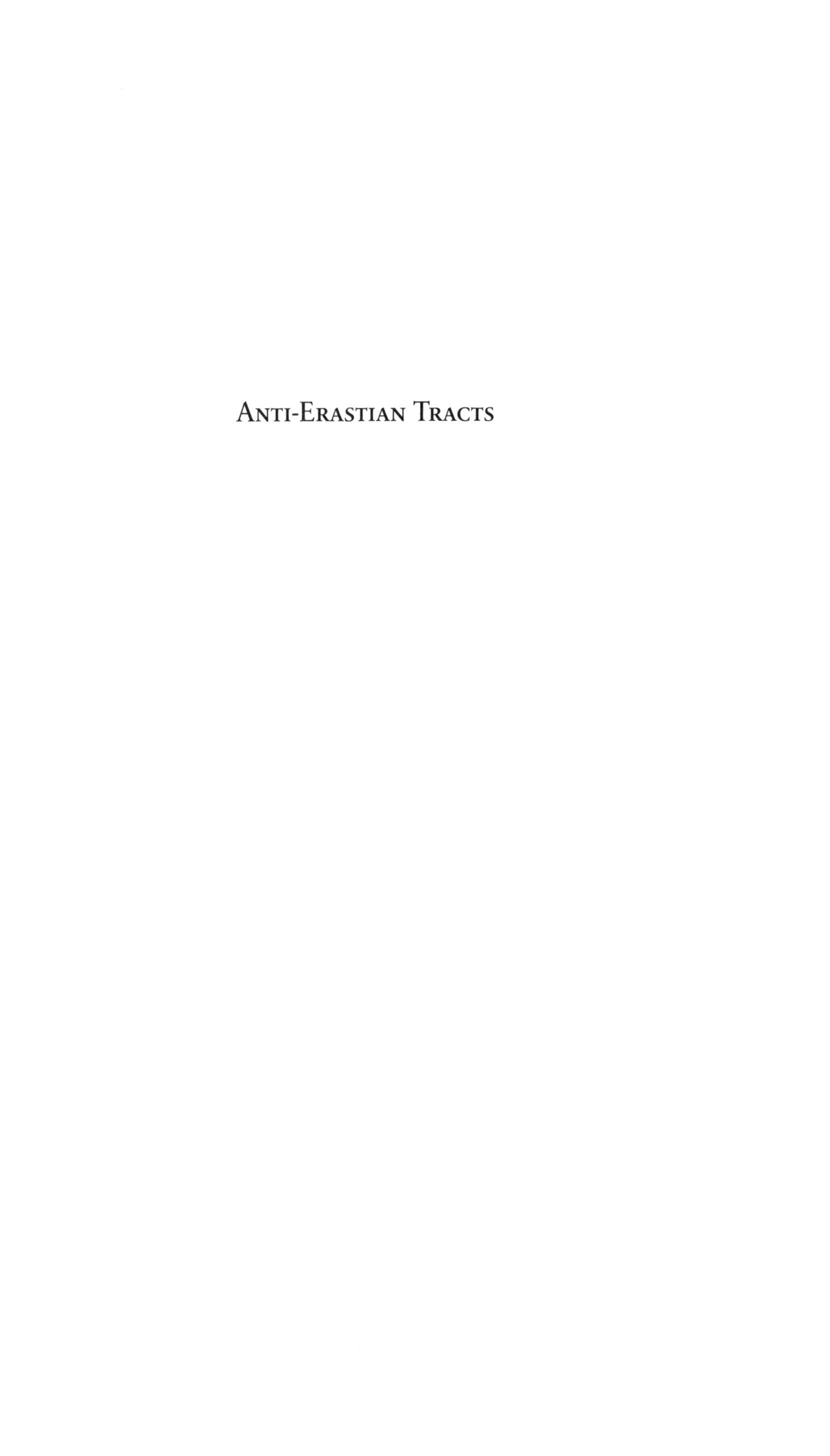

Anti-Erastian Tracts

Preface

George Gillespie and the Scottish Commissioners attending the Westminster Assembly understood well the evils of Erastianism. Long before they met in debate with those wanting to place supreme power over the church in a parliament, they experienced the tyranny of those who would have it rest in the king through his civil-ecclesiastical office-holding bishops in their court of High Commission. This is clear from Gillespie's first work against the *English Popish Ceremonies* and from his *Assertion of the Government*, where he first mentions Erastus by name in print.[1] So, while Gillespie may not have been expecting to run into a government in England intent on claiming Erastian granted powers for itself, he was clearly familiar with and ready to counter the errors of Erastus. In Gillespie's understanding of ecclesiology, "the errors characteristic of Erastianism represented a recent error in the history of ecclesiology and should be considered suspect, in part, because of its late date and 'new-fangled language.'"[2] The clash was not new. The confrontation can be seen as one of a number flowing from the original controversy involving Thomas Erastus in Heidelberg beginning in the late 1560s, which was itself not unique but the most famous clash between the Genevan "two-sphere" and the "single-sphere" Zürich-Bern model of church discipline.[3] The former is the familiar Genevan scheme of discipline resting solely in the church in a presbyterian form in an assembly of elders, while the Zürich model saw no need "to erect separate ecclesiastical" courts when there was a Christian state where the civil government would "supervise morals."[4] The two reforming centers worked hard to avoid conflict in order to present a united front in the continuing Reformation, but controversy ignited when Erastus began pressing his views, which even the favorers of the Zürich model saw as too extreme in his maintaining that church censures, or "the entire concept of excommunication was without

---

1. *English Popish Ceremonies* (1637), pp. 176, 195–197 (Naphtali Press, 2013), pp. 332, 356–358. Gillespie first mentions Erastus in *Assertion of the Government* (1641; repr. NPSE vol. V, 2021), part one, chapter 4, p. 132. He next mentions Erastus in *Dialogue Between a Civilian and a Divine* (1644; repr. NPSE vol. V, 2021), pp. 310, 313, which was in print by October 30, 1644.

2. Chad Van Dixhoorn, "Presbyterian ecclesiologies at the Westminster assembly," in *Church Polity and Politics in the British Atlantic World, c. 1635–66* (Manchester University Press, 2020), ebook, location 3355.

3. Charles D. Gunnoe, *Thomas Erastus and the Palatinate: A Renaissance Physician in the Second Reformation* (Brill, 2011), pp. 136, 165.

4. Gunnoe, pp. 165, 168–169.

theological justification or biblical merit."[5] The controversy exploded into public view when Erastus's theses and defense of them were published after his death in London.[6] In England, there had been continuing efforts by those who wished further reform in the English church, which led to the Puritan movement beginning in the early years of the reign of Elizabeth I. The Presbyterians of the movement had pushed for Genevan reforms, which brought those such as Thomas Cartwright into conflict with the Anglican authorities in the church like John Whitgift, who found support in Erastus's views.[7] The prelates were able to crush the presbyterian movement in 1592, which did not die, but went underground.[8] English presbyterianism would re-emerge at the time of the English Civil War with the opportunity it presented the Puritans to remake the English church government, and Presbyterians of course saw Calvin's Genevan model as the biblical form bearing the *jus divinum* imprint.

GILLESPIE V. COLEMAN

The theological dispute between George Gillespie and Thomas Coleman began in August 1645. The parliament had already shown that it desired to retain control over church censures.[9] The assembly had decided to vote on a second petition to present to parliament to make the case for the divine right of church discipline, "urging them not to adopt a novel Erastian stance toward church-governance," which it began refining and approving in Session 476 on July 28, 1645. The only dissent made came from Coleman, and that was only over a wry line criticizing Thomas Erastus as a more successful physician than a theologian. Because of the monthly fast on July 30, the assembly did not finish the work until July 31.[10] In between the two sessions, Coleman

---

5. Gunnoe, p. 190.

6. Thomas Erastus, *Explicatio gravissimæ quæstionis, utrum excommunicatio* (1589).

7. Gunnoe, p. 397. Whitgift may have supported the publication of Erastus's work.

8. Polly Ha, *English Presbyterianism, 1590–1640* (Stanford University Press, 2011), p. 1. See the Introduction in *Jus Divinum Regiminis Ecclesiastici*, NPSE vol. II (2019), pp. 11–12.

9. The assembly was not comfortable drafting lists of scandalous sins that debar from the Lord's supper to give to the Commons. The means of debarring had not been established and the assembly was pressing for it to be in the hands of the church via elders (March 5, 1645 petition, document 61, *Minutes*, 5.176), at which point clear the relationship between the assembly and the house clearly soured (*Minutes*, 1.31). Simonds D'Ewes in the Commons complained about giving "an arbitrary power" to ministers on March 29 (*Minutes*, 5.188). The first dated use of the term Erastian is on April 25 (Baillie, 2.265) and while the use of the term may have begun as early as the time of the debate between Selden and Gillespie in February of 1644, it seems reasonable that it likely coincided with the increasingly clear unwillingness in the Commons to have an independent church government administering church censures. See the preface to Gillespie's Sermon before the House of Lords, p. 138.

10. See *Minutes*, 3.639–640, and the petition in document 81, 5.228–231. "The assembly petitioned again that ministers and elders be permitted to exercise church discipline. Members

preached against the intent of the petition in his fast sermon before the Commons, intentionally disputing against what the assembly was advocating for in its petition before its intended audience.[11] This was clearly contrary to the rules governing assembly debate.[12] The assembly received a complaint about the sermon on July 31, and Coleman gave an accounting, apology, and promise not to publish on August 1, and the assembly filed a complaint to the Commons about the sermon.[13] However, Coleman retracted what he called his declaration on Monday, August 4. The assembly determined to work on another petition against Erastianism on August 6, which they approved the next day, and a committee carried and presented it to parliament on August 8.[14] On August 9, the House of Commons issued a second order to print Coleman's sermon, which could be seen as a negative response to the assembly's petition the prior day.[15] Two papers of advice regarding discipline and the sacrament were presented to the Commons on August 13 and a paper on the right of elderships to suspend from the sacrament was given in by the assembly on August 18. In addition, the assembly presented the same day an extensive "paper with examples of discipline in other churches," exhibiting what Gillespie might call the best practices of the reformed churches. All this was for naught and the tract war with Coleman had not even begun. On August 20, the "Parliament printed its directions for the election of elders … establishing an Erastian presbyterianism." After considering yet another petition, the assembly moved on over the next several months to work on the confession of faith, revising the Psalter, dealing with the troublesome Independent brethren, and other work.[16]

It is in this context that Gillespie briefly reproved and rebutted comments made in Coleman's sermon before the Commons, when at the next monthly

---

excuse their importunity by pleading the duty of their consciences. The assembly also cited Old Testament examples of God-fearing people who reminded rulers to do their duty, and suggested that Erastus, a medical doctor, was better equipped for healing human bodies than churches." Ibid., 5.228.

11. Coleman, *Hopes Deferred and Dashed* (1645), pp. 24–28.

12. This was a serious breach of the assembly rules. See page 144.

13. The text apparently does not survive, but see the account of it in Document 82 in *Minutes*, 5.231.

14. See *Minutes*, 3.642–645. "In this petition the assembly pleads for the freedom to keep ignorant and scandalous people away from the Lord's table. It argues that other civil governments shared similar concerns with the English parliament about arbitrary ecclesiastical power and yet still permitted elderships to exercise church discipline." Van Dixhoorn, *Minutes*, document 83, 5.232.

15. See the introduction to Gillespie's sermon before the House of Lords, p. 146.

16. There was another petition on November 10, 1645, which the assembly took the occasion of presenting alongside an expanded list of scandalous sins that should preclude one from receiving the Lord's Supper, which the Commons had requested. *Minutes*, document 93, 5.257.

faſt he preached before the House of Lords on Auguſt 27, 1645, and criticized Coleman again in a sermon for a ſpecial faſt before the Commons on September 5. On September 3, in between those two occasions, the Commons' Grand Committee on Religion made reports about suſpension and excommunication and John Selden and Bulſtrode Whitelocke pressed the Eraſtian case hard.[17] Selden made use of Coleman's breech of propriety undermining the assembly and used this single divine's intransigence to say that the assembly was not in agreement and parliament had the right to decide the matter of church government. Whitelocke appealed to the Zürich one ſphere model as juſtification of ſtate control of church censures.

Gilleſpie's sermon on September 5 was not published, but the sermon before the Lords from Auguſt 27 was printed on October 13, along with a tract Gilleſpie had taken some time to prepare entitled *A Brotherly Examination*.[18] Coleman reſponded fairly quickly with a *Brotherly Examination Re-examined*, which the Stationers record for October 27, and Thomason notes that he purchased his copy on November 1, 1645.[19] Gilleſpie reſponded equally quickly, and his *Nihil Reſpondes* appeared around November 13.[20] Coleman's *Malè Dicis Maledicis* appeared by or between December 15, 1645 and January 8, 1646,[21] and Gilleſpie's reſponse, *Malè Audis*, appeared by January 24, 1645.[22] This appears to have ended the tract war between the two. At leaſt there is no evidence that Coleman intended to continue the diſpute in tract form. He surely knew with all of Gilleſpie's forecaſting of it in the shorter tracts that a larger comprehensive reply was in the works. However, he was not in retreat, but would engage again when the time was ripe in the Weſtminſter assembly itself.

---

17. House of Commons Journal 4, p. 262. See Elliot Vernon, *London Presbyterians and the British Revolutions, 1638–64* (Manchester University Press, 2021), pp. 121, 133, 160 n6. The speeches are preserved in the Notebook of Jeremiah Baines, British Library, Add. MS 18780, and parts of them (but with no mention of Coleman) are also in Bulstrode Whitelocke, *Memorials of the English Affairs*, volume 1 (Oxford: University Press, 1853), pp. 504–508. See also Vernon, *Church Polity and Politics in the British Atlantic World, c. 1635–66* (Manchester University Press, 2020), ebook, locations 4118, 4426–4452.

18. For Robert Bostock under October 13, 1645 it is recorded, "Entred ... by order of the Lords' house of Parl., A sermon preached before the ho[ble] house of Lords in the Abbey church of Westm[r], the 27th of August 1645, whereunto is added a brotherly examination of M[r] Colemans sermon on JOB. 11.20. by M[r] Gillespie." *A Transcript of the Regiſters of the Worshipful Company of Stationers from 1640–1708 A.D.*, ed. G.E. Briscoe Eyre, 3 vols. (London, 1913–14), I.197.

19. *A Transcript*, ibid., vol. 1, p. 200. For Thomason, see *English Short Title Catalogue* (ESTC), record R23721.

20. ESTC, record R200413.

21. *A Transcript*, ibid., p. 208. ESTC, record R200513.

22. See *A Transcript*, ibid., p. 212, and ESTC, record R200545. Both record the date of January 24, 1646.

On February 12, 1646, the assembly returned to the need to establish presbyteries nationwide for ordaining ministers and petitioned the parliament. On February 13, the day the petition was presented, the divines received a report on its reception and then "reproved Thomas Coleman in Session 589 for his words in the prior session against the solemn league and covenant, after he had been aggravated by the assembly's petition for presbyterianism."[23] On March 5, the assembly discussed church government in the context of the publication of the parliament's ordinance for keeping the scandalous from partaking of communion, which rested review and adjudication with parliament. The next day on Friday, March 6, in Session 600, with that in view, "the assembly considered inserting a strong statement in the confession of faith about the distinction between officers of the state and of the church."[24]

It is in this Session 600 that a proposition was proposed that would reengage Gillespie and Coleman on the floor of the assembly. The minutes read "Debate about the church, Instituting of ecclesiasticall government," with the proposition for debate, "That Jesus Christ as King and Head of His church has appointed an ecclesiastical government in His church in the hand of church officers distinct from the civil government." Gillespie and Coleman are recorded as speaking in Sessions 601, 603, and 604. There is unrecorded debate in session 605, and in Session 606 Coleman is noted as not present. On March 19, 1646 in Session 607, the assembly was informed that Coleman was not well, and on March 20, 1646, in Session 608, it was reported that Coleman was very ill and had asked that the subject be deferred till he could again attend. A week later on March 27, 1646, in Session 611, the assembly was informed of Coleman's death. The whole assembly attended the funeral on March 30.[25]

The Anti-Erastian Tracts

It would be tedious to outline the argumentation across the handful of publications making up the exchange between George Gillespie and Thomas Coleman. The reader may see the flow of the main points in Gillespie's three tracts presented herein with the provided cross referencing. As to the exchange in general, while Gillespie is not beyond scoring rhetorical points, he is doing some of his best writing in this dispute with Coleman. Walker ranks *Nihil Respondes* and *Malè Audis* as "among his best productions," and Hetherington heaps praise on Gillespie's full performance in the controversy.[26] On the other

---

23. *Minutes*, 3.754. Coleman had made an unrecorded speech the prior day in which he complained "that the covenant is made use of to beat all men with."

24. *Minutes*, 3.765–766.

25. See *Minutes*, 3.766–789, 4.6–32; Baillie, 2.364. On March 20, 1646, the same day Coleman was reported very ill, the assembly's "Protest to both houses of parliament against its ordinance for suspension from the Lord's supper" was presented.

26. James Walker, *The Theology and Theologians of Scotland* (2ND ed., 1888), p. 14. See Hetherington's outline of the tract controversy and assessments following herein beginning on page 203.

hand, Coleman struggles, is evasive and misconstrues things, intentionally or otherwise, and Gillespie often schools him on what was the point in question. While Coleman does attempt to martial support from Reformed theologians, he is less scholarly, more sharp, and resorts to less than commendable tactics. Gillespie's constant complaint is that Coleman simply does not engage the substance of the matter and misuses and misrepresents the sources he does cite. For instance, in his *Malè Dicis*, Coleman piles up quotations from several of the Westminster divines using deferential language toward the Houses of Parliament with regard to their responsibilities toward the church, and exclaims that they are more Erastian than he or even Erastus was![27]

Coleman was clearly smarting from Gillespie's rebukes and he apparently feared his reputation was taking a hit in how his views were cast in Gillespie's responses. That seems to be the only explanation for Coleman spending two pages addressing "is it a fault in me for making the Christian magistrate a governor in the church," and that they "ought to manage their office under" and for Christ, and then citing members of the assembly in their sermons before parliament to show that they were more extreme in granting to the magistrate various work with regard to the church.[28] Not only was this off the subject of the points in debate, the quotations are also taken out of context from what the men cited actually believed (none were Erastian in doctrine), and he does so admitting this is the case. Gillespie merely takes one example from the men cited to show how unfair it was to take comments out of context to what the men really believed and portray them as if they were more Erastian than Erastus.[29] The comments also have to be understood within the context of a fault in the preaching of the time, of which Baillie complains "The way here of all preachers, even the best, has been to speak before the parliament with so profound a reverence as truly took all edge from their exhortations." As William Lamont himself notes, who is hostile toward Gillespie, "these phrases should not be taken at more than face value. Otherwise one could do as one contemporary, Thomas Coleman, did: make a careful collection of all the extravagant praises of the civil magistrate,"[30] which are the very quotations in question that Coleman used to portray himself as less radical than the Presbyterians. This was somewhat

---

27. *Malè Dicis*, p. 38. This is in a brief separate reply to Adoniram Byfield's *A Brief View of Mr. Coleman, his new-modell of church government* (1645).

28. Coleman cites Presbyterians of the Westminster assembly, Anthony Burges, William Gouge, William Spurstow, Thomas Wilson, and Stephan Marshall, "for making the Christian Magistrate a governor in the church." *Malè Dicis*, p. 36–37. He cites for holding that the magistrate "ought to manage their office under Christ and for Christ," Marshall, Burges, and Peter Sterry, who was a congregationalist according to Baillie. *Minutes*, 1.139; Baillie, *Letters & Journals*, 2.110.

29. See herein on page 315.

30. William M. Lamont, *Godly Rule: Politics and Religion, 1603–60* (New York: St. Martin's Press, 1969), p. 81.

of a counterproductive exercise, since Gillespie merely used it to once more make the point that Coleman misused the authors he cited.

Criticisms of Gillespie's Anti-Erastian Writings

As with George Gillespie's other writings, the tract exchange with Thomas Coleman is not without controversy in modern literature. Gillespie's views are not sacrosanct. As Zanchius said with regard to Luther and Calvin, if you think Gillespie could not be wrong, you are making an idol for yourself.[31] However, without getting deeply into theological or exegetical questions, of which this is neither the place nor the writer to do so, some criticisms from within and from without the Presbyterian camp require addressing.

Presbyterian Criticism

From within the Presbyterian camp most of the criticism revolves around the thought by some that Gillespie, in his desire to present overwhelming arguments against Erastianism, was led into novel theological positions and novel use of Scripture in support of them.[32] In his pressing of the case for the twofold nature of Christ's kingdom, Gillespie interprets 1 Corinthians 15:25 to distinguish "the Son's eternal kingdom that 'shall be continued and exercised forever' as distinct from his mediatorial kingdom that 'shall not be continued and exercised forever.'"[33] Whatever one may think of the context in which Gillespie takes this view, it is easily resolved. While it is a minority position in Reformed theology, the view that Christ's mediatorial kingdom shall end is not a novel or heterodox one within Reformed thought, as Dr. Jonathon Beeke demonstrates and as Dr. W. D. J. Mckay acknowledges.[34]

More significant objection is made to the doctrine to which this minority view attaches. First, it has been contended by the later Reformed Presbyterian and some in the Free Church tradition that in combating Erastianism, Gillespie took the novel view of "a twofold Kingdom of Jesus Christ," wherein He rules "a general kingdom as He is the eternal Son of God, the Head of all principalities and powers, reigning over all creatures," "and a particular kingdom as He is Mediator, reigning over the church only,"[35] and failed to take

---

31. Cited in George Gillespie, *English Popish Ceremonies* (2013), p. 192.

32. W. D. J. McKay, *An Ecclesiastical Republic: Church Government in the Writings of George Gillespie*, Rutherford Studies in Historical Theology (Edinburgh: Rutherford House, 1997), page 76.

33. Jonathon David Beeke, "*Duplex Regnum Christi:* Christ's Twofold Kingdom in Reformed Theology (PhD dissertation, University of Groningen, 2021), p. 131. Gillespie first states this view in *Brotherly Examination* (see pages 231–234).

34. See *An Ecclesiastical Republic*, pp. 58–59. Turretin, taking the opposite view, calls it an 'in-house' debate amongst the Reformed. Views similar to Gillespie's were held by David Pareus and Heinrich Alting. See Beeke, ibid., pp. 131–132.

35. Gillespie, book two, chapter five, title, in *Aaron's Rod Blossoming* (1646), p. 194, and in *Works*, p. 90. See tracts herein, pages 231–234, 246, 295, 298, 316.

an undivided view of Christ's mediatorial kingdom and that as mediator Christ is king over all nations.[36] Second, W. D. J. Mckay argues for a unified view of Christ's reign, charging that Gillespie's view "in the area of Christology, explicit and implicit," "is most vulnerable to criticism."[37]

The problem with the first criticism is that it flows from a mistake in historical theology. Dr. Mckay recognizes Gillespie's view was not novel.[38] On the other hand, Dr. McKay at the same time muses that Gillespie may have been drawn to the view of the Twofold Kingdom by his quest to eradicate Erastianism to the fullest. While one may speculate that the desire to eradicate Erastianism led to a piling up of arguments that may have included weaker ones, it is pretty clear that Gillespie had been trained up, accepted, and was refuting Erastianism from within the already accepted distinction of the *Duplex Regnum Christi*.[39] Gillespie may have nuances, but all those who wrote on this subject seem to vary to some degree in addressing particular scriptures and concerns, from the earlier theologians such as Franciscus Junius[40] and Amandus Polanus (the latter whom Gillespie cites in his *Aaron's*

---

36. Cf. George Smeaton, *National Christianity and Scriptural Union: or, an exposition of the union-question. Addressed to the office-bearers, members, and adherents of the Free Church of Scotland* (Edinburgh: Johnstone & Hunter, & Co., 1871), pp. 18–19. John Fairly, *An Humble Attempt in Defence of Reformation Principles; Particularly on the Head of the Civil Magistrate* (Edinburgh: David Paterson, 1770), p. 159. "It may be evident to any judicious and intelligent reader, that Mr. Gillespie hath gone into some particular sentimental extremes in his disputations against the Erastians…. He seems to me to advance some things in defense of the truth he pleads for, really and greatly injurious to the scripture doctrine of the Mediator's supreme and universal headship of power over all persons and things…." Cited in R. Andrew Myers, *King of Nations as well as King of Saints: The Extent and Scope of the Mediatorial Kingship of Christ: Survey and Testimony of what is known as the Reformed Presbyterian (Covenanter) Distinctive* (unpublished paper, 2016), p. 167.

37. McKay, *An Ecclesiastical Republic*, p. 61.

38. Mckay, ibid., pp. 57, 76–77.

39. "The Reformed … tend to attribute the regnum universale specifically to the Second Person of the Trinity and only the regnum oeconomicum to the Godman as Mediator." Richard A. Muller, *Dictionary of Latin and Greek Theological Terms* (Baker Academic, 2017), pp. 308–309. We do not know Gillespie's particular course of theological studies (see "University Studies and Ordination" in *Shorter Writings* volume 1). However, it is very clear that Gillespie was familiar with the development of the *Duplex Regnum Christi*, as exhibited in his history of it (this follows herein beginning on page 211), and in that he was also quite conversant with the theologians who wrote on the subject, such as Polanus (whom he cites on the subject), Junius, Sharp's *Cursus Theologicus*, the Leiden professors' *Synopsis Purioris Theologiæ*, etc. See Beeke, *Duplex Regnum Christi*, throughout. See the bibliography in Gillespie, *A Dispute Against the English Popish Ceremonies* (2013).

40. Junius states the doctrine of the *Duplex Regnum Christi* thus: "For Christ as king, and the kingdom of Christ, is spoken of in two ways: first, with respect to a universal kingdom, which is a divine and eternal kingdom, common to the Father, Son, and Holy Spirit in one

Rod Blossoming), to those post-dating Gillespie, such as Peter van Mastricht, who addressed the question later in the seventeenth century.[41] The twofold nature of Christ's kingdom which restricted His mediatorial kingdom to the church, was the dominant view of the Scottish Presbyterians of the seventeenth century.[42] Later, over the course of the eighteenth century the view developed in the Reformed Presbyterian denomination that Christ's mediatorial reign was not restricted to the church but extends over the nations.[43] It became dogma to such an extent that some Reformed Presbyterian writers made it an interpretive lens to impose this later view back onto the generality of the Scottish Presbyterians of the seventeenth century.[44]

---

essence. Second, with respect to a particular kingdom (*respectu singularis regni*), in which as Mediator-King he obtains royal power over his church in his person. The first he has naturally, the later [*sic* latter] by divine dispensation." Jonathon D. Beeke, "Petrus van Mastricht and the Twofold Kingdom of Christ," in *Petrus van Mastricht (1630-1706): Text, Context, and Interpretation*, ed. Adriaan C. Neele (Göttingen: Vandenhoeck & Ruprecht, 2020), p. 52, n34.

41. See Beeke, *Duplex Regnum Christi*, throughout. See also Beeke, "van Mastricht," pp. 50–51. See Gillespie's chapter on the Twofold Kingdom of Christ in *Aaron's Rod Blossoming*, in *Works* (1846), p. 91. Gillespie writes, "The same distinction of the twofold kingdom of Christ, as God and as Mediator, is frequently to be found in Protestant writers; see [*Synopsis Purioris Theologiæ*], disp. 26, thes. 53 [possibly 52], Gomarus *in* [*Analysis Prophetiae Obadiae, in Francisci Gomari Brugensis viri clariss. Opera theologica omnia, maximam partem posthuma; suprema avtoris volvntate à discipulis edit. cum indicibus necessariis.*, volume 2, (1644), p. 544], the late *English Annotations* [1645] on 1 Cor. 15:24, and many others. Let Polanus speak for the rest" [*Syntagma theologiæ christianæ*, vol. 2 (1609), lib. 6, cap.29, cols. 2860, 2861].

42. Muller and Beeke illustrate the dominance of the view and the distinction of the two kingdoms of Christ. Ibid. See also Travis Fentiman, "All of George Gillespie's Writings on Christ's Mediatorial Kingdom is the Church Only" (2014), pp. 3–4 (https://reformedbooksonline.com/wp-content/uploads/2014/07/gillespie-george-christs-mediatorial-kingdom-is-the-church-only.pdf), and The Scottish Covenanters on Christ's Mediatorial Kingdom is the Church Only, https://reformedbooksonline.com/the-scottish-covenanters-on-christs-mediatorial-kingdom-is-the-church-only/. There is some ambiguity over Rutherford's earlier view but at the time of the Erastian controversy at the Westminster Assembly his view was clearly similar to Gillespie's. McKay, p. 140. See Rutherford, *The Due Right of Presbyteries* (1644), pp. 435–438 and his qualifications of what he wrote there in *The Divine Right of Church Government* (1646), p. 592.

43. David McKay, "From Popery to Principle: Covenanters and the Kingship of Christ, in *The Faith Once Delivered, Essays in Honor of Dr. Wayne R. Spear*, ed. Anthony T. Selvaggio (P&R Publishing, 2007), pp. 135, 156.

44. McKay, who is a minister in the Reformed Presbyterian Church of Ireland, traces the development of the Reformed Presbyterian view in "From Popery to Principle" in *The Faith Once Delivered*. The error of reading into the views and Covenants of the Scots of the seventeenth century the later view that the civil magistrate is formally under the authority of the Kingship of Christ as Mediator is made by Andrew Symington, *Introductory Lecture on the Principles of the Second Reformation* (1841) p. 13 and Johannes Vos, *The Scottish Covenanters*

Dr. McKay, who defends a view of an undivided mediatorial kingdom,[45] fears that Gillespie's views are subject to errors in Christology. This by consequence must apply to the reformed generally in the whole of the Post Reformation,[46] which after the early development of the *Duplex Regnum Christi*, was customarily treated under Christology.[47] So, *if* there are real problems, it is not just to be found in Gillespie. It would certainly be ironic to return to a unitary view as held by Romanists, Arminians, Socinians, Photinians, and Lutherans, against which the *Duplex Regnum Christi* developed in Reformed thought, simply to maintain this later distinctive of Christ reigning over the nations as mediator.[48]

In addition to his view of the twofold kingdom of Christ, some of Gillespie's arguments for it from Scripture have also been criticized. Ephesians 1:21–23 is "a key text in support of the later Covenanting doctrine of the Mediatorial Kingship of Christ over the nations," and not surprisingly, Gillespie's handling of the passage comes under criticism from those holding to that understanding. Gillespie's reading of the Greek which he supports in part from the Syriac version[49] is "That God gave Christ 'to be the head

---

([Shanghai], The author, 1940; repr. Pittsburgh: Crown and Covenant, 1980) p. 226. For a recent RP study, see the paper submitted to the Synod of the Reformed Presbyterian Church in North America, "2020 Report of Synod's Special Committee on Christ's Mediatorial Kingship."

45. McKay, *An Ecclesiastical Republic*, pp. 61–78.

46. This is not to say Dr. McKay is ignorant of broader implications. He is familiar with the development of the twofold view and its acceptance as the norm for the Reformed in the seventeenth century. McKay, *An Ecclesiastical Republic*, p. 57.

47. Beeke, *Duplex Regnum Christi*, pp. 150, 183 and n42. "Certainly by the time of Turretin's composition of his *Institutes of Elenctic Theology*, the preferred locus under which to discuss the *duplex regnum* was Christology, and more particularly within one's outline of the mediatorial office of Christ, the *munus triplex*."

48. For the Photinians (who were pre-Reformation, going back to the early church), Socinians and Lutherans, see Gillespie, *Aaron's Rod* in *Works*, pp. 90–91. See also for the Lutheran view, Heinrich Schmid, "The Regal Office," in *The Doctrinal Theology of the Evangelical Lutheran Church* (Philadelphia: Lutheran Publication Society) pp. 370–376. Rutherford explains the Arminian view in *The Divine Right of Church-Government and Excommunication* (1646), p. 614. On the Romanist view see Richard Crakanthorpe, 'That Christ had no such Temporal Monarchy, as is Now Claimed for the Pope,' in *The Defense of Constantine with a treatise of [against] the Pope's Temporal monarchy* (1621), pp. 28–41, and Thomas Barlow, "Quaeritur, An Dominium fundetur in Gratia," in *Several Miscellaneous & Weighty Cases of Conscience* (London, 1692), pp. 26–38. Thanks are due Travis Fentiman for these sources.

49. There is nothing exceptional or desperate in Gillespie citing the Syriac. It was a learned thing to do and theologians of the time often cited the Syriac to support interpretations of Scripture. Lightfoot cited from the Syriac in the assembly, to which Gillespie cited it back, correcting him (Lightfoot, Journal, p. 67; *Minutes*, 2.388), and Selden cited from it also (February 23, 1644, Session 162, *Minutes*, 2.551).

over all things to the church, which is his body;' which the Syriac reads more plainly, 'And him who is over all he gave to be the head to the church.'" In other words, Gillespie is saying that God gave Christ, who is head over all things as the eternal Son, to the church, which is his body. McKay flatly rejects that the context of the passage permits applying "head over all" to Christ as eternal Son of God. "When Christ is then described as 'head over all things' (*kephalen hyper panta*), it does violence to the context to project this headship back into eternity and ascribe it to the pre-incarnate Son alone, separating it entirely from his mediatorial work to which the rest of the passage refers."[50]

Another Scripture verse Gillespie uses is also found objectionable. Gillespie writes regarding Matthew 28:18,

> He that is Mediator, being God, has, as God, all power in heaven and earth (and this power was given to Him, Matthew 28:18, both by the eternal generation and by the declaration of Him to be the Son of God with power, when He was raised from the dead, Romans 1:4, even as He is said to be begotten when He was raised again, Acts 13:33; He had relinquished and laid aside His divine dominion and power when He had made Himself in the form of a servant, but after His resurrection it is gloriously manifested), and so He that is Mediator, being God, has power to subdue His and His church's enemies, and to make His foes His footstool [cf. Psalm 110:1]. But as Mediator He is only the church's King, Head, and Governor, and has no other kingdom.[51]

McKay objects to this limiting of the power received to Christ as the eternal Son, saying "this interpretation cannot be accepted. The one who stands before the disciples is the one who has all *exousia*, thus this authority is predicated of the God-man, the risen Christ who is also Mediator. He exercises supreme authority over all things. To import ideas of eternal generation and a pre-temporal gift of authority is not to interpret the text in its context. Jesus is making a straightforward claim to universal royal authority: he is king over all things. No distinction is made between a reign as eternal Son and a different reign as Mediator."[52]

It is not surprising that Gillespie adduced these Scripture verses. Passages such as Matthew 28:18, Ephesians 1:21 and 1 Corinthians 15:25 "are used by the Reformed scholastics in support of their essential/mediatorial distinction" in elaborating on the *Duplex Regnum Christi*."[53] So whether on

---

50. McKay, *An Ecclesiastical Republic*, p. 45, 63–64. See herein on pages 233, 246, 297.

51. *Brotherly Examination*, herein p. 231.

52. McKay, *An Ecclesiastical Republic*, p. 63. McKay concludes with a citation from Charles Hodge, "As Theanthropos and as Mediator, all power in heaven and upon earth has been committed to his hands." Charles Hodge, *Systematic Theology*, volume II (London and Edinburgh: Published by Thomas Nelson and Sons, 1872), p. 600.

53. Beeke, *Duplex Regnum Christi* p. 124, n17.

examination of bits of his argument against the Erastians he escapes criticism, or does not, Gillespie's use of these passages must be seen in the context of the Reformed case for the *Duplex Regnum Christi*, who sought to be careful in how these passages applied to Christ to combat the errors of the time they faced.

> The use of I Corinthians 15:27 is especially important in the development of the *duplex regnum Christi* doctrine…. in numerous cases (i.e., Alting, Turretin, Polyander, Thysius, Walaeus, Scharpius, and Dickson) a description and defense of the *duplex regnum Christi* occurred in the context of explaining scriptural passages such as Matthew 28:18–20 and 1 Corinthians 15:24–28. As discussed briefly below, the specific exegesis of these passages in this manner was often linked to the differing polemical concerns of the Reformed orthodox. For example, disputes with the Socinians (who, among other reasons, denied Christ's divinity on the basis that he *received* his kingship and power from the Father) forced the Reformed orthodox to refine their language and description of Christ's twofold reign. As the Socinians looked to passages such as 1 Corinthians 15:24 in support of their view, the Reformed orthodox were compelled to offer an alternative exegesis….[54]

> Mastricht is especially concerned with the Socinian argument that attempted to disprove the deity of Jesus Christ. Mastricht argues against the Socinian interpretation (based on verses such as Matt. 28:18 and Ps. 2:6) which suggested Jesus was not divine because he is a lesser and dependent king. Echoing Junius who also responded to this same Socinian challenge at the turn of the sixteenth century, Mastricht notes that the orthodox (*Orthodoxi*) used a *regnum mediatorium/regnum naturale* distinction to understand these verses. Thus, any scriptures which speak of a derived kingdom or authority held by the Son (such as found in Matthew 28 and Philippians 2) reference not the natural or essential kingdom that the Son holds equally with the Father, but his personal kingdom. According to Mastricht, a proper understanding of the *duplex regnum Christi* thus helps in the exegesis of potentially troublesome verses, and protects the full deity of Christ against those who would introduce heterodox views.[55]

As to these specific criticisms made against Gillespie's use of Scripture, we get some help in his further elaborations in *Aaron's Rod Blossoming*. On Matthew 28:18, one would think given the use of that passage just noted in defense of the *Duplex Regnum Christi*, that Gillespie would not have applied "all power" to the Second Person of the Trinity, and perhaps he might have pulled back on it in the larger work as he continued the argument begun in the Coleman tracts. In one sense he moderates or clarifies himself in that

---

54. Beeke, "van Mastricht," p. 50, n28.
55. Beeke, "van Mastricht," pp. 52–53.

he adduces the normal use in the *Duplex Regnum Christi* in application to Christ as mediator.

> When Christ said, "All power is given unto me in heaven and in earth," it may be understood either as He is Mediator, or as He is the Second Person in the blessed Trinity, the eternal Son of God…. Let it be understood of Christ as God-man, and as Mediator … yet it cannot prove that all power, without exception, and all government, as well without as within the church, as well secular as ecclesiastical, is put in Christ's hand as He is Mediator, and that the civil magistrate holds his office of and under Christ. But the sense must be: 'All power which belongs to the Mediator, and all authority which belongs to the gathering and governing of the church is given to me.' For we must needs expound His meaning as Himself has taught us (John 18:36; Luke 12:14). We must not say that any such power is given to Him as Himself denies to be given to Him, namely, civil power and magistracy.[56]

However, unafraid of minority positions, as Dr. McKay noted with regard to his view that Christ's mediatorial kingdom shall end,[57] Gillespie continued several arguments and defended the use of a second application from Matthew 28:18 to God the Son from the use of it by Gormarus against the Ubiquitaries, in his exposition of that verse in "Quæstio est; An ex hoc loco probati possit, Humanam Christi nautram esse omnipotentem."[58] He therefore, continued to maintain "two different applications of that text."[59]

As with Matthew 28:18, Gillespie did not find himself bound to one application or use of Ephesians 1:21–23. He makes this clear in a response to Mr. Coleman that spreads over the tracts in a rather tedious exchange, and elaborates in response to Mr. Hussey over several pages in *Aaron's Rod Blossoming*.[60] Gillespie's response grants two readings, neither of which would help Mr. Coleman's main point.

> First, Granting all that he says, he concludes nothing against me; for I did from the beginning expound these words [in] Ephesians 1:22, "And gave him to be the head over all things to the church," in this sense: That Christ as Mediator is given only to the church to be her head, but He that is given as Mediator to the church is "over all." So that the giving of Christ there spoken of is as

---

56. Gillespie, *Aaron's Rod Blossoming* (1646), p. 200, and in *Works* (1846), p. 99.

57. McKay, *An Ecclesiastical Republic*, pp. 58–59.

58. Franciscus Gomarus, "Quæstio est; An ex hoc loco probati possit, Humanam Christi nautram esse omnipotentem," in *Illustrium ac Selectorum Ex Euangelio Matthæi, locorum explicatio*, in *Opera Theologica Omnia, Maximam partem; suprema autoris voluntate a discipulis edita* (Amsterdam: Jansson, 1644), p. 189.

59. Gillespie, ibid., p. 199–201.

60. Gillespie, *Aaron's Rod Blossoming*, in *Works*, pp. 104–107. The reader may pursue the unfolding argument in the tracts on pages 233, 246, 297.

> Mediator, and He is given to the church only, which I cleared by the Syriac, "And him who is over all he gave to be the head to the church." But His being "over all" there spoken of, if understood of glory, dignity, excellency over all, so [*then*] Christ is "over all" as Mediator (yea, in regard of the exaltation of His human nature), and this helps not Mr. Coleman, who intends to prove from that place that all government, even civil, is given to Christ as Mediator. But if understood of a kingdom and government "over all," so [*then*] He is "over all" as He is the eternal Son of God or Second Person of the Trinity, and not as Mediator.[61]

By the end of the seventeenth century, there had been continued theological tinkering with the *Duplex Regnum Christi*, introducing a universal aspect to Christ's mediatorial kingdom, presaging perhaps the later Presbyterian view. Petrus van Mastricht held to "the by-then formalized twofold kingship of Christ; as the Son is divine, he holds an essential kingship in common with the Father and Spirit, but as theandric mediator, he is given a governance and kingdom by the Father for the specific purposes of redemption." However, he adds a twofold nature of Christ's power, and "makes the case that it is the mediatorial or personal kingship of Christ that can be considered either universally or particularly. In other words, while it is undoubtedly the case that the Son's essential authority—like the Father's and the Spirit's—is universally over all … Mastricht is equally clear that Christ's personal kingship is also universal; it extends, he says, over all creatures…." Drawing on Ephesians 1:19–23 and other passages, Mastricht "qualifies that the purpose of this universal, mediatorial authority centers on Christ's church." Christ's "personal or mediatorial authority" "is particular," which particular redemptive power of Christ has a threefold distinction; it is evident in this age … at the end of this age … and in the future age …." He then opines cryptically that "with these distinctions it is easy to consider how one might be subject to this kingdom"; in general, "including the world and all things contained in it, or specially … including specifically the church…."[62] From another place we know that Mastricht was familiar with the Erastian controversy in England and considered Rutherford and Gillespie to be heroes. [63] Perhaps he had the English controversy in mind as he teased out his own view of the *Duplex Regnum Christi*. Unfortunately, as said, Mastricht ends the discussion and does not present specific examples of problems his further distinctions might solve,

---

61. *Malè Audis*, herein on page 297.

62. Beeke, "Mastricht," p. 50, 51.

63. Petrus van Mastricht, *Theoretico-practica theologia*, 2 vols. (Utrecht on the Rhine: Thomæ Appels, 1699), 2.1072. "Nata a Thomâ Erasto, olim Medico Heidelbergensi A. 1565. adoptata in Anglia a Colemanno quodam, Cocionatore Londinensi: qui cum diffentientes observaret, Presbyteriales et Independentes; universum Ecclesiae regimen, transtulit ad Magistratum civilem, qui per Intermisticos Consiliarios gubernaret Ecclesiam, cui se fortiter opposuerunt Scoti, interque eos nominatim G. Gillespy, et Samuel Rheturforetes."

to gauge if Gillespie and the seventeenth century Scottish divines may have already addressed them sufficiently without Maßtricht's further dißinctions.

To sum up Presbyterian criticism, Gillespie is not beyond criticism and his views are certainly open to inßpection. However, one does not have to agree with every aßpect of his argumentation to agree with his general case. He is certainly within the Reformed tradition in his underßtanding of the *Duplex Regnum Chrißi* in his dißpute againßt Eraßianism.

CRITICISM FROM OUTSIDE PRESBYTERIANISM

From secular or at leaßt non-Presbyterian writers, there is of course the partisan literature which caßts Coleman for the hero and Gillespie as the evil villain laughing gleefully in triumph at the Eraßian's sudden and unexpected death.[64] Others obsess over the aptness or fairness of the term Eraßian. Juß as the term Independent derived from those defending independent churches in the early 1640s,[65] the term Eraßian was coined at the time of the debates of the Weßtminßter assembly over church government and church discipline to describe that faction of the divines advocating the adoption of the views of Thomas Eraßus.[66] Gillespie appears to be the firß

---

64. Lamont, p. 114. In his account of the origins of Erastianism in *Aaron's Rod Blossoming*, Gillespie says with regard to Coleman, "The Lord was pleased to remove him by death before he could do what he intended in this and other particulars." Lamont characterized this statement as something Gillespie chortled. See herein on page 218.

65. While Gillespie disputed against their views as well, he was far friendlier with the Dissenting Brethren of the assembly, and rarely used the Independent label to which they objected. In contrast, in the sermon preached by Thomas Coleman that sparked the public dispute with Gillespie, Coleman freely used the term Independent before the whole House of Commons to describe the congregationalists of the assembly. Coleman, *Hopes Deferred*, pp. 24, 27. For Gillespie's softer disposition toward the Independents, see Van Dixhoorn, *Minutes*, 1.30, and "Presbyterian ecclesiologies at the Westminster assembly," in *Church Polity*, location 3294.

66. There is no current proof for an earlier use of "Erastian" dating to the time of the debate between Gillespie and Selden in February 1644, or thereafter, though it may have been coined by or before then. It came into use by the time the Commons made clear it did not want church censures out of their own hands (March 5 and March 25, 1645; see prior note 9 on page 184). The assembly debated excommunication with one reference to Erastus in session 225 on May 23, 1644 (*Minutes*, 3.117). The first recorded use of the term is by Robert Baillie who uses it in a letter to Spang as early as April 25, 1645. "It has been a mighty neglect that no man has answered Erastus's reply to Beza. The most of the House of Commons are downright Erastians: they are like to create us much more woe than all the sectaries of England." Gillespie writes in a letter dated May 9, 1645, "The House of Commons has passed other two votes, sore against the mind of the Erastian party." Baillie again writes to his cousin Spang in a letter dated circa May to June 1645. "The Erastian party in the Parliament is stronger than the Independent." He uses it frequently in letters from August 1645 to August 1646. Baillie, 2.265, 267, 277, 307, 315, 318, 506. Baillie uses the term "Erastian-Civilian" and "Erastians" in his *A Dissuasive from the Errours of the Time* (1645), pp. 6, 252,

to use the term in print.[67] John Selden would later complain that the term was imprecise and therefore unfair, and modern writers picking up on that have expressed displeasure with the term by enclosing the word within scare quotes, with some fixating on it as an intentional or tactical slur.[68] Charles Gunnoe gives three definitions of the term Erastian in his definitive study of Thomas Erastus. The first definition describes Tudor dominance of the state over the church, and the third is used in the Hobbesian sense of "the absolute right of the state to determine religious policy, regardless of the theological orthodoxy of the magistrate." The second definition is the primary and "authentic use of the term,"[69] which describes the very English controversy under review. It is true that most of the members of parliament were not doctrinal Erastians. They simply either from fear of a church with authority to discipline morals or from craving the Tudoresque power of the first use of the term, did not want a church government independent from the state. But it seems clear enough that it would only be natural for those opposed to advocates of Erastus's views to call the doctrinal Erastians and those led by them by that term. Certainly, all the men Gillespie engaged were true Erastians in the primary use of the label. That Coleman opposed any government other than state government and would have published Erastus's work, and that Selden, despite complaining about the imprecision of its application, fully defended Erastus's rejection of excommunication, which the Zürich school even found extreme, seems to indicate the label fit them both perfectly well.[70] It was certainly a negative or pejorative term, as are most terms coined to describe error. It was the manner of discourse of the times. Worse things were hurled at the Presbyterians, and the Erastians were not opposed to using labels in high places, such as Coleman's use of "Independent" in his sermon before the House of Commons.[71]

---

which according to Thomason was available in print as early as November 24, 1645 (see ESTC record R200539).

67. Gillespie uses the term in print in *Brotherly Examination,* and then in *Nihil Respondes,* and then in the title and throughout *Male Audis.* See herein on pages, 222, 253, 255, 267, 272, 286, 292, 293, 300, 301, 315, 316. It of course figures in *Aaron's Rod Blossoming* as well. Thomason purchased a copy on August 4, 1646, but Gillespie had copies to hand out in the assembly on July 30. *Minutes,* 4.219–220. ESTC R202013.

68. For instance, Elliot Vernon repeatedly calls the term Erastian a slur, making it a part of the structure of one paper in portraying Coleman as turning Gillespie's intent to prejudice his views into a badge of honor by embracing the term and triumphing through the parliament's taking confidence from his arguments. "They agree not in opinion among themselves': two-kingdoms theory, 'Erastianism' and the Westminster assembly debate on church and state, c. 1641–48," in *Church Polity and Politics in the British Atlantic World,* location 3870, 3750, 4118, 4134. See also, *London presbyterians,* pp. 6, 120.

69. Gunnoe, p. 136.

70. On Selden's "full-blown" embrace of Erastus see Gunnoe, ibid., pp. 406–407.

71. Coleman, *Hopes Deferred,* p. 24.

Another criticism revolves around the question of "who won?" It is claimed that Thomas Coleman triumphed in a manner of speaking for adducing the Zürich "one-sphere" view which gave parliament the theological cover needed to withstand the advice coming from the assembly for recognizing church censures in the hands of the church by divine right.[72] However, Coleman actually does not explicitly marshal this argument from the Zürich divines. The perfect occasion to do so would have been in his remarks in his sermon before the House of Commons in the first place, but he does not. He does not adduce such support until his *Re-examination* in which he responds directly to Gillespie's query in *Brotherly Examination*, "will the brother say that the example of the best reformed churches leads us his way; that is, to have no church government at all distinct from the civil government?" In asking this, did Gillespie set himself up or did he set a trap for Coleman? The latter simply responds with no citations, "The opinions of Gualther, Bullinger, Erastus, Aretius, and others, are known." Coleman did not take the bait. He makes no explicit case for Erastianism from the Zürich model. Perhaps he knew full well that because he took Erastus's view on excommunication, which Bullinger thought extreme, that such sources might prove a double-edged sword. He may also not have wished to undermine the Erastian case made in the Commons two months earlier by Selden and Whitelocke by giving Gillespie an opportunity to counter them. Regardless, Gillespie persisted in his *Nihil Respondes*, and adduced the views of Gualther, Bullinger, and Aretius on excommunication against Coleman's and Erastus's view that "the entire concept of excommunication was without theological justification or biblical merit."[73] As to the milder Zürich view, Gillespie argued that it was practices of churches, not the views of men, and "best" reformed churches at that, which were to be the guide as was spelled out in the Solemn League and Covenant, going on to note why Zürich did not meet that sworn guidance. In response, Coleman still did not explicitly delineate or use the Zürich model but made three additional citations that were beside the point and Gillespie had to remind him once again of the actual question between them.

> The reverend brother, notwithstanding of their plain testimonies, speaking for me and against him in the main controversy between him and me, does still allege that they are for him, not for me (*Malè Dicis*, p. 23), yet he does not so much as offer any answer to their testimonies by me cited, only he brings three other passages of theirs, intimating that there may be a true church without excommunication; that they thought it not necessary where they lived; that they thought it hard, yea impossible … to introduce excommunication in those parts, by which citations the brother has proved nothing against me, but confirmed what I said. Let him remember first,

---

72. Vernon, *Church Polity and Politics*, location 4134; *London Presbyterians*, pp. 120–121.

73. Gunnoe, p. 190.

he himself makes the main controversy between him and me about the scriptural warrants of church censures; now in that, they are clearly against him.[74]

When one compares the tracts in the exchange it is a wonder that anyone would even try to portray Coleman as the victor. Baillie calls Coleman,[75] "a man reasonably learned, but stupid [*dull-witted*] and inconsiderate, half a pleasant [*fool*], and of small estimation. But the lawyers in the Parliament … did blow up the poor man with much vanity;[76] so he is become their champion to bring out in the best way he can Erastus's arguments … for the contentment of the Parliament." Even discounting the insulting nature of Baillie' characterization, it seems clear by simply comparing the tracts of the two, that Thomas Coleman was a bit out of his weight class in this sparring match with George Gillespie.

Clearly Gillespie was the victor in the battle with Thomas Coleman. However, what about the overall war between the assembly and the Commons? In the end, the assembly lost the effort to have church discipline only in the hands of the church.[77] It is claimed that the citation of the Zürich divines by Coleman and the Erastians gave the parliament a successful theological argument to retain the English tradition of subverting the church to the

---

74. *Malè Audis*, p. 312.

75. Baillie, 2.360.

76. While one should always take Baillie's gossipy opinions with a grain of salt, he seems to be on target with pegging vanity as an issue for Coleman. That he had it recorded in the July 31 session after his July 30 fast sermon that he had not given any negative vote against the petition itself but only against the slam against Erastus's learning (that he was a better doctor than a theologian), indicates it may be that it was the implication in the slight against his own learning that motivated him to speak against the assembly in his sermon, and not the petition itself. His appeal to the fact that the Commons had ordered his sermon printed as some sort of imprimatur on his views implies an undue importance attached to that fact when almost everyone's fast sermon was ordered printed and the preacher thanked (see Coleman's *Brotherly Examination Re-examined*, page 3, and *Malè Audis*, herein on page 316). In fact, in a somewhat unusual advertisement for such sermons, the printer of Coleman's *Hopes Deferred* noted at the end of the epistle dedicatory, that Coleman's prior three sermons on public occasions had been so ordered printed also, which he then listed out for the readers' information. Now, perhaps this was all the printer's idea (maybe they needed advertising because sales were slow!), but all these things together seem to comport with Baillie's assessment of some vanity in Coleman.

77. Looking strictly at the result in the parliament to Coleman's vague reference to the Zürich divines (although he does not portray it this way), Vernon opines that Gillespie's response was lame and that Coleman won in effect because the Erastians in the Commons adduced a reformed pattern of government that allowed parliament to keep the authority of church censures in their hands rather than in the church's as the Presbyterians pressed from Scripture and the example of the best reformed churches. *Church Polity*, location 4140.

ſtate.[78] Selden had after all used Coleman's illicitly preached dissent to the assembly's advice in an effort to discredit the divines. Whether or not it was by design and Coleman had been encouraged by Selden or others to make the comments he did in *Hopes Deferred*,[79] it is the case that he was simply a tool for the Eraſtians in the Commons to oppose and negate by any means necessary the advice of the overwhelming majority of the assembly. Because they were the minority, the Eraſtians, like the Independents, circumvented the assembly of divines, which the parliament had appointed as the means to determine the queſtion. Was the appeal to Zürich consequential? Except for maybe salving consciences with a reason members of parliament could point to for rejeċting the assembly's advice, not really. The Commons was never going to agree to a church's right to exercise its own discipline separate from their government.[80] Baillie writes that in addition to the few Independents in the Commons who with their counterparts in the assembly were intent to delay till they obtained a full toleration for congregationaliſt churches, and the several "lawyers" (Selden, Whitelocke, etc.), advocating Eraſtian ſtate control of the church and church censures, "a third party of worldly profane men who are extremely affrighted to come under the yoke of ecclesiaſtic discipline"[81] made up two-thirds or more "of the total membership of Parliament."[82] The parliament had already and persistently refused to grant authority of church discipline to elders and paſtors before Coleman and Gilleſpie had their diſpute, and continued to rejeċt

---

78. Coleman "provided clerical backing for the arguments of those, like Selden and Whitelocke, who were skeptical of the presbyterians' divine right theory." Vernon, *London Presbyterians*, p. 121.

79. See *Malè Audis*, herein page 312, and n123.

80. Vernon writes that doubts remained in the Commons as far as challenging the assembly of theologians they had appointed on this matter. However, the reference he cites in Cliffe is about concerns some in the Commons had about citing the assembly for breach of privilege in April 1646. The passage is not about any great reticence to oppose "the advice and learning of the Westminster assembly on matters of ecclesiastical jurisdiction." As is clear, they had been doing that before, during, and after the Coleman-Gillespie dispute. See J. T. Cliffe, *Puritans in conflict: The Puritan Gentry during and after the Civil Wars* (New York: Routledge, 1988), p. 128–129.

81. See Baillie, 2.336 and Cliffe, p. 123. There were always too few true Presbyterians to make any difference in the parliament. The London Presbyterians outside the assembly would try other means to convince parliament to yield, such as refusing to implement the ordinances they issued, but this was not successful any more than the reasoned arguments of the Westminster divines. See Vernon, *London Presbyterians*, p. 121.

82. Ibid. Apparently the character of Selden and Whitelocke was not any better than Baillie's two-thirds. "An anonymous correspondent in a letter to [Richard] Baxter distinguished men close to Erastus's views, such as Coleman, Lightfoot and Stillingfleet, from 'ill principled men['] such as Selden, Grotius and Hobbes, 'as bad as can be.' Doctor William's Library, Baxter MSS. 59.6, f.192v. Cited in Lamont, pp. 116, 133.

the assembly's plea not to have an Erastian church settlement instead of recognizing the right of the church to exercise her own discipline.[83] The *jure divino* Presbyterians of the assembly simply as a point of faith believed that "Christ's royal law was as binding with regard to church government as it was with regard to doctrine."[84] When the controversy came to a head in April 1646 and the assembly reproved the Commons, telling them their ordinance retaining church censures in the state's hands was "contrary to that Way of Government which Christ hath appointed in His Church, in that it giveth a Power to judge of the Fitness of Persons to come to the Sacrament unto such as our Lord Christ hath not given that Power unto," the assembly received the censure of breach of privilege for their testimony.[85]

The House of Commons complained bitterly that they had given the assembly everything they wanted except for the right of the church to exercise church discipline on her own authority through her elders. Such a complaint stubbornly overlooked the height of impiety it was "to wrest this rule of Christ from him and give it to the counsels, wills, or laws of men."[86]

It is not a wonder that worldly minded politicians would desire such authority over the church, but it is passing strange why any Christian would champion the Erastian view today "considering the repugnance of most Christians to accept the claim the magistrate has the right to settle a nation's religion. Particularly after the totalitarian experiments of the twentieth century, what person of faith would want to give the state carte blanche authority over the church",[87] and even more so given the general hostility to orthodox Christian morality in Western Civilization today? Gillespie did defend a proper role for the civil government in the affairs of the church.[88] If a Christian government limited itself to its own place and the church, from the result of a new revival in the nation, called a national synod, and the government listened to its advice, perhaps the outcome would be a new reformation?

---

83. See the introduction to Gillespie's sermon before the House of Lords, page 138.

84. McKay, "From Popery to Principle," p. 138.

85. For more on the censure, see *Jus Divinum Regiminis Ecclesiastici*, NPSE volume II (2020), pp. 14–19. The Commons went beyond censuring and published nine queries it insisted the assembly must answer "in a public effort to discredit the claim that presbyterian discipline was required by Scripture…." *Minutes*, 1.78. The assembly's answer by proxy can be seen in *Jus Divinum Regiminis Ecclesiastici*. See the authors' argument against Erastianism in part two, chapter nine, pp. 120–145.

86. McKay, "From Popery to Principle," p. 138.

87. Gunnoe, p. 404.

88. See herein, page 230. See *III Propositions*, #94–97 herein on pages 430 and 431, and *Aaron's Rod Blossoming*, in *Works*, page 97–98, and *Aaron's Rod* again in book two, chapter eight, "Of the Power and Privilege of the Magistrate in Things and Causes Ecclesiastical; What it is not, and What it is," pp. 114–124.

The Erastian Controversy

William M. Hetherington[1]

A FULL ACCOUNT of the literature of the Erastian controversy would be an extremely interesting and highly important production; but to attempt anything more than a very brief outline of it here would lead to a digression far beyond our limits. We shall therefore mention almost solely those works which were either written by some of the Westminster Divines, or were closely connected with the proceedings of that venerable Assembly. A few preliminary sentences, however, may be of use to introduce the subject.

During the earliest ages of Christianity the only relationship in which the civil magistrate and the church stood towards each other, was that which exists between persecutors and the persecuted. When at length Constantine avowed himself a Christian, persecution ceased, and the more friendly relation of granting and receiving protection became that between the State and the church. But Christianity had already become deeply tainted with the antichristian leaven; prelacy had raised its haughty head, equally inclined to domineer over what it regarded as the inferior orders of the clergy, and over the people, and to arrogate to itself exemption from the control of the civil magistrate, even in civil matters. A protracted struggle ensued between the imperial and royal powers and the Bishop of Rome, the issue of which was, not merely an exemption of ecclesiastical matters, and even persons, from civil authority, but the establishment of a supremacy over civil rulers and civil matters wielded by the Romish hierarchy, and forming a complete spiritual and civil despotism. This fearful and degrading despotism was overthrown by the Reformation: and although the great and wise Christian divines and patriots by whose instrumentality the Reformation was effected, were unable entirely to perfect their work, yet they all, more or less clearly, indicated their judgment that the two jurisdictions, civil and ecclesiastical, ought to be, and to remain co-ordinate and distinct, mutually supporting and supported, but each abstaining from interference with the other's intrinsic and inherent rights, privileges, and powers. In some countries this high and true theory was clearly developed, in others more obscurely, and in some not at all. In no part of Reformed Christendom was it so distinctly stated, and so fully realized, as in Scotland; and nowhere was it so thoroughly rejected as in England. In England, indeed, the exact counterpoint of the Romish system was established, the king's ecclesiastical supremacy rendering him equally

---

1. [From William M. Hetherington, *History of the Westminster Assembly of Divines* (1843), fifth edition edited by Robert Williamson (New York: Randolph, 1890), pp. 289–302.]

judge of ecclesiastical as of civil matters. It was soon found that in this, as in all other things, extremes meet; the king, by a slight transfer of terms, became a civil pope, and the country was oppressed by a complete civil and spiritual despotism.

In the meantime, the great principle of truth and freedom, the principle of distinct and co-ordinate civil and ecclesiastical jurisdictions, was assailed on the Continent by Erastus, and became a subject of speculative thought and controversial literature. Unfortunately for the cause of truth and freedom, the great men of the Reformation had nearly all departed from the scene of their labors and triumphs before the Erastian theory was fully brought forward, so that it was not at once met and overthrown as it would otherwise have been. And besides, it was too accordant with the views and feelings of men of secular minds not to obtain a ready credence and a hearty welcome from politicians, who can form no higher idea of a church than an engine of State; from lawyers, who can conceive no higher rule than statutory enactments; and from irreligious and immoral men, who equally detest and fear the strict and pure severity of divinely authorized Christian discipline. In England, also, the despotism of the Prelatic hierarchy tended to produce, in the minds of all zealous assertors of freedom, an instinctive dread of ecclesiastical power, and rendered many men Erastians from terror and in self-defense, not because they had studied the theory, and been convinced of its truth. Such men were ready to oppose the establishment of Presbyterian church government on the ground of divine right, not because they were convinced that no system of church government can justly lay claim to an authority so high and sacred; but because they were apprehensive that it would produce a species of spiritual despotism as oppressive as that which they had just been striving to abolish. In vain did the Scottish statesmen and divines answer and refute their objections; their fears were not removed, and fear is a mental emotion that cannot be set aside by argument.

But Selden, Whitelocke, Lightfoot, and Coleman, took up the subject on other grounds, which, though difficult, were not equally unassailable by reason. Their chief argument was one of analogy, although, as they used it, the appearance which it bore was that of identity. They held that the Christian system ought to resemble, or rather to be identical with, the system of the Mosaic Dispensation; and they attempted to prove that there were not two distinct and co-ordinate courts, one civil and the other ecclesiastical, among the Hebrews, but that there was a mixed jurisdiction, of which the king was the supreme and ultimate head and ruler; and that, consequently, the civil courts determined all matters, both civil and ecclesiastical, and inflicted all punishments, both such as affected person and property, and such as affected a man's religious privileges, properly termed church censures. From this they concluded that the civil magistrate, in countries avowedly Christian, ought to possess an equal, or identical authority, and ought consequently to be the supreme and ultimate judge in all matters, both civil and ecclesiastical, inflicting or removing the penalties of church censure equally with those affecting person and property. The arguments on which they most relied were drawn from rabbinical lore, rather than from the Bible itself, although they were very willing to obtain the appearance of its support, by ingenious versions, or perversions of peculiar passages of Scripture. Selden's argument has been already stated,[2] and need not be repeated. The value of Lightfoot's authority may be estimated somewhat lower than is usually done, if we take into consideration, not merely the amount of his learning, but the soundness, or the reverse, of his judgment. As for instance, he strenuously maintained that the Jews are utterly and finally rejected, that those of them who embraced Christianity in the time of Christ and the apostles were the "remnant to be saved," and that there neither then was, nor ever shall be, any universal calling of them."[3] He held also that the expressions, "the keys of the kingdom of heaven," and " binding and loosing," had no reference to discipline, but merely to doctrine; in which opinion he differed from almost every person, both before and since his time. His opinion of the Septuagint was equally at variance with the views of the most eminently learned and judicious men. In short, whatever may be said of his extensive and minute rabbinical lore, it is impossible to regard his judgment as entitled to much deference; consequently his advocacy of Erastian principles will not avail much for their support.

Mention has already been made of Coleman's sermon, preached before the House of Commons, on the 30th of July 1645.[4] That sermon must be noticed as part of the Erastian literature, not so much on account of its own merits, as on account of other works to the composing of which it gave occasion. Towards the end of the sermon, various advices and directions are given, as calculated to promote the peace and welfare of the kingdom; and of these, one point on which Coleman dwelt strongly was, the unity of the church, and the best way to procure that unity. For this he gives several directions, of which the following are the chief:

> 1. Establish as few things jure divino as can well be. Hold out the practice, but not the ground. 2. Let all precepts held out as divine institutions have clear scriptures; an occasional practice, a phrase upon the by, a thing named, are too weak grounds to uphold such a building. I could never yet see how two co-ordinate governments, exempt from superiority and inferiority, can be in one State; and in Scripture no such thing is found that I know of. 3. Lay no more burden of government upon the shoulders of ministers than Christ hath plainly laid upon them; let them have no more hand therein than the Holy Ghost clearly gives them. The ministers will have other work to do, and such as will take up the whole man. I ingeniously profess I have a heart that knows better how to be governed than to govern. I fear an ambitious

---

2. [See Hetherington, *History*, pp. 248–249.]

3. Lightfoot, *Works*, 1.165.

4. [Hetherington, *History*, p. 247.]

ensnarement; and I have cause. I see what raised prelacy and Papacy to such a height; and what their practices were, being so raised. Give us doctrine; take you the government. Give me leave to make this request, in the name of the ministry; give us two things, and we shall do well:—give us learning, and give us a competency. 4. A Christian magistrate, as a Christian magistrate, is a governor in the church. All magistrates, it is true, are not Christians; but that is their fault: all should be; and when they are, they are to manage their office under and for Christ. Christ hath placed governments in His church. Of other governments besides magistracy I find no institution; of them I do. I find all government given to Christ, and to Christ as Mediator; and Christ, as head of these, given to the church. To rob the kingdom of Christ of the magistrate and his governing power, I cannot excuse, no, not from a kind of sacrilege, if the magistrate be His.[5]

Sentiments such as these could not but be agreeable to the Erastian members of Parliament; yet they seem to have thought that Coleman had spoken with more plainness than prudence, for while they ordered the sermon to be printed, as was customary, they did not give him the thanks of the House— an omission which was extremely unusual.[6] But the principles stated in Coleman's sermon were not allowed to remain long unassailed. On the 27TH of August George Gillespie preached a sermon before the House of Lords; and when it was published, he appended to it a small pamphlet of nine leaves, entitled, *A Brotherly Examination of some Passages of Mr. Coleman's late printed Sermon.* In this short treatise, Gillespie not only answered and refuted Coleman, but also completely turned his arguments against himself; proving, *first,* that the proper rule for human conduct in all things, but especially in religious matters, was to obtain as much of divine guidance, or to establish as much by divine right, as possible. He then proceeds to examine in succession Coleman's directions or rules in a very masterly manner, annihilating or reversing each with great strength and clearness of argument. It is proved that Coleman's principle that in every divine institution Scripture must speak expressly, would involve a dangerous tampering with Scripture, and would sweep away several important Christian institutions which were never doubted: and also that whatever, by necessary consequence, is drawn from Scripture, is a divine truth, as well as what is expressly written therein. The argument of coordinate jurisdiction is next taken up, and thoroughly established both by argument and by illustration. And in answer to Coleman's assertion that he can find no institution of any government except magistracy, Gillespie proves from Scripture that obedience is directly commanded to spiritual governors, who are "over us in the Lord," and who must have been

---

5. Coleman's Sermon, pp. 24–28.

6. [Hetherington may have had in view the August 9 second order to print, because it is rather the case that Coleman was indeed thanked by the House of Commons in the usual manner on July 30, 1645. House of Commons Journal, vol. 4, p. 224.]

distinct from the civil magistrate at a time when there was no Christian magistracy. In a short, but very clearly stated argument, Gillespie refutes Coleman's dangerous assertion, "That all government is given to Christ as Mediator, and Christ, as head of these, given to the church;" and states the distinction between Christ's government as God and as Mediator,—by the right understanding of which important idea the whole Erastian controversy must be decided.

Coleman soon afterwards published a pamphlet entitled, *A Brotherly Examination Re-examined*, which is distinguished chiefly by boldness of assertion and feebleness of argument. To this Gillespie replied in another, bearing the title, *Nihil Respondes*, in which he somewhat sharply exposed the weakness of his antagonist's reasoning. Irritated by the castigation he had received, Coleman published a bitter reply, to which he gave the not very intelligible title of *Male Dicis Maledicis*,—meaning, doubtless, that Gillespie's answer was rather of a railing character, or, to use a phrase of modern times, displayed a bad spirit. This Gillespie answered in an exceedingly vigorous pamphlet, entitled, *Malè Audis*, in which he swept rapidly over the whole Erastian controversy, so far as Coleman and some of his friends had brought it forward, convicted him and them of numerous self-contradictions, of unsoundness in theology, of violating the covenant which they had sworn, and of inculcating opinions fatal to both civil and religious liberty. To this Coleman did not attempt to reply, feeling, probably, that he was overmatched.

Several of these controversial pamphlets appeared in the course of the year 1646; and towards the close of the same year,[7] Gillespie published his celebrated work, *Aaron's Rod Blossoming; or, The Divine Ordinance of Church Government Vindicated*. In this remarkably able and elaborate production, Gillespie took up the Erastian controversy as stated and defended by its ablest advocates, fairly encountering their strongest arguments, and assailing their most formidable positions, in the frank and fearless manner of a man thoroughly sincere, and thoroughly convinced of the truth and goodness of his cause. The work is divided into three books; the *first* treating "Of the Jewish Church Government;" the *second*, "Of the Christian Church Government;" and the *third*, "Of Excommunication from the Church, and of Suspension from the Lord's Table." In the first book the five following propositions are demonstrated:

> 1. That the Jewish Church was formerly distinct from the Jewish State. 2. That there was an ecclesiastical sanhedrim and government distinct from the civil. 3. That there was an ecclesiastical excommunication distinct from civil punishments. 4. That in the Jewish Church there was also a public exomologesis, or declaration of repentance, and thereupon a reception or admission again of the offender to fellowship with the church in the holy things. 5. That there was a suspension of the profane from the temple and passover.

---

7. [*Aaron's Rod* appeared earlier than this; see note 67, page 198.]

In this part of his work Gillespie boldly met and completely overthrew the united strength of Selden, Lightfoot, and Coleman, on their own chosen field of Hebrew learning.

In the second book or part of his work, "Of the Christian Church Government," the main element of the controversy which he had to encounter is of a nature so abstract that it requires peculiar clearness of thought and accuracy of reasoning to keep the subject intelligible, and to draw the requisite distinctions. Coleman had in his sermon said that, "a Christian magistrate, as a Christian magistrate, is a governor in the church;" and that "all government is given to Christ as Mediator, and Christ, as head of these, is given to the church:" from this he drew, though not very distinctly, the inference that the Christian magistrate is directly the vicegerent of Christ, and therefore rules in the church; yet when pushed on this point he recoiled and modified his inference so as to state it in the following terms, "that magistracy is given to Christ to be serviceable in His kingdom." But this modified statement would not have answered the purposes of the Erastians; and therefore their principle was more boldly and plainly expressed by Mr. Hussey, minister at Chesilhurst, in Kent. This thorough Erastian boldly maintained, both "that all government is given to Christ as Mediator, and that Christ, as Mediator, has placed the Christian magistrate under Him, and as His vicegerent, and has given him commission to govern the church."[8] It will be at once perceived that the very terms of this proposition involved an inquiry into the nature and extent of Christ's mediatorial sovereignty. To this point, accordingly, Gillespie directed his attention in his answer to Hussey's argument. He draws the distinction between the power and sovereignty of Christ as the Eternal Son of God and as God-man and Mediator. Considered as the Eternal Son of God, as the Word by whom the universe was called into being, He necessarily rules over all, and magistrates derive their power from Him: considered as God-man and Mediator, His direct sovereignty is in and over the church, which is His body; and all power has been given to Him both in heaven and in earth to be wielded by Him for the safety and the extension of His spiritual kingdom. A further distinction is drawn by Gillespie betwixt *power over* and *power in* any kingdom, which are not necessarily identical, although the one may be employed for the purpose of promoting and securing the other. In this argument, some have thought that Gillespie has drawn his distinctions too fine, more so than was necessary for his argument, or than many would be able to follow or willing to admit. Beyond all question, he has overthrown the Erastian theory, "that the civil magistrate is Christ's vicegerent, and appointed to govern the church"; but some have been afraid that one aspect of his argument might seem to countenance the Voluntary theory, and to exempt civil government from the duty and responsibility of giving countenance and support to the church. Certainly no such idea was

---

8. [This is Gillespie's summary of William Hussey's position (*Aaron's Rod*, cf. *Works*, p. 104) citing *A Plea for Christian Magistracy* (1646), pp. 32–33.]

ever in Gillespie's mind, nor is it my opinion that his reasoning, rightly understood, gives it the least shadow of support. Besides, if there be any danger arising from the extreme fineness with which his distinctions are drawn in that branch of his argument, it is completely removed by the succeeding chapter in which he treats "of the power and privilege of the magistrate in things and causes ecclesiastical, what it is, and what it is not."[9] It would be well if magistrates would study carefully the passage alluded to, that they might acquire some information respecting the proper nature and boundaries of their duties and responsibilities *circa sacra*, about religious matters, as distinguished from what they have always been so eager to usurp, power *in sacris*, in religious matters, which forms no part of their peculiar duty, and is not within their province.

The third book, "Of Excommunication from the Church, and of Suspension from the Lord's Table," has the appearance of being an answer to Prynne, who had written largely against the exercise of such power by church-officers. But it is evident that Gillespie had more in view than merely to answer Prynne. He makes no express reference to the Parliament's *jus divinum* queries, but he meets them nevertheless, and gives to them very conclusive answers, while appearing to be merely replying to a less formidable antagonist. The very tenor of Prynne's writings gave him this opportunity, for Prynne kept as closely to the line of the parliamentary queries as he with propriety could, so that Gillespie was both enabled and fairly entitled to answer both at once, so far as they were identical or similar. The work, in short, is a very complete refutation of the whole Erastian theory, taking up its leading points systematically, clearing away all obscurities of language, reducing every argument to its elementary principles, stating these in the form of simple propositions, and in terms strictly defined, so as to preclude sophistry or mere verbal subtleties, and proceeding to refute error and demonstrate truth, in a manner singularly clear and forcible, displaying, each in a very high degree, extensive learning, sound judgment, intellectual acuteness and strength, and the pure and lofty spirit of genuine Christianity.

Another able and elaborate work on the Erastian controversy was written and published also in the year 1646 by Samuel Rutherford, entitled, *The Divine Right of Church Government and Excommunication*. Although Rutherford manifests a thorough understanding of the subject, and treats very fully of all its main elements, exhibiting great learning and extreme minuteness in thought, argument, and illustration, his work is not, upon the whole, so successful as that of Gillespie. It is defective in point of arrangement, and especially for want of a statement of the systematic order which the author meant to follow, though it is perfectly plain that in his own mind there was a system by which he regulated his course of argument. But the very minuteness of his learning and his reasonings is felt to obscure, or rather to overlay the subject; and while tracing out every point of detail, the general

---

9. *Aaron's Rod*, book 2, chapter 8, p. 114–124.

impression is either weakened, or fails to be forcibly conveyed. This, however, is criticism according to modern taste; for the style of the times when
Rutherford wrote, was to exhaust every subject under discussion, and to leave
nothing unsaid upon it that could be said. In this respect, therefore, Rutherford merely followed the spirit of the age in which he lived; and whosoever
will carefully peruse his very elaborate work, will obtain ample materials for
the refutation of Erastianism.

There appeared another work at that time, not indeed written by one of
the Assembly of Divines, but so intimately connected with the controversies
which were agitators among them that it deserves to be mentioned here. This
was a treatise written by the celebrated Apollonius of Middleburg, entitled,
*Consideratio Quarundam Controversiarum ad Regimen Ecclesiæ Dei Spectan-
tium, quæ in Angliæ Regno hodie Agitantur*. When this treatise was published,
a copy of it was sent to each member of the Westminster Assembly. "It was,"
says Baillie, "not only very well taken, but also, which is singular, and so far
as I remember, *absque exemplo*, it was ordered, *nemine contradicente*, to write
a letter of thanks to Apollonius."[10] The spirit of this work is thoroughly Presbyterian, encountering alike the theories of the Independents and the Erastians. It consists of seven chapters, each treating of a separate topic briefly,
but with great clearness and force of reasoning. They are as follow:

> 1. Concerning the qualification of church members. 2. Concerning a church
> covenant. 3. Concerning the church visible and instituted. 4. Concerning
> power ecclesiastical. 5. Concerning ecclesiastical ministry and its
> exercise. 6. Concerning classes (presbyteries) and synods, and their
> authority. 7. Concerning forms or directories of faith and worship.

It will at once be seen that in the discussion of these topics the learned author
must come into direct collision with both the Independents and the Erastians;
yet his work has very little of a merely controversial character, being a calm
and dispassionate, but very clear and able, disquisition concerning these
important theological questions. There is another very valuable work by
the same author written a short time before the meeting of the Westminster
Assembly, but treating very fully of the Erastian theory. Its title is, *Jus Majestatis
Circa Sacra; sive, Tractatus Theologicus de jure Magistratus circa res Ecclesiasticas*.
A translation of this work, for the purpose of general circulation, would be a
very valuable contribution to the cause of religious liberty, which is at present
beset by so many and such formidable enemies.

But we must quit this digression, however alluring the subject, and return to what remains to be stated respecting the concluding labors of the
Westminster Assembly....

---

10. Baillie, 2.246.

Of the Rise, Growth, Decay, & Reviving of Erastianism

By George Gillespie[1]

DIVERS LEARNED men have (to very good purpose) discovered the origin, occasion, first authors, fomenters, rise and growth of errors, both popish and others. I shall, after their example, make known briefly what I find concerning the rise and growth, the planting and watering, of the Erastian error. I cannot say of it that it is *honestis parentibus natus;* it is not born and descended of honest parents. The father of it is the old serpent, who, finding his kingdom very much impaired, weakened and resisted, by the vigor of the true ecclesiastical discipline, which separates between the precious and the vile, the holy and profane, and so contributes much to the shaming away of the unfruitful works of darkness, thereupon he has cunningly gone about to draw men first into a jealousy, and then into a dislike of the ecclesiastical discipline by God's mercy restored in the reformed churches. The mother of it is the enmity of nature against the kingdom of Jesus Christ, which He, as Mediator, does exercise in the government of the church; which enmity is naturally in all men's hearts, but is unmortified and strongly prevalent in some, who have said in their hearts, "We will not have this man to reign over us" (Luke 19[:14]); "Let us break their bands asunder, and cast away their cords from us" (Ps. 2:3). The midwife which brought this unhappy brood into the light of the world was Thomas Erastus, doctor of medicine at Heidelberg, of whom I shall say no more than what is apparent by his own preface to the reader, namely, that as he was once of opinion that excommunication is commanded in the Word of God, so he came off to the contrary opinion, not without a malcontented humor and a resentment of some things which he looked upon as provocations and personal reflections, though it is like[ly] enough they were not really such, but in his apprehension they were. One of these was a public dispute at Heidelberg in the year 1568, upon certain theses concerning the necessity of church government and the power of presbyteries to excommunicate; which theses were exhibited by Mr George Withers, an Englishman, who left England because of the ceremonies and was at that time made doctor of divinity at Heidelberg. And the learned dispute thereupon you may find epitomized (as it was taken the day following from the mouth of Dr. Ursinus) in the close of the second part of Dr. Pareus' *Explication of the Heidelberg Catechism.*[2]

---

1. [This text is taken from book 2, chapter 1 of *Aaron's Rod Blossoming* in *Works: A Presbyterian's Armoury* (1844), pp. 75–79.]

2. [*The Summe of Christian Religion… Lectures upon the Catechisme* (1617), pp. 835–847.]

The Erastian error being born, the breasts which gave it suck were *profaneness* and *self-interest*. The sons of Belial were very much for it, expecting that the eye of the civil magistrate shall not be so vigilant over them, nor his hand so much against them for a scandalous and dissolute conversation, as church discipline would be. *Germanorum bibere est vivere*,[3] in *practice* as well as in *pronunciation*. What great marvel if many among them (for I do not speak of all) did comply with the Erastian tenet? And it is as little to be marveled at if those, whether magistrates, lawyers, or others, who conceived themselves to be so far losers, as ecclesiastical courts were interested in government, and to be greater gainers by the abolition of the ecclesiastical interest in government, were biased that way. Both these you may find among the causes (mentioned by Aretius, *Theol. Probl.*, loc. 133 [*sic*]), for which there was so much unwillingness to admit the discipline of excommunication. *Magistratus jugum non admittunt, timent honoribus, licentiam amant*, etc. "The magistrates do not admit a yoke, are jealous of their honors, love licentiousness." *Vulgus quoque et plebs dissolutior: major pars corruptissima est*, etc. "The community also and people are more dissolute; the greater part is most vicious."[4]

After that this unlucky child had been nursed upon so bad milk, it came at last to eat strong food, and that was arbitrary government, under the name of royal prerogative. Mr John Wemyss (sometime senator of the College of Justice in Scotland), as great a royalist as any of his time, in his book *de Regis Primatu* (lib. 1, cap. 7),[5] does utterly dissent from and argue against the distinction of civil and ecclesiastical laws, and against the synodical power

---

3. ["They [the Germans] are little addicted to Venus and very much to Bacchus, whence the proverb, *Germanorum vivere est bibere*." Peter Heylyn, *Mikrokosmos: A little description of the great world. Augmented and reuised* (Oxford: Lichfield and Short, 1621), p. 253. It appears Gillespie may be linking this to a saying of Scaliger about the people of Gascoigne, who could not pronounce some letters correctly. Perhaps the German proverb may have been in Scaliger's mind? "In the province of Gascoigne in France, the natives substitute the letters *B* and *V* for each other, which occasioned Joseph Scaliger to say [*to joke*] of them—'Felices Populi, quibus *bibere* est *vivere*.'" See Samuel Pegge, *Anecdote of the English Language* (London: J. B. Nichols and Son, 1844), p. 67, and Louis Moreri, Edmund Bohun, *The Great Historical, Geographical and Poetical Dictionary*, volumes 1 and 2 (1694), under "Gascogne" and under "V." See Julius Cæsar Scaliger, *De Causis Linguæ Latinæ* (Lyon, 1540), p. 17; *Pœtice* (1561), lib. iii, cap. cxxvi. See "An Epigram by Julius Cæsar Scaliger," in *A Medium of Intercommunication for Literary Men, General Readers, etc.* Twelfth Series, Volume 1, January–June, 1916 (London: Oxford University Press, 1849), p. 67.

4. [*Sic* Locus 112. Gillespie made the same mistake in *Nihil Respondes* and likely simply copied the mistaken reference from there. See herein page 264. Benedictus Aretius, *Locus LVI. De Exemplis Veteris Testamenti, quatenus scilicet transferenda sint in usum nostrum, S.S. theologiæ problemata: hoc est, Loci commvnes Christianæ religionis, methodice explicati* (Isayas le Preux, 1617), De Excommunitione, Loc. CXII, pp. 638, 639.]

5. [John Wemyss, ΒΑΣΙΛΕΩΣ ΎΠΕΡΟΧΗ. *Sive De Regis primatu. libellus* (1623), De Concilis, seu Synodis Ecclesiæ, p. 60.]

of censures, holding that both the power of making ecclesiastical laws and the corrective power to censure transgressors, is proper to the magistrate.

The tutor which bred up the Erastian error was Arminianism;[6] for the Arminians, finding their plants plucked up and their poison antidoted by classes and synods, thereupon they began to cry down synodical authority and to appeal to the magistrate's power in things ecclesiastical, hoping for more favor and less opposition that way. They will have synods only to examine, dispute, discuss, to impose nothing under pain of ecclesiastical censure, but to leave all men free to do as they list. See their *Examen Censuræ* (cap. 25), and *Vindiciæ* (lib. 2, cap. 6, pp. 131–133).[7] And for the magistrate, they have endeavored to make him head of the church, as the Pope was; yea, so far, that they are not ashamed to ascribe unto the magistrate that jurisdiction over the churches, synods, and ecclesiastical proceedings, which the Pope did formerly usurp. For which see Apollonius in his *Jus Majestatis Circa Sacra*.[8]

But the Erastian error being thus born, nursed, fed and educated, did fall into a most deadly decay and consumption; the procuring causes whereof were these three: First, The best and most (and in some respect all) of the reformed churches refused to receive, harbor, or entertain it, and so left it exposed to hunger and cold, shame and nakedness.

Some harbor it had in Switzerland, but that was looked upon as coming only through injury of time, which could not be helped: the theological and scriptural principles of the divines of those churches being anti-Erastian and presbyterial, as I have elsewhere shown against Mr. Coleman;[9] so that Erastianism could not get warmth and strength enough, no not in Zürich itself. Yea, Dr. Ursinus, in his *Judicium de Disciplina Ecclesiastica et Excommunicatione*, exhibited to the Prince Elector Palatine Frederick III (who had required him to give his judgment concerning Erastus's theses), does once and again observe that all the reformed churches and divines, as well those that did not practice excommunication as those who did practice it, agree, notwithstanding, in this principle that excommunication ought to be in the church;[10] which is a mighty advantage against Erastianism.

---

6. [Lamont cries out that this statement is false, but he writes as though Gillespie spoke here of the Arminianism of the Laudians. As is patently clear, Gillespie is speaking specifically of the actions of the Dutch Arminians. See William M. Lamont, *Godly Rule: Politics and Religion, 1603–60* (New York: St. Martin's Press, 1969), p. 81.]

7. [*Examen Censuræ* in Simon Episcopius, *Apologia pro Confessione* (1629), pp. 287v–308v. Episcopius, *Vedelivs Rhapsodvs, sive Vindiciæ Doctrinæ Remonstrantium* (1633), pp. 131, 133.]

8. [Willem Apollonii, *Jus Majestatis Circa Sacra, sive Tractatus Theologicus, de jure Magistratus circa res ecclesiasticas, Oppositus Cl. D. Professoris Nicolai Vedelii tractatui, de Episcoparu Constantini Magni, ex authoritate, & jussu classis Walachriana adornatum* ([Middelburg]: Iacobum Fierensium bibliopolam, sub insigni Globi, Anno 1642).

9. See *Nihil Respondes*, p. 32, 33, *Male Audis*, pp. 52, 53. [Herein pages 264 and 312.]

10. *In aliis (ecclesiis) ubi aut nulla est excommnnicatio in usu, aut non legitime administratur, ac nihilominus absque omni controversia, in confesso est ac palam doettur, cam merito in ecclesia*

The second cause was a mis-accident from the midwife, who did half stifle it in the birth, from which did accrue a most dangerous infirmity, of which it could never recover. Read the preface of Erastus before the Confirmation of his Theses,[11] also the close of his sixth book: put these together, you will find him yield that all ought not to be admitted promiscuously to the sacrament, but that such admission be according to the custom and rule observed in the church of Heidelberg (and what that was, you may find in the Heidelberg Catechism, quest. 82 and 87,[12] namely, a suspension of profane scandalous persons from the sacrament, and in case of their obstinacy and continuing in their offences, an excommunicating of them). He yields also that these seven sorts of persons ought not to be esteemed as members of the church, and that if any such be found in the visible church, they ought to be cast out: 1. Idolaters. 2. Apostates. 3. Such as do not understand the true doctrine; that is, ignorant persons. 4. Such as do not approve and embrace the true doctrine; that is, heretics and sectaries. 5. Such as desire to receive the sacrament otherwise than in the right manner, and according to Christ's institution. 6. Such as defend or justify

---

vigere debere. [Zacharias Ursinus, in *Opera Theologica*, vol. 3 (Heidelbergæ: Rosa, 1612), col. 804.] Et infra. *Ne etiam celsitudo tua se suasque ecclesias ab aliis omnibus ecclesiis, tam ab iis quæ nullam habent excommunicationem, quam ab iis quæ habent, nova hæc opinione sejungat: siquidem universæ ac singulæ uno ore confitentur, semperque confessæ sunt, merito illam in usu esse debere.* [Ibid., Objection 10, col. 810D]. [See the translations in III *Propositions*, #104, p. 434.]

11. Erast., Præfat. *Nos de illis solis loqui peccatoribus qui doctriuam intelligunt, probant amplectuntur: peccata sua se agnoscere vere atque odisse aiunt, et sacramentis secundum institutionem Christi uti cupiunt. Et lib. 6, cap. 2. Faciunt præterea nobis injuriam (imrao vera calumnia est) cum dicuut nos omnes sine ullo examine velle admitti, quales sint ac esse velint. Quippe sic volumus unumquemque admitti, quomodo ecclesiæ nostræ consuetudo et regula jubet. Et infra. Sine ut idololatram et apostatam, negamus membrum esse ecclesiæ Christi, sic etiam* Nequitiam suam defendentem *negamus inter membra ecclesiæ censendum esse. Et quemadmodum illos ex Christiano cœtu judicamus exterminandos, sic hos quoque putamus in eo cœtu non esse ferendos. Verum neque de his, neque de illis quærunt nostræ theses: sed disputatur in eis, de solis doctrinam amplexantibus, et sacramentis rite cum ecclesia uti cupientibus, hoc est pænitentiam eodem modo quo alii profitentibus.* [Thomas Erastus, *Explicatio gravissimæ quæstionis, utrum excommunicatio* (1589), pp. 67, 348, 349. Gillespie added the emphasis to "Nequitiam suam defendentem."]

12. [QUEST. 82. Are they also to be admitted to this supper, who in confession and life declare themselves to be infidels and ungodly? ANSW. No. For by that means the covenant of God is profaned, and the wrath of God is stirred up against the whole assembly: wherefore the church by the commandment of Christ and His apostles, using the keys of the kingdom of heaven, ought to drive them from this supper, till they shall repent and change their manners. QUEST. 87. Cannot they then be saved, which be unthankful and remain still carelessly in their sins, and are not converted from wickedness unto God? ANSW. By no means. For as the Scripture bears witness, neither unchaste persons, nor idolaters, nor adulterers, nor thieves, nor covetous men, nor drunkards, nor slanderers, nor robbers, shall inherit the kingdom of God. Cf. Ursinus, *The Summe of Christian Religion* (1617), pp. 791, 851.]

their wickedness. 7. Such as do not confess and acknowledge their sins, and profess sorrow and repentance for them, and a hatred or detestation of them. And thus, you see, as Erastianism pleads for no favor to sectaries, or whosoever dissent in doctrine, or whose tenets concerning Christ's institution, or manner of administration, are contrary to that which is received in the church where they live (for it is content that all such, were they never so peaceable and godly, be cast out of the church by excommunication:[13] all the favor and forbearance which it pleads for is to the loose and profane), so neither does it altogether exempt the profane, but such only as do neither deny nor defend their wickedness, but confess their sins, and profess sorrow for them. Let the Erastians of this time observe what their great master has yielded touching the ecclesiastical censure of profane ones, which, though it is not satisfactory to us, for reasons elsewhere given, yet it can be as little satisfactory to them. But whereas Erastus, together with those his concessions (that he may seem to have said somewhat), falls a quarrelling with presbyteries for presuming to judge of the sincerity of that repentance professed by a scandalous sinner, and their not resting satisfied with a man's own profession of his repentance, if his followers will now be pleased to reduce the controversy within that narrow circle—whether a presbytery may excommunicate from the church, or at least suspend from the sacrament, any church member as an impenitent scandalous sinner, who yet does not defend nor deny his sin by which he has given scandal, but confesses it, and professes sincere and hearty repentance for it (which is the point that Erastus is fain to hold at in the issue),—then I hope we shall be quickly agreed and the controversy buried. For we do rest satisfied with the offender's confession of his sin and profession of his repentance, unless his own known words or actions give the lie to his profession of repentance; that is, if he be known to justify and defend his sin in his ordinary discourse, or to continue in the practice of the sin which he professes to the presbytery he repents of. If these or such like sure signs of his impenitency be known, must the presbytery notwithstanding rest satisfied with his verbal profession of repentance? All that fear God (I think) would cry, "Shame, shame," upon such an assertion. And, moreover, let us take it in the case of an idolater, heretic, apostate (for Erastus is content that such be excluded from the sacrament). Suppose such a one does confess his sin and profess repentance, but in the meanwhile is known to be a writer or spreader of books in defense of that idolatry or heresy, or to be a persuader and enticer of others secretly to that way, or if there be any other known infallible sign of his impenitency. Must his verbal profession

---

13. Erastus ib. *Equidom in Thesibus ab initio monui, me dc sola ilia excominunicatione agere, qua aliqui doctrinam intelligentes, probantes, amplexantes, et sacramentis recte uti cupientes, quod ad externum usura attinet ab eiisdera propter anteactae vitae turpitudinem a quibusdam presbyteris repelluntur: quia scilicet non videtur eis scrio dolere, qui lapsus fuit, ac sibi dolere id profitetur.* [Ibid., p. 349.]

to the presbytery in such cases be trusted and taken as satisfactory? I am confident Erastus himself would not have said so. Wherefore, as in the case of a heretic, so in the case of a profane person, or one of a scandalous conversation, there is a necessity that the presbytery examine the real signs of repentance; and the offender's verbal profession is not all.

The third cause which helped forward the deadly malady and consumption of Erastianism, was the grief, shame, confusion, and loss which it sustained by the learning and labor of some divines in the reformed churches, who had to very good purpose taken pains to discover to the world the cursed nature of that unlucky brood, being of the seed of the Amalekites, which ought not to enter into the congregation of the Lord. The divines who have more especially and particularly appeared against it are (to my observation) these:

Beza, *de Excommunicatione et Presbyterio contra Erastum*,[14] which was not printed till Erastus's reply unto it was first printed. Whereunto, as Beza, in a large preface lays the foundation of a duply [*second reply*], so he had prepared and perfected his duply had he not been hindered by the great troubles of Geneva, at that time besieged by the Duke of Savoy, Beza himself being also at that time seventy-one years old: howbeit, for all that, he did not lay aside the resolution and thought of that duply, if he should have opportunity, and see it requisite or called for; all which is manifest from that preface.

Next to him I reckon Zecharias Ursinus, a most solid judicious divine, who did (as I touched before) exhibit to the Prince Elector Palatine Frederick III., *Judicium de Disciplina Ecclesiastica et Excommunicatione* [15] (which you may find in the end of his third vol.), wherein he does soundly confute the theses of Erastus; neither has any reply been made thereto that ever I could learn of. Also in his *Catechetical Explications*, question 85, he plainly disputes against the Erastian principles.[16] The more strange it is that Mr. Hussey, in his Epistle to the Parliament,[17] would make them believe that Ursinus is his, and not ours, in this controversy.

After these, there did others more lately come upon the stage against the Erastian principles, as Casparus Brochmand, a Lutheran, in *System. Theol.*, tom. 2, *Artic. de Disciplina Ecclesiastica*, where he examines the most substantial arguments of Erastus;[18] Antonius Walæus, *de Munere Ministrorum Ecclesiæ et inspectione Magistratus circa illud, et in locis com. de clavivibus et potestate*

---

14. [Théodore de Bèze, *Tractatus pius et moderatus de vera Excommunicatione & christiano Presbyterio … Th. Erasti D. Medici centum manuscriptis thesibus oppositus, & nunc primum, cogente necessitate, editus* (Geneva: Le Peux, 1590; London: Norton {1590}).]

15. [Ursinus, *Opera*, vol. 3, ibid.]

16. [Ursinus, *Opera theologica*, volume 1 (1612), col. 294.]

17. [William Hussey, "To the Right Honoourable, the Lords and Commons assembled in Parliament," in *A Plea for Christian Magistracie: or, An answer to some passages in Mr. Gillespies Sermon, against Mr. Coleman. Also to the Brotherly examination of some passages*, etc. (1646), unnumbered pages 6– 7.]

18. [Caspar Rasmussen Brochmand, "Caput IV. Religionis Christianæ, Religionis

ecclesiastica, et tom. 2, *Disp. de Disciplina Ecclesiastica*;[19] Helmichius, *de vocatione Pastorum et institutione Consistoriorum*;[20] D. Triglandius, *in dissertatione de Potestate Civili et Ecclesiastica*;[21] D. Revius, *in examine libelli de Episcopatu Constantini magni*;[22] D. Apollonii, *Jus Majestatis circa sacra*;[23] D. Cabeliavius, *de libertate Ecclesicæ in exercenda Disciplina Spirituali*;[24] Dr. Voetius, in his *Politica Ecclesiastica*, especially his *Disputationes de Potestate et Politia Ecclesiarum*.[25] Besides Acronius, Thysius, Ludov. à Renesse, who were champions against that unhappy error revived in the Low Countries by Wtenbogard, a proselyte of the Arminians.[26]

But now, while Erastianism did thus lie a dying, and like to breathe its last, is there no physician who will undertake the cure and endeavor to raise it up from the gates of death to life? Yes, Mr. Coleman was the man, who (to that purpose) first appeared publicly; First, by a sermon to the parliament;[27] next, by debating the controversy with myself in writing;[28] and lastly, by

---

Christianæ Articulus de Discplina Ecclesiastica," in *Systematis Universæ Theologiæ*, volume 2 (Lipsiæ: Hallervord et Moltken, 1638), p. 977ff.]

19. [*Works* set "Walæus" as "Walden." Antonius Walæus, *Tractatus de munere ministrorum ecclesiæ: et inspectione magistratus circa illud. Ab Antonio Walæo Belgice conscriptus: nunc a Ludovico Renesse, verbi divini ministro in ecclesia Bredana, in linguam Latinam translatus*, in *Opera omnia*, Tomus secundus (Lugduni Batavorum: Franciscus Hackius, 1643).]

20. [Wernerus Helmichius, *Grondich bericht van de wettelijcke beroepinghe der predicanten ofte kercken-dienaren. Mitsgaders vande noodtwendicheydt des kercken-rædts ofte consistorie* (Delft, Schiedam: Jan Andriesz Cloeting, 1611). The title is given in Latin in the preface to Walæus's *Tractatus de munere ministrorum ecclesiæ*.]

21. [Jacobus Trigland, Sr., *Dissertatio theologica de civili & ecclesiastica potestate, Occasione libelli Vedeliani, de Episcopatu Constantini Magni* (Amsterdam: Janson, 1642).]

22. [Jacobus Revius, *Examen dissertationis D. Nicolai Vedelii de episcopatu Constantini Magni* (Amsterdam: Janson, 1642).]

23. [Willem Apollonii, *Jus Majestatis Circa Sacra*, ibid.]

24. [Pieter Cabeljauw, *Aopolgetica rescriptio pro libertate ecclesiæ in exercenda disciplina spirituali: Ad anonymi brevem responsionem ad solutiones datas ad argumenta D. Maccovii* (Amsterdam: Janson, 1642).]

25. [Gillespie likely is referring to the II part collection, Gisbertus Voetius, *Disputationis ex Politica Ecclesiastica, de Ecclesia Visibili et Instituta, pars prima[-secta]* with *Disputationis ex politica ecclesiastica de potestate et politia ecclesiarum pars prima–quinta* (Trajecti ad Rhenum, 1644–45). No further dissertations under the general title could be found for the timeframe. In the later collection, there are 13 chapters under *De Potestate Ecclesiastica* in *Politicæ Ecclesiasticæ*, volume 4, Parts Tertia & Ultima (Amsterdam: Joannis à Waesberge, 1676), pp. 770ff.]

26. [Ruardus Acronius, *Predicatie, door Johannem Wtenbogart bearbeydet* (Adriæn Cornelisz, 1610). Possibly, Antoine Thysius *Responsio Remonstrantium remonstrantiam* (1617). It is not clear to what work by Lodewijk Gerardus van Renesse Gillespie refers.]

27. [Thomas Coleman, *Hopes deferred and dashed, observed in a sermon to the Honourable House of Commons, in Margarets Westminster, July 30, 1645* (1645).]

28. [Gillespie, *Brotherly Examination* (1645), Coleman, *Brotherly Examination Re-examined*

engaging in a public debate in the reverend Assembly of Divines against this proposition, "Jesus Christ, as King and Head of His church, has appointed a government in the church in the hands of church officers distinct from the civil government."[29] After he had some days argued against this proposition (having full liberty both to argue and reply as much as he pleased), it pleased God to visit him with sickness, during which the Assembly (upon intimation from himself, that he wished them to lay aside that proposition for a time, that, if God should give him health again, he might proceed in his debate), did go upon another matter and lay this aside for that season. The Lord was pleased to remove him by death before he could do what he intended in this and other particulars.[30] One of his intentions was to translate and publish in English the book of Erastus against excommunication. But, through God's mercy, before the poison was ready, there was one antidote ready, I mean Mr. Rutherford's answer to Erastus.[31] But though Mr. Coleman was the first man, he was not the only man that has appeared in this controversy in England. Others (and those of divers professions) are come upon the stage. I shall leave every man to his Judge, and shall judge nothing before the time; only I shall wish every man to consider sadly and seriously, by what spirit and principles he is led, and whether he be seeking the things of Christ, or his own things; whether he be pleasing men, or pleasing Christ; whether sin be more shamed and holiness more advanced, this way or that way; which way is the most agreeable to the Word of God, to the example of the best reformed churches, and so [therefore] to the Solemn League and Covenant. The controversy is now hot: every faithful servant of Christ will be careful to deliver his own soul by his faithfulness, and let the Lord do what seems Him good. The cause is not ours, but Christ's; it stands Him upon His honor, His crown, His laws, His kingdom. Our eyes are towards the Lord, and we will wait for a divine decision of the business; "For the Lord is our judge; the Lord is our lawgiver; the Lord is our king; He will save us" (Isa. 33:22).[32].

(1645), Gillespie, *Nihil Respondes* (1645), Coleman, *Malè dicis maledicis. Or A brief reply to Nihil respondens* (1645 [1646]), Gillespie, *Malè Audis* (1645 [1646]).]

29. [This question was taken up on Friday, March 6, 1645, in Session 600. See page 187.]

30. [Lamont (p. 114), despicably characterized this as chortling at Coleman's death.]

31. [Rutherford, *The Divine Right of Church Government and Excommunication* (1646).]

32. [The text in *Works* omits the reference after the text of Isaiah 33:22.]

A Brotherly Examination of
Some Passages of Mr. Coleman's
Late Printed Sermon upon Job 11:20

In which he hath Endeavoured to strike at the root of
All Church Government

Hieronymus in Epitaphio Fabiolae.
Aliae sunt leges Caesarum, aliae Christi:
aliud Papinianus, aliud Paulus noster praecipit.

A Sermon Preached Before the Right Honorable the House of Lords, in the Abbey Church at Westminster, upon the 27th of August, 1645. Being the day appointed for solemn and public Humiliation. Whereunto is added A Brotherly Examination of some Passages of Mr. Coleman's late Printed Sermon upon Job 11:20. In which he hath endeavoured to strike at the root of all Church-Government.

EDITIONS

1. *A sermon preached before the Right Honourable the House of Lords.... Whereunto is added a brotherly examination of some passages of Mr Colemans late printed sermon upon Iob 11.20. in which hee hath endeavoured to strike at the root of all church-government. By George Gillespie minister at Edinburgh* (London: printed for Robert Bostock dwelling in Pauls Church-yard at the sign of the Kingshead, 1645.). [8], 48 p.; 4⁰. ESTC R200235 (Wing G758). "Wing has 'by F. Neile for Robert Bostock' in imprint. No copy seen has Neile's name in imprint." This appeared in before or around October 13. *A Transcript of the Registers of the Worshipful Company of Stationers from 1640–1708 A.D.*, ed. G.E. Briscoe Eyre, 3 vols. (London, 1913-14), p. 197.

2. *A sermon preached before the Right Honourable the House of Lords.... Whereunto is added a brotherly examination of some passages of Mr. Colemans late printed sermon upon Job 11.20. In which he hath endeavoured to strike at the root of all church-government. By George Gillespie minister at Edenburgh* (London: printed by F. Neile for Robert Bostock dwelling in Pauls Church-yard at the sign of the Kings Head, 1646.). [4], 44 p.; 4⁰. ESTC R30413 (Wing G759).

3. *A Brotherly Examination of some Passages of Mr. Coleman's late Printed Sermon upon Job XI. 20, as it is now printed and published: by which he hath, to the great offence of very many, endeavoured to strike at the very root of all spiritual and ecclesiastical government, contrary to the Word of God, the Solemn League and Covenant, other Reformed Churches, and the votes of the Honourable Houses of Parliament, after advice had with the Reverend and learned Assembly of Divines* (Edinburgh: Robert Ogle and Oliver and Boyd, 1844). In *Works* in *A Presbyterian's Armoury*. 13 pp.; royal octavo.

The Epigraph on the prior page is from the first edition published with Gillespie's sermon preached before the House of Lords. Jerome, *The Eulogy of Fabiola*. "The laws of Cæsar are different, it is true, from the laws of Christ: Papinianus commands one thing; our own Paul another." "Letters and Select Works," in *NPNF2*, v. 6, Letter LXXVII to Oceanus, p. 151, §7.

A Brotherly Examination

of some passages of Mr. Coleman's late Sermon upon Job 11:20, as it
is now printed and published: by which he hath, to the great offence
of very many, endeavoured to strike at the very root of all Spiritual
and Ecclesiastical Government, contrary to the Word of God, the
Solemn League and Covenant, other Reformed Churches, and the
Votes of the Honourable Houses of *Parliament*, after advice had with
the Reverend and Learned Assembly of *Divines*

I HAVE BEFORE touched this purpose in the third branch of the third
application of my second doctrine, and did in my sermon in the Abbey
church express my thoughts of it at some length. But as I was then unwilling
to fall upon such a controversy so publicly, and especially in a fast sermon,
if that which I intend to examine had not been as publicly and upon the
like occasion delivered, so now in the publishing I have thought good to
open my mind concerning this thing distinctly and by itself. That which
had been too late to be preached after sermon is not too late to be printed
after sermon. Others (upon occasion offered) have given their testimony
against his doctrine, and I should think myself unfaithful in the trust put
upon me if, upon such an occasion, I should be silent in this business; and
I believe no man will think it strange that a piece of this nature and strain
get an answer; and I go about it without any disrespect either to the person
or parts of my reverend brother. Only, I must give a testimony to the truth
when I hear it spoken against, and I hope his objections have made no such
impression in any man's mind as to make him unwilling to hear an answer.
Come we therefore to the particulars.

Four rules were offered by the reverend brother as tending to unity and
to the healing of the present controversies about church government. But
in truth his cure is worse than the disease, and instead of making any agreement he is like to have his hand against every man and every man's hand
against him.

The first rule was this, "Establish as few things *jure divino* as can well be;"[1]
which is, by interpretation, as little fine gold and as much dross as can well
be. "The words of the Lord are pure words: as silver tried in a furnace of

---

1. [Thomas Coleman, *Hopes Deferred and Dashed*, p. 24.]

earth, purified seven times" (Ps. 12:6). What you take from the Word of God is fine "gold tried in the fire" (Rev. 3:18), but a holy thing of man's devising is the dross of silver. Can he not be content to have the dross purged from the silver except the silver itself be cast away? The very contrary rule is more sure and safe; which I prove thus:

If it be a sin to diminish or take aught from the Word of God, insomuch that it is forbidden under pain of taking away a man's part out of the book of life, and out of the holy city,[2] then as many things are to be established *jure divino* as can well be. But it is a sin to diminish or take aught from the Word of God, insomuch that it is forbidden under pain of taking away a man's part out of the book of life and out of the holy city; therefore, as many things are to be established *jure divino* as can well be.

It must be remembered, withal, 1. That the question is not now, whether *this or that* form of church government be *jure divino,* but, whether *a* church government be *jure divino;* whether Jesus Christ has thus far revealed His will in His word that there are to be church censures, and those to be dispensed by church officers. The brother is for the negative of this question. 2. Neither is it stood upon by any, so far as I know, that what the parliament shall establish concerning church government must be established by them *jure divino.* If the parliament shall, in a parliamentary and legislative way, establish that thing which really and in itself is agreeable to the Word of God, though they do not declare it to be the will of Jesus Christ, I am satisfied, and I am confident so are others. This I confess, that it is incumbent to parliament men, to ministers, and to all other Christians, according to their vocation and interest to search the scriptures and thereby to inform their own and other men's consciences, so as they may do in faith what they do in point of church government, that is, that they may know they are not sinning, but doing the will of God. And it ought to be no prejudice nor exception against a form of church government that many learned and godly divines do assert it from Scripture to be the will of God. And why should *jus divinum* be such a *noli me tangere?*[3] The reason was given:

> This was the only thing that hindered union in the Assembly (he says). Two parties came biased. The reverend commissioners from Scotland were for the *jus divinum* of the presbyterial, the Independents for the congregational government. How should either move? Where should both meet?[4]

If it was thus, how shall he make himself blameless, who made union in the Assembly yet more difficult because he came biased a third way with the Erastian tenets?

And where he ASKS where the Independents and we should meet, I ANSWER,

---

2. [See Revelation 22:18, 19.]

3. [*Noli me tangere:* "touch me not."]

4. [Coleman, *Hopes Deferred and Dashed,* p. 24.]

in holding a church government *jure divino*, that is, that the pastors and elders ought to suspend or excommunicate (according to the degree of the offence) scandalous sinners. Who can tell but the purging of the church from scandals and the keeping of the ordinances pure (when it shall be actually seen to be the great thing endeavored on both sides), may make union between us and the Independents more easy than many imagine. As for his exceptions against us who are commissioners from the Church of Scotland,[5] I thank God it is but such, yea, not so much as the Arminians did object against the foreign divines who came to the Synod of Dort. They complained that those divines were pre-engaged and biased in regard of the judgment of those churches from which they came, and that therefore they did not help, but hinder, union in that assembly. And might not the Arians have thus excepted against Alexander, who was engaged against them before he came to the Council of Nice? Might not the Nestorians have made the same exception against Cyril because he was under an engagement against them before he came to the Council of Ephesus? Nay, had not the Jewish zealots the very same objection to make against Paul and Barnabas, who were engaged, not in the behalf of one nation, but of all the churches of the Gentiles, against the imposition of the Mosaical rites, and had so declared themselves at Antioch before they came to the synod at Jerusalem? Acts 15:2. It is not faulty to be engaged for the truth, but against the truth. It is not blameworthy, but praiseworthy, to hold fast so much as we have already attained unto.[6] Notwithstanding, we, for our part, have also from the beginning professed, "That we are most willing to hear and learn from the Word of God what needeth further to be reformed in the church of Scotland."[7]

---

5. *Grotii Apologet*, cap. 5. *Extranei autem quorum maximus esse debuerat usus in pace concilianda ex partium altera erant conquisiti. {Et infa} mandata externis data damnationem Remonstrantium prae se ferebant, ut et orationes habitae ante causam cognitam.* [*Works* did not correct the text against the errata of the first edition, which instructed to read "Et infra" for "Et infra Josa." See Hugo Grotius, *Apologeticus eorum qui Hollandiae Vvestfrisiaeque et vicinis quibusdam nationibus ex legibus praefuerunt ante mutationem quae evenit anno 1618* (Paris: Boun, 1622), p. 92–93.] The Arminians in their *Examen Censurae*, cap. 25, p. 286, 287, hold this as a necessary qualification of those that are admitted into synods, that they be not astricted [*restricted*] to any church, not to any confession of faith. [See Simon Episcopius, *Apologia pro Confessione sive declaratione sententiæ eorum* (1629), p. 291v; ibid. (1630), pp. 286, 287.]

6. [Cf. Philippians 3:16, Revelation 2:25, 3:11.]

7. In our first paper presented to the Grand Committee. [Since this is called the first paper, it may have formed a part of and/or informed the report from the Grand Committee to the assembly given on November 14, 1643 by Stephen Marshall. As summarized by Lightfoot, it contains in substance this same statement about the Scots' willingness to be governed by the Word of God and references the testimonies of Brightman and Cartwright (Lightfoot's journal, p. 51; *Minutes*, Session 95, 2.312; cf. 5.160). This first paper or some form of it with similar content was published as *Reformation of church-government in Scotland cleered from some mistakes and prejudices by the commissioners of the general assembly of the Church of*

The second rule which was offered in that sermon was this: "Let all precepts held out as divine inſtitutions have clear scriptures," etc.; "Let the Scripture ſpeak expressly," he says.[8]

I ANSWER. The Scripture ſpeaks in that manner which seemed fitteſt to the wisdom of God; that is, so as it muſt coſt us much searching of the Scripture, as men search for a hid treasure, before we find out what is the good, and acceptable, and perfeᷓt will of God concerning the government of His church [cf. Rom. 12:2]. Will any divine [*theologian*] in the world deny that it is a divine truth which by necessary consequence is drawn from Scripture, as well as that which in express words and syllables is written in Scripture? Are not diverse articles of our profession, for inſtance the baptism of infants, necessarily and certainly proved from Scripture, although it makes no express mention thereof in words and syllables? But let us hear what he has said concerning some scriptures (for he names but two of them) upon which the aᷓts of ſpiritual or ecclesiaſtical government have been grounded. "That place [in] 1 Corinthians 5 takes not hold," he says, "on my conscience for excommunication, and I admire [*marvel*] that Matthew 18 so should upon any." It is ſtrange that he should superciliously pass them over without reſpeᷓt to so great a cloud of witnesses in all the reformed churches, or without so much as offering any answer at all to the arguments which so many learned and godly divines of old and of late have drawn from these places for excommunication, which, if he had done, he should not want [*lack*] a reply. In the meantime, he intermixes a politic consideration into this debate of divine right. "I could never yet see," he says, "how two coordinate governments, exempt from superiority and inferiority, can be in one ſtate."[9] I suppose he has seen the coordinate governments of a general and of an admiral; or, if we shall come lower, the government of parents over their children and masters over their servants, though it fall often out that he who is subjeᷓt to one man as his maſter is subjeᷓt to another man as his father. In one ship there may be two coordinate governments, the captain governing the soldiers, the maſter governing the mariners. In these and such like cases you have two

---

Scotland, now at London (London: Robert Bostock, 1644), pp. 7, 15. Thomason's copy is dated January 23, 1643 [i.e., 1644]. The Grand Committee was the Treaty Committee repurposed with the work of ensuring agreement of England and Scotland on uniformity of religion. It included members of parliament, the assembly, and the Scottish commissioners. Shaw overinflates its directing of the assembly work, and its influence waned after the first year by the fall of 1644. *Minutes,* 1.26. Wayne Spear, *Covenanted Uniformity in Religion: The Influence of the Scottish Commissioners upon the Ecclesiology of the Weſtminſter Assembly* (Reformation Heritage Books, 2013), p. 45. William A. Shaw, *A Hiſtory of the English Church during the Civil Wars and under the Commonwealth* (New York: Longmans, Green, and Co., 1900), 1.152. Jaretha Joy Jimena-Palmer, *Church and Politics During the English Reformation: Ecclesiology and Politics in the Writings of Stephen Marshall* (1595–1655), ebook, location 2503. See Baillie, 2.110.]

8. [Coleman, *Hopes Deferred and Dashed,* pp. 24, 25.]

9. [Coleman, *Hopes Deferred and Dashed,* p. 25.]

coordinate governments, when the one governor is not subordinate to the other. There is more subordination in the ministers and other church officers towards the civil magistrate. For the minister of Christ must be in subjection to the magistrate, and if he be not, he is punishable by the law of the land as well as any other subject. The persons and estates of church officers, and all that they have in this world, are subject to civil authority. But that which is Christ's, and not ours, the royal prerogative of the King of saints in governing of His church according to His own will is not subject to the pleasure of any man living. But the reverend brother might well have spared this. It is not the independency of the church government upon the civil government which he intended to speak against, it is the very thing itself, *a* church government, as is manifest by his other two rules.

I come therefore to his next, which is the third rule: "Lay no more burden of government upon the shoulders of ministers than Christ has plainly laid upon them."[10] He means none at all, as is manifest not only by his fourth rule, where he says that he finds no institution of other governments besides magistracy, but also by the next words, "The ministers have other work to do," he says, "and such as will take up the whole man." [11] He might have added this one word more, that without the power of church government, when ministers have done all that ever they can, they shall not keep themselves nor the ordinances from pollution. Before I proceed any farther, let it be remembered, when he excludes ministers from government: First, It is from spiritual or ecclesiastical government, for the question is not of civil government. Secondly, He excludes ruling elders too, and therefore ought to have mentioned them with the ministers as those who are to draw the same yoke together, rather than to tell us of an "innate enmity between the clergy and the laity." [12] The keeping up of the names of the clergy and laity savors more of a domineering power than anything the brother can charge upon presbyteries. It is a point of controversy between Bellarmine[13] and those that write against him, he holding up, and they crying down those names, because the Christian people are the κλῆρος, the heritage of the Lord as well as the ministers. Thus [*this*] much by the way of that distinction of names. And, for the thing itself, to object an innate enmity between the ministers of the gospel and those that are not ministers, is no less than a dishonoring and aspersing of the Christian religion.

To return, you see his words tend to the taking away of all church government out of the hands of church officers. Now, may we know his reasons? He fetches the ground of an argument out of his own heart: "I have a heart," he

---

10. [Coleman, *Hopes Deferred and Dashed*, p. 25. In the published text of Coleman's sermon this third reason has "2." repeated instead of a "3."]

11. [Coleman, ibid., *Hopes Deferred and Dashed*, p. 25.]

12. [Coleman, *Hopes Deferred and Dashed*, p. 26.]

13. Bellarm., *de Cler.*, lib. 1, cap. 1. [See Bellermine, "Controversiarum de Membros Ecclesiae," Liber Primus, De Clericis, in *Opera Omnia*, Tomus 2 (1870), 2.419.]

says," that knows better how to be governed than govern." I wish his words might hold true in a sense of pliableness and yielding to government. How he knows to govern I know not; but it should seem in this particular he knows not how to be governed; for after both houses of parliament have concluded "that many particular congregations shall be under one presbyterial government,"[14] he still acknowledges no such thing as presbyterial government. I dare be bold to say he is the first divine in all the Christian world that ever advised a state to give no government to church officers, after the state had resolved to establish presbyterian government; but let us take the strength of his argument as he pretends it. He means not of a humble pliableness and subjection (for that should ease him from his fear of an ambitious ensnarement, and so were contrary to his intention), but of a sinful infirmity and ambition in the heart, which makes it fitter for him and others to be kept under the yoke than to govern. And thus his argumentation runs:

> Might I measure others, and I know not why I may not (God fashions men's hearts alike; and as in water face answers face, so the heart of man to man), I ingenuously profess I have a heart that knows better how to be governed than govern: I fear an ambitious ensnarement, and I have cause; I see what raised prelacy and Papacy to such a height, etc.

The two scriptures will not prove what he would. The first of them, Psalm 33:15, "He fashioneth their hearts alike," gives him no ground at all, except it be the homonomy of the English word alike, which in this place notes nothing else but τὸ καθόλου, all men's hearts are alike in this, that God fashions them all, and therefore knows them all *æque*, or alike (that is the scope of the place). The Hebrew *jachad* [*yachad*] is used in the same sense in Ezra 4:3.[15] "We ourselves together will build." They mean not they will all build in the like fashion, or in the same manner, but that they will build all of them together, one as well as another. So Psalm 2:2, "The rulers take counsel together;" Jeremiah 46:12, "They are fallen both together."

The other place, Proverbs 27:19, if you take it word by word as it is in the Hebrew, is thus: "As in water faces to faces; so the heart of man to man." Our translators add the word "answereth," but the Hebrew will suffer the negative reading, "As in water faces answer not to faces." The Septuagints reads: "As faces are not like faces, so neither are the hearts of men alike." The Chaldee paraphrase thus: "As waters and as countenances, which are not like one another, so the hearts of the sons of men are not alike."[16] Thus does Mr. Cartwright, in

---

14. [Shaw, ibid., 1.185–186. House of Commons Journal, volume 4, January 14, 1645, p. 20. House of Lords Journal, volume 7, January 27, 1645, p. 158.]

15. יַחַד *una simul.* from יָחַד *unire.*

16. [The Chaldee paraphrase and Septuagint texts are given in both the Complutensian (1522) and Antwerp Polyglotts (1568–1573). Both polyglots were available to Gillespie in the Westminster Abbey Library (the Antwerp also was held at Sion College and Lambeth

his judicious commentary give the sense: "As in the water face doth not answer fully to face, but in some sort, so there may be a conjecture, but no certain knowledge of the heart of man."[17] But let the text be read affirmatively, not negatively, what shall be the sense? Some take it thus: "A man's heart may be someway seen in his countenance as a face in the water."[18] Others: "As a face in the water is various and changeable to him that looks upon it, so is the heart of man inconstant to a friend that trusts in him."[19] Others thus: "As a man seeth his own face in the water, so he may see himself in his own heart or conscience."[20] Others thus: "As face answers face in the water, so he that looks for a friendly affection from others, must show it in himself."[21]

It will never be proved that any such thing is intended in that place as may warrant this argumentation. There is a particular corruption in one man's heart, for instance, ambition, which makes him unfit to be trusted with government; therefore, the same corruption is in all other men's hearts; even as the face in the water answers the face out of the water so just, that there is not a spot or blemish in the one but it is in the other. I am sure Paul taught us not so when he said, "In lowliness of mind let each esteem other better than themselves" (Phil. 2:3). Nay, the brother himself has taken off the edge of his own argument (if it had any) in his epistle printed before his sermon, where, speaking of his brethren, from whose judgment he dissents in point of government, he has these words: "Whose wisdom and humility (I speak it confidently) may safely be trusted with as large a share of government as they themselves desire."[22] Well, but suppose now the same corruption to be in other men's hearts, that they are in great danger of an ambitious ensnarement if they be trusted with government, is this corruption only in the hearts of ministers, or is it in the hearts of all other men? I suppose he will say "in

---

Palace). See pages 57 and 152. See comments on the two copies of the Complutensian Polyglot that were in the abbey library at the time in *Grand Debate* (Naphtali Press, 2014), p. 390. The Chaldee paraphrase would have been available as well in Buxtorf's great Rabbinical Bible (1618) and the Septuagint in other publications as well.]

17. [Thomas Cartwright, *Commentarii succincti & dilucidi in Proverbia Salomonis* (Amsterdam, 1632), col. 1161.]

18. Maldonate, Mercerus. [Juan de Maldonado, *Commentarii in Praecipuos Sacrae Scripturae Libros Veteris Testamenti* (Paris, 1643), p. 140. Jean Mercier, *Commentarij in Salomonis prouerbia, ecclesiasten, et canticum canticorum* (Geneva, 1573), p. 81.]

19. Melancthon. [Philipp Melanchthon, *Explicatio proverbiorum Salomonis* (1550), p. 195. *Corpus reformatorum: Philippi Melanthonis Opera quae supersunt omnia* (Brunsvigae: C.A. Schwetschke, 1847), volume 14, col. 74.]

20. Jansenius. Diodati. [Cornelius Jansen, *Commentaria in proverbia salomonis* (1568; Antwerp, 1609), p. 207. Giovanni Diodati, *Pious annotations, upon the Holy Bible expounding the difficult places thereof learnedly, and plainly: vvith other things of great importance* (1643), p. 178.

21. D. Jermin. [Michael Jermin, *Paraphrasticall Meditations by way of Commentarie upon the whole booke of the Proverbs of Salomon* (1638), p. 630.]

22. [Coleman, *Hopes Deferred and Dashed*, p. A2.]

all men's hearts," and then his argument will conclude against all civil government. Last of all, Admit that there be just fears of abusing the power and government ecclesiastical; let the persons to be entrusted with it be examined, and the power itself bounded according to the strictest rules of Christ. Let abuses be prevented, reformed, corrected. *The abuse cannot take away the use where the thing itself is necessary.*[23] Why might he not have satisfied himself without speaking against the thing itself? Once, indeed, he seems to recoil, and says, "Only I would have it so bounded, that it might be said, Hitherto shalt thou come, and here shalt thou stay thy proud waves," yet by and by he passes his own bounds and totally renounces the government to the civil power, which I shall speak to anon. But I must first ask, "Whence is this fear of the proud swelling waves of presbyterial government? Where have they done hurt?" Was it upon the coast of France, or upon the coast of Holland, or upon the coast of Scotland, or where was it? Or was it the dashing upon *terra in cognita?*[24] He that would forewarn men to beware of presbyterial usurpations (for so the brother speaking to the present controversy about church government must be apprehended), and to make good what he says falls upon the stories of Pope Paul V and of the Bishop of Canterbury, is not a little wide from the mark. I should have expected some examples of evils and mischiefs which presbyterial government has brought upon other reformed churches.

Well, the reverend brother has not done, but he proceeds thus:

> It was the king of Sodom's speech to Abraham, "Give me the persons, take thou the goods;" so say I, Give us doctrine, take you the government: as is said, Right Honorable, give me leave to make this request in the behalf of the ministry. Give us two things and we shall do well: 1. Give us learning; and, 2. Give us a competency.[25]

This calls to mind a story which Clemens Alexandrinus tells us, when one had painted Helena with much gold, Apelles, looking upon it, "Friend," said he, "when you could not make her fair, you have made her rich."[26] Learning and competency do enrich. The Jesuits have enough of both, but that which makes a visible ministerial church to be "beautiful as Tirzah, comely as Jerusalem,"[27] that which makes fair the outward face of a church, is government and discipline, the removing of scandals, the preserving of the ordinances from pollution. He had spoken more for the honor of God and for the power of godliness if he had said this in the behalf of the ministry:

---

23. [Emphasis added. See the discussion of this in *Popish Ceremonies*, 3.2 (2013), 149ff.]

24. [*Terra in cognita*: unknown land.]

25. [Coleman, *Hopes Deferred and Dashed*, p. 26.]

26. *Paedag.*, lib. 2, cap. 12. [Clement of Alexandria, *Paedagogus*, in PG 8, col. 550. Cf. *ANF* 2, chapter 13, p. 269.]

27. [Cf. Song of Solomon 6:4.]

"It were better for us to want competency and helps to learning, than to partake with other men's sins, by admitting the scandalous and profane to the Lord's table."

His way which he advises will perhaps "get us an able ministry and procure us honor enough,"[28] as he speaks, but, surely, it can neither preserve the purity nor advance the power of religion because it puts no black mark upon profaneness and scandal in church members more than in any others. The king of Sodom's speech cannot serve his turn except it be turned over, and then it will serve him as just as anything, thus: "Give us the goods, take you the persons" (or the souls, as the Hebrew and the Chaldee have it). "Give us a competency," he says. Here he asks the goods. "Take you the government." Here he quits the persons or souls to be governed only by the civil power. However, as at that time Abraham would take nothing that was not his own, insomuch as he answers the king of Sodom: "I will not take from a thread even to a shoe-latchet, and that I will not take anything that is thine" (Gen. 14:23), so this parliament, I trust, shall be so counseled and guided of the Lord that they will leave to the church what is the church's, or rather to Christ what is Christ's. And as Abraham had lift up his hand to the most high God to do that (v. 22), so have the Honorable Houses, with hands lift up to the most high God, promised to do this.

And now, seeing I have touched upon the covenant,[29] I wish the reverend brother may seriously consider whether he has not violated the oath of God in advising the parliament to lay no burden of government upon church officers, but to take the government of the church wholly into their own hands. In the first article of the Solemn League and Covenant, there is thrice mention made of the government of the church; and namely, that we shall endeavor the reformation of religion in the kingdoms of England and Ireland, in doctrine, worship, discipline, and government, according to the Word of God, and the example of the best reformed churches. Where observe, 1. The extirpation of church government is not the reformation of it. The second article[30] is indeed of things to be extirpated; but this of things to be preserved and reformed. Therefore, as by the covenant prelacy was not to be reformed, but to be abolished, so, by the same covenant, church government was not to be abolished, but to be reformed.

2. Church government is mentioned in the covenant as a spiritual, not a civil thing. The matters of religion are put together: doctrine, worship, discipline, and government.[31] The privileges of parliament come after, in the third article.[32]

---

28. [Coleman, *Hopes Deferred and Dashed*, p. 26.]

29. [Covenant: The Solemn League and Covenant (1643). See *The Confession of Faith; the Larger and Shorter Catechisms* ... (Edinburgh: Johnstone and Hunter, 1855), pp. 358–360.]

30. [Ibid., p. 359.]

31. [Ibid., p. 358.]

32. [Ibid., p. 359.]

3. That clause, "According to the Word of God,"[33] implies that the Word of God holds forth such light unto us as may guide and direct us in the reformation of church government.

4. And will the brother say that the example of the best reformed churches[34] leads us his way; that is, to have no church government at all distinct from the civil government?

And so much concerning his third rule.

The fourth was this: "A Christian magistrate, as a Christian magistrate, is a governor in the church."[35] And who denies this? The question is whether there ought to be no other government in the church besides that of the Christian magistrate. That which he drives at is that the Christian magistrate should leave no power of spiritual censures to the elderships. He would have the magistrate to do like the rich man in the parable, who had exceeding many flocks and herds, and yet did take away the little ewe-lamb from the poor man who had nothing save that.[36] The brother says, "Of other governments besides magistracy, I find no institution; of them I do, Romans 13:1–2." I am sorry he sought no better, else he had found more. Subjection and obedience is commanded, as due not only to civil but to spiritual governors, to those that are over us in the Lord, 1 Thessalonians 5:12; so 1 Timothy 5:17, "Let the elders that rule well be counted worthy of double honour;" Hebrews 13:7, "Remember them which have the rule over you, who have spoken unto you the Word of God;" verse 17, "Obey them that have the rule over you, and submit yourselves; for they watch for your souls." And what understands he by "he that ruleth," [in] Romans 12:8? If the judgment of Gwalther and Bullinger have any weight with him (as I suppose it has) they do not there exclude, but take in under that word the ruling officers of the church.[37]

But now, in the close, let the reverend brother take heed he has not split upon a rock and taken from the magistrate more than he has given him; he says

> Christian magistrates are to manage their office under Christ and for Christ. Christ has placed governments in His church, 1 Corinthians 12:28, etc. I find all government given to Christ, and to Christ as Mediator (I desire all to consider it), Ephesians 1:3, 23, and Christ as Head of these, given to the church.

If this be good divinity, then I am sure it will be the hardest task whichever he took in hand to uphold and assert the authority either of pagan or Christian magistrates.

---

33. [Ibid., article 1, p. 359.]

34. [Ibid. article 1, p. 359.]

35. [Coleman, *Hopes Deferred and Dashed*, p. 27.]

36. [See 2 Samuel 12:1–7.]

37. [Cf. Gwalther, *In D. Pauli apostoli epistolam ad Romanos homiliæ* (1566; (Tiguri: Wolphium, 1608), p. 223. Heinrich Bullinger, *Commentarii In omnes Pauli Apostoli Epistolas, atque etiam in Epistolam ad Hebraeos* (1537; Tiguri: Cambierus, 1603), p. 74.]

First, He lets the pagan or infidel magistrate fall to the ground as a usurper who has no just title to reign because all government is given to Christ, and to Him as Mediator. But which way was the authority of government derived from Christ, and from Him as Mediator, to a pagan prince or emperor?

Next, He will make it to fare little better with the Christian magistrate. For if the Christian magistrate be the vicegerent of Christ, and of Christ as Mediator, and if he be to manage his office under and for Christ, then the reverend brother must either prove from Scripture that Christ as Mediator has given such a commission of vicegerentship and deputyship to the Christian magistrate, or otherwise acknowledge that he has given a most dangerous wound to magistracy, and made it an empty title, claiming that power which it has no warrant to assume.

God and nature have made magistrates and given them great authority, but from Christ as Mediator they have it not.

I find in Scripture that church officers have their power from Christ as Mediator, and they are to manage their office under and for Christ, and in the name of the Lord Jesus Christ do we assemble ourselves together (Matt. 18:20); in His name do we preach (Luke 24:47; Acts 4:17, 18; 5:28, 41; 9:27); in His name do we baptize (Acts 2:38; 4:12, 16; 19:5); in His name do we excommunicate (1 Cor. 5:5). But I do not find in Scripture that the magistrate is to rule, or to make laws, or to manage any part of his office in the name of the Lord Jesus Christ. And as the Mediator has not anywhere given such a commission and power to the magistrate, so, as Mediator, He had it not to give; for He was not made a judge in civil affairs (Luke 12:14), and His kingdom is not of this world (John 18:36). How can that power which Christ as Mediator has not received of the Father be derived from Christ to the Christian magistrate? I know that Christ, as He is the eternal Son of God and "thought it no robbery to be equal with God" [Phil. 2:6], does, with the Father and the Holy Ghost, reign and rule over all the kingdoms of the sons of men. He that is Mediator, being God, has, as God, all power in heaven and earth (and this power was given to Him, Matthew 28:18, both by the eternal generation and by the declaration of Him to be the Son of God with power, when He was raised from the dead, Romans 1:4, even as He is said to be begotten when He was raised again, Acts 13:33; He had relinquished and laid aside His divine dominion and power when He had made Himself in the form of a servant, but after His resurrection it is gloriously manifested), and so He that is Mediator, being God, has power to subdue His and His church's enemies, and to make His foes His footstool [cf. Psalm 110:1]. But as Mediator He is only the church's King, Head, and Governor, and has no other kingdom.

The Photinians have defined the kingly office of Christ thus: "It is an office committed to Him by God, to govern, with the highest authority and power, all creatures endued with understanding, and especially men, and the church gathered of them." But those that have written against them have corrected their definition in this particular, because Christ is properly King of His church only.[38]

As for those two scriptures which the brother cites, they are extremely misapplied. He cites 1 Corinthians 12:28 to prove that Christ has placed civil governments in His church.[39] If by the governments or governors there mentioned he understood the civil magistrates, yet that place says not that Christ has placed them, but that God has done it.

Next, The apostle speaks of such governors as the church had at that time; but at that time the church had no godly nor Christian magistrates. This is Calvin's argument whereby he proves that ecclesiastical, not civil governors, are there meant.[40]

Thirdly, I ask, How can we conceive that civil government can come into the catalogue of ecclesiastical and spiritual administrations? For such are all the rest there reckoned forth.

Lastly, The brother, after second thoughts, may think he has done another disservice to the magistrate, in making the magistracy to be below and behind the ministry. The apostle puts them in this order: "God hath set some in the church, first apostles, secondly prophets, thirdly teachers, after that miracles, then gifts of healings, helps, governments," etc. How makes the brother this to agree with his interpretation?

Next, He cites Ephesians 1:21–23,[41] to prove that all government is given to Christ, and to Him as Mediator, and Christ, as Head of these, given to the church. But this place makes more against him than for him; for the apostle says not that Christ is given to the church as the Head of all principalities

---

38. *Religionis Christianae brevis Institutio*, anno 1634, cap. 23. *Quid est regium munus? Resp. Est munus ipsi a Deo commissum omnes creaturas intelligentia praeditas, ac imprimis homines et ex iis collectam ecclesiam, summa cum auctoritate ac potestate gubernandi.* Jac. Martini, *Synops. Relig. Photin.*, cap. 23. *Etiamsi non negemus Christo jam ad dextrum Dei sedenti subjecta esse omnia, […] inimicosque ipsi subjici tanquam Scabellum pedum suorum, &c. Proprie tamen dicitur Rex suae ecclesiae, uti etiam ecclesia, proprie loquendo ejus regnum est. Sic enim de ipso vaticinatus est Zecharias, cap. 9, v. 9, etc. Unde etiam nos cum Hasenreffero officium Christi regium definimus, quo Christus cives suos Verbi ministerio usque ad mundi finem colligit, eosque praeclaris donis ornat, contra hostes (in quorum medio dominatur) fortiter defendit, ac tandem aeterna gloria et honore coronat.* Fr. Gomar. *Anal. prop. Obad.* vers. ult. *Is autem Jesus Christus, in N.T. exhibitus Rex. Qui ut cum patre habet regnum generale omnipotentiae: ita habet speciale, de quo hic agitur, mediationis.* [Fausto Sozzini, *Religionis Christianae Brevis Institutio* (1634), p. 68. *Works* reads "homines et ecclesiam ex iis collectam" [*sic*] and the 1646 second edition omits "ecclesiam." Jacob Martini, *Synopsis totius religionis photinianorum novorum, ex illorum institutione brevi* (Wittebergæ: Bergeri, 1633), pp. 654, 655. Franciscus Gomarus, "Apocalypsis Explicatio, Appendix, ... Analysis Prophetiæ Obadiæ," in *Opera Theologica Omnia*, vol. 2 (Amsterdam: Jansson, 1644), page 544.]

39. [Coleman, *Hopes Deferred and Dashed*, p. 27.]

40. [See John Calvin, *Institutes*, 4.11.1, McNeill and Battles, *Institutes*, 2.1211.]

41. [Coleman, *Hopes Deferred and Dashed*, p. 27–28.]

and powers. The brother says so; and, in saying so, he makes Christ a head to those that are not of His body.

The apostle says far otherwise: That God gave Christ "to be the head over all things to the church, which is his body;" which the Syriac reads more plainly, "And him who is over all he gave to be the head to the church."[42] He is a head to none but the church; but He who is head to the church "is over all, God blessed for ever," Romans 9:5; yea, even as a man, He is over or above all. The very human nature of Christ which was raised from the dead, being set at the right hand of the Majesty of God, is exalted to a higher degree of honor and glory than either man or angel ever was, or ever shall be; so that He that is head of the church is over all, because He does not only excel His own members, but excel all creatures that ever God made. It is one thing to say that Christ is exalted to a dignity, excellency, preeminence, majesty, and glory, far above all principality, and power, and might, and dominion; another thing to say that Christ is head of all principalities and governments, and, as Mediator, exercises His kingly office over these. The apostle says the former, but not the latter.

Shall I need to illustrate this distinction? Is there anything more known in the world? Will any say that he who excels other men in dignity, splendor, honor, and glory, must therefore reign and rule over all those whom he thus excels?

The apostle says indeed, in another sense, that Christ "is the head of all principality and power" (Col. 2:10). But that is spoken of Christ not as He is Mediator, but only as He is God; and the apostle's meaning in those words is nothing but this: That Christ is true God, says Tossanus;[43] that He is omnipotent, says Gwalther;[44] that He, being the natural Son of God, is together with the Father, Lord of all things, says Bullinger.[45]

That this is the meaning will soon appear:

1. From the scope of the place, which is to teach the Colossians not to worship angels because they are but servants, and the Son of God is their Lord and Head.

2. The apostle expounds himself how Christ is the head of all principality and power. Colossians 1:15–17, "Who is the image of the invisible God, the firstborn of every creature: for by him were all things created that are in heaven, and that are in earth, visible and invisible, whether they be thrones, or dominions, or principalities, or powers; all things were created by him,

---

42. [The Antwerp Polyglot added the Syriac text to the texts that had been in the Complutensian. See the text for Ephesians 1:22 in the Antwerp Polyglot, volume 5, p. 336.]

43. [See Daniel Tossanus, Sr., "In Epistolam D. Pauli ad Colossenses," in *Opera*, volume 2 (Hanover, 1604), p. 322.]

44. [Rudolf Gwalther, *Archetypi homiliarum in Epistolas S. Pauli ad Galatas, Ephesios, Philip. Colossens* (Tiguri: Wolphium, 1609), p. 209 *sic* 290.]

45. [Heinrich Bullinger, *In D. Apostoli Pauli ad Galatas, Ephesios, Philippen. et Colossenses epistolas* (Zürich: Christoffel Froschouer, 1535), pp. 248v–249.]

and for him: and he is before all things, and by him all things consist." Now, all this is without controversy to be understood not of the office but of the person of Jesus Christ; not of His governing and kingly office as He is Mediator, but to prove that He is true and very God; therefore, Beza,[46] Zanchius,[47] Gwalther,[48] Bullinger,[49] Tossanus,[50] M. Bayne,[51] and divers other interpreters upon the place do generally agree that the apostle [in] verses 15–17 speaks of the dignity and excellency of the person of Jesus Christ, proving Him to be true God, and that [in] verse 18 he comes to speak of His office as He is Mediator: "And he is the head of the body, the church," etc. So that we may distinguish a twofold headship of Jesus Christ: one, in regard of His Godhead, and so He is head of all principality and power; another, in regard of His office of Mediatorship, and so He is head of the church only. The present question is of the latter, not of the former. The former is common to the Son of God with the Father and the Holy Ghost; the latter is proper to Christ as God and man. The former shall continue forever; the latter shall not continue forever. The former does not necessarily suppose the latter; but the latter does necessarily suppose the former. Christ can reign as God, though He reign not as Mediator; but He cannot reign as Mediator and not reign as God. The object of the former is every creature; the object of the latter is the church gathered out of the world.

This digression concerning the headship of Jesus Christ may for the future prevent diverse objections, so I shall return.

And now (I desire all to consider it) there is not one word in those three last verses of Ephesians [chapter] one, which will give any ground for that which the brother with so much confidence avers.[52] Verse 21 affords this

---

46. [Théodore de Bèze, *Jesu Christi Domini Nostri Novum Testamentum, sive, Novum Foedus* (Cambridge, 1642), pp. 602–603.]

47. [Girolamo Zanchi, "In Epistolam ad Colossenses," in *Omnium opera*, volume 2, part 4–6 (1613), p. 264.]

48. [Gwalther, ibid., pp. 279v–280.]

49. [Bullinger, ibid., pp. 235–238.]

50. [Tossanus, ibid., pp. 312–315.]

51. [Paul Baynes, *A Commentarie vpon the first and second chapters of Saint Paul to the Colossians* (1634), pp. 73–101.]

52. P. Martyr, *Loc. Com.*, clas. 2, cap. 17, p. 293. *Regnare interdum accipi quasi sit, excellere, eminere prae caeteris, et summum locum tenere. Ac ista significatione Christus perpetuo regnabit. Sin vero dicamus regnare idem quod officia regis exercere,* etc. Christus non semper regnabit. ["that to reigne, is sometime taken as it were to excell, to be aboue others, and to hold the highest place. And in this signification Christ shall reigne perpetuallie. But if we saie, that to reigne, is in such sort as to exercise the office of a king, to fight, to defend, to ouercome, and other such like; Christ shall not alwaies reigne" Peter Martyr Vermigli, *Loci communes* (1576; IITH ed., Geneva, 1624), p. 293; trans.: *The Common Places* (1583), p. 607.] Zanchius in Eph. 1:21, expounds the latter part of that verse of the eternity of Christ's kingdom; but he adds: *Finis erit regnandi hoc modo quo jam regnat, tanquam Mediator.* ["finis denique erit regnandi, hoc

argument against him: The honor and dignity of Jesus Christ there spoken of has place "not only in this world, but also in that which is to come." But the kingdom and government which is given to Christ as Mediator shall not continue in the world to come (for when Christ has put His enemies under His feet, He shall deliver up the kingdom to the Father, and reign no longer as Mediator, 1 Corinthians 15:24, 25). Therefore, the government given to Christ as He is Mediator cannot be meant in that place, but the dignifying, honoring, preferring, and exalting of Christ to a higher degree of glory than either man or angel.

Come on now and see whether verse 22 makes any whit more for him. He "hath put all things under his feet;" that is, says Zanchius, all things but the church, which is His body.[53] But this must be meant in respect of the decree and foreknowledge of God, as Jerome expounds the place;[54] and so does the Scripture expound itself. Hebrews 2:8. "But now we see not yet all things put under him." 1 Corinthians 15:25. "He must reign, till he hath put all enemies under his feet." Acts 2:34–35. "Sit thou on my right hand, until I make thy foes thy footstool." Now, when Christ shall have put down all rule, and all authority, and power, and shall put His enemies under His feet, then He shall cease to reign anymore as Mediator (which I have even now proved); but before that be done, He reigns as Mediator. So that it can never be proved that the meaning of these words, "He hath put all things under his feet," is that all government in this world is given to Christ as Mediator; and whoever says so must needs acknowledge that Christ's exercising of government as He is Mediator over all principalities and powers shall continue after all things shall be put under His feet, or that Christ shall not govern as Mediator, "till all things be put under his feet," which is so contrary to the apostle's meaning that Christ shall then cease to reign as Mediator.

The next words, "And he gave him to be the head over all things to the church," do furnish another argument against him. Christ's headship and His government as Mediator are commensurable and of an equal extent. Christ is a head to none but to His church; therefore, no government is given to Him as Mediator but the government of His church.

The last verse does further confirm that which I say; for the apostle, continuing his speech of the church, says, "Which is his body, the fulness of him that filleth all in all." He calls the church Christ's fullness in reference to His headship, that which makes Him full and complete so far as He is a head or king. Having His church fully gathered, He has His complete kingdom, His perfect body, and this being done, He wants [*lacks*] nothing, so far

---

modo, quo iam regnat, tanquam Mediator…." Girolamo Zanchi, "In Epistolam ad Ephesios," in *Omnium opera*, volume 2, part 4–6 (1613), p. 73 *sic* 37.]

53. [Zanchi, ibid., p. 74 *sic* 38.]

54. [See Jerome, *Commentariorum in Epistolam ad Ephesios, Libri Tres*, in PL 26, col. 462; and see *The Commentaries of Origen and Jerome on St. Paul's Epistle to the Ephesians*, trans. Ronald E. Heine (Oxford University Press, 2002), p. 115.]

as He is Mediator: so that the Holy Ghost does here, as it were on purpose, anticipate this opinion, lest any should think all civil government is given to Christ as Mediator. Though, as God, He fills heaven and earth, yet, as Mediator His filling of all in all extends no further than His body, His church, which is therefore called His fullness.

Finally, To avoid the mistake of this place, and upon the whole matter, let these three things be well distinguished in the Mediator Jesus Christ.

1. His ὑπεροχὴ or δύξα, His eminence and highness in respect of the glory and majesty He is exalted to, far above whatsoever is highest among all the creatures. 2. His δύναμις, the power by which He can, and does by degrees, and will more and more subdue His and His church's enemies, and dash them in pieces like a potter's vessel, and break them with a rod of iron [Ps. 2:9]. 3. His Βασιλεία, His kingly power, by which He exercises acts of government. These three are distinguished in an earthly king, the first two being of a larger extent than the third. The conclusion of that prayer which our Lord taught His disciples does distinguish the same three in God: "Thine is the kingdom, and the power, and the glory." Now these being distinguished in the Mediator Jesus Christ, I conclude with these three distinct assertions (the truth whereof I hope I have made to appear): 1. As Mediator, He is exalted and dignified above all creatures, and His glory is above all the earth; 2. As Mediator, He exercises acts of divine power and omnipotence over all creatures in the behalf of and for the good of His church, and restrains, or diverts, or destroys all His church's enemies; 3. As Mediator, He is king, head, and governor to none but His church; neither was all government put in His hand, but that of the church only.

I could enlarge myself further against that most dangerous principle, "That all government, even that which is civil, is given to Christ, and to Him as Mediator," but let these things suffice for the present. The reverend brother's opinion will find better entertainment among the Jews, who expect a temporal monarchy of the Messiah, and among papists, who desire to uphold the Pope's temporal authority over kings, as Christ's vicegerent upon earth.

Nihil Respondes: Or,

A Discovery of the Extreme Unsatisfactoriness of

Mr. Coleman's Piece, Published Last Week under

The Title of *A Brotherly Examination Re-Examined*

Wherein his self-contradictions; his yielding of some things, and not answering to other things objected against him; his abusing of Scripture; his errors in divinity; his abusing of the parliament, and endangering their authority; his abusing of the assembly; his calumnies, namely, against the Church of Scotland and against myself; the repugnancy of his doctrine to the Solemn League & Covenant, are plainly demonstrated

1 Timothy 1:7
Understanding neither what they say, nor whereof they affirm.

Nihil Respondes: or, A Discovery of the extream unsatisfactorinesse of Mr. Coleman's Peece, Published last weeke Under the Title of A Brotherly Examination re-examined. Wherein his self-contradictions; his yeelding of some things, and not answering to other things Objected against him; his abusing of Scripture; his errors in Divinity; his abusing of the Parliament, and endangering their Authority; his abusing of the Assembly; his Calumnies, namely, against the Church of Scotland and against my selfe; the repugnancy of his Doctrin to the solemne League and Covenant, are plainly demonstrated. By Mr. George Gillespie Minister at Edenburgh.

Editions

1. *Nihil Respondes: or, A Discovery of the extream unsatisfactorinesse of Mr. Coleman's Peece, Published last weeke Under the Title of A Brotherly Examination re-examined,* etc. Published by Authority. Printed at London for Robert Bostock dwelling in Pauls Church-yard, at the signe of the Kings head. 1645. [2], 34 p.; 4^0. ESTC R200413 (Wing G755). Thomason, E.309[9]. "Annotation on Thomason copy: 'Nouemb: 13.'"

3. *Nihil Reſpondes: Or A Discovery Of The Extreme Unſatisfaċoriness Of Mr Coleman's Piece, Published Laſt Week Under the Title of "A Brotherly Examination Re-Examined." Wherein his self contradiċions; his yielding of some things, and not answering to other things objeċed againſt him; his abusing of Scripture; his errors in divinity; his abusing of the Parliament, and endangering their authority; his abusing of the Assembly; his calumnies, namely, againſt the Church of Scotland and againſt myself; the repugnancy of his doċrine to the Solemn League and Covenant;—are plainly demonſtrated. By George Gilleſpie, Miniſter At Edinburgh, 1642* (Edinburgh: Robert Ogle and Oliver and Boyd, 1844). In *Works* in *A Presbyterian's Armoury.* 19 pp.; royal octavo.

The Epigraph on the prior page is from the first edition.

A Discovery of the extreme unsatisfactoriness of Coleman's Piece, published last week under the Title of, *A Brotherly Examination re-examined*[1]

AFTER THAT Mr. Coleman had preached and printed such doctrine as I was, in my conscience, fully persuaded was contrary to the covenant of the three kingdoms and destructive (if it were put in practice) to the reformation of religion, he having also flatly and publicly imputed to the Commissioners from the Church of Scotland a great part of the fault of hindering union in the Assembly here, I thought myself obliged in duty and in the trust which I bear, to give a public testimony against his doctrine (which others did also) upon occasion not sought, but by divine providence and a public calling then offered, first for preaching, and after for printing, in either of which I think there did not appear the least disrespect or bitterness towards the reverend brother. The Lord knows my intention was to speak to the matter, to vindicate the truth, and to remove that impediment of reformation by him cast in; and if he, or any man else had in meekness of spirit gravely and rationally, for clearing of truth, endeavored to confute me, I ought not, I should not, have taken it ill; but now, when this piece of his against me, called *A Brotherly Examination Re-examined* (I think he would or should have said *examined*, for this is the first examination of it), I find it more full of *railing* than of *reasoning*, of *gibing*[2] than of *gravity*; and when polemics do so degenerate, the world is abused not edified. He tells me if I have not work enough I shall have more. I confess the answering of this piece is no great work; and the truth is, I am ashamed I have so little to make answer unto; yet, I shall do my best to improve even this work to edification. When other work comes I wish it be work indeed, and not words. *Res cum re, ratio cum ratione concertet,* as the father said:[3] Arguments, sir, arguments, arguments, if there be any: you have affirmed great things, and new things, which you have not proved. The assertions of such as are for a church government *in genere,* and for the presbyterial government *in specie,* are known; their arguments are known, but your solutions are not yet known. If Mr. Prynne's book against the suspension of scandalous persons from the sacrament be the work for the present

---

1. [Thomas Coleman, *A Brotherly Examination re-examined* (1646 *sic* 1645). Thomason's copy is dated November 1, and Gillespie's *Nihil Respondes* is dated November 13.]

2. [*Gibing*: probably in the sense of behaving like a cat, yowling and caterwauling. Perhaps *jibbing*, as in jibber-jabber; to utter nonsense.]

3. [Augustine, *Contra Maximinum Arianorum*, in *PL* 42, col. 772.]

which he means,[4] I hope it shall be in due time most satisfactorily spoken unto, both by others and by myself. I desire rather solid than subitane [*spontaneous; unpremeditated*] lucubrations.[5] In the meanwhile, "Let not him that putteth on his armour boast as he that putteth it off" [1 Kings 20:11]. And let the brother that puts me in mind of other work remember that himself has other work to do which he has not yet done.

I have, for better method and clearness, divided this following discourse into certain heads, taking in under every head such particulars in his reply as I conceive to be most proper to that point.

THAT MR. COLEMAN DOES NOT ONLY PREVARICATE, BUT CONTRADICT HIMSELF, CONCERNING THE STATE OF THE QUESTION

He tells us often that he does not deny to church officers all power of church government, but only the corrective part of government; that the doctrinal and declarative power is in the ministry; see pages 11, 14.[6] He denies that he did "advise the parliament to take church government wholly into their own hands; I never had it in my thoughts," he says, "that the parliament had power of dispensing the Word and sacraments." I must confess it is to me new language, which I never heard before, that the dispensing of the Word and sacraments is a part of church government; surely, the word government is not nor never was so understood in the controversies concerning church government. But if it be, why did the brother in his sermon oppose doctrine and government? "Give us doctrine," he said, "take you the government."[7] But behold now how he does most palpably contradict himself in one and the same page. It is the 11TH [page]. "I know no such distinction of government," he says, "ecclesiastical and civil, in the sense I take government for the corrective part thereof; all ecclesiastical (improperly called) government being merely doctrinal; the corrective or punitive part being civil or temporal." Again, within a few lines, "I do acknowledge a presbyterian government; I said so expressly in my epistle; and do heartily subscribe to the votes of the house." If he heartily subscribes to the votes and ordinances of parliament, then he heartily subscribes that elderships suspend men from the sacrament for any of the scandals enumerated, it being proved by witnesses upon oath: this power is corrective, not merely doctrinal. He must also subscribe to the subordination of congregational, classical, and synodical assemblies in the

---

4. [Coleman refers to finding some other ministers in London who agreed with him. *Brotherly Examination re-examined*, page 2. William Prynne, *A vindication of foure serious questions of grand importance, concerning excommunication and suspention from the sacrament of the Lords Supper* (1645). Thomason records for his copy a date of October 3, 1645.]

5. [*Lucubration*: a piece of writing, typically a pedantic or over-elaborate one (Oxford).]

6. [Unless otherwise noted, page references refer to Coleman's *Re-examination*.]

7. [Coleman, *Hopes Deferred and Dashed*, p. 26.]

government of the church, and to appeals from the lesser to the greater, as likewise to ordination by presbyteries. And, I pray, is all this merely doctrinal? And will he now subscribe heartily to all this? How will that stand with the other passages before cited? Or with page 17, where it being objected to him that he takes away from elderships all power of spiritual censures, his reply neither yields excommunication nor suspension, but admonition alone, and that by the ministers who are a part of the elderships, not by the whole eldership consistorially. Again, page 14, he confesses: "I advised the parliament to lay no burden of government upon them, whom he, this commissioner, thinks church officers, pastors, and ruling elders." Now, I argue thus: He that advises the parliament to lay no burden of government upon ministers and ruling elders, he advises the parliament to do contrary to their own votes and ordinances, and so is far from subscribing heartily thereunto. But Mr. Coleman, by his own confession, advises the parliament to lay no burden of government upon ministers and ruling elders; *Ergo* [*therefore*], etc. How he will reconcile himself with himself, let him look to it.

Page 11. He takes it ill that one while [*one time*] I make him an enemy to all church government, then [another time] *only* to the presbyterial. "Only" is his own addition. But I had reason to make him an enemy to both, for so he has made himself; yea, in opposing all church government, he cannot choose but oppose presbyterial government, for the consequence is necessary, *a genere ad speciem*, negatively though not affirmatively. If no church government, then no presbyterial government.

The particulars in my brief Examination, which Mr. Coleman either
grants expressly, or else does not reply unto

My argument, page 32,[8] proving that as many things ought to be established *jure divino* as can well be, because he cannot answer it, therefore he grants it (page 5).[9]

He had in his sermon called for plain and clear institutions,[10] and let Scripture speak expressly. Now, page 7, he yields that it is not only a divine truth (as I called it) but clear scripture, which is drawn by necessary consequence from Scripture.

He has not yet, though put in mind, produced the least exception against the known arguments for excommunication and church government drawn from Matthew 18, and [for] 1 Corinthians 5, he tells the affirmer is to prove; but the affirmers have proved, and their arguments are known (yea, he himself, page 1, says, "I have had the opportunity to hear almost what man can say in either side," speaking of the controversy of church government); therefore,

---

8. [In this present volume, see *Brotherly Examination*, p. 222.]

9. [*Works* begins the next paragraph with "Page 5," but the first edition is correct.]

10. [Coleman, *Hopes Deferred and Dashed*, p. 24–25.]

he should have made a better answer than to say that those places did not take hold of his conscience; yet if he have not heard enough of those places, he shall, I trust, ere long hear more.

He had said, "I could never yet see how two coordinate governments, exempt from superiority and inferiority, can be in one state," page 35.[11] I gave him three instances: A general and an admiral; a father and a master; a captain and a master of a ship.[12] This, page 8, he does not deny, nor says one word against it; only he endeavors to make those similes to run upon four feet, and to resemble the General Assembly and the Parliament in every circumstance. But I did not at all apply them to the General Assembly and the Parliament; only I brought them to overthrow that general thesis of his concerning the inconsistency of two coordinate governments, which, if he could defend, why has not he done it?

His keeping up of the names of clergy and laity being challenged by me, page 36,[13] he has not said one word in his *Re-examination* to justify it.

I having, pages 37, 38,[14] confuted his argument drawn from the measuring of others by himself, whereby he did endeavor to prove that he had cause to fear an ambitious ensnarement in others as well as in himself, God having fashioned all men's hearts alike, now he quits his ground and says nothing for vindicating that argument from my exceptions.

I showed, page 40,[15] his misapplying of the king of Sodom's speech, but neither in this does he vindicate himself.

That which I had at length excepted against his fourth rule concerning the magistrate, and his confirmation thereof, he has not answered, nor so much as touched anything which I had said against him, from the end of page 42 to the end of page 48, except only a part of page 43 and of page 44, concerning 1 Corinthians 12:28.[16] Some contrary argumentations he has [on] page 21, of which after, but no answer to mine.

Page 10. He digresses to other objections of his own framing, instead of taking off what I had said.

His abusing of the Scriptures

Mr. Coleman did ground an argument upon Psalm 33:15 [and] Proverbs 27:29, which cannot stand with the intent of the Holy Ghost, because contrary to other scriptures and to the truth, as I proved [on] page 38.[17] He answers in

---

11. [Coleman, *Hopes Deferred and Dashed*, p. 25.]

12. [*Brotherly Examination*, herein p. 224.]

13. [*Brotherly Examination*, p. 225.]

14. [*Brotherly Examination*, pp. 225–226.]

15. [*Brotherly Examination*, p. 228.]

16. [*Brotherly Examination*, pp. 230–236, 231–232.]

17. [*Brotherly Examination*, p. 227.]

his *Re-examination*, that my sense may stand, and his may stand too. But if my sense may stand, which is contrary to his, then his argument had no sure ground for it; yea, that which I said was to prove that his consequence drawn from those scriptures did contradict both the Apostle Paul's doctrine and his own profession, which still lies upon him since it is not answered.

Page 14. He cites 1 Corinthians 10:32, "Give none offence, neither to the Jews, nor to the Gentiles, nor to the church of God," to prove that all government is either a Jewish government, or a church government, or a heathenish government, and that "there is no third." Yes, sir, yourself has given a third (for you have told three), but *transeat cum cæteris erroribus*.[18] To the matter: This is a perverting of Scripture to prove an untruth; for the government of generals, admirals, majors, sheriffs, is neither a Jewish government, nor a church government, nor a heathenish government. Neither does the apostle speak anything of government in that place. He makes a distribution of all men who are in danger to be scandalized, not of governments; and if he had applied the place rightly to the Parliament of England, he had said, 'they are either of the Jews, or of the Gentiles, or of the church of God,' and this needs not an answer. But when he says, "The English Parliament is either a Jewish government, or a church government, or a heathenish government," I ANSWER, It is none of these, but it is a civil government.

Page 15. Declaring his opinion of church government he cites Romans 13:4, "To execute wrath upon him that doeth evil," to prove that the punitive part belongs to the Christian magistrate. But what is this to the punitive part which is in controversy—spiritual censures, suspension from the sacraments, deposition from the ministry, excommunication? The punitive part spoken of in Romans 13 belongs to all civil magistrates, whether Christian or infidel.

Page 18. He makes this reply to 1 Thessalonians 5:12, 1 Timothy 17 [*sic* 1:17], [and] Hebrews 13:7, 17: "Why, man, I have found these a hundred and a hundred times twice told, and yet am I as I was." Why, sir, was the argument so ridiculous? I had brought those places to prove another government (and, if you will, the institution of another government) besides magistracy, which he said he did not find in Scripture. Here are some who are no civil magistrates set over the Thessalonians in the Lord (1 Thessalonians 5:12). Paul writes to Timothy of elders that rule well (1 Timothy 5:17). The churches of the Hebrews had some rulers who had spoken to them the Word of God (Hebrews 13:7); rulers that watched for their souls as they that must give an account (v. 17). Now, let the reverend brother speak out. What can he answer? Were these rulers civil magistrates? Did the civil magistrate speak to them the Word of God? If these rulers were not magistrates but ministers, I ask next, is it a matter of indifferency, and no institution, to have a ministry in a church or not? I hope, though he does not acknowledge ruling elders *jure divino*, yet he will acknowledge that the ministers of the Word are *jure divino*; yet these

---

18. [*Transeat cum cæteris erroribus*: Let it go with the other errors.]

were some of the rulers mentioned in the scriptures quoted. Let him loose the knot, and laugh when he hath [*is*] done.

Page 19, 20, He labors to prove from 1 Corinthians 12:28 that Christ has placed civil government in His church, and whereas it is said that though it were granted that civil governments are meant in that place, yet it proves not that Christ has placed them in the church, he replies, "I am sure the commissioner will not stand to this: he that placed governors was the same that placed teachers." But his assurance deceives him; for upon supposition that civil governments are there meant (which is his sense), I deny it, and he does but *petere principium*.[19] God placed civil governments; Christ placed teachers; God placed all whom Christ placed, but Christ did not place all whom God placed.

Next, whereas it was said that governments in that place cannot be meant of Christian magistrates because at that time the church had no Christian magistrates, he replies that Paul speaks of governments that the church had not because in the enumeration [in] verses 29, 30, he omits none but helps and governments. I ANSWER, The reason of that omission is not because these two were not then in being (for God had set them as well as the rest in the church, verse 28), but to make ruling elders and deacons contented with their station, though they be not prophets, teachers, etc. Thirdly, I asked, How comes civil government into the catalogue of ecclesiastical and spiritual administrations? His reply is nothing but an affirmation that Christian magistracy is an ecclesiastical administration and a query whether working of miracles and gifts of healings be ecclesiastical. ANSWER. Hence follow, 1. That if the magistrate ceases to be Christian he loses his administration. 2. That though a worker of miracles ceases to be Christian, yet it is a question whether he may not still work miracles.

Lastly, Where I objected that he puts magistracy behind ministry, he makes no answer but only that he may do this, as well as my rule puts the nobility of Scotland behind the ministry. No, sir, we put but ruling elders behind ministers in the order of their administrations because the apostle does so. It is accidental to the ruling elder to be of the nobility or to nobles to be ruling elders: there are but some so, and many otherwise. That of placing deacons before elders [in] 1 Corinthians 12:28 is no great matter; surely the apostle, Romans 12, places elders before deacons.

HIS ERRORS IN DIVINITY

---

1. Page 21. He admits no church government distinct from civil, except that which is merely doctrinal; and, page 14, he advises the parliament to take the corrective power wholly into their own hands and exempts nothing of ecclesiastical power from their hands but the dispensing of the Word and

---

19. [*Petere principium*: beg the question; assume that which is to be proved.]

sacraments. Hence it follows that there ought to be neither suspension from the sacrament, nor excommunication, nor ordination, nor deposition of ministers, nor receiving of appeals, except all these things be done by the civil magistrate. If he say the magistrate gives leave to do these things, I ANSWER, (1) So does he give leave to preach the Word and minister the sacraments in his dominions. (2) Why does he then in his sermon, and does still in his *Re-examination* (p. 14), advise the parliament to lay no burden of corrective government upon ministers, but keep it wholly in their own hands? It must needs be far contrary to his mind that the magistrate gives leave to do the things above mentioned, they being most of them corrective and all of them more than doctrinal. (3) He gives no more power to ministers in church government than in civil government; for, page 11, he ascribes to them a ministerial, doctrinal, and declarative power, both in civil and ecclesiastical government.

2. Pages 11, 14. He holds that the corrective or punitive part of church government is civil or temporal, and is wholly to be kept in the magistrate's own hands; and in his sermon (p. 25), he told us he sees not in the whole Bible any one act of that church government in controversy performed. All which how erroneous it is appears easily from 1 Corinthians 5:13, "Put away from among yourselves that wicked person" (which Mr. Prynne himself, in his *Vindication*,[20] page 2, acknowledged to be a warrant for excommunication); 2 Corinthians 2:6, there is a "punishment," or censure, "inflicted of many"; 1 Timothy 5:19, "Against an elder receive not an accusation, but before two or three witnesses." Where acts of church government or censures were neglected it is extremely blamed (Rev. 2:14, 15, 20). Was not all this corrective? Yet not civil or temporal.

3. Page 9. Whereas I had said that without church government ministers shall not keep themselves nor the ordinances from pollution, he replies that he understands neither this keeping of themselves from pollution, nor what this pollution of the ordinances is. I am sorry for it, that any minister of the gospel is found unclear in such a point. I will not give my own, but scriptural answers to both. The former is answered [in] 1 Timothy 5:22, be not "partaker of other men's sins: keep thyself pure." It is sin to dispense ordinances to the unworthy, whether ordination or communion in the sacrament. For the other, the pollution of ordinances is the Scripture language. I hope he means not to quarrel at the Holy Ghost's language: Ezekiel 22:26, "Her priests have violated my law, and have profaned mine holy things: they have put no difference between the holy and profane"; Malachi 1:7, "Ye offer polluted bread upon mine altar"; verse 12, "Ye have profaned it"; Matthew 21:13, "Ye have made it a den of thieves"; Matthew 7:6, "Neither cast ye your pearls before swine, lest they trample them under their feet."

4. Page 11. Whereas I had objected to him that he excludes ruling elders as well as ministers from government, he answers that ruling elders are either

---

20. [William Prynne, *A vindication of foure serious questions*, ibid.]

the same for office and ordination with the minister (which, as he thinks, the Independents own, but not I), or they are the Christian magistrate; and so he says he does not exclude them. Mark here, he excludes all ruling elders from a share in church government who are not either the same for office and ordination with the minister or else the Christian magistrate; and so, upon the matter, he holds that ruling elders are to have no hand in church government. Those ruling elders which are in the votes of the Assembly and in the reformed churches, have neither the power of civil magistracy (*qua* elders, and many of them not at all, being no magistrates), nor yet are they the same for office and ordination with the minister; for their office, and consequently, their ordination to that office, is distinct from that of the minister among all that I know. And so, excluding all ruling elders from government who are neither magistrates nor the same with ministers, he must needs take upon him that which I charged him with.

5. Page 21. Where he makes reply to what I said against his argument from Ephesians 1:19–21, he says he will blow away all my discourse with this clear demonstration: "That which is given to Christ, He has it not as God, and Christ as God cannot be given. But this place (Eph. 1:19–21) speaks both of dignity given to Christ and of Christ as a gift given; therefore, Christ cannot be here understood as God." This is in opposition to what I said [on] page 45 concerning the headship and dignity of Christ as the natural son of God, "the image of the invisible God" (Col. 1:15), and [on] page 43 of the dominion of Christ as He is the "eternal Son of God."[21] This being premised, the brother's demonstration is so strong as to blow himself into a blasphemous heresy. I will take the proposition from himself and the assumption from Scripture thus: That which is given to Christ He has it not as God. But all power in heaven and in earth is given to Christ (Matt. 28:18); life is given to Christ (John 5:26); authority to execute judgment is given to Christ (v. 27); all things are given into Christ's hands (John 3:35); the Father has given Him power over all flesh (John 17:2); He has given Him glory (John 17:22): *Ergo*, [*therefore*], by Mr. Coleman's principles, Christ has neither life, nor glory, nor authority to execute judgment, nor power over all flesh, as He is the eternal Son of God, consubstantial with the Father, but only as He is Mediator, God and man. As for the giving of Christ as God, what if I argue thus? If Christ, as He is the eternal Son of God, or Second Person of the ever-blessed Trinity, could not be given, then the incarnation itself, or the sending of the Son of God to take on our flesh, cannot be called a giving of a gift to us. But this were impious to say. *Ergo*[, etc.][22] Again, if Christ as He is the Second Person of the blessed Trinity could not be given, then the Holy Ghost as the Third Person cannot be given (for they are co-essential; and that which

---

21. [See *Brotherly Examination*, herein pp. 231 and 233.]

22. [*Works* rendered this "But this were impious to say. Therefore, again…." However, the *Ergo* belonged to the conclusion of the prior argument, not with the next point beginning with "Again."]

were a dishonor to God the Son were a dishonor to God the Holy Ghost);
but to say that the Holy Ghost cannot be given as the Third Person were to
say that He cannot be given as the Holy Ghost. And what will he then say
to all those scriptures that speak of the giving of the Holy Ghost (Acts 15:8;
Rom. 5:5; 1 John 4:13, etc.)?

Finally, As Mr. Coleman's demonstration has blown away itself, so it could
not hurt me were it solid and good (as it is not), for he should have taken
notice that in my examination I did not restrict the dignity given to Christ
(Eph. 1:21), nor the giving of Christ (v. 22), to the Divine nature only. Nay,
I told, pages 44, 46,[23] that these words of the apostle hold true even of the
human nature of Christ.

6. Page 21. He concludes with a syllogism, which he calls the scope of my
discourse (I know not by what logic, the proposition being forged by himself, and contrary to my discourse); thus it is:

> Whosoever do not manage their office and authority under Christ, and for
> Christ, they manage it under the devil, and for the devil; for there is no middle:
> either Christ or Belial. He that is not with me is against me.

> But, according to the opinion of the commissioner, Christian magistracy does
> not manage the office and authority thereof under Christ, and for Christ.

> Therefore, He believes I shall be hard put to it to give the kingdom a clear
> and satisfactory answer. It is well that this is the hardest task he could set me.

The truth is his syllogism has *quatuor terminos*,[24] and is therefore worthy
to be exploded by all that know the laws of disputation. Those words in
the proposition, "under Christ, and for Christ," can have no other sense but
to be serviceable to Christ, to take part with Him, and to be for the glory
of Christ, as is clear by the confirmation added, "He that is not with me is
against me." But the same words in the assumption must needs have another
sense, "Under Christ, and for Christ;" that is, *vice Christi*, in Christ's stead. For
that which I denied was that magistracy is derived from Christ as Mediator,
or that Christ as Mediator has given a commission of vicegerentship and
deputyship to the Christian magistrate to manage His office and authority
under and for Him and in His name, as is clear in my examination (p. 42).[25]
Nay, Mr. Coleman himself, a little before his syllogism (p. 19), takes notice
of so much. His words are these: "The commissioner says, magistracy is not
derived from Christ: I say, magistracy is given to Christ to be serviceable in
His kingdom; so that, though the commissioner's assertion be sound (which
in due place will be discussed), yet it infringes nothing that I said." Now

---

23. [See *Brotherly Examination*, herein pp. 232 and 234.]

24. [*Quatuor terminos*: four terms.]

25. [See *Brotherly Examination*, herein pp. 231.]

then, *qua fide* [*by what faith*] could he in his argument against me confound these two things which he himself had but just now carefully distinguished? If he will make anything of his syllogism he must hold at one of these two senses. In the first sense it is true that all are either for Christ or against Christ, and it is as true that his assumption must be distinguished. For, *de facto*, the Christian magistrate is for Christ when he does his duty faithfully and is against Christ if he be unfaithful. But, *de jure*, it holds true universally that the Christian magistrate manages his office under and for Christ; that is, so as to be serviceable for the kingdom and glory of Christ. In the second sense (which only concerns me), taking "under and for Christ," to be in Christ's stead as His deputies or vicegerents; so, his assumption is lame and imperfect because it does not hold forth my opinion clearly. That which I did and still do hold is this: That the civil magistrate, whether Christian or pagan, is God's vicegerent, who by virtue of his vicegerentship is to manage his office and authority under God and for God; that is, in God's stead and as God upon earth. But he is not the vicegerent of Christ as Mediator, neither is he by virtue of any such vicegerentship to manage his office and authority under Christ and for Christ; that is, in Christ's stead and as Christ [*Christ's*] Mediator upon earth. This was and is my plain opinion (not mine alone, but of others more learned), and Mr. Coleman has not said so much as γρυ to confute it.[26] So much for the assumption. But in the same sense I utterly deny his proposition as being a great untruth in divinity; for the sense of it can be no other than this: Whosoever does not manage their office and authority in Christ's stead or as deputies and vicegerents of Christ as He is Mediator, they manage it in the devil's stead as the devil's deputies and vicegerents. Now, I assume pagan magistrates do not manage their office as the deputies and vicegerents of Jesus Christ as He is Mediator, *ergo* [*therefore*], as the devil's deputies. Which way was the authority derived to them from Christ as Mediator? Mr. Coleman, page 19, says in answer to this particular, formerly objected, that Christ is rightful king of the whole earth and all nations ought to receive Christ, though as yet they do not. But this helps him not. That which he had to show was that the pagan magistrate, even while continuing pagan and not Christian, does manage his office as Christ's deputy and vicegerent; if not, then I conclude by his principles, a pagan magistrate is the devil's deputy and vicegerent, which is contrary to Paul's doctrine, who will have us to be subject for conscience' sake even to heathen magistrates, as the ministers of God for good (Rom. 13:1–7). By the same argument, Mr. Coleman must grant that generals, admirals, majors,

---

26. [ΓΡΥ or γρῦ: LSJ: Used with the negative, "not a syllable," "not so much as a grunt." "The least trifle" (Charlton T. Lewis, Charles Short, *A Latin Dictionary* {1879}). "Mutter, complain" (Walter Bauer, *Greek English Lexicon of the New Testament and other early Christian Literature*, 2010). "Anything very small, a trifle; a small piece of money; the dirt of the nails, the grunt of a hog; also the muttering of one who is vexed or cross and refuses an answer." John Pickering, *Greek and English Lexicon* (1832), p. 166.]

sheriffs, constables, captains, masters, yea, every man that has an office, is either Christ's vicegerent or the devil's vicegerent, than which what can be more absurd? I might, besides all these, show some other flaws in his divinity, as, namely, pages 9 and 13, he does not agree to this proposition, that "the admitting of the scandalous and profane to the Lord's table makes ministers to partake of their sins;" and he supposes that ministers may do their duty, though they admit the scandalous; but of this elsewhere.

His abusing of the Honourable Houses of Parliament

Most honorable senators, I humbly beseech you to look about you and take notice how far you are abused by Mr. Coleman.

First, While he pretends to give you more than his brethren, he takes a great deal more from you, and so far as in him lies, even shakes the foundation of your authority. The known tenure of magistracy is from God. He is the minister of God (for good, and the powers that are, are ordained of God, says the apostle [Rom. 13:1]). The magistrate is God's vicegerent; but now this brother seeks a new tenure and derivation of magistracy, which takes away the old. He told in his sermon, page 27:

> Christ hath placed governments in his church (1 Cor. 12:28); of other governments besides magistracy I find no institution, of them I do (Rom. 13:1–2). I find all government given to Christ, and to Christ as Mediator (I desire all to consider it), Ephesians 1, three last verses [21–23], and Christ as head of those given to the church.[27]

Here you have these three in subordination: God, Christ, and the Christian magistrate. God gives once all government, even civil, to Christ, and to Him as Mediator. Well, but how comes it then to the magistrate? Not straight by a deputation from God. Mr. Coleman's doctrine makes an interception of the power. He holds that God has put it in Christ's hands as Mediator. How then? The brother holds that Christ as Mediator has instituted and placed the Christian magistrate, yea, and no other government, in His church. This was the ground of my answer that he (p. 42)

> must either prove from Scripture that Christ as Mediator has given such a commission of vicegerentship and deputyship to the Christian magistrate, or otherwise acknowledge that he has given a most dangerous wound to magistracy and made it an empty title, claiming that power which it has no warrant to assume.[28]

---

27. [Coleman, *Hopes Deferred and Dashed*, p. 27.]
28. [*Brotherly Examination*, herein p. 231.]

I added: "As the Mediator has not anywhere given such a commission and power to the magistrate, so, as Mediator, He had it not to give; for He was not made a judge in civil affairs (Luke 12:14); 'And his kingdom is not of this world' (John 18:36)."[29] Now, but what reply has he made to all this? Page 19, he says, granting it all to be true and sound, yet it infringes not what he said. "The commissioner," he says, "says magistracy is not derived from Christ. I say magistracy is given to Christ to be serviceable in His kingdom."[30] But by his good leave and favor, he said a great deal more than this, for he spoke of Christ's being head of all civil governments, and His placing these in His church as He is Mediator. Yea, that fourth rule delivered by him in his sermon did hold forth these assertions:

1. That God gave all government, even civil [government], to Christ, and to him as Mediator.

2 That Christ, as Mediator, has power and authority to place and substitute under and for Him the Christian magistrate.

3. That Christ has placed and instituted civil governments in His church to be under and for Him as He is Mediator.

4. That the Christian magistrate does and all magistrates should manage their office under and for Christ (that is, as His vicegerents), He being, as Mediator, head of all civil government.[31]

Now, instead of defending his doctrine from my just exceptions made against it, he resiles [*withdraws*], and having brought the magistrate in a snare, leaves him there. He endeavors to vindicate no more but this, That magistracy is given to Christ to be serviceable in His kingdom. But if he had said so at first, I had said with him and not against him in that point; and if he will yet hold at that, why does he [on] page 19 refer my assertion to further discussion?

Secondly, He has abused the parliament in holding forth that rule to them in his sermon, "Establish as few things *jure divino* as can well be." And yet now he is made, by strength of argument, to acknowledge, page 5, that this is a good rule, "Establish as many things *jure divino* as can well be."[32]

Thirdly, I having stated the question to be not whether this or that form of church government be *jure divino*, but whether *a* church government be *jure divino*; whether Christ has thus far revealed His will in His word, that there are to be church censures, and those to be dispensed by church-officers,

---

29. [*Brotherly Examination*, ibid.]

30. [Coleman, A *Brotherly Examination re-examined*, p. 19.]

31. [Coleman, *Hopes Deferred and Dashed*, p. 27.]

32. [Coleman, *Hopes Deferred and Dashed*, p. 24.]

I said the brother is for the negative of this question (p. 32).[33] This he flatly denies, pages 5, 6, whereby he acknowledges the affirmative that there is a church government *jure divino*, and that Jesus Christ has so far revealed His will in His word that there are to be church censures, and those to be dispensed by church-officers. But how does this agree with his sermon? "Christ has placed governments in His church. Of other governments," said he, "besides magistracy I find no institution, of them I do."[34] Is magistracy church government? Are magistrates church officers? Are the civil punishments church censures? Is this the mystery? Yes, that it is. He will tell us anon that the Houses of Parliament are church officers; but if that bolt [*arrow*] do any hurt I am much mistaken.

Fourthly, He professes to subscribe to the votes of parliament concerning church government, page 11; and yet he still pleads that all ecclesiastical government is merely doctrinal, page 11, the parliament having voted that power to church officers which is not doctrinal (as I showed before).[35] And he advises the parliament to keep wholly in their own hands the corrective part of church government, page 14, though the Parliament has put into the hands of elderships a power of suspension from the sacrament, which is corrective.

Fifthly, He did deliver in that sermon before the honorable House of Commons divers particulars, which being justly excepted against, and he undertaking a vindication, yet he has receded from them, or not been able to defend them, as that concerning two coordinate governments in one kingdom, and his argument concerning the fear of an ambitious ensnarement in ministers, these being by me infringed, he has not so much as offered to make them good.

Sixthly, Having acknowledged under his own hand that he was sorry he had given offence to the reverend Assembly and to the Commissioners from Scotland, he now appeals to the parliament and tells us they are able to judge of a scandalous sermon and they thought not so of it (p. 3). I know they are able to judge of a scandalous sermon: that they thought not so of it, it is more than I know or believe. However, I know they have a tender respect to the offence of others, even when themselves are not offended, and so they, and all men, ought to do according to the rule of Christ. For his part, after he had acknowledged he had given offence, it is a disservice to the parliament to lay over the thing upon them. For my part, I think I do better service to the parliament in interpreting otherwise that second order of the House, not only desiring, but enjoining Mr. Coleman to print that sermon, as near as he could as he preached it.[36] This was not, as he takes it, one portion of approbation above all its brethren (for I shall not believe that so wise an auditory was not at all scandalized at the hearing of that which was contrary both to

---

33. [*Brotherly Examination*, page 32, see herein page 222.]

34. [Coleman, *Hopes Deferred and Dashed*, p. 27.]

35. [See the prior section on page 240.]

36. [See the preface to the sermon to the House of Lords, page 146.]

the covenant and to their own votes concerning church government, nor at that which he told them out of the Jewish records, that "Hezekiah was the first man that was ever sick in the world, and did recover");[37] but, as I humbly conceive it was a real censure put upon him, his sermon being so much excepted against and stumbled at, the honorable House of Commons did wisely enjoin him to print his sermon that it might abide trial in the light of the world and lie open to any just exceptions which could be made against it abroad and that he might stand or fall to himself.

Seventhly, He abuses the parliament by arrogating so much to himself, as that his sermon "will, in the end, take away all difference and settle union," page 3; and that his model will be, when he is dead, "the model of England's church government," as he says in his postscript.[38] Whether this be prophesying or presuming I hope we are free to judge. And what if the wisdom and authority of the honorable Houses, upon advice from the reverend and learned Assembly, choose another way than this? Must all the synodical debates, and all the grave parliamentary consultations, resolve themselves into Mr. Coleman's way, like Jordan into *Mare Mortuum* [*Dead Sea*]?

Eighthly, He does extremely wound the authority of parliament in making their office to be a church office and of the same kind with the minister's office (page 14). "Do not I hold ministers church officers?" And a little after, "I desire the parliament to consider another presbyterian principle that excludes your honorable Assembly from being church officers."[39] If so, then the offices of the magistrate and of the minister must stand and fall together; that is, if the nation were not Christian the office of magistracy should cease as well as that of the ministry. And if he makes the magistrate a church officer, he must also give him ordination, except, with the Socinians, he deny the necessity of ordination.

HIS ABUSING THE REVEREND ASSEMBLY OF DIVINES

Whereas I had objected that his sermon had given no small scandal and offence, he replies, page 3, "But hath it given offence? To whom? I appeal to the honorable audience." Is this candid or fair dealing, when he himself knew both that he had given offence and to whom? I shall give him no other answer but his own declaration which he gave under his hand after he had preached that sermon.

> For much of what is reported of my sermon I utterly deny; and refer myself to the sermon itself. For what I have acknowledged to be delivered by me, although it is my judgment, yet, because I see it has given a great deal of offence

---

37. [Coleman, *Hopes Deferred and Dashed*, p. 9.]
38. [Coleman, A *Brotherly Examination re-examined*, p. 22.]
39. [Coleman, A *Brotherly Examination re-examined*, p. 14.]

to this Assembly and the reverend Commissioners of Scotland, I am sorry I have given offence in the delivery thereof. And for the printing, although I have an order, I will forbear, except I be further commanded. Tho. Coleman.[40]

Page 33.[41] I had this passage: "And where he asks where the Independents and we should meet, I answer, In holding a church government *jure divino*; that is, that the pastors and elders ought to suspend or excommunicate (according to the degree of the offence) scandalous sinners. Who can tell but the purging of the church from scandals, and the keeping of the ordinances pure (when it shall be actually seen to be the great work endeavored on both sides), may make union between us and the Independents more easy than many imagine."

What reply has he made to this? Page 6. "Sure[ly] I dream" (awake then); "but I will tell you news: The Presbyterians and Independents are" (he should have said may be) "united; nay, more [than],[42] the Lutherans and Calvinists; nay, more yet, the papist and Protestant; nay, more than so, the Turk and Christian. But wherein? In holding that there is a religion wherein men ought to walk."[43] No, sir. They must be united upon the like terms; that is, you must first have Turks to be Christians, and papists to be Protestants; and then you must have them as willing to purge the church of scandals, and to keep the ordinances pure. We will never despair of a union with such as are sound in the faith, holy in life, and willing to a church-refining and sin-censuring government in the hands of church officers. In the meanwhile, it is no light imputation upon the Assembly to hint this much, that the harmony and concord among the members thereof, for such a government as I have now named (though in some other particulars dissenting), can no more unite them than Turks and Christians, papists and Protestants, can be united. And now I will tell you my news: The Presbyterians and Independents are both equally interested against the Erastian principles. He reflects also upon the Assembly in the point of *jus divinum*, page 6. But what his part has been in reference to the proceedings in the Assembly, is more fully, and in divers particulars expressed in the *Brief View of Mr. Coleman's New Model*, unto which he has offered no answer.[44]

---

40. [See *Minutes*, 3.641. For Coleman's words as recorded in the minutes see the preface to the House of Lords sermon, page 145. Gillespie provides a bit more text than the minutes do, particularly Coleman's "except I be further commanded."]

41. [Gillespie, *Brotherly Examination*, herein p. 231.]

42. [In the 1645 text of *Nihil Respondes* (p. 19), the "than" in Coleman's text was omitted. *Works* did not restore it.]

43. [Coleman, *A Brotherly Examination Re-examined*, page 6. In changing the quotation from italics to quotation marks, some of Coleman's words were made Gillespie's in *Works*.]

44. [Adoniram Byfield, *A brief view of Mr. Coleman his new-modell of church government, delivered by him in a late sermon, upon Job 11.20* (1645). Thomason records a date of October 27, 1645 for when he purchased his copy. Coleman dismisses this tract in a postscript to his

His calumnies

1. Page 3. He desires me with wisdom and humility to mind what church-refining and sin-censuring work this church government with all its activity has made in Scotland, in the point of promiscuous communicating. I shall desire him with wisdom and humility to mind what charity or conscience there is in such an aspersion. I dare say divers thousands have been kept off from the sacrament in Scotland, as unworthy to be admitted. Where I myself have exercised my ministry, there have been some hundreds kept off; partly for ignorance, and partly for scandal. The Order of the Church of Scotland and the acts of General Assemblies are for keeping off all scandalous persons, which every godly and faithful minister does conscientiously and effectually endeavor.[45] And if, here or there, it be too much neglected by some Archippus who takes not heed to fulfill the ministry which he has received of the Lord [Col. 4:17], let him and his eldership bear the blame and answer for it.

2. Page 4. I having professed my unwillingness to fall upon such a controversy in a fast sermon, he replies, "How can you say you were unwilling?" But how can you, in brotherly charity, doubt of it after I had seriously professed it? My doing it at two several fasts[46] (the only opportunities I then had to give a testimony to that presently controverted truth) is no argument of the contrary. May not a man do a thing twenty times over, and yet do it unwillingly?

3. Page 5. He slanders those that did in their sermons give a public testimony against his doctrine; the occasion (as he gives out) not being offered, but taken.[47] But had they not a public calling and employment to preach as well as himself? And if a fast was not an occasion offered to them, how was a fast an occasion offered to him to fall upon the same controversy first, and when none had done the like before him?

4. A fourth calumny is this: He had first blamed two parties that they came biased to the Assembly. I answered, How then shall he make himself

re-examination (but he would go on to address it again in his *Malè Dicis*). Published anonymously, it was apparently known to everyone that Byfield wrote the piece, and Coleman wrote: "Be it what it will be, I am contented he shall have the advantage of the last word, and let him make the best of it, I will pass By the Field of such nameless authors, and having held out the thoughts of my heart, I will contend no farther." *Examination Re-examined*, p. 22.]

45. [Cf. *The Book of Common Order of the Church of Scotland* (Edinburgh and London: Blackwood, 1868), p. 123. *The first and second booke of discipline* (1621), pp. 41, 50–54, 59, 79.]

46. [Gillespie addressed Coleman in his Lords sermon and again apparently in his fast sermon for the miseries of Scotland before the Commons on September 5, 1645. See page 148, note 84.]

47. [Coleman complains about four or five who remonstrated against his sermon publicly, one at the election of the Mayor of London, and the other at a public funeral. *Brotherly Examination Re-examined*, p. 5.]

blameless who came biased a third way, which was the Erastian way, and that, for our part, we came no more biased to this Assembly than the foreign divines came to the Synod of Dort, Alexander to the Council of Nice, Cyril to that of Ephesus, and Paul to the synod at Jerusalem. But now, pages 6, 7, instead of doing us right he does us greater injury. For now he makes us biased, not only by our own judgments, but by something adventitious from without, which he denies himself to be (but how truly I take not on me to judge: beholders do often perceive the biasing better than the bowlers);[48] yea, he says that I have acknowledged the bias and justify it. Where, sir? Where? I deny it. It is no bias for a man to be settled, resolved, and engaged in his judgment for the truth, especially when willing to receive more light and to learn what needs to be further reformed. Has he forgotten his own definition of the bias which he had but just now given? But he will needs make it more than probable by the instances which I brought, that the Commissioners from Scotland came not to this Assembly as divines, by dispute and disquisition to find out truth, but as judges to censure all different opinions as errors; for so came foreign divines to Dort, Alexander to the Council of Nice, Cyril to Ephesus. Is it not enough that he slander us, though he do not, for our sakes, slander those worthy divines that came to the Synod of Dort, Alexander also, and Cyril, prime witnesses for the truth in their days? Could no less content him than to approve the objections of the Arminians against the Synod of Dort, which I had mentioned (p. 33)?[49] But he gets not away so. The strongest instance which I had given he has not once touched: it was concerning Paul and Barnabas, who were engaged (not in the behalf of one nation, but of all the churches of the Gentiles) against the imposition of the Mosaical rites, and had so declared themselves at Antioch, before they came to Jerusalem. Finally, Whereas he doubts, though not of our willingness to learn more, yet of our permission to receive more: That very paper[50] first given in by us (which I had cited and unto which he makes this reply), did speak not only of our learning, but of the Church of Scotland's receiving, and, which is more, there is an actual experiment of it, the last General Assembly having ordered the laying aside of some particular customs in that church, and that for the nearer uniformity with this church of England, as was expressed in their own letter to the reverend Assembly of Divines.[51]

5. A fifth calumny there is page 9. 6. [*sic* page 6.] "The commissioner is content that *jus divinum* should be a *noli me tangere*[52] to the parliament,

---

48. [In the game of lawn bowls, the ball is shaped to have a bias and from this the usage came to mean lacking objectivity. Gillespie is saying that as with the game, the observation of bias often is clearer to observers than to the participants.]

49. [*Brotherly Examination*, herein page 223.]

50. [On the Scots' paper, see herein *Brotherly Examination*, p. 223.]

51. [Gillespie refers to the letter he brought back from the General Assembly of the Church of Scotland. See the House of Lords Sermon, p. 134 ,note 32, and p. 137.]

52. [*Noli me tangere*: do not touch me.]

yet blames what himself grants." I was never content it should be *a noli me tangere* to the parliament, but at most a *non necesse est tangere*,[53] for so I explained myself, pages 32, 33.[54] If the parliament establish that thing which is agreeable to the Word of God, though they do not establish it as *jure divino*, I acquiesce; in the meantime, both they and all Christians, but especially ministers, ought to search the scriptures, that what they do in matters of church government, they may do it in faith and assurance, that it is acceptable to God. It was not of parliamentary sanction, but of divines' doctrinal asserting of the will of God that I said, "Why should *jus divinum* be such a *noli me tangere*?

6. [Page 9]. It seems strange to him that I did at all give instance of the usefulness of church government in the preservation of purity in the ordinances and in church members. He says for an Independent to have given this instance had been something; but it seems strange to him that "I should have given an instance of the power and efficacy of government, as it is presbyterial and contradistinct to congregational." This is a calumny against presbyterial government, which is neither privative nor contradistinct, but cumulative to congregational government; and the congregational is a part of that government which is comprehended under the name of presbyterial. But in cases of common concernment, difficulty, appeals, and the like, the preserving of the ordinances and church-members from pollution, does belong to presbyteries and synods.

7. He says of me, page 9, "He ascribes this power of purifying men and means of advancing the power of godliness afterward, to government." A calumny. It was only a *sine quo non*[55] which I ascribed to government thus far, that without it, ministers "shall not keep themselves nor the ordinances from pollution," page 23 [*sic*].[56] But that church government has power to purify men, I never thought it nor said it. That which I said of the power (which he points at) was that his way can neither preserve the purity nor advance the power of religion (p. 40),[57] and the reason is because his way provides no ecclesiastical effectual remedy for removing and purging away the most gross scandalous sins, which are destructive to the power of godliness. God must by His Word and Spirit purify men and work in them the power of godliness. The church government which I plead for against him is a means subservient and helpful, so far as *removere prohibens*,[58] to remove that which apparently is impeditive and destructive to that purity and power.

8. Having told us of the proud swelling waves of presbyterial government, I asked upon what coast had those waves done any hurt. France, or Scotland,

---

53. [*Non necesse est tangere*: you do not need to touch.]

54. [*Brotherly Examination*, herein pages 222–223.]

55. [*Sine quo non*: an essential condition.]

56. [This is page 36 in the first edition, not 23. See *Brotherly Examination*, page 225.]

57. [See *Brotherly Examination*, herein page 229.]

58. [*Removere prohibens*: to remove obstacles.]

or Holland, or *terra incognita?*[59] He replies, page 12, "I confess I have had no great experience of the presbyterial government." Why make you bold then to slander it, when you can give no sure ground for that you say? He tells us his fears arise from Scotland and from London. The reverend and worthy ministers of London can speak for themselves *ætatem habent.*[60] For my part, though I know not the particulars, I am bound in charity not to believe those aspersions put upon them by a discontented brother. But what from Scotland? "I myself," he says, "did hear the presbytery of Edinburgh censure a woman to be banished out of the gates of the city. Was not this an encroachment?" It had been an encroachment indeed, if it had been so. But he will excuse me if I answer him in his own language (which I use not), pages 3, 5: "It is, at the best, a most uncharitable slander," and "There was either ignorance or mindlessness in him that sets it down."[61]

There is no banishment in Scotland but by the civil magistrate, who so far aides and assists church discipline that profane and scandalous persons, when they are found unruly and incorrigible, are punished with banishment or otherwise. A stranger coming at a time into one of our presbyteries and hearing of somewhat which was represented to or reported from the magistrate, ought to have had so much both circumspection and charity as not to make such a rash and untrue report. He might have at least inquired when he was in Scotland and informed himself better whether presbyteries or the civil magistrate do banish. If he made no such inquiry, he was rash in judging; if he did, his offence is greater, when, after information, he will not understand.

9. He makes this to be a position of mine (p. 13): That "a learned ministry puts no black mark upon profaneness more than upon others." A calumny. For, first, He makes me to speak nonsense; secondly, I did not speak it of a learned ministry, but of "his way" (p. 40).[62] How long ago since a learned ministry was known by the name of Mr. Coleman's way! His way is a ministry without power of government or church censures. Of this his way I said, that "it puts no black mark upon profaneness and scandal in church members more than in any other"; and the reason is because the corrective or punitive part of government he will have to be only civil or temporal, which strikes against those that are without as well as those within. But the apostle tells us of such a corrective government as is a judging of those that are within and of those only (1 Cor. 5:12); and this way (which is not only ours, but the apostolical way) puts a black mark upon profaneness and scandalous sins in church members more than in any others.

10. He says of me (p. 17), "The commissioner is the only man that we shall meet with that, forsaking the words, judges of the intentions." A calumny.

---

59. [*Terra incognita*: unknown land.]

60. [*Ætatem habent*: they are of age.]

61. [Coleman, *A Brotherly Examination Re-examined*, pages 3 and 5.]

62. [See *Brotherly Examination*, herein page 229.]

I judged nothing but *ex ore tuo*;[63] but in this thing he himself has trespassed. I will instance but in two particulars. In that very place he says, "Admonition is a spiritual censure in the commissioner's opinion." Whence knows he that to be my opinion? Consistorial or presbyterial admonition given to the unruly may be called a censure; and if this were his meaning, then, ascribing to elderships power of admonition, he gives them some power of spiritual censures, and so something of the corrective part of government, which were contrary to his own principles. But he speaks it of the ministers' admonishing, who are but a part of the elderships, as himself there grants. Now, where did I ever say or write that admonition by a minister is a spiritual censure? Again, page 4, he so judges me that he not only forsakes but contradicts my words, "How can you say you were unwilling?"

11. He says, page 16, "Now the commissioner speaks out, etc. What! Not the Parliament of England meddle with religion?" A horrid calumny! Where have I said it? *Dic sodes*.[64] I never preached before them but I exhorted them to meddle with religion, and that in the first place and above all other things. I shall sooner prove that Mr. Coleman will not have the Parliament of England to meddle with civil affairs because he makes them church officers. It is a non sequitur. Their power is civil, *ergo* [*therefore*], they are not to meddle with religion. It will be a better consequence: They are church officers; so he makes them, page 14; and "Christian magistracy is an ecclesiastical administration"; so he says, page 20—*ergo*, they are not to meddle with civil government.

THE REPUGNANCY OF HIS DOCTRINE TO THE
SOLEMN LEAGUE AND COVENANT

Mr. Coleman, page 13, acknowledges that to assert anything contrary to the Solemn League and Covenant is a great fault in any, in himself more than in divers others, if made out, he having for his own part taken it with the first, and not only so, but having administered it to divers others. Yes; and take this one circumstance more:

In his sermon upon Jeremiah 30:21 at the taking of the covenant, September 29, 1643,[65] he answers this objection against the extirpation of prelacy: "But what if the exorbitances be purged away, may not I, notwithstanding my oath, admit of a regulated prelacy?" For satisfaction to this objection he answers thus: "First, We swear not against a government that is not; Secondly, We swear against the evils of every government, and doubtless many materials of prelacy must of necessity be retained as absolutely necessary;

---

63. [*Ex ore tuo*: out of your mouth.]

64. [*Dic sodes*: please tell me.]

65. [Thomas Coleman, *The Hearts Ingagement: A sermon preached at St. Margarets Westminster, at the publique entering into the Covenant* (1643), see the objections at the end.]

Thirdly, Taking away the exorbitances, the remaining will be a new government and no prelacy." Let the brother now deal ingenuously. What did he understand by those materials of prelacy absolutely necessary to be retained? Did he understand the dispensing of the Word and sacraments, which is common to all pastors? Or did he understand the privileges of parliament? Were either of those two materials of prelacy? And if he had meant either of these, was this the way to satisfy that scruple concerning the extirpation of prelacy? Again, What was that new government which he promised them after the taking away of the exorbitances of the old? Was it the minister's doctrinal part? That is no new thing in England. Was it the parliament's assuming of the corrective part of church government, as he improperly distinguishes, wholly and solely into their own hands, excluding the ministry from having any hand therein? This were [*would be*] a new government, I confess. But, surely, he could not in any reason intend this as a satisfaction to the scruples of such as desired a regulated prelacy, whose scruples he then spoke to, for this had been the way to dissuade them from, not to persuade them to the covenant.

But I go along with his *Re-examination*. Page 14, He explains himself and me thus: "He should have said that I advised the parliament to lay no burden of government upon them whom he, this commissioner, thinks church officers, then had he spoken true." I thank him for his explanation. And, I pray, who were the church officers whom I said he excluded from church government? Were they not pastors and ruling elders? And does not himself think these to be church officers? Yes; of the ministers he thinks so, but of ruling elders he seems to doubt, except they be magistrates. Well, but excluding those church officers from church government he takes with [*acknowledges*] the charge. Why seeks he a knot in the rush?[66] But now how does he explain himself? He will have the parliament to be church officers (of which before), and such church officers as shall take the corrective part of church government wholly into their own hands; yet not to dispense the Word and sacraments, but to leave the doctrinal part to the ministry, and their power to be merely doctrinal, as he says, page 11. Thus you have his explanation. But does this solve the violating of the covenant? Nay, it makes it more apparent; for the government of the church, which the first article of the covenant speaks of, is distinguished from the doctrinal part: "That we shall endeavour the reformation of religion in the kingdoms of England and Ireland, in doctrine, worship, discipline and government."[67] So that, excluding pastors and ruling elders from the corrective part of government and from all power which is not merely doctrinal, he thereby excludes them from that discipline and government which the covenant speaks of as one special part of the reformation of religion. Come on to the reasons.

---

66. [To seek (find) a knot in a (bul)rush. To find difficulties where there are none. *Oxford Dictionary of English Proverbs* (1970), p. 433.]

67. [See the text in *Confession of Faith*, etc. {1855}, pp. 358–359.]

I had given four reasons; he takes notice but of three. This is the second time he has told three for four, yet even these three will do the business.

1. "The extirpation of church government is not the reformation of it."[68] Here the brother adds these words following as mine, which are not mine: "Therefore, he that finds no church government breaks his covenant." His reply is, "We must reform it according to the Word of God, if that hold out none, here is no failing."[69] He adds a simile of a jury sworn to inquire into the felony of an accused person, but finds not guilty; and of three men taking an oath to deliver in their opinions of church government (where, by the way, he lets fall that I hold the national synod to be above all courts in the kingdom; which, if he means of ecclesiastical courts, why did he speak so generally? If he means above all or any civil courts, it is a gross calumny.) But now, if this be the sense which he gives of that first article in the covenant, then,

(1) All that is in the second article might have been put into the first article: for instance, we might, in Mr. Coleman's sense, have sworn "to endeavour the reformation of prelacy, and even of popery itself, according to the Word of God, and the example of the best reformed churches" that is, taking an oath to deliver in our opinions of these things according to the Word of God and to inquire into the evils of church government by archbishops, bishops, deans, etc., whether guilty or not guilty. I strengthened my argument by the different nature of the first and second article. I said, "The second article is of things to be extirpated, but this of things to be preserved and reformed."[70] Why did he not take the strength of my argument and make a reply?

(2) By the same principle of his we are not tied by the first article of our covenant to have any, either doctrine or worship, but only to search the scriptures whether the Word hold out any; for doctrine, worship, discipline and government, go hand in hand in the covenant.

(3) His own simile has this much in it against him. If a jury, sworn to inquire into the felony of an accused person, should, after such an oath, not only find the person not guilty, but further take upon them to maintain that there is no such thing as felony, surely this were inconsistent with their oath, so he that swears to endeavor the reformation of religion in doctrine, worship, discipline, and government, and yet will not only dislike this or that form of government, but also hold that there is no such thing as church government, he holds that which cannot agree with his oath.

(4) This answer of Mr. Coleman, leaving it free to debate whether there be such as church government, being his only answer to my first argument from the covenant, must needs suppose that the government mentioned in the covenant, the reformation whereof we have sworn to endeavor, is understood even by himself of church officers' power of corrective government,

---

68. [Gillespie, *Brotherly Examination*, herein, p. 229.]

69. [Coleman, *Brotherly Examination Re-examined*, pp. 14–15.]

70. [Gillespie, *Brotherly Examination*, herein, p. 229.]

it being the corrective part only, and not the doctrinal part, which he casts upon an uncertainty whether the Word[71] hold out any such thing.

2. "Church government as mentioned in the covenant is a spiritual, not a civil thing. The matters of religion are put together: doctrine, worship, discipline, and government. The privileges of parliament come after in the third article." The reverend brother replies, "What if it be? Therefore, the parliament is not to meddle with it, and why?" And here he runs out against me, as if I held that the parliament is not to meddle with religion, an assertion which I abominate. Princes and magistrates' putting off themselves all care of the matters of religion, was one of the great causes of the church's mischief, and of popish and prelatical tyranny. But is this just and fair, sir, to give out for my opinion that for which you are not able to show the least color or shadow of consequence from anything that ever I said? That which was to be replied unto was whether do not the materials of the first article of the covenant differ from the materials of the third article of the covenant? Or whether are they the same? Whether does the privilege of parliament belong to the first article of the covenant? Whether is that government mentioned in the first article a civil thing or a spiritual? If civil, why is discipline and government ranked with doctrine and worship, and all these mentioned as parts of the reformation of religion? If spiritual, then why does the brother make it "civil or temporal" (p. 11)? To all this nothing is answered but, "What if it be?" Then is my argument granted.

And to put it yet further out of question, I add other two arguments from that same first article of the covenant. One is this: In the first part of that first article we swear all of us to endeavor "the preservation of the reformed religion in the Church of Scotland, in doctrine, worship, discipline, and government," where all know that the words "discipline" and "government" (especially being mentioned as two of the principal things in which the reformed religion in that church does consist) signify church government and church discipline distinct both from doctrine and worship (which, by the way, how Mr. Coleman endeavors to preserve, I will not now say, but leave it to others to judge), therefore, in that which immediately follows, our endeavoring "the reformation of religion in the kingdoms of England and Ireland, in doctrine, worship, discipline and government," the words "discipline" and "government" must needs have the same sense thus far, that it is a church discipline and a church government distinct from the civil power of the magistrate, and distinct also from doctrine and worship in the church; for we cannot make these words, "discipline" and "government" in one and the same article of a solemn oath and covenant to suffer two senses differing *toto genere* [*entirely*] (especially considering that the civil government is put by itself in another article, which is the third), unless we make it to speak so as none may understand it.

The other argument which I now add is this. In the third part of that first

---

71. [*Works* misset "word" as "world" (p. 16).]

article we swear that we "shall endeavour to bring the churches of God in the three kingdoms to the nearest conjunction and uniformity in religion, confession of faith, form of church government, directory for worship and catechising,"[72] where, (1) Church government does agree generically with a confession of faith, directory of worship, and catechizing. I mean all these are matters of religion; none of them civil matters. (2) It is supposed there is such a thing as church government distinct from civil government, and therefore, it is put out of all question that so far there shall be an uniformity between the churches of God in the three kingdoms (and otherwise it were an unswearing of what was sworn in the first part of that article), but it ties us to endeavor the nearest conjunction and uniformity "in a form of church government," which were a vain and rash oath if we were not tied to a church government in general, and that as a matter of religion. (3) The uniformity in a form of church government which we swear to endeavor must needs be meant of corrective government, it being clearly distinguished from the confession of faith and directory of worship. So that Mr. Coleman's distinction of the doctrinal part and of the dispensing of the Word and sacraments cannot here help him.

From these two arguments (besides all was said before) I conclude that the covenant does undeniably suppose and plainly hold forth this thing as most necessary and incontrovertible, that there ought to be a church government which is both distinct from the civil government, and yet not merely doctrinal. And if so, what Apollo can reconcile Mr. Coleman's doctrine with the covenant? And now I go on.

[3.] My last reason formerly brought was this: "Will the brother say that the example of the best reformed churches leads [us] his way?"[73] For the covenant ties us to a reformation of the government of the church both according to the Word of God and the example of the best reformed churches: that as *regula regulans* [*the rule ruling*]; this as *regula regulata* [*rules ruled*].

The reverend brother replies: (1) "The best reformed church that ever was went this way; I mean the church of Israel."

ANSWER. {1} Is the church of Israel one of the reformed churches which the covenant speaks of? {2} Was the church of Israel better reformed than the apostolical churches? Why then calls he it the best reformed church that ever was? {3} That in the Jewish church there was a church government distinct from civil government, and church censures distinct from civil punishments, is the opinion of many who have taken great pains in the searching of the Jewish antiquities; and it may be he shall hear it ere long further proved, both from Scripture and from the very Talmudical writers.[74]

---

72. [*Confession of Faith*, ibid., p. 359.]

73. [*Brotherly Examination*, herein p. 230.]

74. [By April of 1645, Baillie and the Scottish Commissioners understood they had an Erastian problem, not in the assembly, but in Parliament. "The most of the House of Commons are downright Erastians; they are like to create us much more woe than all the sectaries

(2) "I desire," he says, "the commissioner to give an instance in the New Testament of such a distinction (civil and church government) where the state was Christian."

Answer. I desire him to give an instance in the New Testament of these three things, and then he will answer himself. {1} Where was the state Christian? {2} Where had the ministry a doctrinal power in a Christian state? {3} Where does the New Testament hold out that a church government distinct from civil government may be where the state is not Christian, and yet may not be where the state is Christian? Shall the church's liberties be diminished, or rather increased, where the state is Christian?

(3) In the third and fourth place, the brother tells us of the opinions of Gwalther, Bullinger, Erastus, Aretius. The question is of the examples of churches, not of the opinions of men. But what of the men? As for that pestilence that walks in darkness through London and Westminster, Erastus' book against Beza, let him make of it what he can, it shall have an antidote by and by.[75] In the meanwhile, he may take notice that in the close of the sixth book, Erastus casts down that which he has built, just as Bellarmine did in the close of his five books of justification.[76] But as for the other three named by the brother, they are ours, not his, in this present controversy. Gwalther expounds 1 Corinthians 5 all along of excommunication, and of the necessity of church discipline, insomuch that he expounds the very delivering to Satan (the phrase most controverted by Erastus and his followers) of excommunication, and the not eating with the scandalous (ver 9–11) he takes also to import excommunication. He thinks also that ministers shall labor to little purpose except they have a power of government.[77] Bullinger

---

of England" (April 25, 1645, *Letters & Journals*, 2.265). Gillespie's *Nihil Respondes* was written in early November 1645 and in print by November 13, 1645 (the date on Thomason's copy). Here and at the third and fourth point below he refers either to the hoped for responses from continental writers whom Baillie was encouraging to write against Erastianism in letters sent in April, June, and August 1645, or Gillespie had begun to write his larger treatise which would be published as *Aaron's Rod Blossoming*. This would be published eight and a half months later at the end of July, 1646. Gillespie gave copies out to the assembly on July 30, 1645 (*Minutes*, 4.219–220). The London bibliophile George Thomason records obtaining a copy several days later on August 4, 1645 (ESTC R202013). Coleman never saw Gillespie's magnum opus, having taken ill after the March 17 session 605, and died before the March 30 session 612 in which the assembly is noted as having received notice and invitation to his funeral. See the preface to these Anti-Erastian tracts.]

75. [See the prior note.]

76. [See *Aaron's Rod Blossoming*, in *Works*, pp. 76–77.]

77. Gwalther, Archetyp in 1 Cor. 5. 5. *decrevi impurum hunc tradendum esse Satanæ, id est ejiciendum ex Ecclesia, etc. Ratio locutionis quia extra Ecclesiam Satan Regnat.* In ver 6. *Ita vero innuit disciplinam necessariam esse, ne contagium peccandi serpat.* In ver. 9, 10, 11. *Catalogus eorum qui debent excommunicari, ibid. Imo non sufficiunt ministri nisi publica authoritate juventur. Ideo Paulus Corinthios tam multis monet, ut Ecclesiae disciplinam instaurent, et fermentum omne ex*

is most plain for excommunication as a spiritual censure ordained by Christ, and so he understands Matthew 18:17.[78]

Aretius holds that God was the author of excommunication in the Old Testament, and Christ in the New.[79] And now are these three Mr. Coleman's way? Or does not his doctrine flatly contradict theirs? Peradventure he will say, Yet there is no excommunication in the church of Zurich, where those divines lived, nor any suspension of scandalous sinners from the sacrament. I ANSWER. This cannot infringe what I hold, that the example of the best reformed churches makes for us and against him. For, {1} The book written by Lavater, another of the Zurich divines, *de Ritibus et Institutis Ecclesiæ Tigurinæ*, tells us of divers things in that church which will make the brother easily to acknowledge that it is not the best reformed church, such as festival days, cap. 8, that upon the Lord's days, before the third bell, it is published and made known to the people, if there be any houses, fields, or lands, to be sold, cap. 9. They have no fasts indicted, cap. 9, nor psalms sung in the church, cap. 10. Responsories in their Litany at the sacrament, the deacon upon the right hand says one thing, the deacon upon the left hand says another thing, the pastor a third thing, cap. 13.[80]

{2} Yet the church of Zurich has some corrective church government besides that which is civil or temporal, for the same book, cap. 23,[81] tells us that in their synods any minister who is found scandalous or profane in his life, is censured with deposition from his office, *ab officio deponitur*. Then

---

purgent. In ver. 13. Tollite, etc. Si Christiam estis si Ecclesiam vultus habere puram, utimini jurè vestro. [Gwalther, "Ad Corinthios Priorem," in *In Divi Pauli Apostoli Epistolas Omnes* (Zurich: Frosch., 1589), pp. 23r, 23v, 25r, 26r.]

78. Bullinger in 1 Cor. 5. 3, 4, 5. *Viri ergo Apostolici et veteres quique contumaces et Ecclesiastica censura dignos è contubernio Sanctorum abjecerunt, excludentes eos à sacris castibus, et communione corporis et sanguinis mystici.* And a little after, *Quod si his quoque addas ordinationem Christi ex Mathaeo, videbis eam hue quoque spectare, ut publicè mulctetur qui spretis commonitionibus amicis, in honestè perrexerit vivere. Esse enim Ethnicum et Publicanum, est deleri è Catalogo Ecclesiastico et recenseri haberique inter facinorosos quibus nihil neque officii, ueque sinceri tutò committas.* [Heinrici Bullingeri Commentarii In omnes Pauli Apostoli Epistolas, atque etiam in Epistolam ad Hebraeos (Tiguri: Cambierus, 1603), p. 114.]

79. Aret., *Theol. Probl.*, loc. 133 [sic]. *à Deo originem habet, et à Christo confirmata fuit.* And after, *Supra de origine dixi, indicans à Deo indictam fuisse hauc disciplinam, etc. Demum Christus filius Dei eandem ecclesiæ suæ commendavit.* [Benedictus Aretius, *Locus LVI. De Exemplis Veteris Testamenti, quatenus scilicet transferenda sint in usum nostrum, S.S. theologiæ problemata: hoc est, Loci commvnes Christianæ religionis, methodice explicati* (Isayas le Preux, 1617), De Excommunitione, Loc. CXII, pp. 634, 636.]

80. [Ludwig Lavater, *De Ritibus Et Institutis Ecclesiæ Tigurinae opusculum* ([Zürich]: [Christoph Froschauer], 1559), ch. 8, p. 4r–4v, ch. 9, pp. 5r, 8v, ch. 10, pp. 8v–9r, ch. 13, 11v. There is also a 1565 edition by Froschauer that has pagination which is off from the prior by about an additional page.]

81. [Lavater, *De Ritibus Et Institutis Ecclesiæ Tigurinae opusculum*, p. 23r.]

follows, *finita censura*, *singuli decani*, etc. Here is a synodical censure, which I find also in Wolphius,[82] a professor of Zurich, and the book before cited [*de Ritibus et Institutis Ecclesiæ Tigurinæ*], cap. 24, tells us of some corrective power committed to pastors and elders, which elders are distinguished from the magistrates.[83]

{3} The Zurich divines themselves looked upon excommunication as that which was wanting through the injury of the times; the thing having been so horribly abused in popery, and the present licentiousness abounding among people, did hinder the erecting of that part of the church discipline at that time. But they still pleaded the thing to be held forth in Scripture, and were but expecting better times for restoring and settling of excommunication, which they did approve in Geneva and in other reformed churches who had received it. I give you their own words for the warrant of what I say.[84]

I have been the longer upon this point as being the chief objection which can be made by Mr. Coleman concerning that clause in the covenant, "The example of the best reformed churches."

He hath only one thing more, which may well pass for a paradox. He will take an instance, forsooth, from Geneva itself, though presbyterian in practice. And why? Because in the Geneva Annotations upon Matthew 9:16, it said that "the external discipline is to be fitted to the capacity of the church."[85] "This

---

82. Wolphius, Com. in Lib. Esdra, p. 21. *Atque hoc exemplo veteris Testamenti discimus quid facto opus sit in novo: nempe ut crebris synodis ac censuris, in vocationem in doctrinam, in vitam ac mores ecclesiastarum inspiciatur.* [*Esdras: in Esdrae librum primum de reditu populi Iudaei e captivitate Babylonica in patriam, et templi reiquepublicae instautarione commentariorum Ioannis Vvolphii* (Tiguri: Christoph. Froschouerus, 1584), chapter 2, verses 61–65, p. 21v.]

83. *In Ecclesiis ditionis Tigurinae, deliguntur Seniores, qui unà cum pastore vitia corrigant. Postea Magistratus de facinorosis veluti blasphemia, per juris, pœnas sumit.* [Lavater, *De Ritibus Et Institutis Ecclesiæ Tigurinae opusculum*, p. 23v.]

84. Bullinger in 1 Cor. 5. *Et hac tenus de castigatione scelerum Ecclesiastica. Hic tamen diligenter admonitos volo fratres, vigilent, et omni diligentia curent, ut salutare hoc Pharmacum, è cætu sanctorùm Pontificis avaritia eliminatum, reducatur, hoc est ut scelera offendentia plectantur. Hic enim unicus est Excommunicationis finis, ut mores excolatur et floreant sancti, prophani verò coerceantur* [coherceantur], *ne mali porrò impudentia ac impietate grassentur. Nostrum est ista ô fratres, summa cum diligentia curare. Videmus enim et Paulum cessantes hoc loco incitare.* [Bullinger, ibid., pp. 114–115. Aretius, ubi supra: *Magistratus jugum non admittunt, timent honoribus, licentiam amant, etc. Vulgus quoque et pleba dissolutior: major para corruptissima est, etc. Interea non desperandum esse libenter fateor: dabit posterior ætas tractabiliores fortè animas, mitiora pectora, quàm nostra habent secula.* [Aretius, ibid., pp. 638, 639.] Lavater in Nehem, homil. 52: *Quia pontifices Romani excommunicatione ad stabiliendam suam tyrannidem abusi sunt, factum est ut nulla ferè justa disciplina amplius in ecclesiis institui possit. Nisi autem flagitiosi coerceantur, omnia ruant in peius neccesse est.* [Ludwig Lavater, *Nehemias: liber Nehemiae, qui et secundus Ezrae dicitur, homiliis LVIII* (Tiguri: ex Officina Froschoviana, 1586), p. 98.]

85. "La discipline exterieure se doit accommoder à la capacité de L'Eglisè. Manieres de parler allegoriques." Bonaventure Corneille Bertram; Théodore de Bèze; Antoine de La Faye;

is no Scotland presbytery," the brother says. Nay, sir, nor yet Geneva presbytery; for it does not at all concern presbytery. It is spoken in reference to the choosing of fit and convenient times for fasting and humiliation—that as Christ did not, at that time, tie his disciples to fasting, it being unsuitable to that present time, so other like circumstances of God's worship, which are not at all determined to the Word, are to be accommodated to emergent occasions and to the church's condition for the time, which both Scotland, and Geneva, and other reformed churches do.

If I have now more fully and convincingly spoken to that point of the covenant, let the brother blame himself that put me to it.

The Lord guide His people in a right way, and rebuke the spirit of error and division, and give us all more of His Spirit, to lead us into all truth, and into all self-denial, and grant that none of His servants be found unwilling to have the Lord Jesus Christ to reign over them in all His ordinances!

Jean Jacquemot; Simon Goulart; Jean Baptiste Rotan; Francis Fry, *La Bible, qui est toute la saincte Escriture du Vieil et du Nouveau Testament, autrement, l'Anciene et la Nouvelle Alliance: le tout reveu et conferé sur les textes hebrieux et grecs par les pasteurs et professeurs de l'Eglise de Genève* (A Genève: [Jérémie des Planches], 1588), p. 6v.]

Malè Audis: or,

An answer to Mr. Coleman's *Malè Dicis*:

Wherein the repugnancy of his Erastian doctrine to the
Word of God, to the Solemn League & Covenant, and
to the Ordinances of Parliament; also his contradictions,
tergiversations, heterodoxies, calumnies, and perverting of
testimonies, are made more apparent than formerly

Together with some animadversions upon Mr. Hussy's *Plea
for Christian Magistracy*: showing that in divers of the aforementioned particulars he hath miscarried as much as, and in
some particulars more than, Mr. Coleman

Tertullian. De virginibus velandis
*Semel dixerim, una ecclesia sumus. Ita nostrum est, quodcunque nostrorum est.
Cæterum dividis corpus: tam hic, sicut in omnibus varie institutis & dubiis &
incertis fieri solet, adhibenda fuit examinatio, quæ magis ex duabus tam diversis
consuetudinibus disciplinæ dei conveniret.*

Malè Audis: or An answer to Mr. Coleman His Malè Dicis: Wherein the repugnancy of his Erastian Doctrine to the word of God, to the solemne League and Covenant, and to the Ordinances of Parliament: also his Contradictions, Tergiversations, Heterodoxies, Calumnies, and perverting of Testimonies, are made more apparent than formerly. Together with some Animadversions upon Mr. Hussey his Plea for Christian Magistracy: *Shewing, that in divers of the afore mentioned particulars he hath miscarried as much as, and in some particulars more than Mr. Coleman. By Mr. George Gillespie, Minister at Edinbrugh.*

Editions

1. *Malè Audis*, etc. Published by Authority. London: Printed for Robert Bostocke at the Kings head in Paules Church-yard 1646. [8], 56 p.; 4^0. ESTC R200545 (Wing G754). Thomason, E.317[16]. "Annotation on Thomason copy: "Jan: 24 1645"; the second 6 in imprint date crossed out."

3. *Male Audis: or, An answer to Mr. Coleman's Malè Dicis: Wherein the repugnancy of his Erastian doctrine to the Word of God, to the Solemn League & Covenant, and to the Ordinances of Parliament; also his contradictions, tergiversations, heterodoxies, calumnies, and perverting of testimonies, are made more apparent than formerly. Together with some animadversions upon Mr. Hussy's Plea for Christian Magistracy: showing that in divers of the afore-mentioned particulars he hath miscarried as much as, and in some particulars more than, Mr. Coleman. By George Gillespie, Minister At Edinburgh, 1642* (Edinburgh: Robert Ogle and Oliver and Boyd, 1844). In *Works* in *A Presbyterian's Armoury*. 30 pp.; royal octavo.

The Epigraph on the prior page is from the first edition. Jerome, *On the Veiling Of Virgins*. "Let me say it once for all, we are one Church. Thus, whatever belongs to our brethren is ours: only, the body divides us. Still, here (as generally happens in all cases of various practice, of doubt, and of uncertainty), examination ought to have been made to see which of two so diverse customs were the more compatible with the discipline of God." *ANF*, volume 4, page 28.

As I DID NOT begin this present controversy, so I do not desire to hold up the ball of contention, yet having appeared in it (neither alone, nor without a calling and opportunity offered), I hold it my duty to vindicate the truth of Chriſt, the Solemn League and Covenant, the ordinances of Parliament, the Church of Scotland, and myself—For this end was I born, and for this end came I into the world, that I might bear witness to the truth—whereunto I am so much the more encouraged because it appears already in this debate, that *magna eſt vis veritatis*, great is the force of truth, and so great, that my antagoniſts, though men of parts, and such as could do much for the truth, yet, while they have gone about to do somewhat againſt the truth, they have mired themselves in foul errors; yea (so far as in them lies), have moſt dangerously shaken and endangered the authority of magiſtrates, who are God's vicegerents, and particularly the authority of parliament, and of parliamentary ordinances. They have ſtumbled and fallen, and shall not be able to rise but by the acknowledgment of the truth.

In this following reply, I have not touched much of the argumentative part in Mr. Hussey's *Plea for Chriſtian Magiſtracy* [1645], reserving moſt of it to another work, unto which this is a prodromus [*forerunner*][1] (howbeit much of what he says is the same with what I did confute in my *Nihil Reſpondes*, and his book, coming forth a month after, takes no notice of that second piece of mine, but ſpeaks only to the firſt). Meanwhile, let him not believe that his big looking title can like Gorgon's head blockify or ſtonify rational men, so as they shall not perceive the want or weakness of argument. It has ever been a trick of adversaries to calumniate the way of God and his servants, as being againſt authority, but I will, by God's assiſtance, make it appear to any intelligent man that the reverend brother has pleaded very much againſt magiſtracy, and so has fallen himself into the ditch which he has digged for others [Prov. 23:27], whilſt I withal escape.

But now, what may be the meaning of Mr. Coleman's cabaliſtical title, *Malè Dicis Maledicis*? Great philologiſts will tell him that *male dico* is taken in a good sense as well as in a bad, according to the difference of matter and circumſtances.[2] If any kind of malediction be juſtifiable, it is *male dicere maledicis*, to ſpeak evil to evil ſpeakers. For "as he loved cursing, so let it come unto him: as he delighted not in blessing, so let it be far from him" [Ps. 109:17]. But he does

---

1. [This is the first of several allusions in *Malè Audis* to Gillespie's *Aaron's Rod*.]

2. *Math. Martinius in lexi philol. Maledico, malum loquor sivè juſte sive injuria.* [Matthias Martini, *Lexicon philologicum, praecipuè etymologicum* (Bremæ: Villerianis, [1623]), col. 1782.]

worse, and his title, with a transposition of letters, will more fitly reflect upon himself *Malè Dicis de amicus*. You, sir, speak evil of your friends, and of those that never wronged you. For my part, I have not shared with him in evil speaking, nor rendered revilings for revilings. I am sorry that he is so extremely ill of hearing, as to take reason to be railing and good sayings to be evil sayings. He applies to himself the apostle's words, "Being reviled, we bless" [1 Cor. 4:12]. But where to find these blessings of his, those unwritten verities, I know not. I am sure he had spoken more truly if he had said, "Being not reviled, we do revile."

For the matter and substance of his reply, there are divers particulars in it which serve rather to be matter of mirth than of argument, as that a parliament parasite cannot be called an abuser of the parliament, and that passage, "How can a clause delivered in a postscript, concerning my opinion of my way, be abusive to the parliament?"[3] A great privilege either of postscripts or of his opinions, that they cannot be abusive to the parliament. Many passages are full of acrimony, many extravagant, and not to the point in hand, many void of matter. Concerning such, Lactantius gives me a good rule, *Otiosum est persequi singula*, it is an idle and unprofitable thing to prosecute[4] every particular.[5] And much more I have in my eye the apostle's rule, "Let all things be done to edifying" (1 Cor. 14:26). I have accordingly endeavored to avoid such jangling, and such debates as are unprofitable and unedifying, making choice of such purposes as may edify and not abuse the reader.

Peradventure some will think I might have wholly saved myself this labor. I confess I do not look upon that which I make reply unto as if it were like to weigh much with knowing men, yet the apostle tells me that some men's mouths must be stopped [Titus 1:11], and Jerome tells me there is nothing written without skill, which will not find a reader with as little skill to judge, and some men grow too wise in their own eyes when they pass unanswered [Prov. 26:5].[6] Besides all this, a vindication and clearing of such things as I mentioned in the beginning, may, by God's blessing, anticipate future and further mistakes. Read therefore, and consider, and when thou hast done, I trust thou shalt not think that I have lost my labor. I pray the Lord that all our controversies may end in a more cordial union for prosecuting the ends expressed in the covenant and especially the reformation of religion, according to the Word of God and the example of the best reformed churches, and more particularly the practical part of reformation, that the ordinances of Jesus Christ may be kept from pollution, profaneness and scandals shamed away, and piety commended and magnified.

---

3. [Coleman, *Malè dicis maledicis. Or A brief reply to Nihil respondens* (1645 [1646]), p. 17.]

4. [*Works* reads "persecute."]

5. Lib. 2. c. 4. ["It is idle to follow up each particular instance." Lactantius, *Divine Institutes*, in *ANF* 7, p. 46. Some first edition copies may read "lib.c.3. 2.", corrected in the errata.]

6. Hieron. Eustochio. [None of the three letters of Jerome to Eustochium fit the context. If this is a lesson deduced from Jerome, rather than the summary of a quotation, §12 in Letter XLVIII to Pammachius may be more likely. And at §18, Jerome references his letter 22 to Eustachius, which may account for this mistake. *NPNF2*, v6, pp. 72–77.]

Chapter One
That Mr. Coleman does still Contradict Himself in the Stating of this Present Controversy about Church Government

---

It was before both denied and yielded by Mr. Coleman that there is a church government which is distinct from the civil, and yet not merely doctrinal. He did profess to subscribe heartily to the votes of parliament, and yet advised the parliament to do contrary to their votes, as I proved in *Nihil Respondes* (p. 3).[1] He answers now in his *Malè Dicis* (p. 4), "I deny an institution; I assent to prudence; where is the self-contradiction now?" And (p. 5), "The advice looks to *jus divinum*; the parliament votes to prudence." Sir, you have spoken evil for yourself; you have made the self-contradiction worse. Will you acknowledge your own words in your sermon (p. 25), "Lay no more burden of government upon the shoulders of ministers than Christ has plainly laid upon them; have no more hand therein than the Holy Ghost clearly gives them. The ministers have other work to do, and such as will take up the whole man," etc.; "I fear an ambitious ensnarement," etc.; and in your *Re-examination* (p. 14), "He should have said I advised the parliament to lay no burden of government upon them whom he (this commissioner) thinks church officers, then had he spoken true." Now, let the reverend brother take heed to checkmate, and that three several ways (but let him not grow angry, as bad players use to [*commonly*] do). For 1. *Eo ipso* [*by the fact*] that he denies the institution, by his principles he denies the prudence; for he that denies the institution and advises the parliament to lay no more burden of government upon ministers than Christ has plainly laid upon them is against the settling of the thing in a prudential way because it is not instituted. But Mr. Coleman denies the institution and advises the parliament to lay no more burden of government upon ministers than Christ has plainly laid upon them; *ergo* [*therefore*], Mr. Coleman is against the settling of the thing in a prudential way because it is not instituted. And how to reconcile this with his denying of the institution and yielding of the prudence will require a more reconciling head than Manasseh Ben Israel conciliator himself.[2]

2. He that advises the parliament to lay no burden of government upon ministers because they have other work to do which will take up the whole man, and because of the fear of an ambitious ensnarement, is against the laying of any burden of corrective government upon ministers, so much as in a prudential way. But Mr. Coleman advises the parliament, etc.; *ergo*, the consequence in the proposition is necessary, unless he will say that it is agreeable

---

1. [See in this present volume, page 241.]

2. [Rabbi Manasseh Ben Israel, *The Conciliator: A Reconcilement of the apparent contradictions in Holy Scripture* (in Spanish, 1632; Latin, 1633).]

to the rules of prudence to lay upon them more work besides that which will take up the whole man, or to commit that power unto them which is like to prove an ambitious ensnarement.

3. He that advises the parliament to lay no burden at all of corrective government upon ministers and other officers joined with them in elderships, but to keep that power wholly in their own hands, is against the prudence of the thing as well as against the institution of it. But Mr. Coleman advises the parliament to lay no burden at all of corrective government upon these, but to keep that power wholly in their own hands; *ergo*, the proposition is proved by that which himself says, "The parliament votes" look "to prudence." So that the parliament, having voted a power of suspension from the sacrament unto elderships, for so many scandals as are enumerate[d] in the ordinance (which power is a part of that which he calls corrective),[3] he that is against this power in elderships is both against the prudence and against the ordinance of parliament. The assumption I prove from his *Re-examination* (p. 14), where, after his denial of the power to those whom we think church officers, being charged with advising the parliament to take church government wholly into their own hands, his answer was, "If you mean the corrective power, I do so."

And now, after all this, I must tell the reverend brother that he might have saved himself much labor had he in his sermon to the parliament declared himself (as now he does) that he was only against the *jus divinum*, but not against their settling of the thing in a parliamentary and prudential way. Did I not, in my very first examination of his sermon (p. 32),[4] remove this stumbling block?

And, withal, seeing he professes to deny the *jus divinum* of a church government differing from magistracy, why does he hold (p. 19), that the Independents are not so much interested against his principles as the Presbyterians? Did he imagine that the Independents are not so much for the *jus divinum* of a church government and church censures as the Presbyterians? But, says he, "The Independents' church power seems to me to be but doctrinal." But is their excommunication doctrinal? And do they not hold excommunication to be *jure divino*? Either he had little skill in being persuaded, or some others had great skill in persuading him that the Independents' church power is but doctrinal, and that they are not so much interested against the Erastian principles as the Presbyterians are; as if, forsooth, the ordinance of excommunication (the thing which the Erastian way mainly opposes) and a church government distinct from magistracy were not common to them both.

---

3. ["The House of Commons has passed other two votes, sore against the mind of the Erastian party, that elderships shall examine scandals by two witnesses, and that they shall examine the witnesses upon oath." George Gillespie, Letter No. 6. London, May 9, 1645. Baillie, *Letters & Journals*, 2.506.]

4. [See *Brotherly Examination*, herein page 222.]

Laſtly, If the reverend brother deny the inſtitution of church censures, but assent to the prudence, why does he allege the Zurich divines to be so much for him? (*Malè Dicis*, p. 23). For it was upon prudential grounds, and because of the difficulty and (as they conceived) impossibility of the thing, that they were againſt it, ſtill acknowledging the scriptural warrants for excommunication, as I shall show, yea, have showed already; so that, if Mr. Coleman will follow them, he muſt rather say, "I assent to an inſtitution; I deny a prudence."

CHAPTER TWO

A CONFUTATION OF THAT WHICH MR. COLEMAN HAS SAID AGAINST CHURCH GOVERNMENT; SHOWING ALSO THAT HIS LAST REPLY IS NOT MORE BUT LESS SATISFACTORY THAN THE FORMER, AND FOR THE MOST PART IS BUT A TERGIVERSATION AND FLEEING FROM ARGUMENTS BROUGHT AGAINST HIM, AND FROM MAKING GOOD HIS OWN ASSERTIONS AND ARGUMENTS CONCERNING THE DISTINCTION OF CIVIL AND CHURCH GOVERNMENT

---

1. THE REVEREND brother said in his sermon, "I could never yet see how two coordinate governments, exempt from superiority and inferiority, can be in one ſtate."[5] To overthrow this general thesis, I brought some inſtances to the contrary; such as the governments of a general and an admiral, of a maſter and a father, of a captain and a maſter in a ship. He being thus put to his vindication, replies, "The commissioner acknowledges he did not apply them to the Assembly" (I said the General Assembly) "and parliament; yet that was the controversy in hand" (*Malè Dicis*, p. 5). But, by his favor, that was not the controversy; for he was not ſpeaking particularly againſt the diſtinction of the government of the General Assembly and of the government of the parliament (neither had he one syllable to that purpose), but generally againſt the diſtinction of church government and civil government, and particularly againſt excommunication; in all which he excluded presbyteries as well as general assemblies. Wherefore, he does now recede not only from defending his *thesis*, but from applying it againſt the power of presbyteries. And so far we are agreed.

2. I having confuted his argument grounded on Psalm 33:15 [and] Proverbs 27:19, he shifts the vindication of it, and ſtill tells me he grounded no argument on those places, but ſpoke "by way of allusion" (*Malè Dicis*, p. 6). Now, let the reader judge. His words to the parliament were these: "Might I measure others by myself, and I know not why I may not (God fashions men's hearts alike; and as in water face answers face, so the heart of man to man), I ingenuously profess I have a heart that knows better how to be governed than govern; I fear an ambitious ensnarement," etc.[6] This argument, there largely prosecuted, has no other ground but the parenthesis using the

---

5. [Coleman, *Hopes Deferred and Dashed*, p. 25.]

6. [Coleman, Ibid.]

words (though not quoting the places) of Scripture. And now, forsooth, he has served the parliament well, when, being put to make good the sole confirmation of his argument, he tells it was but an allusion. But this is not all. I confuted the whole argument drawn from his own heart to the hearts of others and gave several answers: but neither before, nor now, has he offered to make good his argument.

3. The reverend brother cited 1 Corinthians 10:33 to prove that all government is either a heathenish government, or a Jewish government, or a church government. This I denied, "Because the government of generals, admirals, mayors, sheriffs, is neither a Jewish government, nor a church government, nor a heathenish government."[7] What says he to this? "I deny it; a Jewish general is a Jewish government," etc. (*Malè Dicis*, p. 6). Deny it? No, sir, you must prove (because you are the affirmer) that a Christian general, a Christian admiral, are church governments. For I deny it. You tell us, you are persuaded it will trouble the whole world to bound civil and ecclesiastical jurisdiction, the one from the other (p. 7). You shall have them bounded and distinguished ere long, and the world not troubled neither.[8] Meanwhile, you have not made out your assertion from 1 Corinthians 10:33.

4. The reverend brother had cited Romans 13:4 to prove that the corrective part of church government belongs to the Christian magistrate. And now he brings in my reply thus: that I said he abuses the place, "Because spiritual censures belong not to the civil magistrate," which, says he, begs the question (*Malè Dicis*, p. 7). I replied no such thing upon this argument. Look at my words again. How can the brother answer it, to shape answers of his own devising as if they were mine? My answer was, That the punitive part, Romans 13:4, belongs to all magistrates, whether Christian or infidel, which he takes notice of in the second place, and bids me prove "that Scripture-commands belong to infidels," not observing that the question is not of Scripture-commands, but whether a duty mentioned in this or that Scripture may not belong to infidels. There are two sorts of duties in Scripture; some which are duties by the Law of God written in man's heart at his creation, some principles and notions whereof remain in the hearts of all nations, even infidels by nature; other duties are such by virtue of special commands given to the church, which are not contained in the law of nature. The first sort (of which the punishing of evil doers mentioned [in] Romans 13:4 is one) belongs to those that are without the church as well as those within. The other only to those that are within.

5. The reverend brother had said in his sermon, "Of other governments besides magistracy I find no institution."[9] I cited 1 Thessalonians 5:12, 1 Timothy 5:17, [and] Hebrews 13:7, 17, to prove another government (yea, the institution

----

7. [*Nihil Respondes*, herein p. 243.]

8. [This is a reference to the present argument or this may be one of several forecasts in *Malè Audis* to Gillespie's begun work on *Aaron's Rod Blossoming*.]

9. [Coleman, *Hopes Deferred and Dashed*, p. 27.]

of another government) besides magistracy.[10] And, in my *Nihil Respondes*, I told he had laughed, but had not yet loosed the knot.[11] Now hear his two answers:

First, "for the institution; for the commissioner affirms so much. Had he said that these texts hold out an office or officer already instituted, the words would have borne him out," etc. "But the institution in this place I cannot see" (*Malè Dicis*, p. 8). See the like in Mr. Hussey, pp. 19, 22.[12] I thank them both. That Scripture which supposes an institution and holds out an office already instituted, shall to me (and, I am confident, to others also) prove an institution; for no text of Scripture can suppose or hold out that which is not true. Nay, has Mr. Coleman forgotten that [he] himself proved an institution of magistracy from Romans 13:1, 2? Yet that text does but hold out the office of magistracy already instituted, but the institution itself is not in that place.

Secondly, Mr. Coleman answers to all these three texts. To that [of] 1 Thessalonians 5:12, "Them which are over you in the Lord," he says that these words prove not that it is not meant of magistracy. But he takes not the strength of the argument. My words were, "Here are some who are no civil magistrates set over the Thessalonians in the Lord." This the reverend brother must admit to be a good proof, or otherwise say that the civil magistrates set over the Thessalonians, though they were heathens, yet were set over them in the Lord.

For that of 1 Timothy 5:17, he says it does not hold out ruling elders. Whether it does hold ruling elders or not, does not at all belong to the present question. It is easy to answer something so that a man will not tie himself to the point. The place was brought by me to prove "another government beside magistracy," which he denied. Now, suppose the place to be meant only of preaching elders? Yet here is a rule or government: "Elders that rule well;" and these are no civil magistrates, but such as ""labour in the word and doctrine." Come on now. "But I will deal clearly," says the brother: "These officers are ministers which are instituted not here, but elsewhere, and these are the rulers here mentioned. And so have I loosed the knot." Now, sir, you shall see I will not *male dicere*, but *bene dicere*. My blessing on you for it. You have at last loosed the knot so perfectly that you are come to an agreement with me in this great point, which I thus demonstrate: He that acknowledges ministers to be instituted rulers, acknowledges another instituted government beside magistracy. But Mr. Coleman acknowledges ministers to be instituted rulers. *Ergo* [*therefore*], Mr. Coleman acknowledges another instituted government besides magistracy.

To the other texts [of] Hebrews 13:7, 17, he says nothing against my argument, only expounds the rulers to be guides, as Mr. Hussey also does, of which

---

10. [*Brotherly Examination*, herein page 230.]

11. [*Nihil Respondes*, herein pp. 243, 244.]

12. [William Hussey, *A Plea for Christian Magistracie, or, An answer to some passages in Mr. Gillespies sermon, against Mr. Coleman* (1645), pp. 19, 22. Thomason purchased his copy on December 20, 1645.]

more elsewhere; meanwhile, it is certain that ὁ ἡγουμένος, is usually taken for a name of highest authority,[13] yea, given to emperors; for which see learned Salmasius in his *Walo Messalinus*, pages 219, 220.[14] It is Joseph's highest title to express his government of Egypt (Acts 7:10). It must the rather be a name of government and authority in this place [of] Hebrews 13:17 because subjection and obedience is required: "Obey them that have the rule over you, and submit yourselves." When the word signifies ὁδηγὸν [*guides, leaders*], *seu vice ducem* [*or vice-commander*] (and it is very rarely so used by the Septuagints, but frequently and almost in innumerable places, they use it for a name of rule and authority), obedience and subjection is not due to such a one *qua talis* [*as such*]; for obedience and subjection cannot be *correlata* [*correlated*] to the leading of the way, when it is without authority and government.

6. I having charged Mr. Coleman's doctrine with this consequence, "That there ought to be neither suspension from the sacrament, nor excommunication, nor ordination, nor deposition of ministers, nor receiving of appeals, except all these things be done by the civil magistrate," which things, I said, "are most of them corrective, and all of them more than doctrinal."[15] Instead of making answer, the reverend brother expresses the error, which I objected to him, thus: "That here are no church censures," which is the *Quæsitum* [*the query*], he says (*Malè Dicis*, p. 10). Here, again, he brings an imagination of his own, both for matter and words, instead of that which I said, and does not take the argument right. If the minister's power be merely doctrinal, and government wholly in the magistrate's hands, then all the particulars enumerated—for instance, suspension from the sacrament, and the receiving of appeals (which he must not bring under the *Quæsitum*, except he bring the ordinance of parliament[16] under the *Quæsitum*), shall be wholly in the magistrate's hand; and elderships may not suspend from the sacrament; classes and synods may not receive appeals, which yet, by the ordinance [of parliament], they have power to do. One of the particulars, and but one, the reverend brother has here touched, and it is this: "For ordination of ministers, I say, it is within the commission of teaching, and so appertains to the doctrinal part." This is the effect of his zeal to maintain that all ecclesiastical ministerial power is merely doctrinal. But mark the consequence of it: He that holds ordination of ministers to be within the commission of teaching, and to appertain to the doctrinal part, must hold, by consequence, that the

---

13. [See Luke 22:26 and Acts 14:12.]

14. [Claude Saumaise, *Walonis Messalini De Episcopis Et Presbyteris Contra D. Petavium Loiolitam Dissertatio Prima* (Lugduni Batavorum: Maire, 1641), pp. 219–220.]

15. [*Nihil Respondes*, herein p. 245.]

16. ["*Die Sabbathi 8 Novemb. 1644.* An Ordinance of the Lords and Commons assembled in Parliament, For the Ordination of Ministers." In *An ordinance of the Lords and Commons assembled in Parliament: for giving power to all the classicall presbyteries within their respective bounds to examine, approve, and ordaine ministers for severall congregations. Die Lunæ 10. Novemb. 1645* [*sic*] (1645).]

power of ordination is given *uni* as well as *unitati*; that is, that every single minister has power to ordain, as well as the classes. But Mr. Coleman holds ordination of ministers to be within the commission of teaching, etc. The reason of the proposition is clear, because the commission of teaching belongs to every single minister, so that if the power of ordination be within that commission, it must needs belong to every single minister. *Quid respondes?*[17]

7. The reverend brother having brought an odious argument against me, which did conclude the magistrate to manage his office for and under the devil, if not for and under Christ, I showed his syllogism to have four terms, and therefore worthy to be exploded.[18] I get now two replies:

First, "This is an error (if one) in logic, not divinity. Is it an error in divinity to make a syllogism with four terms?" (*Malè Dicis*, p. 15). See now if he be a fit man to call others to school, who puts an *If* in this business. *If one.* Who did ever doubt of it? And if it be an error in divinity to be fallacious, and to deceive, then it is an error in divinity to make a syllogism with four terms, yea, as foul an error as can be.

Secondly, He admits not my distinction of those words, "Under Christ, and for Christ." I said the Christian magistrate is under Christ and for Christ; that is, he is serviceable to Christ, but he is not under Christ nor for Christ as Christ's vicegerent, *vice Christi*, in Christ's stead, as Christ is Mediator.[19] The reverend brother says, he foresaw that this would be said (the greater fault it was to make his argument so unclear and indistinct), but he rejects the distinction as being *distinctio sine differentia*.[20] "If a magistrate, says he, "be thus far a servant of Christ, as Mediator, that he is to do his work, to take part with him, to be for his glory, then he does it *vice Christi*."[21] He adds the simile of a servant. Hence it follows, by the reverend brother's principles, that the king's cook, because he does work and service for the king, therefore, he does it *vice regis*, and as the king's vicegerent. Likewise, that a servant who obeys his master's wife and executes her commands because it is his master's will and for his master's honor, does therefore obey his master's wife *vice domini*, as his master's vicegerent; and, by consequence, that the duty of obedience to the wife does originally belong to the husband; for the capacity of a vicegerent, which he has by his vicegerentship is primarily the capacity of him whose vicegerent he is. These, and the like absurd consequences, will unavoidably follow upon the reverend brother's argumentation, that he who does Christ service does it *vice Christi*, as Christ's vicegerent, and that to be a man's vicegerent, and to do a man's work or service, which I made two different things, are all one. But, further, observe his tergiversation. I had, page 13, proved my distinction out of these words of his own: "The commissioner

---

17. [*Quid respondes*: what do you answer?]

18. [See *Nihil Respondes*, herein page 247.]

19. [See ibid., p. 247.]

20. [*Distinctio sine differentia*: a distinction without difference.]

21. [*Malè Dicis*, pp. 15–16.]

says magistracy is not derived from Christ. I say magistracy is given to Christ to be serviceable in his kingdom; so that, though the commissioner's assertion be sound (which in due place will be discussed), yet it infringes nothing that I said." I asked, therefore, *qua fide* [*by what faith*] he could confound in his argument brought against me those two things which himself had so carefully distinguished.[22] There is no reply to this in *Malè Dicis*. When the brother thought it for his advantage, he denied that the magistrate's being serviceable to Christ does enter the derivation of his power by a commission of vicegerentship from Christ (for that was the derivation spoken of), and yielded that the magistrate may be said to be serviceable to Christ, though his power be not derived from Christ. Now he denies the very same distinction for substance.

8. Whereas the reverend brother had told the parliament that he sees not in the whole Bible any one act of that church government which is now in controversy, I brought some scriptural instances against his opinion, not losing either the argument from Matthew 18 (concerning which he asks what is become of it), or other scriptural arguments, which I intend, by God's assistance, to prosecute elsewhere.[23] Now, hear what is replied to the instances which were given. First, To that [of] 1 Corinthians 5:13, "Put away that wicked person from among you," his answer is, "I say, and it is sufficient against the commissioner, If this be a church censure, then the whole church jointly and every particular person has power of church censure" (*Malè Dicis*, p. 10). I hope, sir, it is not sufficient against me that you say it, so long as you say nothing to prove it. I told you that Mr. Prynne himself (who holds not that every particular person has power of church censure) acknowledged that text to be a warrant for excommunication,[24] and when you say "every particular person," you say more than the Independents say, and I am sure more than the text will admit; for the text says, "Put away from among you," therefore, this power was given not *uni*, but *unitati*, and this *unitas* was the presbytery of Corinth.[25] The sentence was inflicted ὑπὸ τῶν πλειόνων, by many (2 Cor. 2:6); it is not said by all. I might say much for this, but I will not now leave the argument in hand; for it is enough against Mr. Coleman that the place proves an act of church government, flowing from a power not civil but ecclesiastical. To whom the power belonged is another question.

To the next instance from 2 Corinthians 2:6, which is coincident with the former, a punishment or censure inflicted by many, "It is only a reprehension,"[26]

---

22. [See *Nihil Respondes*, herein pages 248—248.]

23. [Here is another indication that Gillespie had begun work for a definitive larger work against Erastianism, which would be published as *Aaron's Rod Blossoming* at the end of July 1646, six months after the appearance of *Malè Audis*.]

24. [*Nihil Respondes*, herein page 245.]

25. [In other words, "this power was not given to one but to the whole, united body, and that body was the presbytery of Corinth."]

26. [*Malè Dicis*, p. 10.]

says he, "ἐπιτιμία, which by all the places in the New Testament can amount no higher than to an objurgation [*a harsh rebuke*], and so is doctrinal."

Answer. (1) He made it even now an act of the whole church jointly, and of every particular person. Why did he not clear himself in this, how the whole church, men, women, children and all, did doctrinally reprehend him?

(2) If the objurgation must be restricted, To whom? Not to a single minister (yet every single minister has power of doctrinal objurgation), but to the presbytery. It was an act of those πλεὶονες, I spoke of; and this is a ground for that distinction between ministerial and presbyterial admonition, which Mr. Coleman does not admit ([*Malè Dicis,*] p. 22).

(3) If it were granted that ἐπιτιμία in this text amounts to no more but an objurgation, yet our argument stands good; for the apostle having in his first epistle required the Corinthians to put away from among them that wicked person, which they did accordingly resolve to do (which makes the apostle commend their obedience, 2 Corinthians 2:9), no doubt either the offender was at this time actually excommunicated and cast out of the church, or (as others think) they were about to excommunicate him if the apostle had not by his second epistle prevented them and taken them off with this *sufficit*: Such a degree of censure is enough, the party is penitent, go no higher.

(4) When the reverend brother appeals to all the places in the New Testament, he may take notice that the word ἐπιτιμία is nowhere found in the New Testament except in this very text. And if his meaning be concerning the verb ἐπιτιμάω, he may find it used to express a coercive power, as in Christ's rebuking of the winds and waves (Matt. 8:26; Mark 4:39); His rebuking of the fever (Luke 4:39); His rebuking of the devil (which was not a doctrinal, but a coercive rebuke, Mark 1:25; 9:25; Luke 4:35; 9:42). Sometimes it is put for an authoritative charge, laying a restraint upon a man, and binding him from liberty in this or that particular, as Matthew 12:16, Mark 3:12 and 8:30, Luke 9:21. The word ἐπιτιμία I find in the apocryphal Book of Wisdom, chapter 3:10. It is said of the wicked, ἕξουσιν ἐπιτιμίαν, they shall have correction or punishment. The whole chapter makes an opposition between the godly and the wicked, in reference to punishments and judgments. The Hebrew גָּעַר (which, if the observation holds which is made by Arias Montanus, and divers others, following Kimchi, when it is construed with בְ signifies *objurgavit, duriter reprehendit*; when without בְ, it signifies *corrupit, perdidit, or maledixit*), the Septuagints do most usually turn it ἐπιτιμάω and that in some places where it is without בְ, as Psalm 119:21, "Thou hast rebuked the proud that are cursed;" ἐπετίμησας. Pagnini, *disperdidisti*, thou hast destroyed.[27] So the sense is, it is rebuke with a judgment or a curse upon them. The second part of the verse in the Greek is exegetical to the first part, "Thou hast rebuked the proud, ἐπικατάρατοι, cursed are they," etc.; so Zechariah 3:2, "The Lord rebuke (ἐπιτιμήσαι) thee, O Satan." The same phrase is used in

---

27. [Santes Pagnino, *Biblia, … utriusque instrumenti nova tranlatio ædita a Sancte Pagnino* (1527; repr. Anton du Ry, 1528), Psalm 119:21, fol. 27v.]

Jude, verse 9, which must needs be meant of a coercive, efficacious, divine power, restraining Satan. The same original word they render by ἀφορίζω, which signifies to separate and to excommunicate, [in] Malachi 2:3, "Behold I will corrupt your seed," etc. In the preceding words, God told them that He would curse them. The same word they render by ἀιποσκοπακίζω, *extermino*, [in] Isaiah 17:13, a place which speaks of a judgment to be inflicted, not of a doctrinal reproof. Yet Aquila reads there ἀποσκορακιεῖ;[28] likewise the word which the Septuagints render ἀπωλείᾳ, perdition, [in] Proverbs 13:1, and θυμοῦς, wrath, [in] Isaiah 51:20, in other places they render it ἐπιτίμησις [ἐπιτιμήσεώς] Psalm. 76:6, "At thy rebuke, O God of Jacob, both the chariot and horse are cast into a dead sleep;" 80:16, "They perish at the rebuke of thy countenance." These are real rebukes, that is, judgments and punishments.

(4) What says Mr. Coleman to Pasor,[29] who expounds ἐπιτιμία to be the same with ἐπιτίμιον, *mulcta*, and that [of] 2 Corinthians 2:6, it is meant of excommunication; which he proves by this reason: Because, in the same place, the apostle exhorts the Corinthians to forgive him. Add hereunto Erasmus's observation upon the word κυρῶσαι[30] (verse 8, to "confirm your love toward him"), that it implies an authoritative ratification of a thing by judicial suffrage and sentence, which well agrees to the πλειόνες (v. 6); that is, that they who had judicially censured him, should also judicially loose him and make him free. Now, therefore, the circumstances and context being observed, and the practice [in] 2 Corinthians 2:6 compared with the precept [in] 1 Corinthians 5:13, I conclude that, whether this ἐπιτιμία was excommunication already inflicted, or whether it was a lesser degree of censure tending to excommunication, a censure it was, and more than ministerial objurgation. And it is rightly rendered by the English translators [as] punishment or censure; which well agrees with the signification of the verb ἐπιτιμάω given us by Hesychius[31] and by Julius Pollux,[32] who makes ἐπιτιμᾶν, to punish or

---

28. [Aquila of Sinope. Cf. Frederick Field, *Origenis Hexaplorum quæ supersunt; sive, Veterum interpretum Græcorum in totum Vetus Testamentum fragmenta*, volume 2 (Oxford, 1875), p. 461.]

29. [Georg Pasor, *Lexicon Græco-Latin in N. Test.* (1619; Amsterdam, 1641), p. 495, r.]

30. Κυρῶσαι. *Quod propemodum valet ac si dicas, facite ut pondus et auctoritatem habeat charitas erga ilium. Loquitur enim velut ad judices et concionem, quorum suffragiis velit absolvi eum, qui traditus fuerat Satanæ. Nam* κυρία *concionem significat, in qua creantur magistratus, quæ Latini vocant comitia, et diem alicujus rei causa præstitutum, et jus aliquod agendi. Quin et* κύριον *Græci dicunt scriptum authenticum, authoribus Hesychio et Suida. Mihi videtur et ea sententia quæ vicisset in suffragiis dicta fuisse* κυρία. [Desiderius Erasmus, *In Secundam ad Corinthios Epistolam*, in *Opera* (Basel: Froben, 1541), p. 528; cf. Latin and Greek text and annotations in *Desiderii Erasmi Roterodami Opera omnia*, Volume [ordo] 6, Part 8; Volume 8, ed. M.L. van Poll-van de Lisdonk (North-Holland, 2003), p. 346.]

31. Ἐπιτιμᾶ τιμωρεῖται, ἢ τὴν τιμὴν αὔξει. [Hesychius (of Alexandria), *Lexicon* (Jenae, 1867), p. 604, 30.]

32. Julius Pollux, lib. 8, cap. 5, Εἰ δὲ τὴν δίκην καὶ τιμωρίαν χρὴ λέγειν, ῥητίον δίκη, τιμωρία κόλασις, ζηυία, ἰπιζήμιον, τίμημα, πρστίμημα, ἐπιτίμημα. Καὶ ὡς

chastise, and ἐπιτίμημα, punishment or chastisement. Clemens Alexandrinus uses ἐπιτιμία as well as ἐπιτίμιον, *pro poena vel supplicio.*[33] So Stephanus, in *Thes. Ling. Gr.*[34] From all which it may appear that the text in hand holds forth a corrective church government in the hands of church officers; the thing which Mr. Coleman denies.

To the next instance from 1 Timothy 5:19, "Against an elder receive not an accusation, but before two or three witnesses," the reverend brother answers, "It is either in relation to the judgment of charity, or ministerial conviction, as the verses following."[35]

ANSWER. (1) That of two or three witnesses is taken from the law of Moses, where it is referred only to a forensical proceeding. But in relation either to the judgment of charity, or ministerial conviction, it is not necessary that there be two or three witnesses. If a scandalous sin be certainly known to a minister, though the thing be not certified by two or three witnesses, yet a minister, upon certain knowledge had of the fact, may both believe it and ministerially convince the offender. But there may not be a consistorial proceeding without two or three witnesses.

(2) Since he appeals to the following verses, let verse 22 decide it: "Lay hands suddenly on no man." To whom the laying on of hands or ordination did belong, to them also it did belong to receive an accusation against an elder. But to the presbytery did belong the laying on of hands, or ordination, 1 Timothy 4:14; therefore, to the presbytery did belong the receiving of an accusation against an elder. And so it was not the act of a single minister, as ministerial conviction is.

Ἀντιφῶν, ἐπιτίμιον, ἐπιβολὴ, εὐθύνη, ὄφλημα, καταδίκη, κατάγνωσις. Τὰ δὲ ῥήματα, τιμωρεῖσθαι, κολάζειν, ζημιοῦν, τιμᾶσθαι, προστιμᾶν, ἐπιτιμᾶν, etc. [See *Onomasticon cum annotationibus interpretum* (1502; Lipsiae: Kuehn, 1824), vol. 2, p. 121.]

33. Clemens Alexandrinus, *Pædag.*, lib. 1, cap. 10, uses promiscuously ἐπιτίμιον and ἐπιτιμία, in one and the same sentence, to express punishment. Τὸ ἐπιτιμιον τῶν ἁμαρτωλῶν, καὶ τὸ εὐδιαφόρητον αὐτῶν, κὰ τὸ ὑπηνέμιον δείξας ὁ παιδαγωγὸς, ἀπετρέψατο τῆς αἰίας διὰ τῆς ἐπιτιμίας. Which Gentianus Hervetus, his interpreter, reads thus: *Cum peccatorum pœnas, et facilem et tanquam ventis perflabilem eorum dissipationem ostendisset pædagogus, per pœnam a causa dehortatus est.* Again, *Pædag.*, lib. 3, cap. 2, *ad finem:* Ἀλλὰ καὶ Εικιμῖται κολάζονται καταπεπτωκότες, τὴς ἁγίαν ὑβρίζοντες παρθένον. Τάφος ἡ κόλασις αὐτοῖς, καὶ τὸ μνημόσυνον τῆς ἐπιτιμίας εἰς σωτηρίαν παιδαγωγεῖ. The interpreter thus: *Quin etiam Sichimitæ puniuntur, qui lapsi sunt, sanctæ virgini probrum inferentes. Sepulchrum eis est supplicium, et pœnæ monimentum nos ducit ad salutem.* [Gentian Hervet, *Clementis Alexandrini … Omnia quæ quidem extant opera* (1566), pp. 153, 258. Clement of Alexandria, *The Instructor* in *ANF* 2. "By showing the punishment of sinners, and their easy dispersion, and carrying off by the wind, the Instructor dissuades from crime by means of punishment" (p. 233). "The Shechemites, too, were punished by an overthrow for dishonouring the holy virgin. The grave was their punishment, and the monument of their ignominy leads to salvation" (p. 274).]

34. [Henri Estienne, *Thesaurus græcæ linguæ* (1572; repr. Paris: Didot, 1835), vol. 3, p. 1849.]

35. [*Malè Dicis*, p. 10.]

To the laſt inſtance from Revelation 2:14, 15, 20, the reverend brother answers, That he "had ſtriven to find out how church censures might be there
grounded," but "was conſtrained to let it alone."[36] But what is it, in his opinion, which is there blamed in the angels of those churches? Does he imagine
that those who are so much commended by Chriſt Himself for their holding faſt of His name, and of the true faith, did not so much as doctrinally
or miniſterially oppose the foul errors of the Balaamites and of Jezebel? No
doubt but this was done: but Chriſt reproves them because such scandalous
persons were yet suffered to be in the church, and were not caſt out. "I have a
few things againſt thee, because thou haſt there them that hold the doctrine
of Balaam;" and verse 20, "Thou suffereſt that woman Jezebel." And why was
the very having or suffering them in the church a fault, if it had not been a
duty to caſt them out of the church? Which caſting out could not be by banishment, but by excommunication. It did not belong to the angel to caſt out
the Balaamites out of Pergamos, but he might and ought to have caſt them
out of the church in Pergamos.

9. Mr. Coleman has another passage againſt the diſtinction of church censures and civil punishments. "But what are ecclesiaſtical censures," says he?
"Let us take a taſte. Is deposition from the miniſtry? This kings have done,"
etc. (*Malè Dicis*, p. 7). Now, *similia labra lactucis*.[37] But for all that, the taſte
is vitiated, and does not put a difference between things that are different.
Deposition is sometimes taken, improperly, for expulsion, as Balsamon in
Conc. Nicæni, can. 19, does observe.[38] And so the Chriſtian magiſtrate may
remove or put away miniſters when they deserve to be put away, that is, by
a coercive power to reſtrain them, imprison, or banish them, and in case of
capital crimes, punish them with capital punishments. King James, having
once heard a diſpute in St. Andrews about the deposition of miniſters, was
convinced that it does not belong to the civil magiſtrate, "yet," said he, "I can
depose a miniſter's head from his shoulders," which was better divinity than
this of Mr. Coleman. If we take deposition properly, as it is more than the

---

36. [*Malè Dicis*, p. 10.]

37. [*Similes habent labra lactucas* (like lips like lettuce). Gillespie is using this old proverb
recounted in Erasmus's adages to underscore the unsuitableness of the placing of church
censures in the magistrate's hands. "Thistles suit the rough and hard lips of the ass…." Robert
Bland, *Proverbs, Chiefly Taken From The Adagia Of Erasmus* (1814), p. 231. *Adagiorum chiliades
Des. Erasmi* (1551), p. 339. "To sum up, we can use" [this proverb] "whenever dreadful things
befall dreadfull persons and people get what they deserve, even though they think what they
are getting is fine, just as to an ass thistles are like lettuce leaves." *Collected Works of Erasmus:
Prolegomena to the Adages* (University of Toronto Press, 2017), p. 87. "And like lips find like lettuce; nay, the more foolish anything is, the more 'tis admired…." Erasmus, *The Praise Of Folly*,
trans. John Wilson (1688), p. 73.]

38. ["Depositionis nomen hic abusive pro expulsione acceptum est." Theodore Balsamon, *Canones Sanctorum apoſtolorum, Conciliorum generalium et provincialium* (Paris, 1620),
page. 300B.]

expelling, sequestering, or removing of a minister from this or that place, and comprehends that which the Council of Ancyra, canon 18, calls Ἀφαιπεῖθαι τὴν τιμὴν τοῦ πρεσβυτερίου, the honor of presbytership to be taken away,[39] or a privation of that *presbyteratus*, the order of a presbyter, and that ἐξουσία, the authority and power of dispensing the Word, sacraments, and discipline, which was given in ordination, so none have power to depose who have not power to ordain, it belongs not to the magistrate either to make or unmake ministers. Therefore, in the ancient church, the bishops had power of the deposition as well as of the ordination of presbyters, yet they were bound up that they might not depose either presbyter or deacon without the concurrence of a presbytery or synod in the business.[40] Mark, of the *synod*, not of the magistrate. As for the testimonies brought by Mr. Coleman, he does both here and in divers other places, name his authors without quoting the places. It seems he has either found the words cited by others, but durst not trust the quotations, or else has found somewhat in those places which might make against him. However, all that he can cite of that kind concerning deposition of ministers by emperors is meant of a coercive expulsion, not of that which we call properly deposition. And to this purpose let him take the observation of a great antiquary.[41]

And, withal, he may take notice that Protestant writers do disclaim the magistrate's power of deposing ministers,[42] and hold that deposition is a

---

39. [Cf. Balsamon, p. 781.]

40. Concil. Antioch. sub Constantio, can. 4. *Si quis episcopus a synodo depositus, [vel presbyter,] vel diaconus a proprio episcopo, sacrum celebrare ausus fuerit*, etc. [Cf. Balsamon, ibid., pp. 813.] Concil. Hispal. 2, can. 6, *Ut nullus nostrum sine concilii examine, dejicere quemlibet presbyterum vel diaconum audeat. Episcopus enim sacerdotibus et ministris solus honorem dare poteat: auferre solus non potest.* [Cf. *PL* 130, col. 598.] Vide etiam Conc. Afric., can. 20 [Christopher Justel, *Codex canonum ecclesiæ Africanæ* (1614), p. 90]; Conc. Carthag. 4, can. 23. [Bartolomé de Carranza, *Summa Conciliorum* (Venice, 1546; Venice, 1606), p. 84v.]

41. Salmas. *Appar. ad lib. de Primat.*, pp. 298, 299. *Non enim potestatem quam in ordinatione accepit per impositionem manuum, potest eripere princeps, cum nec eam possit dare. Si princeps igitur velit ministrum aliquem ob sua peccata prorsus degradari et* καθαιρεῖσθαι *et ministerium simul cum ejus functione amittere, per pastores ipsos id faciendum debet curare, qui Judices veri ipsius sunt, et auferre soli possunt quod per ordinationem dederunt. Imperatores Romani quos per vim ejicerent, quia intelligebant potestatem ministerii fungendi non aliter iis adimere posse, in exilium eos mittebant. Quod possemus infinitis testimoniis demonstrare. Relegatus hoc modo episcopus remanebat nihilominus episcopus, non ordine excidebat episcopali, nee ad laicorum ordinem redigebatur.* [Claudius Salmasius (Claude de Saumaise), *Salmasii Liborum de Primatu Papae pars prima, cum Apparatu Accessere de eodem Pramatu Nili et Barlaami Tractatus* (Lugd. Batavor: Ex officina Elzeviriorum, 1645), pp. 298, 299.]

42. Gerhard. Loc. Com., tom. 6, p. 201. *Probari nequit illorum pseudo politicorum opinio, qui ad jura regalia magistratus remotionem ministrorum pertinere censent.* [Cf. *Loci theologici: cum pro adstruenda veritate tum pro* (Lipsiae: Hinrichs, 1885), volume 6, p. 117.] See Fr. Junius, *Ecclesiast.*, lib. 3, cap. 3; *et Animad. in Bell. Contr.*, 4, lib. 1, cap. 20, note 8; Balduin., *de Cas. Conscient.*,

part of ecclesiastical jurisdiction: ministers being always punishable (as other members of the commonwealth), according to the law of the land, for any offence committed against law.

CHAPTER THREE
THAT MR. COLEMAN'S & MR. HUSSEY'S OPPOSING OF CHURCH GOVERNMENT NEITHER IS NOR CAN BE RECONCILED WITH THE SOLEMN LEAGUE & COVENANT

MR. COLEMAN's doctrine was by me charged to be a violation of the Solemn League and Covenant. This he acknowledged in his *Re-examination* (p. 13, 17), to be a very grievous charge, and a greater fault in him than in divers others, if made out; and he desired seriously, yea, challenged it by the right of a Christian, and by the right of a minister, that I should prosecute this charge; whereupon I did, in my *Nihil Respondes*, prosecute it so far, that, by five strong arguments I did demonstrate the repugnancy of his doctrine to the covenant.[43] About a month afterward comes out Mr. Hussey's book, wherein the charge itself (before desired to be prosecuted) is declined expressly by Mr. Coleman in the few lines by him prefixed (which are ranked together with the errata),[44] in which he desires that the argumentative part may be so prosecuted as that the charge of covenant-breaking may be laid aside; which, if it be taken up, he lets me know beforehand it shall be esteemed by them a *nihil respondes*. It is also declined by Mr. Hussey (p. 15): "The argument of the covenant is too low to be thought on in the discourse: we are now in an higher region than the words of the covenant,"[45] etc.: a tenet looked upon by the reformed churches as proper to those that are inspired with the ghost of Arminius; for the Remonstrants, both at and after the Synod of Dort did cry down the obligation of all national covenants, oaths, etc., in matters of religion, under the color of taking the Scripture only for a rule.[46] Well, we

---

lib. 4, cap. 5, cas. 12. [Franciscus Junius, *Ecclesiastici sive de natura et administrationibus ecclesiæ Dei: libri tres* (Wechel, 1581); in *Opera* (1613), vol. 1, cols. 1969–1971. Ibid., 2.1064. Friedrich Balduin, *Tractatus Luculentus, Posthumus, Toti Reipublicæ Christianæ Utilissimus De Materia rarissime antehac enucleata, Casibus nimirum Conscientiæ* (Wittenbergæ: Pauli Helwigii, [1628]), pages 1030–1031.]

43. [See *Nihil Respondes*, herein pages 260–265. These are not clearly laid out as five reasons, which may be at least one of the reasons Gillespie enumerates them again in this chapter.]

44. [Hussey, *A Plea for Christian Magistracie* (1645), page facing page 1.]

45. [Hussey, ibid., p. 15.]

46. *Vide apud Synod Dordrac, sess. 25, Conditiones synodi legitime instituendas quas remonstrantes,* etc., *condit. 9.* [*Acta Synodi nationalis, in nomine Domini Iesu Christi* (Lugduni Batavorum: Isaaci Elzevir, 1620), pp. 69–70. Cf. *Acta of the Synod of Dordt*, ed. edited by Christian Moser, Donald Sinnema, Herman J. Selderhuis (Bristol, Ct: Vandenhoeck & Ruprecht, 2014), p. 371.

see the charge declined as nothing. But this is not all. Almost two months after my proof of the charge, Mr. Coleman comes out with his *Malè Dicis*, and declines both the charge itself (which he calls an "impertinent charge," page 22), and my five arguments too, without so much as taking notice of them, or offering replies to them; yea, all that I said in my *Nihil Respondes* (p. 27–34),[47] in prosecution of this argument concerning covenant-breaking, the reverend brother has skipped over *sicco pede*[48] in the half of one page (p. 23); all that follows is new and other matter, wherein he did not mind his own answer to the learned viewer (p. 33), "I will keep you to the laws of disputation, and will not answer but as it is to the matter in hand."[49] I leave it to be judged by men of knowledge and piety whether such a one does not give them some ground to apprehend that he is αὐτοκατάκριτος, that is, self-judged, who first calls so eagerly for making out a charge against him, and then when it is made out, does decline the charge, and not answer the arguments; and such as esteem the charge of covenant-breaking to be a *nihil respondes*, and the argument of the covenant too low to be thought on in a controversy about church government, "O my soul, come not thou into their secret; unto their assembly, mine honour, be not thou united."[50] It is in vain for them to palliate or shelter their covenant-breaking with appealing from the covenant to the Scripture, for *subordinata non pugnant*.[51] The covenant is *norma recta*, a right rule, though the Scripture alone be *norma recti*, the rule of right. If they hold the covenant to be unlawful, or to have anything in it contrary to the Word of God, let them speak out. But to profess the breach of the covenant to be a grievous and great fault, and worthy of a severe censure, and yet to decline the charge and proofs thereof, is a most horrible scandal; yea, be astonished, O ye heavens, at this, and give ear, O earth![52] how small regard is had to the oath of God by men professing the name of God.

As for that little which the reverend brother has replied unto; first, he takes notice of a passage of his sermon at the taking of the covenant, which I had

---

"Ut de controversis articulis non fiat decisio, sed accommodationi studeatur, cuius tamen via et ratio rata non habeatur, nisi accedente utriusque partis consensu. Qua de causa quoque licitum sit singulis partibus cum absentibus deliberare per modum recessus; utque (si forte inter partes convenire nequeat, quod tamen ut fiat in timore Domini serio allaborabitur) magistratus summus dispiciat statuatque, re utrimque cognita, quem ordinem et modum, tum in docendo tum in aliis, in publicis templis obtinere velit." *Early Sessions of the Synod of Dordt*, ed. Donald Sinnema, Christian Moser, Herman J. Selderhuis, Johanna Roelevink (Bristol, Ct: Vandenhoeck & Ruprecht, 2018), pp. 305, 312.]

47. [See *Nihil Respondes*, herein pages 260–265.]

48. [*Sicco pede*: dry foot; i.e., he skipped over the difficult work, avoiding getting his feet wet.]

49. [Coleman, *Malè Dicis*, p. 33.]

50. [Genesis 49:6.]

51. [*Subordinata non pugnant*: subordinates do not fight (strive, conflict).]

52. [Cf. Isaiah 1:2 and Jeremiah 2:12.]

put him in mind of, but he answers only to one particular, viz., concerning that clause, "Doubtless many materials of prelacy must of necessity be retained as absolutely necessary."[53] I asked what he understood by this clause? Now observe his answer: "I answer ingenuously, as he desires, and fully, as I conceive, These materials of prelacy are ordination."[54] Remember you said, "many materials of prelacy." I beseech you, sir, how many is ordination? Ordination, ordination, ordination; tell on till you think you have made many materials; and, withal, tell us (if this be the meaning, that ordination should be retained without any power of ecclesiastical government in the ministry) how was it imaginable that he could hereby satisfy that scruple which then he spoke to, viz., the scruple about the purging away of the exorbitances of prelacy, and retaining a regulated prelacy? And after all this, I shall desire him to expound that other clause (which I desired before, but he has not done it), "Taking away," said he, "the exorbitancies, the remaining will be a new government and no prelacy."[55] Either he means this of a new church government distinct from the civil, so that the ministry should have new power of government, or he meant it of the way which now he pleads for. If the former, I have what I would. Mr. Coleman himself, as well as other men, took the covenant with an intention to have an ecclesiastical government distinct from the civil. If the latter, then let him answer these two things: 1. What good sense there was in applying such an answer to such a scruple, as if the Erastian way, or the appropriating of all ecclesiastical jurisdiction wholly to the civil magistrate, could be the way to satisfy those who scrupled the total abolition of prelacy. 2. How will he reconcile himself with himself; for here, [*Malè Dicis,*] page 22, he says that his way was in practice before I was born, "and the constant practice of England always." This, as it is a most notorious untruth (for the constant practice of England has granted to the clergy, as he calls them, after the popish dialect, a power of deposition and excommunication, whereas his way denies all corrective power or church censures to the ministry), so, if it were a truth, it is utterly inconsistent with that which he said of the remaining part, namely, that it will be a new government. If it be his way, how will he make it the constant practice of England always, and a new government too?

In the next place, the reverend brother makes short work of my five arguments to prove the repugnancy of his doctrine to the Solemn League and Covenant. They were too hot for him to be much touched upon. "All is but this much," says he, "the covenant mentions and supposes a distinct church government."[56] It is hard when arguments are neither repeated nor answered. He repeats a point which was proved (and but a part of that), but

---

53. [Thomas Coleman, *The Hearts Ingagement: A sermon preached at St. Margarets Westminster, at the publique entering into the Covenant* (1643), see the objections at the end. See *Nihil Respondes*, here page 259.]

54. [Coleman, *Malè Dicis*, p. 22.]

55. [Coleman, *The Hearts Ingagement*, ibid.]

56. [Coleman, *Malè Dicis*, p. 23.]

not the proofs; and so he answers (rather to the conclusion than to the arguments) these two things: "First," saith he, "the expressions in the covenant are according to the general apprehensions of the times, which took such a thing for granted, yet I believe Mr. Gillespie cannot make such a supposition obligatory." Now you yield, sir, what before you eagerly contended against, viz., that the covenant does suppose a church government. Remember your simile of the jury sworn to inquire into the felony of a prisoner, which oath does not suppose the prisoner to be guilty of felony, but he is to be tried, guilty or not guilty. We are now so far agreed that the covenant does suppose a church government distinct from the civil government, and yet not merely doctrinal, for that was the point which I proved, and which here he yields. As for the obligation of an oath sworn upon such supposition, I ANSWER, 1. It is more than supposed; the words and expressions of the covenant do plainly hold out the thing as I proved, and as the reverend brother here seems to yield. 2. That which an oath does necessarily suppose, if the oath be lawful, and the thing supposed lawful, is without all controversy obligatory. Now the reverend brother does acknowledge both the covenant itself to be a lawful oath, and that which the covenant supposes, namely, a church government distinct from the civil government, and yet not merely doctrinal, to be a lawful thing; for he professes to yield it (though not *jure divino*, yet) in prudence, which he cannot do if he makes the thing unlawful. 3. That which an oath does suppose is sometimes supposed *vi materice*, or *consequentiæ*, that is, the words of the oath do necessarily imply such a thing, though it be not intended by the swearer. And here I will tell Mr. Coleman one story of Alexander for another.[57] When Alexander was coming against a town to destroy it, he met Anaximenes, who, as he understood, came to make intercession and supplication for sparing the town. Alexander prevented him with an oath that he would not do that thing which Anaximenes should make petition for, whereupon Anaximenes made petition that he would destroy the town. Alexander found himself bound by the plain words of his oath not to do what he intended, and so did forbear.[58] And to add a divine story to a human, Joshua and the princes of Israel did swear to the Gibeonites upon a supposition that was not true, yet they found themselves tied by their oath [Joshua 9:15–18]. So he that swears to his own hurt must not change, the oath being otherwise lawful (Ps. 15:4), yet that self-hurt which is wrapped up in the matter of his oath was not intended in swearing. Sometimes, again, that which is supposed and implied in an oath lies also in the thoughts and intentions of those that swear. Now, where those two are coincident, that is, where the thing supposed in an oath is both implied necessarily in the words of the oath, and is also according to the apprehensions of those that swear (which is the case here in the covenant, and

---

57. [Coleman adduces a story about Alexander at the beginning of *Malè Dici*, page 3.]

58. [Pausanias, *Description of Greece*, Book III, trans. W. H. S. Jones, Loeb Classical Library (Cambridge: Harvard University Press, 1961), p. 107. Errata (1646): "to do" to "not to do."]

is acknowledged by the reverend brother), I should think it most strange how any divine can have the least doubt concerning the obligation of such a thing, except he conceive the thing itself to be unlawful.

His second answer is this: "In my way," says he, "the governments, civil and ecclesiastical, are in the subject matter clearly distinct. When the parliament handles matters of war, it is a military court; when business of state, it is a civil court; when matters of religion, it is an ecclesiastical court." If this hold good, then it will follow: 1. That the parliament, when they deliberate about matters of war or matters of religion, are not, at least formally and properly, a civil court, else how makes he these so clearly distinct? 2. That ministers may be called civil officers, for consider his words in his *Re-examination*, page 11: "I do not exclude ministers, neither from ecclesiastical nor civil government, in a ministerial way, doctrinally and declaratively." Compare this with his present answer, it will amount to thus [*this*] much: That different denominations being taken from the different subject matter, ministers, when they handle doctrinally matters of religion are ecclesiastical ministers, and when they handle doctrinally matters of civil government, which himself allows them to do, they are civil ministers.

But now to apply his answer to the argument: How does all this solve the repugnancy of his doctrine to the covenant? If he had examined my arguments, he had found that most of them prove from the covenant a church government distinct from civil government, *subjective* as well as *objective*; that is, another government besides magistracy; different agents as well as different acts; different hands as well as handling of different matters. I know the Christian magistrate may and ought to have a great influence in matters of religion; and whatsoever is due to him by the Word of God, or by the doctrine either of the ancient or reformed churches, I do not infringe, but do maintain and strengthen it. But the point in hand is that the covenant does undeniably suppose and clearly hold forth a government in the church distinct from magistracy, which is proved by these arguments (which, as they are not yet answered, so I will briefly apply them to the proof of that point which now Mr. Coleman sticks at):

1. The church government[59] mentioned in the covenant is as distinct from the privileges of parliament as the first article of the covenant is distinct from the third article.[60]

2. The church government in the first article of the covenant, the reformation whereof we are to endeavor, differs from church government by archbishops, bishops, etc., mentioned in the second article as much as a thing to be reformed differs from a thing to be extirpated; so that the church government formerly used in the Church of England is looked upon two ways in the covenant, either *qua* church government, and so we swear to endeavor

---

59. [*Works* misset this as "church covenant" (p. 15).]

60. [Covenant: The Solemn League and Covenant (1643). See *The Confession of Faith; the Larger and Shorter Catechisms* ... (Edinburgh: Johnstone and Hunter, 1855), pp. 358–360.]

the reformation of it (which I hope was not meant of reforming that part of the privileges of parliament whereby they meddle with religion in a parliamentary way), or *qua* church government by archbishops, bishops, etc., and so we swear to endeavor the extirpation of it. This difference between the first and second articles, between reformation and extirpation, proves that the covenant does suppose that the church government formerly used in the Church of England, in so far as it was *a* church government,[61] is not *eatenus* [*thus far*] to be abolished, but in so far as it was a corrupt church government, that is, prelatical.

3. Church government in the covenant is matched with doctrine, worship, and catechizing. Now, these are subjectively different from civil government, for the civil magistrate does not act doctrinally nor catechetically, neither can he dispense the Word and sacraments, as Mr. Coleman acknowledges.

4. In the first part of the first article of the covenant, concerning "the preservation of the reformed religion in the Church of Scotland, in doctrine, worship, discipline, and government,"[62] it is uncontroverted that discipline and government are ecclesiastical and subjectively different from civil government, that is, though divers who have a hand in the civil government are ruling elders, yet it is as true that divers members of parliament and inferior civil courts are not church officers, and of the ministry none are civil governors, which makes the two governments clearly distinct subjectively. Now, the second part of that article concerning "the reformation of religion in the kingdoms of England and Ireland, in doctrine, worship, discipline, and government," cannot so far differ from the first part of that article in the sense of the words, "discipline and government," as that the same words in the same article of the same covenant should signify things differing *toto genere*, which will follow, unless "discipline and government" in the second branch, and "form of church government" in the third branch, be understood of the power of church officers and not of the magistrate.

5. We did swear to "endeavor the reformation of religion in the kingdoms of England and Ireland, in doctrine, worship, discipline, and government, according to the Word of God and the example of the best reformed

---

61. [As on page 222 and 250, though not noted in those places, the emphasis has been added for clarity of the arguement (*a* church government).]

62. [Article one of the Solemn League and Covenant: "That we shall sincerely, really, and constantly, through the grace of GOD, endeavour, in our several places and callings, *the preservation of the reformed religion in the Church of Scotland, in doctrine, worship, discipline, and government*, against our common enemies; *the reformation of religion in the kingdoms of England and Ireland, in doctrine, worship, discipline, and government, according to the word of GOD, and the example of the best reformed Churches*; and shall endeavour to bring the Churches of GOD in the three kingdoms to the nearest conjunction and uniformity in religion, confession of faith, form of church government, directory for worship and catechising; that we, and our posterity after us, may, as brethren, live in faith and love, and the Lord may delight to dwell in the midst of us." *Confession*, etc. (1855), pp. 358–359. Emphasis added.]

churches."[63] Now, the Word of God holds forth another government besides magistracy; for Mr. Coleman himself has acknowledged that he finds in the New Testament ministers to be rulers, yea, instituted rulers; and the example of the best reformed churches, without all doubt, lead us to an ecclesiastical government different from magistracy. Neither has the reverend brother so much as once adventured to allege the contrary, except of the church of Israel, which, as it is heterogeneous, being none of the reformed churches mentioned in the covenant, so it shall be discussed in due place;[64] from all which reasons I conclude that the wit of man cannot reconcile Mr. Coleman's doctrine with the covenant.

6. I add a confutation of him out of himself, thus: No such church government as Mr. Coleman casts upon an uncertainty, whether the Word hold out any such thing, can be, by his principles, the power of magistracy in things ecclesiastical, but another government beside magistracy. But the church government mentioned in the first article of the covenant is such a church government as Mr. Coleman casts upon an uncertainty whether the Word hold out any such thing; therefore, the church government mentioned in the first article of the covenant cannot be, by his principles, the power of magistracy, but another government besides magistracy. The proposition he will easily admit, unless he alters his assertions; the assumption is clear from his *Re-examination* (p. 15).

---

63. [See the text in the previous note.]

64. [By in due place, Gillespie means in due course in another piece of writing, which was his *Aaron's Rod Blossoming*. This is a third or fourth time at this point that Gillespie has made note of this work in progress in *Malè Audis*. Gillespie addresses this extensively in book one, chapters two through nine under five topics in *Aaron's Rod* (*Works*, p. 3). "It hath been by some (with much confidence and scorn of all who say otherwise) averred, that excommunication and church government distinct from the civil hath no pattern for it in the Jewish church. "I am sure," saith Mr. Coleman in his *Brotherly Examination Re-examined*, p. 16, "the best reformed church that ever was, went this way, I mean the church of Israel, which had no distinction of church government and civil government." Hast thou appealed unto Caesar? Unto Caesar shalt thou go. Have you appealed to the Jewish church? thither shall you go. Wherefore I shall endeavour to make these five things appear: 1. That the Jewish church was formerly distinct from the Jewish state. 2. That there was an ecclesiastical sanhedrim and government distinct from the civil. 3. That there was an ecclesiastical excommunication distinct from civil punishments. 4. That in the Jewish church there was also a public exomologesis, or declaration of repentence, and, thereupon, a reception or admission again of the offender to fellowship with the church in the holy things. 5. That there was a suspension of the profane from the temple and passover."]

Chapter Four
Mr. Coleman & Mr. Hussey's Errors In Divinity

Mr. Hussey all along calls for divinity schools: I confess himself has much need of them, that he may be better grounded in his divinity, and that if he will plead any more for Christian magistracy, he may not involve himself into such dangerous heterodoxies as have fallen from his pen in this short tractate. I instance in these:

First, In his epistle to the parliament he has divers passages against synodical votes; he will have no putting to the vote: "For votes" says he [on] page 6, "are of no other use but to gather parties, and ought nowhere to be used but by those that have the power of the sword." And [on] page 3, he will have the business of assemblies to be only doctrinal, and "by dispute to find out truth. Their disputes ought to end in a brotherly accord, as in Acts 15, much disputing, but all ended in accord, no putting to the vote." And [on] page 5, he will have things carried "with strength of argument and unanimous consent of the whole clergy." [65] Behold how he joins issue with the Remonstrants against the Contra Remonstrants, to introduce not only an academical, but a sceptical and Pyrrhonian dubitation and uncertainty,[66] so that there shall never be an end of controversy, nor any settlement of truth and of the ordinances of Jesus Christ, so long as there shall be but one tenacious disputer to hold up the ball of contention. One egg is not liker another than Mr. Hussey's tenet is like that of the Arminians, for which see the Synod of Dort, session 25.[67] It was the ninth condition which the Arminians required in a lawful and well-constituted synod, that there might be no decision of the controverted articles, but only such an accommodation as both sides might agree to. And generally, they hold that synods ought not to meet for decision or determination, but for examining, disputing, discussing; so their *Examen Censuræ*, cap. 25; and their *Vindiciæ*, lib. 2, cap. 6, pp. 131, 133.[68]

Secondly, In that same epistle to the parliament [on] page 4, he has this

---

65. [William Hussey, "To the Right Honoourable, the Lords and Commons assembled in Parliament," in *A Plea for Christian Magistracie: or, An answer to some passages in Mr. Gillespies Sermon, against Mr. Coleman. Also to the Brotherly examination of some passages*, etc. (1646), unnumbered pages 3, 5, 6.]

66. [Pyrrhonian doubt or hesitation. Pyrrhonism was a philosophy of skepticism founded by Pyrrho of Elis, which taught that wisdom was based in suspending judgment and rejected the pursuit of certain knowledge. (Britannica).]

67. *Ut de controversis articulis non fiat decisio, sed accommodationi studeatur: cujus tamen via et ratio rata non habeatur, nisi accedente utriusque partis consensu.* [See the prior note in chapter three, page 284.]

68. [*Examen Censuræ* in Simon Episcopius, *Apologia pro Confessione sive declaratione sententiæ eorum* (1629), pp. 287v–308v. Episcopius, *Vedelivs Rhapsodvs, sive Vindiciae Doctrinæ Remonstrantium* (1633), pp. 131, 133.]

passage: "Will-worship is unlawful, I mean in matters that are essential to God's worship, which are matters of duty; as for circumstantials of time and place, except the Sabbath, which are matters of liberty, in these the commonwealth may vote, etc.; and this is your Christian liberty, that in matters of liberty ye make rules and laws to yourselves, not crossing the ends that you are tied to in duty." And is the Sabbath only a circumstantial of time contradistinct from matters of duty? It seems he will cry down not only the *jus divinum* of church censures with the Erastians, but the *jus divinum* of the Sabbath with the Canterburians. And if will-worship be unlawful only in the essentials of God's worship, why was the argument of will-worship so much tossed, not only between prelates and nonconformists, but between papists and Protestants, even in reference to ceremonies? And whether has not Mr. Hussey here engaged himself to hold it free and lawful to the Christian magistrate, yea, to private Christians (for he calls it Christian liberty, not parliamentary liberty; now, Christian liberty belongs to all sorts of Christians), to make laws to themselves for taking the sacrament anniversarily on Christmas, Good-Friday, and Easter, or to appoint a perpetual monthly fast or thanksgiving; yea, another parliament may, if so it should seem good to them, impose again the surplice and cross in baptism, fonts, railing of communion tables,[69] the reading of divers passages of Apocrypha to the congregations, doxologies, anthems,[70] responsories, etc., as heretofore they were used; or they may appoint all and every one to sit in the church with their faces towards the east, to stand up at the epistles and gospels, etc.; yea, what ceremonies, Jewish, popish, heathenish, may they not impose, provided they only hold the foundation, and keep to those essentials which he calls matters of duty? By restraining the unlawfulness of will-worship to the essentials, he leaves men free to do anything in religion, *præter verbum* [*beside the Word*], so that it appear not to them to be *contra verbum* [*contrary to the Word*]; anything they may add to the Word, or do beside the Word, so that the thing cannot be proved contrary to the Word.

Thirdly, Mr. Hussey, ibid., p. 4, 5, says that the parliament may require such as they receive for preachers of truth, "to send out able men to supply the places, and that without any regard to the allowance or disallowance of the people," where, in the first part of that which he says, there is either a heterodoxy or a contradiction. A heterodoxy, if he means that ministers are to be sent out without ordination; a contradiction if he means that they must be ordained; for then he gives classis a work which is not merely doctrinal. But most strange it is that he so far departs from Protestant divines in point of the church's liberty in choosing ministers. He tells us [on] page 14, that Mr. Herle, "for want

---

69. [*Railing*: rails for kneeling at the communion table. *Fonts*: The Directory for Worship notes that baptism is to be administered "in the place of publick worship, and in the face of the congregation, where the people may most conveniently see and hear; and not in the places where fonts, in the time of Popery, were unfitly and superstitiously placed. *Confession*, etc. (1855), p. 382. See Gillespie, Notes, p. 89; *Minutes*, 3.379; Lightfoot, Journal, p. 315.]

70. [*Anthem*: a short religious song for a choir, often with an organ (Oxford).]

of skill and theological disputations," has granted to people a right to choose their minister. Mr. Herle's skill, both logical and theological, is greater than it seems he can well judge of;[71] neither can this bold arrogant censure of his derogate from Mr. Herle's, but from his own reputation. For the matter itself, it is one, and not the least, of the controversies between the papists and Protestants, what right the church has in the vocation of ministers. Read Bellarmine, *de Cleric*, and those that write against him, and see whether it be not so.[72] The Helvetic Confession tells us that the right choosing of ministers is by the consent of the church, and the Belgic Confession says, "We believe that the ministers, seniors and deacons, ought to be called to those their functions, and by the lawful elections of the church to be advanced into those rooms." See both these in the *Harmony of Confessions*, section 11.[73] I might here, if it were requisite, bring a heap of testimonies from Protestant writers; the least thing which they can admit of is that a minister be not obtruded *renitente ecclesia. Factum valet, fieri non debet*.[74] It may be helped after it is done, without making null or void the ministry; but in a well-constituted church there ought to be no intrusion into the ministry; the church's consent is requisite; for which also I might bring both Scripture and antiquity, but that is not my present business. One thing I must needs put Mr. Hussey in mind of, that when the prelates did intrude ministers, without any regard to the disallowance of the people, it was cried out against as an oppression and usurpation, and we are often warned by Mr. Prynne, by Mr. Coleman, and by myself, to cast away the prelates' usurpation with themselves. But who lords it now over the Lord's inheritance, the Presbyterians or the Erastians? Nay, he who will have ministers put in churches "without any regard to the allowance or disallowance of people," falls far short of divers prelatical men, who did much commend the ancient primitive form of calling ministers, not without the church's consent. See Dr Field, *Of the Church*, lib. 5, cap. 54;[75] Bilson, *de Gubern. Eccl.*, cap. 15, p. 417;[76] the author of *The History of Episcopacy*, part 2, p. 360.[77]

Fourthly, Mr. Hussey, Epistle, page 7, says that upon further consideration he found "the minister charged only with preaching and baptizing." The like he has afterwards [on] page 39, "Let any man prove that a minister has any more to do from Christ than to teach and baptize." And again, page 44, he propounds

---

71. [Charles Herle, a Presbyterian, was one of the most active members of the Westminster Assembly. Hussey cited no work and appears to have simply made a personal attack.]

72. [Robert Bellarmine, *De Clericis*, in *Opera omnia* (1870), pp. 415–497. See the animadversiones of Franciscus Junius in *Opera*, volume 2 (1613) and William Ames, *Bellarminus enervatus*, 4 vols (Amsterdam: Jan Jansson, 1630), volume 1, book 3, pp. 73–140.]

73. [*An Harmony of the Confessions of the Faith* (1643), pp. 236, 258.]

74. [I.e., this should not be done with the resistance of the church. *Factum valet, [quod] fieri non debet*: "what should not be done, yet being done, shall be valid."]

75. [Richard Field, *Of the Church, five books* (1628), p. 686ff.]

76. [Thomas Bilson, *De Perpetua Ecclesiae Christi Gubernatione* (1611), p. 417.]

77. [Peter Heylyn, *The History of Episcopacy: the 2. part* (1642), p. 360.]

this query, "Whether Christ gave any more government (he should have said any more to do, for preaching and baptizing are not acts of government) than is contained in preaching and baptizing," and he holds the negative. If only preaching and baptizing, then not praying and reading in the congregation, ministering the Lord's supper, visiting the sick and particular families.

Fifthly, He holds [on] page 20, that a heathen magistrate is unlawful, "and for his government, if sin be lawful, it is lawful." A gross heterodoxy. The apostle exhorts to be subject even to heathen magistrates, Romans 13, for there were no other at that time, and to pray for them, 1 Timothy 2; so that by Mr. Hussey's divinity, the apostle would have men to be subject unto and to pray for an unlawful government. It is an anabaptistical tenet that a heathen magistrate is not from God, which Gerhard, *de Magistratu Politico*, pp. 498, 499, fully confutes.[78]

Sixthly, He says of Christ, page 40, "He does nothing as Mediator which He does not as God or as man." It is a dangerous mistake, for take the work of mediation itself, He neither does it as God, nor as man, but as God-man.

Seventhly, He says, page 35, "Nothing can be said of Christ as second person in Trinity, in opposition to Mediator, but in opposition to man there may." So that he will not admit of this opposition: Christ as the Second Person in the Trinity is equal and consubstantial to the Father, but as Mediator he is not equal to His Father, but less than His Father, and subject and subordinate to his Father, a distinction used by our divines against the Anti-Trinitarians and Socinians. Now by his not admitting of this distinction, he does by consequence mire himself in Socinianism; for Christ, as Mediator, is the Father's servant (Isa. 42:1), and the Father is greater than He (John 14:28); and as the head of the man is Christ, so the head of Christ is God (1 Cor. 11:3). If, therefore, it cannot be said of Christ, as He is the Second Person in the Trinity, that His Father is not greater than He, and that He is not subordinate to God as His head, then farewell Anti-Socinianism. I dare boldly say, it is impossible to confute the Socinians, or to assert the eternal Godhead of Jesus Christ, except somewhat be affirmed of Him as the Second Person of the Trinity, which must be denied of Him as He is Mediator, and something be denied of Him as He is the Second Person in the Trinity, which must be affirmed of Him as He is Mediator.

Eighthly, He says, page 36, that Christ, "by His mediation, has obtained from the Father that He shall not judge any man according to rigor, but as they are in or out of Christ; all deferring of judgment from the wicked is in and for Christ, which otherwise the justice of God would not allow." Then, Christ did thus far make satisfaction to the justice of God in the behalf of

---

78. [This is a reference to Gerhard, Locus XXIV, "de Magistratu Politico" in *Loci theologici*, volume 6, chapter three, first part, §79 (first ed., 1619; second ed., 1626). Gillespie is citing from the 1639 third edition. See *Locorum Theologicorum, Cvm Pro Adstruenda Veritate… In quo continentur hæc capita: 26. De Ministerio Ecclesiastico. 27. De Magistratu Politico* (1639), cols. 498–499. Cf. *Loci theologici: cum pro adstruenda veritate tum pro* (Lipsiae: Hinrichs, 1885), volume 6, 298–299.]

the wicked, and die for them, that judgment might be deferred from them, and thus far perform acts of mediation for the savages and Mohammedans, and for them that never heard the gospel, that by such mediation He has obtained of the Father that they shall be judged not according to rigor, but by the gospel. Which intimates that Christ has taken away all their sins against the law, so that all men shall now go upon a new score, and none shall be condemned or judged by the law, but by the gospel only; for if Christ has not taken away their sins against the law, the justice of God will judge them according to the rigor of the law. Must not every jot of the law be fulfilled? And is there not a necessity that everyone undergo the curse and rigor of the law, or else that the Mediator has undergone it for them?

Ninthly, He propounds this query [on] page 44: "Whether ministers have any right to those privileges which are given to the church more than another Christian," and he holds the negative. Now, the preaching of the Word, the administration of the sacraments, and the power of the keys, are privileges given to the church, that is, for the church's good: "For all things are yours," says the apostle, "whether Paul, or Apollos," etc. (1 Cor. 3:21, 22). Therefore, by Mr. Hussey's divinity, any other Christian has as much right to administer Word, sacraments, keys, as the minister.

Come on now to Mr. Coleman's errors in divinity, not to repeat what was expressed in my *Nihil Respondes*, but to take off the *Malè Dicis* in the main points.

[Tenthly,] The tenth heterodoxy shall therefore be this, That whatsoever is given to Christ, He has it not as the eternal Son of God. Into this ditch did Mr. Coleman first fall, and then Mr. Hussey, after him (page 25). I said this tenet leads to a blasphemous heresy. For the better understanding whereof let it be remembered what I did promise in my *Nihil Respondes*, page 11, in reply to his proposition, "That which is given to Christ, He has it not as God." "This," said I," "is in opposition to what I said, page 45, concerning the headship and dignity of Christ, 'as the natural Son of God, the image of the invisible God' (Col. 1:15), and page 43, of the dominion of Christ 'as He is the eternal Son of God.' This being premised," etc. Mr. Coleman, without taking the least notice of that which I did purposely and plainly premise, begins to speak of God essentially, and that if something may be given to Christ as God, then something may be given to God, and then God is not absolutely perfect, etc., *Malè Dicis*, pages 13, 14. Thus, he turns over to the essence and nature of God what I spoke of the Second Person in the Trinity, or of Christ as He is the eternal Son of God. Was not the question between him and me, Whether the kingdom and dominion over all things may be said to be given to Christ as He is the eternal Son of God? This is the point which he did argue against because it takes off his argument first brought to prove that all government, even civil, is given to Christ as He is Mediator. And still from the beginning I spoke of Christ as the Second Person in the Trinity, or the eternal Son of God. Thus therefore the case stands: The reverend brother, to prove that a universal sovereignty and government over all things is given to Christ as He is Mediator, and to confute my assertion that it is given to Christ as He is the eternal Son of God, does frame this argument againſt me, "That which is given to Chriſt, He has it not as God. But here dignity is given to Chriſt; therefore, not here to be taken as God;" where there is more in the conclusion than in the premises. For the conclusion which naturally follows had been this, Therefore, Chriſt has not here dignity as God. It seems he was ashamed of the conclusion, yet not of the premises, which infer the conclusion. But this by the way. I ſpeak to his proposition, "That which is given to Chriſt, he has it not as God." These words "as God," either he underſtands οὐσιωδῶς, *essentially*, or ἐπιστατικῶς, *personally*; that is, either in regard of the nature and essence of God, which is common to the Son of God with the Father and the Holy Ghoſt, and in reſpect whereof They three are one; or in regard of the person of the Word, as Chriſt is the Second Person in the Trinity, and personally diſtinct from the Father and the Holy Ghoſt. If in the former sense, then he muſt lay aside his whole argument as utterly impertinent and making nothing at all againſt my thesis, which affirmed that a universal dominion and kingdom over all things is given to Chriſt, not as He is Mediator (in which capacity He is only King of the church), but as He is the eternal Son of God. In opposing of which assertion, as the reverend brother was before *nihil reſpondens*, so now he is twice nought. But if in the other sense he underſtands his proposition (which I muſt needs suppose he does, it being in opposition to what I said), then I ſtill aver his proposition will infer a blaſphemous heresy, as I proved before by a clear demonſtration: That which is given to Chriſt, He has it not as God. But life, glory, etc., are given to Chriſt; therefore, Chriſt has not life, glory, etc., as God. The reverend brother says, "I acknowledge the conclusion unsound, and I deny not but that the major is mine own, and the minor is the very Scripture." Yet he denies the conclusion, and clears himself by this simile, "That which was given this poor man he had not before. But a shilling was given this poor man; therefore, he had not a shilling before, where both propositions are true, yet the conclusion is false," says he, "contrary to the axiom, *Ex veris nil nisi verum*." You are extremely out, sir. Your syllogism of the poor man is *fallacia ab amphibolia*.[79] The major of it is ambiguous, dubious, and fallacious, and cannot be admitted without a diſtinction. But here you acknowledge the major of my argument to be your own, and so not fallacious in your opinion. You acknowledge the minor to be Scripture. You have not found four terms in my premises, nor charged my major or minor with the leaſt fault in matter or form, and yet, forsooth, you deny the conclusion, and do not admit that incontrovertible maxim in logic, *Ex veris nil nisi verum*; or, as Kekerman has it, *Ex veris præmissis falsam conclusionem colligi eſt impossibile*, "It is impossible that a false conclusion should be gathered from true premises."[80] Now, let us hear what he would say againſt my conclusion; it is concerning the sense of the word *hath*: "For *hath*," says he, "by me is used for receiving or having by virtue of the gift, but by him for having fundamentally, originally." You

---

79. [In other words, Coleman has committed the logical fallacy of amphiboly.]

80. *Syſtem. Log.*, lib. 3, cap. 5. [Bartholomäus Keckermann, *Syſtema Logicæ*, in *Syſtema Syſtematum*, volume 1 (Hanover: Apud Hæredes Guilielmi Antonii, 1613), p. 242, §12.]

are still out, sir. I take it just as you take it. For though the Son of God, as God essentially, or in respect of the nature and essence of God, which is common to all Three Persons in the blessed Trinity, has originally of Himself a kingdom and dominion over all, yet, as He is the Second Person in the Trinity, begotten of and distinct from the Father, He has the kingdom and dominion over all not of Himself, but by virtue of the gift of His Father. So that the reverend brother is still *nihil respondens*, and therefore he shall be concluded in this syllogism: He who holds that whatsoever is given to Christ, He has it not by virtue of the gift as He is the eternal Son of God or Second Person in the Trinity, but only as Mediator, he holds, by consequence, that Christ has not glory by virtue of His Father's gift, as He is the eternal Son of God or Second Person in the Trinity. But Mr. Coleman holds the former; *ergo*, Mr. Coleman holds the latter. The consequence in the proposition is proved from John 17:22, "The glory which thou gavest me." The assumption he will own, or else quit his argument against my distinction of the double kingdom given to Christ, as He is the eternal Son of God, and as Mediator. The conclusion which follows is heretical; for whereas the Nicene Creed said of Christ,[81] in regard of His eternal generation, that He is *Deus de Deo, Lumen de lumine*, God of God, Light of light, Mr. Coleman's argument will infer that He is not only *ex seipso Deus*, but *ex seipso Filius*; and so deny the eternal generation of the Son of God, and the communication of the Godhead, and the sovereignty, glory, and attributes thereof, from the Father to the Son. For if Christ, as He is the eternal Son of God, has not glory by virtue of His Father's gift, then He has it not by virtue of the eternal generation and communication, but fundamentally and originally of himself.

As for the other branch of Mr. Coleman's argument, tending to prove that Christ, as He is the eternal Son of God, cannot be given, which he endeavors to vindicate [on] pages 14, 15, I answer these two things:

First, Granting all that he says, he concludes nothing against me; for I did from the beginning expound these words [in] Ephesians 1:22, "And gave him to be the head over all things to the church," in this sense: That Christ as Mediator is given only to the church to be her head, but He that is given as Mediator to the church is "over all." So that the giving of Christ there spoken of is as Mediator, and He is given to the church only, which I cleared by the Syriac, "And him who is over all he gave to be the head to the church."[82] But His being "over all" there spoken of, if understood of glory, dignity, excellency over all, so [*then*] Christ is "over all" as Mediator (yea, in regard of the exaltation of His human nature), and this helps not Mr. Coleman, who intends to prove from that place that all government, even civil, is given to Christ as Mediator. But if understood of a kingdom and government "over all," so [*then*] He is "over all" as He is the eternal Son of God or Second Person of the Trinity, and not as Mediator.

Secondly, The question which the reverend brother falls upon, concerning

---

81. [The 1646 errata corrected "that Christ" to "of Christ."]

82. [*Brotherly Examination*, herein page 233.]

the personal inhabitation of the Holy Ghost, will never follow from anything which I said, more than God's giving of His Son to us will infer a personal inhabitation of the Son of God in us. That which I said was to this intent: That both the Son of God and the Holy Ghost are given, not as God essentially; that is, in respect of the Godhead itself, or as they are one in nature with the Father (for so the Father that gives, and the Holy Ghost which is given, could not be distinguished), but the Son is given as the Son proceeding from the Father, and the Holy Ghost is given as the Holy Ghost proceeding and sent from the Father and the Son. Whether He be given to dwell personally in us, or by His gracious operations only, is another question, which has nothing to do with the present argument, and therefore, I will not be led out of my way.

[Eleventhly,] The eleventh heterodoxy is this: "I see no[83] absurdity to hold that every man in authority is either Christ's vicegerent, or the devil's" (*Malè Dicis*, p. 16). Here I make this inference: Heathen and infidel magistrates, either, 1. They are not men in authority;[84] or 2. They are Christ's vicegerents; or 3. They are the devil's *maledicis*. If he say they are not men in authority, he shall contradict the Apostle Paul, who calls them higher powers (Rom. 13:1), and men in authority (1 Tim. 2:2), speaking in reference even to the magistrates of that time, who were infidels. If he says they are Christ's vicegerents, then, 1. He[85] must say that Christ, as Mediator, reigns without the church, and is a king to those to whom He is neither priest nor prophet. 2. He must find a commission given by Christ to the infidel magistrate. 3. Whom in authority will he make to be the devil's vicegerents if infidel magistrates be Christ's vicegerents? If he says that they are the devil's vicegerents, then it follows, 1. That they who resist the devil's vicegerent resist the ordinance of God, for they that resist an infidel magistrate and do not submit to his lawful authority (which his infidelity takes not away), is said to resist the ordinance of God (Rom. 13:2). 2. That the Apostle Paul bade pray for the devil's vicegerent (1 Tim. 2:1, 2). The reverend brother does but more and more wind himself into a labyrinth of errors, while he endeavors to take away the distinction of the twofold kingdom and the twofold vicegerentship of God and of Christ.

[Twelfthly,] The twelfth heterodoxy follows: "Now it is true that Christ, being God as well as man, has of Himself originally, as God, whatsoever He has by virtue of gift as Mediator" (*Malè Dicis*, p. 13). Now subsume, Christ has by virtue of gift as Mediator, the priestly office; therefore, by Mr. Coleman's principles, Christ has of Himself originally, as God, the priestly office. And if Christ has it of Himself originally as God, then the Father and the Holy Ghost have it also; so that by his doctrine the Father and the Holy Ghost shall be the priests of the church as well as Christ, for Christ has nothing of Himself originally as God which the Father and the Holy Ghost have not likewise.

[Thirteenthly,] The thirteenth and last error concerns the office of deacons.

---

83. [The first edition errata instructed to change "an absurdity" to "no absurdity."]

84. [The errata instructed to change "activity" to "authority."]

85. [The errata instructed to change "I" to "he."]

Not only a widow[86] but a deacon is denied to be a church officer, or to have any warrant from Scripture. "I hold not a widow a church officer," he says, "no more do I a deacon; both having a like foundation in Scripture, which is truly none at all" (*Malè Dicis*, p. 9). If this was his opinion formerly, why did he not in so main a point enter his dissent from the votes of the Assembly concerning deacons, together with his reasons?[87] Well, his opinion is so now, whereby he runs contrary not only to the reformed churches (which it seems weigh not much in his balance), but to the plain Scripture, which speaks of the office of a deacon, 1 Timothy 3:10; and this could be no civil office, but an ecclesiastical office, for the deacons were chosen by the church, were ordained with prayer and laying on of hands, and their charge was to take special care of the poor; all which is clear [in] Acts 6. If he had given us the grounds of his opinion he should have heard more against it.[88]

CHAPTER FIVE
The Prelatical way and tenets of Mr. Coleman & Mr. Hussey, Repugnant also, in divers particulars, to the Votes & Ordinances of Parliament

---

1. MR. COLEMAN, in his *Re-examination* (p. 14), makes the parliament to be church governors and church officers to the whole kingdom. It was an argument used against the prelates that ecclesiastical and civil government, spiritual and secular administrations, are inconsistent in the same persons, either of which requires the whole man. It was another exception against the prelate that he assumed the power of church government and ecclesiastical jurisdiction over the whole diocese, which was much more than he could discharge. How will Mr. Coleman avoid the involving the parliament into prelatical guiltiness by his principles, which we avoid by ours?

2. The prelates sought great things for themselves rather than to purge the church of scandals. What other thing was it when Mr. Coleman, in his third rule, instead of exhorting to the purging [of] the church, called only for learning and competency, and told it out that this will "get us an able

---

86. [On December 29, 1643, Coleman does object to the idea that "Widows are church-officers." See *Minutes*, 2.12; 5.58; Gillespie, Notes, p. 5, and Lightfoot's much longer account, p. 93ff.]

87. [As Gillespie notes here, Coleman entered no dissent to the institution of such an office in the New Testament. In Session 108 on December 5, 1643, "the assembly voted that the scriptures teach that there is an office of deacon." *Minutes*, 2.405. On December 20, 1643, in session 119, there was an unresolved debate over the perpetuity of the office of deacon because the minutes for session 120 (indeed, all the minutes through session 154) are missing. However, document 19, which records votes by the assembly on the first draft of the directory for church government, records that this was affirmed in session 120. *Minutes*, 2.476, 488, and 5.60.]

88. [Coleman does not defend his view but only notes it. *Malè Dicis*, p. 9.]

ministry, and procure us honor enough." Mr. Hussey, in his epistle to myself,[89] tells me that our attending on reading, exhortation and doctrine (without government) will obtain the magistrate's love, "more honor, more maintenance," something for shame he behooved to add of the punishing of sin (yet he will not have the minister called from his study to be troubled or to take any pains in discipline), but behold the love of the magistrate; more honor and more maintenance are strong ingredients in the Erastian electuary.

3. Mr. Hussey will have ministers placed "without any regard to the allowance or disallowance of the people," Epist. to the Parliament.[90] This is prelatical, or rather more than prelatical.

4. The prelates were great enemies to ruling elders; so are Mr. Coleman and Mr. Hussey, who acknowledge no warrant from the Word of God for that calling, nor admit of any ruling elders who are not magistrates, a distinction which was used by Saravia and Bilson in reference to the Jewish elders, and by Bishop Hall in reference to the elders of the ancient church who were not preaching elders, *Assert. of Episcop. by Divine Right*, pages 208, 209, 221.[91] And now, forsooth, Mr. Hussey, in his Epistle to the Parliament, does earnestly beseech them to "set up classes [*classis*] consisting only of ministers, whose work should be only to preach the Word," etc.[92] Such classes, I dare say, the prelates themselves will admit of. Sure[ly] the Scottish prelates, when they were at their highest, yielded as much.

5. Mr. Coleman and Mr. Hussey hold[93] that ruling elders and a church government distinct from the civil government in the times of persecution and under pagan magistrates can be no warrant for the like where the state is Christian. This plea for Christian magistracy was Bishop Whitgift's plea against the ruling elders, *Answer to the Admon.*, p. 114.[94]

6. Mr. Hussey says that granting the incestuous Corinthian to be excommunicated (p. 22), "the decree was Paul's and not the Corinthians," and that it no way appertained to them under the notion of a church. This is Saravia's answer to Beza, *de Tripl. Epist. Genere,* pages 42, 43,[95] yea, the papists' answer to Protestant writers, by which they would hold up the authority and sole jurisdiction of the prelates as the apostles' successors to excommunicate. They do not more agree with the prelatical principles than they differ from the votes and ordinances of parliament, which is the other point

---

89. [Hussey, *A Plea*, To the Reverend Commissioner of Scotland, Mr. George Gillespie, second unnumbered page after A3.]

90. [Hussey, *Plea*, pp. a3v–{a4r}.]

91. [Joseph Hall, *Episcopacie by Divine Right* (1640), pp. 208, 209, 221. Cf. Adrian de Saravia, *Diversi Tractatus Theologiæ: De Diversis Ministrorum Evangelli gradibus* (1601), pp. 166–176. Thomas Bilson, *The Perpetual Government of Christ's Church* (1593; repr. 1842), chaps. 7, 10, 11.]

92. [Hussey, *Plea*, pp. {a4r}.]

93. [*Works* omitted the numbering for point five.]

94. [John Whitgift, *An answere to a certen Libel intituled, An admonition* (1572), p. 114.]

95. [Adrian de Saravia, *Examen Tractatus de Episcopatuum Triplici Genere* (1610), pp. 42, 43.]

that I have here undertaken to discover; and I shall do it by the particular instances following:

First, The ordinance of the Lords and Commons assembled in Parliament for the calling of an assembly of divines, begins thus: "Whereas, among the infinite blessings of Almighty God upon this nation, none is, or can be, more dear unto us than the purity of our religion, and for that as yet many things remain in the liturgy, discipline, and government of the church, which do necessarily require a further and more perfect reformation than as yet has been attained; and whereas it has been declared and resolved by the Lords and Commons assembled in Parliament, that the present church government, by archbishops, bishops, etc., is evil and justly offensive, etc.; and that, therefore, they are resolved that the same shall be taken away, and that such a government shall be settled in the church as may be most agreeable to God's holy Word, and most apt to procure and preserve the peace of the church at home, and nearer agreement with the Church of Scotland, and other reformed churches abroad."[96] After it was resolved and voted in both the honorable houses of parliament, and sent as one of the propositions to the treaty at Uxbridge, "That many particular congregations shall be under one presbyterial government."[97] Now, therefore, what can be more contrary to the votes and ordinances of parliament than that which Mr. Coleman and Mr. Hussey hold, that there ought to be no ecclesiastical government besides civil magistracy, except we please to take preaching and baptism under the name of government, as if, forsooth, the parliament had meant by presbyterial government parliamentary government; or as if by the purity of religion in point of the discipline of government of the church, they had intended nothing but their civil rights and privileges; or as if the wise and honorable houses had understood themselves no better than to intend that for a nearer agreement with the Church of Scotland and other reformed churches, which is the widest difference from them, to wit, the Erastian way.

Secondly, In the same ordinance of parliament for the calling of an assembly of divines, it is ordained that the assembly, after conferring and treating among themselves touching the liturgy, discipline, and government of the church, or vindication and clearing of the doctrine of the same, shall deliver their opinions or advices of or touching the matters aforesaid to both

---

96. [*An ordinance of the Lords and Commons assembled in Parliament. For the calling of an assembly of learned, and Godly divines to be consulted with by the Parliamen,...* June 20, 1643 (1643). See *Minutes*, vol. 1, appendix 1, pp. 162–169.]

97. [At the time Gillespie and other Scots Commissioners were planning to depart for General Assembly on January 6, 1645, the commissioners representing the Scottish government asked the Treaty committee of parliament for a report accounting parliament's actions on church government to present at negotiations at Uxbridge. The parliament rushed and ultimately passed propositions including "that many particular congregations may be under one Presbyterial government." The negotiations ultimately failed. See Shaw, *A History of the English Church During the Civil Wars*, vol. 1 (1900), pp. 184–187.]

or either of the houses of parliament, yet Mr. Hussey (*Epist. to the parliament*, pp. 3, 6),[98] will not have classes [*classis*] to put anything to the vote, but to hold on the disputes till all end in accord and in unanimous consent of the whole clergy. But how can the Assembly, after disputes, express their sense and deliver their opinions and advice to the parliament, as they are required, except they do it by putting to the vote? Mr. Coleman himself has consented, yea, sometime called to put things to the vote; and as for classes [*classis*], will any man imagine that when both houses of parliament did vote "that many particular congregations shall be under one presbyterial government," their meaning was that the classical presbytery shall only school-wise dispute and put nothing to the vote, or that the classical presbytery shall in common dispense the Word and sacraments to many congregations, and that either the classical presbytery shall go to the several congregations successively, or the many congregations come to the classical presbytery for preaching and baptizing? I admire [*marvel*] what opinion Mr. Hussey can have of the parliamentary vote concerning presbyterial government.

Thirdly, Mr. Hussey will have ministers placed (*Epistle to the parliament*, p. 4–5),[99] "without any regard to the allowance and disallowance of the people," yet the ordinance of parliament for giving power to classical presbyteries to ordain ministers does appoint that he who is examined and approved by the presbytery shall be "sent to the church or other place where he is to serve (if it may be done with safety and conveniency), there to preach three several days and to converse with the people, that they may have trial of his gifts for their edification, and may have time and leisure to inquire into and the better to know his life and conversation," after which the ordinance appoints public notice to be given and a day set to the congregation to put in what exceptions they have against him.

Fourthly, Mr. Hussey in that epistle to the parliament says (p. 5), "Oh that this honorable court would hasten to set up classes [*classis*] consisting only of ministers whose work should be only to preach the Word, and weekly meet in schools of divinity!" Here is a double contradiction to the ordinances of parliament, for in the directions of the Lords and Commons for choosing of ruling elders and speedy settling of presbyterial government, it is appointed that ruling elders shall be members both of classes and synodical assemblies, together with the ministers of the Word.[100]

Again, the ordinance about suspension of scandalous persons from the

---

98. [Hussey, *Plea*, the third and sixth unnumbered pages of the epistle. *Works* rendered this incorrectly as "p. 36."]

99. [Hussey, *Plea*, the fourth and fifth unnumbered pages of the epistle to parliament.]

100. [See *Minutes*, document 71 and 72, pp. 193–197, and *Directions of the Lords and Commons assembled in Parliament after advice had with the Assembly of Divines, for the electing and choosing of ruling-elders in all the congregations, and in the classicall assemblies for the cities of London and Westminster, and the several counties of the kingdom, for the speedy setling of the Presbyteriall-Government*. August 19, 1645 (June 20, 1645).]

sacrament appoints other work to classes [*classis*] besides preaching and disputing, namely, the receiving and judging of appeals from the congregational eldership.[101] Mr. Coleman in *Malè Dicis*, page 12, professes that he excludes ruling elders from church government, yet he can hardly be ignorant that as the parliament has voted "that many particular congregations shall be under one presbyterial government," so their votes do commit that government to pastors and ruling elders jointly.

I will not here repeat the particulars wherein I showed in my *Nihil Respondes*[102] that Mr. Coleman has abused the honorable houses of parliament, unto which particulars he has answered as good as nothing. The honorable houses in their wisdom will soon observe whether such men, whose avouched tenets are so flatly repugnant to the parliamentary votes and ordinances, are like to be good pleaders for Christian magistracy.

Chapter Six
Mr. Coleman's Wronging of the Church of Scotland

Mr. Coleman ends his *Malè Dicis* with a resentment of accusations charged upon him by a stranger, a commissioner from another church.[103] The lot of strangers were very hard,[104] if, when they are falsely accused to authority, they may not answer for themselves. He may remember the first accusation was made by himself, when in his sermon to the parliament he did flatly impute to the commissioners from the Church of Scotland a great part of the fault of hindering union in the Assembly of Divines, as having come biased with a national determination; his doctrine also at that time being such, as did not only reflect upon the government of the Church of Scotland, but tend to the subversion of the covenant in one principal point, without which there can be small or no hopes of attaining the other ends of the covenant.[105]

Since that time he did in his *Re-examination*, and now again in his *Malè Dicis*, fall foully upon the Church of Scotland, not only by gross mistakes and misrepresentations of our way, but by most groundless aspersions and most uncharitable and unjust calumnies. I am sure I am not so much a stranger to this doctrine as he is to the Church of Scotland, of which notwithstanding he boldly speaks his pleasure in divers particulars, which he will never be able to make good.

---

101. [*An ordinance of the Lords and Commons assembled in Parliament: Together with rules and directions concerning suspention from the sacrament of the Lords Supper in cases of ignorance and scandall. Also the names of such ministers and others that are appointed triers and judges of the ability of elders in the twelve classes within the province of London. Die Lunæ 20. Octob. 1645* (1645), p. 7.]

102. [See *Nihil Respondes*, herein pages 249ff.]

103. [*Malè Dicis*, pp. 20ff.]

104. [In other words, "the condition of strangers would be very hard…."]

105. [Coleman, *Hopes Deferred*, p. 24. See *Brotherly Examination*, herein page 222.]

[I.] First, He has aspersed that church in the point of promiscuous communicating. This I confuted in my *Nihil Respondes*,[106] and told him both of the order of the church and practice of conscientious ministers to the contrary. Now what replies he?

"First, This refining work, I think, is not one year old in Scotland, or much more. I was lately informed that in Edinburgh it is begun: whether anywhere else I know not" (*Malè Dicis*, p. 20). Are not these now good grounds of censuring and aspersing a reformed church (whose name has been as precious ointment among other churches abroad), "I think; I was informed; whether it be otherwise I know not?" He will sit in Cornhill[107] and tell the world what he imagines or hears of the Church of Scotland, and that, forsooth, must be taken for a truth. Yet there were both rules and practice in the Church of Scotland for debarring ignorant and scandalous persons from the sacrament before he was born, though all was put out of course under the prelates.

Secondly (says the reverend brother), "It is not a very effectual sin-censuring and church-refining government, under which, after fourscore years' constant practice, divers thousands in the kingdom, and some hundreds in one particular parish, because of ignorance and scandal, are yet unfit to communicate" (*Malè Dicis*, p. 20).

ANSWER. 1. It is notoriously false that there has been fourscore years' constant practice of presbyterial government in Scotland; for the prelates there were above thirty years' standing. 2. "Shall the earth be made to bring forth in one day, or shall a nation be born at once?" saith the prophet (Isa. 66:8). It is no easy matter to get a whole nation purged of ignorant and scandalous persons. 3. He may take notice that the Apostle Paul, almost in all his epistles, makes mention of scandalous persons among those to whom he wrote, warning them not to have fellowship with such, to note them, to avoid them. If the apostolic churches were not free of such, what great marvel if we be not? 4. Before he objected promiscuous communicating. This being cleared to be a calumny, now he objects that there are such as are unfit to communicate. But while he thus seeks a quarrel against church government, he does upon the matter quarrel the preaching of the gospel itself; for he that imputes it as a fault to the church government that there are still divers thousands who by reason of ignorance or scandal are unfit to communicate, does by consequence, yea, much more, impute it as a fault to the preaching of the gospel in England, Scotland, Ireland, France, Germany, the Low Countries, Switzerland, Sweden, Poland, that in all these, and other reformed churches, after fourscore years' constant preaching of the gospel (which is appointed of God to turn unconverted and unregenerate persons from darkness to light, and from the power of Satan to God), there are not only divers thousands, but divers millions, who, by reason of ignorance or

---

106. [*Nihil Respondes*, herein page 254.]

107. [After the prior rector was turned out and the parsonage sequestered, Coleman was appointed by the Commons to be the preacher at St. Peters, Cornhill, London.]

scandal, are yet unfit to communicate. If the Word does not open the eyes of the ignorant and convert the scandalous, what marvel that church government cannot do it? Church government is not an illuminating and regenerating ordinance as the Word is. But this church government can and will do, yea, has done, where it is duly executed: It is a most blessed means for keeping the ordinances from visible and known pollution, which does very much honor God, shame sin, and commend piety; it puts a visible difference between the precious and the vile, the clean and the unclean, the silver and the dross, and may well be, therefore, called a church-refining ordinance.

[II.] The second calumny was this, "I myself," said he, "did hear the presbytery of Edinburgh censure a woman to be banished out of the gates of the city."[108] I answered him in his own language, "It is at the best a most uncharitable slander,"[109] and told him there is no banishment in Scotland but by the civil magistrate, and that he ought to have inquired and informed himself better.

Now he does neither adhere to his calumny, or offer to make it good, nor yet quit it, or confess he was mistaken, but propounds three new queries (*Malè Dicis*, p. 21), still forgetting his own rule of keeping to the laws of disputation and matter in hand.

For the particular in hand he only says thus [*this*] much, "I did make inquiry, and from the presbytery itself I received information, but not satisfaction." He tells not what information he received. If he will say that he received information that the banishment was by the magistrate, how could he then report that it was by the presbytery? If he says that the information he had from the presbytery gave him any ground for the report which he has made, let him speak it out and the world shall know the untruth of it. He may remember, withal, that by his principles an accusation may not be received against an elder (much less against an eldership), in reference either to the judgment of charity, or to ministerial conviction, except under two or three witnesses. If, therefore, he would have his accusation believed, let him find two or three witnesses.[110]

[III.] Thirdly, Whereas I had rectified a great mistake of the reverend brother when I told him, "It is accidental to the ruling elder to be of the nobility, or to nobles to be ruling elders; there are but some so, and many otherwise,"[111] he is not pleased to be rectified in this, but replies, "I say, first, It is continually so; secondly, The king's commissioner in the General Assembly, is his presence accidental?" (*Malè Dicis*, p. 10). See now here whether he understands what he says or whereof he affirms [1 Timothy 1:7]. That which he says is continually so, is almost continually otherwise; that is, there are continually some ruling elders who are not nobles, and there are continually

---

108. [Coleman, *Brotherly Examination Re-examined*, p. 12.]

109. [*Nihil Respondes*, herein page 257.]

110. [*Malè Dicis*, p. 10.]

111. [*Nihil Respondes*, herein page 244.]

some nobles who are not ruling elders. So that, if anything be accidental, this is accidental, that an elder be of the nobility, or nobles be elders; they are neither nobles *qua* elders, nor elders *qua* nobles. It is no less accidental that the king's commissioner be present in the General Assembly; for there have been General Assemblies in Scotland, both before the erection and since the last casting out of prelacy, in which there was no commissioner from the king. And when the king sends a commissioner, it is accidental that he be of the nobility; for the king has sent commissioners to General Assemblies who were not of the nobility.

[IV.] A fourth injury not to be passed in silence is this: Mr. Coleman has endeavored to make the world believe that the commissioners from the Church of Scotland came to the assembly biased with something adventitious from without, which he calls a national determination,[112] and that we are not permitted by those that sent us to receive any further light from the Word of God. I shall say no more of the bias, because, as I told him before, the standers-by see well enough which way the bias runs.[113] But most strange it is, that after I had confuted his calumny, not only from our paper first presented to the grand committee, but from the General Assembly's own letter to the Assembly of Divines, showing that they had ordered the laying aside of some particular customs in the Church of Scotland for the nearer uniformity with the church of England, so much endeared unto them,[114] yet he still adheres to his former calumny (*Malè Dicis*, p. 20), without taking notice of the evidence which I had given to the contrary. And not content with this, he still quarrels with my allegation of certain parallel examples, which are by him so far disesteemed, that he has not stuck to pass the very same censure upon the foreign divines who came to the Synod of Dort which the Arminians did. The same he says of Alexander's coming to the Council of Nice, and of Cyril's coming to the Council of Ephesus; all these, I say, he still involves under the same censure with us; for, whereas he had alleged that I justified the bias, this I denied, and called for his proof.[115] His reply now is thus: "Is not the allegation of the examples of the like doing a justification of the act done?" (*Malè Dicis*, p. 20). This reply can have no other sense but this: That I justified the thing which he thinks our bias because I justified those other divines who (as he holds) came also biased in like manner. I am persuaded this one particular, his joining with the Arminians in their exceptions against the Synod of Dort, would make all the reformed churches, if they could all speak to him *uno ore* [*with one accord*], to cry *Malè audis*. And I am as firmly persuaded that the confession which I have extorted from him in this place, that he knows no adventitious engagements those divines had, makes him

---

112. [*Malè Dicis*, p. 20.]

113. [Gillespie had said that "beholders do often perceive the biasing better than the bowlers." *Nihil Respondes*, herein page 255. See Brotherly Examination, herein page 222.]

114. [See *Brotherly Examination*, herein page 223; *Nihil Respondes*, herein pages 255, 255.]

115. [*Nihils Respondes*, herein page 255.]

irreconcilably to contradict himself; for he made them but just now biased in the same manner as he thinks us, and made my allegation of their examples to be a justification of the bias charged by him upon us: as, therefore, he does must uncharitably and untruly judge us to be biased with adventitious engagements, so does he judge of them. Neither can he assoil [*absolve from sin*] them while he condemns us; for the articles concerning predestination, the death of Christ, grace, free will, and perseverance, were determined before the Synod of Dort by most (if not by all) of those reformed churches who sent commissioners thither, as much as presbyterial government was determined in the Church of Scotland before the reverend Assembly of Divines was called. And this pre-engagement and predetermination of those reformed churches was the main objection of the Arminians against the foreign divines who came to the Synod of Dort.

To conclude this point, Mr. Coleman himself in his *Re-examination* (p. 7), avouches roundly that the foreign divines came to Dort, not as divines, by dispute and disquisition to find out truth, but as judges to censure all different opinions as erroneous.

CHAPTER SEVEN
CALUMNIES CONFUTED, AND THAT QUESTION BRIEFLY CLEARED, WHETHER THE MAGISTRATE BE CHRIST'S VICEGERENT

MR. HUSSEY, in his title page, tells us he has prosecuted the argumentative part without any personal reflections,[116] yet I could instance divers personal reflections in his book which any moderate impartial man will extremely dislike; but what should this be to the edifying of my reader, the end which, next to the glory of God and the promoting of reformation, I have proposed to myself? Yet I must needs take notice of some calumnies.

First, In his Epistle (p. 8),[117] he offers it to be examined whether I was not beside my text, Malachi 3:2, when I pressed from it reformation by ecclesiastical discipline: whether that refiner's fire and fuller's soap does not point at another and a nearer operation upon the souls and spirits of men by the blood, Word, Spirit, and grace of Christ, and whether such handling of a similitude in a text be to preach the mind of God, or men's own fancy. It is no discontent to me, but I shall rejoice in it, that men of piety and judgment examine my doctrine by the Word of God, and hold fast what they find agreeable to the Scriptures and no more. But is this brotherly, or fair, or conscionable dealing, to offer my sermon to be examined under such a notion, when he has not only said nothing to confute any of my doctrines as not arising from my text,

---

116. [Hussey, *A Plea for Christian Magistracie … wherein the Argumentative part of the controversy is calmely and midly, without any personall reflections, prosecuted* (1646).]

117. [Hussey, *A Plea*, "To the Right Honorable, the Lords and Commons assembled in Parliament."]

or any of my applications as not arising from my doctrines, but has also untruly represented my sermon as coming short of or not expressing that which indeed it has most principally and most expressly in it? That of reformation was but a part of my sermon, and that of church censures against scandalous sinners was but the least part of that part.[118] And why should not the fuller's soap in the house of God take off those spots in our feasts? Why should not the refiner's fire purge away the wicked of the earth like dross? So David calls them [Psalm 119:119]. That reformation is one part of the Holy Ghost's intendment in that text is Gwalther's opinion as well as mine, yet he thinks Gwalther his own.[119] Nay, I proved it from comparing Scripture with Scripture, which is the best way that I know to clear Scripture. Why did he not answer my proofs? But besides all that I said of reformation, had I not other three doctrines out of that text comprehending all that which Mr. Hussey hints as omitted by me, and yet intended in the text? Dare he say that I did not take in purgation by the Word? (though I confess he does not well prove it from the words which he cites, "Is not my word an hammer?" [Jer. 23:29]. But it is proved by the words which he cites not, "Is not my word like as a fire?"). Did I not expressly say that Christ is to us as a refiner's fire and as fuller's soap three ways: by reformation, by tribulation, by mortification? Did I not handle the last two as well as the first? Oh let no more such gross calumnies be found among those who profess to be brethren!

Secondly, Mr. Hussey in his epistle to myself, gives it out that I say, "We have leave from the civil magistrate to preach the gospel,"[120] which he interprets as if I denied that we preach the Word with authority from Christ. It was *de facto, not de jure*, that I spoke it. The magistrate has power in his hand to hinder both doctrine and discipline if he be an adversary, though it be the will of Christ that there be both doctrine and discipline, and the authority of both is from Christ. When the magistrate assists or countenances, or so much as does not[121] hinder the preaching of the gospel, then he gives leave to it.

Thirdly, Mr. Coleman in his *Malè Dicis* says (p. 3), "I am confident the Church of Scotland sent this commissioner to dispute down our reasons, not to revile our persons." Why did he not, if he could, give instance of some reviling word written by me against his person? I have not so learned Christ. The Lord rebuke every railing and reviling spirit. I have given him reason against railing; he has given me railing against reason; I spoke to his doctrine; he speaks to my place and relation, which is both the alpha and omega of his *Malè Dicis*.

Fourthly, "Knowledge," he says, "is only with Mr. Gillespie; others understand neither what they say, nor whereof they affirm" (p. 3). He will sooner bring water out of flint than prove this consequence out of [the epigraph

---

118. [See the House of Lords Sermon herein on page 172.]

119. [Hussey, *A Plea*, page 3.]

120. [Hussey, *A Plea*, "To the Reverend Commissioner," etc., second unnumbered page.]

121. [The 1646 errata corrected "as he doth" to "as doth."]

on] my titlepage [p. (237)]. Although I confess himself has affirmed divers things of the Church of Scotland which he does not understand, as I have made plainly to appear. If he takes a review of the title page of his *Re-examination*, he gives more ground for this consequence: that Mr. Coleman is the only man that denies himself; others seek great things for themselves. Or from the title-page of his *Malè Dicis*, this consequence will be as good, that Mr. Coleman is the only man that blesses; others are revilers.

Fifthly, Thus says Mr. Coleman, "O ye honorable house of parliament, take you notice that you manage that great place of yours under Christ and for Christ: He is your head, and you are his servants; and take you notice withal that Mr. Gillespie accounts this your reproach" (*Malè Dicis Maledicis*, p. 17). But O ye honorable house of parliament, be pleased to take notice of my own plain expression of my mind in my *Nihil Respondes* (p. 13): "The Christian magistrate manages his office under and for Christ, that is, so as to be serviceable for the kingdom and glory of Christ." And now judge whether it be suitable to the sincerity and candor of a minister of the gospel to endeavor to make me odious to authority by imputing to me that which not only I did not say, but the contrary whereof I did plainly express. The thing which I charged his doctrine with was this: That by holding all government to be given to Christ as Mediator and from Him as Mediator derived to the magistrate as His vicegerent, he shakes the foundation of magistracy. I am sure that which I hold, that all lawful magistrates are powers ordained by God and are to be honored and obeyed as God's vicegerents is a firm and strong foundation for magistracy. But that which Mr. Coleman and Mr. Hussey hold, viz., that the Christian magistrate holds his office of, under, and for Christ as He is Mediator, and does act *vice Christi*, as Christ's vicegerent, gives a most dangerous wound to Christian magistracy, which I can demonstrate in many particulars. I shall now give instance only in these few:

First, They must prove from Scripture that Christ as Mediator has given a commission of vicegerentship to Christian magistrates, and appointed them not only to be serviceable to Him, and to do His work (for that they must serve Christ, and be for His glory is not controverted, nay, can never enough be commended to them), but also to govern *vice Christi*, in Christ's stead, and that not only as He is God, which is not controverted neither, but as He is Mediator. This, I say, they must prove, which they will never be able to do, or otherwise they do by their doctrine lead the magistrate into a snare and leave him in it. For how shall he be acknowledged for a vicegerent who can show no commission nor warrant for his vicegerentship?

Secondly, Their doctrine tends to the altering of the surest and best known tenure of magistracy, which is from God; for they hold that God has put all government, and all authority civil, and all, into the hands of Christ as Mediator; if the tenure from Christ fail, then, by their doctrine, the tenure from God shall fail too.

Thirdly, The vicegerent cannot act in that capacity, nor assume that power which his sovereign, whose vicegerent he is, ought not to assume if he were personally present; so that by their principles it will follow that the Christian magistrate can act no further, nor assume any other power of government, than Christ Himself might have assumed when He was on earth, or might now assume and exercise as Mediator if He were on earth. But Christ Himself, when He was on earth, neither did exercise, nor was sent to exercise civil judgment (Luke 12:14), and the temporal sword (John 18:36), nor external observation and state (Luke 17:20, 21); and He declined to be an earthly king (John 6:15). Therefore, by their principles the Christian magistrate ought to forbear and avoid all these.

A fifth calumny[122] is this: Mr. Coleman, descanting upon the governments mentioned [in] 1 Corinthians 12:28, charges me with a circular argumentation: "He circularly argues," says he, "they are civil because God placed them there, and God placed them there because they are civil" (*Malè Dicis Maledicis*, p. 9). I neither argued the one nor the other; they are both, sir, of your own forging. But this is not your first allegation of this kind. I sometime admire what oscitancy [*drowsiness; dullness*] or supine negligence (to judge it no worse) this can be, to fancy to yourself that I have said what you would, and then to bring forth your own apprehensions for my arguments.

CHAPTER EIGHT

THAT MR. COLEMAN DOES GREAT VIOLENCE, BOTH TO HIS OWN WORDS
& TO THE WORDS OF OTHERS WHOM HE CITES

THE REVEREND brother has offered extreme violence to his own declaration, of which let the reader now judge, comparing his declaration with his interpretation.

Declaration: "For much of what is reported of my sermon I utterly deny, and refer myself to the sermon itself, for what I have acknowledged to be delivered by me, although it is my judgment, yet because I see it has given a great deal of offence to this assembly and the reverend commissioners of Scotland, I am sorry I have given offence in the delivery thereof; and for the printing, although I have an order, I will forbear, except I be further commanded.[123] THO. COLEMAN."

---

122. [*Works* reads "sixth."]

123. [This is the apology Coleman made to the assembly in writing after he had preached his fast sermon *Hopes Deferred*. Coleman made the apology in a Friday session and made a retraction on Monday at least as to the promise not to publish (session 479, August 4, 1645). The minutes do not indicate a retraction of the apology but seem to focus on the promise not to print. "either to release me of my promise or take order for the[?] occasion[?]. I protest it to be unconsidered and null and voyd." *Minutes*, 3.642. Coleman declared it pertained to the full declaration. *Malè Dicis*, p. 18. In his August 27 House of Lords sermon, Gillespie had preached that Coleman's comments in *Hopes Deferred* had given offense to many, and said the same in the title of *Nihil Respondes*. Coleman chose to make an issue of this and began disputing the

Interpretation: "It is a truth, and a Scripture truth, which I have delivered, and because I see a Scripture truth has given offence to the commissioners of Scotland, etc., I am sorry. This must needs be the sense; I am sure this was the sense intended." *Malè Dicis, Maledicis* (p. 18).

Surely if such Orleans glosses be admitted upon men's declarations,[124] signed with their hands, and if he who has subscribed himself sorry that he has given offence in the delivery of such a doctrine, shall be allowed to expound himself thus; that he meant he was sorry others had taken offence at a Scripture truth, that is, he was sorry for our fault, not for his own, I know not how men shall trust one another's declarations, or how we can practically, as well as doctrinally, confute the Jesuitical equivocations and mental reservations.[125] And if this must needs be the sense which now the reverend brother gives, and was the sense intended, why says he that he did publicly recall that declaration? He might make a revocation of it, in the sense wherein I understood it, but how could he make a revocation of it as himself understood it, and as he says the sense must needs be? Was this his sorrow for our taking offence at a Scripture truth a sorrow to be sorrowed for? Why did he not rather make a second declaration the next day interpreting the former? And whereas he thinks that his revocation ought to have been mentioned together with his declaration, because the whole truth is to be told as well as the truth, his own heart knows that he himself has not told the whole truth, for he could tell much more if he pleased, how he was brought

---

point of offence in his *Re-examination* (p. 3). He questioned to whom he gave offense, not to the Commons, to whom he appealed as best to judge of a scandalous sermon. Gillespie in response cited the apology in *Nihil Respondes* to make it clear Coleman very well knew who he had offended since he apologized to them. Coleman complained in *Malè Dicis* that Gillespie did not give the full truth in omitting that he had made a retraction. Here Gillespie focuses on Coleman's own apparent partial accounting and spinning of his apology after the fact.]

124. ["The practices of the schools of Orleans, famous for their commentaries on ancient authors, gave rise to the saying 'we freely admit that the gloss of Orleans destroys the text here' (on dit voulentiers que la glose/D'Orleans si destruit le texte)." Jacqueline Cerquiglini-Toulet, *A New History of Medieval French Literature*, trans. Sara Preisig (The Johns Hopkins University Press, 2011), p. 127.]

125. ["The doctrine of equivocation and mental reservation says that it is always sinful to tell an outright lie, but it is permissible to deceive a malevolent interlocutor when a life or property is threatened. One option is equivocation, the use of words with double meaning, where the listener is expected to understand the false sense, but the speaker intends a hidden meaning that is true. Or, more conventionally, one can use a mental reservation, in which the speaker adds a silent condition to what he or shay says. The spoken words are false, but are true if understood with a silent condition." "The Jesuit priest Henry Garnet, for example, when convicted for his part in the gunpowder plot of 1606, was shown to have written a manual for Catholic priests in England on the use of equivocation." Emily Corran, *Lying and Perjury in Medieval Practical Thought: A Study in the History of Casuistry* (Oxford University Press, 2018), p. 22.]

upon the business, and particularly upon that revocation.[126] Why will he challenge others for not telling the whole truth, when [he] himself does it not? I should have thought that this revocation was neither here nor there as to the point of scandal, for proof whereof his declaration was brought; and that, as it was not to the business in hand, so it might rather serve for impairing his credit than for anything else. But seeing himself thinks it more for his credit to tell the world of his saying and unsaying, declaring and undeclaring, let him be doing.

In the next place, Will you see how much violence he offers to divines whom he cites? I had cited plain and full testimonies of the Zurich divines, showing that Gwalther expounds 1 Corinthians 5 all along of excommunication; that Bullinger holds excommunication to be instituted by Christ (Matt. 18); that Aretius says God was the author of excommunication in the Old Testament, and Christ in the New, all which see in *Nihil Respondes*, p. 32.[127]

The reverend brother, notwithstanding of their plain testimonies, speaking for me and against him in the main controversy between him and me, does still allege that they are for him, not for me (*Malè Dicis*, p. 23), yet he does not so much as offer any answer to their testimonies by me cited, only he brings three other passages of theirs, intimating that there may be a true church without excommunication; that they thought it not necessary where they lived; that they thought it hard, yea impossible (*arduum nec non impossibile*)[128] to introduce excommunication in those parts, by which citations the brother has proved nothing against me, but confirmed what I said. Let him remember first, he himself makes the main controversy between him and me about the scriptural warrants of church censures; now in that, they are clearly against him. Next, Aretius, who thought it hard, yea impossible, to bring in excommunication at that time, says also, *Dabit posterior ætas tractabiliores forte animas*,[129] "peradventure the following age shall bring forth more tractable souls." And thereupon he advises not to despair of the restitution of excommunication. I cited also other testimonies to show that the Zurich divines did endeavor and long for the discipline of excommunication, though as things stood then and there, they

---

126. [By "business," Gillespie may mean the apology and retraction, but it seems that there was a broader intrigue, which at the least may point to some members of the Commons persuading him to make the retraction, and perhaps may point to similar influence to make the remarks in his sermon in the first place. See the introduction to the House of Lords sermon, herein page 144.]

127. [See *Nihil Respondes*, herein pages 263–265.]

128. [Benedictus Aretius, Locus 112, in *De Exemplis Veteris Testamenti, quatenus scilicet transferenda sint in usum nostrum, S.S. theologiæ problemata: hoc est, Loci commvnes Christianæ religionis, methodice explicati* (Isayas le Preux, 1617), De Excommunitione, p. 638.]

129. [See ibid, p. 639. Gillespie makes the same reference to this passage in *Aaron's Rod Blossoming* (1646, p. 541 *sic* 341; *Works*, p. 157), but the reference mistakenly directs to loci 132 rather than 112.]

did prudentially supersede the restoring of it where they lived, because of the difficulty and apprehended impossibility of the thing. If Mr. Coleman will follow the Zurich divines, he must change his tone and quite alter the state of the question and make it thus: Whether, as things now stand, it be expedient to settle excommunication in the church of England. Now, if he makes this the state of the question, then he must make a revocation of that word, "I deny an institution, I assent to a prudence." For the tables were turned with the Zurich divines; they assented to an institution; they denied a prudence; they held an affirmative precept for excommunication, but that it does not bind *ad semper;* that the thing is not at all times, nor in all places necessary; that weighty inconveniences may warrant the superseding of it.

The reverend brother brings another testimony out of Aretius against suspension from the sacrament. "And further," he says, "for this grand desired power, suspension from sacrament, these are his words," etc.; a testimony three ways falsified: 1. Aretius speaks not at all in that place of the power or duty of church officers, of which suspension is a part, but he speaks of private Christians, and what is incumbent to them. 2. He speaks of separation, not of suspension from the sacrament; that a man is not bound to withdraw and lie off [*lay off*] from the sacrament because everyone who is to communicate with him is not in his opinion a saint. 3. He speaks against separation from both Word and sacrament because of the mixture of good and bad in hearing and in communicating; but scandalous sinners are invited to, not suspended from the hearing of the Word, wherefore take Aretius's words as they are,[130] and then let the reverend brother consider what he has gained.

What hath this now to do with church officers' power of suspension from the sacrament?

Observe another testimony which he adds out of Augustine, *lib. de Fide*, *Excommunicatio debet supplere locum visibilis gladii*, which he Englishes thus: "Excommunication comes in only to supply the want of the civil sword." But how comes in your *only*, sir? Augustine says no such thing. And when I have expunged that word, I must tell you further, that I can find no such passage in Augustine's book *de Fide*;[131] but I find somewhat to this purpose in another book of his, which is entitled *De Fide et Operibus*, a book which he wrote against the admission of such persons to baptism, as being instructed in the faith, are, notwithstanding, still scandalous in their lives

---

130. Aret., *Probl. Theol.*, loc. 8. *Privatis satis est ferre utrinque utrosque* (infirmos et palam sceleratos) *emendare autem quoties fert exemplo et doctrina. Si parum vel nihil etiam proficiat, non habet ob id causam secedendi. Nec est quod contaminationem metuat, modo non consentiat sceleribus,* etc., *nihil ad me attinet in communione coenae Domini, in coetu publico cum audio verbum Dei* (which last clause Mr. Coleman leaves out without so much as etc.), *quales singuli sint mecum participantes.* [Gillespie has inserted some context (placed here in the Roman face). Ibid., p. 51.]

131. [Gillespie may have thought Coleman meant *De fide et symbolo*.]

(which, by the way, will hold *à fortiori*, for the exclusion of notorious scandalous sinners from the Lord's supper; for they who ought not to be admitted to the sacrament of initiation, ought much less to be admitted to the sacrament of confirmation). Now, because divers scriptures speak of a mixture of good and bad in the church, Augustine takes there occasion to reprove those who abused these scriptures against the exercise of discipline and church censures, the necessity whereof he shows to be the greater because the magistrate does not punish by death all such crimes as under the law were punished by death, as, namely, adultery, the scandal chiefly by him insisted upon. As for that passage concerning excommunication supplying the place of the sword,[132] it plainly holds forth excommunication under Christian emperors and magistrates, for such they were at that time, so far it is from making against us. For these are the words which say no such thing as Mr. Coleman would make them say: "And Phinehas the priest did thrust through the adulterous persons found together with the avenging sword, which signified that it should be done by degradations and excommunications in this time, when, in the discipline of the church, the visible sword was to cease."

If the reverend brother had let me know where to find his other testimonies of Origen[133] and Chrysostom,[134] peradventure I had given him as good

---

132. Aug., *de Fide et Operibus*, cap. 2, Et Phinees sacerdos adulteros simul inventos ferro ultore confixit. Quod utique degradationibus et excommunicationibus significatum est esse faciendum in hoc tempore, cum in ecclesiae disciplina visibilis fuerat gladius cessaturus. [Cf. Migne, *PL* 40, col. 199. "And Phinees, the priest, thrust through with the avenging sword the adulterers whom he found together. Which very thing it was signified was to be done by degradations and excommunications at this time, when in the discipline of the Church the visible sword was to lie by." *Seventeen Short Treatises of S. Augustine* (Oxford, 1847), p. 38.]

133. [While Gillespie was unable to locate the quotation, he clearly could have challenged the Origen and Chrysostom citations as misused. The citation reads: "Qui vocatur ad Episcopalum, non vocatur ad principatum, sed servitute totius Ecclesiae," which he translated as "He that is called to the ministry, is not called to government, but to be a servant to the whole Church." *Malè Dicis*, p. 25. The sentence is found in Origin's work on Isaiah (cf. *PL* 24, col. 957). "It is good not to hasten toward those posts that are from God, offices of honor and chief positions and ministerial posts [note: office of a preacher] in the Church. If only we would imitate Moses and say with him: 'Provide another whom you may send.' For he who wants to be saved does not come to rule over the Church, even if he has charge, but he comes in order to serve, if it is proper to speak also from the Gospel: 'Indeed, the leaders of the people rule over them, and those who have power over them are called the magistrates, yet it will not be like this for you.' 'For the leaders [of the Church] do not have absolute rule over you, but whoever from among you wants to be greater, he will be the least of all; whoever wants to be first, he will be the last of all.' *Accordingly, he who is called to the office of the bishop is not called to rulership but to service to the whole Church.*" Emphasis added. Origen, *Homilies on Isaiah*, trans. Elizabeth Ann Dively Lauro (CUA Press, 2021), p. 89.]

134. ["Episcopatus tempore Apostolorum, ne bonos quidem tum fuit sed merum onus,

an account of them. Tertullian's words which he cites, *Præsident probati seniores*, I know very well where to find; and I know also, that if there be a passage in all antiquity against the Erastians, that is one. Which therefore, I here offer as it is to be considered.[135]

One instance more of his misalleging and perverting of testimonies. In the close,[136] he cites a passage of Mr. Case's sermon, Aug. 22, 1645.[137] "He" (Christ) "is king of nations and king of saints. As king of nations he has a temporal kingdom and government over the world," etc., "and the rule and regiment of this kingdom he has committed to monarchies," etc. "Here is Erastianism," says Mr. Coleman ([*Malè Dicis*,] p. 38), "a step higher than ever I or Erastus himself went. And I desire to know of Mr. Gillespie, if he will own this as good divinity?" Yes, sir, I own it for very good divinity; for my

---

meræ eura et sollicitudo." "The ministry in the times of the apostles, was not an honor, but a mere burden and care." *Malè Dicis*, p. 25. Coleman appears to be drawing on some summary; at least an exact match to these words could not be found. It appears to come from Nicolaus Vedel's Exercitations contra Bellarmine and Baronius on Ignatius's letter to the Trallians chapter 9. "Et certe voces hae sapiunt nullo modo auream illam ætatem *Apostolicam*, qua Ignatius visit, ubi *Episcopatus* non fuit imperium aut potestas, sed ministerium. Imo, ut Chrysostom dicit in Act. cap. 1. *ne honos quidem tum fuit, sed merum onus, mera cura et sollicitudo.*" Emphasis added. If this is not Coleman's source, perhaps this was reduced to what he cited in some other work. See *S. Ignatii Episcopi Antiocheni … quae extant omnia, in duos libros distincta, Quorum Prior Continet Epistolas genuinas, alter suppositias, Cum XII exercitationibus in eundem Ignatium pro antiquitate Catholica adversus Baronium et Bellarminum, auctore Nicolas Vedelio* (1623), p. 34. See Chrysostom, *PG* 60, cols. 39–40 and *The Homilies of S. John Chrysostom, on the Acts of the Apostles*, Part 1 (Oxford: Parker, [1851]), p. 46.]

135. Tert., *Apologet., cap.* 39. *Ibidem etiam exhortationes, castigationes, et censura divina. Nam et judicatur magno cum pondere, ut apud certos de Dei conspectu: summumque futuri judicii præjudicium est, si quis ita deliquerit, ut a communicatione orationis, et conventus, et omnis sancti commercii relegetur. Præsident probati quique seniores, honorem istum non pretio sed testimonio adepti.* ["In the same place also exhortations are made, rebukes and sacred censures are administered. For with a great gravity is the work of judging carried on among us, as befits those who feel assured that they are in the sight of God; and you have the most notable example of judgment to come when any one has sinned so grievously as to require his severance from us in prayer, in the congregation and in all sacred intercourse. The tried men of our elders preside over us, obtaining that honour not by purchase, but by established character." *Apology*, in *ANF* vol. 3, p. 46.]

136. [This is in the section specifically answering Adoniram Byfield's *A brief view of Mr. Coleman his new-modell of church government*, where Coleman addressed Gillespie's objection directly via this quotation from Thomas Case's thanksgiving sermon.]

137. [Thomas Case, *A sermon preached before the Honourable House of Commons at Westminster, August 22. 1645. Being the day appointed for their solemn thanksgiving unto God for his several mercies to the forces of the Parliament in divers parts of the kingdome, in the gaining of the towns of Bath and Bridgewater, and of Scarborough-Castle, and Sherborn-Castle, and for the dispersing of the Clubmen, and the good successe in Pembroke-shire* (1645), p. 26.]

reverend brother, Mr. Case, says not that Christ, as Mediator, is king of nations, and has a temporal kingdom in the world, and has committed rule and regiment to monarchies or other lawful magistrates (which is the point that you and Mr. Hussey contend for, being a great heterodoxy in divinity), but he says of the Son of God that He is king of nations, and has committed rule to monarchies, which I own with all my heart. The distinction of the twofold kingdom of Christ, a universal kingdom, whereby He reigns over all things as God, and a special economical kingdom, whereby He is king to the church only, and rules and governs it, is that which, being rightly understood, overturns, overturns, overturns the Erastian principles. Let Mr. Coleman but own this distinction, and that which Mr. Case adds concerning the kingdom, which Christ, as king of saints (and so as Mediator), does exercise both invisibly in the conscience, and visibly in the church: First, By conquering a people and visible subjects; secondly, By giving them laws distinct from all the laws and statutes of all the kingdoms and republics in the world (Isa. 33:22); thirdly, By constituting special officers in the church not only to promulgate these laws (Matt, 18:19), but to govern His people according to them (Acts 20:28; Rom. 12:8; 1 Cor. 12:28; 14:32); fourthly, In that He has commanded all His people to obey these ecclesiastical officers (Heb. 13:7, 17); fifthly, And hath appointed censures proper to this government (Matt. 18:17; 1 Cor. 5:13): I say, let Mr. Coleman but own this doctrine of Mr. Case, which was printed by order of the honorable House of Commons as well as his was,[138] then we are agreed. And so much for this time.

---

138. [It was pro forma for both houses of parliament to order the sermons preached before them printed as the preacher desired. Coleman seems to have placed a lot of emphasis on this order, as if it were a peculiar stamp of approval, which it was not as Gillespie notes, since it was customary, and all the orders follow the same form in the parliamentary journals. What was unusual was that the House of Commons issued a second order to print because the assembly complained to them about Coleman's sermon. See the introduction to Gillespie's House of Lords sermon on page 146.]

Acts of the General Assembly
of the Church of Scotland
Edinburgh, February 1645

Preface

As noted in a prior preface, George Gillespie and Robert Baillie had taken a break from the Westminster assembly to present the work accomplished to that point before the General Assembly of the Church of Scotland meeting beginning on January 22, 1645. The Scottish commissioners attended the next day and both spoke and presented a letter from the assembly, as well as the Directory for Public Worship, propositions regarding church government and ordination as they stood at that point, and other work.[1] While, apart from his speech, Baillie seems to have largely played the role of observer, to whom we owe thanks for some facts about this assembly, Gillespie took quite an active role. He appears to have been the author of at least one if not two acts, as well as *A Solemn & Seasonable Warning* issued by the General Assembly. Hetherington writes in the expanded version of his history of the Scottish church,

> "The Assembly met on the 22d of January 1645, earlier than had been intended, on account of urgent business which demanded its attention. Baillie, Gillespie, and Warriston had come to give an account of the progress made by the Westminster Assembly; and Montrose was spreading terror and devastation through the kingdom, which was comparatively defenceless in consequence of its most experienced generals and best troops being in England. The report of the Commissioners was received with great approbation, and the directory for public worship which they brought with them received the sanction of the Assembly. A very important act was passed for the advancement of learning, the principles and regulations of which reflect great credit on the enlightened men by whom it was framed. Another very remarkable act was that entitled "A Solemn and Seasonable Warning," &c., in which a clear and strong view is taken of the causes of the national disasters by which they were at that time agitated and alarmed. A remonstrance was also written, addressed to the King, in which the Assembly expressed the most earnest desire for peace on religious terms; and letters were sent to the Westminster Assembly."[2]

---

1. See the background in the preface to Gillespie's sermon before the House of Lords herein on page 134. See the letter from the Westminister Assembly in *Minutes*, 5.160–164.

2. William M. Hetherington, *History of the Church of Scotland: From The Introduction of Christianity to the period of the Disruption, May 18, 1843. Seventh edition with ecclesiastical map* (Edinburgh: Johnstone and Hunter, [1852]), p. 372.

The Solemn & Seasonable Warning was issued with approval of the Assembly in its eighteenth session on February 12, 1645. Robert Baillie credits George Gillespie as the author of this exhortation to the Scottish people, in a letter to his cousin William Spang about this General Assembly meeting.[3] After detailing losses to the Earl of Montrose, he writes,

> The country was exceedingly exhaust[ed] with burdens; and, which was worst, a careless stupid lethargy had seized on the people, so that we were brought exceedingly low. In this lamentable condition, we took ourself to our old rock; we turned ourself to God. The Assembly sent out a printed Warning to the country, very well penned by Mr. Gillespie.

This is apparently a little known fact missed by many historians, though it is noted by Florence N. McKoy in her work on Robert Baillie, and by C. G. M'Crie in his book on public worship in Scotland.[4] Hetherington does not

---

3. See Robert Baillie, *Letters & Journals*, 2.263. The text was first published as *A Solemne and Seasonable Warning to the Noble-men, Barons, Gentlemen, Burrows, Ministers, and Commons of Scotland: As also to our Armies without and within this Kingdome: From the Generall Assembly met at Edinburgh the 12 day of February, 1645* (Edinburgh: Printed by Evan Tyler, Printer to the Kings most Excellent Majestie, 1645). It was republished in London as *A Solemne and Seasonable Warning To the Noblemen, Barons, Gentlemen, Burrows, Ministers, and Commons of Scotland: As also to the Scotish Armies without and within that Kingdom. From the Generall Assembly, 12 Feb. 1645. And the humble Remonstrance of the aforesaid Assembly to the King, 13. Feb. 1645. According to the Copy printed at Edinburgh* (London, Printed by J. Raworth, 1645). It appears in *A True Copy of the Whole Printed Acts of the General Assemblies of the Church of Scotland, beginning at the Assembly holden at Glasgow the 27. day of November 1638; and ending at the Assembly, holden at Edinburgh the 6. day of August. 1649. Diligently compared, and exactly reprinted conforme to the foresaid printed Acts. By a welwisher of the Church of Scotland* (1682), pp. 270–284. This was reprinted in 1691. See also *Records of the Kirk of Scotland: containing the acts and proceedings of the General Assemblies, from the year 1638 downwards, as authenticated by the clerks of assembly: with notes and historical illustrations*, ed. Alexander Peterkin (1843), pp. 423–426, and *Acts of the General Assembly of the Church of Scotland 1638–1842, Reprinted from the original edition, under the superintendence of The Church Law Society*, Preface by Thomas Pitcairn, Convener of Committee of Church Law Society, May 15, 1843 (Edinburgh: The Edinburgh Printing and Publishing Company, 1843), pp. 122–128.

4. C. G. M'Crie, *The Public Worship of Presbyterian Scotland: Historically Treated* (Edinburgh and London: William Blackwood and Sons, [1892]), p. 190. F. N. McKoy, *Robert Baillie and the Second Scots Reformation* (Berkeley: University of California Press, 1974), p. 99 n12. McKoy notes, "The Solemn League and Covenant had caused a rift among the Covenanters, the first of many. Some had become disaffected; some, like Montrose, had gone over to the royalist cause. Baillie apparently did not want any apostate Covenanters in key positions at this important General Assembly, which would be dealing with the results of that Solemn League and Covenant. An indication of the seriousess [*sic*] of the rift is seen in the action of the General Assembly when, on February 12, it ordered that "A Solemn and Seasonable Warning,"

appear to have been aware of this fact and the piece is not noticed in the nineteenth century collected works of Gillespie. It has clear similarities to Gillespie's manner and style. Given Hetherington's high praise of the piece, it is a pleasure to present it in these shorter writings with full attribution to its author.

At this same assembly, Gillespie appears to have played the primary role in drafting the Act approving the Directory for Public Worship issued in Session 10 on February 3, 1645. Baillie writes,

> On Thursday we were brought to the Assembly. I spoke what you have in the enclosed. Mr. Gillespie spoke thereafter much to the same purpose. Because of the longing desire of all to know what we brought, and to deliver the minds of some from their fears, lest we had other things than we at first would bring forth, all was presently read: the letters of the English Assembly, our Commissioners' letters, the Directory from end to end, the Directory for Ordination, the votes of Government so far as had past the assembly, and some other papers. All was heard with great applause and contentment of all. It was one of the fairest assemblies I had seen; the choice of the ministry and elders of all Scotland well convened; almost the whole parliament, nobles, barons, burrows, and all the considerable persons who were in town. Our message to all was exceeding opportune and welcome. It was a great refreshing to them in a time of languishing and discouragement. A numerous committee was appointed to examine all punctually, which we were desired to attend. In five or six days we went through, and, by God's assistance, gave all men satisfaction in everything. The brethren, from whom we expected most fashery [*trouble*], were easily satisfied; all did lovingly condescend to the alterations I had so much opposed, whereof I was very glad: only Mr. And. R[amsay] was oft exceeding impertinent with his ostentation of antiquity, and Mr. D. Cald[erwood] was oft faschious [*troublesome*]with his very rude and humorous opposition. Yet we got them also at last contented, and the Act, which Mr. Gillespie drew very well, consented to, in the committee first, and thereafter in the Assembly, with a joy unspeakable, blessed be God.
>
> Thereafter we gave to the Committee like satisfaction anent [*about*] the other papers, whereupon they were to have the assembly's opinion, but no act till they had passed the Houses of the English Parliament. When we had this far proceeded, I went to Glasgow to see my family and friends, after sixteen months absence....5

---

written by George Gillespie, be printed and distributed throughout Scotland. In it, warning was given to those who spoke against the Covenant or who attempted to divide the Scots and English parliamentary forces, with Montrose specifically mentioned. 'He that is not with us, is against us,' it concluded."

5. See Robert Baillie, *Letters & Journals*, 2.259–260.

Baillie refers to one act. However, Alexander Turner writes that Gillespie was the author of the act "approving the Propositions concerning Kirk Government and Ordination of Ministers," which passed in session 16 on February 10, 1645.[6] Given the acts are a week apart there is reason to suspect this is a mistake since Baillie refers to a singular act. That this is a mistake seems further confirmed in that it is the later act on ordination to which Baillie refers that has the note appended that these should not be printed until the English concur in passing the same propositions on government and ordination. Also, Baillie writes that the passing of the act he was describing caused great joy in the assembly and it is the act pertaining to the directory of worship that mentions "much joy and thankfulness." However, both troublesome men named by Baillie are mentioned in the brief notes Gillespie has for the committee appointed to examine these propositions on February 7, 1645,[7] so it is not absolutely outside the realm of possibility that Baillie may have collapsed the narrative in his later recap of the Assembly written to Spang on April 25, 1645. The reader may judge in comparing the two acts presented.

The briefer act concerning government and ordination is presented here and the longer act approving the directory for worship follows standing alone, since the attribution is surer for it to stand as Gillespie's work. It should be noted that both acts appear as part of the text of both directories

---

6. Alexander Turner, *The Scottish Secession of 1843: Being an Examination of the Principles, and Narrative of the Contest, which led to that remarkable event* (Edinburgh: Paton and Ritchie, [1859]), p. 58. Turner writes, "It must also be kept in mind that Gillespie drew up the Act of Assembly 1645, which required parties objecting to put in the grounds of their exceptions." This language is in the Act concerning the propositions on church government and ordination. "And now, the Assembly having thrice read, and diligently examined the propositions (hereunto annexed) concerning the Officers, Assemblies, and Government of the Kirk; and concerning the Ordination of Ministers, brought unto us as the results of the long and learned debates of the Assembly of Divines sitting at Westminster, and of the treaty of uniformity with the Commissioners of this Kirk there residing; after mature deliberation, and after timeous calling upon, and warning of all who have any exceptions against the same, to make them known, that they might receive satisfaction, doth Agree to, and Approve the propositions aforementioned, touching kirk government and ordination...." There is similar but not quite the same language in the act approving the directory for worship, but the context in Turner makes it difficult to see he had that act in view. However, the similarity in this may indicate Gillespie had a hand in the shorter act as well. See *The Confession of Faith, the Larger and Shorter Catechism … Covenants, National and Solemn League* (Edinburgh: Johnstone and Hunter, 1855; repr. Free Presbyterian Publications, 1990), pp. 396.

7. "Mr. D. Calderwood confessed, That the people's consent ought to be had, but that the presbytery is to choose give a list to the people to take one of that number. Mr. Andrew Ramsey said, They had also election in the ancient church." "Notes of Proceedings at the General Assembly at Edinburgh, 1645," in *Notes of Debates and Proceedings of The Assembly of Divines and other Commissioners at Westminster*, in *Works*, p. 120.

in the standard Scottish collection of the Westminster Standards,[8] and thus at least in the one case if not both, text exclusively by Gillespie forms a part of those historic statements of presbyterian doctrine and practice, including it might be added, the famous qualification regarding the Scottish practice of celebrating the Lord's Supper about the communion table.

> Session 16, February 10, 1645, post meridiem.—Act of the General Assembly of the Kirk of Scotland, approving the Propositions concerning Kirk Government and Ordination of Ministers.

The General Assembly, being most desirous and solicitous, not only of the establishment and preservation of the form of kirk government in this kingdom, according to the Word of God, Books of Discipline, Acts of General Assemblies, and National Covenant, but also of an uniformity in kirk government betwixt these kingdoms, now more straightly and strongly united by the late Solemn League and Covenant; and considering, that as in former times there did, so hereafter there may arise, through the nearness of contagion, manifold mischiefs to this Kirk from a corrupt form of government in the Kirk of England: Likeas the precious opportunity of bringing the Kirks of Christ, in all the three kingdoms, to an uniformity in kirk government, being the happiness of the present times above the former; which may also, by the blessing of God, prove an effectual mean, and a good foundation to prepare for a safe and well-grounded pacification, by removing the cause from which the present pressures and bloody wars did originally proceed. And now, the Assembly having thrice read, and diligently examined the propositions (hereunto annexed) concerning the Officers, Assemblies, and Government of the Kirk; and concerning the Ordination of Ministers, brought unto us as the results of the long and learned debates of the Assembly of Divines sitting at Westminster, and of the treaty of uniformity with the Commissioners of this Kirk there residing; after mature deliberation, and after tymous [*timely*] calling upon, and warning of all who have any exceptions against the same, to make them known, that they might receive satisfaction, does Agree to, and Approve the propositions aforementioned, touching kirk government and ordination; and does hereby authorize the Commissioners of this Assembly, who are to meet at Edinburgh, to agree to and conclude, in the name of this Assembly, an uniformity betwixt the Kirks in both kingdoms in the aforementioned particulars, so soon as the same shall be ratified, without any substantial alteration, by an ordinance of the Honorable Houses of the Parliament of England; which ratification shall be timely intimate[d] and made known by the Commissioners of this Kirk residing at London. Provided always, that this act shall be no ways prejudicial to the further discussion and examination of that Article which holds forth, that the Doctor or Teacher has power of the administration of the Sacraments as well as the Pastor; as also

---

8. *The Confession of Faith*, ibid., pp. 371–72, 396.

of the diſtinct rights and intereſts of Presbyteries and People in the Calling of Miniſters—but that it shall be free to debate and discuss these points, as God shall be pleased to give further light.

The propositions of Government and Ordination, mentioned in the preceding act, are not to be here printed; but after the ratification thereof by the Parliament of England, they are to be printed by warrant of the Commissioners of this Assembly.

John Calvin. Sermons on the Book of Micah
*For if we hope to worship God in the manner that is acceptable to him,
we must divest ourselves of all silly superstitions and frivolous inventions,
renounce all idolatry in order to worship God in spirit and in truth (as God
commands us), and cling to the simplicity that we observe in his Word*

Act of the General Assembly of the Kirk of Scotland, for the establishing and putting in Execution of the Directory for the Publick Worship of God in *A Directory for the Publike Worship of God, throughout the three kingdoms of Scotland, England, and Ireland. With an act of the Generall Assembly of the Kirk of Scotland, for establishing and observing this present directory. Together with an act of the Parliament of the Kingdom of Scotland approving and establishing the same: an act of the Committee of Estates concerning the printing thereof: and an act of the Commission of the Generall Assembly for the printing, and for the present practice of it throughout the said Kingdom of Scotland.*

Editions

1. *A Directory*, etc. (Edinburgh: Evan Tyler, 1645). [14], 65, [1] p.; 4⁰. ESTC R31329 (Wing D1549). This act appeared in this first Scottish edition of the directory after England had approved it and the Commission of the General Assembly had reviewed that printing and authorized Scottish publication of it on May 27, 1645. Along with the directory it became a customary part of the traditional Scottish collection of standards set by the Reformed Presbyterian version published by Lumisden and Robertson in 1728. See *The Confession of Faith, Larger and Shorter catechisms*, etc. (Edinburgh: Printed by Thomas Lumisden and John Robertson…, 1728); and Coldwell, "*Antiquary*: The Development of the Traditional Form of The Westminster Standards," *The Confessional Presbyterian* journal, volume 1 (2005): 171. See *The Confession of Faith, the Larger and Shorter Catechism … Covenants, National and Solemn League* (Edinburgh: Johnstone and Hunter, 1855; repr. Free Presbyterian Publications, 1990), pp. 371–372.

    The text also appears in the Acts of the General Assembly. See the text in *A True Copy of the Whole Printed Acts of the General Assemblies of the Church of Scotland, beginning at the Assembly holden at Glasgow the 27. day of November 1638; and ending at the Assembly, holden at Edinburgh the 6. day of August. 1649. Diligently compared, and exactly reprinted conforme to the foresaid printed Acts. By a welwisher of the Church of Scotland* (1682), pp. 256–259. This was reprinted in 1691. See also *Records of the Kirk of Scotland: containing the acts and proceedings of the General Assemblies, from the year 1638 downwards, as authenticated by the clerks of assembly: with notes and historical illustrations*, ed. Alexander Peterkin (1843), pp. 418–419, and *Acts of the General Assembly of the Church of Scotland 1638–1842, Reprinted from the original edition, under the superintendence of The Church Law Society*, Preface by Thomas Pitcairn, Convener of Committee of Church Law Society, May 15, 1843 (Edinburgh: The Edinburgh Printing and Publishing Company, 1843), pp. 115–116.

The Epigraph on the prior page has been added for this volume. John Calvin, *Sermons on the Book of Micah*, translated by Benjamin W. Farley (Phillipsburg, NJ : P&R, 2003), p. 364.

Whereas a happy unity and uniformity in religion amongst the Kirks of Christ in these three kingdoms, united under one Sovereign, have been long and earnestly wished for by the godly and well-affected amongst us—was propounded as a main article of the large treaty,[1] without which band and bulwark no safe, well-grounded, and lasting peace could be expected—and, afterward, with greater strength and maturity revived in the Solemn League and Covenant of the three kingdoms, whereby they stand straightly obliged to endeavor the nearest uniformity in one form of Church Government, Directory of Worship, Confession of Faith, and Form of Catechizing—which have also before and since our entering into that covenant been the matter of many supplications and remonstrances, and sending commissioners to the king's Majesty, of declarations to the Honorable Houses of the Parliament of England, and of letters to the Reverend Assembly of Divines, and others of the ministry of the Kirk of England—being also the end of our sending commissioners, as was desired from this Kirk, with commission to treat of uniformity in the four particulars aforementioned, with such committees as should be appointed by both Houses of the Parliament of England, and by the Assembly of Divines sitting at Westminster—and besides all this, it being, in point of conscience, the chief motive and end of our adventuring upon manifold and great hazards for quenching the devouring flame of the present unnatural and bloody war in England, though to the weakening of this kingdom within itself, and the advantage of the enemy which has invaded it, accounting nothing too dear to us, so that this our joy be fulfilled. And now this great work being so far advanced, that a Directory for the Public Worship of God in all the three kingdoms being agreed upon by the Honorable Houses of the Parliament of England, after consultation with the divines of both kingdoms there assembled, and sent to us for our approbation, that being also agreed upon by this Kirk and Kingdom of Scotland, it may be, in the name of both kingdoms, presented to the king, for his royal consent and ratification. The General Assembly having most

---

1. "Articles of the large treaty concerning the establishing of the peace between the king's majesty and his people of Scotland" (1641). See page 487.

seriously considered, revised, and examined the Directory aforementioned, after several public readings of it, after much deliberation, both publicly and in private committees, after full liberty given to all to object against it, and earnest invitations of all who have any scruples about it to make known the same, that they might be satisfied, do unanimously, and without a contrary voice, Agree to and Approve the following Directory, in all the heads thereof, together with the preface set before it; and does require, discern, and ordain, that, according to the plain tenor and meaning thereof, and the intent of the preface, it be carefully and uniformly observed and practiced by all the ministers and others within this kingdom whom it doth concern; which practice shall be begun upon intimation given to the several presbyteries from the commissioners of this General Assembly, who shall also take special care for the timeous [*prompt*] printing of this Directory, that a printed copy of it be provided and kept for the use of every kirk in this kingdom; also that each presbytery have a printed copy thereof for their use, and take special notice of the observation or neglect thereof in every congregation within their bounds, and make known the same to the provincial or General Assembly, as there shall be cause. Provided always, that the clause in the Directory, of the administration of the Lord's Supper, which mentions the communicants sitting about the table, or at it, be not interpreted as if in the judgment of this kirk it were indifferent and free for any of the communicants not to come to and receive at the table; or as if we did approve the distributing of the elements by the minister to each communicant, and not by the communicants among themselves. It is also provided that this shall be no prejudice to the order and practice of this kirk in such particulars as are appointed by the Books of Discipline and Acts of General Assemblies, and are not otherwise ordered and appointed in the Directory.

Finally, the Assembly does with much joy and thankfulness acknowledge the rich blessing and invaluable mercy of God, in bringing the so much wished for uniformity in religion to such a happy period, that these kingdoms, once at so great distance in the form of worship, are now by the blessing of God brought to a nearer uniformity than any other reformed Kirks, which is unto us the return of our prayers and a lightning of our eyes and reviving of our hearts, in the midst of our many sorrows and sufferings, a taking away in a great measure the reproach of the people of God, to the stopping of the mouths of malignant and disaffected persons, and an opening unto us a door of hope, that God has yet thoughts of peace towards us, and not of evil, to give us an expected end [cf. Hosea 2:15; Jer. 29:11]. In the expectation and confidence whereof we do rejoice, beseeching the Lord to preserve these kingdoms from heresies, schisms, offences, profaneness, and whatsoever is contrary to sound doctrine and the power of godliness, and to continue with us, and the generations following, these His pure and purged ordinances, together with an increase of the power and life thereof, to the glory of His great name, the enlargement of the kingdom of His Son, the corroboration of peace and love between the kingdoms, the unity and consent of all His people, and our edifying one another in love.

A Solemn and Seasonable Warning

Shall the Watchmen of Zion be silent, when Israel is in trouble?

A Solemne and Seasonable Warning to the Noble-men, Barons, Gentlemen, Burrows, Ministers, and Commons of Scotland: As also to our Armies without and within this Kingdome: From the Generall Assembly met at Edinburgh the 12 day of February, 1645.

EDITIONS

1. *A Solemne and Seasonable Warning to the Noble-men, Barons, Gentlemen, Burrows, Ministers, and Commons of Scotland: As also to our Armies without and within this Kingdome: From the Generall Assembly met at Edinburgh the 12 day of February, 1645* (Edinburgh: Printed by Evan Tyler, Printer to the Kings most Excellent Majestie, 1645). [4], 19, [1] p.; 4⁰. ESTC R39980 (Wing C4259G).

2. *A Solemne and Seasonable Warning To the Noblemen, Barons, Gentlemen, Burrows, Ministers, and Commons of Scotland: As also to the Scotish Armies without and within that Kingdom. From the Generall Assembly, 12 Feb. 1645. And the humble Remonstrance of the aforesaid Assembly to the King, 13. Feb. 1645. According to the Copy printed at Edinburgh* (London, Printed by J. Raworth, 1645). 16 p.; 4⁰. ESTC R200167 (Wing C4259H). "Annotation on Thomason copy: 'July 24.'" A reason for the long delay in printing the title in England was not found.

The warning was reprinted in the Acts of the General Assembly. See the preface and note 3 on page 320.

The Epigraph on the preceding page comes from the London edition noted above published by J. Raworth. It likely draws from passages such as Isaiah 62:1, 6–7, Ezekiel 3:16–21, and Ezekiel 33:6.

A Solemn And Seasonable Warning
To the Noblemen, Barons, Gentlemen, Burrows, Ministers,
and Commons of Scotland: As also to the
Scottish Armies without and within that Kingdom
From the General Assembly, 12 Feb. 1645

Session 18, February 12, 1645, afternoon.

The General Assembly after mature deliberation, having found it most necessary that this whole nation be timely warned and duly informed of their present dangers, and the remedies to be used and duties to be done for preventing and removing thereof, does ordain this warning to be forthwith printed and published, and sent to all the presbyteries in this kingdom, as also to the presbyteries that are with our armies. And that each presbytery, immediately after the receipt hereof, take speedy course for the reading of it in every congregation within their bounds upon the Lord's day after the forenoon's sermon, and before the blessing, and that they give account of their diligence herein to the commissioners of the General Assembly, who have hereby power and warrant to try and censure such as shall contemn or slight the said warning, or shall refuse or neglect to obey this ordinance. *Extracted forth of the Warrands and Records of Parliament, by me Sir Alexander Gibsone of Durie, Knight, Clerk of his Majesty's Register and Rolls, Under my Sign and Subscription Manual. Alex Gibsone, Cler. Registri.*

A Solemn and Seasonable Warning to the Noblemen, Barons, Gentlemen, Burrows, Ministers, and Commons of Scotland; as also to our Armies without and within this Kingdom. {From the Generall Assembly, February 12, 1645.}[1]

The cause of God in this kingdom, both in the beginnings and progress of it, has been carried through much craft and mighty opposition of enemies, and through other perplexities and dangers, God so disposing for the greater glory of His manifold and marvelous wisdom and His invincible power, and for our greater trial.

These dangers, both from without and from within, together with the remedies thereof, have been from time to time represented and held forth

---

1. This final part of the subtitle was omitted in the 1682, 1838, and 1843 texts of the acts of the assembly, respectively pages 271, 423, and 122. See page 320, footnote 3.

in the many public supplications of this kirk and kingdom to the king, and in their many declarations, remonſtrances, letters, acts, and other public intimations, particularly, by a necessary warning published by the commissioners of the General Assembly in January 1643, and by the remonſtrance of the same commissioners to the Convention of Eſtates in July thereafter, concerning the dangers of religion and the remedies of these dangers; which warning and remonſtrance at that time had by the blessing of God very good and comfortable effects. And now, the General Assembly itself, being by a ſpecial providence and upon extraordinary occasions called together, while God is writing bitter things againſt this land in great letters, which he that runs may read[2]—and knowing that we cannot be answerable to God nor our own consciences, nor the expectation of others, if from this chief watchtower we should give no seasonable warning to the city of God; while we think of these things, "for Zion's sake we will not hold our peace, and for Jerusalem's sake we will not reſt;"[3] truſting that God will give, though not to all, yet to many, a seeing eye, a hearing ear, and an underſtanding heart;[4] for "who is wise, and he shall underſtand these things, prudent, and he shall know them; for the ways of the Lord are right, and the juſt shall walk in them; but the transgressors shall fall therein," and "the wicked shall do wickedly, and none of the wicked shall underſtand."[5]

That which we principally intend is to hold forth (so far as the Lord gives us light) how this nation ought to be affected with their present mercies and judgments, what use is to be made of the Lord's dealings, and what is required of a people so dealt with.

Had we been timely awaked [*awakened*] and taken warning, either from the exemplary judgments of other nations, or from God's threatenings by the mouths of His servants amongſt ourselves, or from our own former visitations, and namely, the sword threatened and drawn againſt us both at home and from abroad, but at that time, through the forbearance of God, put up in the sheath again, we might have prevented the miseries under which now we groan. But the cup of trembling before taken out of our hands[6] is again come about to us, that we may drink deeper of it; and although, when these bloody monſters, the Irish rebels, together with some degenerate, unnatural, and perfidious countrymen of our own, did firſt lift up their heads and enter this kingdom in a hoſtile way, it was looked upon as a light matter, and the great judgment which has since appeared in it not apprehended. Yet now we are made more sensible that they are "the rod of God's wrath, and the ſtaff in their hand," which has ſtricken us these three times, is [*sic*]

---

2. Habakkuk 2:2. All footnotes are editorial. No Scripture references were in the original text. Unless otherwise noted, all references are to the Authorized Version.

3. Cf. Isaiah 62:1.

4. Proverbs 20:12; 1 Kings 3:9, 12.

5. Hosea 14:9 and Daniel 12:10.

6. Cf. Isaiah 51:22.

"his indignation."[7] He "hath shewed his people hard things, and made us to drink the wine of astonishment."[8] Take we, therefore, notice of the hand that smites us; "for affliction cometh not forth of the dust, neither doth trouble spring out of the ground."[9] "There is no evil in the city" nor country "which the Lord hath not done;" He it is that "formeth the light, and createth darkness; who maketh peace, and createth evil;" He it is that has given a charge to the sword, "so that it cannot be still;" He it is that has His other "arrows ready upon the string to shoot at us," the pestilence and famine.[10]

In the next place, let us apply our hearts to know, and to search, and to seek out wisdom, and the reason of things, and to understand the language of this present judgment, and God's meaning in it. For though the Almighty "giveth not an accompt [*account*] of any of his matters," and has "his way in the sea, and his path in the deep waters,"[11] which cannot be traced; yet He is pleased by the light of His Word and Spirit, by the voice of our own consciences, and by that which is written and engraven upon our judgment, as with the point of a diamond and a pen of iron,[12] to make known in some measure His meaning unto his servants. "God hath spoken once, yea twice, yet man perceiveth not;"[13] therefore, now has He made this rod to speak aloud the third time,[14] that we may "hear the voice of the rod, and who hath appointed it;"[15] that which the rod points at is not any guilt of rebellion or disloyalty in us, as the sons of Belial do slander and belie the Solemn League and Covenant of the three kingdoms, which we are so far from repenting of, that we cannot remember or mention it without great joy and thankfulness to God, as that which has drawn many blessings after it, and unto which God has given manifold and evident testimonies. For no sooner was the covenant begun to be taken in England, but sensibly the condition of affairs there was changed to the better; and though a little before the enemy was coming in like a flood, yet as soon as the Spirit of the Lord did lift

---

7. Cf. Isaiah 10:5.

8. Cf. Psalm 60:3.

9. Cf. Job 5:7.

10. Cf. Amos 3:6; Isaiah 47:5; apparently an allusion to Jeremiah 47:6; and Psalm 21:12.

11. Job 33:13. Cf. Isaiah 43:16.

12. Gillespie made use of Jeremiah 17:1 before in *English Popish Ceremonies* (1637), part 3, chapter two, §17, p. 31; Naphtali Press critical edition (2013), p. 168, and in his sermon before the House of Commons (herein on page 106).

13. Psalm 62:11.

14. This is a reference to Covenanter losses in battle against Montrose's forces at Tippermuir on September 1, 1644, at Aberdeen on September 13, and just a week before the approval of this warning, at Inverlochy on February 2, 1645. Montrose would go on in a second campaign to win three more battles before General Leslie returned from England with his forces and defeated him at Philipbaugh on September 13, 1645. See the preface to Gillespie's sermon before the House of Lords, pp. 136, 137, and 149.

15. Cf. Micah 6:9.

up the ſtandard againſt him, from that day forward the waters of their deluge did decrease.[16]

And for our part, our forces sent into that kingdom in pursuance of that covenant, have been so mercifully and manifeſtly assiſted and blessed from heaven (though in the mids [*midſt*] of many dangers and diſtresses, and much want and hardship,) and have been so far inſtrumental to the foiling and scattering of two principal armies—firſt, the Marquesse of Newcaſtle, his army, and afterward Prince Rupert's and his together; and to the reducing of two ſtrong cities, York and Newcaſtle[17]—that we have what to answer the enemy that reproaches us concerning that business, and that which may make iniquity itself to ſtop her mouth.[18] But which is more unto us than all victories, or whatsomever [*whatever*] temporal blessing, the reformation of religion in England and uniformity therein between both kingdoms (a principal end of that covenant) is so far advanced that the English Service-Book, with the Holy-Days and many other ceremonies contained in it, together with the prelacy, the fountain of all these, are abolished and taken away by ordinance of Parliament, and a Directory for the Worship of God in all the three kingdoms agreed upon in the assemblies and in the parliaments of both kingdoms, without a contrary voice in either; the government of the kirk by congregational elderships, classical presbyteries, provincial and national assemblies, is agreed upon by the Assembly of Divines at Weſtminſter, which is also voted and concluded in both Houses of the Parliament of England; and what is yet remaining of the intended uniformity is in a good way; so that, let our lot fall in other things as it may, "the will of the Lord be done."[19] In this we rejoice, and will rejoice, that our Lord Jesus Chriſt is no loser, but a conqueror; that His ordinances take place, that His cause prevails, and the work of purging and building His temple goes forward and not backward. Neither yet are we so to underſtand the "voice of the rod"[20] which lies heavy upon us, as if the Lord's meaning were to pluck up what He has planted, and to pull down what He has built in this kingdom,[21] to have no more pleasure in us, to remove our candleſtick,[22] and to take His kingdom from us; nay, before that our God caſt us off, and the "glory depart from Israel,"[23] let Him rather consume us by the sword, and the famine, and

---

16. Cf. Isaiah 59:19 and Genesis 8:5.

17. The forces of William Cavendish, Marquis of Newcastle and Prince Rupert were defeated at Marston Moor on July 2, 1644. York surrendered on July 16, and Newcastle on October 27, 1644. The first defeat of Cavendish may refer to his abandoning engaging the Covenanter forces in County Durham to fall back to defend York in April 1644.

18. Cf. Psalm 55:12 and Psalm 107:42.

19. Acts 21:14.

20. Cf. Micah 6:9.

21. Cf. Jeremiah 45:4.

22. Cf. Revelation 2:5.

23. Cf. Ezekiel 10:18.

the pestilence, so that He will but keep His own great name from reproach and blasphemy, and own us as His people in covenant with Him. But "now there is hope in Israel concerning this thing,"[24] we will believe "that we shall yet see the goodness of the Lord in the land of the living."[25] We will not cast away our confidence of a blessed peace, and of the removing of the scourge and casting it in the fire, when the Lord has by it performed "his whole work upon Mount Zion and Jerusalem,"[26] much more will we be confident of the continuance of the blessings of the Gospel, "that glory may dwell in our land."[27] "This is the day of Jacob's trouble, but he shall be saved out of it."[28] And the time is coming when a new song shall be put in our mouths[29] and we shall say, "This is our God; we have waited for him, and he hath saved us."[30] Though the Lord smite us, it is the hand of a father, not of an enemy. He is not consuming us, but refining us, that we may come forth as gold out of the fire.[31] "We are troubled on every side, yet not distressed; we are perplexed, but not in despair; persecuted, but not forsaken; cast down, but not destroyed."[32] We know assuredly there is more mercy in emptying us from vessel to vessel, then [*than*] in suffering us to settle on our lees, whereby our taste should remain in us, and our sent [*scent*] not be changed.[33]

These things premised, we come to the true language of this heavy judgment, and to the real procuring causes thereof. "For the transgression of Jacob is all this, and for the sins of the house of Israel."[34] God is hereby showing to great and small in this land their work and their transgression, that they have exceeded. "He openeth also their ear to discipline, and commandeth that they return from iniquity."[35] We leave every congregation in the land, every family in every congregation, and every person in every family, to examine their own hearts and ways, and to mourn for congregational, domestical, and personal sins: Cursed shall they be who have added fuel to the fire, and now bring no water to extinguish it, who had a great hand in the provocation, and bear no part in the humiliation.

Let every one commune with his own conscience, and repent of his, even his wickedness, and say, What have I done?[36] We shall here touch

---

24. Ezra 10:3.

25. Cf. Psalm 27:13.

26. Isaiah 10:12.

27. Psalm 85:9.

28. Cf. Jeremiah 30:7.

29. Cf. Psalm 40:3.

30. Isaiah 25:9.

31. Cf. Isaiah 43:2 and Job 23:10.

32. 2 Corinthians 4:8–9.

33. Jeremiah 48:11.

34. Micah 1:5.

35. Job 36:10.

36. Jeremiah 8:6.

only the national sins, or at least more public ones, than those of a family or congregation, which we also intend for chief causes of a public fast and humiliation. If among our nobles, gentry, and barons, there have been some studying their own private interests more than the public, and "seeking their own things more than the things of Christ," or oppressing and defrauding the poorer sort and the needy,[37] "because it was in the power of their hand;"[38] and if, among our ministry there have been divers time-servers, "who have not renounced the hidden things of dishonesty, whose hearts have not been right before God, nor steadfast in his covenant,"[39] who have been secretly haters of the power of godliness, and of mortification, shall not God search all this out, "who will bring to light the hidden things of darkness, and will make manifest the counsels of the hearts"?[40] In these also, leaving all men to a judging and searching of themselves, there are many other provocations which are apparent in all or many of this nation, from which, "though they wash with nitre, and take much soap,"[41] yet they cannot make themselves clean. "Because of these the land mourneth,"[42] and at these the sword strikes.

As, first, the contempt, neglect, and disesteem of the glorious gospel; our unbelief, unfruitfulness, lukewarmness, formality, and hardness of heart, under all the means of grace; our not receiving of Christ in our hearts, nor seeking to know Him and glorify Him in all His offices. The power of godliness is hated and mocked by many to this day, and by the better sort too much neglected, and many Christian duties are not minded; as, "the not speaking of our own words, nor finding of our own pleasure upon the Lord's day;"[43] holy and edifying conference,[44] both on that day, and at other occasions; the instructing, admonishing, comforting, and rebuking one another, as divine providence ministreth [*ministers*] occasion. In many families, almost no knowledge nor worship of God [is] to be found; yea, there are among the ministers [those] who have strengthened the hearts and hands of the profane more than of the godly, and have not taken "heed to the ministry which they have received of the Lord to fulfill it."[45]

Next, God has sent the sword to avenge the quarrel of His broken covenant;[46] for, besides the defection of many of this nation under the

---

37. Philippians 2:21. Possibly allusions to Psalm 12:5, Ezekiel 18:12; 22:29, and/or Amos 4:1.

38. Cf. Micah 2:1.

39. 2 Corinthians 4:2, Psalm 78:37.

40. 1 Corinthians 4:5.

41. Jeremiah 2:22.

42. Cf. Jeremiah 23:10.

43. Cf. Isaiah 58:13.

44. Conference: conferring with one another about the Scriptures. Cf. Nicholas Bownd, *The True Doctrine of the Sabbath* (1595; 1606; critical edition, 2015), pp. 378–384.

45. Colossians 4:17.

46. Cf. Leviticus 26:5.

prelates from our first National Covenant,[47] a sin not forgotten by God, if not repented by men as well as forsaken, our latter vows and covenants have been also foully violated by not contributing our uttermost assistance to this cause, with our estates and lives, by not endeavoring with all faithfulness, the discovery, trial, and condign punishment of malignants and evil instruments,[48] yea, by complying too much with those who have not only borne arms and given their personal presence and assistance, but also drawn and led on others after them in the shedding of our brethren's blood, therefore is our sin made our punishment, and "we are filled with the fruit of our own ways."[49] These horns now push the sides of Judah and Jerusalem because the carpenters,[50] when they ought and might, did not cut them off, and yet to this day the course of justice is obstructed. The Lord Himself will execute justice if men will not. But, above all, let it be deeply and seriously thought of, that our covenant is broken by the neglect of a real reformation of ourselves and others under our power; let everyone ask his own heart what lust is mortified in him, or what change wrought in his life since, more than before the covenant? Swearing, cursing, profanation of the Lord's day, fornication, and other uncleanness, drunkenness, injustice, lying, oppression, murmuring, repining, and other sorts of profaneness still abound too much both in the country and in our armies; yea, there is no reformation of some members of public judicatories, which is a great dishonor to God, and a foul scandal to the whole nation.

Thirdly, We have not glorified God according to the great things which He has done for us, nor made the right use of former mercies; since He loved us (a nation not worthy to be beloved),[51] He has made us precious and honorable, but we have not walked worthy of his love.[52] We "waxed fat and kicked," "forsaking God who made us, and lightly esteeming the rock of our salvation."[53] And this great unthankfulness fills up our cup.

Fourthly, Notwithstanding of so much guiltiness, we did send forth our armies and undertake great services presumptuously, without repentance and making our peace with God, like the Children of Israel, who, trusting to the goodness of their cause, minded no more, but "which of us shall go up first."[54]

---

47. The National Covenant of 1580, subscribed again in 1590 and again in 1638, and approved by General Assemblies in 1638 and 1639. See The National Covenant or Confession of Faith in *The Confession of Faith, the Larger and Shorter Catechism*, ibid., pp. 347–354.

48. *Malignants*: supporters of the king who opposed the covenants and goals of the Second Reformation in Scotland. See article four of the Solemn League and Covenant, in *Confession of Faith*, ibid., p. 359.

49. Proverbs 1:31.

50. Cf. Zechariah 1:18–21.

51. See Zephaniah 2:1 (Geneva Bible) and Isaiah 43:4 (KJV).

52. Cf. Isaiah 43:4; Colossians 1:10 and Ephesians 5:2.

53. Cf. Deuteronomy 32:15.

54. Judges 20:18.

It is now high time, under the feeling of so great a burden, both of sin and wrath, to humble our uncircumcised hearts, to put our mouth in the dust, if so be there may be hope, to wallow ourselves in ashes, to clothe ourselves with our shame as with a garment, to justify God's righteous judgments, to acknowledge our iniquity, to make our supplication to our Judge, and to seek His face, that He may pardon our sin and heal our land.[55] The Lord roars, and shall not His children tremble?[56] The God of glory thunders, and "the Highest uttereth his voice, hailstones and coals of fire;"[57] who will not fall down and fear before Him? The fire waxes hot and burns round about us, and shall any sit still and be secure? The storm blows hard, and shall any sluggard be still asleep? This is a day of trouble, and of rebuke, and of blasphemy;[58] who will not take up a lamentation? Let the watchmen rouse up themselves and others, and strive to get their own and their people's hearts deeply affected, and even melted before the Lord. Let everyone turn from his evil way and cry mightily to God, and give Him no rest till He repent of the evil and smell a savor of rest,[59] and say, "It is enough."[60] He has not said to the seed of Jacob, Seek ye me in vain.[61] We do not mourn as they that have no hope,[62] but we "will bear the indignation of the Lord, because we have sinned against him, until he plead our cause, and execute judgment for us."[63] And what though our candles be put out, so that our sun shine? What though our honor be laid in the dust, so that God work out His own honor, yea, our happiness out of our shame? In vain have we trusted to the arm of flesh; in the Lord our God is the salvation of Israel.[64] No flesh must glory before Him, but "he that glorieth must glory in the Lord."[65]

These duties of humiliation, repentance, faith, amendment of life, and fervent prayer, though the principal, yet are not all which are required at the hands of this nation, but men of all sorts and degrees must timely apply themselves to such other resolutions and actions as are most suitable and necessary at this time; which that all may the better understand and be excited and encouraged to act accordingly, let it be well observed that the present state of the controversy and cause is no other but what has been formerly professed before God and the world, that is, the reformation and preservation of religion, the defense of the honor and happiness of the king,

---

55. Cf. 2 Chronicles 7:14.

56. Cf. Hosea 11:10.

57. Psalm 18:13.

58. See 2 Kings 19:3 and Isaiah 37:3.

59. Cf. Ezekiel 20:41; Ezekiel 16:19. "I will accept you with your sweet savour" (savor of rest).

60. 1 Chronicles 21:15.

61. Isaiah 45:19.

62. Cf. 1 Thessalonians 4:13.

63. Cf. Micah 7:9.

64. Cf. Jeremiah 17:5; 3:23.

65. 1 Corinthians 1:29, 31.

and of the authority of the parliament, together with the maintenance of our laws, liberties, lives, and estates.[66] We are not changed from our former principles and intentions, but these who did fall off from us to the contrary party have now made it manifest that these were not their ends when they seemed to join with us. "Therefore are they gone out from us, because they were not of us."[67] And as our cause is the same, so the danger thereof is not less, but greater than before, and that from two sorts of enemies. First, from open enemies, we mean those of the popish, prelatical, and malignant faction, who have displayed a banner against the Lord and against His Christ in all the three kingdoms, being "set on fire of hell,"[68] and by the special inspiration of Satan, who is full of fury, because he knows he has but a short time to reign.[69] The cockatrice before hatched is now broken forth into a viper.[70] The danger was before feared, now it is felt—before imminent, now incumbent—before our division, now our destruction is endeavored—before the sword was furbished and made ready, now the sword "is made fat with flesh, and drunk with blood,"[71] and yet it hungers and thirsts for more. The queen is most active abroad, using all means for strengthening the popish, and suppressing the Protestant party; insomuch, that malignants have insolently expressed their confidence that her journey to France shall prove a successful counsel and that this island, and particularly this kingdom, shall have a greater power to grapple with before the next summer than any which yet we have encountered with. The Irish rebels have offered to the king to send over a greater number into both the kingdoms.[72] The hostile intentions of the King of Denmark, if God be

---

66. Gillespie is summarizing from various parts of the Solemn League and Covenant.

67. 1 John 2:19.

68. James 3:6.

69. Cf. Revelation 12:12.

70. Cf. Isaiah 59:5.

71. Cf. Isaiah 34:5–7 and Deuteronomy 32:42.

72. It is unclear if this was rumor due to Montrose's activities and boasts or if the word of the king's new focus in just the prior month in January 1645 to pursue Irish aid had leaked out or been surmised. When not enough troops from his Protestant forces in Ireland arrived, "in January 1645 the king adopted a new and more perilous scheme to get Irish aid. He gave Edward Somerset, the Earl of Glamorgan, a virtual *carte blanche* to go to Ireland and make peace with the rebels." "Even if the price included the repeal of Poynings' Law and punitive legislation against Catholics 'we shall not think it a hard bargain,' since the benefits would be even greater. By the end of March the king told his wife, 'I am confidently assured of considerable and sudden supply of men from Ireland.'" Christopher Durston, *Charles I* (1983; second edition, Routledge, 1995; digital printing, 2007), p. 280. The plan would end in failure later in the year after a copy of the first treaty Glamorgan made with the Irish was discovered and published (*The Kings cabinet opened: or, certain packets of secret letters & papers, written with the Kings own hand, and taken in his cabinet at Nasby-Field, June 14. 1645 By victorious Sr. Thomas Fairfax; wherein many mysteries of state, tending to the justification of that cause, for which*

not pleased ſtill to divert and disable him, do plainly enough appear from his own letters ſent not long since to the eſtates of this kingdom.[73] In the meantime, the hellish crew, under the conduᴄt of the excommunicated and forefaulted[74] Earl of Montrose, and of Alaſter MacDonald,[75] a papiſt and an outlaw, does exercise such barbarous, unnatural, horrid, and unheard

---

Sir Thomas Fairfax joyned battell that memorable day are clearly laid open; together, with some annotations thereupon. Published by ſpeciall order of the Parliament [London: Bostock, 1645]). *Poynings' Law*: "Under the terms of Poynings' Law, all Irish Bills had to be submitted by the English chief governor in Ireland to the King and Privy Council, via the English Parliament. There they could be amended and approved, or rejected. Only Bills approved and returned to Ireland under the Great Seal of England were presented to the Irish Parliament." Parliament.uk (accessed August 15, 2022).

73. The King of Denmark was Charles' uncle. The Scots were particularly concerned that Christian IV of Denmark not get involved and transport troops to fight on Charles's behalf (Steve Murdoch, *Scotland and the Thirty Years' War: 1618–1648* [Leiden: Brill, 2001], p. 94). Queen Henrietta Maria was active in the English Civil War and opposed any settlement of peace. She led a convoy of ships from Denmark laden with ammunition in February 1643, which successfully arrived in Oxford. On hearing of plans to capture her as a bargaining chip to force her husband's hand, she fled to France and landed at Brest on July 16, 1644. Whitelocke notes that letters from the Queen and others were recovered on February 4, 1645. Letters from Henry Jermyn and Colonel George Goring and others, spoke of a "great army from France to be ready against the Spring, to come over to the King, that Montrose and the King would join and march into the West." Bulstrode Whitelocke, *Memorials of the English Affairs* (1682), p. 197. The particular correspondence from the King of Denmark could not be identified.

74. *Forefault*: To forfeit, to deprive of rights or property, esp. as a penalty for treason (*DSL*).

75. See the preface to Gillespie's sermon before the House of Lords, pp. 136, 137. James Graham, Marquis of Montrose (1612–May 21, 1650), a royalist, had originally supported the Covenanter cause and its dual goal of reform of the church and establishment of a constitutional monarchy, which had broad support amongst the clergy, nobility and populace. He signed the renewal of the National Covenant in 1638 (I. B. Cowan, "The Covenanters: a revision article," *The Scottish Hiſtorical Review*, 47, #143, part one [Apr., 1968]: 40). He was "a front-rank Covenanter," raising money and forces for the cause (Laura A. M. Stewart, *Rethinking the Scottish Revolution: Covenanted Scotland, 1637–1651* [Oxford University Press, 2016], pp. 188–189). The subsequent agreement with England in a Solemn League and Covenant proved too much of an attack on the monarchy for royalists such as Graham. Baillie affirms there was strong opposition to the covenant with England amongst many of the nobility (Baillie, 2.102, Cowan, ibid., p. 40). Graham raised an army and did significant damage to the Covenanters' military prestige in the eyes of the English, who lost multiple battles to Montrose in Scotland. The royalist allies in Ireland sent Alasdair MacColla (Sir Alexander MacDonald, 1610–November 13, 1647) with 2000 soldiers to aid Montrose. For more on the campaigns of Montrose in Scotland see James King Hewison, *The Covenanters: A Hiſtory of the Church in Scotland from the Reformation to the Revolution*, 2 volumes, second revised and corrected edition (Glasgow: John Smith and Son, 1913), and

of cruelty, as is above expression, and (if not repressed) what better usage can others, not yet touched, expect from them, being now hardened and animated by the success which God has, for our humiliation and correction, permitted unto them? And if they shall now get leave to secure the Highlands for themselves, they will not only from thence infest the rest of this country, but endeavor a diversion of our forces in England from the prosecution of the ends expressed in the covenant of the three kingdoms, toward which ends, as their service has been already advantageous, so their continuance is most necessary.

The second sort of enemies from which our present dangers arise, are secret malignants and dis-covenanters, who may be known by these and the like characters:

—their slighting or censuring of the public resolutions of this kirk and state;

—their consulting and laboring to raise jealousies and divisions, to retard or hinder the execution of what is ordered by the public judicatories;

—their slandering of the covenant of the three kingdoms and expedition into England as not necessary for the good of religion or safety of this kingdom, or as tending to the diminution of the king's just power and greatness;

—their confounding of the king's honor and authority, with the abuse and pretence thereof, and with commissions, warrants, and letters, procured from the king by the enemies of this cause and covenant, as if we could not oppose the latter without encroaching upon the former;

—their whetting of their tongues to censure and slander those whom God has honored as His chief instruments in this work;

—their commending, justifying, or excusing the proceedings of James Graham, some time Earl of Montrose, and his complices [*accomplices*];

—their conversing or intercommuning, by word or writ with him, or other excommunicate[d] Lords, contrary to the nature of that ordinance of Christ, and to the old Acts of General Assemblies;

—their making merry, and their insolent carriage, at the news of any prosperous success of the popish and malignant armies in any of these kingdoms;

—their drawing of parties and factions to the weakening of the common union;

—their spreading of informations that uniformity in religion and the presbyterial government is not intended by the Parliament of England;

—their endeavors, informations, and solicitations tending to weaken the hearts and hands of others, and to make them withhold their assistance from this work.

Let this sort [*these sorts*] of bosom enemies and disaffected persons be well marked, timely discovered, and carefully avoided, lest they infuse the

---

John Buchan, *Montrose: A History* (Boston and New York: Houghton Mifflin Company, The Riverside Press Cambridge, 1928).

poison of their seducing counsels into the minds of others; wherein let ministers be faithful and presbyteries vigilant and unpartial [*impartial*], as they will answer the contrary to God, and to the General Assembly or their commissioners.

The cause and the dangers thereof being thus evidenced, unless men will blot out of their hearts the love of religion and the cause of God, and cast off all care of their country, laws, liberties, and estates, yea, all natural affection to the preservation of themselves, their wives, children, and friends, and whatsoever is dearest to them under the sun (all these being in the visible danger of a present ruin and destruction), they must now or never appear actively, each one stretching himself to, yea, beyond his power. It is no time to dally nor go about the business by halves, nor by almost, but altogether zealous: "Cursed be he that doth the work of the Lord negligently, or deals falsely in the covenant of God."[76] If we have been so forward to assist our neighbor kingdoms, shall we neglect to defend our own? Or shall the enemies of God be more active against His cause than His people for it? God forbid. If the work, being so far carried on, shall now miscarry and fail in our hands, our own consciences shall condemn us and posterity shall curse us; but if we stand stoutly and steadfastly to it, the pleasure of the Lord shall prosper in our hands and all generations shall call us blessed.

Let ministers stir up others by free and faithful preaching, and by admonishing every one of his duty as there shall be occasion; and if it shall be the lot of any of them to fall under the power of the enemy, let them, through the strength of Christ, persevere in their integrity, choosing affliction rather than sin,[77] glorifying God, and not fearing what flesh can do unto them.[78]

Let our armies beware of ungodliness and worldly lusts, living godly, soberly, and righteously,[79] avoiding all scandalous carriage, which may give occasion to others to think the worse of their cause and covenant; and remembering that the eyes of God, angels, and men, are upon them. Finally, renouncing all confidence in their own strength, skill, valor, and number, and trusting only to the "God of the armies of Israel,"[80] who has fought and will fight for them.

Let all sorts, both of high and low degree in this kingdom, call to mind their solemn covenants, and pay their vows to the Most High; and, namely, that article of our first covenant, which obliges us not to stay nor hinder any such resolution as by common consent shall be found to conduce for the ends of the covenant,[81] but by all lawfull means to further and promove

---

76. Cf. Jeremiah 48:10; Psalm 44:17.

77. Cf. Hebrews 11:25.

78. Cf. Psalm 56:4.

79. Cf. Titus 2:12.

80. 1 Samuel 17:45.

81. See the National Covenant in *Confession of Faith*, ibid., p. 353.

[*advance*] the same; which lies as a bond upon people's consciences, readily to obey such orders, and willingly to undergo such burdens as by the public and common resolution of the Estates of Parliament are found necessary for the prosecution of the war; considering that the enemy cannot be suppressed without a competent number of forces, and forces cannot be kept together without maintenance, and maintenance cannot be had without such public burdens, which, however, for the present not joyous but grievous,[82] yet it shall be no grief of heart afterwards, even unto the common sort, that they have given some part of their necessary livelihood for assisting so good a work. It is far from our thoughts that the pinching of some should make others superfluously to abound. It is rather to be expected of the richer sort that they will spare and defalk [*deduct; subtract*], not only the pride and superfluity both of apparel and diet, but also a part of their lawful allowance in these things, to contribute the same as a free-will offering, besides what they are obliged to by law or public order, after the example of godly Nehemiah, who, for the space of twelve years, while the walls of Jerusalem were a-building [*being built*], did not eat the bread of the governor, that he might ease by so much the people's burdens and bondage.[83]

In our last covenant there is another article, which (without the oblivion or neglect of any of the rest) we wish may be well remembered at this time, namely, that we shall assist and defend all "that enter into this League and Covenant, in the maintaining and pursuing thereof, and shall not suffer ourselves, directly or indirectly, by whatsoever combination, persuasion, or terror, to be divided and withdrawn from this blessed union and conjunction, whether to make defection to the contrary part, or to give ourselves to a detestable indifferency or neutrality in this cause,"[84] according to which article, men's reality and integrity in the covenant will be manifest and demonstrable, as well by their omissions as by their commissions; as well by their not doing good as by their doing evil. "He that is not with us is against us, and he that gathereth not with us scattereth."[85] Whoever he be that will not, according to public order and appointment, adventure his person, or send out those that are under his power, or pay the contributions imposed for the maintenance of the forces, must be taken for an enemy, malignant, and covenant-breaker, and so involved both into the displeasure of God and censures of the kirk, and no doubt into civil punishments also, to be inflicted by the state.

And if any shall prove so untoward and perfidious, their iniquity shall be upon themselves, and they "shall bear their punishment."[86] Deliverance and good success shall follow those who with purpose of heart cleave unto the

---

82. Hebrews 12:11.

83. Nehemiah 5:14.

84. Solemn League and Covenant, article 6, ibid., p. 359.

85. Cf. Matthew 12:30 and Luke 11:23.

86. Cf. Ezekiel 14:10.

Lord,[87] and whose hearts are upright toward His glory. When we look back upon the great things which God has done for us,[88] and our former deliverances out of several dangers and difficulties, which appeared to us insuperable, experience breeds hope; and when we consider how in the midst of all our sorrows and pressures, the Lord our God has given us a nail in His holy place, and has lightened our eyes[89] with the desirable and beautiful sight of His own glory in His temple, we take it for an argument that He has yet "thoughts of peace,"[90] and a purpose of mercy toward us; "though for a small moment he hath forsaken us, yet with great mercies he will gather us."[91] He has lifted up our enemies that their fall may be the greater, and that He may cast them down into desolation forever. Arise, and let us be doing;[92] "the Lord of Hosts is with us; the God of Jacob is our refuge."[93]

87. Cf. Acts 11:23.

88. Cf. Psalm 126:2, 3; 1 Samuel 12:24, etc.

89. Cf. Ezra 9:8.

90. Jeremiah 29:11.

91. Cf. Isaiah 54:7.

92. 1 Chronicles 22:16.

93. Psalm 46:7, 11.

Acts of the General Assembly
of the Church of Scotland
Edinburgh, August 1647

Preface

After Thomas Coleman's death at the end of March 1646, the sparser notes of the Westminster Assembly only record Gillespie speaking twice, once in response to Lightfoot, who briefly took up Coleman's fallen torch for Erastianism, on April 3, 1646, and once on April 9, 1646, for the proofs of the proposition of a divine right of churches to govern themselves.[1] The minutes mention him thrice more on July 30, 1646, when he presented copies of *Aaron's Rod Blossoming* to the assembly, and on December 24, 1646, about the desire of the Scots to present a paper to the Grand Committee before some of them were to depart, and then a final time in giving notice of Gillespie's own final departure on July 16, 1647.[2] It seems clear from April to July 1646 that Gillespie was involved in finishing and producing *Aaron's Rod*, but there are few specifics about what Gillespie did for the final year of his stay in London. He surely remained active at the assembly but it is unfortunate the briefer notes for the final volume of minutes record so little about him. He likely had additional occasions to preach, but it is again lamentable that the volume of sermons he collected were destroyed, which might have given some clues about this final year in London.

The next Gillespie items of interest all tie into the August 1647 meeting of the General Assembly of the Church of Scotland, for which he had again departed London in order to attend and give the latest report on the work of the Westminster divines. As with the February 1645 assembly meeting, Gillespie played a key role in some of the productions and the proceedings at this August gathering. Gillespie and Baillie, who had returned in January, both gave speeches, and in this instance Gillespie's was preserved as well as Baillie's. Baillie alludes to Gillespie and his fellow Scottish Commissioners and their work in his own speech.

My Speech in The General Assembly [at Edinburgh,] Giving Account of our Labors at London, August 6th 1647.

It is one of the Lord's promises to us that they who sow in tears shall reap in joy; that they who go out weeping and carry precious seed, shall return with rejoicing and bring their sheaves [Ps. 126:5–6]. It was the General Assembly's pleasure some four years ago to send some of us, their weak brethren and servants, to that very venerable and worthy Synod at Westminster, to sow in

---

1. *Minutes*, 4.47, 53. Lightfoot's and Gillespie's notes end in December 1644 and January 1645.

2. *Minutes*, 4.218, 376–377, 644–45.

that famous place some of the precious seed, not of our church, as enemies do slander, but of God, the Father of all light and truth. Our poor labors in that service were so blessed by the good hand of our God that, although the sowing of the seed was often accompanied with much solicitude and perplexity of mind, yea, sometimes with great grief of heart, and tears in a good measure, yet the visible appearance of a fair harvest did bring a sensible joy not only to ourselves but to many thousands more on both side [of] the seas. The last assembly wherein my present colleague and I did appear in this place, we brought with us a bundle of so goodly sheaves, as did revive the hearts of many in that very sad time. This day the Lord has sent us again to the same place, loadened [*loaded*] with more of these precious fruits, which we trust shall help to refresh all honest spirits, though otherwise exceedingly sadded [*saddened*] with the late unhappy and much unexpected occurrences.[3]

---

3. Baillie's comment here and elsewhere, as well as comments by Gillespie in his speech and in his "Declaration and Brotherly Exhortation" to England, reflect the considerably soured relation between England and Scotland at this point. In desperation Charles I had put himself in the hands of the Scottish forces in England and they were loath to give him over to the English. However, they also had not ever been paid, had had to forage the land to the grief of the locals; the Scottish forces and cause were no longer welcome in England. All sides wearied of the king's dogged intent to retain his divine right episcopacy under every negotiation attempt, and finally the Scots gave up the king on February 3, 1647 in order to receive a partial payment, and marched out of England. With the departure of the Scottish forces there was very little the Scots could do to influence events and the radicals of the New Model Army and amongst the Sects and Independent factions, were doing all they could to malign the Scots and Presbyterianism. "The hue and cry which followed the surrender—The traitor Scot Sold his king for a groat'—was a political libel intended to intensify the English hatred of Presbyterianism, and to mitigate the odium resting on the southern regicides." James King Hewison, *The Covenanters* (1913), 1.441. John Willcock further explains: "The circumstances attending the departure of the Scotch army from England augured ill for the prospect of peaceable relations being maintained between the two countries.... The alliance from which so much had been hoped had proved abortive. The uniformity in religion, which the people of Scotland had had in view in concluding that alliance, had not been secured, and there seemed but little hope that it would be eventually established. In the meantime their troops had been paid off very much as if they had been hired fighters whose services were no longer needed, and whose claim to have a voice in the further settlement of affairs was both absurd and offensive. The last of the soldiers who left Newcastle for their homes in the north heard as their parting greetings insults and taunts in which they were described 'as nothing but Jews, people who had sold their King and their honour;' and we are told that 'the English officers had considerable trouble, with blows and threats, to prevent the women of the town from following the Scottish troops and throwing stones at them while they were leaving it.'" John Willcock, *Life and Times of Archibald, 8th Earl, and 1st (and only) Marquess of Argyll (1607–1661)* (Edinburgh and London: Oliphant Anderson & Ferrier, 1903), p. 201. Also at this time the House of

Right Honorable and Reverend, you remember that all your ecclesiastic desires from your brethren of England, that all the commissions and instructions laid upon us your servants, were only for the obtaining of uniformity in four particulars,—in the Worship of God, in the Government of the Church, in a Confession of Faith, and Catechism. For the first, the Directory we presented in the forenamed assembly gave good and ample satisfaction. It was then your pleasure to cause both of us [to] return for the assistance of our other colleagues in pressing your three remnant desires. As for the Government of the Church, the goodness of our God gave us to obtain not only these initial propositions, whereof at our last appearance we gave an account to the good liking of all then present, but also a full and perfect model of discipline, which by the blessing of God may make in a short time the churches in the three kingdoms in all considerable parts of government, not only uniform, but well near one, as you may see when you shall think it convenient to take that model of discipline into consideration.

In your third desire, the Lord made our success no less prosperous; a large Confession of Faith is perfyted [*perfected*] with far greater unanimity than any living could have hoped for, among so many learned divines, in so distempered a place and distracted a season. I am confident if the judgment of many my wiser do not deceive, this piece of work is so fine and excellent, that whenever you shall be pleased to look upon it, the sight of it shall draw from the most censorious eye a good acceptation.

For your fourth and last desire, the catechism, my reverend colleague, I know, is instructed to give satisfaction therein. I stayed till some good progress was made into it, but long three years and sundry odd months peregrination from my country, and absence from my particular charge, wakened, I confess, in me a great languor to return; yea, all of us fell very desirous to be at home, and jointly did press the Commission of the Kirk for a liberty. At last, it was their favor to permit to ourselves the permission of someone, by the providence of God, and equity of the brethren there, the lot fell upon me. I was glad to be a carrier of a Confession of Faith; also of a Psalter, which

---

Commons had a discontented New Model Army on its hands, which refused to disband at the end of the first English Civil War. The parliament had been as remiss in paying its own army as it had been in paying the Scottish forces and the army was dissatisfied at the slow pace in reaching a settlement with Charles I. It also displeased them to hear parliament and the City of London were attempting to raise and pay a new army while not paying what was owed the New Model Army, which began a slow march to London. Presbyterians attempted to wrest control of parliament and the Westminster Assembly offered to mediate between the factions and the army (*Minutes*, 5.331). However, the New Model Army occupied London on August 6, 1647, and restored the Independent faction to power. On June 4, 1647, the army had issued its grievances it wished to be met, which Gillespie references as being of concern in his exhortation to the English.

to my knowledge had coſt the Assembly some considerable pains, and is like to be one necessar [*necessary*] part of the three kingdoms' uniformity. I brought likewise a good assurance of a perfect catechism to follow with all convenient diligence. This message made me, in January laſt, to obtain from the Commission of the Kirk that welcome which is my earneſt desire may in due time be ratified and approven by this venerable assembly; for after the approbation of God and teſtimony of conscience, their allowance of my mean endeavors is that which I wish; not as a reward for some labors and dangers I know I have undergone in your service, but as an encouragement to return with cheerfulness to my private charge, after so long a diversion. This is all I desire for myself, which, if I may obtain, I shall be desirous to be thankful to God and your reverences.

For my colleagues, may I make bold, with permission, to offer some few of my thoughts. That glorious soul of blessed memory,[4] who now is crowned with the reward of all his labors for God and for us, I wish his remembrance may be fragrant among us, so long as free and pure assemblies remain in this land, which we hope shall be to the coming of our Lord. You know he ſpent his ſtrength and wore out his days; he breathed out his life in the service of God and of this church. This binds it on our back, as we would not prove ungrate [*ungrateful*] to pay him his due. If the thoughts of others be conform to my inmoſt sense, in duty and reason he ought to be accounted by us and the poſterity the faireſt ornament after John Knox of incomparable memory that ever the Church of Scotland did enjoy. For my other colleague,[5] who yet remains in the place of our long toil, my desire is that this reverend meeting may not forget him, but, according to his very great worth and deservings, may take him to their wise consideration.

For my present moſt dear brother,[6] all I now entreat is that he may find in this place such an open ear and ready attention as ordinarily [*commonly*], I know, he had in the English Assembly, where, indeed, no man was wont to find a greater attention and audience. I hope the Lord shall enable him to give you so clear an account of the true eſtate of affaires, whereof, since my departure, he has been an eye and ear witness, as shall make it visible and palpable to all that we have no reason to repent of any of the labors of our love towards our neighbor church and kingdom; that the great work we do intend there is so well-grounded, and so far advanced among them, that the ports of hell, and the greateſt power of man, shall never be able to overturn it; yea, that the present ſtorm, how terrible soever, which the prime inſtruments of Satan this day on earth, and our greateſt adversaries, the sectaries, have raised, shall, by the goodness, wisdom, and power of God, be

---

4. Alexander Henderson had died a year earlier, August 16, 1646.

5. Samuel Rutherford was then the remaining Scottish divine at the Westminster assembly.

6. George Gillespie.

turned over as the unreasonable rage and folly of the prelates lately was, to be a happy means of hastening the accomplishment of all our desires. I am very hopeful that the present earthquake, though it shake the foundation, and threaten the swallowing up of both church and state, yet it shall prove a near antecedent to the settling of all the three kingdoms and the churches in them, in that peace and happiness which some cannot believe till they see and feel it.

It is my heart's wish, with which now I close, that the hands of our church and state, which God has made very instrumental in the laying the ground and helping up every part of the wall of this exceeding great and glorious work, may not now be deficient in the end, when the top-stone alone is to be laid, and deficient we must needs be if ever we open a door to the devil of division to enter in, especially among us of the ministry. This evil is so great and destructive, that the fears of it in zealous brethren, though never so causeless, are very pardonable. It has often been my great comfort since my return, that, when I have searched so far as my mean knowledge can reach, I could find no real ground at all for division in our church as yet. It ought to be all our prayers that long it may so continue, for the old serpent is lying at all our doors; but the man with whom he shall first prevail to make himself a ringleader, upon whatsoever cause, to divide and trouble the Kirk of Scotland, let me speak prophecy unto him: Were he this day of never so high a price, and great fragrancy among us, yet he shall become a cursed soul, and his memory shall stink to all generations. But trusting that our God will avert this, and all other mischiefs from us, I give place to that large and comfortable accompt [*account*] which we expect from my Reverend Brother. Finis.

In addition to Gillespie's speech, we know from Baillie that he was solely responsible for a declaration passed without objection entitled, "A Declaration and Brotherly Exhortation of the General Assembly of the Church of Scotland to their Brethren of England." We also learn from the same letter to William Spang, that Gillespie's famous *111 Propositions* were prepared while he was still in London, and that he had undertaken them at the request of Gisbertus Voetius. They were formally laid before the assembly for approval. It is not clear what prompted Voetius's request, but it may be this was in response to having received a copy of Gillespie's *Aaron's Rod*. Baillie writes,

We agreed, *nemine contradicente*, to that declaration, which was committed to Mr. Gillespie and me, but was drawn by him alone; also, after much debate in the committee, to the confession of faith and to the printing of the directory for government, for the examination of the next general assembly; of the catechise [catechism] also, when the little that remains shall come down; likewise for printing, to that same end, two or three sheet[s] of Theses against Erastianism, committed to Mr. Gillespie and me, but done by him at London, at Voetius's motion; which we mind, when approven here, to send to him; who is hopeful to get the consent of your universities, and of the General Assembly of France to them, which may serve for good purpose....[7]

While it is likely these propositions would not have taken Gillespie more than a few days to draft, it is good to learn of something he put his hand to work on in his last year at the Westminster Assembly in London. We also learn from Voetius of a couple of objections or qualifications he had to the *111 Propositions*, and at the same time he thoughtfully preserved the letter written to him by George Gillespie. Written in Latin months after the August assembly,[8] it is a pleasure to present this letter in English translation for these collected shorter writings. In the section in question, Voetius is discussing the question (Problem II),[9] "Does the church have its own polity and intrinsic government, and is this necessary; or rather, where the magistrate is the nursing father of the church, does their extrinsic government in and about the church alone suffice?" After giving reasons for affirming the first and denying the second, Voetius lists resources "on the utility and necessity of polity," at the end of which he adduces the correspondence with Gillespie.

III PROPOSITIONS & GEORGE GILLESPIE'S LETTER TO GISBERTUS VOETIUS

It will not be unsuitable for me to insert here the approbation, written by our theological faculty at the request of the brethren in Scotland, of the III theorems in which, with the assent of the National Synod of Scotland, the most renowned divine of Edinburgh, George Gillespie, had learnedly delineated the necessity, distinction, and form of the government and discipline of the churches. The formula of approbation, drawn up then by me in the name of our faculty, reads thus:

"Inasmuch as it seemed good to the reverend and most learned divine Dr. George Gillespie to share with brotherly affection with our faculty in this Academy of Utrecht III *Theorems on Church Ministry and Government* (printed in Edinburgh by Evan Taylor, 1647), and to seek our judgment in regard to them, we could not refuse this fulfillment, however small, of our duty to this our reverend brother. Therefore, having read and duly weighed them all, we give our declaration and assessment that in the aforementioned theorems the controversy on church ministry and government has been determined in a manner learned and agreeable to the Holy Scripture, as well as to the common doctrine and discipline of our churches in the Netherlands.

---

7. Baillie, 3.20–21.

8. The months delay in writing Voetius was likely because Gillespie and his family took some time to settle into his return to pastoral work in Edinburgh (see p. 441).

9. Translated by Michael Spangler from the text in Gisbertus Voetius, *Politica Ecclesiastica*, Pars I, Lib. I, Tract. II, Cap. VII, §5 (Amsterdam: Wæsberge, 1663), pp. 246–249.

"However, we candidly advise that it seems to us that out of an abundance of caution, in Theorem 3 a fuller explanation thus should be made of the assertion regarding *sending* or *ordination*, leſt that be thought, as something diſtinct from *election*, to be absolutely or simply necessary to the essence or accounting of a legitimate calling. Besides this, in Theorem 76 should be added a treatment addressing in what manner and to what extent the power of the church, whether proper or direct, or analogical and indirect, is or is not occupied with the church's incomplete members (so to ſpeak), that is, those baptized in infancy, and all other catechumens, indeed also any that are auditors. Laſtly, in Theorem 7 and 75, limits should be drawn so that the whole body of the people, as diſtinct from the consiſtory, may not be excluded absolutely from all participation in church power, in regard to its possession and its use, in every circumſtance and case. For this matter has been explained otherwise by us (with all due reſpect to their judgment) from the Scriptures and the consensus of the ancients, and has been observed otherwise throughout the Dutch churches, as our previously published writings and diſputations manifeſt.

"Utrecht, April 4, 1648. Subscribed by: Gisbertus Voetius, Carolus de Mæts, Johannes Hoornbeeck."

The letter by which Dr. Gilleſpie sought the approbation of our faculty reads thus:

"Reverend and moſt renowned man, brother in the Lord (who is the moſt greatly to be honored),

"I received your letter sent April 8, 1647, and I rejoice within me fervently, firſt at your singular humanity which would receive so small a gift so favorably,[10] then at your diſtinguished teſtimony and support againſt Eraſtianism, which your moſt learned letter showed me. But now I would beg leave to trouble you about another matter, inasmuch as it was you who counseled and encouraged me to think of it: affairs have so progressed that it seemed good to our recent National Synod to bear a public teſtimony againſt the moſt dangerous and deſtructive errors of Eraſtianism, Independency, and liberty of conscience (be it falsely so-called, for we would much more fittingly give it the name of license). As these three in our present age have become the moſt severe impediments, and nearly the sole hindrances, to eſtablishing religion in our Isle in accordance with the Word of God and the example of the churches that are moſt reformed, accordingly if they should ſtrike deeper root in England, it can hardly happen otherwise than that from thence as time goes on the other reformed churches, even those across the sea, muſt risk a lethal wound, and be caſt into a moſt dangerous crisis. For if it happen not (though

---

10. It is possible that Gillespie had sent a copy to Voetius of *Aaron's Rod Blossoming.*

the Lord has promised that it will) that when the enemy rush on as a river, the Spirit of Jehovah run against him, the baleful influence of such errors as they pour themselves forth far and wide cannot but in a short time reach to other reformed churches. All the rest of the reformed churches are cut down and wounded through this attack upon our flank; nor does this only happen thus obliquely, but by open warfare also is assailed, with most determined zeal, the government of all reformed churches everywhere.

"Besides this, not a few things which are taught openly in the reformed churches' confessions of faith are reprehended, censured, and condemned by these sectarians, for against them they do daily speak, and snarl in public; indeed, against the received truth they often itch to write, and publish pasquinades, haughtily claiming as their own prerogative nothing less than the changing of the times, and (since they strive after novelties) the abrogation of the most well-approved laws, in addition holding each and every reformed church to be not reformed, indeed deformed, and also (horrible to say) labeling Christ's churches with the byname 'Antichristian.' Meanwhile, they who will not give their names to support any of these sects are treated in the most shameful ways. Yet upright and prudent men judge it better to wage war with the sects, be there a thousand of them, than to give their hand to covenant-breaking, treacherous sworn enemies of catholic and Christian truth.

"Wherefore, lest this evil creep more broadly (if it could), lest this gangrene of error pour out and propagate itself further, and lest this pestilent contagion spread, these Theses now sent to you were prepared, and were ratified by the decree of the National Synod (which is sent to you together with the Theorems) as regards the heads themselves of the doctrine contained in them, about which express and individual mention is made in the Synod's decree itself. They put off and deferred a more full and thorough, a more exact and careful approbation of the Theses until the next National Synod, to be held in July of this year just begun (that is, 1648), God willing.

"At which time, they determined that[11] together with the approbatory judgments of our country's four theological faculties (to which the matter was most excellently committed and entrusted),[12] the assenting vote of your own most honored Academy should be added to these theorems, in a manner timely enough that it may be brought out and brought forth before that National Synod.

"I trust that the result of this matter, by God's blessing, will be abundant and fruitful, namely for the more sure establishing of that so necessary part

---

11. *Quo tempore hi* …. Something is missing in the sentence, in both printed editions, and the addition of the verb "determined" seemed the best of the possible emendations.

12. Four theological faculties: St. Andrews, Edinburgh, Glasgow, and Aberdeen.

of Christian doctrine, and its more firm corroboration by the harmonious consent and holy unanimity of so many and such weighty orthodox and most learned men in diverse kingdoms and republics. Hence also, this most agreeable outcome will be able, in God's kindness (for all is not yet lost in this affair), to obtain that not a few who now think opposite could be by such a great concourse of minds persuaded to embrace catholic and orthodox truth.

"For which cause, by the eloquent advice and prompting of not a few prudent and learned brethren, I humbly offer you these Theses, that you might examine them, seeking and beseeching eagerly that these Theorems, to the extent and degree that they be approved by you as in agreement with the Word of God and useful for the church's edification, may not lack your testimony and support, whereby they may be confirmed in others' judgment.

"These things are what I had to communicate and commend to you, most learned man, and what I would see effected and accomplished by your help. May God grant that our brethren also across the sea, being stirred up by our troubles as if by their own, and weighing earnestly the woeful and lamentable condition of affairs in England, grieving at the wounded and imperiled British covenant,[13] may be ready at all such opportunities (as I assure myself with certainty) to give timely help, and to run willingly to quench this universal conflagration, that at the least they may deliver their own souls, and enjoy this most sweet comfort: we did what we could, for we did not shun bearing even public testimony against the spreading errors of our time.

"I am persuaded that the end of all this turmoil will be happier than the beginning seems to promise. God will be favorable to us, if we flee with sincere hearts to Him for refuge, nor will He let such great contempt of His own name and covenant go unavenged for long.

"I wish upon you, with your most learned colleagues, most full health. May God most richly bless you all, and your studies and endeavors. R. T.[14]

"Most devoted in all service, George Gillespie

"Written in Edinburgh, January 31, 1648."

---

13. The news of the agreement between Charles I and some of the Scottish leadership known as The Engagement had become known and the English Parliament voted to cut off negotiations with the king on January 18, 1648. The agreement essentially meant the two countries which had been bound by a mutual covenant, would be at war if Scottish forces entered England on essentially a mission to rescue the king from the English.

14. It is not certain whether "R.T." stands for some unusual Latin phrase in closing, possibly the initials of a secretary who penned the letter for Gillespie, or what exactly is the significance of its placement here.

> The superscription was: "To the reverend and most renowned man, Doctor of Divinity Gisbertus Voetius, Professor of Most Holy Theology in the Academy of Utrecht, and most vigilant pastor there."

Hetherington writes of these propositions: "The celebrated Hundred and Eleven Propositions were prepared before he left London, and laid before the General Assembly on his return to Scotland in the summer of 1647. Perhaps it is not possible to obtain a clear conception of Erastianism better than by the study of these propositions."[15] The propositions received tentative approval at the August 1647 assembly, but the assembly deferred final approval till after the four universities had examined them. The assemblies of 1648 and 1649 did not address the issue again and after Cromwell's conquest there was not an assembly again until 1690.

It is in the seventh and seventy-fifth propositions to which Voetius objected above, that we see a change from the view Gillespie articulated in his *Dispute Against the English Popish Ceremonies*, and which Dr. Van Dixhoorn identifies as the third of five building blocks of Gillespie's ecclesiology, which he held rather consistently in his publications for most of his short life. The third element of that ecclesiology was that "Christ has delivered to the whole church, including local congregations, the keys of the kingdom, both doctrine and discipline."[16] He goes on to note that the *111 Propositions* are "contrary to his publications prior to 1647," in which "Gillespie, without qualification, appears to source the power of church government in the officers of the church [alone] rather than in the membership and eldership of the church jointly."[17] This apparent change was noted in a footnote by James Bannerman in his classic work on presbyterianism,

---

15. Memoir by W. M. Hetherington, in *The Shorter Writings of George Gillespie*, vol. 1, p 43.

16. Chad Van Dixhoorn, "Presbyterian ecclesiologies at the Westminster assembly," in *Church Polity and Politics in the British Atlantic World, c. 1635–66* (Manchester University Press, 2020), ebook, location 3309.

17. Hunter Powell claims this change was made as early as 1641, but Van Dixhoorn writes that weighty evidence points to a late change. See Van Dixhoorn, ibid. See Hunter Powell, *The Crisis of British Protestantism: Church Power in the Puritan Revolution, 1638–44* (Manchester University Press, 2015), pp. 47–49, 194. There was significant opposition among the Scots Presbyterians, such as David Calderwood, against the sectarianism and congregationalism coming out of England. Calderwood had already early on in May of 1644 written the commissioners at the Westminster Assembly and chastised them for concessions too close to congregationalism and had an ongoing dispute with Gillespie over the latter's view of excommunication (Baillie, 2.182; see Powell, p. 112, 215–216). In this very same August 1647 assembly were passed the directions for family worship penned by Robert Blair, which cracked down on multiple families gathering together for family worship, so concerned was the church for any hint of independent conventicles arising, even though such had been used profitably in Ireland by men such as John Livingstone and Robert Blair himself. It may be the case that the strong opposition to anything smacking of congregationalism within the kirk

Gillespie, in his masterly work, *A Dispute against the English Popish Ceremonies*, first published in 1637, maintains the view stated above,—namely, that both the office-bearers and the members of the Church are alike the proper and primary subject of Church power, although in different ways and for different ends (p. 166, in *Presbyt. Arm.* vol. i.).[18] After witnessing, however, along with Rutherford and Baillie, the state of matters in England at the time of the Westminster Assembly, he seems, to a certain extent, to have shared with them in their strong recoil from the ecclesiastical democracy of the Independents. In his *CXI. Propositions concerning Church Government*, Gillespie makes statements somewhat inconsistent with his own former position (Prop. 7 and 75); although it might perhaps be held doubtful, from the wording of the first of the Propositions referred to, whether it is not only the exercise of Church power in all ordinary circumstances which he restricts so decidedly to the ministers and elders of the Church. These CXI. Propositions were not sanctioned immediately by the General Assembly of our Church to which they were submitted, from lack of time fully to consider them. They were referred for judgment to the Theological Faculties of the four Scottish Universities, and were also sent abroad for the consideration of foreign Churches. And Voetius, in the name of the Theological Faculty of Utrecht, while bestowing high praise on the learning, ability, and soundness in the faith evinced by the author of [the] Propositions, put his finger at once on the 7th and the 75th. "There ought," he said, "to be some limitation put on these two theorems, lest the whole body of the people, as distinct from the consistory of office-bearers, should seem to be excluded absolutely, and under all circumstances whatsoever, from any share of Church power, both as regards the possession and the use of it." Voetius, *Pol. Eccles.*, tom. i., lib. i., tract. ii., cap. v., Qu. 11-33, where his correspondence with Gillespie is given.[19]

It is a pity Gillespie died so young or we may have had more from his pen reconciling the differences of this apparent change in view regarding "to whom Christ, as Head of the Church, has committed, in the first instance, the gift of ecclesiastical power, and in whom the right to such power primarily resides."[20] He surely would have also interacted with Voetius's concerns.

---

had influenced Gillespie as much as his experiences in London, at least as far as the form of Propositions 7 and 75. "He [Calderwood], and others of his acquaintance, came with resolution to make great din about privy meetings and novations, being persuaded, and willing to persuade others, that our church was already much pestered with schism. My mind was clean contrary, and now, when we have tried all to the bottom, they are found to be much more mistaken than I; for they have obtained, with the hearty consent of these men whom they counted greatest patrons of schism, all the acts they pleased against that evil, wherein the wisdom and authority of Mr. Blair has been exceeding serviceable." Baillie, 3.20.

18. See Gillespie, *Dispute* (2013), pp. 325–326.

19. James Bannerman, *The Church of Christ*, 2 vols. (1868), 1.274, note.

20. Bannerman, 1.262.

However, at the point that he wrote Voetius at the end of January 1648, Gillespie had less than a year left of his earthly pilgrimage. Just the month before, a royalist faction had agreed to rescue Charles I and restore him to rule without any significant concessions, and Gillespie would be called upon to use up his remaining strength in several more services to the Church of Scotland opposing The Engagement.

The Speech of George Gillespie
Before the General Assembly of the
Church of Scotland,
Meeting at Edinburgh, August 1645

Zechariah 4:10

For who hath despised the day of small things? for they shall rejoice, and shall see the plummet in the hand of Zerubbabel with those seven; they are the eyes of the LORD, which run to and fro through the whole earth.

"Mr. George Gillespie's Speech in the General Assembly at Edinburgh, 6TH August 1647." Wodrow MSS, 4to, Vol. XXVI., No. 12.

EDITIONS

1. Published in *The Letters and Journals of Robert Baillie, 1637–1662*, Volume 3, edited by David Laing (Edinburgh: Alex Laurie & Co., 1842), pp. 450–454.

The Epigraph on the previous page has been added for this volume.

Mr. George Gillespie's Speech

in the General Assembly at Edinburgh,

August 6, 1647

[Moderator.]

Sir, I have been long desirous to return here, that I might as wait upon my particular charge, so also give a further account to this honorable and learned assembly of our employments with the Assembly of Divines at London. I speak ingenuously, the Lord knows, that I was altogether insufficient for so great a work, and such an employment. My colleagues indeed, have been both painful and successful. Only this I would desire to profess, that with some uprightness of heart I have studied to lay hold on occasions of promoving [*advancing*] the work of God there, and the service of His church in this land. Neither have our labors been altogether without success, which we ascrive [*ascribe*] wholly to the blessing of God, and therefore desire that as prayers have been made to God in behalf of our commissioners and that assembly of divines, so thanks may be given in behalf of both for their good success and peaceable setting about the work wherein the Lord has employed them.

You know we have acted in a double capacity according to our commission. We have gone on in a way of treating with the Committee of Parliaments and Divines jointly, and have given in many papers, as concerning the officers of the kirk excluding scandalous persons from the kirk sacrament, the growth of heresies, and such things, as in your judgment and ours, was defective among them. We have acted in another capacity, debating with and assisting the Assembly of Divines, their debates. Much of their time has been taken up with the trial of ministers, for presbyteries not being established in that land, ministers to be admitted in several places behooved to be tried by them; yet the heads of our commission have been carried on to no small measure of perfection.

The Confession of Faith is framed, so as it is of great use against the floods of heresies and errors that overflow that land. Nay, their intention of framing of it was to meet with all the considerable errors of the present time: the Socinian, Arminian, popish, antinomian, Anabaptistian, Independent errors, etc. The Confession of Faith sets them out and refutes them, so far as belongs to a confession. This Confession of Faith has been, to my knowledge, very much commended of them that had occasion to see it, even by some of the prelatical party too. It is not yet fully approven by the Houses of Parliament. The House of Lords have approved it; the House of Commons

361

have approved the first chapter of it, and was going on in consideration of the rest of it at that time when they were taken off by the late commotion there and emergent differences.[1]

For the next head of our commission, you know the Directory for Worship is settled long ago by the parliaments of both kingdoms. I confess it is not yet observed by all there so as it ought, yet it is observed by many to the great good of that land. We shall only add to that head, the matter of the Psalms; all grant that there is a necessity of the change of the old paraphrase. This new paraphrase was done by a gentleman very able for the purpose,[2] but afterward it was revised by a committee of the Assembly of Divines according to the original, and was approven by the whole Assembly. The House of Commons has given it a full approbation. The House of Lords has not as yet, many desiring and pressing other paraphrases also to be made use of in congregations, if they please.[3] All the animadversions sent by you were taken in due consideration. There are also here some new amendments made by the gentleman himself. Here is the book, the perfect copy and *ultima cura* of it.[4]

The third head was church government, which, as it was the most controverted of the rest, so it has suffered maniest obstructions. There was a practical directory for church government drawn forth without scriptural propositions, but because some thought a model of church government could not be framed, which were *Jure Divino*, there was another directory for government drawn up in propositions with Scriptural truths, proving the same. Here they are both.[5]

Now, in relation to this head of church government, there was a Committee of the Assembly and Parliament appointed to see if the Dissenting Brethren might been drawn to agree upon a common rule, according to the Word of God, peace of the Kirk, and the Covenant. There was some hopes of an Accommodation,[6] but because of some difficulties, especially for that they would have had a liberty of gathering their separate churches out of

---

1. See the note on page 349.

2. The Assembly used as the basis of their work the paraphrase of the psalms by Francis Rous. "A stepbrother and colleague of John Pym and ardent supporter of presbyterianism until 1649, Rous is the most frequent assembly speaker from the Commons...." *Minutes*, 1.134.

3. See *Minutes*, 5.259–261, 303.

4. Gillespie likely had in hand a copy of the edition printed in London circa February 10 to 16, 1647 with subsequent changes made by hand by Rouse. The assembly itself declared itself done with the work on the Psalter in November 1645. See the account in document 94, *Minutes*, 5.259.

5. See the discussion of documents 45, 58 and 77 in *Minutes*, 5.127, 168, and 204. The directory with scripture proofs was published in Scotland after this August meeting, sometime before November 1, 1647. *Concerning Church-Government and Ordination of Ministers* (Edinburgh: Evan Tyler, 1647).

6. See herein pages 56, 133, 138, 139, and *Grand Debate* (2015), pp. 305ff.

others already constitute[d], upon this it brake [*broke*] up. Only a new motion was made of it for establishing that Committee of Accommodation before I came away, and their differences are yet lasting, and their ways, as I conceive, inconsistent.[7]

Now, the erecting of presbyterial government has been opposed by diverse parties. First, By these that deny all governments. These are Erastians. Secondly, By these that would have another form of government than the presbyterial; of those some have studied to get in a moderate prelacy, and a model of that sort has been put in the hands of some parliament men, as I have seen. Others labor mightily for Independency. Third, It has been obstructed and received many wounds by those that would have a church government framed in a prudential way by the wisdom of the state, and limited as they shall think meet, as the parliament has studied to do in the point of suspension from the sacrament. They have made a great deal of restrictions in that business, which the Assembly and godly ministry there dare not condescend to in conscience; whereupon the Assembly, sticking to that that they conceive agreeable to the truth, they presented a Petition accordingly. The Petition was casten [*cast away*], being conceived a breach of privilege.[8] Among other incongruities, they [*parliament*] urged a double number of ruling elders, at least to that of ministers, and if they please, four times more, so that all what ministers do say may be made null by the major part of ruling elders. To this we gave in our reasons to the contrary. It was upon the occasion of this prudential model that the Nine Queries were sent to the Assembly by the House of Commons, that the Assembly might be put to it for a particular model of church government, which was expected by many they could never do it, and so this might be a ground to go on in their intended prudential way. These Nine Queries, as I am very confident they may have a full and satisfactory answer from Scripture, so I believe they (would) have gotten ere now, were it not the Assembly had been necessarily diverted by other things, put in their hands by the Parliament.[9] There is a fourth impediment that did hinder much the presbyterial government, because there be many that would be content of it, so being it were with Liberty of Conscience that, if they pleased, they might come under it, otherways not. This is become a common plea, not only to sectaries, but also to the prelatical party. Doctor Taylor, the king's chaplain, has written a large book for the defense of Liberty of Conscience.[10]

---

7. This committee for accommodation is not noted in the assembly minutes.

8. See the preface to the House of Lords Sermon, pp. 146, 147. For greater background, see John R. de Witt, *Jus Divinum: The Westminster Assembly and the Divine Right of Church Government*, pp. 169–208. See *Jus Divinum Regiminis Ecclesiastici, or, the Divine Right of Church Government*, NPSE volume ii (Naphtali Press and RHB, 2019), pp. 14ff.

9. See *Minutes*, 1.[214]–216, 5.300–302. See *Jus Divinum Regiminis Ecclesiastici*, NPSE volume ii (2020), pp. 14–17.

10. Jeremy Taylor, Θεολογια εκλεκτικη *a discourse of the liberty of prophesying: shewing the*

The last head of our commission was the catechism. The framing of this the Assembly have been very laborious in, and have found great difficulty how to make it full, such as might be expected from an Assembly, and, upon the other part, how to condescend to the capacity of the common and unlearned. Therefore, they are a-making two distinct catechisms, a short and plain one for these, and a larger one for those of understanding. They have had no time yet to do anything in the latter [*sic* former], but here is the copy of the greater, which is almost complete.

Now, to add to these particulars the dangers threatening religion, as affairs now stand, which are very great, and though the wisdom of this assembly can very well judge of them without great information, yet, since you are pleased to desire an accompt [*account*] of affairs there, I shall shortly express what we conceive to be the greatest dangers hindering the advancement of the desired reformation in that land, and these we conceive are growing greater, when we were in expectation they were growing less than before. The disease was in the body; now it is broken forth in the spirits before the gross humors were purged away, and so the danger is double. There is a conjunction of interests among those that have been averse from the covenant, and those that have been aiming [at] a reformation of religion hitherto, the prelatical party and Independent. There is a great deal of endeavor used to unite them, although, I believe, that by this time they see that their interests and principles are inconsistible [*unable to agree*].

2. A second danger there is, which needs must be great, because there is a recidivation [*relapse*] which is worse than the first disease; that which has been built up is now a-casting down, and that which has been a-casting down is a-building up. The Service Book,[11] which we thought had been buried, is now allowed at court [*at the king's residence*], and the sequestrat[ed] ministers are by this means animated to intrude themselves in their former places, and sundry are received.

3. Before, our difference was with the prelates and sectaries, so much as we knew only concerning church government, scarce imagining other differences; but now they are grown to that, that there is not an article of the Christian Faith but it is controverted; and some have drunk in that principle, the more fundamental the point denied or controverted, the more it ought to be tolerated, because being the more remote from sense and reason, and so the deniers or affirmers of it ought the less to be controlled.

4. As the Solemn League and Covenant was justly conceived to be a sovereign remedy against the former evils, so when that is cast aside, it must make the dangers the more and greater. Many refuse to subscrive [*subscribe*] that League and Covenant, and it is no wonder, seeing it has not a civil

---

unreasonablenes of prescribing to other mens faith, and the iniquity of persecuting differing opinions (London: R. Royston, 1647). Thomason purchased a copy on June 28, 1647.

11. This refers to the liturgy known as Laud's service book, the imposition of which, among other things, sparked the Second Reformation in Scotland.

sanction urging it upon the people. The king has not agreed to it. The Parliament, though it has enjoined the subscription of it in all the kingdom, yet there is no penalty charged upon the not-subscrivers [*nonsubscribers*] of it; and so by many is not only slighted, but also it is written against, of late, by the whole University of Oxford, which has not as yet gotten an answer, but I hope it shall shortly.[12]

5. The present commotions there make the cause to be in a great hazard. Now there is a division between them that have taken the covenant, as there was formerly between them that took it and them that took it not. As for the army, it is true they do profess in their public papers that it is not their intention to oppose presbyterial government. They take God to witness their intention is not against the covenant. What is the *intentio mentis* we know not, or the *intentio operantis*, but *intentio operis* looks far otherways. Nevertheless of the forementioned dangers, yet, on the other part, there is hope in Israel concerning this thing. We want not our grounds of encouragement for hoping better things.

1. The hand of God that has done very great things for us already, gives us strong hope to believe that He will do great things still; and I have heard many godly both ministers and people there say that if the Kirk of Scotland, which has had so many great proofs of an Almighty hand working for them, should distrust the thorow-bearing [*support*] of this work, their sin were greater than of any others. Now, as God's honor is engaged in it, so has He given many hearts to pray for the carrying on of the work, and, to my certain knowledge, assuredly to believe the full satisfaction of their prayers, and a happy closure of the work.

2. Next, we have grounds of confidence from the petitions of many, especially of London. You may understand very well the hearts of many by the petitions that have been occasionally from time to time published.

3. There is hope from that that is put in execution already. You know there is no government owned by the parliament but the presbyterial; although they have not come up so far as the Assembly of Divines have holden forth to them, yet that is the only government owned by them, and is put in execution in sundry places in England. They have classical congregations, presbyteries, and synods in London; and elsewhere there are beginnings. There is a parochial eldership in Yarmouth and other some in Suffolk. They have received appeals from parochial elderships, as the superior judicatory from the inferior. There is so much done as is more than a day of small things [Zech. 4:10], so much as we would have greatly accounted of, if we might have hoped for it ten years ago, when we were a-coming out of Egypt.

4. There is encouragement to us from the great discovery of the ways of sectaries. Many who by their being very plausible gained ground before, are

---

12. *Reasons of the present judgement of the University of Oxford, concerning the Solemn league and covenant, the negative oath, the ordinances concerning discipline and worship. Approved by generall consent in a full convocation, 1 Jun. 1647* (1647).

now down in the opinions of many, and their army, though now they prosper very much, yet have lost very many of their friends by their carriage of late, being fully persuaded their ways are not of God.

5. From the Assembly of Divines: God has blessed that assembly very much, and they do resolve that whatsoever others shall do, or whatever dangers or fears shall arise, that they shall not suffer themselves to be led away from the prosecution of that Solemn Covenant, and the ends of it; that they will adhere to that confession of faith, directory of government and worship, which, according to the written word, they have resolved upon.

And truly, Sir, they have desired me to assure this assembly of their solid resolution of adhering to presbyterial government, and the other ends of our commission from this church. I speak with warrant from the Prolocutor of the Assembly, as is clear in this paper, which, for my memory's sake in the premises, I have here, being subscribed by the Prolocutor and the Clerk; and withal, their desire was to make their excuse for their not giving answer to diverse letters from the parliament and Assembly of Scotland; for that they being only assembled for giving advice by the parliament, not being a national assembly as you are, they were loath to interrupt the parliament, whose warrant they behooved to procure, the parliament being now otherways most seriously employed. I shall only add, friends in England do bless God for this assembly's writing at such a seasonable time, and expects so much shall come forth from you as shall refresh their saddened hearts, and advance the opposed work of reformation.

A Declaration and Brotherly Exhortation of
The General Assembly of the Church of Scotland,
Met at Edinburgh, August 20, 1647
To their Brethren of England

Psalm 44:17

All this is come upon us; yet have we not forgotten thee,
neither have we dealt falsely in thy covenant.

A Declaration and Brotherly Exhortation of the General Assembly of the Church of Scotland to their Brethren of England.

EDITIONS

1. *A Declaration and Brotherly Exhortation of the General Assembly of the Church of Scotland to their Brethren of England* (Edinburgh: Printed by Evan Tyler, Printer to the Kings most Excellent Majestie, 1647). 22 p.; 4⁰. ESTC R35584 (Wing C4205).

2. *A Declaration and Brotherly Exhortation of the Generall Assembly of the Church of Scotland, to their brethren of England* (London: printed for Rob. Bostok at the signe of the Kings Head in Paul's Church-yard, 1647). [2], 14 p.; 4⁰. ESTC R204642 (Wing C4204). "Annotation on Thomason copy: Sept. 18. Variant: R204643 (Wing C4204A).

3. Reprinted in *A True Copy of the Whole Printed Acts of the General Assemblies of the Church of Scotland, beginning at the Assembly holden at Glasgow the 27. day of November 1638; and ending at the Assembly, holden at Edinburgh the 6. day of August. 1649. Diligently compared, and exactly reprinted conforme to the foresaid printed Acts. By a welwisher of the Church of Scotland* (1682), pp. 329–342. This was reprinted in 1691. See also *Acts of the General Assembly of the Church of Scotland 1638–1842, Reprinted from the original edition, under the superintendence of The Church Law Society, Preface by Thomas Pitcairn, Convener of Committee of Church Law Society, May 15, 1843* (Edinburgh: The Edinburgh Printing and Publishing Company, 1843), pp. 148–154.

The Epigraph on the previous page has been added for this volume.

A Declaration and Brotherly Exhortation of
The General Assembly of the Church of Scotland,
Met at Edinburgh, August 20, 1647,
To their Brethren of England

Sess. 15, August 20, 1647, ante meridiem.—A Declaration and Brotherly Exhortation of the General Assembly of the Church of Scotland to their Brethren of England.[1]

The conscience of our duty to God obliging us to give a testimony to His truth, and to the kingdom of His Son Jesus Christ, now so much resisted and opposed by many, and so little owned by others—the laudable custom and example of correspondency between neighboring churches, exhorting, encouraging, and (in case of public scandal) admonishing in love one another, as well as single brethren ought to admonish one another in love, in the case of private offence—our nearer relation and more special affection to our brethren of England, making us to sympathize with them in their danger and affliction as our own, both kingdoms being united as one entire body in one covenant, for pursuing the common cause and ends therein expressed—yea, common reason and experience itself teaching us that we have no cause to conceive our religion, the liberties of this church, or ourselves, to be in a condition of safety whenever the enemies of our religion and liberties are growing to a prevalency in the neighbor kingdom. Any one of these considerations, much more all of them together, cry aloud upon us to break our silence in this present juncture of affaires; yet we hope to express ourselves both concerning the present dangers and present duties, as in a conscionable and brotherly freedom, so in a fair and inoffensive way; for we have no pleasure nor purpose to provoke any person or party whatsoever, nor to increase, but to endeavor the allaying and composing of the present unhappy differences. If any shall offend at our discharging our conscience and doing our duty, yet we shall rather choose to take our hazard of that, than

---

1. The editor of the 1843 edition of the Acts of the General Assembly notes that this declaration was "Drawn up by Mr. George Gillespie." This appears to be based upon Baillie's attribution. "We agreed, *nemine contradicente*, to that declaration, which was committed to Mr. Gillespie and me, but was drawn by him alone…." *Letters & Journals*, 3.20. While it is not absolutely clear, the only action of the August General Assembly of 1647 styled a declaration is this one. It clearly has the evidence of Gillespie's writing.

of displeasing God by neglect of duty. But we hope better things than to be misunderstood or misinterpreted by such as desire a candid interpretation of their own actions or expressions.

First of all, whatsoever the present discouragements, difficulties, or dangers are, or whatsoever for the future they may be, we cannot but commemorate, to the glory of God, and we doubt not it shall be remembered to His glory in the church throughout all ages, how great a salvation His mighty hand and outstretched arm has wrought for these three kingdoms—how He stirred up the spirits of His people in this kingdom ten years ago, to begin to shake off the yoke of prelatical tyranny, and of popish ceremonies obtruded upon us, contrary to the laws of God and men—how He led us on from so small beginnings, and from one degree to another, till we were united in a National Covenant—how He gave us a banner to be displayed for the truth, and so blessed us in the prosecution of that covenant, that the king's Majesty was graciously pleased, upon the humble petitions of his loyal subjects in this nation, to indict a general assembly and parliament for healing the grievances of church and state respectively, as likewise to grant his royal consent for confirming and ratifying by acts of parliament our National Covenant, and the government and liberties of this church. After which the new troubles raised against us by the malice and treachery of our enemies did occasion the first expedition of this nation into England (upon which followed the calling of the parliament there, and the large treaty[2]), and, in the issue, the return of that army was with an olive branch of peace, and not without the beginnings of a reformation in England; in which work, while the parliament was interrupted and opposed, and a bloody war begun with great success on that side which opposed the parliament and the begun reformation, from whence also did accrue great advantage to the popish party (whereof the cessation of arms concluded in Ireland may be instead of many testimonies), commissioners were sent hither from both Houses, earnestly inviting and persuading to a nearer union of the kingdoms, and desiring assistance from this nation to their brethren in that their great distress; and this, by the good hand of God, produced the *Solemn League & Covenant* of the three kingdoms, to the terror of the popish and prelatical party, our common enemies, and to the great comfort of such as were wishing and waiting for the reformation of religion, and the recovery of just liberties. And although, for the conjunction of the kingdoms in covenant and arms (being a special means tending to the extirpation of popery, and strengthening the true reformed religion), this kingdom has been invaded and infested by the bloody Irish rebels,[3]

---

2. "Articles of the large treaty, concerning the establishing of the peace between the king's majesty and his people of Scotland" (1641). See page 487.

3. The king's forces led by Montrose in league with Irish rebel forces, had made a number of victories in Scotland before the return of the main Scottish army put their successes to an end. See herein on pages 136–137, 149, 319–321, 333, 339–340. Sadly, the Covenanter forces under

aided and strengthened by some degenerate and perfidious countrymen of our own; although, also, in England there were not wanting incendiaries, who, hating and envying nothing more than the union of the kingdoms in such a covenant, were very vigilant to catch, and active to improve, all occasions of making divisive motions, and creating national differences; yet God has been graciously pleased to break our enemies' strength at home, when it was greatest, and to guide us through these jealousies and differences, fomented by disaffected persons, between the kingdoms; so that, instead of a splitting upon these rocks (the thing hoped for by our enemies), there was a peaceable and friendly parting; since which time God has further blessed our army at home, to the expelling of the enemy out of our own borders. Nor can we pass in silence the happy progress which has been made in the reformation of the Church of England. He that has brought the children to the birth, can also give strength to come forth,[4] and He whose hand did cast out prelacy and the Book of Common Prayer (although strongly rooted in standing laws), and who inclined the Parliament of England to own no other church government but the presbyterial (though it be not yet fully settled according to the Word of God and the example of the best reformed churches), can as easily incline, when He thinks good, both the king and them, and the body of that kingdom, to a thorough and perfect reformation. He that made the Assemblies and Parliaments of both kingdoms to agree upon one Directory for the Public Worship of God, can also, when He will, make an agreement in the other parts of uniformity, Confession of Faith, Form of Church Government, and Catechism; in all which there has been also a good progress made in the reverend and learned Assembly of Divines through the good hand of God so long upon them.

Having now seen so much of God, both in the beginning and progress of this His great work, and His hand having done so wondrous things for His people in their greatest extremities of danger; and having discovered and defeat[ed] the plots of enemies, making them fall even by their own counsels, these things we resolve to keep still fixed in our hearts, and as memorials before our eyes, that remembering the works of the Lord, and the years of the right hand of the Most High,[5] we may neither want matter of praises and thanksgivings, nor experience to breed hope. Although the building of the house of the Lord in England be not yet after so long expectation finished, and now also the work ceases, yet we do from our hearts bless the Lord for the laying of the foundation, and for so much progress as has been made in the work; having still confidence in the Almighty, to whom nothing is impossible or too hard, that every mountain which does or shall stand in the

---

Leslie behaved no better than the Irish rebels in slaughtering men, women, and children. See King Hewison, *The Covenanters*, 1.411–442.

4. Cf. 2 Kings 19:3 and Isaiah 37:3.

5. Cf. Psalm 77:10–11.

way shall become a plain, and that the headstone shall be brought forth[6] with shoutings of joy, "Grace, grace unto it."[7]

Nevertheless, we are also very sensible of the great and imminent dangers into which this common cause of religion is now brought by the growing and spreading of most dangerous errors in England, to the obstructing and hindering of the begun reformation, as namely (beside many others), Socinianism, Arminianism, Anabaptism, Antinomianism, Brownism, Erastianism, Independency, and that which is called (by abuse of the word) Liberty of Conscience, being indeed liberty of error, scandal, schism, heresy, dishonoring God, opposing the truth, hindering reformation, and seducing others; whereunto we add those nullifidians,[8] or men of no religion, commonly called Seekers. Yea, we cannot but look upon the dangers of the true Reformed religion in this island as greater now than before, not only for that those very principles and fundamentals of faith which, under prelacy, yea, under popery itself, were generally received as uncontroverted, are now, by the skepticism of many sectaries of this time, either oppugned or called in question; but also, because instead of carrying on the reformation towards perfection, that which has been already built is in part cast down, and in danger to be wholly overthrown through the endeavors of sectaries to comply with many of the prelatical and malignant,[9] and even the popish party; and their joining hand in hand, and casting in their lots, and interweaving their interests together in way of combination against the covenant and presbyterial government; yea, the unclean spirit which was cast out, is about to enter again, with seven other spirits worse than himself, and so the latter end like to be worse than the beginning.[10]

We are extremely sorry that we have cause to aggravate these evils from the crying sin of breach of covenant, whereof if we should hold our peace, yet, according to the Word of the Lord, other nations will say, and many among them do say, Wherefore has the Lord done thus unto this people? And what means the heat of this great anger? And they answer one another, "Because they have forsaken the covenant of the Lord their God."[11] We would not be understood as if we meant either to justify this nation, or to charge such a sin upon all in that nation. We know the covenant has been in divers particulars broken by many in both kingdoms—the Lord pardon it and accept a sacrifice; and we do not doubt but there are many seven thousands in England,[12] who have not only kept themselves unspotted, and retained

---

6. "brought for" *sic*: *Acts of the General Assembly* (Scottish Law Society, 1843), p. 149.

7. Cf. Jeremiah 32:27; Luke 1:37; Matthew 17:20; Zechariah 4:7.

8. The term nullifidian is used frequently by Gillespie. See *English Popish Ceremonies*, pages xlv, 3, and *Shorter Writings*, vol. 1, pages 275, 283, 316, 374 and especially page 338.

9. *Malignants*: those who had taken up arms for the king against the Covenanter cause.

10. See Matthew 12:45 and Luke 11:26.

11. Cf. Jeremiah 22:9.

12. Cf. 1 Kings 19:18 and Romans 11:4.

their integrity in that business, but do also mourn and groan before the Lord for that sin of others; yet we should but deny our own sense and betray the truth, if we should not resent so great a sin and danger, as is the breach of a solemn covenant, sworn with hands lifted up to the Most High God; which breach, however varnished over with some colorable and handsome pretexts, one whereof is the liberty and common right of the free people of England, as once Saul broke a covenant with the Gibeonites, "in his zeal to the children of Israel and Judah",[13] yet God could not then, and cannot now, be mocked; yea, it is too apparent and undeniable, that among those who did take the covenant of the three kingdoms, as there are many who have given themselves to a detestable indifferency or neutrality, so there is a generation which has made defection to the contrary part, persecuting, as far as they could, that true Reformed religion, in doctrine, worship, discipline, and government, which by the covenant they ought to preserve against the common enemies—hindering and resisting the reformation and uniformity which by the covenant ought to be endeavored—preserving and tolerating those cursed things which by the covenant ought to be extirpate[d], heresy and schism—encroaching upon, yea offering violence unto the rights, privileges, and authority of magistracy—protecting and assisting such as by the covenant ought to have been brought to condign trial and punishment—and persecuting those who by the covenant ought to be assisted and defended—endeavoring also a breach instead of a firm peace and union between the kingdoms, so that there is not any one article of the *Solemn League & Covenant* which has not been sinfully and dangerously violated before God, angels, and men. Now, if a covenant for the preservation and reformation of religion, the maintenance and defense of liberties, was justly thought a fit and excellent means, not only to strengthen and fortify the kingdoms against the common enemy of the true Reformed religion, public peace, and prosperity, but also, "to acquire the favor of Almighty God towards the three kingdoms of England, Scotland, and Ireland," as is expressed in the Ordinance of the Lords and Commons for the taking of the covenant, dated February 2, 1643,[14] surely, then, the authors and chief instruments of the breach of that covenant are to be looked upon as those who strengthen the hands of the common enemy, and provoke the wrath of Almighty God against these kingdoms. Yea, if this covenant was the "sovereign and only means of the recovery" of these embroiled bleeding kingdoms, as is expressed in the Exhortation of the Assembly of Divines to the taking of the covenant, approved and ordered to be printed by the House

---

13. See 2 Samuel 21:2.

14. *An Ordinance of the Lords and Commons assembled in Parliament; with instructions for the taking of the leagve and covenant in the kingdom of England, and dominion of Wales. With An exhortation for the taking of the covenant; and for satisfying such scruples as may arise thereupon* ([London]: Printed for E. Husbands, and are to be sold at his shop in the Middle-Temple, [1644]).

of Commons, the despising, refusing, and casting aside of that remedy must needs render the disease much more desperate.[15] And if by the Declaration of both kingdoms joined in arms, anno 1643, such as would not take the covenant were declared "to be public enemies to their religion and country, and that they are to be censured and punished as professed adversaries and malignants,"[16] who sees not now a strange falling away from these first principles and professions among these who either magnify and cry up, or at least connive at and comply with such as have not taken the covenant, yea, are known enemies to it, and cry down such as are most zealous for it?

In this case, while in the neighbor kingdom, the staves of beauty and bands, covenant and brotherhood, are broken by many, the horn of malignants and sectaries exalted, the best affected borne down, reformation ebbing, heresy and schism flowing, it can hardly be marveled at, by any person of prudence and discretion, if we be full of such fears and apprehensions as use to be [*commonly is*] in those who dwell near a house set on fire, or a family infected, especially being taught, by the sad experience of these prelatical times, how easily a gangrene in the one-half of this island may spread through the whole; knowing also the inveterate and insatiable malice of the enemies of this cause and covenant against this church and kingdom, which we cannot be ignorant of, unless we would shut our eyes and stop our ears.

Our present purpose leads us to touch somewhat of the proceedings of the army in England this summer,[17] so far as religion is therein concerned. As we are confident divers have gone along with them in the simplicity of their hearts—and we presume not to judge the thoughts and intentions of any, it being God's own prerogative to bring to light the hidden things of darkness, and to make manifest the counsels of the hearts—so it cannot be denied that upon these passages and proceedings has followed the interrupting of the so much longed-for reformation of religion, of the settling of presbyterial government, and of the suppressing of heresies and dangerous errors (which works the Parliament had taken in hand), the retarding and delaying

---

15. "An Exhortation to the taking of the Solemn League and Covenant, for Reformation and Defence of Religion, the Honour and Happiness of the King, and the Peace and Safety of the three Kingdoms of England, Scotland, and Ireland." See *An Exhortation to the taking of the Solemn League and Covenant* (1644), and in John Rushworth, *Historical Collections*, fifth volume (1721), p. 475.

16. *The Declaration of the kingdomes of England and Scotland, ioyned in armes for the vindication and defence of their religion, liberties, and lawes, against the popish, prelaticall, and malignant party* (London: Printed for Iohn Wright in the Old-baily, Februar. 1. 1643 [i.e. 1644]). See Rushworth, 5.499.

17. See the note on pages 348–349. Gillespie appears to be citing from proposals presented by the army to parliament on August 1, 1647. See *The Heads of Proposals, agreed on by his Excellency Sir Thomas Fairfax, and the Councell of the Armie.: Tendred to the commissioners of Parliament residing with the Armie* (1647). See Rushworth, second edition, volume 7 (1721), pp. 731–736 [errors in pagination].

the relief of Ireland, the sowing of the seeds of another war in England, the strengthening of the hand of the malignant and episcopal party, the weakening and wounding both of magistracy and ministry; in all which, whether the army be blameless and innocent from ministering occasion to so great evils, or whether there be not cause for them to repent and do the first works, and to practice more of that love, moderation, and meekness of spirit, and of that zeal against malignants and prelatical persons, which they have from the beginning professed, and the want whereof (when suspected in others) they did so much censure; or whether there be such a thing among them as adjoining with those against whom, and against those with whom the covenant was taken;—we leave them in all these to the search and examination of their own consciences, that they may stand or fall unto God. For our part, we cannot conceive how the proposals of that army for settling of a peace, do in point of religion consist with the *Solemn League & Covenant*, or with the propositions of peace formerly agreed upon by both kingdoms, there being so considerable omissions of divers material desires contained in those former propositions, concerning the abolition of prelacy—concerning the enjoining of the taking of the covenant by all his Majesty's subjects, under such penalties as the parliaments should agree upon—concerning the settling of religion in England and Ireland according to the covenant, in such manner as both Houses of Parliament shall agree on, after advice had with the Assembly of Divines concerning the settling of uniformity between the Churches of God in both kingdoms, according to the covenant, in such manner as shall be agreed on by both Houses of the Parliament of England, and by the Church and Kingdom of Scotland, after advice had with the divines of both kingdoms—also concerning an act of parliament to confirm the calling and sitting of the Assembly of Divines: All which, with some other particulars concerning religion, expressed in the former propositions, if they should now be omitted in the settling of a peace, the progress already made, not only in the Assembly of Divines, but in the Houses of Parliament in settling presbyterial government, with the Confession of Faith, yea, the Directory of Public Worship (though agreed upon by the Assemblies and Parliaments of both kingdoms), shall be but so much lost labor. But, besides these omissions, it may be justly doubted whether there be not in these proposals of the army somewhat for episcopacy and against the covenant; for we cannot understand the eleventh proposal in any other sense,[18] but that it supposes the continuance of the ecclesiastical office of bishops or prelates, as well as of any other church officers, and takes no more from the prelates but coercive power or jurisdiction, extending to civil penalties, which, indeed, belongs

---

18. Eleventh proposition: "An act to be passed to take away all Power, authoritie and jurisdiction of Bishops, and all other Ecclesiasticall Officers whatsoever extending to any Civill penalties upon any; And to repeale all Laws whereby the Civill Magistracie hath been, or is bound, upon any Ecclesiastical Censure to proceed (Exofficio) unto any Civill penalties against any person so censured." *Heads of Proposals*, p. 8. Rushworth, p. 334 [*sic* 734].

to no ecclesiastical officers. In the twelfth proposal,[19] we do not see how it can avoid or shun the toleration of popery, superstition, heresy, schism, profaneness, or whatsoever works of darkness shall be practiced by such as despise the public worship of God in the church, and have the most unlawful and wicked meetings elsewhere, under a profession of religious duties, exercises, or ordinances. From the thirteenth proposal,[20] we can make no other result, but that instead of enjoining the taking of the covenant, under such penalties as the parliaments in their wisdom shall agree upon, the former ordinance of parliament, enjoining the taking of it is desired to be repealed; and then what may be the danger of those that have taken, or shall take, an oath of that kind, not enjoined nor ratified by authority, we leave it to be judged by those who know best the laws of that kingdom.

One thing more we cannot pass, that whereas in the army's declaration or representation to the parliament, dated June 14, 1647,[21] they mention their brethren of Scotland as having proceeded in the vindication and defense of their just rights and liberties, much higher than that army has done, we are necessitated to say this much for clearing of these proceedings in this nation reflected upon. They of this church and kingdom who joined together and associated themselves in this cause, first by humble petitions, and afterwards by covenant, were so far from slighting or breaking that covenant which was taken, that it was the special visible character by which the friends of the cause were distinguished from the enemies thereof, and they were so far from crying down the ministry and ecclesiastical assemblies, or from disobeying any orders or commands of parliament, that a general assembly of the church and a parliament were two chief heads of their petitions and desires at that time, when they had neither; and when they had

---

19. Twelfth Proposal: "That there be a repeale of all Acts, or clauses in any Act enjoyning the use of the book of Common Prayer, and imposing any penalties for neglect thereof, as also of all acts or clauses in any act imposing any penaltie for not comming to Church, or for meetings else-where, for Prayer, or other Religious duties, Exercises or Ordinances, and some other Provision to be made for discovering of Papists and Popish Recusants, and for disabling of them, and of all Jesuits, and Priests, from disturbing the State." *Heads of Proposals*, p. 8. Rushworth, ibid.

20. "That the taking of the Covenant be not inforced upon any, nor any penalties imposed upon the refusers, whereby men might be constrained to take it against their Judgements or consciences, but all Orders or Ordinances to that purpose to be repealed." *Heads of Proposals*, p. 8. Rushworth, ibid.

21. *A Declaration from Sir Thomas Fairfax, and the Army under his command. As it was humbly tendered to the Right Honourable the Lords and Commons assembled in Parliament: as also to the Honourable the Lord Mayor, aldermen, and Common-Councell of the City of London. Concerning the just and fundamentall rights and liberties of themselves and the kingdome: with some humble proposals and desires. Printed by the speciall appointment of His Excellency Sir Thomas Fairfax, and souldiery of the Army under his command. St. Albans, June 14. 1647. Signed by me, John Rushvvorth* (London: for L. Chapman, and L. Blacklocke, 1647), pp. 5–6.

obtained a General Assembly and Parliament, they cheerfully submitted to both respectively.

And now the dangers of religion in this island being so great, as there has been lately a solemn humiliation throughout this land, upon occasion of these great and growing dangers,[22] so, we cannot but still look upon them as matters of frequent prayer and humiliation to ourselves, as well as our brethren in England, there being much sin in both kingdoms procuring all this evil, and justly deserving these and heavier judgments. And as we desire, in the first place, to be humbled for our own sins, and the sins of this nation, so we trust our brethren will be willing to be put in mind of the necessity of their humiliation and repentance for the national sins of that kingdom, which we shall wish rather to be sadly considered by them then expressed by us. One thing we are confident of, that God has had a special controversy against His people of old, for the sin of a broken covenant, and unwillingness to be reformed and purged according to the Word of the Lord; and that till these sins were acknowledged and repented His controversy did not take an end. We are no less confident that the godly and well-affected will, in tenderness of conscience, timely search out, weigh well, mourn for, and study to remove, all the causes of the Lord's present controversy against that nation. What the Honorable Houses of Parliament have to be humbled for, and to reform or amend, they have been (and we trust still are) put in mind by such as are ambassadors to them in Christ's stead, at their solemn humiliations.

---

22. Gillespie and Rutherford wrote from London to the Commissioners of the Church of Scotland on June 4, 1647, "Only we humbly move and offer it to be considered by you whether it were not very fit to have a general fast and humiliation in Scotland as soon as can be upon occasion of these new clouds, commotions, and disturbances in this kingdom." *The Records of the Commissions of the General Assembly of the Church of Scotland Holden in Edinburgh in the Years 1646 and 1647*, ed. Alexander F. Mitchell and James Christie (Edinburgh: T. and A. Constable for the Scottish History Society, 1892), pp. 274–275. A fast was called for July 25, 1647. "Causes of a public fast and solemn humiliation to be kept throughout the Church of Scotland upon the last Sabbath of this instant month of July, being the 25 day thereof 1647. 1. That notwithstanding of our solemn engagement in the covenant, our obligations from great and singular mercies, and our many warnings from judgments of all sorts, yet not only do we come far short of that sobriety, righteousness, and holiness that becometh the gospel of Jesus Christ, but ungodliness and worldly lusts abound everywhere throughout the land, unto the grieving of the Lord's Spirit, and provoking the eyes of His glory, because we continue to walk contrary unto Him. 2. That the Lord's hand is still stretched out against us in the judgment of the pestilence, which spreads not only in several places of the country, but continues and increases in many of the most eminent cities in the kingdoms. 3. The great danger that threatens religion and the work of reformation in these kingdoms, from the number, policy, and power of the sectaries in England, which are like not only to interrupt the progress of uniformity, and the establishing of the ordinances of God in their beauty and perfection, but to overturn the foundation already laid, and all that has been built thereupon, with the expense of so much blood and pains." See ibid., pages 285–288.

A Declaration and Brotherly Exhortation   377

For our part, as we have always mentioned them in our prayers, with thanksgivings also in their behalf, so we now must humbly beseech the Lord to direct and bless them, and in their present difficulties to keep them by His grace from all sinful compliance, especially from establishing iniquity by a law; to show them why He contends with them, that the true cause of His controversy may be removed, and that the glory of His name, the kingdom, crown, and scepter of His Son Jesus Christ, with His word, laws, ordinances, truth, ministers, may be yet more set by in their eyes, that they also may find a further performance of the word of the Lord: "Exalt her, and she shall promote thee;" and "Them that honour me, I will honour."[23]

We shall now, by the mercies of God, and in the bowels of Jesus Christ, earnestly beseech all those, of whatsoever quality or condition, in England, who have entered into the same League and Covenant with us, and especially the Houses of Parliament, the city of London, and Assembly of Divines, that, with sound humiliation, fervent prayer, and making sure their peace with God, they may join all care, faithfulness, and zeal, to hold fast the profession of their faith without wavering, against the many heresies and errors of these times; that they may, according to their places and callings, endeavor to the utmost of their power to prevent or hinder the laying aside or slighting of the covenant, the re-establishment of episcopacy, and the toleration of popery, prelacy, heresy, schism, superstition, or profaneness, and not suffer themselves, directly or indirectly, by whatsoever combination, persuasion, or terror, to be divided and withdrawn from that blessed union and sacred covenant, either to the contrary side, or to a neutrality in this cause, which so much concerns the glory of God, the good of the kingdoms, and the honor of the king; but all the days of their lives zealously and constantly continue therein, against all opposition, and promote the same according to their power, against all lets [*hindrances*] and impediments whatsoever; which things both they and we have solemnly, and in the sight of God, sworn unto. And as we desired them to rest confident of the constancy of their brethren in this nation, in adhering to that covenant, in all the articles thereof, which we shall, by the grace of Christ (without which we are nothing), sincerely, really, and constantly,[24] pursue and promote, so far as concerns our places and callings—using our utmost endeavors towards the suppression of those errors which have so dangerously hurt religion in this island; so, we expect confidently the like of our brethren in England united in covenant with us, and that whatever they may have cause to fear, or be called to suffer, yet the Lord will so strengthen them by His grace, as that they may be able to say, "All this is come upon us; yet have we not forgotten thee, neither have we dealt falsely in thy covenant."[25] And here is the wisdom and patience of the

---

23. Proverbs 4:8 and 1 Samuel 2:30.

24. In this paragraph Gillespie is drawing from the Solemn League and Covenant. See *Confession of Faith*, etc. (1855), pp. 358–360.

25. Psalm 44:17.

saints,[26] to choose affliction rather than iniquity, to do duty in the worst of times, and to trust God with events, and in so doing, to hope to the end, and wait upon the Lord, until He plead their cause, and execute judgment for them;[27] so shall they be more purified, and not made blacker (as, alas! some are), but whiter in times of trial.

More particularly, we do desire that presbyterial government may be settled and put in practice throughout that kingdom, according to the Word of God and example of the best reformed churches; for without this we know no other proper and effectual remedy against the present dangers of religion there, or for purging the church from scandals, which are destructive either to sound doctrine or to godliness; and herein we are confident the experience of all the reformed churches will bear witness with us. Nor do we doubt but in England also time and experience will more and more commend, not only the beautiful order, but the great utility, yea, necessity of this government, and dispel all the clouds of aspersions and prejudices which it lies under among such as know it not, who ought, therefore, to beware of speaking evil of the things they understand not. Yet we would not have our zeal for presbyterial government misunderstood, as if it tended to any rigor or domineering over the flock, or to hinder and exclude that instructing in meekness them that oppose themselves, which the apostolical rule holds forth; or as if we would have any such to be entrusted with that government as are found not yet purged, either from their old profaneness, or from the prelatical principles and practices, which were but to put a piece of new cloth unto an old garment, and so to make the rent worse; or to put new wine into old bottles, and so to lose both wine and bottles.[28] Yea, who knows whether this may not be one of the causes (and not the least) why the present reformation succeeds the worse, even because of so little repentance, either for the profaneness or prelatical errors and corruptions of divers who have acted in it; nevertheless, the right hand of fellowship is to be given to all such as bring forth fruits meet for repentance, whatsoever their former errors or failings were. And to our great joy, we understand that there are many learned, able, godly, and prudent ministers in that kingdom, fit to be employed in that government, together with such able and pious men as are to be joined with them in the capacity of ruling elders. It shall be a part of our prayers that the Lord of the harvest may send forth many more laborers in that kingdom, where the harvest is so great and the laborers so few proportionably; and in the meanwhile, that such as He has already thrust out may not be unemployed, as to the point of discipline and government.[29]

Nor, lastly, does our zeal for the covenant and presbyterial government abate or diminish anything at all from our loyalty and duty to the king's

---

26. Cf. Revelation 14:12.

27. Cf. Micah 7:8.

28. Cf. Matthew 9:16–17, Mark 2:21–22, and Luke 5:36–37.

29. In other words, may those put out of office not escape church discipline.

Majesty, although incendiaries and enemies spare not to reproach this church and kingdom with disloyalty. Yet such calumnies will easily be repudiate[d] by all who will examine the whole course of the public proceedings in this nation in reference to the king, and particularly the Declaration of the Parliament of this kingdom, dated January 16, 1647.[30] Wherefore, passing all such calumnies, which cannot but be hateful to God and good men, we do clearly and candidly profess, that the covenant and presbyterial government are so far from hindering or excluding our duty to the king, that it is thereby very much strengthened and supported; for our giving to God what is God's, does not hinder us, but help us, to give unto Cæsar what is Cæsar's. And we earnestly wish his Majesty's royal heart may be graciously inclined to the just desires of his good subjects in both kingdoms, and to that happy settlement of truth and peace, religion and righteousness, which may be as well for the establishment of his own throne as for the good of his people.

Now the Prince of Peace Himself grant His afflicted people, tossed with tempests, and not comforted, a safe and well grounded peace, bring light out of the present darkness, and order out of all these confusions—give unto all who are waiting for the consolation of Israel "good hope through grace, comfort their hearts, stablish them in every good word and work,"[31]—make His cause to triumph at last over all opposition, and the enemies' foot to slide in due time, and so put a new song of praise in the mouths of His people.[32]

Amen.

---

30. *A Letter of the Parliament of Scotland to both Houses of the Parliament of England. Together with the declaration of the Parliament of Scotland, concerning His Majestie: their desires; and the answer of the Parliament of England* ([London]: Printed at Edinburgh by Evan Tyler, printer to the Kings most excellent Majestie: and re-printed at London for Robert Bostock, at the signe of the Kings head in Pauls Church-yard, 1647). "A reissue, with cancel title page, of the edition ostensibly printed by Evan Tyler in Edinburgh but in fact probably a London forgery; the title pages are mostly in the same setting." ESTC R203720.

31. Cf. 2 Thessalonians 2:16–17.

32. Cf. Psalm 40:3.

CXI Propositions

Concerning the Ministery &
Government of the Church.

Hebrews 13:7, 17, 24

Remember them which have the rule over you, who have spoken unto you the word of God: whose faith follow, considering the end of their conversation.… Obey them that have the rule over you, and submit yourselves: for they watch for your souls, as they that must give account, that they may do it with joy, and not with grief: for that is unprofitable for you.… Salute all them that have the rule over you, and all the saints. They of Italy salute you.

Editions

1. *CXI Propositions Concerning the Ministerie and Government of the Church* (Edinburgh: Printed by Evan Tyler, Printer to the Kings most Excellent Majesty, 1647). [6], 43, 30–31, [1] p.; 4^0. ESTC R21587 (Wing G752).
2. *A Form for Church Government and Ordination of Ministers, contained in CXI propositions, propounded to the late Generall Assembly at Edinburgh, 1647. Together with an Act concerning Erastianisme, Independencie, and Liberty of Conscience. Published by authority* (London: Printed for Robert Bostock, at the King's Head in Pauls Church-yard, MDCXLVII [1647]). [6], 45, [1] p.; 4^0. ESTC R202292 (Wing G749). Annotation on Thomason copy: "Nov. 30."
3. *Theoremata CXI de Ministerio & Regimine Ecclesiastico* (Edinburgi: Excudebat Evanus Tyler, Regiæ Majestatis typographus, 1647). [2], 44 p.; 4^0. ESTC R21700 (Wing G760).
4. *Theoremata CXI. de Ministerio & Regimine Ecclesiastico* ([Edinburgh]: juxta exemplar quod Edinburgi excudebat Evanus Tyler, Regiæ Majestatis Typographus, 1648). [2], 62 p.; 8^0. ESTC R177417 (Wing G760A).
5. *The Hundred and Eleven Propositions Concerning the Ministry and Government of the Church, drawn up by order of the General Assembly 1645* [sic]… *together with a remarkably full and candid acknowledgment of the sins of the ministry, drawn up by the Commission in 1651. Reprinted at the desire of a theological society* (Edinburgh: Printed by Gavin Alston, [1778]). 48 pages; 19 cm.
6. *The Hundred and Eleven Propositions Concerning the Ministry and Government of the Church, drawn up by order of the General Assembly 1645* [sic], etc. (Glasgow: Printed by E. Miller, 1797). 39, 1 unnumbered page ; 20 cm.
7. *One Hundred and Eleven Propositions Concerning the Ministry and Government of the Church*, in *Works: A Presbyterian's Armoury* (Edinburgh: Robert Ogle and Oliver and Boyd, 1844). 23 pp.; royal octavo.

The Epigraph on the previous page has been added for this volume.

ACT Approving Eight General Heads of Doctrine
Against the Tenets of Erastianism, Independency,
& Liberty of Conscience, Asserted in the
One Hundred and Eleven Propositions, which are to be
Examined against the next Assembly[1]

BEING TENDER of so great an engagement by Solemn Covenant, sincerely, really, and constantly to endeavor in our place and callings the preservation of the Reformed religion in this Kirk of Scotland, in doctrine, worship, discipline, and government, the reformation of religion in the Kingdoms of England and Ireland in doctrine, worship, discipline, and government, according to the Word of God and the example of the best reformed Kirks, and to endeavor the nearest conjunction and uniformity in all these, together with the extirpation of heresy, schism, and whatsoever shall be found contrary to sound doctrine; and, considering withal that one of the special means which it becometh us in our places and callings to use in pursuance of these ends, is, in zeal for the true Reformed religion, to give our public testimony against the dangerous tenets of Erastianism, Independency, and which is falsely called Liberty of Conscience, which are not only contrary to sound doctrine but more special lets and hindrance[s], as well to the preservation of our own received doctrine, worship, discipline, and government, as to the work of reformation and uniformity in England and Ireland. The General Assembly, upon these considerations, having heard publicly read the 111 following Propositions,[2] exhibited and tendered by some brethren who were appointed to prepare articles or propositions for the vindication of the truth in these particulars, does unanimously approve and agree unto these eight general heads of doctrine therein contained and asserted, viz.:—

---

1. The *Acts* shorten this to "Act concerning the Hundred and Eleven Propositions therein mentioned." This act appears in the published collection of acts of the General Assembly of the Church of Scotland (1682; 1691, Peterkin 1838/43, Church Law Society, 1843), as well as in *The Confessions of Faith, Catechisms, Directories, Form of Church-Government, Discipline*, etc. *of public authority in the Church of Scotland: Together with The Acts of Assembly, concerning the Doctrine, Worship, Discipline, and Government*, etc. (Edinburgh: Thomas Lumisden and John Robertson, [1725]), pp. 552–555. It also prefaces the 1647 Edinburgh and London editions and is given in Latin in the 1647 and 1648 Latin editions. As neither the act nor the Latin translation of it are authored by Gillespie, it is only given in English in this printing.

2. The Acts note, "Not that they are to be here printed, but because they being to be printed severally, this Act is to be prefixed to them."

1. That the ministry of the Word and the administration of the sacraments of the New Testament, Baptism and the Lord's Supper, are standing ordinances instituted by God Himself, to continue in the church to the end of the world.

2. That such as administer the Word and sacraments ought to be duly called and ordained thereunto.

3. That some ecclesiastical censures are proper and peculiar to be inflicted only upon such as bear office in the kirk; other censures are common and may be inflicted both on ministers and other members of the kirk.

4. That the censure of suspension from the sacrament of the Lord's Supper, inflicted because of gross ignorance, or because of a scandalous life and conversation, as likewise the censure of excommunication, or casting out of the kirk flagitious or contumacious offenders, both the one censure and the other is warrantable by and grounded upon the Word of God, and is necessary (in respect of divine institution) to be in the kirk.

5. That as the rights, power, and authority of the civil magistrate are to be maintained according to the Word of God and the Confessions of the Faith of the Reformed kirks, so it is no less true and certain that Jesus Christ, the only Head and only King of the kirk, has instituted and appointed a kirk government distinct from the civil government or magistracy.

6. That the ecclesiastical government is committed and entrusted by Christ to the assemblies of the kirk made up of the ministers of the Word and ruling elders.

7. That the lesser and inferior ecclesiastical assemblies ought to be subordinate and subject unto the greater and superior assemblies.

8. That notwithstanding hereof, the civil magistrate may and ought to suppress by corporal or civil punishments, such as, by spreading error or heresy, or by fomenting schism, greatly dishonor God, dangerously hurt religion, and disturb the peace of the kirk;
—which heads of doctrine (howsoever opposed by the authors and fomenters of the foresaid errors respectively), the General Assembly does firmly believe, own, maintain, and commend unto others, as solid, true, orthodox, grounded upon the Word of God, consonant to the judgment both of the ancient and the best Reformed kirks. And because this assembly (through the multitude of other necessary and pressing business) cannot now have so much leisure as to examine and consider particularly the foresaid 111 Propositions: Therefore, a more particular examination thereof is committed and referred to the Theological Faculties in the four universities of this kingdom, and the judgment of each of these faculties concerning the same is appointed to be reported to the next General Assembly. In the meanwhile, these Propositions shall be printed, both that copies thereof may be sent to presbyteries, and that it may be free for any that please to peruse them, and to make known or send their judgment concerning the same to the said next Assembly. A[ndrew] Ker, [Clerk of the General Assembly].

CXI Propositions

Concerning the Ministry and Government of the Church

1. As our Lord Jesus Christ does invisibly teach and govern His church by the Holy Spirit,[1] so in gathering, preserving, instructing, building, and saving thereof, He uses ministers as His instruments, and has appointed an order of some to teach and others to learn in the church, and that some should be the flock and others the pastors.

Quemadmodum Dominus noster Jesus Christus ecclesiam invisibiliter per Spiritum Sanctum docet et ducit, ita in ea colligenda, instruenda, ædificanda, et salvanda, administris tanquam organis suis utitur, ordinemque docentium et discentium in ecclesia constituit, atque ut alij quidem sint oves, alij vero pastores.

2. For besides these first founders of the church of Christ extraordinarily sent and furnished with the gift of miracles, whereby they might confirm the doctrine of the gospel, He appointed also ordinary pastors and teachers for the executing of the ministry, even until His coming again unto judgment (Eph. 4:11–13). Wherefore also, as many as are of the number of God's people, or will be accounted Christians, ought to receive and obey the ordinary ministers of God's Word and sacraments (lawfully though mediately called) as the stewards and ambassadors of Christ Himself.

Enim vero præter primos illos ecclesiæ Christianæ fundatotes extra ordinem missos, donoque miraculorum, quo doctrinæ evangelicæ veritatem confirmarent, instructos; ordinarios etiam pastores et[2] doctores ad opus ministerii, tantisper dum ad judicium redierit, obeundum destinavit act dedit (Eph. 3:11–13).[3] Quocirca et ordinarios verbi divini ac sacramentorum administratores, legitime utut mediate vocatos, veluti ipsius Christi œconomos atque legatos recipere iisque aucultare[4] debent quotquot se Dei populo adnumerant, vel Christiani haberi volunt.

---

1. The English text is presented in modern form, along with the Latin text, which presumably is also by Gillespie. While some corrections along with those noted by an early collator of the two Latin editions are noted, there is no intent to present a critical text of the Latin. There is minor editing and the mock accents have not been retained, which were not consistently used in both editions (à, â, á, etc.). N.B. The Latin offers more Greek than the English.

2. The 1647 Latin edition omitted the "et". In the example in Early English Books (EEB), an "et" has been inserted by hand by someone who must have been comparing it to the 1648 edition. It is less likely that the mark-up was for that 1646 printing, but it cannot be ruled out.

3. 1647: "11.13." 1648: "11.12.13."

4. 1647: aucultare. 1648: auscultare.

3. It is not lawful for any man how fit soever and how much soever enriched or beautified with excellent gifts, to undertake the administration either of the Word or sacraments by the will of private persons, or others who have not power and right to call, much less is it lawful by their own judgment or arbitrament, to assume and arrogate the same to themselves. But before it be lawful to undergo that sacred ministry in churches constituted, a special calling, yea besides, a lawful election (which alone is not sufficient), a mission, or sending, or (as commonly it is termed) ordination, is necessarily required, and that both for the avoiding of confusion, and to bar out or shut the door (so far as in us lies) upon impostors; as also by reason of divine institution delivered to us in the holy Scripture (Rom. 10:15; Heb. 5:4. Titus 1:5; 1 Tim. 1:14).

Nemini quantumvis idoneo, præclarisque donis ditato ac exornato, vel verbi vel sacramentorum administrationem, ex privatorum, aliorumve penes quos non est jus vocandi, arbitrio,[5] obire, nedum ex proprio judicio sibi assumere aut arrogare fas est; sed priusquam cuipiam sacrosanctum illud ministerium obire liceat, in ecclesiis jam constitutis, specialis vocatio; et quidem præter[6] legittimam electionem (quæ[7] sola non sufficit) missio, seu (ut vulgo nuncupatur) ordinatio necessario requritur: Idque tum ad vitandam confusionem, atque januam impostoribus (quantum in nobus est) præcludendam; tum propter institutionem divinam in sacra Scriptura nobis traditam (Rom. 10:15; Heb. 5:4; 1 Titus 1:5 [*sic*]; Tim. 4:14 [*sic*]).[8]

4. The church ought to be governed by no other persons than ministers and stewards preferred and placed by Christ, and after no other manner than according to the laws made by Him; and therefore, there is no power on earth which may challenge to [*claim for*] itself authority or dominion over the church. But whosoever they are that would have the things of Christ to be administered not according to the ordinance and will of Christ revealed in His Word, but as it likes [*suits*] them, and according to their own will and prescript, what other thing go they about to do than by horrible sacrilege to throw down Christ from His own throne?

Ecclesia nec ab aliis quam administris ac œconomis a Christo præfectis et adscitis, nec aliter quam juxta leges ab ipso latas regi debet ac proinde nulla est in terris potestas, cui imperium aut dominium[9] in ecclesiam sibi vendicare liceat. Quicunque vero sint qui illa quæ Christi sunt, non juxta Christi ordinationem et[10] volutatem in vero suo retectam, sed ut ipsis libet, atque ad ipsorum nutum ac præscriptum administrari velint; quid aliud moliuntur quam infando quodam sacrilegio, Christum de solio suo deturbare?

---

5. The 1647 edition omitted the comma after "arbitrio".

6. 1647: preter.

7. 1647: que.

8. The errors in the Scripture references were corrected in the 1648 edition.

9. 1647 "Dominum" [*sic*].

10. 1648: "et et" [*sic*].

5. For our only lawgiver and interpreter of His Father's will, Jesus Christ, has prescribed and fore-appointed the rule according to which He would have His worship and the government of His own house to be ordered. To wrest this rule of Christ laid open in His holy Word to the counsels, wills, manners, devices, or laws of men, is most high impiety. But contrarily, the law of faith commands the counsel and purposes of men to be framed and conformed to this rule, and overturns all the reasonings of worldly wisdom, and brings into captivity the thoughts of the proud swelling mind to the obedience of Christ. Neither ought the voice of any to take place or be rested upon in the church, but the voice of Christ alone.

Unicus enim legislator noster, Paternæque voluntatis interpres, Jesus Christus regulam juxta quam cultum suum, domusque suæ gubernationem institui vult, præfixit et præfinivit. Hanc Chrisi regulam, in verbo suo sancto promulgatam, ad consilia, voluntates, mores, instituta, vel leges hominum inflectere, summa est impietas: Sed contra, lex fidei consilia et instituta hominum regulæ isti conformari jubet, omnesque secularis sapientia λογισμοὺς everit, animique intumescentis æstus et cogitationes in captivitatem redigit ad obediendum Christo. Neque enim in ecclesia ullius hominis, sed solius Christi vox obtinere debet.

6. The same Lord and our Savior Jesus Christ, the only head of the church, has ordained in the New Testament not only the preaching of the Word and administration of Baptism and the Lord's Supper but also ecclesiastical government distinct and differing from the civil government, and it is His will that there be such a government distinct from the civil in all His churches everywhere, as well those which live under Christian as those under infidel magistrates, even until the end of the world (Heb. 13:7, 17, [24];[11] 1 Tim. 5:17, 19; Rom. 12:8; 1 Cor. 12:28; 1 Thes. 5:12; Acts 1:20, 28 [*sic* 20:28]; Luke 12:42; 1 Tim. 6:14. Rev. 2:25).

Idem Dominus ac salvator noster Jesus Christus, unicum ecclesiæ caput, non solum verbi annunciationem, verum etiam regimen ecclesiasticum a politico distinctum ac discretum in Novo Testamento instituit; atque in omnibus suis, ubique terrarum ecclesiis, tam sub Christiano quam sub infideli magistratu degentibus, vigere, et ad finem usque seculi locum habere voluit (Heb. 13:7, 17, 24; 1 Tim. 5:17, 19; Rom. 12:8; 1 Cor. 12:28; 1 Thess. 5:12; Acts 20:28; Luke 12:42;[12] 1 Tim. 6:14; Rev. 2:25).

7. This ecclesiastical government distinct from the civil is from God committed not to the whole body of the church or congregation of the faithful, or to be exercised both by officers and people, but to the ministers of God's Word, together with the elders which are joined with them for the care and government of the church (1 Tim. 5:17). To these, therefore, who are over the church in the Lord, belongs the authority and power, and it lies upon them by their office according to the rule of God's Word to discern

---

11. The 1647 and 1648 Latin editions add Hebrews 13:24, which in not in the English text.

12. The 1647 Latin has Luke 12:42, 43, which the 1648 corrects(?) in omitting verse 43.

and judge between the holy and profane, to give diligence for amendment of delinquents, and to purge the church (as much as is in them) from scandals, and that not only by enquiring, inspection, warning, reproving, and more sharply expostulating, but also by acting in the further and more severe parts of ecclesiastical discipline, or exercising ecclesiastic jurisdiction, even unto the greatest and weightiest censures, where need is.

Regimen illud ecclesiasticum a politico discretum, non toti ecclesiæ, seu cœtui fidelium; sed verbi divini ministris, una cum senioribus, qui ipsis ad ecclesiæ curam ac gubernationem adjuncti sunt, divinitus commissum est (1 Tim. 5:17). Istis itaque, qui ecclesiæ in Domino præsunt, potestas est, simulque ex officio incumbit, secundum verbi Dei normam inter sanctum et prophanum discernere ac judicare, delinquentium emendationi operam dare, ecclesiamque a scandalis (quoad ab iis fieri potest) repurgare: idque non solum inquirendo, inspiciendo, monendo, increpando, duriusque expostulando; sed et ulteriores ac severiores disciplinæ ecclesiasticæ partes obeundo; seu jurisdictionem ecclesiastico-forensem, usque ad censuras maximas ac gravissimas (ubi opus est) exercendo.

8. None that are within the church ought to be without the reach of church law and exempt from ecclesiastic censures; but discipline is to be exercised on all the members of the church without respect or consideration of those adhering qualities which use to [*which commonly*] commend a man to other men, such as power, nobility, illustrious descent, and the like; for the judgment cannot be right where men are led and moved with these considerations. Wherefore, let respect of persons be far from all judges, chiefly the ecclesiastical. And if any in the church do so swell in pride that he refuses to be under this discipline, and would have himself to be free and exempt from all trial and ecclesiastic judgment, this man's disposition is more like the haughtiness of the Roman Pope than the meekness and submissiveness of Christ's sheep.

Nemo qui in ecclesia est, exlex, aut a censuris ecclesiasticis exemptus esse debet; sed in omnia ecclesiæ membra exercenda est disciplina, absque respectu seu consideratione qualitatum illarum adhærentium, quæ homini apud alios homines favorem conciliare solent: cujusmodi sunt, potentia, nobilitas, stemmatum spendor, opes, et id genus alia. Neque enim apud eos qui his moventur salva esse poterit judiciorum æquitas. Quare ab omnibus judicibus præsertim autem ecclesiasticis longissime absit προσωπολημψία illa. Si vero cujuspiam in ecclesia animus adeo superbe intumescat, ut huic disciplinæ subesse recuset; atque se ab omni examine et judicio ecclesiastico immunem et exlegem esse velit; illius genius, Pontificis Romani fastui, quam ovium Christi subjectioni et mansuetudini similior est.

9. Ecclesiastical censure, moreover, is either proper to be inflicted upon the ministers and office bearers only, or with them common to other members of the church. The former consists in suspension or deposition of ministers from their office (which in the ancient canons is called καθαίρεσις); the latter consists in the greater and lesser excommunication (as they speak).

Whatsoever in another brother deserves excommunication, the same much more in a minister deserves excommunication. But justly sometimes a minister is to be put from his office and deprived of that power which by ordination was given him, against whom, nevertheless, to draw the sword of excommunication, no reason does compel.

Censura porro ecclesiastica est vel ministrorum propria, vil iis cum aliis ecclesiæ membris communis. Illa in suspensione vel depositione (quæ in vetustis canonibus καθαίρεσις) dicitur) ministrorum ab officio: Ista in excommunicatione minore (quam vocant) et majore consistit.[13] Quicquid in alio fratre, id multo magis in ministro ecclesiæ excommunicationem meretur: ast merito quandoque minister quispiam exauthorandus et abdicandus est, ac ea potestate quæ per ordinationem data fuit, privandus; contra quem tamen, excommunicationis gladium vibrare, nulla ratio cogit.

10. Sometimes also it happens that a minister having fallen into heresy, or apostasy, or other grievous crimes, if he shows tokens of true repentance, may be justly received into the communion of the church, whom notwithstanding, it is no way expedient to restore into his former place or charge; yea, perhaps it will not be found fit to restore such a one to the ministry in another congregation, as soon as he is received into the bosom of the church, which surely is most agreeable as well as to the Word of God (2 Kings 23:9; Ezek. 44:10–14), as to that ecclesiastical discipline, which in some ages after the times of the apostles was in use.

So true is it that the ministers of the church are liable as well to peculiar as to common censures, or that a minister of the church is censured one way, and one of the people another way.

Interdum etiam accidit ut in hæresin vel apostasiam, vel aliud grande crimen prolapsus minister, ad ecclesiæ communionem si veræ respiscentiæ signa ostendat, jure recipiatur; quem tamen in pristinum locum, sorte[14] etiam in ministeri dignitatem alibi restitui, simul atque in sinum ecclesiæ receptus est, haud quaquam expedit quod sane, tam verbo Dei (2 Kings 23:9; Ezek. 44:10–14). Quam antiquæ disciplinæ ecclesiasticæ quæ seculis aliquot post apostolorum tempora in usu fuit; maxime consentaneum est. Adeo verum est, ministros ecclesiæ tam peculiaribus quam communibus censuris obnoxios esse, seu aliter quandoque ministrum ecclesiæ, aliter ex plebe quempiam ἀφορίζεσθαι.

11. Ecclesiastical censure, which is not proper to ministers but common to them with other members of the church, is either suspension from the Lord's Supper (which by others is called the publican's excommunication) or the cutting off of a member, which is commonly called excommunication. The distinction of this twofold censure (commonly, though not so properly passing under the name of the lesser and greater excommunication) is not only much approved by the Church of Scotland and the Synod now

---

13. 1647: consistsit [*sic*].

14. The 1648 appears to read "forte."

assembled at Westminster, but also by the Reformed Churches of France, the Low Countries, and of Poland, as is to be seen in the book of the *Ecclesiastic Discipline of the Reformed Churches in France* (chap. 5, Art. 9),[15] in the *Harmony of the Belgic Synods* (chap. 14, Art. 8, 9),[16] in the canons of the general Synod of Torn, held in the year 1597 [*sic*].[17]

Censura ecclesiastica quæ non est ministrorum propria, sed iis cum aliis ecclesiæ membris communis, est vel suspensio a cœna dominica (quæ ab aliis *excommunicatio publicani* nuncupatur) vel membri abscissio, quæ proprie excommunication dicitur. Duplicis hujus censuræ vulgo (quanquam non ita proprie) sub nomine excommunicationis minoris et majoris ventilatæ, distinctio, non tatum Ecclesiæ Scoticanæ Synodoque Westmonasteriensi hodiernæ; sed et Ecclesiis Reformatis Gallicis, necnon Belgicis et Polonicis vehementer probatur; ut videre est in Libello *Ecclesiasticæ Disciplinæ Reformatarum Ecclesiarum in Gallia*, cap. 5, art. 9, in *Harmoniæ Synodorum Belgicarum*, cap. 14, art. 8, 9, *in Canonibus Toruniensis Synodi Generalis* Anno Dom. 1595, celebratæ.

12. That the distinction of that twofold church censure was allowed also by antiquity, it may be sufficiently clear to him who will consult the sixty-one canon of the sixth general Synod, with the annotations of Zonaras and Balsamon; also the thirteenth canon of the eighth Synod (which is termed the first and second) with the notes of Zonaras;[18] yea, besides, even the penitents also themselves of the fourth degree, or οἱ ἐν συστασεῖ, that is, which were in the *consistency*,[19] were suspended from the Lord's Supper, though as to other things of the same condition with the faithful; for, to the communion also of prayers, and so to all privileges of ecclesiastical society, the eucharist alone excepted, they were thought to have right. So sacred a thing was the eucharist esteemed. See also besides others, Cyprian book 1, epist. 11,[20] that Dionisius, the author of the *Ecclesiastic Hierarchy*, chap. 3, part. 3.[21] Basil, Epist.

---

15. *The Ecclesiastical Discipline of the Reformed Churches in France* (London: 1642), p. 18.

16. Festus Hommius, *Harmonia synodorum Belgicarum* in *Specimen Controversiarum Belgicarum Seu Confessio Ecclesiarum Reformatarum in Belgio* (Elzeviriana, [1618]), p. 158.

17. Both Latin editions read 1595. See *Acta et Conclusiones Synodi Generalis Toruniensis* (Thorn(?), 1595); cf in *Consensus in Fide et Religione Christiana … Accesserunt in hac editione Acta et Conclusiones Synodi Generalis Toruniensis* (Heidelberg: Voegelinianis, 1605), p. 71

18. Cf. Theodore Balsamon, *Canones SS. Apostolorum Conciliorum Generalium [et] Prouincialium* (Paris, 1620), pp. 431–434. Johannes Zonaras, *In canones SS. Apostolorvm & sacrorum conciliorum* (Paris, 1618), pp. 176–177. See *NPNF2*, vol. 14, *The Seven Ecumenical Councils*, p. 393. Zonaras, ibid., pp. 254–255.

19. *Consistency:* A consistent or penitent in the Eastern Church is one "who took their station with the faithful, but were not admitted to communion" (*OED*).

20. Gillespie is using the numbering of Cyprian's letters by Erasmus. See Cyprian, Migne, *PL* 4, cols. 364–372. See *ANF* 4, pp. 364–372.

21. See John Parker, *The Works of Dionysius the Areopagite, now first translated into English, from the original Greek*, 2 vols. (London: James Parker and Co., 1897), 2.91.

to Amphilochius, can. 4.[22] Ambrose, lib. 2, *De officiis*, chap. 27.[23] Augustine, in his book against the Donatists, after the conference, cap. 4.[24] Chrysostom, homily 83 in Matthew.[25] Gregory the Great, *Epist.*, lib. 2, chap. 65 and 66.[26] Walafridus Strabo, *Of Ecclesiastical Matters*, chap. 17.[27]

Duplicis illius ἀφορισμοῦ distinctionem vetustati quoque probatum fuisse satis liquere poterit consulenti sextæ Synodi œcumenicæ canonem 61. Cum annotatis Zonaræ et Balsamonis, item octavæ synodi (quæ prima et secunda nuncupatur) canonem 13. Cum Notis Zonaræ. Quid quod etiam ipsi pœnitentes quarti gradus, seu oi ἐν[28] συστασει, a cœna Domini suspensi erant: etsi quoad cætera, ejusdem conditionis cum fidelibus: nam ad communionem orationum, adeoque ad omnia societatis ecclesiasticæ privilegia, una excepta eucharistia, jus habere censebantur: adeo sacrosancta res existimabatur eucharistia. Consule item, præter alios, Cyprianum, lib. 1. Epist. 11. Dionysium illum *Ecclesiasticæ Hierarchiæ* authorem. Cap. 3, part 3. Basilium, *Epist. ad Amphilochium*, can. 4. Ambrosium, lib. 2, *De Officiis*, cap. 27. Augustinum, lib. *contra donatistas post collationem*, cap. 4. Chrysostomum, Hom. 83, in Matth. Gregorium magnum, *Epist.*, lib. 2, cap 65 & 66. Walafridum Strabonem, *de rebus Ecclesiasticis*, cap. 17.

13. That first and lesser censure by Christ's ordinance is to be inflicted on such as have received Baptism and pretend to be true members of the church, yet are found unfit and unworthy to communicate in the signs of the grace of Christ with the church, whether for their gross ignorance of divine things,

---

22. See Basil, Letter CLXXXVIII to Amphilochius, concerning the Canons, *NPNF2*, vol. 8, pp. 225–226.

23. See Ambrose, On the Duties of the Clergy, *NPNF2*, vol. 10, p. 64.

24. This seems to refer to Augustine, *Contra Donatistas post conlationem* [*Contra Partem Donati post gesta*]. See the text in *Scriptorum contra Donatistas pars III*, ed. M. Petschenig, *CSEL* 53/3 (Vienna: Tempsky, 1910), pp. 100–104.

25. Chrysostom, *Expositio in Euangelium secundùm Matthæum* (Vorlageform des Erscheinungsvermerks: Ex Officina Commeliniana, 1602), pp. 698–706. See Homily 82 (not 83) in *NPNF1*, vol. 10, pp. 491–497.

26. This reference is unclear not only from the use of chapter instead of epistle, but the letters 65 and 66 in book 2 do not seem to the point. Epistles 65 and 66 in other books were difficult to discern as matches either. See the index under excommunication—none of which entries list any letters numbered 65 or 66—for other letters in Gregory Magnus, *Opera*, Tom. 4 (1613), p. 1011. See the book 2 letters 65–66 on pages 179–181. See also Gregory to John, Bishop of Syracuse, October 598, Book 9, Letter 25 in *The Letters of Gregory the Great*, trans. John R. C. Martyn (Pontifical Institute of Mediaeval Studies, 2004), pp. 560–561. Martyn does not follow the numbering in Migne nor the old numbering.

27. Walafried Strabo, *De Rebus Ecclesiasticis*, Caput XVII, De virtute sacramentorum, et cur ab eis criminosi suspendantur, *PL* 114, cols. 957–958.

28. The 1647 example from EEB has corrections in hand of spelling errors and here notes that ἐν was misspelled. While crossed out, it appears to have been αν. ESTC does not note any errata for any edition of the Propositions.

the law namely, and goſpel, or by reason of scandal either of false doctrine or wicked life. For these causes therefore, or for some one of them, they are to be kept back from the sacrament of the Lord's Supper (a lawful judicial trial going before) according to the interdiction of Chriſt, forbidding that that which is holy be given to dogs, or pearls be caſt before swine (Matt. 7:6); and this censure of suſpension is to continue till the offenders bring forth fruits worthy of repentance.

Prior, illa minorque censura ex inſtituto Chriſti irroganda eſt in ejusmodi homines qui baptismum susceperunt, seque pro veræ ecclesiæ membris gerunt; indonei tamen ac indigni depræhenduntur qui signis gratiæ divinæ cum ecclesia communicent; sive propter rerum divinarum, legis scilicet et evangelii crassam ignorantiam; sive propter scandalum doctrinæ pravæ, vel vitæ improbæ: Propter has ignitur causas, vel harum aliquam, a sacramento cœnæ Domini, præcunte legitima cognitione, arcendi sunt; juxta interdictum divinum, quo [illud]²⁹ quod santum eſt, canibus dari, vel margaritas coram porcis proiici prohibetur (Matt. 7:6). Idque tantiſper dum tulerint καρποὺς ἀξίους τῆς μετανοίας.³⁰

14. For the asserting and defending of this suſpension there is no small accession of ſtrength from the nature of the sacrament itself, and the inſtitution and end thereof. The Word of God indeed is to be preached, as well to the ungodly and impenitent that they may be converted, as to the godly and repenting, that they may be confirmed. But the sacrament of the Lord's Supper is by God inſtituted not for beginning the work of grace, but for nourishing and increasing grace, and therefore, none³¹ is to be admitted to the Lord's Supper who by his life teſtifies that he is impenitent and not as yet converted.

Suſpensioni huic asserendæ haut exiguum robur accedit ex ipsius sacramenti natura, inſtitutione et fine. Annunciandum eſt quidem verbum Dei tam impiis et impœnitentibus ut convertantur, quam piis et pænitentibus, ut confirmentur: Sacramentum vero Cœne Domini divnitus inſtitutun eſt, ad gratiam nutriendam et augendam, non item ad gratiam inchoandam; ac proinpe nemo ad S., Cœnam addmictendus eſt, qui vita [sua]³² teſtatur se impœnitentem et impium esse.

15. Indeed, if the Lord had inſtituted this sacrament that not only it should nourish and cherish faith, and seal the promises of the goſpel, but also should begin the work of grace in sinners and give regeneration itself as the inſtrumental cause thereof, verily even the moſt wicked, moſt unclean, and moſt unworthy were to be admitted. But the Reformed churches do otherwise judge of the nature of this sacrament, which shall be abundantly manifeſt by the gleaning of these following teſtimonies [Propositions 16–18].

---

29. The 1648 Latin edition adds a missing "illud" (that).

30. 1647: μεταν ίας. 1648: μετανο ίας.

31. *Works* (1844): "no one."

32. The 1648 Latin edition omits "sua."

Profecto si ad id instituisset Dominus hoc sacramentum ut non tantum fidem foveat atque alat, promissionesque evangelii obsignet; sed etiam opus gratiæ in peccatoribus inchœt, ac ipsam regenerationem (tanquam causa illius instrumentalis) exhibeat; omnio ad mensam Domini admittendi forent impurissimi etiam et indignissimi homines. Atqui aliter sentiunt ecclesiæ Reformatæ de natura hujus sacramenti; quod ex sequenti specilegio quantulocunque satis superque manifestum erit.

16. The Scottish Confession, Article 23. But we confess that "the Lord's Supper belongs only to those of the household of faith, who can try and examine themselves, as well in faith, as in the duties of faith towards their neighbors. Whoso abides without faith and in variance with their brethren, do at that holy table eat and drink unworthily. Hence it is that the pastors in our church do enter on a public and particular examination both of the knowledge, conversation, and life of those who are to be admitted to the Lord's table."[33] The Belgic Confession, Article 35. "We believe also and confess that our Lord Jesus Christ has ordained the holy sacrament of His supper that in it He may nourish and uphold them whom He has already regenerated." [34]

Confessio Scoticana Art. 23. *Cœnam vero Domini tantum Domesticis [fidei] qui se examinare et probare possunt tam in fidei quam in fidei officiis erga proximos, pertinere confitemur. Qui sine fide aut qui cum fratribus suis in dissentione manentes, in sacra illa mensa edunt et bibunt, idigne edunt. Hinc est quod in ecclesia nostra pastores publicum et particulare examentum cognitionis tum conversationis ineunt, eorum qui ad Cœnam Domini Iesu sunt admittendi.* Confessio Belgica, Art. 35. *Credimus etiam et confitemur D. Jesum Christum servatorem nostrum, Sacrsanctum cœnæ suæ sacræmentum instituisse, ut in eanutriat ac sustentet eos quos jam regeneravit.*

17. The Saxon Confession, Article 15, Of the Lord's Supper. "The Lord wills that every receiver be particularly confirmed by this testimony, so that he may be certified that the benefits of the gospel do appertain to himself, seeing the preaching is common, and by this testimony, by this receiving, he shows that thou art one of his members, and washed with his blood." And by and by, "Thus therefore we instruct the church that it behooves them that come to the Supper to bring with them repentance or conversion, and (faith being now kindled in the mediation of the death, and resurrection, and the benefits of the Son of God) to seek here the confirmation of this faith."[35] The very same things are set down, and that in the very same words, in the consent of the Churches of Poland in the Sendomirian Synod, Anno 1570, Article of the Lord's Supper.[36]

---

33. Compare with James T. Dennison, Jr., *Reformed Confessions of the 16th and 17th Centuries in English Translation*, 4 vols. (Reformation Heritage Books, 2008–2014), 2.204.

34. Compare with *Reformed Confessions of the 16th and 17th Centuries*, 2.245–246.

35. See *An Harmony of the Confessions of the Faith of the Christian and Reformed Churches* (1643), pp. 335, 336.

36. Dennison, 3.239–244.

Confessio Saxonica, Art. 5. De Cœna Domini. *Vult* (Dominus) *quemlibet sumentem hoc teſtomonio singulariter confirmare, ut ſtatuat ad se pertinere beneficia evangelii, cum Concio sit communis: et hoc teſtimonio, hac sumptione, oſtendit te ipsius membrum esse, et te ablutum esse sanguine suo. Et mox.*[37] *Sic igitur erudimus ecclesiam, accessuros ad Cœnam Domini oportere pænitentiam seu conversionem adferre: et accensa iam fide in cogitatione de morte et resurreƈtione et beneficiis filii Dei, querere hic confirmationem hujus fidei.* Hæc eadem habentur, et quidem ἀυτολεξεὶ {in concensu Poloniæ faƈto}[38] in Synodo Sendomiriensi Anno, 1570, Art. De Cœna Domini.

18. The Bohemian Confession, Article 11. "Next our divines teach that the sacraments of themselves, or as some say, *ex opere operato*, do not confer grace to those who are not firſt endued with good motions and inwardly quickened by the Holy Spirit; neither do they beſtow juſtifying faith, which makes the soul of man in all things obsequious, truſting, and obedient to God; for faith muſt go before (we ſpeak of them of ripe years) which quickens a man by the work of the Holy Spirit, and puts good motions into the heart."[39] And after: "But if any come unworthily to the sacraments, he is not made by them worthy or clean, but does only bring greater sin and damnation on himself.

Confessio Bohemica, Art. 11. *Docent deinde (noſtri) quod Sacramenta per se, vel ut quidam dicunt, ex opere operato, his qui prius bono motu non sunt præditi, et intus per Spiritum Sanƈtum vivificati, non conferunt gratiam; nec fidem illam juſtificantem quæ mentem hominis Deo per omnia obsequentem, fidentem ac morigerum reddit, largiuntur. Præcedere enim fidem oportuit (de adultis loquimur) quæ hominem per Spiritum Sanctum vivficet, et Cordi bonos motus iniciat. Et infra. Enim vero, si quis indigne ad sacramenta accesserit, non is per ea dignus aut mundus redditur: sed inde sibi tantum majus peccatum et damnationem accersit.*

19. Seeing, then, in the holy Supper, that is, in the receiving the sacramental elements (which is here diſtinguished from the prayers and exhortations accompanying that aƈtion), the benefits of the goſpel are not firſt received, but for them being received are thanks given; neither by partaking thereof does God beſtow the very ſpiritual life, but does preserve, cherish, and perfeƈt that life. And seeing the Word of God is accounted in the manner of letters patents, but Sacraments like seals (as rightly the Helvetian Confession says, chap. 19),[40] it plainly follows that those are to be kept back from the Lord's Supper, which by their fruits and manners do prove themselves to be ungodly or impenitent, and ſtrangers or aliens from all communion with Chriſt. Nor are the promises of grace sealed to any other than to those to whom these promises do belong, for otherwise the seal annexed should contradiƈt and gainsay the letters patents, and by the visible Word those should be loosed

---

37. The 1648 Latin reads "Dt mox."

38. The text between braces was omitted in the 1648 Latin edition.

39. The Bohemian Confession of 1573, article 11, in Dennison, 3.361.

40. See Dennison, 2.859.

and remitted, which [*who*] by the audible Word are bound and condemned. But this is such an absurdity, as that if any would, yet he cannot smooth or heal it with any plaſter.

Cum igitur in Sacra Cœna non primum accipiantur beneficia evangeli, sed pro acceptis gratiæ agantur; nec per illius participationem Deus largiatur ipsam vitam Spiritualem, sed vitam illam conservet, foveat et perficiat: cumque verbum Dei habeatur inſtar tabularum vel literarum; Sacramenta vero inſtar sigillorum, ut reĉte ait Confessio Helvetica, cap. 19. Plane consequitur, quod ab ea arcendi sint qui fructibus moribusque suis, se impios vel impœnitentes, atque ab omni cum Chriſto communione alienos esse, certo probant: Neque enim promissiones gratiæ aliis obsignantur quam illis ad quos promissiones illæ pertinent: alioqui sigillum appensum repugnaret et contradiceret ipsi diplomati: ac verbo *visibili* solverentur qui *audibili* ligantur: atqui hoc absurdum ejusmodi eſt, ut si quis emplaſtro quocunque lenire velit, handquaquam poterit.

20. But as known, impious, and unregenerate persons have no right to the holy table, so also ungodly [*sic* godly][41] persons by reason of a grievous scandal are juſtly for a time deprived of it; for it is not lawful or allowable that the comforts and promises which belong only to such as believe and repent, should be sealed unto known unclean persons, and those who walk inordinately, whether such as are not yet regenerate, or such as are regenerate but fallen and not yet reſtored or risen from their fall. The same discipline plainly was shadowed forth under the Old Teſtament, for none of God's people during their legal pollution were permitted to enter into the Tabernacle, or to have access to the solemn sacrifices and society of the church. And much more were wicked and notorious offenders debarred from the Temple ever until by an offering for sin, together with a solemn confession thereof, being cleansed, they were reconciled unto God (Num. 5:6–8; Lev. 5:1–7; Lev. 6:1–8).

Quemadmodum autem manifeſto impii ac irregeniti[42] nihil juris ad sacram mensam adepti sunt: ita et pii jure illo, propter grave scandalum ad tempus merito privantur. Neque enim cognitis ac notatis hominibus impuris, illisive qui ambuland ἀτάκτως (sive nondum renati fuerint, sive renati lapsi, at nondum inſtaurati, nec a lapsu resurgentes) promissiones ac consolationes illas quæ credentibus ac resipiscentibus[43] saĉtæ suut, obsignari fas eſt. Iſtiusmodi plane disciplina sub veteri Teſtamento adumbrata fuit; Nemo enim ex Dei Populo, durante immunditie legali, tabernaculum ingredi, aut ad Sacra Solemnia et commercium ecclesiæ accedere permittebatur: Ac multo magis templi aditu arcebantur impii et scelerati, tantiſper

---

41. The Latin texts of 1647 and 1648 and the context both indicate that this should read "godly" rather thant "ungodly," which is incorrect in both the Edinburgh and London 1647 English editions and in *Works* (1844).

42. 1647: irregentii. This was corrected by hand in the margin similar to the prior errors mentioned.

43. 1648: resipistibus.

dum oblatione pro delicto una cum solemni ejusdem confessione, rite expiati Deo reconciliarentur (Num. 5:6-8; Lev. 5. ad vers. 7 cum Lev. 6 ad vers. 8).

21. Yea, that those who were polluted with sins and crimes were reckoned among the unclean in the Law, Maimonides proves out of Levitcus 20:3, 18:24; Numbers 35:33–34 (*in More Nevochim*, Part. 3. Chap. 47).[44] Therefore, seeing the shedding of man's blood was rightly esteemed the greatest pollution of all, hence it was that as the society of the leprous was shunned by the clean, so the company of murderers by good men was most religiously avoided (Lament. 4:13–15). The same thing is witnessed by Ananias the high priest in Josephus *Of the Jewish War*, book 4, chapter 5,[45] where he says that those false Zealots of that time, bloody men, ought to have been restrained from access to the Temple by reason of the pollution of murder. Yea, as Philo the Jew witnesses in his book *Of the Offerers of Sacrifices*, whosoever were found unworthy and wicked, were by edict forbidden to approach the holy thresholds.[46]

Sed et immundis sceleribus pollutos ex lege accenseri, Maimonides *in More Nevochim*, part 3, cap. 47, probat, ex Lev. 20:3, Lev. 18:24, Num. 35:33–34. Itaque cum sanguinis insontium profusio, longe maxima pollutio jure existimaretur; hinc erat quod sicut leprosi consortium a viris sanis, ita homicidæ consortium a viris probis religiosissime divitabatur; Lament. Jer. 4:13–15. Testis porro est Ananus ponifex,[47] apud Josephum *de bello Jud.*, lib. 4, cap. 5. Pseudozelotas illius temporis, homines sanguinarios, templi aditu arcendos fuisse, propter τὴν μιαιφωνίαν. Quin et teste Philone, lib. *de offrentibus victimas*, edicto prohibebantur sacra adire limina quotquot indigni ac improbi deprehenderentur.

22.   Neither must that be passed by which was noted by Zonaras, Book 4 of his *Annals*[48] (whereof see also Scaliger agreeing with him, in *Elench. Triheres. Nicserrar.* Cap. 28),[49] namely that the Essenes were forbidden the holy place as being heinous and piacular transgressors, and such as held other opinions, and did otherwise teach concerning sacrifices than according to the Law, and observed not the ordinances of Moses, whence it proceeded that they

---

44. Moses Maimonides, Johann Buxtorf, *Rabbi Mosis Majemonidis liber* מורה נבוכים *Doctor perplexorum ... Rabbi Mosis Majemonidis liber [Moreh nevukhim] Doctor perplexorum: ad dubia & obscuriora Scripturæ loca rectiùs intelligenda veluti clavem continens, prout in præfatione, in quâ de authoris vitâ, & operis totius ratione agitur, pleniùs explicatur* (Basiliæ, 1629), page 493.

45. "The Jewish War," in *The Works of Josephus*, volume 4, trans. William Whiston (1737; repr. New York: Armstrong & Son, 1889), book 4, chapter 3, §13, p. 99.

46. See *The Works of Philo Judæus*, trans. C. D. Yonge, volume 3 (London: Bohn, 1855), p. 230. *Works* (1844) has "threshold."

47. 1648 Latin text: "ponfex."

48. See Johannes Zonaras, *Corpus Universæ Historiæ, præsertim Bizantinæ: Ioannis Zonaræ Annales* (Lutetiæ: Apud Gulielmum Chaudiere, 1567), p. 43v.

49. Joseph Juste Scaliger, *Elenchus Trihæresii Nicolai Serarii* (Franekeræ: Radeus, 1605), p. 228. "Itaque non mirum, si tanquam εξαγεῖς et piaculares aditu Templi prohibebantur."

sacrificed privately. Yea, and also the Essenes themselves did thrust away from their congregations those that were wicked. Whereof see Drusius, of the three sects of Jews, Lib. 4. cap. 22.[50]

Nec præteriri oportet quod a Zonara, *Annal.*, tom 1, annotatum est (de qua re, vide etiam suffragantem Scaligerum, in *Elench. Trihæres. Nic. Serrar.*, cap. 28). Nempe Essænos tanquam εξαγεῖς et piaculares (ut qui aliter sentirent et docerent de sacrificiis quam juxta legem, nec ritus Moisaicos observarent) communi sacrario prehibitos fuisse, nec intra Templum admissos, proptereaque privatim sacraficasse. Quid, quod ipsi etiam Esseni, quos deprehenderant improbos, a sua congregatione depulerint? De quo vide, Drusium *de tribus sectis Judæorum*, lib. 4, cap. 22.

23. God verily would not have His Temple to be made open to unworthy and unclean worshippers, nor was it free for such men to enter into the Temple. See Nazianzen, Orat. 21.[51] The same thing is witnessed and declared by divers late writers, such as have been and are more acquainted with the Jewish antiquities. Consult the annotations of Vatablus and of Ainsworth, an English writer, upon Psalm 118:19–20;[52] also Constantius L'Empereur, *Annotat., in Cod. Middoth*, cap. 2, pages 44, 45;[53] Cornelius Bertramus, *Of the Common-wealth of the Hebrews*, cap. 7;[54] Henrie Vorstius, *Animadvers. in Pirk. Rab. Eliezer*, page 169.[55] The same may be proved out of Ezekiel 23:38–39, Jeremiah 7:9–12, whence also it was that the solemn and public society in the Temple had the name of the Assembly of the Righteous and Congregation of Saints (Ps. 89:5, 7; Ps. 111:1; Ps. 147: 1). Hence also is that [in] Psalm 118:19–20 of the gates of righteousness by which the righteous enter.

Noluit sane Deus Templum suum patere indignis ac impuris cultoribus; nec instiusmodi hominibus Templum ingridi liberum fuit. Ita Nazianzenus, Orat. 21. Ita etiam perhibent neoterici, Hebræorum[56] monumentis reserandis assuetiores.

---

50. Johannes Drusius, *De Sectis Judaicis Commentarii, Trihæresio et Minervali Nic. Serarii opposite* (Arnhemiæ: Jansonium, 1619), pp. 181–201.

51. Gregory Nazianzen, Oration 21, On the Great Athanasius, Bishop of Alexandria, in *NPNF2*, vol. 7, pp. 269–280.

52. See François Vatable, in *Liber Psalmorvm Davidis: Tralatio duplex, vetus et nova. Hæc posterior, Sanctis Pagnini … ex Francisci Vatabli Hebraicarum literarum professoris quondam Regii eruditissimis prælectionibus emendata et expolita*, etc. (Liva Rob. Stephani, [1556]), p. 415. Henry Ainsworth, *Annotations upon the five bookes of Moses, the booke of the Psalmes, and the Song of Songs, or, Canticles*, etc. (1627; repr. 2 vols., Glasgow: Blackie, 1843), 2.641.

53. Constantine L'Empereur, *Talmudis Babylonici codex Middoth* (Elzevir, 1630), pp. 44–45.

54. Bonaventure Corneille Bertram, *De Republica Ebræorum* (Lugduni Batavorum: Ex officina Ioannis Maire), pp. 81–86.

55. Willem Henricus Vorstius, *Capitula R. Elieser continentia imprimis succinctam historiæ sacræ recensionem circiter 3400 ann. sive à creatione usque ad Mardochæiætatem cum veterum rabbinorum commentariis. Ex Hebræo in Latinum translata* (Lugduni Batavorum: Maire, 1644), page 169.

56. 1648: "Ha bræorum."

Consule Vatabili et Answorthi Angli annotata in Psal. 118:19–20.[57] Item Cornelium Bertramum de *Repub. Ebær.*, cap. 7. Constantinum L'Empereur, *Annotat. in Cod. Middoth*, cap. 2, pp. 44, 45. Henricum Vorstium, *animadv. in Pirke R. Elieser*, pag. 169. Idem evinci potest ex Ezech. 23:38–39; Jer. 7:9–11. Unde etiam cœtus solemnis et publicus in Templo, nomine cœtus justorum, et congregationis sanctorum potitus fuerat (Psal. 89:5–7; Psal. 111:1; Psal. 147:1. Hinc et illud, Psal. 118:19–20). De portis justitiæ; per quas justi intrant.

24. That which is now driven at is not that all wicked and unclean persons should be utterly excluded from our ecclesiastical societies, and so from all hearing of God's Word. Yea, there is nothing less intended. For the Word of God is the instrument as well of conversion as of confirmation, and therefore is to be preached as well to the not converted [*the unconverted*] as to the converted, as well to the repenting as the unrepenting. The Temple indeed of Jerusalem had special promises, as it were pointing out with the finger a communion with God through Christ (1 Kings 8:30, 48; Dan. 6:10; 2 Chron. 6:16, etc.,[58] 7:15–16. But it is far otherwise with our temples or places of church assemblies, "because our temples contain nothing sacramental in them, such as the Tabernacle and Temple contained," as the most learned Professors of Leyden said rightly in *Synopsis Purioris Theologiæ*, Disputatio 48. Thes. 47.[59]

Id jam non agitur, ut prorsus a cœtibus nostris ecclesiasticis, adeoque a verbi divini auditu, omnes impii ac impuri excludantur. Nihil minus: est enim verbum Dei

---

57. 1648: Psal. 118:12–10 [*sic*].

58. Both Latin texts correct the "and" to "and etc.," i.e., verse 16 and following, rather than placing the "and" with the next reference, which full context required.

59. Antonius Walæus (1573–1639), Andreas Rivetus (1572–1651), Antonius Thysius (1603–1665), John Polyander (1568–1646), *Synopsis Purioris Theologiæ* (Leyden: 1625; 3rd ed., Lugdunum Batavorum: Elzevier, 1642), pp. 721–722. See *Synopsis Purioris Theologiæ / Synopsis of a Purer Theology: Latin Text and English Translation*, Volume 3, Disputations 43–52 (Brill, 2020), pp. 401. "But although in the first church it was customary to exclude even from the buildings those who were excommunicated,[32] we nevertheless hold the view that this is not necessary under the New Testament, since our temples in and of themselves possess nothing sacramental (such as the tabernacle and temple of the Old Testament possessed) nor hold any special promises of grace above other places, as the papal teachers superstitiously believe contrary to Christ's assertion in John 4:21, 23.[33] Secondly, because those who have been excommunicated are not to be excluded from either the public or private hearing of the Word, since it contains the warnings and encouragements unto faith and repentance, and because prayers for their conversion are offered by the church in it. In the same way we see in 1 Corinthians 14:23 that even unbelievers were admitted to the gatherings of Christians for that purpose, and that Christ Himself associated with sinners and tax collectors for that purpose; and the apostle expressly warns in 2 Thessalonians 3:15: "That we not treat that sort of man as an enemy, but that we admonish him as a brother." See pages 395 and 401 for references 32 (which directs to fn24) and 33 which provides background on the early church and the papal church practice.

tam conversionis quam confirmationis organum, ac proinde tam conversis quam resipiscentibus annunciandum eſt. Templum Hierosolymitanum ſpeciales quidem habuit promissiones, quasi digito monſtrantes communionem cum Deo per Christum (1. Reg. 8:30, 48; Dan. 6:10; 2 Paral. 6:16 &c.; 7:15–16). De Templis noſtris diſpar eſt ratio: *Quia Templa noſtra nihil in se sacramentale continent?* ut quidem recte doctissimi professores Leidenses,[60] in *Synops. Pur. Theol.*, Diſp. 48, Thes. 47.

25. Wherefore, the point to be here considered as that which is now aimed at is this: that howsoever even under the New Teſtament, the uncleanness of those to whom the Word of God is preached be tolerated, yet all such of what eſtate or condition soever in the church as are defiled with manifeſt and grievous scandals, and do thereby witness themselves to be without the inward and ſpiritual communion with Chriſt and the faithful, may and are to be altogether discharged from the communion of the Lord's Supper, until they repent and change their manners.

Quamobrem is jam scopus reſpici debet, ut sub novo etiam Teſtamento, utcunque feratur impuritas illorum quibus annuncitur verbum divinum: omnes tamen cujuscunque ſtatus vel conditionis ecclesia, qui manifeſtis gravibusque scandalis contaminati, se extra internam et ſpiritulem[61] cum Chriſto et fidelibus communiionem esse teſtantur: a Cœnæ Dominicæ communion plane arceantur, quoad resipuerint et mores mutaverint.

26. Besides, even those to whom it was not permitted to go into the holy courts of Israel and to ingyre[62] themselves into ecclesiaſtical communion, and who did ſtand between the court of Israel and the utter [*outer*] wall, were not therefore to be kept back from hearing the Word. For in Solomon's Porch, and so in the *intramurale*, or court, of the Gentiles, the goſpel was preached, both by Chriſt (John 10:23) and also by the apoſtles (Acts 3:11 and 5:12); and that of purpose, because of the reason brought by Pineda, *Of the Things of Solomon* (book 5, chap. 19),[63] because a more frequent multitude was there and somewhat larger opportunity of sowing the goſpel. Wherefore, to any whomsoever, even heathen people meeting there, the Lord would have the Word to be preached, who, notwithſtanding, purging the Temple, did not only overthrow the tables of moneychangers and chairs of those that sold doves, but also caſt forth the buyers and sellers themselves (Matt. 21:12); for He could not endure either such things or such persons in the Temple.

Quid quod illi etiam quibus sacra Iſrælis atria adire, adeoque sese in communionem

---

60. 1648: "Leidensis."

61. 1648: "spiritulam."

62. *Ingyre*: "To push (oneself) in, obtrude (oneself), chiefly intrusively or presumptuously. Also, to insinuate (oneself)" (*DSL*). *Works* (1844) renders this "ingratiate." This passage in Gillespie is one of the examples of this usage (*DSL* cites the English edition of 1647).

63. *Joannis de Pineda Hiſpalensis e Societate Jesu Ad suos in Salomonem Commentarios* (Moguntiæ: Hierati, [1613]), p. 450.

ecclesiasticam ingerere concessum non erat, quique consistebant in Interemurali, non propterea ab omni verbi divini auditu arcendi fuerant? Nam in porticu Solomonis, adeoque in Intermurali seu atrio gentium, annunciatum fuit evangelium, tum a Christo (Joh. 10:23) tum ab apostolis (Act. 3:11 et 5:12). Idque consulto, ob rationem allatam a Pineda, *de Rebus Solomonis* (lib. 5, cap. 19). Quia ibi densior erat multitudo, et ampliuscula seminandi evangelii occasio, quare, quibusvis ibi convenientibus, etiam ethnicis, verbum prædicari voluit Dominus: qui tamen Templum repurgans, non solum mensas numulariorum, et Cathedras vendentium subvertit: sed et ipsos vendentes ac ementes ejecit (Math. 21:12). Neque enim vel personas istiusmodi in Templo ferre potuit.

27. Although, then, the gospel is to be preached to every creature, the Lord in express words commanding the same (Mark 16:15), yet not to everyone is set open an access to the holy supper. It is granted that hypocrites do lurk in the church, who hardly can be convicted and discovered, much less repelled from the Lord's Supper. Such, therefore, are to be suffered till by the fan of judgment the grain be separate[d] from the chaff; but those whose wicked deeds or words are known and made manifest, are altogether to be debarred from partaking those symbols of the covenant of the gospel, lest that the name of God be greatly disgraced, whilest sins are permitted to spread abroad in the church unpunished; or, lest the stewards of Christ by imparting the signs of the grace of God to such as are continuing in the state of impurity and scandal, be partakers of their sins. Hitherto of suspension.

Etsi igitur omni creaturæ annunciandum sit evangelium, id mandante Domino disertis verbis (Marc. 16:15), non tamen quibusvis in ecclesia patet accessus ad sacram cœnam. Id quidem hand diffitendum est, delitescere in ecclesia hypocritas, qui vix redargui, nedum a mensa Domini arceri possunt: tales igitur ferendi sunt, donec ventilabro judicii granum a palea separetur. Ast illi quorum impia πράγματα vel ῥήματα innotescunt; a symbolorum istorum fœderis evangelici participatione omnio arcendi sunt, ne Dei nomen summua contumelia afficiatur, dum scelera impune in ecclesia grassari permittuntur; neve œconomi Christi signa gratiæ Dei illis, in statu impuritatis ac scandali perseverantibus, impertiendo, peccatis illorum communicent. Hactenius de suspensione.

28. Excommunication ought not to be proceeded unto except when extreme necessity constrains. But whensoever the soul of the sinner cannot otherwise be healed, and that the safety of the church requires the cutting off of this or that member, it behooves to use this last remedy. In the Church of Rome, indeed, excommunication has been turned into greatest injustice and tyranny (as the Pharisees abused the casting out of the synagogues, which was their excommunication) to the fulfilling of the lust of their own minds; yet the ordinance of Christ is not therefore by any of the Reformed Religion to be utterly thrust away and wholly rejected. What Protestant knows not that the vassals of Antichrist have drawn the Lord's Supper into the worst and most pernicious abuses, as also the ordination of ministers and other ordinances of

the gospel? Yet, who will say that things necessary (whether the necessity be that of command or that of the means or end) are to be taken away because of the abuse?[64]

Ad excommunicationem, non nisi extrema necessitate cogente, procedendum est: at quotiescunque delinquentis anima aliter sanari nequit, ecclesiæque salus membri hujus vel illius abscissionem flagitat, ultimo hoc remedio uti oportet. In ecclesia quidem Romana excommunicatio in summam injustitiam et tyrannidem conversa est; quemadomodum etiam Pharisæi ejectione ex synagoga (quæ illis excommunicatio plane fuit) ad explendam animi sui libidinem abutebantur: Non tamen proptera Sanctum Christi institutum, a Reformatis ullis exterminandum aut explodendum est. Quis Reformatus nescit, Antichristi mancipia in pessimos et perniciosissimos abusus rapuisse Cœnam Domini, ordinationem ministrorum, aliaque instituta evangelica? At quis dixerit res necessarias (sive necessitas sit præcepti, sive medii finisve) propter abusum, e medio tollendas esse?

29. They, therefore, who with a high hand do persevere in their wickedness after foregoing admonitions stubbornly despised or carelessly neglected, are justly by excommunication in the name of the Lord Jesus Christ cut off and cast out from the society of the faithful, and are pronounced to be cast out from the church, until being filled with shame and cast down, they shall return again to a more sound mind, and by confession of their sin and amendment of their lives, they shall show tokens of repentance, Matthew 18:16–18, 1 Corinthians 5:13, which places are also alleged in the Confession of Bohemia, Article 8,[65] to prove that the excommunication of the impenitent and stubborn, whose wickedness is known, is commanded of the Lord. But if stubborn heretics or unclean persons be not removed or cast out from the church, therein do the governors of the church sin and are found guilty (Rev. 2:14, 20).

Igitur qui elata manu in sua pravitate perseverant, post prævias admonitiones procaciter despectas, vel socorditer neglectas, ex cœtu fidelium, in nomine Domini nostri Iesu Christi, per excommunicationem merito exscinduntur et ejiciuntur, ejectique ab ecclesia esse pronunciantur; donec pudore suffusi et dejecti ad saniorem mentem redierint, atque criminis confessione seu exomologesi[s],[66] morumque emendatione, vere resipiscentiæ signa ostenderint: Matth. 18:15–18; 1 Cor. 5:13. Atque hæc quidem loca allegantur etiam in Bohemica Confessione, Art. 8. Ut probetur,

---

64. See Gillespie's sermon before the Commons and *Brotherly Examination*, herein on pages 105 and 228. See the discussion in *A Dispute Against the English Popish Ceremonies*, 3.2 (2013), pp149ff.

65. See the Bohemian Confession of 1573 in Dennison, 3.352.

66. Both Latin editions leave off the final "s." Interestingly, the scribe noting errors in the 1647 EEB example underlined the passage but did not note a specific correction. If he were strictly comparing the two texts, there is no obvious reason to do this, and something more significant may be at work with this scribe's corrections (e.g., checking the Latin against the English, etc., actually preparing for the 1648 reissue, etc.).

excommunicationem impœnitentium et contumacium, quorum nota est impietas, a
Domino præceptam esse. Quod si contumaces hæretici, vel impuri homines ecclesia
non moveantur, in eo peccant atque rei peraguntur ecclesiæ rectores. Apoca. 2:14, 20.

30. But that all abuse and corruption in ecclesiastical government may be
either prevented and avoided, or taken away, or lest the power of the church,
either by the ignorance or unskillfulness of some ministers here and there, or
also by too much heat and fervor of mind, should run out beyond measure
or bounds, or contrariwise, being shut up within straiter [*stricter*] limits
than is fitting, should be made unprofitable, feeble, or of none effect: Christ
the most wise Lawgiver of His church has foreseen and made provision to
prevent all such evils which He did foresee were to arise, and has prepared
and prescribed for them intrinsical and ecclesiastical remedies, and those also
in their kind (if lawfully and rightly applied) both sufficient and effectual:
some whereof He has most expressly propounded in His Word, and some
He has left to be drawn from thence by necessary consequence.

Atqui ut omnis regimine ecclesiastico abusus ac corruptela vel vitetur vel ausera-
tur; ac ne potestas ecclesiastica, vel nonnullorum sparsim administrorum inscitia
seu imperitia, aut etiam præfervido ingenio ac nimio animi æstit, terminos ac me-
tas exuperet atque excurrat; vel e contra, intra[67] arctiores, quam par est, cancellos
conclusa, inutilis, elumbis, ac frustranea reddatur: Christus sapientissimus ecclesiæ
Legislator exorituris ejusmodi malis omnibus prospexit, iisque remedia intrinseca
seu ecclesiastica, et quidem in suo genere (si rite recteque adhibeantur) tum suffi-
cientia tum efficacia aptavit ac præstituit; eorumque nonnula diserte admodum in
verbo suo proposuit, alia per necessariam consequentiam inde deducenda reliquit.

31. Therefore, by reason of the danger of that which is called *clavis errans*, or
a wrong key, and that it may not be permitted to particular churches to err or
sin licentiously, and lest any man's cause be overthrown and perish, who in
a particular church had perhaps the same men [as] both his adversaries and
his judges; also that common businesses which do belong to many churches,
together with the more weighty and difficult controversies (the deciding
whereof in the consistories of particular churches is not safe to be adventured
upon) may be handled and determined by a common counsel of presbyteries.
Finally, that the governors of particular churches may impart help mutually
one to another against the cunning and subtle enemies of the truth, and may
join their strength together (such as it is) by an holy combination, and that
the church may be as a camp of an army well-ordered, lest while everyone
strives singly all of them be subdued and overcome, or lest by reason of the
scarcity of prudent and godly counselors (in the multitude of whom is safety)
the affairs of the church be undone: For all those considerations particular
churches must be subordinate to classical presbyteries and synods.

Igitur propter clavis (quod ajunt) errantis periculum, atque ut particularibus

---

67. 1647: intar (corrected in the margin in the EEB example).

ecclesiis aberrandi et peccandi licentia non fiat; nec de illius causa actum sit, qui in ecclesia particulari eosdem forte habuit adversarios et judices; ut etiam communia negotia quæ ad multas ecclesias spectant; necnon controversiæ graviores et difficiliores, quas in particularium ecclesiarum consistoriis decidi minime tutum est, communi presbyterorum consilio tractentur et definiantur; Denique ut ecclesiarum rectores sibi mutuo, contra pervigiles ac astutos veritatis hostes, auxilium impendant, viresque suas, quantæ quantæ illæ sint, sancta conspiratione jungant, sitque ecclesia veluti castrorum acies ordinata; ne dum singuli pugnant, universi vincantur; neve piorum ac prudentum consiliariorum (in quorum multitudine salus est) penuria, res ecclesiasticæ corruant; particulares ecclesias, earumque consistoria, presbyteriis classicalibus et synodis subordinari ac subjici oportet.

32. Wherefore, it is not lawful to particular churches or (as commonly they are called) parochial, either to decline the authority of classes or synods, where they are lawfully settled, or may be had (much less to withdraw themselves from that authority if they have once acknowledged it), or to refuse such lawful ordinances or decrees of the classes or synods as, being agreeable to the Word of God, are with authority imposed upon them (Acts 15:2, 6, 22–24, 28–29. Acts 16:4).

Quapropter ecclesiis particularibus, seu (ut vulgo nuncupantur) parochialibus, nec ipsarum classium synodorumqe (ubi illa legitime constituuntur, vel haberi possunt) auctoritatem declinare; nedum ab ea semel agnita sese subducere, nec classium vel synodorum legitima ac verbo Dei consentanea statuta, aut decreta, quæ cum autoritate iis imponuntur, respuere fas est (Act. 15:2, 6, 22–24, 28–29. Act. 16:4).

33. Although synods assemble more seldom, classes and consistories of particular churches more frequently, yet that synods, both provincial and national, assemble at set and ordinary times, as well as classes and parochial consistories, is very expedient, and for the due preservation of church policy and discipline, necessary. Sometimes, indeed, it is expedient they be assembled occasionally, that the urgent necessity of the church may be the more speedily provided for, namely when such a business happens, which without great danger cannot be put off till the appointed time of the Synod.

Etsi synodi rarius, classes et particularium ecclesiarum consistoria frequentius et sæpius conveniant; synodos tamen tum provinciales tum nationales, non minus quam classes et parochialia consistoria, statis et ordinariis temporibus coire summopere expedit, et politiæ ecclesiasticæ rite conservanda necessarium est: Nonnunquam sane pro re nata eas cogi expedit, ut urgenti ecclesiarum necessitati ocyus occurratur; puta quando tale obvenit negotium, quod absque gravi periculo in præstitutum synodi tempus differri nequit.

34. But that, besides occasional synods, ordinary synods be kept at set times, is most profitable, not only that they may discuss and determine the more difficult ecclesiastical causes coming before them, whether by the appeal of some person aggrieved, or by the hesitation or doubting of inferior assemblies

(for such businesses very often fall out), but also that the state of the churches whereof they have the care, being more certainly and frequently searched and known, if there be anything wanting or amiss in their doctrine, discipline, or manners, or anything worthy of punishment, the slothful laborers in the vineyard of the Lord may be made to shake off the spirit of slumber and slothfulness, and be stirred up to the attending and fulfilling more diligently their calling, and not suffered any longer to sleep and snort[68] in their office; the stragglers and wanderers may be reduced [*called back*] to the way; the untoward and stiff necked, which scarce or very hardly suffer the yoke of discipline, as also unquiet persons which devise new and hurtful things, may be reduced to order. Finally, whatsoever does hinder the more quick and efficacious course of the gospel, may be discovered and removed.

Ast insuper ordinarias synodos statis temporibus haberi utilissimum est; non modo ut difficiliores causas ecclesiasticas, quæ ad eas, sive per gravati cujuslibet appellationem, sive per inferiorum conventuum απορίαν ac hæsitationem devolvuntur (ejusmodi autem negotia sæpissime obveniunt) discutiant ac definiant: Verumentiam ut ecclesiarum, quarum cura eis est, statu certius, et quidem non ita raro explorato et cognito, si quid sit quod in illarum doctrina disciplina vel moribus desideretur aut animadversione dignum sit; desidiosi in venea Domini operarii, excusso tandem incuriæ veterno, ad vocationem diligentius obeundam excitentur, nec diutius in officio suo stertere sinantur; a veritate aberrantes et deviantes reducantur; pervicaces ac cervicosi, qui jugum disciplinæ vix ac ne vix quidem patiuntur; nec non inquieti homines qui nova ac noxia moliuntur, in ordinem, redigantur; Denique quæcunque liberiorem tranquilliorem aut efficaciorem evangelii cursum impediunt, retegantur et amoveantur.

35. It is too too manifest (alas for it) that there are [those], which [*who*][69] with unwearied diligence do most carefully labor that they may oppress the liberties and rights of synods, and may take away from them all liberty of consulting of things and matters ecclesiastical, at least of determining thereof (for they well know how much the union and harmony of churches may make against their designs). But so much the more it concerns the orthodox churches to know, defend, and preserve this excellent liberty granted to them by divine right, and so to use it that imminent dangers, approaching evils, urging [*provocative*] grievances, scandals growing up, schisms rising, heresies creeping in, errors spreading, and strifes waxing hot, may be corrected and taken away, to the glory of God, [and] the edification and peace of the church.

Nimis quidem (proh dolor) in propatulo est, non deese qui studio indefesso id unice satagunt, ut synodorum jura ac libertates opprimant, omnemque de rebus et negotiis ecclesiasticis delibrandi, saltem definiendi potestatem eis præripiant. Neque enim eos latet quantum possit contra ipsorum molimina ecclesiarum unio

---

68. *Works* (1844) replaced "snort" with "snore."

69. *Works* (1844) inserted "those" without comment, and customarily that editor also replaces "which" with "who" as appropriate, without notice.

et συμφωνια. Aſt eo magis ecclesiarum ortodoxarum intereſt, præclaram hanc libertatem sibi divinitus concessam scire, asserere, conservare, eaq; sic uti, ut imminentia pericula, ingruentia mala,[70] urgentia gravamina, suppullulantia scandala, exorientia schismata, irrepentes hæreses, errores semet diffundentes, gliscentes denique lates corrigantur ac auferantur, ad Dei gloriam ecclesiæque ædificationem ac pacem.

36. Besides provincial and national synods, an oecumenical [*ecumenical*] (so called from ἀπὸ τῆς ὀικουμένης,[71] that is from the habitable world) or more truly a general, or if you will, a universal synod, if so be it be free and rightly conſtituted and no other commissioners but orthodox churches be admitted (for what communion is there of light with darkness, of righteousness with unrighteousness, or of the Temple of God with idols [1 Cor. 6:14–16]); such a synod is of ſpecial utility, peradventure also such a synod is to be hoped for, surely, it is to be wished that for defending the orthodox faith, both againſt popery and other heresies, as also for propagating it to those who are without, eſpecially the Jews, a more ſtrait and more firm consociation may be entered into. For the unanimity of all the churches as in evil it is of all things moſt hurtful, so on the contrary side, in good it is moſt pleasant, moſt profitable, and moſt effeᴄtual.

Præter synodos provinciales ac nationales, concilii etiam œcumenici (ἀπὸ τῆς ὀικουμένης, i.e., ab orbe habitato nuncupati) seu verius generalis, vel si lubet universalis, siquidem liberum sit ac reᴄte inſtitutum, nec aliarum quam orthodoxarum ecclesiarum delegati admittantur (quæ enim communio luci cum tenebris, juſtitiæ cum injuſtitia, aut Templo dei cum idolis?) summa eſt utilitas; forte etiam ſperandum, certe optandum eſt ejusmodi concilium; pro fide orthodoxa tum contra Papatum, reliquasque hæreses asserenda, tum ad extraneos, presertim vero Judæos propaganda, arᴄtior firmiorque consociatio {ac combinatio}[72] fœliciter ineatur. Etenim ecclesiarum omnium ὁμόνοια ut in malo rerum omnium perniciosissima eſt; ita ex adeverso, in bono gratissima, utilissima et efficacissima eſt.

37. Unto the universal synod also (when it may be had) is to be referred the judgment of controversies, not of all, but of those which are *controversiæ juris*, controversies of right; neither yet of all these, but of the chief and moſt weighty controversies of the orthodox faith, or of the moſt hard and unusual cases of conscience. Of the controversies of faᴄt there is another and different consideration to be had; for besides that it would be a great inconvenience that plaintiffs, persons accused, and witnesses be drawn from the moſt remote churches to the general or universal council, the visible communion itself of all the churches (on which the universal council is built, and whereupon as on a foundation it leans) is not so much of company, fellowship, or conversation, as of religion and doᴄtrine. All true churches of the world do indeed profess

---

70. The 1648 Latin edition omits "mala, urgentia."

71. *Works* (1644) set the Greek as simply "ὀικουμένη."

72. The 1648 Latin edition omitted the words between braces.

the same true religion and faith; but there is besides this a certain commixture and conjunction of the churches of the same nation, as to a more near fellowship, and some acquaintance, conversing, and companying together, which cannot be said of all the churches throughout the habitable world.

Ad Synodum etiam universalem (quando ea haberi poteſt) devolvendum eſt Judicium de controversiis, non quidem omnibus, sed de iis quæ controversiæ juris dicuntur: neque vero de universis ac singulis controversiis juris, sed de præcipuis ac gravissimis controversiis quæ sunt de fide orthodoxa, vel de difficillimis ac insolitis casibus conscientiæ: De controversiis faſti diſpar et longe alia ratio eſt. Præterquam enim quod grave foret incommodum, aſtores, reos, teſtes ex remotissimis etiam ecclesiis ad concilium œcumenicum trahi; ipsa ecclesiarum omnium visibilis communio (cui tanquam fundamento innititur concilium universale) non tam consortii ac conversationis, quam religionis ac doſtrinæ eſt. Omnes quidem totius orbis veræ ecclesiæ eandem veram religionem et fidem profitentur. Aſt ecclesiarum ejusdem nationis vel regni eſt insuper quædam ἀνάμιξις, συνήθεια ac προσδιατριβή quod de omnibus τῆς ὁικουμένης ecclesiis dici non poteſt.

38. And for this cause, as in doſtrinal controversies which are handled by theologues [*theologians*][73] and casuiſts, and in those which belong to the common ſtate of the orthodox churches, the national synod is subordinate and subjeſted to the universal lawfully conſtituted synod, and from the national to the oecumenical synod (when there is a juſt and weighty cause) an appeal is open. So there is no need that the appeals of them who complain of injury done to them through the exercise of discipline in this or that church, should go beyond the bounds of the national synod; but it is moſt agreeable to reason that they should reſt and acquiesce within those bounds and borders, and that the ultimate judgment of such matters be in the national synod, unless the thing itself be so hard and of so great moment, that the knot be juſtly thought worthy of a greater decider. In which case, the controversy which is carried to the universal synod is rather of an abſtraſt general theological proposition, than of the particular or individual case.

Idcirco ut incontroversiis doſtrinalibus quæ a theologis ac casuiſtitis traſtantur, atque in iis quæ communem ecclesiarum orthodoxarum ſtatum ſpeſtant, synodo universali legitimæ subordinatur et subjacet synodus nationalis, ac ab iſta ad illam (ubi gravis subeſt causa) provocatio patet; ita non opus eſt ut provocationes illorum qui disciplinæ ecclesiaſticæ exercitio in hac vel illa ecclesia injuriam sibi faſtam esse queritantur, synodi nationalis terminos transiliant; sed rationi maxime consentaneum eſt, ut intra terminos ac cancellos illos conquiescant, ibidemque ultimum de iis judicium fiat; nisi res ipsa tam ardua, tantive momenti sit, ut nodus majore vindice dignus merito exiſtimetur; atque tum demum, de thesi potius quam de hypothesi inſtituitur ea controversia, quæ ad synodum universalem defertur.

39. Furthermore, the adminiſtration of the ecclesiaſtic power in consiſtories,

---

73. *Works* (1844) renders this "theologists."

classes, and synods, does not at all tend to weaken in anywise, hurt, or minish [*diminish*] the authority of the civil magistrate, much less to take it away or destroy it; yea, rather, by it a most profitable help comes to the magistrate, forasmuch as by the bond of religion men's consciences are more straitly [*strictly*] tied unto him. There have been, indeed, phantastical[74] men, who under pretence and cloak of Christian liberty, would abolish and cast out laws and judgments, orders also, degrees and honors out of the commonwealth, and have been bold to reckon the function of the magistrate armed with the sword, among evil things and unlawful. But the Reformed churches do renounce and detest those dreams, and do most harmoniously and most-willingly confess and acknowledge it to be God's will that the world be governed by laws and policy, and that He Himself has appointed the civil magistrate, and has delivered to him the sword to the protection and praise of good men, but for punishment and revenge on the evil, that by this bridle men's vices and faults may be restrained, whether committed against the first or against the second table [of the Law].

Cæterum potestatis ecclesiasticæ administratio in consistoriis, classibus et syondis, haudquaquam eo tendit ut magistratus politici auctoritatem ullatenus labefactet, ladat vel minuat, nedum tollat aut destruat: quinimo utilissimum ex ea adjumentum magistratui accedit; quatenus religionis vinculo hominum conscientiæ arctius illi devinciuntur. Non defuerunt quidem fanatici, qui sub libertatis Christianæ prætextu, jura ac judicia, ordines item, gradus ac dignitates ex republica ejicire et abolere voluerint, atque magistratus gladio armati functionem rebus malis ac illicitis accensere ausi fuerint. Ecclesiæ autem Reformatæ somnia illa respuunt ac detestantur, atque consentientibus calculis lubentisssime confitentur et agnoscunt, Deum velle mundum legibus ac politia gubernari, atque constituisse magistratum politicum, eique gladium tradidisse in protectionem ac laudem proborum, in malorum autem pœnam et vindictam; ut hoc fræno cœrceantur hominum vitia ac delicta, sive contra primum sive contra secudam tabulam commissa.

40. The Reformed churches believe also and openly confess the power and authority of emperors over their empires, of kings over their kingdoms, of princes and dukes over their dominions, and of other magistrates or states over their commonwealths and cities, to be the ordinances of God Himself, appointed as well to the manifestation of His own glory, as to the singular profit of mankind: And withal, that by reason of the will of God Himself revealed in His Word, we must not only suffer and be content that those do rule which are set over their own territories, whether by hereditary or by elective right, but also to love them, fear them, and with all reverence and honor embrace them as the ambassadors and ministers of the most high and good God, being in His stead, and preferred for the good of their subjects, to pour out prayers for them, to pay tributes to them, and in all business of

---

74. *Phantastical*: a. Irrationally formulated or conceived; unreal. b. Fanciful; extravagant (*DSL*). *Works* (1844): fantastical.

the commonwealth which are not against the Word of God, to obey their laws and edicts.

Credunt etiam et palam profitentur Reformati, potestatem et authoritatem imperatorum in sua imperia, regum in sua regna, principum et ducum in sua dominia, aliorumque magistratuum[75] seu ordinum in suas respublicas ac civitates, esse ipsius Dei ordinationem, tam ad gloriæ ipsius manifestationem, quam ad singularem humani generis utilitatem destinatam: simulque oportere propter ipsius Dei voluntatem in verbo suo revelatam, non tantum pati ut ii dominentur qui ditionibus suis, sive hæreditario sive electivo jure præficiuntur, verum etiam eos tanquam Deo optimo maximo legatos ac ministros, ipsius vicem gerentes, ac in bonum subditorum præfectos amare, timere, omnique reverentia et honore prosequi, preces[76] pro iis fundere, vectigalia ac tributa iis pendere, atque in omnibus reipublicæ negotiis quæ verbo Dei non repugnant, legibus vel edictis eorum parere.

41. The orthodox churches believe also, and do willingly acknowledge, that every lawful magistrate, being by God Himself constituted the keeper and defender of both tables of the Law, may and ought first and chiefly to take care of God's glory, and (according to his place, or in his manner and way) to preserve religion when pure, and to restore it when decayed and corrupted; and also to provide a learned and godly ministry, schools also, and synods, as likewise to restrain and punish as well atheists, blasphemers, heretics and schismatics, as the violators of justice and civil peace.

Credunt porro et lubentes agnoscunt orthodoxi, quod omnis legitimus magistratus, utpote, utriusque tabulæ legis custos ac vindex divinitus constitutus, de Dei Gloria imprimis curare, atque more modoque suo religionem recte constitutam conservare, ac collapsam vel depravatam instaurare; adeoque de docto pioque ministerio, de scholis etiam et synodis prospicere; itidemque tam atheos, blasphemos, hæreticos ac schismaticos, quam justitiæ pacisque civilis temeratores cœrcere ac plectere possit ac debeat.

42. Wherefore, the opinion of those sectaries of this age is altogether to be disallowed, who, though otherwise insinuating themselves craftily into the magistrate's favor, do deny unto him the authority and right of restraining heretics and schismatics, and do hold and maintain that such persons, how much soever hurtful and pernicious enemies to true religion and to the church, yet are to be tolerated by the magistrate, if so be he conceive them to be such as no way violate the laws of the commonwealth, and in no wise disturb the civil peace.

Qua propter illorum hujus seculi sectariorum, qui cætera magistratus favorem aucupantes, ei denegant jus cœrcendi hæreticos vel schismaticos, eosque quantumlibet veræ religioni ecclesiæque noxios et exitiales, a magistratu (modo eos jure reipub.

---

75. 1647: magistratum (the person making corrections in the EEB example has inserted a "u" in the margin).

76. 1647: præces (corrected to an "e" in the margin in the EEB example).

neutiquam violare, pacemque civilem nullatenus perturcare judicet) tolerandos esse contendunt, dogma omnino improbandum eſt.

43. Yet the civil power and the ecclesiaſtical [power] ought not by any means to be confounded or mixed together. Both powers are indeed from God and ordained for His glory, and both to be guided by His Word, and both are comprehended under that precept, "Honour thy father and thy mother," so that men ought to obey both civil magiſtrates and ecclesiaſtical governors in the Lord; to both powers their proper dignity and authority is to be maintained and preserved in force. To both also is some way entruſted the keeping of both Tables of the Law, also both the one and the other do exercise some jurisdiction and give sentence of judgment in an external court or judicatory. But these, and other things of like sort, in which they agree notwithſtanding, yet by marvelous vaſt differences are they distinguished the one from the other, and the rights of both remain diſtinct, and that *eight manner of ways,*[*] which it shall not be amiss here to add, that unto each of these adminiſtrations, its own set bounds may be the better maintained.

Poteſtas tamen civilis et poteſtas ecclesiaſtica haudquaquam commisceri vel confundi debent. Utraque quidem poteſtas eſt a Deo, et adipsius gloriam inſtituta, ipsiusque verbo dirigenda, atque[77] sub præcepto illo morali, *Honora Patrem et Matrem,* comprehensa; adeo ut tum magiſtratibus politicis, tum gubernatoribus ecclesiaſticis obediendum sit in Domino. Utrique poteſtati asserenda eſt sua dignitas et auctoritas. Utrique etiam utriusque legis tabulæ cuſtodia aliqua commissa eſt. Utraque itidem jurisdictionem quandam exercet, judiciumque fert in foro exteriori. Hisce tamen, et id genus aliis in quibus conveniunt, non obſtantibus, immani discrimine inter se distinguuntur, diſtinctaque manent utriusque jura. Etquidem octo fere modis, quos hic adjicere non pigebit, ut utrique muneri termini sui præfigantur.

44. *Firſt*[*] of all, therefore,[78] they are differenced the one from the other in reſpect of the very foundation and the inſtitution. For the political or civil power is grounded upon the Law of Nature itself, and for that cause it is common to infidels [as] with Chriſtians. The power ecclesiaſtical depends immediately upon the positive Law of Chriſt alone. That [*civil*] belongs to the universal dominion of God the Creator over all nations, but this unto the ſpecial and oeconomical Kingdom of Chriſt the Mediator, which He exercises in the church alone, and which is not of this world [cf. John 18:36].

Primo igitur a se invicem discernuntur reſpectu ipsius fundamenti ac inſtitutionis. Poteſtas enim politica in ipso jure naturali fundatur, proptereaque infidelibus ac Chriſtianis communis eſt: poteſtas ecclesiaſtica a Chriſti solius inſtitution ac lege positiva immediate pendet. Illa ad universale Dei conditoris in omnes gentes dominum: iſta ad ſpeciale et œcumenicum Chriſti Mediatoris regnum, quod in ecclesia sola exequitur, quodque non eſt ex hoc mundo, pertinet.

---

77. 1647: atqæ (the correcter has "u" in the margin).

78. *Works* (1844) omits "of all." [*]Italics added for clarity.

45. The *second** differences [*sic* difference is] in the object,[79] or matter about which. The power politic or civil is occupied about the outward man, and civil or earthly things, about war, peace, conservation of justice, and good order in the commonwealth; also about the outward business or external things of the church, which are indeed necessary to the church, or profitable, as touching the outward man, yet not properly and purely ſpiritual, for they do not reach unto the soul, but only to the external ſtate and condition of the miniſters and members of the church.

Secunda differentia eſt in objecto, seu materia circa quam poteſtas politica versatur circa hominem externum, ac res civiles seu terreſtres; circa bellum pacem, atque justitiæ, bonique ordinis in repub., conservationem, item circa τα[80] ἔξω τῆς ἐκκλησίας, id eſt, circa ea quæ sunt quidem ecclesiæ necessaria vel commoda quoad externum hominem, non tamen proprie et pure ſpiritualia: neque enim ad animam pertingunt, sed solummodo ad miniſtrorum et membrorum ecclesiæ ſtatum externum.

46. For the better underſtanding whereof, it is to be observed that so far as the miniſters and members of the church are citizens, subjects, or members of the commonwealth, it is in the power of the magiſtrate to judge, determine, and give sentence concerning the diſposing of their bodies or goods, as also concerning the maintenance of the poor, sick, the banished, and of others in the church which are afflicted; to regulate (so far as concerns the civil order) marriages, burials, and other circumſtances which are common both to holy and also to honeſt civil societies; to afford places fit for holy assemblies and other external helps by which the sacred matters of the Lord may be more safely, commodiously, and more easily in the church performed; to remove the external impediments of divine worship or of ecclesiaſtical peace, and to repress those which exalt themselves againſt the true church and her miniſters, and do raise up trouble againſt them.

Nimirum quatenus miniſtri et membra ecclesiæ sunt cives ac membra Reipub. Penes magiſtratum eſt, de illorum corporibus ac bonis diſponendis, necnon de pauperibus ægrotis exulibus, aliisque in ecclesia afflictis sublevandis; De nuptiis, de sepulturis, deque aliis circumſtantiis, quæ tum sacris, tum aliis honeſtis societatibus communes sunt (quoad ordinem politicum) ordinandis et moderandis; De locis sacræ synaxi idoneis, aliisque externis adminiculis, quibus sacra Domini negotia tutius, facilius, et commodius in ecclesia peragi poterunt, subminiſtrandis; Denique de omnibus externis cultus divini, vel pacis ecclesiaſticæ impedimentis removendis; deque eis qui adversius[81] veram ecclesiam, ejusque miniſtros sese extollunt, illisque moleſtiam concitant, reprimendis, judicare, ſtatuere et sententiam ferre.

47. The matter may further be thus illuſtrated: There is almoſt the like reſpect

---

79. The London 1647 and *Works* (1844) have "difference is," which the Latin supports.

80. The 1647 Latin text set this incorrectly. It has been corrected to "τα" in the margin by hand in the EEBO copy and as his wont, the original is heavily marked out (possibly τὸ).

81. The 1647 Latin text: adversùs; 1648: adversius.

and consideration of the magistrate as he is occupied about the outward things of the church, and of the ecclesiastic ministry as it is occupied about the inward or spiritual part of civil government; that is, about those things which in the government of the commonwealth belong to the conscience. It is one thing to govern the commonwealth and to make political and civil laws; another thing to interpret the Word of God and out of it to show to the magistrate his duty, to wit, how he ought to govern the commonwealth, and in what manner he ought to use the sword. The former is proper and peculiar to the magistrate (neither does the ministry intermeddle or entangle itself into such businesses), but the latter is contained within the office of the ministers.

Res porro sic illustrari potest. Parilis ferre ratio est magistratus, dum versatur circa τὰ ἔξω τῆς ἐκκλησίας, et ministerii ecclesiastici versantis circa τὰ ἔισω[82] τῆς πολιτείας, id est, circa ea quæ in Reipub. Administratione ad conscientiam pertinent. Aliud est Rempub. administrare ac leges polticas ferre: aliud verbum Dei interpretari, atque ex eo magistratui officium commonstrare: puta quomodo Rempub. administrare et qua ratione gladio uti debeat. Illud magistratui proprium et peculiare est (nec ejusmodi negotiis sese immiscet vel implicat minmisterium) Istud autem in munere ministrorum ecclesiæ continetur.

48. For to that end also is the holy Scripture profitable, to show which is the best manner of governing a commonwealth, and that the magistrate as being God's minister may by this guiding star be so directed, as that he may execute the parts of his office according to the will of God, and may perfectly be instructed[83] to every good work; yet the minister is not said properly to treat of civil businesses, but of the scandals which arise about them, or of the cases of conscience which occur in the administration of the commonwealth. So also, the magistrate is not properly said to be exercised about the spiritual things of the church, but rather about those external things which adhere unto and accompany the spiritual things.

Nam ad id etiam utilis est Scriptura sacra, ut ostendat, quæ sit optima Reipub. administratio, atque ut magistratus tanquam Dei minister, hac cynosura ita dirigatur, ut muneris sui partes juxta Dei voluntatem exequatur, et ad omne opus bonum perfecte instructus sit. Neque tamen ministerium proprie dicitur tractare de civilibus negotiis, sed de scandalis, quæ circa ea oboriuntur, vel de casibus conscientiæ, quæ in Reipub. administratione occurrunt. Ita et magistratus non tam circa spiritualia, quam circa τὰ ἔξω quæ spiritualibus adjacent versari proprie dicitur.

49. And in such external matters of the church, although all magistrates will not, yet all, yea, even heathen magistrates may and ought to aide and help the church. Whence it is that by the command of God, prayers are to be made

---

82. The 1647 Latin text mispelled ἔισω. The correcter we have been noting has blackened out what should have been an ω and noted the ω in the margin.

83. The London 1647 edition misset this as "instituted."

also for a heathen magistrate, that the faithful under them may live a quiet life with all godliness and honesty (1 Tim. 2:1–2).

Atque in ejusmodi quidem externis ecclesiæ negotiis, etsi non omni magistratui opem ei ferre peræque allubescat; omnis tamen, etiam ethnicus ei auxiliari potest ac debet. Unde est, quod ex præcepto divino, pro ethnico etiam magistratu preces fieri oportet, ut fideles sub eo vitam tranquillam et quietam degant, cum omni pietate et honestate (1 Tim. 2:1–2).

50. Unto the external things of the church belongs not only the correction of heretics and other troublers of the church, but also that civil order and way of convocating and calling together synods which is proper to the magistrate; for the magistrate ought by his authority and power both to establish the rights and liberties of synods assembling together, at times appointed by the known and received law, and to indict and gather together synods occasionally, as often as the necessity of the church shall require the same; not that all or any power to consult or determine of ecclesiastic or spiritual matters does flow or spring from the magistrate as head of the church under Christ, but because in those things pertaining to the outward man, the church needs the magistrate's aid and support.

Ad τὰ ἔξω τῆς ἐκκλησίας pertinet non tantum hæreticorum, aliorumque ecclesiæ turbonum castigatio; sed et ordo ille modusque politicus synodos convocandi qui magistratui proprie[84] competit. Magistratus enim ex officio tenetur, tum synodorum, statis temporibus ex lege ordinaria coëuntium, jura ac libertates, auctoritate et sanctione sua stabilire; tum synodos pro re nata quotiescunque ecclesiæ necessitas id[85] postult, indicere ac cogere. Non quod potestas vel omnis, vel ulla de rebus spiritualibus ac ecclesiasticis deliberandi, easque definiendi, a magistratu tanquam ecclesiæ sub Christo capite fluat vel promanet, sed quia in iis quæ sunt exterm hominis, ecclesia magistratus subsidio ac suppetiis eget.

51. So that the magistrate calls together synods, not as touching those things which are proper to synods, but in respect of the things which are common to synods with other meetings and civil public assemblies; that is, not as they are assemblies in the name of Christ, to treat of matters spiritual, but as they are public assemblies within his territories; for to the end that public conventions may be kept in any territory, the license of the lord of that place ought to be desired. In synods, therefore, a respect of order, as well civil as ecclesiastical, is to be had. And because of this civil order, outward defense, better accommodation, together with safe access and recess, the consent and commandment of him who is appointed to take care of and defend human order, does intervene.

Itaque synodos convocat magistratus, non quoad ea quæ synodorum propria sunt, sed quoad ea quæ synodis cum comitiis, aliisque conventibus civilibus publicis

---

84. 1648: proprè.

85. 1648: ad.

communia sunt id est, non quatenus sunt congregationes in nomine Christi, de rebus spiritualibus tractaturæ, sed quatenus sunt congregationes publicæ in sua ditione: ut enim publici conventus in ditione aliqua habeantur, licentia Domini illius loci merito expeti debet. In synodis igitur ratio habenda est ordinis tam politici quam ecclesiastici: atque ordinis istius politici, externæ tutelæ, melioris accommodationis, salvi denique accessus et recessus gratia, intervenit consensus ac mandatum ejus, qui humani ordinis curator ac vindex constitutus est.

52. Moreover, when the church is rent asunder by unhappy and lamentable schisms, while they who have raised the troubles and have given cause of solemn gathering a synod (whether by their heresy, or schism, or tyranny, or any other fault of others) use to [*commonly*] place the great strength and safeguard of their cause in declining and fleeing the trial and sentence of a free synod, as being formidable to them, who sees not that they cannot be drawn to a public and judicial trial, nor other disobedient persons be compelled to obedience, without the magistrate's public mandate and help?

Præterea, quando ecclesia infausto et lugendo schismate dilaceratur, cum illi qui turbas excitarunt, atque concilio celebrando sive hæresi, sive schismate, sive tyrannide, aliave aliqua culpa sua[86] causam dederunt in eo unicum causæ suæ præsium ponere soleant, ut liberi concilii examen ac decretum, tanquam ipsis formibabile declinent; quis non videt eos non posse ad jus trahi, nec alios immorigeros ad obedientiam cogi, absque magistratus diplomate et subsidio.

53. The object of ecclesiastical power is not the same with the object of the civil power, but much differing from it; for the ecclesiastical power does determine and appoint nothing concerning men's bodies, goods, dignities, civil rights, but is employed only about the inward man, or the soul; not that it can search the hearts, or judge of the secrets of the conscience, which is in the power of God alone. Yet notwithstanding, it has for its proper object those externals which are purely spiritual, and do belong properly and most nearly to the spiritual good of the soul; which also are termed, τὰ ἔισω τῆς ἐκκλησίας, "the inward things of the church."

Objectum potestatis ecclesiasticiæ non est idem cum objecto potestatis politicæ, sed longe diversum. Nihil enim statuit illa in hominum corpora, bona, dignitates, ac jura civilia, sed versatur solummodo circa hominem internum seu animam; non quod corda scrutari, aut de arcanis conscientiæ judicare possit, quod solius Dei est, sed quod habeat pro objecto proprio externa illa quæ pure spiritualia, et ad animæ bonum spirituale proprie et maxime spectant quæ etiam τὰ ἔισω τῆς ἐκκλησίας nuncupantur.

54. Those things, then, wherein the ecclesiastical power is exercised, are the preaching of the Word, the administration of sacraments, public prayer and thanksgiving, the catechizing and instructing of children and ignorant

---

86. 1648: omits "suâ."

persons, the examination of those who are to come to the holy communion, the ecclesiastical discipline, the ordination of ministers, and the abdication, deposing, and degrading of them (if they become like unsavory salt), the deciding and determining of controversies of faith and cases of conscience, canonical constitutions concerning the treasury of the church and collections of the faithful, as also concerning ecclesiastical rites, or indifferent things, which pertain to the keeping of decency and order in the church, according to the general rules of Christian love and prudence contained in the Word of God.

Ea igitur, in quibus versatur potestas ecclesiastica, sunt verbi divini prædicatio; sacramentorum administratio, publica ac solennis divini nominis invocatio, atque gratiarum actio, puerorum, rudiorumque catechisatio et institutio, illorum qui ad sacram communionem accessuri sunt exploratio et probatio, disciplinæ ecclesiasticæ exercitium, ministrorum ordinatio, eorundemve (si instar salis infatuati fuerint) abdicatio, depositio, vel degradatio, controversiarum fidei, casuumque conscientiæ ex Dei verbo decisio ac determinatio, de ærario ecclesiase et collectis fidelium, nec non de ritibus ecclesiasticis, seu de adiaphoris quæ ad ordinem et decorum in ecclesia servandum pertinent, secundum Christianæ charitatis et prudentiæ regulas generales in verbo Dei contentas, canonica constitutio.

55. It is true that about the same things the civil power is occupied, as touching the outward man, or the outward disposing of divine things in this or that dominion, as was said, not as they are spiritual and evangelical ordinances piercing into the conscience itself, but the object of the power ecclesiastical is a thing merely and purely spiritual; and insofar as it is spiritual (for even that jurisdiction ecclesiastical which is exercised in an outward court or judicatory, and which inflicts public censures, forbids from the use of the holy supper, and excludes from the society of the church), does properly concern the inward man, or the repentance and salvation of the soul.

Circa eadem quidem potestas politica versatur, quoad ea quæ sunt externi hominis, seu quoad externam rerum divinarum dispositionem, in hac vel illa ditione, ut dictum est; non autem quatenus sunt spiritualia ac evangelica instituta ad ipsam animam et conscientiam penetrantia. Atqui objectum potestatis ecclesiæ est res pura puta spiritualis, et in quantum spiritualis est: nam et ea jurisdictio ecclesiastica, quæ in foro exteriori exercetur, quæque censuras publicas irrogat, usu sacræ cœnæ interdicit, a consortio ecclesiæ excludit, proprie respicit hominem interiorem seu animam, ejusque resipiscentiam ad salutem.

56. Surely the faithful and godly ministers, although they could do it unchallenged and uncontrolled, and were therein allowed by the magistrate (as in the prelatical times it was), yet would not usurp the power of life and death, or judge and determine concerning men's honors, goods, inheritance, division of families, or other civil businesses, seeing they well know these things to be heterogeneous to their office. But as they ought not to entangle themselves with the judging of civil causes, so if they should be negligent and slothful in their own office, they shall in that be no less culpable.

Certe fideles et pii ministri, etiamsi impune et cum bona venia magistratus (prout prælatorum seculo mos invaluerat) possent, nollent tamen potestatem vitæ ac necis usurpare, vel de hominum dignitatibus, bonis, hæredatibus, herciscunda familia, alisve negotiis civilibus, judicare aut sententiam serre; cum hæc a munere suo aliena esse probe norint. Atqui ut causarum civilium diiudicationi sese immiscere non debent; ita si in suo officio desides et socordes fuerint, non minus in eo culpabiles erunt.

57. To the object also of ecclesiastical power belongs the assembling of synods, so far as they are spiritual assemblies proper to the church, and assembled in the Holy Ghost; for being so considered, the governors of churches after the example of the apostles and presbyters, Acts 15, in a manifest danger of the church, ought to use their own right of meeting together and convening, that the churches endangered may be relieved and supported.

Ad objectum potestatis ecclesiasticæ pertinet etiam synodorum convocatio, quatenus sunt conventus spirituales, ecclesiæ proprii, ac in Spiritu Sancto congregati: Sic enim ecclesiarum rectores, juxta exemplum apostolorum et presbyterorum, Act. 15, in manifesto ecclesiæ periculo jure suo cœundi et una conveniendi uti debent, quo laborantibus ac periclitantibus ecclesiis spiritualiter subveniatur.

58. *Thirdly,** Those powers are differenced in respect of their forms, and that three ways: For first, the civil power, although in respect of God it be ministerial, yet in respect of the subjects it is lordly and magisterial. Ecclesiastical power is indeed furnished with authority, yet that authority is liker [*more like*] the fatherly than the kingly authority; yea, also it is purely ministerial, much less can it be lawful to ministers of the church to bear dominion over the flock.

Tertio distinguuntur munia illa respectu formæ, idque trifariam. Nam primo potestas politica, quamvis respectu Dei, ministerialis sit, respectu tamen subditorum est δεσποτικὴ. Potestas ecclesiastica auctoritate quidem instructa est, verum enimvero illa auctoritas paternæ quam regali similior est: quin etiam ὑπηρετικὴ est, seu pure ministerialis; tantum abest, ut ministris ecclesiæ in gregem dominari liceat.

59. Emperors, kings, and other magistrates are indeed appointed fathers of the country, but they are withal lords of their people and subjects, not as if it were permitted to them to bear rule and command at their own will and as they list [*wish*] (for they are the ministers of God for the good and profit of the subjects), yet it belongs to their power truly and properly to exercise dominion, to hold principality, to proceed imperiously. It is indeed the duty of ministers and rulers of the church to oversee, to feed as shepherds, to correct and rectify, to bear the keys, to be stewards in the house of Christ, but in no wise to be lords over the house, or to govern as lords, or lord-like to rule. Yea, in brief, this is the difference between the civil magistrate and the ecclesiastical ministry in respect of those which are committed to their trust, that the lot of the former is to be served or ministered unto, the lot of the latter to minister or serve.

Imperatores, reges, aliique magiſtratus supremi, patres quidempatriæ conſtituti sunt; sed sunt insuper populorum ac subditorum domini; non quod illis pro libitu vel arbitratu imperare concessum sit (sunt enim Dei miniſtri subditorum bono ac utilitati) penes illos tamen eſt vere et proprie κυριεύειν, dominari, principatum obtinere, imperiose agere. Miniſtrorum ac antiſtitum ecclesiæ eſt quidem ἐπισκοπεῖν, ποιμάινειν, κατορθοῦν, κλειδοῦν, ὀικονομεῖν; nequaquam vero ὀικοδεσποτεῖν, vel κυριεύειν. Adeoque hoc intereſt inter magiſtratum politicum et miniſterium ecclesiſticum, reſpeᥴtu hominum qui utrique procurationi commissi sunt, quod illius fors sit διακονηθῆναι iſtius διακονῆσαι.

60. Now we have one only Lord which governs our souls. Neither is it competent to man, but to God alone to have power and authority over consciences. But the Lord has appointed His own ſtewards over His own family, that according to His commandment they may give to everyone their allowance or portion, and to diſpense His myſteries faithfully. And to them He has delivered the keys, or power of letting in into His house, or excluding out of His house those whom He Himself will have let in or shut out (Matt. 16:19, and 18:18; Luke 12:42; 1 Cor. 4:1; Titus 1:7).

Unum autem habemus dominum qui animas noſtras gubernat; neque enim hominibus, sed soli Deo competit jus et autoritas in conscientias. Conſtituit vero dominus œconomos suos supra familitium suum, ut juxta ipsius mandatum dent unicuique demensum, ac ipsius myſteria fideliter diſpensent: iisque tradidit claves, seu poteſtatem intromittendi in domum, vel ex domo eiiciendi, quos ipse vel intromitti vult, vel eiici (Matth. 16:19 et 18:18; Luc. 12:42; 1 Cor. 4:1; Titus 1:7).

61. Next, the civil power is endued with authority of compelling; but it belongs not to the miniſtry to compel the disobedient. If any compulsion be in or about ecclesiaſtical matters, it is adventitious from without, to wit, from the help and assiſtance of the magiſtrate, not from the nature of ecclesiaſtical power, from which it is very heterogeneous. And therefore, if any suſpended or excommunicate[d] person should be found who shall be so ſtiff-necked, and so impudent, that at once he caſt off all shame, and make no account at all of those censures, but scorn and contemn the same, or peradventure shall insolently or proudly ingyre [*ingratiate*][87] and obtrude himself upon the sacrament, or being also filled with devilish malice do more and more contradiᥴt and blaſpheme, the ecclesiaſtical miniſtry in such cases has nothing more to do by way of jurisdiᥴtion. But the magiſtrate has in readiness a compelling jurisdiᥴtion and external force, whereby such ſtubborn rebellious and undaunted pride may be externally repressed.

Deinde poteſtas civilis cogendi poteſtate, seu imperio ac dominio inſtruᥴta eſt. At penes miniſterium non eſt immorigeros cogere: si qua vero sit circa res ecclesiaſticas

---

87. *Ingyre*: "To push (oneself) in, obtrude (oneself), chiefly intrusively or presumptuously. Also, to insinuate (oneself). b. To take it upon oneself, presume (to do something presumptuous)" (*DSL*). *Works* (1844) renders this "ingratiate." .

coactio, ea aliunde accedit, nempe a magistratus ope et subsidio; nam a natura potestatis ecclesiasticæ prorsus aliëna est. Proinde si abstentus vel excommunicatus quispiam reperiatur, qui sit tam ferreæ cervicis, tamque perfrictæ frontis, ut omnem semel pudorem abstergat et deponat, atque censuras illas susque deque habeat, contemnat, rideat, ac forsan tentet sese proterve aut per superbiam ingerere et obtrudere vel etiam Santanica malitia repletus, indies magis magisque contradicat et blasphemet; hihil istic habet ministerium ecclesiasticum quod ultra agat per modum jurisdictionis; habet autem in promptu magistratus jurisdictionem cogentem ac vim externam, qua cotumax rebellio et infracta superbia externe coërceatur.

62. Last of all, the power of the magistrate works only politically or civilly, according to the nature of the scepter or sword, makes and guards civil laws, which sometimes also he changes or repeals, and other things of that kind he effects with a secular power. But the ecclesiastical power deals spiritually and only in the name of our Lord Jesus Christ, and by authority entrusted or received from Him alone; neither is it exercised without prayer or calling on the name of God; nor lastly, does it use any other than spiritual weapons.

Postremo potestas magistratus politice {tantum et}[88] civiliter agit, pro ratione sceptri vel gladii, leges civiles fert et munit, interdum etiam mutat vel abrogat, pœnas civiles infert, præmia civilia confert, bellæ gerit, hostes vi repellit, et id genus alia brachio seculari operatur. Potestas vero ecclesiastica agit spiritualiter, et non nisi in nomine Domini nostri Iesu Christi, ac auctoritate ab eo solo demandata, nec sine Dei invocatione; nec denique aliis quam spiritualibus armis utitur.

63. The same sin, therefore, in the same man may be punished one way by the civil, another way by the ecclesiastical power; by the civil power under the formality of a crime, with corporal or pecuniary punishment; by the ecclesiastical power under the notion and[89] nature of scandal, with a spiritual censure, even as also the same civil question is one way deliberate[d] upon and handled by the magistrate in the senate or place of judgment; another way by the minister of the church in the presbytery or synod; by the magistrate so far as it pertains to the government of the commonwealth, by the minister so far as it respects the conscience; for the ecclesiastical ministry also is exercised about civil things spiritually, insofar as it teaches and admonishes the magistrate out of the Word of God what is best and most acceptable unto God;[90] or as it reproves freely unjust judgments, unjust wars, and the like, and out of the Scripture threatens the wrath of God to be revealed against all unrighteousness of men [Rom. 1:18]; so also is the magistrate said to be occupied civilly about spiritual things.

Idem igitur peccatum in eodem homine aliter a potestate politica, aliter a potestate ecclesiastica; ab illa scilicet sub formalitate criminis, pœna coporali pecuniaria;

---

88. The words between braces were omitted in the 1648 text.

89. 1647 London text: "or nature."

90. 1647: "Gods."

ab ista sub formalitate scandali, censura spirituali, puniri nil vetat: quemadmodum etiam de eadem quæstione politica aliter deliberat et tractat magistratus in senatu et dicasterio, aliter minister ecclesiæ in presbyterio: ille quatenus ad Reip. administrationem, hic quatenus ad conscientiam pertinet: Nam et circa civilia spiritualiter versatur ministerium ecclesiasticum, quatenus magistratum ex Dei verbo docet et monet quid optimum Deoque acceptum sit: vel quatenus παρρησιάζων, injusta judicia, injusta bella et istiusmodi alia ex sacra Scriptura redarguit, iramque Dei adversus omnem hominum injustitiam revelandam comminatur; sic et politice circa spiritualia versari dicitur magistratus.

64. Therefore, all the actions of the civil magistrate, even when he is employed about ecclesiastical matters, are of their own nature and essentially civil. He punishes externally idolaters, blasphemers, sacrilegious persons, heretics, profaners of holy things, and according to the nature and measure of the sin he condemns to death or banishment, forfeiture of goods, or imprisonment. He guards and underprops [*upholds*] ecclesiastical canons with civil authority, gives a place of habitation to the church in his territory, restrains or expels the insolent and untamed disturbers of the church.

Ergo omnes magistratus politici actiones, etiam quando versatur circa ecclesiastica, sunt sua natura et formaliter civiles: idololatras,[91] blasphemos, sacrilegos, hæreticos, sacrorum temeratores externe punit, atque pro ratione mensuraque delicti, morti, exilio, mulctæ facultatum, vel vinculis adjudicat; canones ecclesiasticos civili sanctione munit et fulcit; ecclesiæ hospitium in sua ditione præbet; protervos ac indomitos ecclesiæ turbatores cohibet, vel loco expellit.

65. He takes care also for maintaining the ministers and schools, and supplies the temporal necessities of God's servants, by his command assembles synods when there is need of them, and summons, calls out, and draws to trial the unwilling, which without the magistrate's strength and authority cannot be done, as has been already said. He makes synods also safe and secure, and in a civil way presides or moderates in them (if it so seem good to him) either by himself or by a substitute commissioner. In all which the power of the magistrate, though occupied about spiritual things, is not for all that spiritual but civil.

De ministris item ac scholis alendis curat, ac servorum Dei necessitatibus humanis suppetias fert; synodos quando vis opus est pro imperio cogit, atque dissentientes invitosque citat, evocat, ad jus trahit; quod nisi magistratus ope et præsidio fieri nequit, ut jam dictum est. Synodos etiam securas ac tutas reddit, eisque (si ita visum fuerit) vel per se, vel per delegatum in ordine politico præsidet, in quibus potestas magistratus ut,[92] ut circa spiritualia occupata, nequaquanm tamen spiritualis sed civilis est.

---

91. 1647: idolatras (the 1647 correcter inserts the missing "lo" in the margin).

92. 1647: "magistratus, ut…." The person correcting the 1647 text by hand in the example in EEB, inserts the additional "ut" after "magistratus" in the margin.

66. *Fourthly,*[*] they differ in the end. The immediate nearest end of civil power is that the good of the commonwealth may be provided for and procured, whether it be in time of peace, according to the rules of law and counsel of judges, or in time of war according to the rules of military prudence; and so the temporal safety of the subjects may be procured, and that external peace and civil liberty may be preserved, and being lost, may be again restored.

Quarto differunt fine. Potestatis politicæ finis immediatus et proximus est, ut Reip. bono, sive pacis tempore, juxta regulas prudentiæ togatæ, sive belli tempoore, juxta regulas prudentiæ militaris, consulatur et prospiciatur, adeoque subditorum salus temporalis procuretur, atque pax externa et libertas civilis conserventur, vel amissæ[93] postiliminio restituantur.

67. But the chiefest and last end of civil government is the glory of God the Creator; namely, that those which do evil being by a superior power restrained or punished, and those which do good getting praise of the same, the subjects so much the more may shun impiety and injustice, and that virtue, justice and the Moral Law of God (as touching those eternal duties of both tables, unto which all the posterity of Adam are obliged) may remain in strength and flourish.

Finis autem illius summus et ultimus est gloria Dei Creatoris, nempe ut refrenatis vel punitis a potestate supereminente,[94] qui, quod malum est, faciunt; laudem vero ab ea obtinentibus, qui, quod bonum est, faciunt, eo magis impietatem et injustitiam fugiant subditi; atque virtus, iustitia, ipsaque lex divina moralis (quoad externa illa utriusque tabulæ officia, ad quæ omnes Adami posteri obligantur) vigeat et efflorescat.

68. But whereas the Christian magistrate does wholly devote himself to the promoting of the gospel and kingdom of Christ, and does direct and bend all the might and strength of his authority to that end, this proceeds not from the nature of his office or[95] function, which is common to him with an infidel magistrate, but from the influence of his common Christian calling into his particular vocation.

Quod autem magistratus Christianus promovendo evangelio, regnoque Jesu Christi se totum impendat, omnesque auctoritatis suæ nervos et vires istruc dirigat ac intendat: id non est ex natura ipsius officii seu muneris, quod illi cum magistratu infideli commune est; sed ex communis seu Christianæ vocationis in particularem ipsius vocationem influxu.

69. For every member of the church (and so also the faithful and godly magistrate) ought to refer and order his particular vocation, faculty, ability, power, and honor to this end, that the Kingdom of Christ may be propagated

---

93. 1647: amislæ.

94. 1647: superminente. 1648: supereminente. Again, by hand, someone has corrected the 1647 EEB example by inserting the missing "e" in the margin.

95. The London edition changed "or" to "and."

and promoted, and the true religion be cherished and defended: So that the advancement of the gospel and of all the ordinances of the gospel, is indeed the end of the godly magistrate, not of a magistrate simply, or (if you will rather) it is not the end of the office itself, but of him who does execute the same piously.

Unumquodque enim ecclesiæ Christi membrum (ac proinde etiam magistratus fidelis et pius) particularem suam vocationem, facultatem, poteentiam et dignitatem unice in hunc scopum referre ac derigere debet, ut regnum Jesu Christi propagetur. Itaque evangelii, omniumque institutorum evangelicorum promotio est, quidem finis pii magistratus, {non autem magistratus}⁹⁶ simpliciter; vel (si mavis) non est finis ipsius muneris, sed ejus qui munus illud pie exequitur.

70. But the end of ecclesiastical power, yea, the end as well of the ministry itself, as of the godly minister, is that the kingdom of Christ may be set forward, that the paths of the Lord be made straight, that His holy mysteries may be kept pure, that stumbling-blocks may be removed out of the church, lest a little leaven, leaven the whole lump [1 Cor. 5:6; Gal. 5:9], or lest one sick or scabbed sheep infect the whole flock, that the faithful may so walk as it becometh [*befits*] the gospel of Christ, and that the wandering sheep of Christ may be converted and brought back to the sheepfold.

Potestatis vero ecclesiasticæ finis, et quidem tam ipsius ministerii quam pii ministri, est, ut regnum illud Christi promoveatur; ut Domini semitæ complanentur; ut sacra ipsius mysteria intemerata serventur: ut offendicula ex ecclesia auferantur, ne modicum fermentum totam massam corrumpat, neve morbida pecus totum inficiat gregem: ut fideles in omnibus se gerant ut convenit evangelio Christi: ut errantes Christi oves convertantur et ad ovile reducantur.

71. And seeing this power is given of the Lord, not to destruction but to edification, therefore, this same scope is propounded in excommunication (which is the greatest and last of ecclesiastical censures); namely, that the soul of an offending brother may be gained to Christ, and that being stricken with fear, and the stubborn sinner filled with shame, may by the grace of God be humbled, and may (as a brand plucked out of the fire) be snatched out of the snare of the devil, and may repent unto salvation; at least the rest may turn away from those which are branded with such a censure, lest the soul infection do creep and spread further.

Cumque potestas hæc a Domino data sit, non ad destructionem sed ad ædificationem: idcirco ad hunc scopum refertur etiam excommunicatio, quæ est censurarum ecclesiasticarum maxima et summa: nempe, ut peccantis fratris anima Christo lucrifiat; atque ut metu perculsus et pudore suffusus contumax peccator per Dei gratiam humilietur, et ex diaboli laqueo, veluti titio ex igne, eripiatur, ac ad salutem

---

96. The 1647 Latin edition omitted the text within braces, which, as in prior cases, someone has corrected the EEB example by inserting the text in the margin (now partially missing due to a trimmed margin).

respiscat: saltem ejusmodi censura insignitos reliqui aversentur, ne animarum contagio latius serpat.

72. *Fifthly,** they are distinguished by the effect. The effect of civil power is either proper or by way of redundance [*advantage*]. The proper effect is the safety temporal [*temporal safety*] of the commonwealth, external tranquility, the fruition of civil liberty, and of all things which are necessary to the civil society of men. The effect by way of redundance is the good of the church, to wit, insofar as by execution of justice and good laws, some impediments that usually hinder and disturb the course of the gospel are avoided or taken away.

Quinto distinguuntur effectu. Potestatis politicæ effectus est vel proprius, vel per modum redundantiæ. Effectus proprius est salus reipub. temporalis, seu tranquillitatis externæ, libertatis civilis, omniumque, quæ civili hominum societati necessaria sunt, fruitio. Effectus per modum redundantiæ est bonum ecclesiæ, puta, in quantum justitiæ ac bonarum legum executione. Remoræ nonnullæ quæ evangelii cursum sæpiuscule interturbant et impediunt, vitantur, vel e medio tolluntur.

73. For by how much the more faithfully the magistrate executes his office in punishing the wicked, and cherishing and encouraging good men, taking away those things which withstand the gospel, and punishing or driving away the troublers and subverters of the church, so much the more the orthodox faith and godliness are reverenced and had in estimation, sins are hated and feared. Finally, all[97] the subjects contained (as much as concerns the outward man) within the lists of God's Law, whence also by consequence it[98] happens by God's blessing, that the church is defiled with fewer scandals, and does obtain the more freedom and peace.

Nam quo fidelius officium suum exequitur magistratus, sceleratos pœnis afficiendo, probos fovendo ac in honore habendo, ea quæ religioni externe obstant auferendo, ecclesiæque subversores ac turbones plectendo vel propulsando; eo magis fides orthodoxa et pietas coluntur ac in pretio habentur, scelera odio habentur et metuuntur, omnes denique subditi intra legis divinæ[99] repagula (quantum quidem ad externum hominem spectat) continentur. Unde et ex consequenti evenit, Dei beneficio, quod eo paucioribus scandalis ecclesia inquinetur, eoque majorem sortiatur libertatem ac pacem

74. But the proper effect of the ecclesiastical power, or keys of the kingdom of heaven, is wholly spiritual; for the act of binding and loosing, of retaining and remitting sins, does reach to the soul and conscience itself (which cannot be said of the act of the civil power). And as unjust excommunication is void, so ecclesiastical censure being inflicted by the ministers of Christ and His stewards according to His will, is ratified in heaven (Matt. 18:18), and

---

97. The London edition reads "and all."

98. The London edition reads "in," which is a clear mistake.

99. 1647: divini (corrected by hand with an æ in the margin in the EEB copy).

therefore ought to be esteemed and acknowledged in like manner as inflicted by Christ Himself.

Atqui potestatis ecclesiasticæ, seu clavium regni cœlorum effectus proprius est παντελῶς spiritualis: actus namque ligandi vel solvendi retinendi vel remittendi peccata, ad ipsam animam ac conscientiam pertingit; quod de actu potestatis politicæ dici nequit. Atque sicut injusta excommunicatio est irrita, sic censura ecclesiastica quæ a Christi administris ac œconomis, juxta ipsius voluntatem infligitur, in cœlis rata habetur (Matth. 18:18). Ideoque perinde ut ab ipso Christo irrogata æstimari et agnosci debet.

75. *Sixthly,*[*] they are also differenced in respect of the subject. The politic power is committed sometimes to one, sometimes to more, sometimes by right of election, sometimes by right of succession. But the ecclesiastical power is competent to none under the New Testament by the right of succession, but he who has it must be called by God and the church to it; neither was it given by Christ to one either pastor or elder, much less to a prelate, but *to the church*, that is, to the consistory of presbyters. It is confessed indeed (and who can be ignorant of it?), that the power (as they call it) of order does belong to particular ministers, and is by each of them apart lawfully exercised. But that power which is commonly called of jurisdiction is committed not to one, but to the unity, that is, to a consistory; therefore, ecclesiastical censure ought not to be inflicted but by many (2 Cor. 2:6).

Sexto, Respectu subjecti etiam discriminantur. Potestas politica, quandoque uni, quandoque pluribus, quandoque jure[100] electionis, quandoque jure successionis, merito demandatur. Potestas autem ecclesiastica nemini sub novo Testamento jure successionis competit, sed a Deo et ecclesia vocatum esse oportet qui ea potitur: Nec uni alicui, sive pastori sive seniori, nedum[101] pseudœpiscopo, sed τῇ ἐκκλησια, id est Presbyterorum consessui a Christo data est. Potestatem quidem quam vocant *ordinis* singulis ministris competere, ab iisque καθ' ἕκαστον legitime exerceri, quis potis est ignorare? Ea vero potestas quæ *jurisdictionis* vulgo dicitur, non *uni*, sed *unitati*, id est, consessui demandata est. Proinde censura ecclesiastica non nisi ὑπὸ τῶν πλείονων irrogari debet[102] (2 Cor. 2:6).

76. *Seventhly,*[*] they differ as touching the correlative. God has commanded that unto the civil power, every soul, or all members of the commonwealth, of what condition and estate soever, be subject; for what have we to do with the papists, who will have them whom they call the clergy or ecclesiastical persons, to be free from the yoke of the civil magistrate? The ecclesiastical power extends itself to none other subjects than unto those which are called brethren, or members of the church.

Septimo, differunt quoad correlatum, potestati politicæ omnem animam seu

---

100. 1647: jurie (corrected by hand in the margin of the EEBO example).

101. 1647: nedunt (corrected by hand in the margin of the EEBO example).

102. 1648: deber.

omnes cives cuiuscunque status et conditionis subiici mandavit dominus: quid enim nobis cum pontificiis, qui clericos (quos vacant) seu ministros ecclesiasticos a jugo magistratus politici immunesesse volunt? Potestas ecclesiastica ad nullos alios cives se extendit, nisi ad eos qui fratres seu ecclesia membra nominantur.

77. *Eighthly,*[*] there remains another difference in respect of the distinct and divided exercise of authority. For either power ceasing from its duty, or remitting punishment, that does not (surely it ought not) prejudice the exercise of the other power; namely, if the magistrate ceases to do his duty, or does neglect to punish with secular punishment those malefactors which by profession are church members. Nevertheless, it is in the power of the governors of the church by the bridle of ecclesiastical discipline to curb such men; yea, also by virtue of their office they are bound to do it. And on the other part, the magistrate may and ought to punish in life and limb, honors or goods, notwithstanding of the offender's repentance or reconciliation with the church.

Octavo, restat et alia differentia quoad distinctum ac diversum auctoritatis exercitium: Utralibet enim potestate ab officio cessante vel pænam remittente, id alterius potestatis exercitio præjudicium non parit, certe parere non debet. Nimirum si magistratus cesset officium suum facere, vel facinorosos, qui fratribus in ecclesia accenseri volunt, pænis secularibus afficere negligat; nihilominus disciplinæ ecclesiasticæ fræno eiusmodi homines cohibere est penes τους προϊσταμένους ecclesiæ, etiamque vi muneris eos cohibere tenentur. Et vicissim pœnæ, quæ necem vel noxam corporis, vel dignatatum bonotumve amissionem inferunt, a magistratu merito infliguntur, infligique debent, non obstante[103] illius qui scelus perpetravit resipiscentia, vel cum ecclesia reconciliatione.

78. Therefore, the one sword being put up in the scabbard, it is free and often necessary to draw the other. Neither power is bound to cast out or receive him whom the other does cast forth or receive. The reason whereof is because the ecclesiastical ministry does chiefly respect the repentance to salvation and gaining of the sinner's soul; wherefore it also embraces all kinds[104] of wicked men repenting, and receives them into the bosom of the church. The magistrate proposes to himself another and much differing scope; for even repenting offenders are by him punished, both that justice and the law may be satisfied, as also to terrify others. Hence it is that absolution from ecclesiastic censure frees not at all the delinquent from civil judgment and the external sword.

Itaque altero gladio in vaginam recondito, alterum evaginare liberum, sæpe etiam necesse est. Neutra potestas eiicere vel receipere tenetur quem altera eiicit vel recipit. Cujus rei ratio inde petenda est quod ministerium ecclesiasticum in lapsorum resipiscentiam et lucrifactionem ad salutem potissimum respicit; quare et omnigenos

____

103. 1647: abstante (corrected by hand in the margin of the EEBO example).
104. The London text reads "kind."

sceleratos pœnitentiam agentes amplectitur, et in sinum ecclesiæ receipit. Diversum
plane scopum sibi proponit magistratus; nam et respiscentes facinorosi ab illo plec-
tuntur, tum ut justitiæ et legibus satisfiat, tum ad terrorem aliis incutiendum. Hinc
est quod absolutio a censura ecclesiastica nequaquam deliquentem liberet a judicio
civilii et gladio externo.

79. Seeing, then, there are so many and so great differences of both offices,
and seeing also that the function of ministers and elders of the church is
not at all contained in the office of the magistrate, neither, on the other part,
this is [*is this*] comprehended within that, magistrates shall no less sin in
usurping ecclesiastical power, ministering holy things, ordaining ministers, or
exercising discipline ecclesiastical, than ministers should sin in rushing into
the borders of the magistrate, and in thrusting themselves into his calling.

Cum igitur utriusque muneris tot tantæque sint differentiæ, cumque munus ministrorum ac seniorum ecclesiæ haudquaquam in munere magistratus contineatur;
nec vice versa istud in illo comprehendatur, tam peccarent magistratus, potestatem
ecclesiasticam usurpando, sacra ministrando, ministros ordinando, vel disciplinam
ecclesiasticam exercendo quam ministri in magistratus fines irruendo, in ejusque
vactionem sese ingerendo.

80. Neither are those powers more mingled one with other, or less
distinguished, where the magistrate is a Christian, than where he is an infidel;
for as in a believing father and in an infidel father, the rights of a father are
the same, so in a Christian magistrate and in an infidel magistrate the rights of
magistrates are the same. So that to the magistrate converted to the Christian
faith, there is no accession of new right, or increase of civil power, although
being endued with true faith and piety, he is made more fit and willing to
the undergoing of his office and the doing of his duty.

Neque vero magis permiscentur, aut minus distinguuntur illæ potestates, ubi magistratus est Christianus, quam ubi est infideles. Sicut {enim}[105] in patre fideli et patre
infideli, jura paterna: sic in magistratu Christiano, et magistratu infideli jura magistratus eadem sunt: Ita ut magistratui ad fidem Christianam converso, nihil novi juris,
nullum politicæ potestatis incrementum accedat, utut vera fide ac pietate imbutus,
tum demum maxime idoneus lubensque efficiatur ad officium suum obeundum.

81. So, then, the Word of God and the Law of Christ, which by so evident
difference separates and distinguishes ecclesiastical government from the
civil, forbids the Christian magistrate to enter upon or usurp the ministry
of the Word and sacraments, or the juridical dispensing of the keys of the
kingdom of heaven, to invade the church government, or to challenge to
[*claim for*] himself the right of both swords, spiritual and corporal. But if
any magistrate (which God forbid) should dare to arrogate to himself so
much, and to enlarge his skirts so far, the church shall then straightway be

---

105. 1648: The text between braces was omitted.

constrained to complain justly and cry out that, though the Pope is changed, yet Popedom remains still.

Magistratus itaque Christanus verbi vel sacramentorum ministerium, claviumque regni cælorum admistrationem adoriri vel usurpare, et ecclesiæ gubernacula inuadere, adeoque utriusque gladii, spiritualis et corporalis jus sibi vendicare, jure divino et lege Christi (regimen ecclesiasticum a regimine politico tam evidenti discrimine separante et distinguente) prohibetur. Si vero magistratus quispiam (quod absit) tantum sibi arrogare, ac finibrias suas usque adeo dilatare audeat; mox cogetur[106] ecclesia jure queritari et exclamare, mutatum iam else Papam, manere autem papatum.

82. It is unlawful, moreover, to a Christian magistrate to withstand the practice and execution of ecclesiastical discipline (whether it be that which belongs to a particular church, or the matter be carried to a class or synod). Now, the magistrate withstands the ecclesiastic discipline, either by prohibitions and unjust laws, or, by his evil example, stirring up and inciting others to the contempt thereof, or to the trampling it under foot.

Magistratui Christiano, insuper, nefas est disciplinæ ecclesiasticæ praxi et executioni (sive ea fit quæ ecclesiæ particulari competit, sive ad classem synodumve res devolvatur) obniti, eamve impedire. Obnititur autem disciplinæ ecclesiæ magistratus sive prohibitionibus ac legibus iniquis, sive exemplo suo malo, alios ad eam contemnendam ac proculcandam incitando atque extimulando.

83. Surely the Christian magistrate (if at any time he give any grievous scandal to the church), seeing he also is a member of the church, ought no ways disdain to submit himself to the power of the keys. Neither is this to be marveled at, for even as the office of the minister of the church is no ways subordinate and subjected to the civil power, but the person of the minister, as he is a member of the commonwealth, is subject thereto, so, the civil power itself, or the magistrate as a magistrate, is not subjected to ecclesiastic power; yet that man who is a magistrate ought (as he is a member of the church) to be under the church's censure of his manners, after the example of the Emperor Theodosius,[107] unless he will despise and set at naught ecclesiastic discipline, and indulge the swelling pride of the flesh.

Sane magistratus Christianus, si quando grave scandalum ecclesiæ præbuerit, cum et ipse sit ecclesiæ membrum, potestati clavium sese subjicere neutiquam dedignari debet. Nec id mirum. Nam quemadmodum ipsum ministrorum ecclesiæ munus nequaquam subordinatur ac subjicitur potestati politicæ, sed persona ministri, qua civis est, ei subjicitur; ita ipsa potestas politica, seu magistratus qua magistratus potestati ecclesiasticæ non subjicitur; attamen homo ille qui est magistratus, quatenus est ecclesiæ membrum, censuræ morum ecclesiasticæ, juxta Theodosii Imperatoris exemplum, subesse debet, nisi disciplinam ecclesiasticam aspernari ac despicari, carnisque typho indulgere velit.

---

106. 1647: cogeur (corrected by hand in the margin of the EEBO example).

107. Ambrose excommunicated Theodosius for the massacre at Thessalonica.

84. If any man should again object that the magistrate is not indeed to resist ecclesiastical government, yet that the abuses thereof are to be corrected and taken away by him, the answer is ready. In the worst and troublesome times, or in the decayed and troubled estate of things, when the ordinance of God in the church is violently turned into tyranny, to the treading down of true religion, and to the oppressing of the professors thereof, and when nothing almost is sound or whole, divers things are yielded to be lawful to godly magistrates, which are not ordinarily lawful for them, that so to extraordinary diseases extraordinary remedies may be applied. So also, the magistrate abusing his power unto tyranny, and making havoc of all, it is lawful to resist him by some extraordinary ways and means, which are not ordinarily to be allowed.

Si quis regerat, regimini quidem ecclesiastico minime resistendum esse a magistratu ejusdem tamen abusus a magistratu corrigendos ac tollendos esse. Responsio in promptu est. Pessimis quidem et turbulentissimis temporibus, seu in collapso ac perturbato {rerum}[108] statu, quando ordo divinitus in ecclesia institutus in tyrannidem rapitur, ad veram religionem conculcandam ejusque professores opprimendos, et οὐδέν ὑγίες; piis et fidelibus magistratibus varia quæ ordinarie licita non sunt, aggredi et præstare concessum esse, quo extraordinariis malis extraordinaria remedia adhibeantur. Ita et magistratui potestate sua ad tyrannidem abutenti omniaque devastanti, modis ac mediis quibusdam extraordinariis (utut ordinarie non probandis) obniti licet.

85. Yet ordinarily and by common or known law and right in settled churches, if any man have recourse to the magistrate to complain, that through abuse of ecclesiastic discipline injury is done to him, or if any sentence of the pastors and elders of the church, whether concerning faith or discipline, do displease or seem unjust unto the magistrate himself, it is not for that cause lawful to draw those ecclesiastical causes to a civil tribunal, or to bring in a kind of political or civil popedom.

Ordinarie tamen, et ex jure communi, in ecclesiis constitutis, si quis ad magistratum confugiat ac apud cum conqueratur, disciplinæ ecclesiasticæ abusu injuriam sibi factam esse; vel si ipsi magistratui displiceat vel iniqua videatur sententia aliqua, sive de disciplina, sive de fide a pastoribus ac senioribus ecclesiæ lata; non ideo causas illas ecclesiasticas ad civile tribunal trahere, vel papatum quendam politicum introducere fas est.

86. What then? Shall it be lawful ordinarily for ministers and elders to do what they list, or shall the governors in the churches, glorying in the law, by their transgression dishonor God? God forbid. For first, if they shall trespass in anything against the magistrate or municipal laws, whether by intermeddling in judging of civil causes, or otherwise disturbing the peace and order of the commonwealth, they are liable to civil trial and judgments, and it is in the power of the magistrate to restrain and punish them.

---

108. The text between braces was omitted in the 1648 Latin edition.

Quid igitur? an ordinarie in ecclesia quidvis licebit ministris ac senioribus? vel anne in ecclesiis constitutis, antistites in lege gloriantes prævaricatione sua Deum dedecorabunt? absit. Primum enim, si quid in magistratum legesve politicas deliquerint, sive causarum civilium dijudicationi sese immiscendo, sive pacem ordinemque reipub. aliter turbando, judiciis civilibus obnoxii sunt, ac penes magistratum est illos coërcere et plectere.

87. Again, it has been before shown that to ecclesiastical evils ecclesiastical remedies are appointed and fitted, for the church is no less than the commonwealth, through the grace of God, sufficient to itself in reference unto her own end. And as in the commonwealth, so in the church, the error of inferior judgments and assemblies, or their evil government, is to be corrected by superior judgments and assemblies, and so still by them of the same order, lest one order be confounded with another, or one government be intermingled with another government. What shall now the adversaries of ecclesiastical power object here, which those who admit not the yoke of the magistrate may not be ready in like manner to transfer against the civil judicatories and government of the commonwealth, seeing it happens sometimes that the commonwealth is no less ill governed than the church?

Deinde malis ecclesiasticis remedia ecclesiastica destinata atque aptata esse prius ostensum est. Est enim ecclesia non minus quam respublica per Dei gratiam sibi sufficiens in ordine ad suum finem: et sicut in repub. sic in ecclesia, inferiorum judiciorum ac conventuum aberratio, malave, administratio, a superioribus judiciis ac conventibus corrigenda est, adeoque ab illis qui sunt ejusdem ordinis; ne ordo ordini, vel regimen regimini permisceatur. Quid amabo hic regerent potestatis ecclesiasticæ adversarii, quod non pariter in judicia politica et reipub. administrationem congerere ac transferre parati fuerint illi qui magistratus jugum non admittunt? cum rempub. etiam non minus quam ecclesiam male administrari sæpiuscule contingat.

88. If any man shall prosecute the argument, and say that yet no remedy is here shown, which may be applied to the injustice or error of a national synod, surely he stumbles against the same stone, seeing he weighs not the matter with an equal balance; for the same may in like sort fall back and be cast upon parliaments, or any supreme senate of a commonwealth. For who sees not the judgment of the supreme civil senate to be nothing more infallible, yea, also in matters of faith and ecclesiastical discipline, more apt and prone to error (as being less accustomed to sacred studies) than the judgment of the national synod? What medicines then, or what sovereign plasters shall be had which may be fit for the curing and healing of the errors and miscarriages of the supreme magistrates and senate? The very like, and besides all this, other and more effectual medicines by which the errors of national synods may be healed, are possible to be had.

Si quis adhuc obstrepat, nullum saltem commonstrari hic remedium, quod synodi nationalis iniquitati vel errori adhiberi possit; næ ille in eundem impingit lapidem, cum non æqua lance hanc rem perpendat: nam et istud pariter in regni comitia, vel reipub. senatum summum recidere ac retorqueri posset. Judicium enim supremi senatus politici, nihilo magis infallbile esse; quinetiam in rebus fidei ac disciplinæ ecclesiasticæ, ad lapsum proclivius (utpote studiis sacris minus assuetum) quam judicium synodi nationalis, quis non videt? Quæ igitur pharmaca, quæve resinaria malagmata summi magistratus vel senatus lapsibus medendis ac sanandis idonea habebuntur? Paria plane, immo ulteriora ac efficaciora medicamenta, quibus fanentur synodi nationalis errores haberi poterint.

89. There wants not a divine medicine and sovereign balm in Gilead [Jer. 8:22]; for although the popish opinion of the infallibility of councils be worthily rejected and exploded, yet it is not in vain that Christ has promised He shall be present with an assembly, which indeed and in truth meets together in His name. With such an assembly verily He useth to be [*commonly is*] present by a spiritual aide and assistance of His own Spirit to uphold the falling, or to raise up the fallen. Whence it is that divers times the errors of former synods are discovered and amended by the latter. Sometimes also, the second or after thoughts of one and the same synod are the wiser and the better.

Non deest sane φαρμακό θεον ac opobalsamum in Gilhade: nam etsi merito explosum sit dogma pontificium de infallibilitate conciliorum; non frustra tamen Christus cœtui servorum ἀληθῶς in nomine suo coëuntium se adfuturum pollicitus est. Tali certe cœtui adesse solet, speciali spiritus sui subsidio ac adjutorio, ad sustentandum cadentes, vel ad erigendum lapsos. Unde est quod non ita raro priorum synodorum lapsus a posterioribus ultro recludantur ac emendentur; interdum etiam unius ejusdemque synodi ἀι δευτέραι φροντίδες σοφώτεραι.

90. Furthermore, the line of ecclesiastical subordination is longer and further stretched than the line of civil subordination. For a national synod must be subordinate and subject to a universal synod in the manner aforesaid, whereas yet there is no oecumenical parliament or general civil court acknowledged, unto which the supreme civil senate in this or that nation should be subject. Finally, neither is the church altogether destitute of nearer remedies, whether a universal council may be had or not.

Adhæc, longius ulteriusque porrigirur subordinationis ecclesiasticæ quam politicæ linea; nam, synodum nationalem synodo œcumenicæ, eo quo dictum[109] est modo, subordinari ac subjici oportet; cum tamen nulla agnoscantur comitia œcumenica quibus subjiciatur supremus in hac vel illa natione senatus politicus. Denique neque proximioribus remediis prorsus destituitur ecclesia; sive concilium œcumenicum haberi possit, sive non.

91. For the national synod ought to declare, and that with greatest reverence, to the magistrate, the grounds of their sentence and the reasons of their proceedings, when he demands or enquires into the same, and desires to be satisfied. But if the magistrate nevertheless does dissent, or cannot by contrary

---

109. 1647: distinctum; corrected by hand (distinctum) in the EEBO example.

reasons (which may be brought, if he please) move the synod to alter their judgment, yet may he require and procure that the matter be again debated and canvassed in another national synod; and so, the reasons of both sides being throughly [*thoroughly*] weighed, may be lawfully determined in an ecclesiastical way.

Magistratui enim offenso ac inquirenti vel interroganti synodus ipsa nationalis sententiæ suæ fundamenta, factique sui rationes, et quidem cum summa, ut par est, reverentia, explicare debet. Quod si magistratus nihilominus diffentiat, aut rationibus in contrariam partem[110] (si ita ei visum fuerint) allatis illos a sententia flectere nequeat; postulare tamen et procurare potest, ut in alia synodo nationali res resumatur et recognoscatur,[111] sique judicio ecclesiastico perpensis utriusque partis rationibus legittime determinetur.

92. But as there is much indeed to be given to the demand of the magistrate, so is there here a twofold caution to be used. For first, notwithstanding of a future revision, it is necessary that the former sentence of the synod, whether concerning the administration of ecclesiastic discipline, or against any heresy, be forthwith put in execution, lest by lingering and making of delays, the evil of the church take deeper root, and the gangrene spread and creep further; and lest violence be done to the consciences of ministers if they be constrained to impart the signs and seals of the Covenant of Grace to dogs and swine, that is, to unclean persons wallowing in the mire of ungodliness; and lest subtle men abuse such interims or intervals, so as that ecclesiastical discipline altogether decay, and the very decrees of synods be accounted as cobwebs, which none fear to break down.

Atqui ut magistratus postulatui multum quidem dandum est; ita duplicem hic adhiberi oportet cautelam. Primo enim non obstante futura revisione, priorem synodi sententiam, sive circa disciplinæ ecclesiasticæ administrationem, sive contra hæresin aliquam latam, executioni confestim mandari necesse est; ne cunctando et moras nectendo, ecclesiæ malum altiores radices agat, ac gangræna latius serpat, neve ministrorum conscientiis vis fiat, si signa gratiæ divinæ canibus et porcis, impuris scilicet hominibus in cœno impietatis volutantibus impertiri cogantur; denique ne talibus interspirationibus ac intervallis versuti homines sic abutantur, ut disciplina ecclesiastica penitus flaccescat, atque synodorum etiam decreta habeantur quasi aranearum telæ, quas nemo perrumpere metuit.

93. Next, it may be granted that the matter may be put under a further examination, yet upon condition that when it is come to the revision of the former sentence, regard may be had of the weaker which are found willing to be taught, though they doubt, but that unto the wicked and contentious tempters, which do mainly strive to oppress our liberty which we have in Christ, and to bring us into bondage, we do not for a moment give place

---

110. 1647: patrem (corrected by hand in the margin in the EEBO example).

111. 1647: recognoscatar (corrected by hand in the margin in the EEBO example).

by subjecting ourselves; for what else seek they or wait for, than that under the pretence of a revising and of new debate, they cast in lets [*hindrances*] and impediments ever and anon, and that by cunning lyings in wait they may betray the liberty of the church, and in process of time may by open violence more forcibly break in upon it, or at least constrain the ministers of the church to weave Penelope's web,[112] which they can never bring to an end.

Deinde concedi potest ut ulteriori examine res subjiciatur; ea tamen lege, ut cum ad superioris sententiæ revisionem venitur, infirmiorum quidem, qui dociles tametsi subdubitantes inveniuntur, ratio habeatur: improbis vero exploratoribus qui libertatem nostram quam in Christo habemus opprimere, atque in servitutem nos adigere unice annituntur, ne ad momentum quidem subjiciendo cedamus. Quid enim aliud illi quærunt ac præstolantur, quam ut sub revisionis vel recognitionis prætextu, remoras et compedes subinde injiciant; ac structis insidiis ecclesiæ libertatem prodant, et clam subvertant, atque cum tempore, aperto marte validius in eam irruant: vel saltem ministros Christi cogant Penelopes telam texere, quam nunquam absolvere poterunt?

94. Moreover, the Christian magistrate has then only discharged his office in reference to ecclesiastical discipline, when not only he withdraws nothing from it, and makes no impediment to it, but also affords special furtherance and help to it, according to the prophecy, Isaiah 49:23, "and kings shall be thy nursing fathers, and queens thy nursing mothers."

Porro magistratus Christianus tum demum officio functus est circa disciplinam ecclesiasticam, quando illi non modo nihil detrahit, nullumve obicem ponit: sed etiam insigne adjumentum impendit, juxta prophetiam, Isai. 49:23, *Et erunt reges nutritii tui, et reginæ eorum nutrices tuæ.*

95. For Christian magistrates and princes embracing Christ and sincerely giving their names to Him, do not only serve Him as men, but also use their office to His glory and the good of the church. They defend, stand for, and take care to propagate the true faith and godliness; they afford places of habitation to the church, and furnish necessary helps and supports, turn away injuries done to it, restrain false religion, and cherish, underprop, and defend the rights and liberties of the church, so far they are from diminishing, changing or restraining those rights; for so [*for otherwise*] the condition of the church were in that respect worse, and the liberty thereof more cut short under the Christian magistrate than under the infidel or heathen.

Princepes enim ac magistratus Christianum exosculantes, eique nomina sua sincere dantes, non tantum ut homines Christo serviunt sed et munere suo ad gloriam Christi et ecclesiæ bonum utuntur: veram fidem ac pietatem defendunt, propugnant et propagari curant ecclesiæ dant hospitium, necessariaque adminicula subministrant:

---

112. In *The Odyssey*, Penelope is to choose a new husband after completing the weaving of Laertes's burial shroud, but she unweaves the work each day to forestall the suitors. Thus, to "weave Penelope's web" is to regularly undo work so that progress cannot be made.

injurias ei illatas depellunt, falsamque religionem coërcent, jura denique et libertates ecclesiæ sovent, fulciunt, vindicant; tantum abeſt ut jura illa mutent, minuant vel reſtringant: sic enim deterior eatenus foret ecclesiæ conditio, ejusque libertas magis accisa sub Chriſtiano magiſtratu, quam sub infideli seu ethinico.

96. Wherefore, seeing these nursing fathers, favorers, and defenders can do nothing againſt the truth, but for the truth, nor have any right againſt the goſpel, but for the goſpel, and their power in reſpect of the church whereof they bear the care, being not *privative* or *deſtructive*, but *cumulative* and *auxiliary*, thereby it is sufficiently clear that they ought to cherish, and by their authority ought to eſtablish the ecclesiaſtical discipline; but yet not with implicit faith, or blind obedience; for the Reformed churches do not deny to any of the faithful, much less to the magiſtrate, the judgment of Chriſtian prudence and discretion concerning those things which are decreed or determined by the church.

Quare cum nutritii illi, fautores ac defensores nihil possint adversus veritatem, sed pro veritate, nec quicquam juris contra evangelium, sed pro evangelio nacti sint; illorumque poteſtas, reſpectu ecclesiæ cujus curam gerunt, non sit *privativa* vel *deſtructiva*, sed *cumulativa* et *auxiliaris;* exinde satis liquet, eos disciplinam ecclesiaſticam fovere ac sanctione sua ſtabilire debere. Minime id quidem fide implicita, vel cœca obedientia: nemini enim fideli, nedum magiſtratui judicium Chriſtianæ prudentiæ ac discretionis de iis quæ ab ecclesia decernuntur vel ſtatuuntur Reformati denegant.

97. Therefore, as to each member of the church reſpectively, so unto the magiſtrate belongs the judgment of such things, both to apprehend and to judge of them. For although the magiſtrate is not ordained and preferred of God, that he should be a judge of matters and causes ſpiritual, of which there is controversy in the church, yet is he queſtionless judge of his own civil act about ſpiritual things; namely, of defending them in his own dominions, and of approving or tolerating the same; and if in this business he judges and determines according to the wisdom of the flesh, and not according to the wisdom which is from above, he is to render an account thereof before the supreme tribunal.

Igitur sicut unicuique ecclesiæ membro, prout cujusque intereſt, sic et magiſtratui de ejusmodi rebus competit judicium tum apprehensivum tum discretivum: etsi enim magiſtratus nequaquam ad id a Deo sit conſtitutus et præfectus, ut sit judex refum ſpiritualium de quibus in ecclesia lis mouetur: eſt tamen proculdubio judex politci sui actus circa ſpiritualia, de iis scilicet in sua ditiones tuendis, approbandis, vel tolerandis. Atque si in hoc negotio secundum id quod sapit caro, non autem secundum sacræ Scripturæ amussim, ac sapientiam quæ superne eſt, judicet atque ſtatuat, de eo coram superno tribunali rationem redditurus eſt.

98. However, the ecclesiaſtical discipline, according as it is ordained by Chriſt, whether it be eſtablished and ratified by civil authority or not, ought to be retained and exercised in the society of the faithful (as long as it is free

and safe for them to come together in holy assemblies), for the want of civil authority is unto the church like a *ceasing gain*,[113] but not like *damage* or *loss ensuing*; as it superadds nothing more, so it takes nothing away.

Utut sit, disciplina ecclesiastica, prout a Christo instituta est sive sanctione civili stabilita ac ratificata fuerit, sive non, in cætu fidelium (quandiu eis in cœtus sacros coire liberum vel tutum est) reteneri ac exerceri debet. Sanctionis enim civilis carentia est ecclesiæ instar *Lucri cessantis*, non autem instar *damni emergentis*: utique, sicut nihil superaddit, ita nihil detrahit.

99. If it further happen (which God forbid) that the magistrate does so far abuse his authority that he does straitly [*strictly*] forbid what Christ has ordained, yet the constant and faithful servants of Christ will resolve and determine with themselves that any extremities are rather to be undergone than that they should obey such things, and that we ought to obey God rather than men; yea, they will not leave off to perform all the parts of their office, being ready in the meantime to render a reason of their practice to everyone that demands it,[114] but specially unto the magistrate (as was said before).

Si porro contingat (avertat autem Deus) magistratum eousque auctoritate sua abuti, ut severe prohibeat quod Christus instituit; cordati tamen et fidi Christi servi, extrema quævis potius subeunda esse, quam ut pareatur; deoque magis quam hominibus obediendum esse apud se statuent; adeoque officii sui partes omnes obire non cessabunt; parati interim omni interroganti, præsertim vero magistratui (ut supra dictum est) rationem suæ praxeos reddere.

100. These things are not to that end and purpose proposed, that these functions should be opposed one against another in a hostile posture, or in terms of enmity, than which nothing is more hurtful to the church and commonwealth, nothing more execrable to them who are truly and sincerely zealous for the house of God (for they have not so learned Christ), but the aim is, first and above all, that unto the King of kings and Lord of lords Jesus Christ, the only Monarch of the church, His own prerogative royal (of which also Himself in the world was accused, and for His witnessing a good confession thereof before Pontius Pilate, was unjustly condemned to death)[115] may be fully maintained and defended.

Hæc non eo animo proponuntur ut munia ista inter se committantur, aut quasi ad dimicandum sese accingentes adversis frontibus opponantur; quo nihil tum ecclesiæ tum reipub. perniciosus, nihil iis, qui sincero et sancto pro domo Dei zelo accensi sunt, execrabilius (neque enim ita didicerunt Christum), sed ante omnia ut Regi regum et Domino dominantium Iesu Christo unico ecclesiæ monarchæ sua gloria et prerogativa regalis (de qua etiam ipse in mundo accusatus, proque ejusdem

---

113. *Lucrum cessans* (Scots Law): a ceasing gain, as opposed to actual loss (*damnum datum*).
114. Cf. Acts 5:29; 1 Peter 3:15.
115. Cf. 1 Timothy 6:13; Mark 15:2; Luke 23:3; Matthew 27:11; John 18:33–36.

confessione, ac præclara coram Pontio Pilato professione, ad mortem injuste condemnatus fuit) in solidum asseratur et vindicetur.

101. Next, this debate tends also to this end, that the power as well of ecclesiastical censure as of the civil sword being in force, the licentiousness of carnal men, which desire that there be too slack ecclesiastical discipline or none at all, may be bridled, and so men may sin less, and may live more agreeably to the gospel. Another thing here intended is that errors on both sides being overthrown (as well the error of those who under a fair pretence of maintaining and defending the rights of magistracy do leave to the church either no power, or that which is too weak; as the error of others, who under the veil of a certain suppositious and imaginary Christian liberty, do turn off the yoke of the magistrate), both powers may enjoy their own privileges; add hereto that both powers being circumscribed with their distinct borders and bounds, and also the one underpropped and strengthened by the help of the other, a holy concord between them may be nourished, and they may mutually and friendly embrace one another.

Denique et huc collimat dissertatio ista, ut tam censura ecclesiasticæ, quam gladii civilis potestate vigente; carnalium hominum qui vel nullam esse, vel nimis laxam disciplinam ecclesiasticam cupiunt, licentia frænetur: a deoque minus peccetur, magisque evangelice vivatur. Præterea hic etiam scopus ob oculos habetur; ut confossis utrinque erroribus tam illorum, qui sub specioso prætextu asserendi et vindicandi jura magistratus, vel nullam vel nimis debilem potestatem ecclesiæ relinquunt; quam aliorum, qui sub putativæ cujusdam Christianæ libertatis velo magistratus jugum aversantur, utraque potestas privilegiis suis fruatur. Adhæc, ut utraque suis cancellis et limitibus circumscripta: necnon altera ope alterius fortius suffulta et statuminata, facta inter eas alatur concordia, atque sese mutuo amice complectantur.

102. Last of all, seeing there are not wanting some unhappy men who cease not to pervert the right ways of the Lord, and with all diligence go about to shake off the yoke of the ecclesiastical discipline, where now it is about to be introduced, yea, also where it has been long ago established, and as yet happily remains in force, it was necessary to obviate their most wicked purposes; which things being so, let all which has been said pass with the good leave and liking of those orthodox churches in which the discipline of excommunication is not as yet in use; neither can any offence easily arise to them from hence; yea (if the best conjecture does not deceive), they cannot but rejoice and congratulate at the defense and vindication of this discipline.

Postremo, cum non desint quidam male feriati homines qui non cessant pervertere vias Domini rectas, ac disciplinæ ecclesiasticæ (ubi jam introducitur, quinetiam ubi pridem stabilita fuit, et etiamnum fœliciter obtinet) jugum excutere omni opera conantur, pessimis illorum consiliis obviam iri oportuit. Quæ quidem cum ita sunt, cum bona venia ac pace ecclesiarum illarum orthodoxarum, apud quas nondum in usu est excommunicationis disciplina, hæc dicta sunto: neque enim facile ullum eis offendiculum hinc nasci potest: quinetiam nisi fallat conjectura, non poterunt non sibi gratificari de istius disciplinæ vindiciis.

103. For those churches do not deny but acknowledge and teach that the discipline of excommunication is most agreeable to the Word of God, as also that it ought to be restored and exercised. Which also heretofore the most learned Zachary Ursine in the declaration of his judgment concerning excommunication, exhibited to Prince Frederick the Third, Count Elector Palatine, the title whereof is, *Judicium de Disciplina Ecclesiastica & Excommunicatione*, etc.[116]

Neque enim illæ ecclesiæ inficiantur, sed agnoscunt et docent disciplinam excommunicationis verbo Dei maxime consentaneam esse, adeoque revocari ac in usu esse debere. Quod et antehac observavit et monuit vir doctissimus Zacharias Ursinus in declaratione suæ de excommunicatione sententiæ, principi Frederico tertio Electori Palatino exhibita, cui titulus est, *Judicium de disciplina {ecclesiastica}*[117] *& Excommunicatione.*

104. For thus he, "In other churches where either no excommunication is in use, or it is not lawfully administered, and nevertheless without all controversy it is confessed and openly taught that it ought justly to be received and be of force in the church." And a little after, "Lest also your highness by this new opinion do sever yourself and your churches from all other churches, as well those which have not excommunication, as those which have it; forasmuch as all of them do unanimously confess and always confessed that there is reason why it ought to be in use."[118]

Ita enim ille. *In aliis* (ecclesiis) *ubi aut nulla est excommnnicatio in usu, aut non legitime administratur, ac nihilominus absque omni controversia, in confesso est ac palam docttur, cam merito in ecclesia vigere debere.* [119] Et infra. *Ne etiam celsitudo tua se suasque ecclesias ab aliis omnibus ecclesiis, tam ab iis quæ nullam habent excommunicationem, quam ab iis quæ habent, nova hæc opinione sejungat: siquidem universæ ac singulæ uno ore confitentur, semperque confessæ sunt, merito illam in usu esse debere.*

105. To the same purpose it tends, which the highly esteemed Philip Melancthon in his *Commonplaces*, chapter of civil magistrates, does affirm: "Before," says he, "I warned that civil places and powers are to be distinguished from the adhering confusions which arise from other causes, partly from the malice of the devil, partly from the malice of men, partly from the common infirmity of men, as it comes to pass in other kinds of life and government

---

116. Zacharias Ursinus, *Judicium de Disciplina Ecclesiastica & Excommunicatione*, in *Opera Theologica*, vol. 3 (Heidelbergæ: Rosa, 1612), cols. 801–812.

117. The text between braces was omitted in the 1648 Latin edition.

118. Ursinus, ibid. Gillespie cited the passages in his survey of the origins of Erastianism. See herein on pages 211, 214.

119. 1647: debet(?) (corrected by hand in the EEBO example; original ending obscured).

ordained of God. No man doubts that ecclesiastical government is ordained of God, and yet how many and great disorders grow in it from other causes."[120] Where he mentions a church government distinct from the civil, and that *jure divino*, as a thing uncontroverted.

Eodem fere recidit quod asserit vir summus Philippus Melanchton in locis theolog. cap. de magistratibus civilibus. *Supra* (inquit) *monus ordinem politicum discernendum esse a confussionibus quæ aliunde admiscentur, partim a diabolo, partim ab hominum malitia, partim a communi infirmitate hominum; ut fit in aliis vitæ generibus ac gubernationibus a Deo ordinatis; nemo dubitat ecclesiasticam gubernationem a Deo institutam esse, at quantum accedit confusionum aliunde?* Ubi de gubernatione ecclesiastica, a munere magistratus jure divino distincta ac discreta, tanquam de re non controversa loquitur.

106. Neither were the wishes of the chief divines of Zürich and Bern wanting for the recalling and restoring of the discipline of excommunication. So Bullinger upon 1 Corinthians 5. "And hitherto," he says, "of the ecclesiastical chastising of wickedness, but here I would have the brethren diligently warned that they watch and with all diligence take care that this wholesome medicine thrown out of the true church by occasion of the Pope's avarice, may be reduced; that is, that scandalous sins be punished. For this is the very end of excommunication, that men's manners may be well ordered and the saints flourish, the profane being restrained, lest wicked men by their impudencey and impiety increase and undo all. It is our part, O brethren, with greatest diligence to take care of these things; for we see that Paul in this place does stir up those that were negligent in this business."[121]

Nec defuerunt florentiorum Theologorum Tigurinorum et Bernensium vota pro disciplina excommunicationis revocanda et instaurandia. Ita Bullingerus in 1 Cor. 5. *Et hactenus* (inquit) *de castigatione scelerum ecclesiastica. Hic tamen diligenter admonitos volo fratres, vigilent, et omni diligenta curent, ut salutare hoc pharmacum, e cœtu sanctorum Pontificis avaritia eliminatum, reducatur, hoc est ut scelera offendentia plectantur. Hic enim unicus est excommunicationis finis, ut mores excolatur et floreant sancti, prophani vero coërceantur, ne mali porro impudentia ac impietate grassentur. Nostrum est ista O fratres, summa cum diligentia curare. Videmus enim et Paulum cessantes hoc loco incitare.*

107. Aretius agrees hereunto. *Problem. Theolog.*, loc. 33. "Magistrates do not admit the yoke, they are afraid for their honors, they love licentiousnesse, etc. The common people is too dissolute, the greatest part is most corrupt, etc. In the meanwhile, I willingly confess that we are not to despair, but the age following will peradventure yield more tractable spirits, more mild

---

120. Philipp Melanchthon, *Loci communes*, in *Opera*, in *Corpus Reformatorum*, vol. 21 (Brunsvigæ: Schwetschke, 1854), p. 1003.

121. *Heinrici Bullingeri Commentarii In omnes Pauli Apostoli Epistolas, atque etiam in Epistolam ad Hebræos* (Tiguri: Cambierus, 1603), pp. 114–115. See this citation in *Nihil Respondes* on page 265.

hearts than our times have."[122] See also Lavater agreeing in this, Homil. 52. on Nehem. "Because the Popes of Rome have abused excommunication for the establishing of their own tyranny, it comes to pass that almost no just discipline can be any more settled in the church, but unless the wicked be restrained, all things must of necessity run into the worst condition."[123] See besides, the opinion of Fabricius upon Psalm 149:6–9, of spiritual corrections, which he grounds upon that text compared with Matthew 16:19 and 18:18, John 20:23.[124]

Annuit Aretius Problem. Theol. Loc. 33. *Magistratus Jugum non admittunt, timent honoribus, licentiam amant, vulgus quoque et plebs dissolutior, major pars corruptissima est etc. Interea non desperandum esse libenter fateor; dabit posterior ætas tractæhiliores forte animas, mitiora pectora quam nostra habent secula.* Astipulantem quoque ecce Lavaterum Hom. 51 in Nehem. *Quia Pontifices Romani excommunicatione ad stabiliendam suam tyrannidem abusi sunt, factum est ut nulla fere justa disciplina amplius in ecclesiis institui possit. Nisi autem flagitiosi coërceantur, omnia ruant in peius neccesse est.* Videatur præterea D. Fabricii in Psal. 149:6-9, de spiritualibus castigationibus sententia; ex illo textu cum Matth. 16:19 et 18:18, Joh. 20:23, collato deprompta.

108. It can hardly be doubted or called in question, but besides these, other learned and godly divines of those churches were and are of the same mind herein, with these now cited; and indeed the very Confession of Faith of the Churches of Helvetia, Chapter 18,[125] may be an evidence hereof. "But there ought to be in the meantime a just discipline amongst ministers for the doctrine and life of ministers is diligently to be enquired of in synods. Those that sin are to be rebuked of the elders, and to be brought again into the way, if they be curable; or to be deposed, and like wolves driven away from the flock of the Lord, if they be incurable." That this manner of synodical censure, namely of deposing ministers from their office for some great scandal, is used in the Republic of Zürich, Lavater is witness in his book *Of the Rites and Ordinances of the Church of Zürich*, Chapter 23.[126] Surely, they could not be of that mind that ecclesiastical discipline ought to be exercised upon delinquent ministers only, and not also upon other rotten members of the church.

---

122. Benedictus Aretius, *Locus LVI. De Exemplis Veteris Testamenti, … hoc est, Loci commvnes Christianæ religionis, methodice explicati* (Isayas le Preux, 1617), De Excommunitione, Loc. CXII, pp. 638–639. See *Nihil Respondes*, herein page 265.

123. Ludwig Lavater, *Nehemias: liber Nehemiæ, qui et secundus Ezræ dicitur, homiliis LVIII* (Tiguri: ex Officina Froschoviana, 1586), p. 98. See *Nihil Respondes*, herein page 265.

124. The Edinburgh and London texts (1647) and *Works* (1844) misspell Fabricius as Fabritius. Stephanus Fabricius, *Sacræ Conciones in centum quinquaginta Psalmos Davidis*, etc. (Geneva: Petri et Jacobi Chouët, 1620), pp. 1093–1094.

125. Dennison, *Reformed Confessions*, 3.858–859.

126. Ludwig Lavater, *De Ritibus et Institutis Ecclesiæ Tigurinæ opusculum* ([Zürich]: [Christoph Froschauer], 1559), p. 22. See *Nihil Respondes*, herein page 264.

Eundem aliis ejusmodi ecclesiarum doctis et piis theologis fuisse et esse animum vix quidem in dubium vocari potest: et quidem indicio esse poterit ipsa Confessio Fidei Ecclesiarum Helveticarum, cap. 18. *Atqui debet interim esse inter ministros disciplina. Inquirendum enim diligenter, in doctrinam et viram ministrorum, in Synodis. Corripiendi sunt peccantes a senioribus, et in viam reducendi, si sint sanabiles, aut deponendi et veluti lupi abigendi sunt per veros pastores a grege dominico, si sint incurabiles.* Hunc morem censuræ synodicæ, deponendi scilicet ab officio ministros propter grave aliquod scandalum in ecclesiis ditionis Tigurinæ vigere, testis est Lavaterus in libello *de Ritibus & Institutis Ecclesiæ Tigurinæ*, cap. 23. Ea certe non potuit esse illis mens, in delinquentes solum ministros, non itidem in putida ecclesiæ membra disciplinam ecclesiasticam exerceri debere.

109. Yea, the Helvetian Confession in the place now cited, does so tax the inordinate zeal of the Donatists and Anabaptists (which are so bent upon the rooting out of the tares out of the Lord's field, that they take not heed of the danger of plucking up the wheat), that withal it does not obscurely commend the ecclesiastical forensical discipline as distinct from the civil power. "And seeing," say they, "it is altogether necessary that there be in the church a discipline, and among the ancients in times past excommunication has been usual, and ecclesiastical courts have been among the people of God, among whom this discipline was exercised by prudent and godly men, it belongs also to ministers according to the case of the times, the public estate and necessity, to moderate this discipline; where this rule is ever to be held, that all ought to be done to edification, decently, honestly, without tyranny and sedition. The Apostle also witnesses, 2 Cor. 13 [*sic* 10:8], that to himself was given of God a power unto edification and not unto destruction."[127]

Quid quod Confessio Helvetica, loco jam citato, Donatistarum et Anabatistarum (qui lolio eradicando ex agro dominico usque adeo intensi sunt, ut a periculo evellendi etiam triticum non caveant) inordinatum zelum ita prestringit, ut simul etiam disciplinam ecclesiasticam a potestate politica distinctam non obscure commendet. *Cumque omnino* inquiunt, *oporteat esse in ecclesia disciplinam et apud veteres quondam usitata fuerit excommunicatio, fuerintque judicia ecclesiastica in populo Dei, quibus per viros prudentes et pios exercebatur hæc disciplina, ministrorum quoque fuerit ad ædeficationem, disciplinam moderare hanc, pro conditio ne temporum, status prublici, ac necessitatis; ubi semper tenenda est regula omnia fieri debere ad ædificatiœm, decenter, honeste, sine tyrannide et seditione: Apostolus etiam testatur. 2 Cor. 13 [sic], sibi a Deo traditam esse in ecclesia potestatem ad ædificationem, et non ad destructionem.*

110. And now what rests [*remains*] but that God be entreated with continual and ardent prayers, both that he would put into the hearts of all magistrates zeal and care to cherish, defend, and guard the ecclesiastic discipline, together with the rest of Christ's ordinances, and to stop their ears against

---

127. Dennison, ibid., p. 858.

the importunate suits of whatsoever clawbacks[128] which would ſtir them up againſt the church, and that also all governors and rulers of churches, being everywhere furnished and helped with the ſtrength of the Holy Spirit, may diligently and faithfully execute this part also of their funcſtion, as it becometh [*befits*] the truſty servants of Chriſt, which ſtudy to please their own Lord and Maſter, more than men.

Quod supereſt, orandus eſt Deus assiduis et ardentibus precibus, tum ut universis ac singulis magiſtratibus indat zelum ſtudiumque, disciplinam ecclesiaſticam, una cum reliquis Chriſti inſtituis, fovendi, tuendi ac muniendi; auresque suas palponum quorumlibet illos in ecclesiam concitantium solicitationibus obſtruendi: tum ut omnes ubique ecclesiarum præfecſti et recſtores, Spiritus sui sancſti viribus inſtrucſti et adjuti, hanc etiam muneris sui partem sedulo et fidelter exequantur, ut decet fidos Chriſti servos, qui Domino suo magis quam hominibus placere ſtudent.

III. Finally, all those who are more averse from ecclesiaſtic discipline, or ill affecſted againſt it, are to be admonished and entreated through our Lord Jesus Chriſt, that they be no longer entangled and inveigled with carnal prejudice to give place in this thing to human affecſtions, and to measure by their own corrupt reason ſpiritual discipline, but that they do seriously think with themselves and consider in their minds, how much better it were that the luſts of the flesh were as with a bridle tamed, and that the repentance, amendment, and gaining of vicious men unto salvation may be sought, than that sinners be left to their own diſposition, and be permitted to follow their own luſts without controlment, and by their evil example to draw others headlong into ruin with themselves. And seeing either the keys of discipline muſt take no ruſt, or the manners of Chriſtians will certainly contracſt much ruſt, what is here to be chosen, and what is to be shunned, let the wise and godly, who alone take to heart the safety of the church, judge.

Monendi denique et rogandi sunt per Dominum noſtrum Iesum Chriſtum quotquot a disciplina ecclesiaſtica alieniores vel adversus eam iniquiores sunt ne divitius carnis præjudicio fascinati, humanis hac in re affecſtibus indulgeant; corruptaque sua ratione disciplinam ſpiritualem metiantur; sed ut probe sibi in animum revocent et inducant, quanto præſtet ut carnis cupiditates, quasi fræno[129] injecſto domentur, hominumque vitiis deditorum resipiscentia emendatio ad salutem quæratur; quam ut peccantes ingenio suo relinquantur, {ac}[130] cupiditatibus suis impune obseqi, alisque exemplo suo malo in ruinam præcipites secum trahere pemittantur. Cumque vel claves disciplinæ rubiginem nullam vel mores Chriſtianorum rubiginem multam contrahere oporteat: quid hic eligendum, quid cavendum sit, penes prudentes ac pios quibus salus ecclesiæ maxime cordi eſt, judicium eſto.

---

128. *Clawback*: sycophant, flatterer, parasite (*OED*).

129. 1648: foæno.

130. The text between braces was omitted in the 1648 Latin edition.

ANTI-ENGAGEMENT WRITINGS, 1648

PREFACE

GEORGE GILLESPIE'S rise to leadership in the Church of Scotland had begun with "his astonishing learned *Dispute Against the English Popish Ceremonies*,"[1] which, smuggled into Scotland from Holland, arrived just in time to give the theological case for the Second Reformation.[2] This virtuoso performance along with his connections to the leadership of the Covenanter movement led to his appointment to be one of the Scottish delegation sent to the Westminster Assembly of Divines in London. His reputation only grew in London and the additional work he did for the General Assemblies to which he and Robert Baillie brought the productions of the divines, brought him to the highest prominence as one of the leaders of the Scottish Church, if only for a brief and turbulent year.

> With his return from the Westminster Assembly, Gillespie emerged as one of the undisputed leaders of the Church of Scotland. As a result, on 22 September 1647 the Edinburgh town council transferred Gillespie from Greyfriars to St. Giles, to succeed Alexander Henderson, and he was admitted soon thereafter. On 24 November 1647 the town council voted to make Gillespie a burgess and gildbrother "gratis."

> For the next year, between the Assemblies of 1647 and 1648, Gillespie actively served on the Commission of the General Assembly, which had become increasing powerful since its inception in 1642. Now that he was back in Scotland, he could and did regularly attend committee meetings and took part in the work of the Commission. At these meetings the Commission

---

1. This is Chad Van Dixhoorn's assessment and one shared by those from the very time of the first publication of *English Popish Ceremonies*, when Gillespie was twenty-two, giving as Professor Cunningham said, "a most astonishing proof of precocious talent and learning…." Baillie marveled at the work as one far beyond that of a twenty-two year old, even if he had aid from "the chief of that side" (it is unclear if this refers to Rutherford or Calderwood). Van Dixhoorn, "Presbyterian ecclesiologies at the Westminster assembly," in *Church Polity and Politics in the British Atlantic World, c. 1635–66* (Manchester University Press, 2020), ebook, location 3294. *Report of the Great Public Meeting held in the Assembly rooms, Edinburgh, on Thursday Evening, Dec. 20, 1838, to commemorate the restoration of civil and religious liberty, and of Presbyterian Church Government, as secured by the Glasgow Assembly of 1638. Taken in short-hand by S. Macgregor* (Edinburgh: Edinburgh Printing and Publishing Company, 1838), p. 51. Baillie, *Letters & Journals*, 1.90.

2. See Introductory Essays in *The Shorter Writings of George Gillespie*, volume 1, pp. 71–79.

441

appointed Gillespie to numerous sub-commissions to deal with practical matters relating to furthering the cause of reforming the Church of Scotland.[3]

The work of the last year of Gillespie's life and ministry was driven by the breakdown of the relationship between England and Scotland and a division amongst the Scots over "the Engagement." This slow moving disaster began with a secret agreement on December 26, 1647, between the king and a royalist faction led by James, First Duke of Hamilton, his brother William, the Earl of Lanark, and John Maitland, second earl of Lauderdale, agreeing to invade England, rescue the king from the antimonarchist New Model Army, and restore Charles to the throne, in exchange for relatively weak concessions and no insistence he agree to the Solemn League and Covenant.[4]

---

3. James Kevin Culberson, B.A., M.A. "'For Reformation and Uniformity': George Gillespie (1613–1648) and the Scottish Covenanter Revolution," Dissertation Prepared for the Degree of Doctor of Philosophy, University of North Texas (2003), p. 67.

4. "When in December the Scottish parliament signed the Engagement with the king, the Commission of the General Assembly stood firmly opposed to the Engagement. Many in Scotland felt loyal to the king and worried about the increasing anti-monarchical radicalism of the English army, so they supported parliament's Engagement with the king. On the other hand, the radical side of the Scottish Covenanters dominated the Commission of the General Assembly, and they believed that rapprochement with King Charles could not take place until he signed the Solemn League and Covenant and agreed to abide by its conditions" (Culberson, pp. 66–68). "When the New Model Army captured the king in June 1647 [away from the English parliamentary guards], the possible terms of settlement were thrown wider and rendered more contentious than ever before. Unilateral peace proposals, known as the Four Bills, were put forward in late November by an English parliament whose Presbyterian grouping had been humbled by demonstrations of military strength [of the New Model Army] in the City." "Fearing justifiably that a treaty inimical to Scottish interests would soon be agreed [between the English and the king], the three parliamentary commissioners, Lanark, Loudoun, and Lauderdale, hurriedly concluded an Engagement with Charles on 26 December 1647. In return for parliamentary confirmation of the Covenants in both kingdoms, Charles was offered military assistance from Scotland to regain his British throne. Charles was not required to take the Covenants and none of his English subjects would be pressed to do so against their consciences…. The key political issue for the Engagement's opponents was its failure to safeguard the principal war aim of 1643: the Presbyterianization of England and Ireland. While the Engagement safeguarded the Covenanted constitution, it opened a path towards divergent religious settlements in the two kingdoms that clearly contradicted the stated aims of the Solemn League. Intervention in England had been promoted by the Solemn Leaguers, at a colossal price to Scotland's people, on the justifiable premise that the future security of the kingdom depended on establishing religion and liberties through the archipelago…. Many Scottish Covenanters were undoubtedly right to fear that the comparatively generous terms of the Engagement risked the undoing of their achievements to date. Robert Baillie's private

On the question of the Covenant Charles accepted a compromise. He agreed to confirm it by an Act of Parliament, so far as to give security to those who had taken it, but he refused to allow any one to be constrained to take it in future…. The Presbyterian system was to be established for three years, during which time plans for a final settlement of all Church questions were to be discussed in the Assembly of Divines, reinforced by twenty members appointed by himself, though no resolution of this body was to have any binding force till it had received his assent and that of the two Houses. The solution here proposed, as the commissioners could not fail to perceive, was not likely to make the Church of England permanently Presbyterian.

On the 27TH, the three Scottish commissioners declared under their signatures their personal acceptance of the Engagement, and their confidence that it would be adopted in Scotland. The King then took them to witness that he did not bind himself in any way to forward the Presbyterian government in England, or to cause any to suffer for rejecting it, excepting those who were excepted in the clause against toleration. [5]

"The terms of the treaty [for the Engagement] were initially made known only to a small circle of leading politicians…."[6] However, the English knew something was up and had sent commissioners to Edinburgh to try to sway the Scots from anything rash. At the same time, Gillespie and other Scottish ministers, fearing a covenant-breaking plan in the works, preached vigorously against any rapprochement with the king. Even before the church was told exactly what the Scottish Parliament was planning, there was fear it involved invading England, and Gillespie in particular had been preaching frequently against such a plan in the first half of February if not also in January 1648. In a letter dated February 15, 1648, the French diplomat Jean De Montereul wrote, "The clergy of this town continue to preach against the intention that they think the Scots have of invading England and of joining with the friends of their king. Gillespie, who has had seven or eight sermons on this subject, prayed God last Sunday that he would preserve them from the latest surprises

---

reflections to David Dickson on England's 'lame Erastian Presbyterie' are frequently quoted by historians who ignore later public statements made in very different political circumstances. A Covenanted union, Baillie informed his colleagues in the 1647 general assembly—meeting as the New Model Army took control of London—had made the churches 'not only uniforme, but weell near one.' Divisions amongst the ministry, Baillie continued, and 'our greatest adversaries, the Sectaries,' risked destroying all that had been achieved [Baillie, 2.362, 3.11–13]. An act of war against England would breach the Solemn League." (Laura A. M. Stewart, *Rethinking the Scottish Revolution: Covenanted Scotland, 1637–1651* [Oxford University Press, 2016], pp. 258–259).

5. Samuel Rawson Gardiner, *History of the Great Civil War, 1642–1649*, Volume 4 (London: Longmans, Green, and Co., 1901), pp. 39, 41.

6. Stewart, p. 267.

of the King of England, and filled his prayer with sundry imprecations against his prince."7 Parliament finally disclosed the plan to the Commission of the Kirk on February 22. The church commissioners "immediately decried it as 'destructive to the Covenant' and set about drawing up a declaration against it."8 The commission appointed the moderator and clerk, Robert Douglas and Andrew Ker, and whomever they pleased to help them, to draw up the declaration the next day on February 23. On February 25, no doubt to underscore and send a clear but respectful warning against the plan, the commission appointed George Gillespie to preach the customary sermon at the opening of the next meeting of the Scottish Parliament on March 2. Gillespie preached on Psalm 2:10–12, in which he briefly but directly alludes to resolving the controversy. "… let our choice care be for the fame of Jesus Christ and His truth and His honor, for He is our head, and rather let us expose kings and kingdoms, and lives and estates to the hazard, before we put one point of His glory or interest to hazard. And if this were respected it might soon end most of our present differences. Do for your honor, for your lands and for anything else you please, so be the honor of Jesus has the first room."9

We do not know if Gillespie had a significant hand in the commission's *Declaration*, but he, Douglas the moderator, David Dickson, Samuel Rutherford, Robert Blair, John Livingstone and James Guthrie were appointed to a committee to revise the wording on the last day of February. On March 1, the Commission of the Kirk approved the declaration. Present from parliament were leaders for the Engagement, Lauderdale and Lanark, and the leaders of the Anti-Engager opposition party, Archibald Campbell, First Duke of Argyll, and John Kennedy, Sixth Earl of Cassilis, Gillespie's old patron.10 As they learned of what was in the *Declaration*, the Hamilton party in the Committee of Estates11 made clear that they did not want the commission of the church to publish it. However, by early April they learned the kirk commissioners had sent it out to be read in presbyteries and churches, and the controversy between parliament and the kirk commission became public and unavoidable.12

---

7. *The Diplomatic Correspondence of Jean De Montereul and the Brothers De Bellièvre: French Ambassadors in England and Scotland, 1645–48, edited with an English translation, introduction and notes by J. G. Fotheringham.* Publications of the Scottish History Society, volume 29–30 (Edinburgh: T. and A. Constable for the Scottish History Society, 1898–99), 2.402.

8. Stewart, p. 268.

9. A good portion of this sermon on Psalm 2:10–12 preached before the Scottish Parliament was preserved in notes by Sir George Maxwell. See page 461.

10. See *Shorter Writings of George Gillespie*, volume 1, pp. 23, 70–74.

11. Much like the work of the Commission of the Kirk, which did the work of the General Assembly of the Church of Scotland when it was not in session, the Committee of Estates governed the state when the Scottish Parliament was not sitting.

12. Stewart, *Rethinking the Scottish Revolution*, page 269. *Records of the Commissions of the*

Since Gillespie had some hand in it, and since he subsequently defends it, this *Declaration* is presented as follows.[13]

A Declaration of the Commissioners of the General Assembly to the whole Kirk and Kingdom of Scotland, concerning present dangers and duties relating to the Covenant and Religion.

If in a time of so great and imminent danger to religion and of the cause of God, the trumpet in Zion should give no certain sound, nor the watchmen's tower any seasonable warning, it might be justly charged upon us as a sinful neglect of duty, and the blood of many thousand souls might be required at our hands. Therefore, so far as we have discovered the dangerous plots and snares of the malicious and crafty adversaries of this cause, we shall freely and faithfully make the same known, trusting that all who would not make shipwreck of faith[14] and a good conscience, will carefully avoid as well hid as manifest rocks when they are warned of them.

After the Solemn League and Covenant of the three kingdoms had so prospered against the enemies and opposers thereof as made them despair of overthrowing it in any such way of a direct opposition, they began with much wit and industry to endeavor a dividing of the ends of the covenant, and an altering of the first principle and state of the cause. Upon the one hand, the sectaries in England (according as is formerly represented by the late General Assembly in their Declaration to their brethren of England, and by our Remonstrance to the Committee of Estates of the 13 of October last)[15] have by fraud and violence endeavored the subversion of religion, whose exorbitant insolency, being now in arms, is so unsupportable, that no man

---

General Assemblies of the Church of Scotland holden at Edinburgh in the years 1646 and 1647, edited from the Original Manuscript by Alexander F. Mitchell, D.D., LL.D. And James Christie, D.D. (Edinburgh: Printed at the University by T. and A. Constable for the Scottish History Society, 1892), pp. 364, 367, 372, 373.

13. *A Declaration of the Commissioners of the General Assembly to the Whole Kirk and Kingdom of Scotland concerning present dangers and duties relating to the covenant and religion* (Edinburgh, London: Printed by Evan Tyler, Re-printed for Robert Bostock, 1648). The text presented here in modern form is taken from that in the minutes of the commission. *Records, 1646 and 1647*, pp. 373–382. Slight variations with the published text are not noted.

14. Cf. Ezekiel 33:2–6, 1 Corinthians 148; 1 Timothy 1:19.

15. *A Declaration and Brotherly Exhortation of the Generall Assembly of the Church of Scotland met at Edinburgh, August 20, 1647, to their Brethren of England* (Edinburgh: Evan Tyler, 1647); see also in the printed Acts of the Assembly, the edition by the Church Law Society [1843], pp. 148–154. October 13. "To the right honourable the Committee of Estates the Humble Remonstrance of the Commissioners of the Generall Assembly," October 13, 1647, *Records in the years 1646 and 1647*, pp. 314–318.

can doubt but all the articles of the covenant are in danger by them; the vile errors, wicked heresies, and intolerable blasphemies, daily growing amongst them, can hardly be reckoned up; all which are mightily aggredged [*made worse*] by the lawless and godless toleration thereof. And lest parliamentary authority should curb this monstrous insolency, they have not only refused orders for disbanding,[16] but have forced orders for their own standing, and do overrule parliament, king, city, and country, to the trampling underfoot all government, civil and ecclesiastical, and to the terror, oppression, and apparent ruin of all the truly godly and sound lovers of the Solemn League and Covenant. On the other hand, the prelatical and malignant party have catched at and studied to make advantage of some parts and clauses of the covenant, without keeping all the links of that golden chain fast together.

This design of receding from the former principles, and stating the public cause otherwise than it was stated by both kingdoms when they joined in Covenant and arms, may be abundantly discovered by two instances. First, the design has been so fast and so far driven on, that although the fourth article of the League and Covenant[17] was clearly framed and intended against the malignant party, and although there was one express article in the treaty between the kingdoms for swearing and subscribing the League and Covenant by both kingdoms, as a more near tie and conjunction of both, for their defense against the popish, prelatical, and malignant party and their adherents,[18] and although in the declaration of both kingdoms in the year 1643, it was declared that all such as would not speedily take the covenant and join with all their power in the defense of this cause,[19] are to be censured and punished as professed adversaries and malignants, yet some are not ashamed to plead for the malignant party as if they were friends rather than enemies to this cause, and as none were now to be looked upon as dangerous enemies to the cause but the sectaries only; whereas the Word of God, and the experience of former times, not only teaches us to beware of dangers from the fraud, as

---

16. This refers to the New Model Army.

17. See *Confession of Faith*, etc. (1855), p. 359.

18. "Articles of the Treaty agreed upon betwixt the Commissioners of both Houses of the Parliament of England, having Power and Commission from the said honourable Houses, and the Commissioners of the Convention of the Estates of the Kingdom of Scotland, authorized by the Committee of the said Estates, concerning the Solemn League and Covenant, and the Assistance demanded in pursuance of the Ends expressed in the same." See *Three Late Treaties Between the Kingdoms of England & Scotland* (London: Husband, [1646]), and see Rushworth, *Historical Collections*, volume fifth (1721), p. 485.

19. *The Declaration of the Kingdoms of England and Scotland, Joyned in Arms for the Vindication and Defence of their Religion, Liberties, and Laws, Against the Popish, Prelaticall, and Malignant Party* (1643); reprinted in *An exhortation to the taking of the Solemne league and covenant for reformation and defence of religion, the hononr [sic] and happinesse of the king, and the peace and safety of the three kingdomes of England, Scotland, and Ireland* (London: Ralph Smith), p. 26.

well as the force, from the plots as well as from the power of enemies, but also sets before us sad examples of great unexpected miseries and mischiefs brought upon the people of God from enemies once broken and quashed, when they got again the power of the sword, and opportunity to act whatsoever cruelties their inveterate malice and enraged spirits put them upon.

The other instance is that, although in the covenant the duty of preserving and defending the king's Majesty's person and authority be joined with and subordinate unto the duty of preserving and defending the true religion and liberties of the kingdoms, and although from the beginning of this cause the good, safety, and security of religion have been principally sought after and insisted upon, yet solicitations, persuasions, and endeavors have not been nor are wanting for his Majesty's restitution to the exercise of his royal power, and for espousing his Majesty's quarrel, notwithstanding his not granting of the public desires concerning the covenant and religion. And this course is clearly contrary to the declared resolution of the parliament of this kingdom, after advice desired from us, upon the case concerning the king then propounded to us; and it is no less contrary to the principles and professions of the Convention and of the Committee of Estates, before any such advice was desired or had from us. Yea, all along, and in the whole course of the public proceedings, the settling and securing of religion have been so much stood upon, that malignants who intended a new state of the cause did well perceive how great difficulty, and how small hopes, there was of satisfying this kirk and kingdom with anything else, while unsatisfied in the point of religion; and therefore, all possible care has been taken by them whereby to have some specious and fair pretenses of satisfaction in the business of religion.

And here, as we do not disapprove but highly commend the worthy pains of such as did indeed endeavor to bring the king's Majesty a greater length, even to give full satisfaction in point of religion, so we cannot but take notice of that report which many did lately entertain and spread in this country, namely, that his Majesty has given satisfaction to the desires of this kirk and kingdom in point of the covenant and religion.

If his Majesty had indeed given such satisfaction, we should rejoice at it as much as any, and however shall not cease to pray for his Majesty that God would give him repentance and remission of sins, and incline his heart to the love of the true religion and reformation, and that his royal person may be preserved from all harm and violence. And being now (as we formerly remonstrate[d] on the 13 of October)[20] very sensible of the present danger his Majesty's person and monarchical government is into, by that prevalent party of sectaries, we shall, so far as concerns the duty of our places and callings, endeavor the preservation of monarchical government in his Majesty and his

---

20. "Humble Remonstrance," *Records in the years 1646 and 1647*, pp. 314–318.

posterity according to the covenant, not being ignorant what confusions and calamities use to [*commonly*] attend the change either of the government itself or of the royal line. Nevertheless, the country being so generally possessed with so dangerous a mistake and misunderstanding of so great a business, and his Majesty himself professing in his letter to us, dated at Carisbrooke Castle, the 27 of December last,[21] that he has resolved so far to agree to the desires of this kirk and kingdom, concerning the covenant and settling religion, as he is confident shall give us satisfaction, if now we should be silent we might be understood as tacitly consenting and acquiescing. We are therefore necessitated for undeceiving the nation, and for acquitting ourselves, to declare that a narrative of the state of public affairs having been made to us by those who were entrusted for that effect, and since delivered to us in writing, we have more especially taken to our serious thoughts so much of that narrative as was from his Majesty made known unto us, as his resolutions for satisfaction in point of religion. The first article whereof is as follows:

1. For the covenant,[22] his Majesty giving belief to the professions of those who have entered into the League and Covenant, and that their intentions are real for preservation of his Majesty's person, according to their allegiance, and no ways to diminish his just power and greatness, is content, so soon as he can with freedom, honor, and safety be present in a free parliament, to confirm the said League and Covenant by act of parliament in both kingdoms, for security of all those who have taken or shall take the said covenant, provided that none who is unwilling shall be constrained to take it.

Which article has nothing in it of his Majesty's affection to, or liking and approbation of, the Covenant, but only what he is content to yield in order to his own interest. Yea, an act of parliament for security of those who have taken, or shall take, the covenant, does or may suppose some fault, or somewhat justly challengeable in the taking of the covenant, which needs an act of indemnity. Next, the offer is but conditional, and has in the bosom of it a complication of such and so many conditions as might open a door to some evasion or other, by multiplying exceptions, difficulties, and various notions, either concerning the professions of those who have entered into the League and Covenant, or concerning his Majesty's just power and greatness, or concerning his freedom, honor, and safety, or concerning a free parliament. And although the concession were certain and absolute, it amounts to no more but to a leaving of the covenant arbitrary, which is contrary to the Acts of the General Assembly and Parliament in this kingdom, to the declaration of both kingdoms before cited, and to one of the chief propositions of religion once

----

21. See *Records of the Commissions for 1646 and 1657*, p. 356.

22. The Commission is citing the agreement of the Engagement. See the text in Samuel Rawson Gardiner, *The Constitutional Documents of the Puritan Revolution, 1625–1660* (Oxford: Clarendon Press, 1906), pp. 347–352.

agreed upon by both kingdoms for a safe and well-grounded peace, viz., the proposition concerning his Majesty's swearing and signing of the League and Covenant, and enjoining by act of parliament in both kingdoms, the taking thereof by all the subjects in the three kingdoms, with such penalties as shall be agreed upon by both kingdoms. So that the first article of his Majesty's offer is a most manifest altering of the state of this cause. It is also a strengthening of the hearts and hands both of the sectaries and of the malignant party, a partaking in, and conniving at, the sin of all those in the three kingdoms who have refused, or shall refuse, to enter into the League and Covenant, an introducing of a detestable indifferency or neutrality in this cause which so much concerns the glory of God, the good of the kingdom, and the honor of the king; and therefore, we have judged this article not only unsatisfactory, but destructive to the covenant. Neither are we moved with that objection which is hinted concerning the constraining or enforcing of men's consciences. They refuse a necessary duty who refuse to take the covenant, and the penalty or punishment of such refusal is no constraining of the conscience, more than the penalty or punishment of a subject who refuses to take the oath of allegiance is a constraining of the conscience to loyalty, or more than the punishment of idolaters, blasphemers, and seducers, mentioned so often in Scripture, can be called a constraining of the conscience to the fear of God.

2. The words of the second article are these,[23] "His Majesty will likewise confirm by act of Parliament in England presbyterial government, the directory for worship, and Assembly of Divines at Westminster, for three years, so that his Majesty and his household be not hindered from using that form of divine service he has formerly practiced, and that a free debate and consultation be had with the Divines at Westminster (twenty of his Majesty's nomination being added unto them) and with such as shall be sent from the Church of Scotland, whereby it may be determined by his Majesty and the two Houses how the church government, after the three years, shall be fully established according to the Word of God."

For aught we know, the conditions couched in the first article are also to be understood in this and the following articles. However, this second article, as it is but the same in substance with some of his Majesty's concessions in former messages, so that which is proposed in it is but a toleration of presbyterial government in England, and that but for three years, and is a direct allowance at least of the Book of Common Prayer in his Majesty's household. And, moreover, by the second article not only a door is left open for reestablishing prelacy and the Service Book, but the happy progress already made in the reformation and uniformity of religion according to the covenant in a confession of faith, directory of worship, form of church government, and catechism is set aside as so much lost labor in order to a future settlement.

---

23. Cf. Gardiner, *Constitutional Documents*, p. 348.

Free debate with any of the prelatical party nominated by his Majesty (when there was any such occasion) has not been declined; but we have great cause to be tender of unsettling and razing a good foundation already laid in the work of reformation. And whereas his Majesty will have it determined by himself and the two Houses how the church government, after the said three years, shall be established according to the Word of God, this does at once cut off three of the most material and most necessary propositions concerning religion formerly agreed upon by both kingdoms, and from both tendered to his Majesty (though some of them be now laid aside by the two Houses of the Parliament of England)—namely, the third proposition for abolishing archbishops, bishops, etc.;[24] the fifth proposition, that reformation of religion according to the covenant be settled by act of Parliament in such manner as both Houses have agreed or shall agree upon, after consultation had with the Assembly of Divines;[25] and the sixth proposition, that such unity and uniformity in religion according to the covenant as, after consultation had with the divines of both kingdoms assembled at Westminster, is, or shall be, jointly agreed by both Houses of the Parliament of England and by the Church and Kingdom of Scotland, be confirmed by acts of parliament of both kingdoms respectively:[26] of which three propositions there can be no hopes (as to his Majesty's consent or concurrence) if the offer now made concerning a determination by his Majesty and the two Houses be compared with his Majesty's claiming of a negative voice, and with his message of November 16, in which he declared that both in relation as he is a Christian and as a king he cannot give his consent to the abolishing [of] archbishops, bishops, etc.,[27] believing that this order was placed in the church by the apostles themselves, and that his Majesty is also bound by his coronation oath to maintain it. And this message of November 16, his Majesty adheres unto in his answer to the bills and propositions presented to him at Carisbrooke Castle, which answer is dated December 28,[28] and so after his Majesty's letter to us. Upon these and the like considerations we have found the said second article of his Majesty's offers in point of religion to be destructive to presbyterial government, the directory of worship, and the uniformity intended according to the covenant.

3. For the third article delivered to us in these words—"And for suppressing of schism and heresies his Majesty is content and most willing that an effectual course be taken by act of parliament, and all other ways needful and expedient,

---

24. "The Propositions of the Houses Presented to the King at Oxford, and subsequently discussed at the Treaty of Uxbridge, November 24, 1644," in Gardiner, page 275.

25. Ibid., p. 276.

26. Ibid., p. 276.

27. Letter of Charles I to the Speaker of the House of Lords, Received November 17, 1647, in Gardiner, *Constitutional Documents*, p. 328.

28. "The King's Reply to the Four Bills and the accompanying Propositions," in Gardiner, *Constitutional Documents*, p. 355.

for suppressing the opinions and practices of Antitrinitarians, Arrians, Socinians, Antiscripturists, Antinomians, Anabaptists, Arminians, Familists, Brownists, Separatists, Independents, Libertines, and Seekers, and generally for suppressing all blasphemy, heresy, schism, and all such scandalous doctrine or practices as are contrary to the light of nature or to the known principles of Christianity (whether concerning faith, worship, or conversation), or to the power of godliness, or which may be destructive to order or government or to the peace of church or kingdom."

As we do approve of the suppression of the particular heresies and schisms enumerat[ed] in his Majesty's offer, so we see not how it can be reconciled with his Majesty's message of November 16, in which there was a concession of toleration to all such as differ from presbyterial government: And do further find the article dangerous and defective in omitting Erastianism and other dangerous errors, especially popery and prelacy, which may prove destructive to the covenant in ministering the occasion to papists and prelates to plead for a toleration, although the covenant binds us to endeavor the extirpation both of popery and prelacy.

Having now discovered the snares and dangers, we shall in the next place most humbly and seriously propose and recommend some wholesome, seasonable, and pious counsels to all the members of this church and kingdom, especially to the Honourand [*sic* Honourable] High Court of Parliament and to the brethren of the ministry, which may also serve to express our sense concerning the whole matter contained in that narrative delivered to us in writing, so far as is competent and fit for us to give any judgment thereupon.

First of all, we exhort all and everyone to make more conscience of endeavoring a real reformation of themselves and their families, and of the places in which they live, than ever yet they have done; to be more serious in searching their hearts, considering their ways, and purging themselves from all filthiness of the flesh and spirit to perfect holiness in the fear of God; to oppose wickedness and profaneness, promote the practice and power of godliness, and to be deeply humbled before the Lord for neglecting these things so much and so long; with all employing and improving Christ's all-sufficiency, and striving to exercise faith in Him for the grace of mortification and sanctification, as well as for remission of sin and peace with God; that, being implanted and rooted in Him, we may grow up as trees of righteousness, the planting of the Lord, that He may be glorified; for without amendment of life and bringing forth of better fruit, the fierce wrath of the Lord cannot turn away from us.

Secondly. As men desire they may not be led into temptation, but may be guided in safe and right paths in the midst of so great difficulties, let them avoid the company and counsel of the ungodly, whereby even good men have been oft times most dangerously ensnared; let all that fear God choose the testimonies of the Lord for their counselors, be much in prayer and searching the mind of God in His Word, without leaning to their own understanding or consulting with flesh and blood in cases of conscience.[29]

Thirdly. Seeing it is no act of wisdom but of folly so to shun one danger as to run upon another as bad or worse, let us therefore avoid enemies and beware of dangers on all hands. We cannot see but the cause of God, the true religion, the covenant, presbyterial government, this church and kingdom, and whatsoever is dearest to us will be in as great danger if the prelatical party prevail, as now they are into, by the power and prevalency of sectaries in England, who have made the covenant and begun reformation to be laid aside, and hindered the promoting thereof. So that there is a necessity to be apprehensive of dangers and attentive to remedies on both sides, and to beware of compliance with and connivance at sectaries upon the one hand, and malignants upon the other.

Fourthly. When we speak of malignants, we desire that the distinction may be remembered which was made in the Solemn Warning to the Kingdom from the General Assembly in February 1645, viz.,[30] that the cause is in very great danger from two sorts of malignant enemies; first, from such as have openly displayed a banner, or joined in arms and professed hostility against the cause, and such as adhered thereunto; secondly, from secret malignants, dis-covenanters, and bosom enemies. This second sort may be still known by some characters given both at that time and before that time, as by their slandering or censuring the covenant of the three kingdoms, and expedition into England in the year 1643, as not necessary for the good of religion or safety of this kingdom, or as tending to the diminution of the king's just power and greatness, by their confounding of the king's power and just authority with the pretence and abuse thereof by commissions, warrants, or letters, procured from his Majesty by the enemies of this cause and covenant; as if none were faithful and loyal to the king who oppose such men and their ways; by their spleen, malice, and calumnies against such as God has made eminently instrumental in this cause, and who resolve to be constant to the end in their first principles, as if such men were the king's enemies who are most zealous for the good and safety of religion; by their commending, justifying, or excusing other known malignants, and by their conversing or inter-communing with excommunicat[ed] delinquents. Unto which characters time and experience give us occasion to add some others, as, namely, their unwillingness and declining to reckon malignants among the enemies of this cause from whom danger is to be apprehended; their disjoining and dividing the duty of endeavoring the king's Majesty's preservation and restitution from the duty of preserving, defending, settling, and securing religion, as if we might

---

29. See the *Solemn Warning* penned by Gillespie herein on page 331.
30. Cf. Psalm 119:24, Proverbs 3:5, Galatians 1:16.

and ought to pursue the former without the latter, while both are in danger; their maligning of and uttering malicious words against faithful and zealous ministers, and against this meeting and judicatory, appointed by the General Assembly; lastly, their crying up or down of parties or persons, and even of the sectaries themselves, according as they have more or less hopes of advantage from them to their own designs. For it is not long since such men made light account of any dangers which were apprehended from the prevalent faction of the sectaries in England, there being then some hopes of a compliance and combination between them and the malignants, which is an infallible demonstration that such men's pretended zeal against those sectaries now is not from the right principle. Wherefore, let all such dangerous persons as we have here deciphered and described be carefully observed and avoided, as men would keep themselves pure and free of snares. And let presbyteries be diligent to discover, try, and censure any of this kind in their bounds, that they may be able herein to give a good account of their diligence; as also that they be careful to discover, try, and censure any trafficking sectaries, and all such as favor their opinions and ways.

Fifthly. Though we esteem that prevalent faction of sectaries, with their abettors and adherents, presumptuous and malicious enemies to religion, king, and government, yet we hold it is our duty to labor to remove and prevent all occasions of jealousies and suspicions betwixt the kingdoms, and to do or say nothing that may breed misunderstandings, break of [*sic* off] correspondence, weaken the confidence, or infringe the union and peace betwixt the two kingdoms, so happily established in his Majesty's presence, and with his royal consent in both parliaments; a caution as necessary now as when it was given abone [*above*] five years ago, in a Warning from the Commissioners of the General Assembly met in this same place, January the fourth, 1643.[31] And generally, we desire that all the articles and clauses of the Solemn League and Covenant may be kept inseparably and inviolably linked together, and that there may be great tenderness and care to avoid everything which may be interpreted as a contradicting or abandoning of the former principles, proceedings, petitions, protestations, remonstrances, and declarations of this kirk and kingdom, in the pursuance of this cause; and more especially to take good heed that Scotland's desires do not mount higher for the king and fall lower in the point of religion, than they were at our first undertaking and engagement in this cause.

Finally. We do most seriously obtest [*charge*] all the people of God in this nation, and especially the Estates of Parliament, by their love to the cause of God, by their solemn vows and covenants, by their first principles and professions, by their former zeal and sincerity, by the many blessings of God,

---

31. *A Necessary Warning to the Ministerie of the Kirk of Scotland, From the meeting of the Commissioners of the Generall Assembly At Edinburgh 4. Jan. 1643* (Edinburgh: Evan Tyler, 1643).

and His great works done for us, when our zeal and integrity was greateſt in this cause, and by all the curses and judgments of God which His Word denounces againſt backsliders and covenant breakers, that they may all the days of their lives continue firm, ſteadfaſt, and faithful in their covenant with God, and one with another, and make good their former professions in a time of tentation [*temptation*] and difficulty, without wavering or falling off to the right-hand or to the left. And as many as walk according to this rule, peace be on them, and mercy, and upon the Israel of God [cf. Gal. 6:16].

After a month of parliamentary debate, the Scottish Parliament issued an answer to the Commission of the Kirk's Declaration on April 18, *A Declaration of the Parliament of Scotland.* The Commission selected Gilleſpie to answer Parliament's paper. "The Commission desires Mr. Hew Mackall to preach for Mr. George Gillaſpie upon the Sabbath, and Mr. Robert Blair upon Mononday [*sic*], in reſpect of his present diſtraction in preparing an answer to the Parliament's Declaration." This paper was presented to the parliament by a contingent from the Commission which included Robert Blair, Samuel Rutherford, Robert Baillie, Zachary Boyd, James Guthrie, and Moderator Robert Douglas. It was published as *The Humble Representation of the Commission of the Generall Assembly, To the Honourable Eſtates of Parliament upon their Declaration lately communicate to us. Edinburgh, 28 Aprile 1648* (London: Edward Griffen for J. R...., 1648).[32] Undeterred, on May 4 the parliament issued "inſtructions for levying new forces." A formal schism between parliament and the kirk commission came the next day on May 5, when the latter "declared the Engagement unlawful and immediately published its judgement, in both Edinburgh and London, as the *Short Information.*[33] This document was sent out to the presbyteries for dissemination from parish pulpits, complete with a compendium of papers that provided a fuller explanation of how and why the kirk had reached its decision. In the preamble, the commission explained that the Engagement was 'contrary to the Word of God, to the Solemn Covenants, firſt Principles and publique Professions of this Kirk and Kingdom' and demanded that all miniſters, and 'any other whatsoever' forbear from supporting the Engagement in any way."[34]

---

32. See herein following Gillespie's sermon on Psalm 2.

33. "The conviction that Charles was a more imminent threat to archipelagic Presbyterianism than the New Model Army underpinned the church's decision, published 5 May, to condemn the Engagement as 'unlawful'—a judgement that referred not only to statute but also to God's law." Laura A. M. Stewart, *Rethinking the Scottish Revolution: Covenanted Scotland, 1637–1651*, p. 259.

34. Stewart, p. 270. *A Short Information from the Commission of the Generall Assembly, concerning the declaration of the Honourable Court of Parliament, lately emitted to the Kingdom* ([Edinburgh?: s.n.], Printed in the year 1648); *A Short Information from the Commission of the Generall Assembly, concerning the declaration of the Honourable Court of Parliament, lately emitted*

As the controversy between the parliament and commission of the church continued through the summer months, the Engager party in parliament may have held out hope that the General Assembly meeting in July might not approve of the actions and papers of the Kirk's Commission. However, that was not the case. George Gillespie was elected moderator of the July 1648 General Assembly and all the work of the commission was approved.

> The General Assembly convened at Edinburgh July 12. The Committee of Estates then sitting, laboured by all means possible to hinder the Assembly to approve the proceedings of the Commission of the former Assembly against the engagement, but all in vain; for the Assembly having examined the proceedings of the Commission, especially their Declarations, Remonstrances, Representations, Petitions, Vindication, and other papers relating to the present engagement, did unanimously find that in all their proceedings they had been zealous, diligent, and faithful in discharge of the trust committed to them; ratifying and approving the whole proceedings, acts and conclusions of the said Commission, and particularly all their papers relating to the said engagement, and their judgment of the unlawfulness thereof. The General Assembly (beside other papers relating to the engagement), did emit a declaration concerning the present dangers of religion, and especially the unlawful engagement in war against the kingdom of England, together with many necessary exhortations and directions to all the members of the Kirk of Scotland. Also they did emit a Declaration and Exhortation of the General Assembly of the Church of Scotland to their brethren in England; though they were desired by the Committee of Estates not to emit any papers.[35]

After the assembly with the meeting of the new Commission on August 2, Gillespie was elected to succeed Robert Douglas as moderator of the Commission of the Assembly. They already had work to do because after

---

to the kingdom ([London]: Imprinted at Edenburgh, and re-printed at London for Joseph Hunscot, 1648). The declaration sent out to the presbyteries was published as *The Declaration of the Commission of the General Assembly, to this whole Kirk and Kingdom of Scotland of the fifth of May: concerning the present publike proceedings towards an engagement in warre, so farre as religion is therein concerned. Together with their desires and petitions to the honourable court of Parliament, the Parliaments answers, Their humble returnes and representations, and other papers that may give full and cleare information in the matter* (London: Printed for Ralph Smith, at the sign of the Bible in Cornhill near the Royall Exchange, 1648). See the text also in *Records of the Commissions … 1646 and 1647* (1892), pp. 520–526.

35. *The Life of Mr. Robert Blair, Minister of St. Andrews containing his autobiography from 1593 to 1636 with supplement to his life, and continuation of the history of the times to 1680, by his son-in-law, Mr. William Row, Minister of Ceres,* edited by Thomas M'Crie, D.D. (Edinburgh: Printed for the Wodrow Society, [1848]), pp. 202–203.

the meeting of the assembly closed on August 11 with the order renewing the commission, a reference was presented "from the late Assembly to this Commission, for answering the *Observations of the Committee of Estates upon the Assembly's Declaration*, which the Assembly being about to close and end had no time to Answer, the Commission appointed Messrs. Robert Douglas, John Smith, James Hamiltoun, James Guttrie, Andro Cant, David Dickson, Robert Ramsay, Earl of Cassills, Scotiscraige, Dudistoun, with the Moderator, to be a Committee for considering the said Observations, and drawing a draught of an answer thereunto, and to report; as also that they consider some expressions in the petition of the late Assembly to the king, which the late Assembly recommended to be revised and helped by this Commission. The next meeting upon Tuesday at 2 afternoon"[36]

The parliamentary paper referenced was issued on August 10, 1648, and it was entitled *Some Few Observations by the Committee of Estates of Parliament, upon the Declaration of The General Assembly of the last of July*. The assembly's declaration had been issued as *A Declaration of the Generall Assembly concerning the present dangers of Religion, and especially the unlawfull engagement in War, against the Kingdom of England; together, with many necessary exhortations and directions to all the members of the Kirk of Scotland* (July 31, 1648).[37] August 12 was a Saturday and we are told that the committee charged with answering the parliament's observations tasked Gillespie with making the draft, and he had to work on it on the Lord's Day and presumably Monday in order to have the draft ready for the next assembling of the commission on Tuesday, August 15, 1648. Mitchell and Christie note that "This paper was at once published under the following title, *The Answer to the Commissioners of the Generall Assembly unto the Observations of the Honourable Committee of Estates upon the Declaration of the late Generall Assembly, August 15, 1648*. Edinburgh. Printed by Evan Tyler, Printer to the King's most excellent Majesty, 1648. Internal evidence points decidedly to George Gillespie, the Moderator, as the main author of this paper, and it is one of the most terse and pithy he ever wrote." We learn from Gillespie's cousin Andrew Simson, "The last paper he wrote, was 'The Commission of the Kirk's Answer to the State's Observations on the Declaration of the General Assembly anent the Unlawfulness of the Engagement.' The Observations were penned (as my relator supposes) by Mr. William Colville, who wrote all these kind of papers for the Committee of Estates, and printed during the Assembly whereof he [Gillespie] was moderator. They could not overtake it, but remitted it to the Commission to sit on Monday,[38] and

---

36. *The Records of the Commissions of the General Assemblies of the Church of Scotland Holden in Edinburgh the Years 1648 and 1649*, ed. Alexander F. Mitchell, and James Christie (Edinburgh: T. and A. Constable for the Scottish History Society, 1896) pp. 7–8.

37. There is similar language in this declaration and *Answer of the Commissioners* (v. 1, p. 52n). This is because Gillespie defends the declaration; there is no evidence he helped draft it.

38. This was actually Tuesday per the adjournment. Simson may have misremembered or

Mr. Gillespie wrote the answer on Saturday and the Sabbath, when he (the thing requiring haste) stayed from sermon, and my informer, Mr. Patrick Simson, transcribed it against Monday at ten, when it passed without any alteration. And just the week after, he went over to Fife, where he died. He was not full ten years in the ministry."[39]

This was the last major paper of any sort that Gillespie wrote. Patrick Simson recalled that Gillespie had been in great weakness of body from the start of 1648, which no doubt was the effect of the tuberculosis which would take his life. Simson wrote that "the next Wednesday after the rising of the Assembly, he went with his wife over to Kirkaldy," to try to recover his health.[40] This must have been the Wednesday of August 16, the day after the commission passed his answer to parliament's observations. As his recovery never materialized, Gillespie's final writings were a letter written to the Commission on September 8, 1648, and a testimony against association and compliance with malignant enemies of the truth and godliness written two days before he died on December 17, 1648. He also wrote a will on September 1, a portion of which was published with the testimony.[41]

The Engagement was a dismal failure. Unpopular at home and led by the Duke of Hamilton who was not a great military man, the Scottish forces were destroyed by Cromwell's New Model Army at Preston on August 19, 1648, just three days after Gillespie retired to Kirkcaldy.

As with many or even most of his other publications, Gillespie's Anti-Engagement writings divide historians. In keeping with many writers' penchant to use few or questionable facts in order to take Gillespie down a notch or two in estimation, Campbell's assessment goes beyond them all to sheer character assassination.

> Gillespie wrecked the Engagement. If the Kirk could have been reasonably sure of Charles' promises being kept, disillusioned as her leaders were with the

---

perhaps Gillespie met with the committee on Monday so all could look at the draft.

39. Cited by Hetherington from Robert Wodrow's *Analecta*, 1.159–160. See *Shorter Writings of George Gillespie*, volume 1, pp. 51–52.

40. See the account accompanying Hetherington's Memoir in *Shorter Writings* vol.1, pp. 48.

41. These appeared in print in Edinburgh and London editions along with *An Usefull Case of Conscience, Discussed, and Resolved. Concerning associations and confederacies with idolaters, infidels, hereticks, or any other known enemies of truth and godlinesse. By Master George Gillespie, late minister at Edinburgh. Whereunto is subjoyned a letter written by him to the commissioners of the Generall Assembly, in the time of his sicknesse; together with his testimony unto this truth, written by him two dayes before his death.* Thomason purchased the London edition on January 25, 1648 [i.e., 1649]. ESTC records two Edinburgh variants (R213029 and R7619). Since *The Usefull Case of Conscience* appears as chapter 14 in *The Miscellany Questions*, and was apparently extracted from that collection published later in the year about July 16, 1649 (Thomason's date), that text with any notes of variation in the known editions will appear with that larger work in the third and final volume of *The Shorter Writings*, D.V.

Cromwellian regime, they might have entered the battle on the Engagers' side on the grounds that the Rump had broken the Solemn League and Covenant. At one point in the negotiations between representatives of the Church and State, Lanark had well nigh won the Church round when Gillespie entered into the debate and turned the tide against him. Led by him the Church encouraged the boycott of supplies, discountenanced enlistment and deprived them of David Leslie as a general. Ill-led, ill-fed and semi-conscript, the army's fate at Preston was a foregone conclusion. Lanark blamed Gillespie most of all for the fiasco. Yet Gillespie did what Henderson would have done. The people were war-weary, the land had suffered from Montrose's campaigns, Charles' word was utterly false and the Kirk knew it. To keep united and wait was the only practical course. So far he showed clear judgment and wise leadership, but he had not Henderson's gift of soothing hurt feelings and smoothing ugly disputes. Breaches between former allies were needlessly widened by his bitter tongue and even his friends could sometimes ill abide it. Never could it be said more truly that the evil men do lives after them. With his dying breath in that last publication he had ordered his Church to purge herself. His arrogant soul seems to have had a perverted delight in excommunication as a weapon of discipline. Desperately the Church carried out his dying orders. Engagers were excommunicated ecclesiastically, worse still, the Act of Classes was a political excommunication, and the strife engendered by this Act was to split the Kirk. Henderson led her out of bondage, the dying Gillespie led her into the wilderness.

Such was the career of Mr. George Gillespie. He was the least lovable of the great quartet at Westminster. He was ambitious, vain and sly in ways unknown to Henderson and Rutherford. Clever and capable, he attracted attention and liked to attract it. "No man was wont to find a greater attention and audience," says Baillie.[42] A triumph for a Scot at Westminster! The bitter tongue of his later years was due partly to failing health, partly to the super-sensitive temperament that goes with clever, vain people, and partly to the impatience with the intellectually inferior in whatever arena he might be confronted by them. Yet in his hey-day at Westminster his contemporaries smiled quietly as he preened himself and delighted in his success.[43] He was a man all through and died fighting; he was upright in all his political

---

42. Baillie says this in his assembly speech as a compliment. Baillie, 3.12–13.

43. This line in particular is fantasy, not history. There are no accounts to support it and it flies in the face of actual comments at the time, such as the thanks given Gillespie by the Prolocutor on behalf of the Westminster Assembly, as well as statements collected by Robert Wodrow given in Hetherington's Memoir showing Gillespie's awareness of both his gifts and failings. Such self-awareness and humility belies the picture of Gillespie that Campbell painted. See the comment by Rowat in footnote 49 at the end of this preface and see the Memoir in *Shorter Writings of George Gillespie*, volume one, pages 46–49. See also Gillespie's speech on leaving the assembly the first time and the thanks he received in this present

conduct; he forsook no cause he sponsored. He gave of the uttermost he had, even to his life in the cause he served; if he never spared anyone, least of all did he spare himself. If the standards of government and worship ultimately framed at Westminster are predominantly Scottish in character, they owe that character to this young man who could so ably debate them through an assembly of the age's most brilliant theological pundits. Twisse, Goodwin, Arrowsmith, Calamy, Marshall, Vines, Seaman, Burgess and Hearle were not men to be readily browbeaten or easily convinced. His particular gift to us is, I think, the formulation of the Scottish doctrine of the Eldership and its powers. His fatal gift was the emphatic prominence he gave to the doctrine and practice of excommunication. He was a young man in his power, with the pride, the intolerance, the rashness, the courage, the unsparingness, the eagerness of youth. Baillie's is no bad epitaph; "Certainly he was as able a man as our Kirk had; of a clear judgment, that which some misliked in him, would easily have been bettered by experience and years."[44] His brother Patrick gained both and died with his armour tarnished. George Gillespie died with his sword drawn and his armour bright.[45]

It is unfortunate that William M. Campbell remains an oft-cited source in Gillespie studies, and "although dated and prejudiced, still provides the best examination of Gillespie's life and the context of his writings."[46] Certainly, earlier writers suffer from hagiographic bias to the positive side, yet on "the other extreme, William Campbell's biographical essay exudes hostility toward Gillespie, whom in one place he describes as having a 'violent and impulsive temperament' and in another as being 'ambitious, vain and sly."[47] James Culberson is preferred to end this preface to Gillespie's Anti-Engagement writings with a truer assessment of this "Hammer of the Malignants."

> During the last year of his life, Gillespie and the church party took an unequivocal stance against the Engagement with the king. Gillespie and other Church leaders strenuously opposed the Engagement, which they believed violated the terms of the Covenant because it proposed to create a political alliance with the king without requiring him to subscribe to the Covenant. Gillespie spent his final days preaching and writing letters[48] and tracts against the Engagement.

---

volume, page 135, and Baillie's appreciation of Gillespie expressed to the Assembly in his speech herein on page 350.

44. See Baillie, 3.12.

45. William M. Campbell, "George Gillespie," in *Records of Scottish Church History Society* 10 (Edinburgh, 1949), pp. 122–123. Campbell did not footnote well, which makes for difficult tracing of some of his statements. Culberson, p. 22.

46. Culberson, p. 22.

47. Culberson, p. 22.

48. Two letters written by Gillespie against the Engagement survive in manuscript, and it

While others joined him in this anti-Engagement fervor, he gave eloquent expression to their rejection of compromise…. In his anti-Engagement writings Gillespie expressed the view that the king's subjects can lawfully resist him when he threatens true religion, and they have exhausted all peaceful means of redress. These ideas became the immediate legacy of Gillespie. It was this Gillespie, defender of the Covenant and "Malleus Malignantium," who influenced subsequent generations of Covenanters, including Resolutioners, Protesters, Cameronians, and other heirs of the Scottish Covenanter tradition.[49]

What follows in this last section of this second volume of *The Shorter Writings of George Gillespie* are:

1. The Sermon on Psalm 2:10–12 preached before the Scottish Parliament on March 2, 1648.
2. *The Humble Representation of the Commission of the Generall Assembly, To the Honourable Estates of Parliament upon their Declaration lately communicate to us. Edinburgh, 28 Aprile 1648.*
3. *The Answer to the Commissioners of the Generall Assembly unto the Observations of the Honourable Committee of Estates upon the Declaration of the late Generall Assembly, August 15, 1648.*
4. Letter to the Commission of the General Assembly, September 8, 1648, with *The Testimony of Mr. George Gillespie Against Association and Compliance with Malignant Enemies of the Truth and Godliness,* and an extract from George Gillespie's will.

---

is hoped that these may be included in the collection of correspondence that will appear in the third and final volume of *The Shorter Writings of George Gillespie,* D.V.

49. Culberson, pp. 12–13. *Malleus Mallignantium*: Hammer of the Malignants. "When Mr. Gillespie was busy studying his sermon [on Psalm 2] that he was to preach before the Parliament tomorrow, the ministers sent privately for Mr. Gillespie, whom he observed to come in very quietly, and when Lauderdale, Glencairn, and some others, rose up and debated very strongly for the engagement, Mr. Gillespie rose up and answered them so fully and distinctly, firstly, secondly, and thirdly, that he fully silenced them all; and Glencairn said, 'There is no standing before this great and mighty man!' I heard worthy Mr. Rowat say, that Mr. Gillespie said, 'The more truly great a man is, he was really the more humble and low in his own eyes,' as he instanced in the great man Daniel; and, said he, 'God did not make choice of some of us as his instruments in the glorious work of Reformation, because we were more fit than others, but rather because we were more unfit than others.' He was called *Malleus Mallignantium,* and Mr. Baillie, writing to some in this church anent Mr. George Gillespie, said, 'He was truly an ornament to our church and nation.' And Mr. James Brown, late minister of Glasgow, told me that there was an English gentleman said to him, that he heard Mr. Gillespie preach, and he said, he believed he was one of the greatest Presbyterians in the world." Hetherington, Memoir, in *Shorter Writings,* volume I, p. 47.

Sermon on Psalm 2:10–12

At Divine Service Prior to the Opening of Parliament,

March 2, 1648

Acts 4:25–28

*And when they heard that, they lifted up their voice to God with one accord, and
said, Lord, thou art God, which hast made heaven, and earth, and the sea, and all
that in them is: Who by the mouth of thy servant David hast said, Why did the
heathen rage, and the people imagine vain things? The kings of the earth stood up,
and the rulers were gathered together against the Lord, and against his Christ. For
of a truth against thy holy child Jesus, whom thou hast anointed, both Herod, and
Pontius Pilate, with the Gentiles, and the people of Israel, were gathered together,
For to do whatsoever thy hand and thy counsel determined before to be done.*

"By Mr Geo.Gilleſpie|at the par|liament sit|ting down| march 2. | 1648. Ps. 2. v. 10 ~~121~~
11. 12," Collection, Maxwells of Pollok, Glasgow and Renfrew, 16 items/notebooks;
T-PM 114/1, Glasgow City Archives, Mitchell Library, Glasgow; Sir George Maxwell,
Summaries of sermons at Cathcart, Glasgow and elsewhere, 10 Aug. 1647(?)–31 Dec.
1648;* in reverse, notes on Genesis, c.i.–xxxi. *The year is supplied by the Mitchell
Library from the contents and the question mark is theirs.

.

Editions

1. Transcription and modernized text in parallel columns, Introduction by
   W. D. J. McKay, The Sermon Manuscript by Chris Coldwell, in "*Antiquary:
   A Transcription from Manuscript of a Sermon on Psalm 2:10–12*," *The
   Confessional Presbyterian* Journal 14 (2018): 249–262.

The Epigraph has been added for this volume.

Introduction[1]

When the ailing George Gillespie preached before the Scottish Parliament on 2 March, 1648, the Covenanters were facing some of their most difficult and testing days. Not so long before it had seemed very different. Although the Westminster Assembly continued to meet in London until 1649, in August 1647 Gillespie and Robert Baillie had appeared before the General Assembly of the Church of Scotland to present the confessional documents produced by the Westminster Assembly, for approval by the Scots. The Confession of Faith, the Larger and Shorter Catechisms, with the Directory for the Public Worship of God and the Form of Presbyterial Church Government would together provide the constitutional foundations and framework for the Church of Scotland with the approval of the General Assembly and of the Scottish Parliament. Dark clouds, however, were gathering.

Charles I, having been handed over by the Scots, was a prisoner of the English Parliament. Having fled from Hampton Court on 11 November, 1647, the king ended up in Carisbrooke Castle on the Isle of Wight. His aim during this period was to foment division among his enemies and to garner enough support for a renewed campaign to restore him to his throne. The Scots were strongly wedded to monarchy, despite Charles' past actions, and in his view offered the most likely source of support if an agreement could be reached with at least some of the political leaders in Scotland.

It was out of this complex background that the notorious Engagement emerged. Many Scots, still loyal to the king and wary of Cromwell and the Parliamentarians, were willing to do what they could for Charles, short of an actual breach of the Solemn League and Covenant. This bond, signed in 1643, committed the Three Kingdoms of England, Scotland, and Ireland to political alliance and religious reformation and had been the warrant for the Scots sending troops to support the English Parliament in the First Civil War. It would be within the bounds of that covenant that Scottish help would be offered.

Three of the leading Scots royalist nobles, Loudon, Lauderdale and Lanark, were able to visit Charles at Carisbrooke Castle: the "Engagement" was the result of their negotiations with the wily and unscrupulous monarch. Acting on behalf of the Marquis of Hamilton and his royalist faction in Scotland,

---

1. This introduction is by Dr. W. D. J. McKay, Professor of Systematic Theology, Ethics and Apologetics at the Reformed Theological College, Belfast, and Minister of Shaftesbury Square Reformed Presbyterian Church, Belfast. It is slightly modified from the text that appeared in *The Confessional Presbyterian* 14 (2018): 249–253.

the three commissioners reached an agreement with Charles which would lead to practical military support from Scotland for the king's restoration. For his part Charles agreed to have the Solemn League and Covenant confirmed by the English Parliament, although it would not be imposed on anyone, including the king. Presbyterian church government would be implemented in England for a period of three years, after which the matter would be settled by an assembly of divines, members of parliament and royal representatives. The king would also suppress sectaries, heretics, and schismatics.

Taken as a whole, the Engagement was a far cry from the original vision of the Covenanters for "covenanted uniformity." Although Charles had at first been told that he would have no Scottish assistance without making concessions on religion, in the end it was the "Engagers" who made concessions without the sanction of Parliament or General Assembly. On 26 December, 1647, the Engagement was signed and the commissioners returned to Edinburgh to seek the approval of Parliament.

The Estates—the Scottish Parliament—met on 2 March and it was on this occasion that Gillespie preached his sermon on Psalm 2:10–12. The reaction of strict Covenanters to the Engagement was, as we would expect, one of vigorous opposition. The agreement was a betrayal of what they had fought for. As James King Hewison vividly puts it, "The preachers generally, and George Gillespie in particular, stormed in every pulpit and hurled imprecations at the king and the Hamiltonians."[2] This is the immediate context for Gillespie's sermon on Psalm 2.

We might note that the recorder of this sermon was Sir George Maxwell of Auldhouse and Pollock, a staunch Covenanter from the late 1640s until his death in 1677. He was actively involved in the courts of the church and in the business of parliament, and was Rector of Glasgow University from 1654 to 1660. Not only did he oppose the Engagement, but he was to be found among the "Protestors" in the controversy with the Resolutioners in the early 1650s, and he was the victim of heavy fines after the Restoration.

This, sadly incomplete, sermon from 1648 is of particular significance because only two other sermons by Gillespie have survived.[3] Both were fast day sermons preached during Gillespie's time at the Westminster Assembly. The first, on Ezekiel 43:11, was preached before the House of Commons on 27 March, 1644, and the second, on Malachi 3:2, was preached before the House of Lords on 27 August, 1645. Although searching in their exposure of the sins of both church and nation which aroused the wrath of God, both also look to glorious days ahead for both England and Scotland. In expounding Ezekiel's vision of the New Temple Gillespie states, "There are very good

---

2. James King Hewison, *The Covenanters. A History of the Church in Scotland from the Reformation to the Revolution* (Glasgow: John Smith and Son, 1908; Revised and Corrected, 1913), 1.445.

3. See the text of the two sermons preached before the Houses of Parliament in this present volume.

grounds for hope to make us think that this new temple is not far off. And (for your part) that Christ is to make a new face of a church in this kingdom, a fair and beautiful temple for His glory to dwell in. And He is even now about the work."[4] Similarly, in introducing his sermon on Malachi 3:2 he says "Scotland shall yet be a crown of glory in the hand of the Lord, and a royal diadem in the hand of thy God (Isa 62:3,4); and shall be called Hephzi-bah and Beulah."[5]

Of particular significance for understanding Gillespie's sermons, especially this fragment on a "royal" psalm, Psalm 2, is Gillespie's doctrine of the Kingship of Christ. Much could be said on this crucial doctrine,[6] but a few comments may be made to highlight the central elements of Gillespie's approach.

Gillespie set out his view of the Kingship of Christ in a number of his published works. In 1645–46 he engaged in an exchange of polemical pamphlets with the Erastian theologian Thomas Coleman which produced three works from Gillespie's pen: *A Brotherly Examination*, *Nihil Respondes*, and *Male Audis*.[7] He also deals with the subject in his great work of 1646, *Aaron's Rod Blossoming*. His formulation of the doctrine of Christ's Kingship is neatly summed up in the title of chapter five of Book 2 of the latter work:

> Of a twofold kingdom of Jesus Christ: a general Kingdom, as He is the eternal Son of God, the head of all principalities and powers, reigning over all creatures; and a particular Kingdom, as He is Mediator reigning over the church only.

In no way is Gillespie seeking to deny that Christ is supreme over all things, nations included, but his concern is to make what he considers to be a scriptural distinction between the ways in which He reigns over nations and over the church. Civil rulers are not under Christ as Mediator but under Christ as the eternal Son (along with the Father and the Holy Spirit). They have nevertheless a duty to promote the welfare of the church, Christ's mediatorial kingdom. These distinctions are clearly evident in Gillespie's exposition of Psalm 2:10-12.

Despite Gillespie's warnings and exhortations to the Parliament, the Engagement was approved and Scotland was set on a road leading to warfare, suffering, and further division. By this time Gillespie's fragile health was broken, yet he continued to pour his remaining energy into opposing the Engagers. He was appointed Moderator of the 1648 General Assembly which sat from 12 July until 12 August. Afterwards he went to Kirkcaldy to seek

---

4. See herein on page 121.

5. See herein on page 155.

6. W. D. J. McKay, *An Ecclesiastical Republic. Church Government in the Writings of George Gillespie* (Edinburgh: Rutherford House, 1997), chapter 2. See the discussion in this present volume on pages 189–197.

7. See the three tracts against Coleman in this present volume.

relief from the consumption (tuberculosis) which was ravaging his body. The hope was unfulfilled. In his final hours, as death approached, his wife said to him, "The time of your relief is now near, and hard at hand." His final words were, "I long for that time. O, happy they that are there." Shortly afterwards he went to meet his King. When he died on 17 December, 1648, he was a month short of his thirty-sixth birthday, having made in those years a profound contribution to Scottish Presbyterianism of abiding significance.

The Sermon Manuscript[1]

It is truly a notable find to have discovered even an incomplete manuscript of notes of a sermon preached by George Gillespie, and even more significant that the sermon was preached at such a key point in Scottish history and on such a text as the last portion of Psalm 2. It is unfortunate that it is half or less of a full sermon, and not Gillespie's own manuscript. However, because all his sermons delivered while in London that were left in manuscript there to be published about this same time were destroyed by malicious sectaries, and because until now the only known examples were the two sermons before the English Houses of Parliament, one must appreciate finding even a portion of another example of his preaching. It is generally known that George Gillespie prayed, preached, and advocated keenly against the Engagement, but it seems to have been largely unknown and omitted from the history books that Gillespie preached before the meeting of the parliament that would approve it.[2] One can find the fact that he was appointed to preach on this occasion buried in the records of the Commissions of the General Assemblies edited by Mitchell and Christie, which were not transcribed and published until 1892. And since that time, it still seems to have escaped notice. This record, and the provenance of the note taker, confirm that the sermon is genuine. "Edinburgh, 25 Februarij 1648." "The Comission appoints Mr. George Gillaspie to preach befor the Parliament the day of their first meiting."[3]

This sermon appears in a manuscript notebook belonging to George Maxwell.[4] The volume is a small leather bound notebook in good condition, with four raised bands on the spine, simple double blind tooling in double fillets, with two clasps, size 17 cm x 13 cm. The pages are not numbered. The length is approximately 390 leaves pages, with a considerable blank

---

1. This introduction is by Chris Coldwell and Matthew A. Vogan. The text is slightly modified from the form in which it first appeared in *The Confessional Presbyterian* 14 (2018): 249–253.

2. The parliament record merely states, "After divine service." The Records of the Parliaments of Scotland to 1707, ed. K.M. Brown et al. (St Andrews, 2007–2018), 1648/3/1. Date accessed: 19 March 2018, http://rps.ac.uk/trans/1648/3/1.

3. *The Records of the Commissions of the General Assemblies of the Church of Scotland holden in Edinburgh the Years 1646 and 1647*, edited by Alexander F. Mitchell and James Christie (Edinburgh: Printed at the University Press by A. Constable for the Scottish History Society, 1892), 367. Wodrow also mentions it. "When Mr Gillespie was bussy studying his sermon that he was to preach before Parliament to-morrow …." *Analecta*, vol. 3 (1843), III.

4. See the bibliographical data on page 462.

section from f.268 to the Genesis material in the back which is in reverse order. There is a wide margin generally and there are not the same amount of contractions, cross-outs and general scrappiness that would reflect notes taken at the time of delivery. Sermons by or presumably by John Carstares at Cathcart most frequently appear. Carstares was minister at the time for that parish. In addition to the sermon preached by George Gillespie before the parliament, there are notes of sermons by David Dickson, James Durham, Patrick Gillespie and others. The Genesis notes are by Maxwell himself and are mathematical calculations on the genealogies.

Sir George Maxwell (1622–1677) was of the Scottish gentry at the time of the Engagement and a Protester in the subsequent Protester-Resolutioner division in the Scottish church. He was also one of the leading figures that drafted the Remonstrance "which pledged that they would not fight for the king [Charles II] until he had supplied concerete (sic) evidence of genuine repentance for his past sins and until he abandoned the company and councils of malignants."[5] In February of 1648, he inherited his grandfather's estate in Nether Pollock, three miles from the parish church in Cathcart. He was advanced to heir by his aged grandfather, George Maxwell (d. 1648), over his father, John (d. 1666), because both were clergymen and the elder George believed his grandson had the business acumen the two lacked. Maxwell "was young, highly educated, an active man of business, and well qualified to represent the ancient house of Pollok." He maintained personal diaries in small palm-sized notebooks, as well as notebooks of sermons and lectures he attended.[6] Maxwell had a distant relation through marriage to two famous ministers of the time. Maxwell's grandmother's brother's daughters married John Carstares, his parish minister, and James Durham.[7]

George Maxwell, who was knighted in 1649, sat as a member of part of the 1648–1649 meeting of the Scottish Parliament, attending sessions 2–5 representing the shire of Renfrewshire ("Maxuell of Nethir Pollock,

---

5. John Roach Young, *The Scottish Parliament, 1639-1661: a political and constitutional analysis*, Ph.D. thesis, University of Glasgow (October, 1993), p. 429. With others, he later felt compelled to renounce the Remonstrance. Cf. Kyle D. Holfelder, *Factionalism in the Kirk during the Cromwellian Invasion and Occupation of Scotland, 1650 to 1660: The Protester-Resolutioner Controversy*, Ph.D thesis, The University of Edinburgh (December 31, 1998), pp. 71, 122. See his life in William Fraser, *Memoirs of the Maxwells of Pollok*, 2 volumes (Edinburgh: Privately printed, 1863), 1.61–77.

6. Diaries do not survive in the collection for the same period as this sermon.

7. George Maxwell the elder married Jean Mure, the daughter of William Mure of Glanderstone. Jean's brother, also William Mure, had through two marriages a number of children including half-sisters Jean and Elizabeth Mure, who became, respectively, Mrs. Carstares and Mrs. Durham. Cf. *A Genealogical and Heraldic History of the Commoners of Great Britain and Ireland Enjoying Territorial Possessions or High Official Rank*, volume 1 (London: Henry Colburn, 1834), p. 455.

Renfrewshire).[8] However, given the great importance of the opening session and the issue at ſtake (approving or not approving the Engagement), he muſt have been in attendance when parliament opened for the firſt session on March 2, 1648,[9] along with others such as Robert Baillie.[10] He presumably was in attendance for the worship service appointed prior to the opening of Parliament and took these notes of Gilleſpie's sermon.[11] It seems less likely he copied the sermon from another's notes, but took them himself. The notes record some use by Gilleſpie of Greek and Hebrew, and it is clear from his other notes and books that Maxwell had some familiarity with these languages. It is moſt likely he took draft notes as Gilleſpie preached, either in pencil or with ink and quill on a portable writing desk, which may have been in shorthand or abbreviated or 'scrappy' with cross outs as would be usual for such notes. He then would have put these notes in finer form as he copied them into his notebook. For some reason he ſtopped copying, leaving blank pages to apparently come back later to fill in and complete the sermon. There is no clue as to why he never did. Presumably the six leaves (f89–f94) were enough ſpace for the remainder, but if not, perhaps this was a factor? The pages left blank do suggeſt he had more of the sermon he could fill in, rather than that his original notes were incomplete.

Gilleſpie comments on or adduces verses from Psalm 2 elsewhere in this volume (see pages 97, 155, 211, 236). He also ſpecifically adduces verses 10–12 in his *English Popish Ceremonies*.

> At the reading of these passages in Saravia and Camero,[12] horror and amazement have taken hold on me. O wisdom of God, by whom kings do reign and princes decree juſtice, upon whose thigh and veſture is written,

---

8. "Pollok is a well-known area on the south side of Glasgow. The lands are now Pollok Country Park where the Burrell Collection is located, the estate was given to the City of Glasgow in 1966. The present Pollok House dates from 1752 but Haggs Castle is still standing." Cited from a draft life of Sir George Maxwell, by Matthew Vogan.

9. March 2 through 10 June 10, 1648.

10. Baillie was in Edinburgh for some eight weeks and during that time attended the Parliament meetings with others such as Dickson and Gillespie, until he needed to return to Glasgow for meeting of the synod and other matters in late March. Letter to William Spang, March 27, 1648, in Baillie, *Letters & Journals*, 3.35.

11. *Members of Parliament: Return of the Names of Every Member Returned to Serve in Each Parliament from the Year 1696 Up to 1876, Specifying the Names of the County, City, University, Borough or Place for Which Returned: Also Return from so Remote a Period As Can Be Obtained Up to Year 1696, of the Surnames, Chriſtian Names, and Titles of All Members of the Lower House of Parliament of England, Scotland and Ireland, with the Name of the Conſtituency Represented and Date of Return of Each*, 2 volumes (London: Ordered by The House of Commons to be Printed, 1878–79), volume 2, "Parliaments and conventions of the Estates of Scotland," 1357–1707, p. 571.

12. *A Diſpute Againſt the English Popish Ceremonies* (Naphtali Press, 2013), pp. 281–282.

"King of kings and Lord of Lords," make the kings of the earth to know that their laws are but *regulæ regulatæ* [*regulated rules*], and *mensuræ mensuratæ* [*measured measures*]! "Be wise now, therefore, O ye kings: be instructed, ye judges of the earth. Serve the Lord with fear, and rejoice with trembling. Kiss the Son" (Ps. 2:10–12), and lay down your crowns at the feet of the Lamb that sits upon the throne,[13] *discite justitiam moniti.*[14] And remember that this is the beginning of wisdom, by casting pride away, to addict yourselves to the dominion of Christ; who, albeit He has given the kingdoms of this world to your hands, and *non aufert mortalia, qui regna datio cælestia,*[15] yet has He kept the government of His church upon His own shoulder (Isa. 9:6; 22:21). So that *rex non est proprie rector ecclesiæ sed reipublicæ; ecclesiæ vero defensor est.*[16]

Presented here is a refined modernized text of George Gillespie's Sermon before the opening of Parliament, March 2, 1648.[17] Anything in doubt in the transcription or other editorial comments are given in footnotes in the text presented on the following pages.

---

13. Calvin in Psalm 2:12. Cf. *Commentaries*, IV, 2.22–27.

14. Virgil, *The Aeneid* (VI, 620). "Having been warned, learn justice."

15. *In distributing heavenly authority, he does not remove mortal things.* Cf. Cœlius Sedulius, *Hymnus*, line 31–32; Migne, *PL* 19.765.

16. *The king is not properly the ruler of the church, but of the state; but he is the defender of the church.* Gillespie may be referencing the words of Isaac Casaubon's *De Libertate Ecclesiastica* ([Paris]: 1607; repr. Rotterdam, [1709]), p. 176. "Rex proprie non est Rector Ecclesiae; sed Reipublicae προηγουμήνως et primarie; ecclesiae vero, quatenus pars est republicae et κατι πακολούθημα at ibiden et passim, audit Rex Defensor Ecclesiae, proprie."

17. The plain transcription in parallel with a modernized text is given in *The Confessional Presbyterian*, volume 14 (2018): 253–262.

Sermon on Psalm 2:10–12

At Divine Service Prior to
The Opening of Parliament,
March 2, 1648

Psalm 2:10. *Be wise now therefore, O ye kings: be instructed, ye judges of the earth. 11. Serve the Lord with fear, and rejoice with trembling. 12. Kiss the Son, lest he be angry, and ye perish from the way, when his wrath is kindled but a little. Blessed are all they that put their trust in him.*

THIS PSALM IS an evangelical psalm concerning Christ Jesus and His kingdom. There are three parallel places [to this Psalm] in the New Testament applied to Christ. 1. The first two verses [in] Acts 4.25–26: "who by the mouth of thy servant David hast said, why did the heathen rage and the people imagine vain things? The kings of the earth stood up and the rulers were gathered together against the Lord and against his Christ. For of a truth against thy holy child Jesus whom thou hast anointed, both Herod and Pontius Pilate with the Gentiles and the people of Israel were gathered together,"—and another place, verse 7, "thou art my son this day have I begotten thee," is also applied to Christ [in] Hebrews 1:10. [2.] And a third place, verse 9, "Thou shalt break them with a rod of iron; thou shalt dash them in pieces as like a potter's vessel." Christ speaks it of Himself [in] Revelation 2:27, "And he shall rule them with a rod of iron; as the vessels of a potter shall they be broken to shivers: even as I received of my Father." And [also in] Revelation 19:15, "And out of his mouth goeth a sharp sword, that with it he should smite the nations: and he shall rule them with a rod of iron."

And now the prophet after he has laid open the attempt of the wicked world, and of the kings and princes of the earth against the kingdom and government of the Son of God in the three first verses, he shows then how God laughs all their designs to scorn, and how in despite of all their malice God will establish the kingdom of Christ, he concludes with this exhortation, *be wise now therefore o ye kings, be instructed ye judges of the earth,* which is not so much spoken to these mad counselors and wicked conspirers against Christ, [as] there was less hope of these, but "be wise O kings," "be instructed all ye judges of the earth," as the Septuagint reads it [to say], take example from Christ's opposers and see their tragic end, how God *speaks to them in His wrath and vexes them in His sore displeasure.* And this is the scope of the text.

471

Four particulars are [here] considerable. I. The person exhorted, the *kings and judges of the earth.* II. The thing exhorted, *to be wise, be instructed.*[1] III. The reason of the exhortation, *be wise therefore, be instructed therefore.* The original is rendered by Tremellius, "nunc ergo:"[2] *now therefore.* IV. The opportunity of the exhortation, *now, be wise now, be instructed now,* lest otherwise thereafter it be too late.

I. The exhortation is spoken to the kings and judges of the earth. The Holy Ghost gives magistrates the titles and dignities done to their places; therefore, the Holy Ghost is no Leveller.[3] I say the Holy Ghost is no Leveler, either if we compare magistrates with God, or with the Mediator, or with their subjects or with the saints.[4] In all of these appears no leveling. 1. In regard of God, magistrates are God's ministry and deputies. They are the ministry of God for good (Rom. 13:4).

2. If we compare them with Jesus the Mediator, though magistrates indeed be not properly the vicegerents of Christ as mediator, yet they are not coordinate, but subordinate. Christ is the only king of His Church and they are His servant[s].[5] So there is no leveling. For if they rebel,[6] He will set His feet upon their necks—"bring hither" these "mine enemies," that "would not that I should reign over them" (Luke 19:27).

3. Compare kings with their subjects, there are higher and lower powers, and where there be some higher and some lower there is no leveling.

4. Compare kings with the saints, and that either as they are inhabitants of the world, and so they must be subject as well as others; Christian liberty does not exeem[7] them from subjection to magistracy, but lays on firmer ties and bands; or, if we look on the saints as they are *municeps cælorum,* burgesses of heaven, there is yet no leveling. When it comes to their eternal privilege, they shall judge the world and kings amongst the rest. "Do ye not know," says the apostle, "but the saints shall judge the earth" (1 Cor. 6:2). And kings are here the judges of the earth. Understand earth in a threefold notion. (1) "Terra quam terimus," the earth we tread upon. (2) "Terra quam gerimus," the earth we carry about us, and that is our bodies. Both these are subject to the magistrate, even as well in regard of the saints as well as other men; that is, the lands, goods and bodies of the saints are subject to kings, though not in an arbitrary way. (3) There is "terra quam querimus,"

---

1. The notes end abruptly before the third and fourth points are reached.

2. See Emmanuel Tremellius, Franciscus Junius, and Théodore de Bèze, *Testamenti Veteris Biblia Sacra* (1579; Hanover: 1602), p. 475.

3. *Leveller*: Advocates for removing social and other societal distinctions, and for popular sovereignty.

4. This last clause is inserted in the left margin in the manuscript.

5. See the introduction regarding this distinction and see the discussion in this present volume on pages 189–197.

6. A second "if" before "He will" appears to be struck out in the manuscript.

7. *Exeem*: To exempt from an obligation, duty, jurisdiction, punishment, etc. (*DSL*).

the earth we seek after; our heavenly inheritance; and in that respect the saints shall be Christ's assessors, and kings shall be judged by them. They shall bind their nobles "with chains" and their princes "with fetters of iron" (Psalm 149:8).

I will make no further use of this than to take away that old calumny, which was the calumny of the prophets and apostles, and of Christ himself, and no wonder if it be also the calumny of godly ministry nowadays, that they are unfriends to magistrates. But we have not so learned Christ [cf. Eph. 4:20]. Those are best subjects to the king that are best subjects to God. And let profane men say what they please, when a temptation and their interest meet together, they shall be found but rebels to kings who are rebels to God. Let it not be started (i.e. startled) at when religion is made use of to say it is a way not to give Cæsar his own.

II. The second particular we promised to speak of was the duty exhorted unto, *be wise, be instructed*. And from this I OBSERVE three things.

OBSERVATION ONE. There is here a parity and a kind of leveling, and in this sense the Holy Ghost is a leveler, though in the sense now last spoken of the Holy Ghost is no leveler. There is a leveling, albeit not of places and powers, yet there is a leveling of hearts and spirits, which even in kings and judges must be as much brought in subjection under the yoke of Christ. For these words, *be instructed, be wise,* are applied to magistrates as well as others, because they stand as much in need of wisdom as others, but that they stand as much in need of instruction would be further chosen. The Septuagint uses a word παδει ρα (*sic* παιδεύθητε), which is a disciplinary word, "be nurtured, be disciplined," and the Hebrew word comes from a root יסר (yasar),[8] which signifies binding: "but thou O son of man behold they shall put bands upon thee, and shall bind thee with them" (Ezk. 3:25); "to bind their kings with chains and their nobles with fetters of iron" (Ps. 149:8). And by a metaphor it is drawn to signify reproofs and rebukes. "He that reprooves a scorner getteth to himself shame: and he that rebuketh a wicked man getteth himself a blot" (Prov. 9:7). Usually it signifies chastising, Psalm 6 at the beginning, "Lord in thy wrath reproove me not, neither chasten me in thy hot displeasure;" Psalm 118:18, "The Lord hath chastened me sore: but he hath not given me over to death." Therefore in a word, kings and judges must be content to subject themselves to discipline as well [as] others and had need of it as well as others. And there is a laying low of great spirits when the mighty potentates and rulers of the earth must lay down their neck to the yoke of Christ as much as the meanest underling in Christ's kingdom. The gates of heaven are not laid wider open for kings and for parliament men nor [*than*] it is for others, but they must be emptied of themselves and must stoop as low as Lazarus [cf. Luke 20:20–31]. Otherwise, no entry. And so there is here a leveling of hearts and spirits, for

---

8. The Hebrew font dropped out in the text presented in *The Confessional Presbyterian* 14 (2018): 257.

whosoever will "not receive the kingdom of God as a little child [he] shall not enter therein" (Mark 10:15).

OBSERVATION TWO. The second point observable is the pertinence of this exhortation, *be wise O ye kings, be instructed O ye judges.* Surely if such another as this had come from us[9] and not from the Holy Ghost, it should have been esteemed very impertinent. "Are we fools that you bid us be wise, or bairnes [*children*] that we had need of instruction?" This is a part of the language of the time, but the Holy Ghost says *be wise now O ye kings.* "Et nunc Reges ad mentem redite."[10] Turn to your wits again, as if they had been out of their wits, and so they were when they thought to shake the cords of Christ from off their shoulders. Job 32:9. "Great men are not always wise," and no more are kings, "neither do the aged understand judgment." And, Revelation 17:17, it was no great piece of wisdom when the kings choose rather to give their crowns to the beast than to Jesus,[11] but, 1 Corinthians 3:18, "if any man among you seemeth to be wise in this world, let him become a fool, that he may be wise. For the wisdom of this world is foolishness with God." And therefore, this exhortation is so much the more pertinent, as kings and great men think themselves less to stand in need of it. But yet they ought to think themselves fools, till they take the testimonies of the Lord for their counsel.[12] If it had been said, "be religious," or sober or temperate, many would have thought the exhortation the more pertinent; yet the Spirit of God lights on that wherein kings think themselves learned enough.

OBSERVATION THREE. Religion is no enemy to wisdom, only it distinguishes true spiritual wisdom from carnal and sensual understanding. [The] sum of all wisdom is [in] Job 28 at the end, after he has said wisdom is not to be found in the earth, nor in the depth of the floods, nor in the land of the living, he concludes, "unto man he said, behold the fear of the Lord, that is wisdom, and to depart from evil is understanding." Many pitch upon that place, Matthew 10:16, "be wise as serpents," and do hereby allow unto themselves

---

9. In other words, "if such words like this had come from us…."

10. This is the Latin of verse 10 as Calvin renders it. Cf. "Commentarium in librum Psalmorvm, in *Iohannis Calvini Opervm Omnivm Theologicorvm, Tomus Tertius* (Geneva: Johannem Vignon, Petrum and Jacobum Chouët, 1617), p. 7. Cf. CR 31 (CO 11), col. 49.

11. Revelation 17:14–18: "These shall make war with the Lamb, and the Lamb shall overcome them: for he is Lord of lords, and King of kings: and they that are with him are called, and chosen, and faithful. 15. And he saith unto me, The waters which thou sawest, where the whore sitteth, are peoples, and multitudes, and nations, and tongues. 16. And the ten horns which thou sawest upon the beast, these shall hate the whore, and shall make her desolate and naked, and shall eat her flesh, and burn her with fire. 17. For God hath put in their hearts to fulfil his will, and to agree, and give their kingdom unto the beast, until the words of God shall be fulfilled. 18. And the woman which thou sawest is that great city, which reigneth over the kings of the earth."

12. Cf. Psalm 119:24.

a great deal of latitude in policy, and extend it even to dissimulation.[13] And therefore, I will take the more pains to open up the true meaning. There is one part of the serpent's wisdom whereby it preserves itself, and this is imitable; and another part of its wisdom whereby it lays snares against man to do him evil, and this is not to be imitated. Therefore, it is expressly added in that same place, "be simple as doves."

The imitable part of the serpent's wisdom has been pointed out in five particulars by ancient writers. The first two are expressed by Epiphanius (Her. 27 [*sic*]).[14] 1. And the first is, which Jerome also observes, when the serpent is pursued, saith, he knows that his life is in his head, therefore he wraps his whole[15] body about his head, and so exposes his whole body to a stroke rather than the head. Therefore, if we will follow this piece of serpent

---

13. It is not clear if Gillespie has in view Scottish politicians with which he and other ministers had conversations about the Engagement leading up to the opening of Parliament, or particular books advocating for this policy of dissimulation, or both. Machiavelli's idea that the prince must be "a great pretender and dissembler" had been in print for more than a century (1532; cf. *The Prince*, trans. W. K. Marriott {1908}, chapter 18, p. 143). Saavedra has three essays on the prince's use of dissimulation. This work appeared in Spanish in 1640 and in Latin in 1643. Published in Amsterdam, the work would have been available in London at the time of the Westminster Assembly (cf. *The Grand Debate* {Naphtali Press, 2014}, Appendix: Westminster Abbey Library: And Other Theological Resources of the Assembly of Divines (1643–1652), p. 402). Saavedra alludes to some of the same actions of the serpent but not with the detail that Gillespie does. "… Serpents, the emblem of carefull and prudent Majesty, and in the sacred Writs the Hieroglysick of Prudence, for their cunning in defending their heads, in stopping their Ears against all Inchantments…." And he alludes to Matthew 10:16, "The greater the Prince is, the greater care he ought to be crown'd with, not the Sincerity of Innocent Doves, but the prudence of subtle Serpents." Diego de Saavedra Fajardo, *Idea principis christiano-politici symbolis* (Amstelodami: apud Joannem Jacobi fil. Schipper, 1659), Essays 43–45, pp. 324–343; English: *The Royal Politician represented in one hundred emblems*, trans. Sir James Astry, 2 vols. (1700), 1.305, 317. Bacon was comfortable with some "seasonable use" of dissimulation in his *Essays* (1597). "Of Simulation and Dissimulation," in *The Essays: Or, Counsels Civil and Moral of Francis Bacon*, ed. Fred Allison Howe 1908), p. 18. Daniel Tuvill (Toutevill, Tutevl) wrote under D.T., *The Dove and the Serpent* (1614), expanding upon "Bacon's own combination of 'serpentine wisdom with the columbine innocency…'" *Essays Politic and Moral and Essays Moral and Theological*, ed. John L. Lievsay (Charlottesville: Published for the Folger Shakespeare Library [by] the University Press of Virginia, 1971), p. xi.

14. See "37. Against Ophites," in *The Panarion of Ephanius of Salamis, Book I Sects 1–46*, translated by Frank Williams (2ND ed., Leiden: Brill, 2009), pp. 267–268. See *The Homilies of Saint Jerome, Volume 1, 1–59 On the Psalms*, translated by Sister Marie Liguori Ewald, Fathers of the Church (Washington, D.C.: The Catholic University of America Press, 1964; 1981; 2001), 363–364. "Just as a serpent that sees someone coming to strike it instinctively makes a coil of its entire body and protects its head, even so these heretics hide themselves in the winding utterances of Aristotle and the other philosophers and so shield and defend themselves."

15. The text here runs to the edge of the page but the "who" appears to be "whole."

wisdom, let our choice care be for the fame of Jesus Christ and His truth and His honor, for He is our head, and rather let us expose kings and kingdoms, and lives and estates to the hazard, before we put one point of His glory or interest to hazard. And if this were respected it might soon end most of our present differences.[16] Do for your honor, for your lands and for anything else you please, so be the honor of Jesus has the first room.

2. It is added there also by the same Epiphanius,[17] that neither the serpent comes out of his holes to the water, lest he should poison the water, he leaves his poison behind him, so before we come to hearing or prayers or any other exercise of religion, let us leave our profanity and wickedness behind us.

3. Augustine on Psalm 58 tells us of a third point of the serpent's wisdom, that fearing enchantments, he lays the one ear to a stone or to the ground and stops the other with his tail.[18] The Holy Ghost points at it in these words: like the deaf adder which will not hear the voice of the charmer, "charming never so wisely" (Ps. 58:4–5).[19] Would [to] God we could stop our ears at the voice of the charmers. For there be charmers that charm indeed very wisely, but look who amongst you all is wisest if you make no conscience to avoid the company of men who are not for God and religion, but walk by the rules of crooked carnal policy. You shall be stolen off your feet, and led off forth with the workers of iniquity.[20]

---

16. This is a reference to the difference over what would be called the Engagement.

17. Epiphanius, ibid., p. 268.

18. Cf. *Works of St. Augustine: A Translation for the Twenty-First Century*, edited by J. E. Rotelle, 42 volumes (Hyde Park, N.Y.: New City Press, 1995), volume 3/17. "Just as snakes, you see, in order to avoid bursting out and leaving their dens when they are being charmed, are said to press one ear to the ground and block the other with their tails." Cited from *Ancient Christian Commentary on Scripture*, edited by Thomas C. Oden, *Old Testament VIII, Psalms 51–150*, edited by Quentin F. Wesselschmidt, (IVP, 2007), p. 35.

19. Psalm 48:1–5: "To the chief Musician, Altaschith, Michtam of David. Do ye indeed speak righteousness, O congregation? do ye judge uprightly, O ye sons of men? 2. Yea, in heart ye work wickedness; ye weigh the violence of your hands in the earth. 3. The wicked are estranged from the womb: they go astray as soon as they be born, speaking lies. 4. Their poison is like the poison of a serpent: they are like the deaf adder that stoppeth her ear; 5. Which will not hearken to the voice of charmers, charming never so wisely."

20. "As for such as turn aside unto their crooked ways, the LORD shall lead them forth with the workers of iniquity…" (Ps. 125:5). This carnal policy was noted in the 1648 renewal of the covenant and confession of sins, some months after this sermon. "Besides these, and many other breaches of the articles of the Covenant in the matter thereof, which it concerneth every one of us to search out and acknowledge before the Lord, as we would wish His wrath to be turned away from us; so have many of us failed exceedingly in the manner of our following and pursuing the duties contained therein; not only seeking great things for ourselves, and mixing of our private interests and ends concerning ourselves, and friends, and followers, with those things which concern the publick good; but many times preferring such to the honour of God, and good of His cause, and retarding God's work, until we

4. Augustine in another place tells of a fourth particular of the serpent's wisdom: he thrusts himself through a hole or cleft of a rock and by this means rubs off his old skin and gets a new one.[21] He applies it to our entering in at the strait and narrow gate. Pliny (lib. 3. cap. 27),[22] says that he scratches himself amongst the juniper bushes. We must go through the briers of mortification.

5. Plinius in that same place adds that whither the serpent has contracted a dimness of sight, he anoints his eyes with an herb, which he calls "marara," and this recovers the clearness of his sight. Let us of our blindness seek of Jesus, that eye salve whereby we may be cured, that they that see not may see and they that see may be made blind [cf. Rev. 3:18; John 9:39].

Another branch of the exhortation[23] is *be instructed,* or disciplined. This points at five things in the context. 1. *Be instructed.* Say not as Christ's rebels (v. 3), *Let us break their bands asunder and cast their cords from off us,* but

---

might carry along with us our own interests and designs. It hath been our way to trust in the means, and to rely upon the arm of flesh for success, albeit the Lord hath many times made us meet with disappointment therein, and stained the pride of all our glory, by blasting every carnal confidence unto us: we have followed, for the most part, the counsels of flesh and blood, and walked more by the rules of policy than piety, and have hearkened more unto men than unto God." ("A Solemn Acknowledgment of Publick Sins, and Breaches of the Covenant," October 6, 1648, in *The Confession of Faith,* etc. {Edinburgh: Johnstone and Hunter, 1855}, p. 366). This was penned by Archibald Johnson, Lord Wariston, who later condemned The Engagement at length in *Causes of the Lord's Wrath* (1653).

21. Cf. Augustine, *Christian Instruction,* translated by John J. Gavigan, in The Fathers of the Church, volume 2 (Washington, D.C.: The Catholic University of America Press, 1947; 2002), pp. 82–83. "It is well known that a serpent exposes its whole body, rather than its head, to those attacking it, and how clearly that explains the Lord's meaning when He directed us to be 'wise as serpents.' We should, therefore, expose our body to persecutors, rather than our head, which is Christ. Thus, the Christian faith, the head so to speak, may not be killed in us, as it would be if, preserving our body, we were to reject God! There is also the belief that, having forced itself through a small opening in disposing of its old skin, the serpent gains renewed vigor. How well this agrees with imitating the wisdom of the serpent and stripping off the 'old man' that we may put on the new, as the Apostle expresses it; and we must strip it off passing through narrow places, since the Lord says: 'Enter by the narrow gate.'"

22. Pliny, *Natural History, Volume III: Books 8–11,* translated by H. Rackham, Loeb Classical Library (Harvard University Press, 1940; 1983), pp. 71–73. "When a snake's body gets covered with a skin owing to its winter inactivity it sloughs this hindrance to its movement by means of fennel-sap and comes out all glossy for spring; but it begins the process at its head, and takes at least 24 hours to do it, folding the skin backward so that what was the inner side of it becomes the outside. Moreover as its sight is obscured by its hibernation it anoints and revives its eyes by rubbing itself against a fennel plant, but if its scales have become numbed it scratches itself on the spiny leaves of a juniper."

23. Rather than finish the word, it appears Maxwell strikes out and adds a period, apparently to note the abbreviation of "exhortation."

serve the Lord with fear. It is God and not man you have to do with. Either you must admit what flesh and blood counts heavy, else you close not kindly with Jesus on His own terms. So this is one point of instruction.

2. A second is *bee instructed* and *serve the Lord with fear* (v. 11); that is, make not bold with respecting Christ's cause and kingdom or His glory or servants, but seek *the Lord with fear.*

2 Chronicles 31:20–21

*And thus did Hezekiah throughout all Judah, and wrought that which was good
and right and truth before the LORD his God. And in every work that he began in
the service of the house of God, and in the law, and in the commandments, to seek
his God, he did it with all his heart, and prospered.*

"The Humble Representation of the Commission of the Generall Assembly, To the Honourable Estates of Parliament upon their Declaration lately communicate to us. Edinburgh, 28 Aprile 1648," in *The Records of the Commissions of the General Assemblies of the Church of Scotland Holden in Edinburgh in the years 1646 and 1647, Edited from the Original Manuscript by Alexander F. Mitchell, D.D., LL.D. and James Christie, D.D. with an Introduction by the forme*r (Edinburgh: Printed at the University Press by T. and A. Constable for the Scottish History Society, 1892), pp. 489–512.

.

EDITIONS

1. *The Humble Representation*, etc. (London: Edward Griffin for I.R. at the Sun in Pauls-Church-yard, 1648). 28 p.; 4^0. ESTC R21600 (Wing G750). Attributed by Wing to George Gillespie.

2. *The Humble Representation*, etc. (London: Printed for Luke Fawne, and are to be sold at his shop at the sign of the Parrot in Pauls Church-yard, 1648). 24 p.; 4^0. ESTC R235030 (Cf. Wing C4229AD). Copies exist per ESTC but an example was not filmed for Early English Books and it was not examined. However, it is one of a group of variants where the printer is not given but "printed for" Fawne and Dallom, etc.

3. *The Humble Representation*, etc. (London: printed for John Dallom dwelling in Black-friers, 1648). 24 p.; 4^0. ESTC R235029 (Wing C4229AD).

4. *The Humble Representation*, etc. (London: printed for John Dallom, dwelling in Black Fryers, 1648). 24 p.; 4^0. ESTC R23892 (Wing C4229AD). Also identified as R1102. Annotation on Thomason copy: "May. 15". "L copy filmed on UMI 'Tract supplement' reel E1 (Harl. 5936[409]): title page only." This is a variant that has a comma after Dallom on the title page, whereas #3 does not.

5. *The Humble Representation*, etc. (Printed at York: T. Broad, 1648). 24 p.; 4^0. ESTC R173935 (Wing C4229AE). While still 24 pages, this is a unique edition set from C4229AD. They share the same error noted herein on page 491.

The Epigraph on the previous page has been added for this volume.

THE HUMBLE REPRESENTATION OF THE COMMISSION OF
THE GENERAL ASSEMBLY TO THE HONORABLE ESTATES OF PARLIAMENT,
UPON THEIR DECLARATION LATELY COMMUNICATE TO US,
EDINBURGH, 28 APRIL 1648

SEEING YOUR Lordships have been pleased in your answer to us of the twenty [*twentieth*] of this month[1] to remit us to your *Declaration* to the kingdom,[2] for satisfaction to our eight desires formerly presented to your Lordships,[3]

---

1. See "Answers of Parliament to the Desyres given in to them be the Commissioners of the Generall Assemblie, and to their papers given in be them upon the 13 and 18 dayes of this moneth," in *Records of the Commissions, 1646 and 1647*, p. 462. Spelling original.

2. "A Declaration of the Parliament of Scotland to his Majesty's good subjects of this kingdom concerning their resolutions for religion, king and kingdoms in pursuance of the ends of the covenant," in *The Acts of the Parliaments of Scotland*, volume 6, April 19, 1648 (1819), pp. 305–309. See also in *Records of the Commissions, 1646 and 1647*, pp. 463–471.

3. Gillespie was on the committee that drafted the paper of eight desires, to which the parliament gave an answer and to which the commission responded. *Records of the Commissions, 1646 and 1647*, pp. 400, 403–405, 416–420, 420–423. The eight desires are appended to the Kirk Commission's May 5, 1648 Declaration (See note, page 455). The Kirk Commission's eight desires were (text modernized): "To the right honorable the Estates of Parliament, The humble desires of the Commission of the General Assembly: Whereas we were desired to appoint a conference with some of your Lordships, which did go on towards an agreement till it was obstructed by a vote of Parliament of the 16TH of this instant, and having already shown by our papers of the 17TH and 20TH, the reasons of our not proceeding in that conference, and that the cause was not in us, we do now, as the servants of Jesus Christ, for our own exoneration, for preventing of mistakes, and for a clear understanding between your Lordships and us, represent these our humble desires, which we recommend to your lordships' serious thoughts:—1. That the grounds and causes of undertaking a war may be cleared to be so just, as that all who are well affected may be satisfied in the lawfulness and necessity of the engagement, and that nothing be acted in reference to a war before the lawfulness of the war and state of the question be agreed upon. 2. That as the breaches of the covenant by the prevalent party of sectaries *in England* [omitted in the published text] are evident, so we desire and hope that according to the treaty it may be condescended upon and declared by the parliament what are these breaches of peace which they take to be a ground of war, and the reparation thereof may be sought. 3. That there be no such quarrel or ground of the war as may break the union between the kingdoms, or may discourage and disoblige the presbyterian party in England who continue firm in adhering to the League and Covenant. 4. That if the popish, prelatical, or malignant party shall again rise in arms, this nation and their armies may be so

481

as likewise to our other desire concerning applications to be made to the king as well as to the Parliament of England, and seeing your Lordships in the same paper answering our desire to be satisfied in the whole matter, were pleased again to remit us to the *Declaration* as containing the grounds and resolutions of the parliament on the whole matter, we have therefore taken to our serious consideration your Lordships' *Declaration*, to look after [*look for*] satisfactory answers to these our desires, and to be satisfied on the whole matter. But instead thereof, our fears and dissatisfactions are not a little increased by your Lordships' *Declaration*. We shall not search into some particulars in matter of fact, mentioned in the narrative part, neither shall we be curious after the reason why in so large a *Declaration* concerning public dangers, duties, and remedies, there is no expression for preservation of monarchical government in his Majesty's posterity as well as in his own person.

---

far from joining or associating with them, that on the contrary they may oppose them and endeavor to suppress them as enemies to this cause and covenant on the one hand, as well as sectaries on the other. 5. Seeing your Lordships' undertaking should be in the first place for religion, we desire that his Majesty's late concessions and offers concerning religion, as they have been by the church, so may be by the parliament, declared unsatisfactory: Whereby your Lordships may give further evidence of the reality of your intentions for the good and safety of religion. 6. That your Lordships may be pleased not to fix or settle upon any such state of a question as does not contain security and assurance to be had from his Majesty by his solemn oath under his hand and seal, that he shall for himself and his successors, consent and agree to Acts of Parliament enjoining the League and Covenant, and fully establishing presbyterial government, directory of worship, and confession of faith, in all his Majesty's dominions, and that his Majesty shall never make opposition to any of these, or endeavor any change thereof, and that this security be had from his Majesty before his restitution to the exercise of his royal power. Which desire we propone for no other end but because we cannot see how religion, which has been, and we trust shall be the principal end of all the undertakings of this nation, can be otherwise secured, but that without this security it shall be left in very great hazard. 7. That for the same end of securing religion (which is professed to be the principal cause of engagement), and for securing all other ends of the covenant, such persons may only be entrusted by your Lordships to be of your committees and armies as have given constant proof of their integrity and faithfulness in this cause, and against whom there is no just exception or jealousy, that so we may the more constantly encourage our flocks and congregations to follow the cause of God in their hands, and not to doubt of the fidelity of those who shall be entrusted by your Lordships. 8. That there may be no engagement without a solemn oath, wherein the church may have the same interest which they had in the Solemn League and Covenant, the cause being the same.—All which desire being duly pondered by your Lordships in an equal balance, will, we trust, be found just and necessary, and do not doubt but satisfaction from your Lordships therein may be a happy and effectual means for facilitating the state of the question, for uniting this nation in an unanimous undertaking of such duties as are requisite for the reformation and defense of religion, the honor and happiness of the king, the peace and safety of the Kingdoms."

To the preface we shall only say this much, that we could have wished your Lordships had been pleased to express yourselves more plainly who are those obstructers and traducers of your Lordships' proceedings: those deceivers and abusers of the people, which your Lordships (we suppose) point at in reference to this kingdom,[4] the *Declaration* being intended for the subjects of this kingdom, whom your Lordships call the abused people. If your Lordships meaning be that the people are abused by the lies and calumnies of malignants, how comes it that so much favor and forbearance is granted to such men? If any others than the malignant party in the kingdom be meant, we should be glad they were made known.

In the first part of the narrative concerning the necessity, occasion, and consequence of the conjunction of both kingdoms, we cannot but take notice of that which your Lordships say of those common enemies, by whose counsels and practices the composing of differences in the beginning was hindered, and what evils this kingdom might have expected if these counsels and advices which gave first life and motion to these dissensions, should have been still prevalent. We desire it may not be forgotten who were these common enemies and whose counsel it was that did prevail about his Majesty in the beginning of these troubles, and whether there ought not to be a jealous and watchful eye over any such, if even after their joining in the covenant they be found in a way of compliance with known malignants, and in a way of opposition to such as have been most active and zealous in the cause from the beginning.

Your Lordships add that in pursuance of the covenant this kingdom joined in arms with their brethren of England, and did prosecute these ends till their common enemies were subdued, and most of them brought to such condign punishment as the respective parliaments thought fit. We shall here pass your Lordships' omitting of the treaty between the kingdoms, which may be thought to have had a near and immediate influence in reference to the conjunction of these kingdoms in arms, although the covenant was the chief foundation thereof. But whereas your Lordships seem to intimate that the cloud of malignancy was then sufficiently dissipat[ed], or at least that the covenant was sufficiently performed in bringing delinquents to such condign punishment as the respective parliaments thought fit, we are sorry that we have cause to remember what forbearance, yea, favor and friendship has been granted to many such, and we are so far from thinking the danger from these former common enemies past and gone, that we still see malignancy upon the one hand, as sectarisim [*sectarianism*] upon the other, springing up like roots of bitterness to trouble, yea, to defile many in these kingdoms. These are the

---

4. "We the Estates of Parliament, in the first Session of this second Triennial Parliament, finding the strong endeavours and attempts of disaffected persons and Enemies of Truth, to blast and obstruct our Labours in the performance of our Duties, in order to all our Relations, by traducing and calumniating our proceedings; are therefore obliged to undeceive the abused People…." A Declaration of the Parliament," *The Acts*, volume 6, ibid., p. 305.

horns which yet push Judah and Jerusalem on both sides. The Lord prepare such carpenters as may cut off both the one and the other [Zech. 1:19–21].

As for the breaches of covenant which your Lordships insist upon in the following part of your narrative,[5] we wish your Lordships to remember a passage in the declaration of the General Assembly, and how cautiously they speak of the breach of covenant in England. The words are these:

> We would not be understood as if we meant either to justify this nation, or to charge such a sin upon all in that nation; we know the covenant has been in diverse particulars broken by many in both kingdoms (The Lord pardon it and accept a sacrifice), and we do not doubt but there are many seven thousands in England who have not only kept themselves unspotted and retained their integrity in that business, etc.[6]

That the covenant has been foully and shamefully broken by as many of the prevalent party of sectaries and their adherents as ever took the covenant, is clear and undeniable, and by their means has come the resisting and hindering of reformation, connivance at heresy and schism, and other things contrary to the covenant; but it can as little be doubted of, that there are dangerous breaches of covenant by malignants, both at home and abroad; and your Lordships know, true zeal against breach of covenant should strike equally on both hands, beginning to reform at home. Your Lordships say well that the not takers of the covenant are by the joint declaration of both kingdoms declared to be public enemies to religion and country, and are to be punished as professed adversaries and malignants,[7] but we wish your Lordships may not forget to apply that passage of the said declaration to those who have not to this day taken the covenant in England, and that therefore, they may be looked upon by your Lordships as common enemies which ought to be suppressed and punished.[8]

The laying aside of the covenant out of the new propositions sent to his Majesty to the Isle of Wight we utterly disapprove, and are heartily sorry for it.[9] But we wish there had not been some guiltiness of this same kind

---

5. *The Acts of the Parliaments of Scotland*, volume 6, April 19, 1648 (1819), p. 306.

6. Gillespie is citing from his *A Declaration and Brotherly Exhortation*, which he authored for the August 1647 General Assembly. See herein page 372.

7. "A Declaration of the Parliament," in *The Acts of the Parliaments of Scotland*, volume 6, April 19, 1648 (1819), p. 306.

8. *The Declaration of the Kingdoms of England and Scotland, Joyned in Arms for the Vindication and Defence of their Religion, Liberties, and Laws, Against the Popish, Prelaticall, and Malignant Party* (1643); reprinted in *An Exhortation to the taking of the Solemne League and Covenant for Reformation and Defence of Religion, the honour [sic] and happinesse of the king, and the peace and safety of the three kingdomes of England, Scotland, and Ireland* (London: Ralph Smith), p. 26.

9. This presumably refers to the "Four Bills" passed by the English Parliament on December 14, 1647, and presented to the king at the Isle of Wight. See "The Four Bills with the

at home, when it was carried in the Committee of Estates that there should be no mention of the covenant in the public desires sent up in August last to his Majesty.[10] And whereas your Lordships do enumerate amongst these breaches of covenant "that they who ought to be brought to trial and condign punishment for hindering the reformation of religion, dividing the king from his people, or one of the kingdoms from another, or making any faction or party among the people, contrary to the League and Covenant, have been protected and assisted,"[11] we shall here only desire your Lordships

---

Propositions accompanying them," in Gardiner, *The Constitutional Documents of the Puritan Revolution, 1625–1660*, pp. 335–347. "On 18 December the Scots presented a long complaint to the House of Lords bemoaning the English Parliament's lack of consultation over the four bills and Parliament's apparent abandonment of the Solemn League and Covenant." Elliot Vernon, *London presbyterians and the British revolutions, 1638–64* (Manchester University Press, 2021), p. 196.

10. This may refer to debates in the Estates which Baillie reports on August 20, 1647, "Yesterday, and this night, our State, after much irreconcileable difference, as appeared, are at last unanimously agreed to send the Chancelor and Lanark to the King and Parliament of England, to comfort and encourage both to keep our Covenant, and not to agree to the propositions of the army." Baillie, 3.15. Argyll, the head of the Covenanters (or radical party as historians term them) in the Committee of Estates, was "outmaneuvered" by Hamilton, the leader of the royalist faction, and this likely is the August 1647 vote to which Gillespie refers. The records for the estates for August 1647 are not published, but John Roach Young summarizes them. "Although Charles I had been abducted by the New Model Army in June 1647 and although the Independents had gained control of the English Parliament, the Committee of Estates was remarkably slow in responding to that situation and in formulating an effective counter-policy. In May 1647 the Scottish diplomatic commissioners had announced that a coup by the New Model Army or the Independents would mean a Scottish invasion to secure the king. It was not until August 1647, several months later, that the Committee of Estates began to decide on the issue, despite the fact that they had called special diets to discuss the issue on 11TH June.... On 19TH August instructions were issued to those Scottish diplomatic commissioners presently in London.... In contradiction of the Scottish diplomatic warning of May 1647 relating to a military invasion of England, the Committee of Estates enacted on 20TH August that the instructions issued on 19TH August were neither intended to infer a military engagement nor weaken the union between the two kingdoms. This enactment was passed primarily because Hamilton managed to out manoeuvre Argyll. Argyll had interpreted the diplomatic instructions as too royalist and had protested that they should not be taken to imply a military engagement or a weakening of the union between the kingdoms. Hamilton counter-protested that the instructions should not be detrimental to the king's interest and it was this that secured the support of the majority of the committee, despite further attempts by Argyll to get it suppressed. John Roach Young, "The Scottish Parliament, 1639-1661: A Political and Constitutional Analysis," PhD thesis (University of Glasgow, 1993), pp. 312–313, 337 notes 6, 7 (citing Scottish Record Office, Committee of Estates Registers and warrants, 1640–51, PA11/5).

11. "A Declaration," in *The Acts of the Parliaments of Scotland*, volume 6 (1819), p. 306.

to remember that all this is true of malignants as well as of sectaries,[12] and for our part (whatsoever liberty there be in the manner or circumstances), we do not doubt but the thing itself is necessary, both by the Word of God and Solemn Covenant, viz., that justice be done and condign punishments inflicted on all hinderers of reformation and peace, and all who make factions contrary to the covenant, whether they be sectaries or malignants. But if it was sufficient that the most part of the malignants were brought to such condign punishment as the respective parliaments thought fit, which your Lordships gave us a touch of in the precedent part of your narrative, we leave it to your Lordships' consideration whether you do not hereby furnish such a retortion [*reply*] to those that favor the sectaries in England, as that they may plead from that principle in your Lordships' *Declaration*, that the punishment of sectaries is to be referred simply to the Parliament of England as they think fit, and that your Lordships must allow them the same latitude of favor toward the sectaries, as before you have allowed both to yourselves and them towards the malignants. Your Lordships add as another breach of covenant, that instead of a firm union and peace between the kingdoms, a breach has been endeavored,[13] which cannot be denied to be a breach of covenant, and therefore a rock to be the more carefully avoided; it is our grief that there is also cause to complain of the malignant party at home, as no less guilty of endeavoring a breach between the kingdoms.

The attempts, injuries, and violences of that party of sectaries against his Majesty's royal person, and the hard condition he is reduced unto by their means, we are very sensible of; and, as we have often before professed, our prayers and endeavors according to our place and calling have not been neither shall be wanting for the preservation of his Majesty's person and authority, in the preservation of the true religion and liberties of the kingdoms. And we leave it to be pondered by your Lordships, whether they that obstruct and hinder the requiring of satisfaction and security from his Majesty in point of religion before his restitution to the exercise of his royal power, do not upon the matter and by consequence obstruct and hinder his Majesty's deliverance and restitution, whereof such security and assurance had from his Majesty might be a powerful and effectual means.

As we know not whom your Lordships mean when you speak of such as had warrant from the parliament of this kingdom for access to his Majesty, and yet were debarred, and as no violence nor injury offered to a public minister of another kingdom can be excused, so we are informed that the soldiers act in removing once the Earl of Lauderdale from Wooburn,[14] was

---

12. Malignants (royalists) and sectaries (sects and fanatics) both opposed the covenant.

13. "A Declaration," ibid., p. 306.

14. Lauderdale had been forced by the English army to depart Wooburn without taking leave of the king. See *A Letter from the Commissioners of Scotland representing the hard usage of the Earle of Lauderdaill by the souldiers of the army at Wooburn and desiring his Majesties speedy coming to London in safety, honour, and freedom* (London: Robert Bostock, [1647]. Thomason

not only disclaimed, but his Lordship often thereafter permitted free access to his Majesty.

Your Lordships insist upon three instances of the breach of treaties, one of the large treaty, and two other breaches of the treaty, 1643. As to the first (which for order's sake we begin at), we cannot say that it holds forth any convincing clearness to us. Yea, so far as we understand, the thing whereunto the Kingdom of England was bound by the treaty, was not insisted upon by the commissioners of this kingdom at London, but an alternative for assistance against the rebels by forces or moneys; after which the parliament of this kingdom made a desire of assistance by moneys, which the Parliament of England promised to take into their consideration; and seeing your Lordships in this same *Declaration* waive breaches of treaty in money-matters, even where the money was due by treaty, we hope your Lordships will find it the more inexpedient to insist upon the not obtaining of that assistance by moneys against the rebels, being a way not provided by the treaty.[15]

Concerning the other two breaches which pitch upon the Treaty, 1643: First, your Lordships say that according to the first article of that treaty,[16] the covenant should have been taken by both kingdoms, but that now by the prevalent party of sectaries and their adherents, it is not only laid aside in the new propositions, and no execution of public orders for taking it throughout the country, but many in places of trust have never taken it, neither are urged to take it. Certainly, such slighting of the covenant is a great sin against God, and a high contempt of the covenant, and it is very fit that this kingdom should desire the Parliament of England to press it, not only upon persons of trust, but universally on all the subjects of that kingdom.

---

dates his copy August 1, 1647, so the publication of the letter postdates Gillespie's piece and the incident by several months. Not dissuaded by the Kirk Commission, the letter was part of the Scottish Parliament's plan to justify invading England via the Engagement. As noted by Gillespie, after the particular incident things were sorted out and Lauderdale had access to the King subsequently. The House of Lords records the letter on the same date it was published. *Journals of the House of Lords*, volume 9 (1767–1836), p. 367.

15. "Articles of the large treaty concerning the establishing of the peace between the king's majesty and his people of Scotland and between the two kingdoms agreed upon by the Scottish and English commissioners at the city of Westminster, 7 August 1641," *The Records of the Parliaments of Scotland to 1707*, ed. K.M. Brown et al. (St Andrews, 2007–2022), 1641/8/21 (http://www.rps.ac.uk/trans/1641/8/21. Date accessed: 30 July 2022). The later Treaty of November 29, 1643, hired a Scottish army to fight the king on the English Parliament's behalf for £30,000 a month. On the monetary nature of Scotland's involvement in England, see Laura A. M. Stewart, "English Funding of the Scottish Armies in England and Ireland, 1640–1648." *The Historical Journal* 52, no. 3 (2009): 573–593.

16. See article 8 in "Articles of the Treaty agreed upon betwixt the Commissioners of both Houses of Parliament of England, having Power and Commission from the said honourable Houses, and the Commissioners of the Convention of the Estates of the Kingdom of Scotland," etc., November 29, 1643, in Rushworth, *Historical Collections*, volume 5 (1721), p. 486.

Yet, we are not convinced of any just ground of war against that kingdom in that which has been instanced by your Lordships, especially considering that the covenant was taken by the representatives, and other chief corporations in England, whereupon both the General Assembly and the Parliament of this kingdom have frequently mentioned in their acts, letters, and declarations, the union and conjunction of both kingdoms by Solemn Covenant. Neither are we without hopes, if things be carried on in a fair and right way that the kingdom of England may be brought a further length in the performance of this duty, whereof we are the more confident because of the famous and frequent testimonies given to the covenant and against the errors of the time by the ministry in diverse provinces in England. As for the last breach, which your Lordships conceive to be against the eighth article of the same treaty, 1643,[17] we heartily wish that the joint way of applications to the king by both kingdoms once begun, had been continued, and do conceive very much prejudice to the cause by the divided way. Only we offer it to your Lordships' further consideration, whether this breach be not at least disputable, there being no mention at all in that article of proposals, propositions, or bills, but only of cessation, pacification and agreement for peace; so that it may justly be doubted whether the sending of those proposals and bills to the king without the consent of this kingdom, has in it that certainty and clearness of a breach of treaty between the kingdoms as may be a ground of war. And if it be a breach of the treaty for either kingdom singly and dividedly to send propositions to his Majesty, we shall crave leave that we may desire to be informed how this consists with that latitude which your Lordships leave afterwards in this same *Declaration* in the manner of presenting bills or acts of parliament to the king, for your Lordships desire assurance of his Majesty to agree to such acts or bills "as shall be presented to him by his parliaments of both or either kingdoms, respective."[18] We might also insist upon some papers and propositions presented to his Majesty from this kingdom at Newcastle, and much more upon the pacification concluded there, with his Majesty, in reference to the disbanding and removing of the rebels in this kingdom, and that in a single way (as we conceive) without the knowledge and concurrence of the Parliament of England.

But we shall come to that which your Lordships make the result upon all these breaches of covenant and treaties, viz., that they call upon your Lordships to a duty to God, your king, and country, and to your oppressed brethren in England, which your Lordships speak more plainly in the next clause, giving us to understand that those differences or breaches are such as, if not repaired by amicable endeavors, may otherwise necessitate this

---

17. See article 8 in "Articles of the Treaty," in Rushworth, *Historical Collections*, volume 5 (1721), p. 487.

18. "A Declaration of the Parliament of Scotland," in *The Acts of the Parliaments of Scotland*, volume 6 (1819), p. 308.

kingdom to engage in a war, but that first your Lordships intend to send the three desires (next mentioned in the *Declaration*)[19] to the Parliament of England: And this is all the satisfaction we find to our second desire, which was, "that according to the treaties it may be condescended upon and declared by the Parliament, what are those breaches of peace which they take to be a ground of war, and that reparation thereof may be sought."[20] But as we see no breach of peace instanced in the *Declaration*, and as the three breaches of treaties insisted upon by your Lordships seem to be at least debatable, so we hear nothing of any resolution of parliament that such breaches as are or shall be condescended upon by your Lordships, shall be made known and sent to the Parliament of England as we expected and they have desired by their commissioners here. Only we hear of three desires to be sent to the Parliament of England for religion, his Majesty, and the good and peace of these kingdoms. We conceive it is the best and most justifiable way of proceeding, that public as well as private injuries be declared and made known to those whom it concerns to give satisfaction therein. Besides all this, we fear your Lordships will hardly avoid a national quarrel against the Parliament of England if the three instances before mentioned be insisted upon as breaches of treaty to infer a war; because when the Houses were most free, and when there was no such overawing influence of the sectaries party, even then they did not suppress the Irishes [*Irish*] in this kingdom, they did not enforce the covenant on all their officers, much less on all English subjects, neither would they then admit that they were obliged by treaty not to send propositions or bills to the king without the concurrence of this kingdom.

In all this that we have said, it is far from our meaning to assume any judgment of the treaties between the kingdoms; only, because your Lordships have remitted us to the *Declaration* for satisfaction to our consciences as in other particulars, so in this of the breaches we have humbly represented to your Lordships wherein we are not clear and satisfied in our consciences, to consent and concur for our part upon such grounds. And withal, seeing it is not only our desire as messengers of peace, but your Lordships' professed resolution in this *Declaration*, that you will assay all brotherly and amicable ways for repairing differences and making up breaches, we recommend it to your Lordships' serious thoughts whether it will not be most agreeable to that brotherly way of proceeding between two kingdoms in covenant together, to desire a treaty with the Parliament of England concerning the breaches and demands mentioned in this your *Declaration*, especially seeing the way of treaty was the way thought fit to be used in the years 1639 and 1640, before the kingdoms were joined in covenant—how much more now, being so conjoined, are all possible and lawful ways to be tried for preventing the effusion of more blood.

---

19. Ibid., p. 307.

20. *Records of the Commissions, 1646 and 1647*, p. 404.

In your Lordships' first demand which concerns religion, there are some things where with we cannot in our consciences be satisfied, as namely,[21]

1. Because the first two particulars therein contained, viz., concerning the taking of the covenant and practicing of the Directory of Worship, are pressed only upon subjects, which may be interpreted as tending to exempt the king's Majesty not only from taking the covenant (which yet was laudably desired in the propositions of both kingdoms),[22] but from having the Directory of Worship practiced in his family, which was a liberty that his Majesty reserved to himself in his late concessions sent to us, and in diverse messages before sent to the Houses of Parliament at Westminster.

2. We find nothing in this demand of any application to be made at or about the same time to the king for obtaining assurance from his Majesty for his royal consent; but of this we have expressed ourselves more fully in answer to your Lordships' paper of the twentieth of this month.[23]

3. Although this is the second time your Lordships cite in this *Declaration* a passage of the joint declaration of both Kingdoms,[24] by which all that would not take the covenant were declared to be public enemies to their religion and country, and that they are to be censured and punished as professed adversaries and malignants, yet we find no such thing declared or resolved by your Lordships in this *Declaration* in reference to those who have not to this day taken the covenant, as that you will hold them all for professed adversaries and malignants. We hope your Lordships will not think it just nor equal to press such a rule upon the Parliament of England except your Lordships be pleased to walk according to that rule yourselves.

4. Your Lordships do simply and absolutely desire that the Confession of Faith transmitted from the Assembly of Divines at Westminster to the Houses, be approven,[25] whereas the act of the last General Assembly approving that Confession of Faith has in it some necessary cautions, provisos, and explanations, which as the General Assembly judged necessary to be added in their act,[26] so we do not think that part of your Lordships' demand as it stands

---

21. See article 1 in "A Declaration of the Parliament of Scotland," etc., in *The Acts of the Parliaments of Scotland*, volume 6, April 19, 1648 (1819), p. 307.

22. "The humble Desires and Propositions for a safe and well-grounded Peace, agreed upon by the mutual Advice and Consent of the Parliament of both Kingdoms, united by Solemn League and Covenant, to be presented to His Majesty," in Rushworth, *Historical Collections*, volume 5, p. 796. See also Gardiner, *Constitutional Documents*, p. 291.

23. "Edinburgh, 25 Aprill 1648, 'The Humble Return of the Comission of the Generall Assembly to the Answer of the Honorabill and High Court of Parliament to our 8 Desires, and to our papers of the 13 and 18 of this moneth,'" in *Records of the Commissions, 1646 and 1647*, pp. 475–480.

24. "Declaration," in *The Acts of the Parliaments of Scotland*, volume 6 (1819), p. 307. See page 484 and footnote 8.

25. Ibid., p. 307.

26. "The provisoes were, 'that the not mentioning in this Confession the several sorts of

without any such caution to be safe enough, which among other things shows the danger and inconvenience of your Lordships' taking resolutions in things concerning religion without our advice and consent.

5. As we desire that reformation of and uniformity in religion may be endeavored by your Lordships in all fair, lawful, and brotherly ways, according to the covenant, and heartily approve any such desire as your Lordships shall send to the Parliament of England by the advice and consent of this kirk, for enjoining the covenant, and for bringing the churches of Chri∫t in the three kingdoms to the neare∫t conjunction and uniformity in one confession of faith, directory of worship, and presbyterial government, so we would be very cautious and tender when such desires are turned into causes of war if not obtained, which is the present case as we under∫tand by your Lordships' expression in the precedent paragraph.[27]

Your Lordships second demand is, "That the King's Maje∫ty may come to some of his houses in or near London, with honor, freedom, and safety, that applications may be made to him by parliaments of both kingdoms, for attaining[28] his royal assent to such desires as shall be by them presented to him for e∫tablishing religion as is abone [*above*][29] expressed, and settling a well grounded peace."[30]

This demand we conceive to be of dangerous consequence to religion and the covenant for the reasons and considerations following, which we humbly offer to be considered by your Lordships:

1. All applications and desires to his Maje∫ty for religion are su∫pended till he come with honor, freedom, and safety to some of his Houses, in or near London; we know not what length of time this may draw to, or how much danger there may be in the delay.

2. The e∫tablishing of religion here mentioned, as that which your Lordships intend to desire of his Maje∫ty, is according to that which is abone [*above*] expressed, where we doubt not your Lordships refer to your fir∫t demand which went before; whereas the e∫tablishing of religion in such

---

ecclesiastical Officers and Assemblies shall be no prejudice to the truth of Christ in these particulars,' and that certain parts of Chapter xxxii, sect. 2, respecting the power of summoning Synods, were to be understood as applying only to Churches not fully settled or constituted." *Records, 1646 and 1647*, p. 497, note 1. See *Confession of Faith*, etc. (1855), p. 15.

27. The variant printings grouped under Wing 4229AD, where no printer is given but title pages changed to read "printed for John Dallom," and "printed for Luke Fawne" misset this as "paraphrase" (Fawne presumably, though a copy was not located to examine). The edition in York by "T. Broad" also is incorrect. Presumably the York edition was set from the London printing. The edition by Edward Griffin is correct (Wing G750). There may be other differences but a collation of the full texts of all the editions has not been attempted.

28. As Mitchell and Christie note, the original text of Parliament's Declaration reads "obtaining." *Records, 1646 and 1647*, page 497, note 2.

29. The English printings of the text change the Scottish "abone" to "above."

30. "Declaration," in *The Acts of the Parliaments of Scotland*, volume 6 (1819), p. 307.

a manner as is there expressed, we do not think safe, for the reasons before given.

3. We conceive that this second demand amounts to no less than the restitution of his Majesty to the exercise of his royal power before applications made and desires presented to him, much more before assurance and security had from him for the settling of religion in the right manner, and according to the covenant. For besides what we have expressed in our last paper presented to your Lordships,[31] that this honor, freedom, and safety is conceived by your Lordships to be such as may enable his Majesty to effectuate his concessions concerning religion; and what is that less than the exercise of his royal power restored? This we further add, that we humbly conceive his Majesty's honor may comprehend, or may be made use of as comprehending, not only the possession of his revenues, but also the exercise of his royal government. Next, being in freedom, he may repair to any part of his dominions in Scotland, England, or Ireland; and lastly, being restored to be in a condition of safety, he may provide forces for guarding himself against all apprehended dangers; for if guards should be set about him by his parliament, it will be said to be contrary to the condition of freedom. So that being restored to some of his houses in or near London, with honor, freedom, and safety, we do not conceive what he shall want of the exercise of his royal power, considering withal, that neither himself, nor any others will conceive the honor, freedom, and safety to be kingly, and such as becomes [*befits*] his royal person, if he shall want the exercise of his royal power. Yet this restitution of his Majesty to the exercise of his royal power, before security had from him for settling religion, your Lordships know by our eight desires, and otherways [*otherwise*], is conceived by us to be inconsistent with the safety and security of religion.

4. If his Majesty were once come with honor, freedom, and safety to some of his houses in or near London, we know not what influences he may have upon the Houses of Parliament to obstruct and hinder their presenting of bills to him, for enjoining the covenant, abolishing prelacy and the Book of Common-prayer, establishing the confession of faith, directory of worship, and presbyterial government; or what strength his Majesty so restored may again attain by the assistance of the popish, prelatical, and malignant party, for a new and bloody war, to the devastation of these kingdoms and the ruin of our religion and liberties. Which things we have the more cause to fear and apprehend, his Majesty having declared and professed that he is obliged in conscience to improve all the power which God shall put in his hands for the establishment of episcopacy.

5. To insist upon the bringing of his Majesty to some of his houses in or

---

31. "Edinburgh, 25 Aprill 1648, 'The Humble Return of the Comission of the Generall Assembly to the Answer of the Honorabill and High Court of Parliament to our 8 Desires, and to our papers of the 13 and 18 of this moneth,'" in *Records of the Commissions, 1646 and 1647*, pp. 475–480.

near London, before satisfaction and security had from him in point of religion, and in such other things as are necessary for the safety of the kingdoms, could not as we conceive but be an exceeding great discouragement and offence to the Presbyterians in England, who will conceive (if such a thing be pressed upon them) that the remedy propounded in your demand is worse than the disease. And we have also heard that the Parliament of England, when they were as free as ever they were, would never agree to his Majesty's coming to London with honor, freedom, and safety, without security first had from him in such things as are necessary for religion and the safety of the kingdom.

6. Seeing your Lordships are obliged by the third article of the covenant to defend his Majesty's person and authority in the preservation and defense of the true religion, and liberties of the kingdoms, we conceive your Lordships should not demand from nor press upon the kingdom of England his Majesty's restitution with honor, freedom, and safety, except with that qualification in the covenant, and with a subordination to religion and the liberties of the kingdoms. And how can this subordination according to the covenant be said to be observed in your Lordships' demand as it stands? For, if his Majesty be brought to some of his houses in or near London, with honor, freedom, and safety, before so much as applications be made to him for establishing religion and peace, we then leave it to your Lordships' consciences whether his Majesty shall not be restored to his honor before Jesus Christ be restored to His honor, and set upon His throne of government in His church, whether his Majesty shall not be in a condition of liberty before the ordinances of Christ have a free course, and whether his Majesty's safety shall not be provided for and secured before either church or kingdom can say they are in a condition of safety. And is this to endeavor the settling of religion before all worldly interests, or rather to make it come after the king's interest?

7. We fear that if after so many instructions from the Parliament, Convention, and Committee of Estates to their Commissioners at London, from time to time, for endeavoring in the first place the settlement of religion, and then to endeavor the removing of the civil differences and the restitution of the king, upon his first giving satisfaction in religion and the grounds of a solid peace, and if after it was declared by this kingdom (during his Majesty's being at Newcastle) that they could not admit of his Majesty's coming to Scotland in freedom, unless his Majesty granted the proposition concerning the covenant and religion, and gave a satisfactory answer to the rest of the propositions—likewise, if after such a declaration of the parliament of this kingdom, January 16, 1647,[32] for his Majesty's being in some of his houses, with such attendance as the two Houses should think fit, until he give satisfaction in the propositions—if after all this it be now insisted upon that his Majesty may be restored with honor, freedom, and

---

32. See "Declaration of the Kingdome of Scotland, concerning the Kings Majesties Person," in *The Acts of the Parliaments of Scotland*, volume 6, April 19, 1648 (1819), p. 307.

safety, before such satisfaction had from him, we fear it shall lie as a great scandal upon this kingdom, and as too sensible and apparent a change of their former principles and professions in a point so much concerning the security of religion.

8. We are very apprehensive that your Lordships urging the disposal of the king's person in England in such a way as that he may come to London with honor, freedom, and safety, without his Majesty's giving or your Lordships' desiring his Majesty to give satisfaction and security in religion, and in such things as belong to the safety of the kingdom (without which there can be no lasting security expected to religion), as it is a far different point from the urging of a joint interest in the disposing of the king's person by both kingdoms for the good of both, so it will be judged by most of all parties in England that ever concurred in this cause, to be so prejudicial to their national rights and liberties, and such an encroachment thereupon (though your Lordships declare you have no such intention), as that it will unite them all in opposition to this kingdom, and consequently alienate them from the intended uniformity in religion according to the covenant. As these reasons make us conceive your Lordships' second demand to import no small danger to religion, so we would not be understood as if we had any thoughts to decline the restoring of his Majesty to the same condition he was in, by the agreement of both kingdoms, when he was taken away by a party of the army under the command of Sir Thomas Fairfax, that both kingdoms may freely make their applications to him.

Concerning your Lordships' third demand, that the present army of sectaries may be disbanded, for the ends expressed in the demand, as we think no persons whatsoever fit to be employed or entrusted in the armies of either kingdom who[33] have not taken the covenant, and that all sectaries in England that are in arms should be disbanded and disarmed, so we conceive there is also reason for your Lordships to foresee and provide against the danger of the rising again of the popish, prelatical and malignant party in arms, and the rather because of the late commotions begun by some of them both in England and Ireland, there being also some both in Wales and Ireland actually in arms, who have discovered and declared their principles and ends to be very malignant, wherein we are informed they are the more animated and encouraged upon confidence of some agreement between his Majesty and this kingdom. It is further to be considered that this demand being joined with the second, the present army in England disbanded, and his Majesty brought to London with honor, freedom, and safety, how easily may all the malignant, popish, and prelatical party in his Majesty's dominions flock unto him? Which how prejudicial it may be, his Majesty keeping still his principles, is easy to be judged.

As for the exceptions added in your Lordships' demand,[34] to pass the

---

33. The English edition by Griffin, which is the edition put out in text by Early English Books Online, has "we" for "who" (Wing G750).

34. "Declaration," in *The Acts of the Parliaments of Scotland*, volume 6 (1819), p. 308.

ambiguity thereof, your Lordships except from the said disbanding the garrisons necessary to be kept in England, and desire that these garrisons may be commanded by such as have or shall take the covenant, and are well affected to religion and government, but do not desire any such thing concerning the garrisons themselves, which may be understood as a tacit confession on your part that all the garrisons to be kept in England may be of such as have not taken nor shall take the covenant, nor are well affected to religion and government, provided that those garrisons be commanded by such as your Lordships describe.

We have but one point more to add concerning this third and last demand, for we cannot conceal our fears and apprehensions that your present resolutions and proceedings, and the entertainment of English soldiers, whereof many are papists and malignants, and some eminent in malignancy, is not the way to further, but to retard and hinder the disbanding of the present army in England, and to frustrate the ends your Lordships propose in your *Declaration* for the disbanding of that army.

And whereas your Lordships declare that it is not your intention at all to make a national engagement against the Parliament and Kingdom of England, but for them, as we shall not presume to speak of the national rights and privileges of another kingdom, so we cannot see how the principles of your Lordships' *Declaration* can consist with the first part of our third desire, which was that there may be no such quarrel or ground of the war as may break the union between the kingdoms. For we conceive there are diverse such quarrels in the *Declaration* as fall directly and necessarily upon the votes and proceedings of the Houses of Parliament, even when they were most free.

Concerning that which your Lordships add in reference to the latter part of our third desire, and to our whole fourth desire, we humbly conceive it is very far short of that which is no less your Lordships' duty than our desire, for:

1. Your Lordships only declare against "association and conjunction of forces with those who shall refuse to swear and subscribe the covenant,"[35] which does not exclude association of forces with such as neither have taken, nor shall take the covenant, so that they be not urged thereto, and so not reckoned amongst refusers. This we have the more reason to take notice of because your Lordships have before in this same *Declaration* complained that there is no urging of the covenant in England nor no execution of public orders for taking of the same. Which being so, how shall your Lordships find the malignants in England to be refusers of the covenant, except your Lordships enforce it upon them, which we suppose your Lordships intend not to do?

2. Your Lordships do not declare that if any who have not taken and shall not take the covenant, nay, not so much as they that shall refuse the covenant, if they rise in arms, your Lordships will oppose them and endeavor

---

35. "Declaration," in *The Acts of the Parliaments of Scotland*, volume 6 (1819), p. 308.

to suppress them; only your Lordships say, you will not associate nor join forces with them.

3. Whereas your Lordships say, "That you will be so far from joining,[36] or associating with the popish, prelatical, or malignant party, if they shall again rise in arms, either to oppose or obstruct all or any one of the ends of the covenant, that you will oppose and endeavor to suppress them as enemies to the cause and covenant,"[37] we beseech your Lordships to consider whether this part of your *Declaration* does not reserve a latitude that if the popish, prelatical, or malignant party shall rise in arms for the king's restitution, and can but have so much cunning (which is more nor [*than*] probable)[38] as to conceal their intentions of obstructing or opposing all, or any one of the ends of the covenant, in such a case it may be free to your Lordships instead of opposing or endeavoring to suppress them, that you shall both protect their persons and estates, and also join or associate forces with them. In all which we have the more cause to be full of fears and apprehensions, because of so many English malignants even now protected and entertained in this kingdom in hopes of military employments, yea, diverse of them (as we are informed) such as have served against this cause and covenant.

As to that which follows relating to our seventh desire concerning such as are to be entrusted in armies and committees, we shall need to say no more than was expressed in our Humble Representation, March 29,[39] namely, that your Lordships omit in your answer some of the qualifications expressed in our desire, viz., such as have given constant proof of their integrity and faithfulness in this cause, and against whom there is no just cause of jealousy, that so we may the more confidently encourage our flocks to follow the cause of God in their hands, and not to doubt of their fidelity; which qualifications being contained in our desire, and omitted in your Lordships' answer, we are not without fears that this omission may be made use of by some as if your Lordships had not meant to agree fully to that desire, and so take occasion to deal for employing and entrusting such in the committees and armies as may be justly excluded by the qualifications contained in our said desire.

These things having been before represented to your Lordships, and there being nothing in your Lordships' *Declaration* to satisfy or take off these our fears, but such expressions insisted upon as keep aloof from the qualifications desired by us, all that are unbiased may easily judge whether we have not herein some real ground to be unsatisfied.

---

36. Mitchell and Christie note that this is "joying" in the manuscript of the records, but they render it "joyning" as did all the English printings.

37. "Declaration," in *The Acts of the Parliaments of Scotland*, volume 6 (1819), p. 308.

38. *Nor*: than (Scottish). Of the English printed texts, Griffin (Wing G750) retains the "nor," but the others replace it with "then" (i.e., "than").

39. "A Humble Representation of the sense of the Commissioners of the General Assembly, To the Honourable Estates of Parliament upon their Lordships Answer to the Desires lately presented to their Lordships," in *Records, 1646 and 1647*, pp. 420, 422.

That which follows in the *Declaration* concerning the rescuing of His Majesty's person, that he may come with honor, freedom, and safety to or near London, where both kingdoms may make their applications to him for settling religion and peace, we have before spoken fully to it. And whereas your Lordships add a kind of salvo in satisfaction to our fifth and sixth desires,[40] it will plainly appear that these desires are not satisfied by anything here expressed in your Lordships' *Declaration*. Your Lordships say you resolve "not to put in his Majesty's hands or in any others whatsoever, any such power whereby any of the ends of the covenant may be obstructed or opposed."[41] But may it please your Lordships to give us leave to put you in mind:

1. That your Lordships' words may be understood either in this sense, that you are not resolved to put any such power in his Majesty's hands, and if so, your Lordships know what you resolve not now you may resolve afterwards; or in this sense, that your Lordships are resolved that you shall put no such power in his Majesty's hands, and if so, then there remains some doubt how far that power extends, which your Lordships conceive shall not be able to obstruct or oppose any of the ends of the covenant, or endanger religion and presbyterial government, or whether it be meant to be extended to his Majesty negative voice.[42]

2. When your Lordships say that you are not resolved to put any such power in his Majesty's hands, this needs not hinder your Lordships' yielding and acquiescing if others put such power in his Majesty's hands; for resolutions not to do a thing may stand with resolutions not to hinder it.

3. When your Lordships have resolved to oppose the putting of any such power in his Majesty's hands as may be destructive to religion, yet upon supposition that his Majesty is come to London with honor, freedom, and safety, we doubt whether it may not prove impossible to your Lordships to hinder the putting of such a power in his Majesty's hands.

Your Lordships add what assurance you intend to crave from his Majesty for satisfaction in point of religion; but withal, we observe three limitations or qualifications joined therewith, which (so far as we are able to judge) leave this great point in a very dangerous uncertainty.

First,[43] Your Lordships resolve that his Majesty give this assurance for religion, "before any agreement or condition to be made with his Majesty,"[44] which is the expression chosen by your Lordships in head of that clause in our sixth desire, "Before his restitution to the exercise of his royal power."[45]

---

40. *Records of the Commissions, 1646 and 1647*, p. 404.

41. "Declaration," in *The Acts of the Parliaments of Scotland*, volume 6 (1819), p. 308.

42. *Negative voice*: the king's veto power over parliament.

43. The text in *Records* has "1." (p. 504), which Griffin follows (Wing G750, p. 20), but the other English editions render it "first."

44. "Declaration," in *The Acts of the Parliaments of Scotland*, volume 6 (1819), p. 308.

45. See Eight Desires, #6, in *Records, 1646 and 1647*, p. 404–405.

If your Lordships' expression were only a more smooth one, with the like security to religion (such as your Lordships' Answer, March 27,[46] did put us in hopes of), we should have cheerfully acquiesced. But we are so far from perceiving the like security to religion, that we rather fear your Lordships' qualification may make void and frustrate the security that we desired. For first, It clearly supposes that his Majesty shall come with honor, freedom, and safety to London before any agreement or condition to be made with him; for such agreement or condition to be made with his Majesty being posterior to the assurance to be made[47] [*sic* had] from him for religion, must be much more posterior to his Majesty's coming to or near London with honor, freedom, and safety, according to the method of proceedings proposed in the *Declaration*. Now, being once at London, with honor, freedom, and safety, and that without any agreement or condition made with him, it is not probable to us that his Majesty will then desire any agreement or condition unless it be for some concessions on his Parliaments' part, and among other concessions, probably somewhat for episcopacy too, for establishing whereof He conceives himself obliged in conscience to make use of his power as was before observed. The result of this point that we humbly conceive is that notwithstanding of that clause, "before any agreement or condition to be made with His Majesty,"[48] or anything else in the *Declaration*, his Majesty may be restored to the humble exercise of his royal power before security had from him for religion as we desired.

The next qualification added by your Lordships immediately is in these words, "having found his late concessions and offers concerning religion not satisfactory,"[49] where first, the words "having found," may be variously understood, either, "when his Majesty shall have found," or, "when your Lordships shall have found," or, "because his Majesty has found," or, "because your Lordships have found."

Next, the words, "not satisfactory," are as doubtful and may be interpreted in several senses, either that his Majesty's late concessions and offers concerning religion, "are not satisfactory in themselves," or, "that they are neither satisfactory to your Lordships, nor to us," or the meaning may be only, "that they are not satisfactory to us," which doubtfulness in the sense of the words we have more cause to observe because your Lordships have not hitherto returned us any clear or positive answer to our fifth desire: "That his Majesty's late concessions and offers concerning religion, as they have been by the church, so may be by the parliament declared unsatisfactory";[50] only your Lordships are pleased here to make a light

---

46. See "Answers of Parliament to the Desires of the Comissioners of the Generall Assembly represented by them to the Parliament," *Records, 1646 and 1647*, pp. 416–420.

47. The English printings render this "to be had." See *Records, 1646–1647*, p. 505, note 1.

48. "Declaration," in *The Acts of the Parliaments of Scotland*, volume 6 (1819), p. 308.

49. "Declaration," in *The Acts of the Parliaments of Scotland*, volume 6 (1819), p. 308.

50. See Eight Desires, #5, in *Records, 1646 and 1647*, p. 404.

transition over that which we conceived to be unto us a grave subject of a solemn declaration.

The third qualification in the assurance to be required from his Majesty, is that he shall agree to such act or acts of parliament, and bills, as shall be presented unto him by his Parliament [Parliaments][51] of both or either kingdoms respectively, for enjoining the covenant, and establishing the presbyterial government, directory of worship, and confession of faith in all his Majesty's dominions. But we humbly conceive it were more for the glory of God, good of religion, and his Majesty's own happiness, that his Majesty should after the example of the godly reforming Kings of Judah, and of the best Christian Emperors of old in the Christian church, declare his own zeal and forwardness for the reformation and settling [of] religion, and that your Lordships should do well to solicit and incite his Majesty hereunto, rather than to seem to yield so far as that his Majesty shall be free for his part till his Parliaments of both or either kingdoms respectively agree what acts or bills to present to him, the preparing and presenting whereof, how much it may be retarded and obstructed by the prevalency both of malignants and secretaries, we know not. Seeing therefore, his Majesty owes a duty both to God and to his people for the reformation and settlement of religion, your Lordships may do better to solicit his Majesty, and to desire that he will positively declare himself willing and ready for his part and for that duty which is incumbent to his Majesty, and that he give assurance for the same in the particulars.

Your Lordships further declare in reference to our eighth[52] and last desire, that you "are willing to subjoin to the ground of" your "undertaking an oath, wherein both in the framing thereof and otherwise" your Lordships "are willing the church shall have their due interest as formerly in the like cases,"[53] where, as we know not how far your Lordships' meaning does reach in the word "otherways" [*otherwise*], and in the word "due," so we know not why your Lordships did not think fit to agree to our desire as it was conceived, and as the words stood, viz., "That there may be no engagement without a solemn oath, wherein the kirk may have the same interest which they had in the Solemn League and Covenant,"[54] which desire is so far unsatisfied, that for our interest in the matter of the oath, and in the grounds of the undertaking, we do not see it allowed or preserved to us, but rather that the *Declaration* holds forth the grounds of the undertaking already resolved upon by your Lordships, only leaving us an interest in the form of an oath to be subjoined, and that not without some uncertain and dubious qualifications, as has been touched. Meanwhile, we see only a *Declaration* without

---

51. As Mitchell and Christie note, the English printings correctly change this to "Parliaments."

52. Eight Desires, #8, *Records*, ibid, p. 405.

53. "Declaration," in *The Acts of the Parliaments of Scotland*, volume 6 (1819), p. 308.

54. Eight Desires, #8, *Records*, ibid, p. 405.

The Humble Representation, 28 April 1648

an oath, and as declarations are alterable by parliaments, and their proceedings sometimes not agreeable to their declarations (which the experience of these times has taught us), so if there were an oath subjoined to the grounds of undertaking expressed in this *Declaration*, we could not account it a lawful oath, but that it would make the business worse.

Your Lordships add somewhat further relating to the matter of our first and second desires, namely, "That your Lordships are resolved not to engage in any war before the necessity and lawfulness thereof be declared [*sic* cleared],[55] so as all who are well affected may be satisfied therewith, and that reparation to such breaches and injuries as are or shall be condescended upon, shall be demanded in such a just and fit way as shall be found most lawful and expedient."[56] This clause, as likewise that which follows, that many of the dangers with the grounds and resolutions, are by this *Declaration* of your Lordships made known to this kingdom, seems to hold us in suspense till all the dangers, grounds, and resolutions be made known, and till the lawfulness and necessity of the war be cleared, and the way of seeking reparation resolved upon; yet your Lordships may be pleased to remember that in that part of your Answer to us of the twentieth,[57] which is a return to our desire of knowing fully your Lordships' resolutions, and being satisfied on the whole matter, we were remitted to the *Declaration* as containing the grounds and resolutions of the Parliament on the whole matter.

As to that which follows concerning a present putting of the country in a posture of defense as in Anno 1643, we should be glad it were made to appear really that the grounds, principles, and ends were the same now as they were in the year 1643. Otherwise, the like act upon different grounds, and for different ends, makes it not the same cause. Your Lordships do indeed speak of the principles expressed in the *Declaration* as the same with the first principles contained in our National Covenant and in the Solemn League and Covenant, but what reason we have to conceive they are new and different principles may appear by the several particulars before mentioned. We cannot here pass a new interpretation which the *Declaration* puts upon the Solemn League and Covenant, viz., "That we did solemnly swear and promise before God and His angels to endeavor reformation of and uniformity in religion and church government in all his Majesty's dominions, according to the Word of God and the example of the best reformed churches,"[58] where we pass your Lordships' limiting and restricting of uniformity more than

---

55. The original text of the Declaration reads "cleared," as Mitchell and Christie note (p. 507, note 1), and the text here simply makes an error in citing it. The English printings correct it to read "to be cleared."

56. Declaration," in *The Acts of the Parliaments of Scotland*, volume 6 (1819), p. 308.

57. "Answers of Parliament to the Desyres given in to them be the Commissioners of the Generall Assemblie, and to their papers given in be them upon the 13 and 18 dayes of this moneth," in *Records of the Commissions, 1646 and 1647*, pp. 462.

58. See "Declaration" in *Records, 1646 and 1647*, pp. 470–471.

the covenant does, which may infer that uniformity in church government between the churches of Christ in these three covenanted kingdoms, is not to be urged in any other manner or measure than we have a precedent of in other reformed kirks, but that which here we chiefly aim at in [*sic* is][59] the following clause of the *Declaration*, viz., "And not only to the utmost of our power with our means and lives to stand to the defense of our dread sovereign, his person and authority in the preservation of the true religion and liberties of the kingdom, but also in every cause which may concern his Majesty's honor, to concur according to the laws of this kingdom and duty of good subjects."[60] Yet your Lordships know that no such interpretation has been made by the assemblies of the kirk of the Solemn League and Covenant, as your Lordships are pleased here to make of it. If it be said that your Lordships meaning was only of our National Covenant, yet it may be observed withal, that the plain and grammatical construction of the words will carry that interpretation either upon the Solemn League and Covenant only, or both upon it and upon our National Covenant. However, although our National Covenant only were here fixed upon, concerning which there is such an expression in the supplication of the General Assembly, Anno 1639, to his Majesty's commissioner and the Lords of Secret Counsel,[61] yet there are some weighty considerations which we humbly offer against the application of that supplication of the assembly to the present business. For:

1. His Majesty was at that time giving satisfaction to the public desires of this kirk concerning religion. We heartily wish we might say the like now.

2. We do not see the cause stated in the *Declaration* to be for his Majesty's honor, and so to fall within that duty expressed in the declaration of the General Assembly. And as one of the ends of the covenant was his Majesty's honor and happiness, and your Lordships also have acknowledged in your oath of parliament that the honor, happiness, and greatness of the king's Majesty does depend on the purity of religion as it is now established in this kingdom, so whatsoever crosses or prejudices the grounds of the covenant, or any of the ends thereof, cannot with us find any such commendation as to be a cause which concerns his Majesty's honor.

3. Whatsoever we owe to the king in civil matters distinct from the cause of religion, sure[ly] all these other duties are with a subordination to the glory of God and good of religion, and we are very confident it was and will be far from the thoughts of the General Assembly, under color of his Majesty's honor, to concur with him, or any in his name, in a cause which is hurtful and prejudicial to the good of religion and to the other ends of the Solemn League and Covenant, yet the cause stated in the *Declaration* we humbly conceive to be such.

---

59. *Records, 1646–1647*, notes "*is* for *in* in 4to print," which is true in all the variants examined.

60. Declaration," in *The Acts of the Parliaments of Scotland*, volume 6 (1819), p. 309.

61. "The Supplication of the Assembly to his Majesty's High Commissioner, and the Lords of secret Council," in Rushworth, *Historical Collections*, volume 3 (1721), p. 961.

4. It may be remembered that the *Crosse-petition*[62] having cited the same clause of the said Petition of the General Assembly, and making use thereof in order to an engagement in war in his Majesty's quarrel against the Parliament of England, was declared against by the Commission of the General Assembly, Anno 1643.[63] And among other particulars, it was then declared that the limitations expressly mentioned in the words cited out of the Assembly's supplication, viz., "according to the laws of this kingdom, and duty of good subjects," were interpreted by some that spoke at the time in the General Assembly to be all one, as if it had been said, *"within this kingdom,"* we not knowing of any laws of this kingdom or further extent.[64] It was also then observed and may now be applied and remembered that the National Covenant having been subscribed in the years 1581 and 1590 before King James was King of England and being qualified in the particular heads and articles by express limitations and restrictions to this kirk and kingdom, to the religion, laws, and liberties of Scotland, can no more be extended to municipal debates and to the laws and liberties of England unto which we are strangers, than the kingdom of England can judge of our laws and determine our differences, the two kingdoms being still independent each on other, and not subordinate one to[65] another,[66] as the first article of the large Treaty fully declares.[67]

As to that we find in the close of the *Declaration*, that this "kingdom of Scotland will now make it evident, as they have often declared, that their

---

62. "A petition presented by some noblemen and gentlemen to the Privy Council on 10TH January 1643, in opposition to one by 'the Commission of the Assembly and certain noblemen, barons, and burgesses', and declared by them to 'tend to the hindrance of their proceedings and endeavors in this public work committed to them by the king's Majesty and Parliament', and declared by the Commission 'to be nothing else but a secret plot and subtle undermining of all the present designs of this kirk and kingdom for unity of religion, and of all the work of God in this land'. See the representation against it published by the Commission under the title, 'A Declaration against a Crosse Petition, wherein some secret lets of the intended Reformation are discovered', etc. Edinr., Evan Tyler, 1643." *Records, 1646 and 1647*, page 509.

63. *A Declaration against a Crosse Petition: wherein some secret lets of the intended reformation are discovered, by the Commissioners of the Generall Assembly* (Edinburgh: Evan Tyler, 1643).

64. *A Declaration against a Crosse Petition*, p. 12.

65. Griffin (Wing G750): "independent each on other, and not subordinate one to another." The other English editions read: "independent each on other, and not subordinate unto another…."

66. *A Declaration against a Crosse Petition*, pp. 11–12.

67. See the opening paragraph in "Articles of the Large Treaty concerning the establishing of the peace between the king's majesty and his people of Scotland and between the two kingdoms agreed upon by the Scottish and English commissioners at the city of Westminster, 7 August 1641," *The Records of the Parliaments of Scotland to 1707*, K.M. Brown et al eds (St Andrews, 2007–2022), 1641/8/21 (http://www.rps.ac.uk/trans/1641/8/21. Date accessed: 30 July 2022).

quietness, stability, and happiness does depend upon the safety of the king's Majesty's person and maintenance of his greatness, and royal authority, who is God's vicegerent set over us, for maintenance of religion, and ministration of justice,"[68] we shall only put your Lordships in mind that your National Covenant joins with his Majesty's safety his good behavior in his office, and says, "That the quietness and stability of our religion and kirk does depend upon the safety and good behavior of his Majesty, as upon a comfortable instrument of God's mercy granted to this country for the maintenance of His kirk, and Ministration of justice."[69] Otherwise, if a king do not his duty for the maintenance of the true religion, and ministration of justice, it is not his safety alone that make his people to be in quietness and happiness; withal, as our quietness and happiness depends on his Majesty, and his doing of his duty as an instrument and minister of God for good, so the honor, greatness, and happiness of the king's royal Majesty, and the welfare of the subjects, depend upon the purity of religion, as is well expressed in your Lordships' oath of parliament.[70]

And now we shall with your Lordships' favor and permission make this conclusion upon the whole matter, that as we neither were nor are against an engagement with this kingdom in war, but have been and shall be willing to consent thereto, if once satisfied in our conscience concerning the clearness, lawfulness, and necessity of the cause and quarrel, and concerning our calling, manner of proceeding, instruments to be entrusted, security to be had for religion, and other particulars contained in our former papers not yet satisfied by your Lordships,[71] so we are necessitate[d] to profess and declare to your Lordships that we cannot, we dare not in our consciences agree to an engagement upon such grounds, and in such a way as is stated in your Lordships' *Declaration*, and therefore, for our exoneration do dissent from the whole complex business in the said *Declaration*, as not containing clear and convincing grounds of undertaking of a war, not providing for the security of religion, nor clearly disclaiming his Majesty's late concessions and offers as unsatisfactory, nor tending to the suppression of the malignant party, but rather to compliance with them, as we humbly conceive, nor preserving the

---

68. Declaration," in *The Acts of the Parliaments of Scotland*, volume 6 (1819), p. 309.

69. See the "National Covenant" in *Confession of Faith*, p. 349.

70. "For so much, as the honour, greatnesse, and happinesse of the Kings Royall Majestie, and the wealfare of the Subjects, dependeth on the purity of Religion, (as it is now established in this Kingdome) the Lawes, Liberties, and Peace thereof, which ought to be sought after by all good Christians, loyall Subjects, and true Patriots; And to be furthered and maintained by them, against all such as by any meanes indevoure to shake or subvert the same." See *The Oath to bee taken by all members of the Parliament 1641 and in all Parliaments hereafter, before they proceed to any act or determination* (Edinburgh: James Bryson, 1641), first page.

71. All the papers of the commission and the Estates' responses regarding the subject of the Engagement are in *Records, 1646 and 1647*, which subject is also discussed in the Introduction to that volume.

liberties and known intere∫t of the kirk, nor proposing the way of treaties, and all other possible ways of peace to be sought and assayed before a war. For which reasons, and others before mentioned upon the particular heads of the *Declaration*, we plainly declare our dissent from the complex circum-∫tantiate ∫tate of the present business contained in the said *Declaration*, and take to witness, God, angels, and men, that your Lordships have not wanted warning from the watchmen, and that we shall be free of all the di∫tractions, confusions, miseries and blood, which may follow upon your Lordships' proceeding to an engagement in war, upon the grounds of the *Declaration*. We further call to record the Searcher of all hearts, and the righteous Judge of all the world, that our not concurring proceeds not from want of zeal again∫t sectaries, nor from any remissness in that which may concern his Maje∫ty's true honor and happiness, and the preservation of monarchical government in him and his po∫terity, nor from any want of tenderness of the privileges of parliament, nor from any want of sympathy with our afflicted and oppressed brethren in England, in reference to all which our proceedings have been and shall be (we tru∫t) real te∫timonies of our affection and sincerity; but our not concurring proceeds merely from tenderness in the point of security of religion and union between the kingdoms, and from the unsatisfactoriness of the grounds of your Lordships' *Declaration*, as has been expressed in the particulars. Wherefore, we humbly beseech your Lordships to interpret favorably and charitably any liberty which we have used (the matter being such as lies sad and weighty upon our consciences), and that your Lordships would also be pleased to be mindful of making good that passage of your *Declaration* where you say that you resolved "not to engage in any war, before the necessity and lawfulness thereof be cleared, so as all who are well affected may be satisfied therewith;"[72] which if your Lordships shall be pleased to do, there is a door of hope[73] yet open, and we shall not cease to pray unto the Lord (as He shall assi∫t us) that a ∫pirit of counsel and under∫tanding and of the fear of the Lord may be upon you [cf. Isa. 11:2], and that God would graciously rid both your Lordships and us out of all hid and lurking snares, and so guide your Lordships as that there may be yet a sweet and harmonious joining of hearts and hands upon right principles, grounds and motives, in a right way, and for the right ends.

---

72. "A Declaration," in *The Acts of the Parliaments of Scotland*, volume 6 (1819), p. 308. See also in *Records of the Commissions, 1646 and 1647*, p. 471.

73. "Door of hope." This likely draws from Hosea 2:15. See similar use at the end of the Act approving the Directory for Worship, herein on page 328.

The Answer of the Commissioners
Of the Generall Assembly unto the Observations of the
Honourable Committee of Estates upon the Declaration of
The Late Generall Assembly, August 15, 1648

Exodus 23:33. *They shall not dwell in thy land, lest they make thee sin against
me: for if thou serve their gods, it will surely be a snare unto thee.*
Exodus 34:12. *Take heed to thyself, lest thou make a covenant with the inhabitants of the land whither thou goest, lest it be for a snare in the midst of thee....*
Judges 2:2a. *And ye shall make no league with the inhabitants of this land;
ye shall throw down their altars....*

"The Answer of the Commissioners of the Generall Assembly unto the Observations of the Honourable Committee of Estates upon the Declaration of the Late Generall Assembly," in *The Records of the Commissions of the General Assemblies of the Church of Scotland holden in Edinburgh the years 1648 and 1649, edited by Alexander F. Mitchell and James Christie* (Edinburgh: Printed at the University Press by T. A. Constable for the Scottish History Society, 1896), pp. 8–26.

EDITIONS

1. *The answer of the Commissioners of the Generall Assembly unto the observations of the Honourable Committee of Estates upon the Declaration of the late Generall Assembly, August 15 1648* (Edinburgh: Printed by Evan Tyler, printer to the Kings most excellent Majesty, 1648). [2], 28, [2] p.; 4^0. ESTC R35583 (Wing C4201). "Pages 2 and 18 are misnumbered 4 and 1 respectively." The Commission of the General Assembly of 1648 assigned George Gillespie the task of creating the draft of *The Answer*, which was approved with no changes by the Commission. Patrick Simson also gives testimony to his cousin authoring it, the last paper he wrote. See pages 456–457.

The Epigraph on the prior page has been added for this volume.

The Answer of the Commissioners

Of the General Assembly unto the Observations of the Honorable Committee of Estates upon the Declaration of the Late General Assembly, August 15, 1648

ALTHOUGH there were other three papers delivered in to the Honorable Committee of Estates from the General Assembly,[1] besides the assembly's *Declaration*, yet nothing was returned from their Lordships, except only some *Observations* upon a part of the *Declaration*;[2] which *Observations* being sent to the General Assembly, while they were hastening to a close after so long attendance, were read and considered, and declared unanimously to be no wise satisfactory to the assembly, who did therefore appoint us their commissioners to prepare a particular answer thereunto. And this we are the rather willing to do, lest by our silence we should seem to be satisfied with such observations. And this only we shall further premise, that both we and the people of God in the land who expect information from us, are put upon this disadvantage, that while many of their Lordships' papers are printed and spread to the detriment of religion and the cause of God, the

---

1. "Sess. 14, July 25, 1648, ante meridiem. The Assembly's Answer to the Paper sent from the committee of Estates of 24TH July." "Sess. 22, August 1, 1648, ante meridiem. The Generall Assemblie's Answer to the Paper sent from the Honourable Committee of Estates, of the date July 28, 1648." "Sess. 25, Eodem die, post meridiem. The humble Supplication of the Generall Assembly to the Right Honourable the Committee of Estates." There was also, "Sess. 18, July 28, 1649, ante meridiem. Act and Declaration against the Act of Parliament and Committee of Estates, ordained to be subscribed the 10TH and 12TH of June, and against all new Oathes or Bands in the common Cause, imposed without consent of the Church." See *Acts of the General Assembly of the Church of Scotland, 1638–1842, Reprinted from the original edition, under the superintendence of The Church Law Society* (Edinburgh: The Edinburgh Printing and Publishing Company, [1843]), pp. 168–188.

2. *Some Few Observations by the Committee of Estates of Parliament, upon the Declaration of The General Assembly of the last of July* (Edinburgh: printed by Evan Tyler, printer to the Kings most Excellent Majestie, 1648). The assembly's paper to which the Estates objected is *A Declaration of the Generall Assembly concerning the present dangers of Religion, and especially the unlawfull engagement in War, against the Kingdom of England; together, with many necessary exhortations and directions to all the members of the Kirk of Scotland* (July 31, 1648); see *Acts*, ibid., pp. 171–181. The text in citations from *Some Few Observations* and *A Declaration*, etc., have been modernized in spelling, grammar, usage, etc.

507

press is not patent [*open*] to our papers, whereby we desire to clear the truth. And now to come to the particulars.

Whereas their Lordships are pleased to say that the offers of the Committee of Estates for securing of religion have not been accepted by the General Assembly at the suggestion of some disaffected persons,[3] they may be pleased to remember that the General Assembly did in some former papers demonstrate to their Lordships by good and solid reasons (never yet answered) that their Lordships offers are so far from securing religion, that they are inconsistent with the security of religion; in all which (we bless the Lord) we had never a more unanimous general assembly, and more free of

---

3. "Albeit the offers of the Committee of Estates for securing of religion have not been accepted by the General Assembly (at the suggestion of some disaffected persons), yet the Committee resolves never to leave pursuing of their duties for preserving the same according to the Solemn League and Covenant." *Some Observations*, page 1, spelling modernized and corrected. Gillespie was almost certainly at least one of the persons in view and Gillespie likely knew this and thus made the challenge to speak plainly. As noted in the preface (p. 443), Gillespie was singled out by name by one reporter of events as preaching strongly and at least eight times against the idea of the Engagement in January and February (or at least February). Gilbert Burnet, born in 1643 and but a child at this time, son of a royalist and hardly an unbiased writer, wrote in his history, "Those in Scotland being advertised by their commissioners of all that passed, failed not to make good use of it, to stir up the affection and duty of all to appear for his majesty; which prevailed generally; and even the ministers begun, both from their pulpits and by their remonstrances, to complain of the prevailings of the sectarian party, and of the force that was put on the king's person. But the old language of the covenant and presbytery was still in their mouths; yet all were pretty forward for a real resentment of the late disorders in England. Only Mr. George Gillespie, who was indeed of good parts, but bold beyond all measure, withstood these inclinations, and represented that the greatest danger to religion was to be feared from the king and the malignant party. He was suspected of correspondence with the sectaries, which some letters in my hand written in cipher give good grounds to believe. Certain it is that he proved a very ill instrument, and marred that great design [i.e., The Engagement], by which all former errors might have been corrected" (Gilbert Burnet, *The Memoirs of the Lives and Actions of James and William, Dukes of Hamilton and Castle-herald* (Oxford: At the University Press, 1852), p. 406). Clearly, if Burnet could actually read the letters in cipher he would have cited them to prove this charge. It is preposterous to think the man whose sermons preached in London were destroyed by sectaries, and who still wrote strongly against them in these anti-Engagement writings, would be secretly conniving with them! The charge is totally inconsistent with all of his writings. His "sin" was rightly seeing the greater danger in the malignant/royalist party, clearly perceiving the hypocrisy and covenant-breaking in the Engagement plan, and consistently pointing out that the Engagers had failed to even try to get any real assurances from the king about religion and reformation. The Engagers, in seeking to restore Charles to power without any such assurances, and who in fact made clear he would defend episcopacy with his royal power, were putting all the achievements of the Second Reformation in peril.

the suggestions of disaffected persons; and we heartily wish their Lordships may be as free of the hearkening to the suggestions of disaffected persons as the general Assembly was. Neither shall we judge anything before the time concerning these *Observations*, but shall leave it to Him who will bring to light the hidden things of darkness and dishonesty, what suggestions have been made to their Lordships in that business. As likewise, whether their Lordships did from a real desire to be informed and edified, or for some other ends call for proofs from Scripture of the unlawfulness of the present engagement in war. However, we shall answer to the *Observations* as they are offered to us. We understand not why the five arguments in the assembly's declaration brought to prove the sinfulness and unlawfulness of the present engagement are by their Lordships reduced to four classes, but we come to the matter.

The substance of the FIRST ARGUMENT used by the assembly was this: In all lawful wars of the people of God, the end principally intended and driven at is that wherein the glory of God is chiefly concerned. But in this present war, the end principally intended and driven at is not that wherein the glory of God is chiefly concerned. Therefore, it is not a lawful war of the people of God.[4] Their Lordships do not deny the proposition of the argument; only they answer to one of the scriptural proofs thereof, that the wars of God's people were called the wars of the Lord, because as they were undertaken by warrant from God's vicegerents, so for an honest cause and for the glory of God.[5] We suppose their Lordships mean for the glory of God principally, and so yield the point; yet it shall not be amiss here to put their Lordships in mind of the other two reasons why the wars of God's people were called the wars of the Lord; namely. 1. Because their wars were not undertaken without consulting of God and His will revealed by his Ministers, as is manifest from Numbers 27:21,[6] and diverse other places. 2. Because their wars were to be managed and ordered according to the Law of God. As to that which their Lordships say concerning the assumption of the Assembly's argument,[7] We answer:

------

4. *A Declaration*, in *Acts*, ibid., pp. 174–175.

5. *Some Few Observations*, p. 2–3.

6. Numbers 27:21: "And he shall stand before Eleazar the priest, who shall ask counsel for him after the judgment of Urim before the LORD: at his word shall they go out, and at his word they shall come in, both he, and all the children of Israel with him, even all the congregation."

7. "To the first we answer by acknowledging and believing that all the wars of the people of God should be the wars of God, undertaken at the command of these who have lawful authority under God, as were the wars by the command of Moses, Joshua, the Judges and Kings of Judah, and as undertaken by warrant from God's Vicegerents, so for an honest cause, for the glory of God; but whereas it is assumed that this Engagement is not such, we deny it, because it has the warrant of lawful authority, The Estates of Parliament, and the cause being honest to do a duty commanded of God to our prince, God is glorified by

1. Their Lordships say nothing to it as it stands in the assembly's *Declaration* with the proofs thereof; but passing all this, they form another assumption which they deny, and bring some reasons for their denial of it. The Assembly did clearly prove in their declaration, that the end principally intended and driven at in this engagement is not that wherein the glory of God is chiefly concerned; and this was proved by the parliament's not satisfying of the desires of the kirk concerning the safety and security of religion, as likewise by their resolutions of bringing his Majesty to some of his houses in or near London with safety, freedom, and honor, before any security had or sought from him for religion and the covenant, which is a manifest postponing of the safety of religion to his Majesty's safety, of the freedom of the gospel to his Majesty's freedom, and of the honor of God to his Majesty's honor. But all this their Lordships are pleased to pass in silence; and as if the assembly had denied all duty to the king, they go about to prove that it is a duty incumbent to subjects to undertake a war for his Majesty's freedom and honor (we know not why their Lordships omit his safety). And several texts of Scripture are cited by their Lordships to this end, whereas they touch not the point in controversy, viz., whether religion being in so great danger by his Majesty's opposition thereunto, it be the subjects' duty to make war for his Majesty's freedom and honor before security sought and had from him for religion?

2. Their Lordships instead of weakening the assembly's first argument, do indeed add no small strength to it; for while they are answering that very argument which challenges the neglect of the glory of God and of religion in this engagement, they mention nothing of religion, but only the king's freedom and honor as the cause of undertaking the present war.

3. The Kirk of Scotland has ever been and is most willing to resent any injuries done to his Majesty, and to perform every duty for his Majesty's freedom and honor in the right way and order, that is, giving to God in the first place what is God's. But it has not been the mind of kirk or state in this land to make war for his Majesty in an absolute way, and without any qualification, or to the detriment and hurt of religion. For in the year 1643, this kingdom was solicited by his Majesty to undertake war for him; but because he was engaged in a course against religion and the liberties of the kingdoms, therefore all giving of assistance to him was declined, although at that time the kingdoms were not joined in covenant. How much less is it the subjects' duty, after such a covenant, and after so much bloodshed by the means of his Majesty's opposing the covenant and reformation, and his Majesty's adhering still to his former principles, yet notwithstanding of all this, to engage in war for him, and to espouse his quarrel before security desired and had from him for religion?

4. The three scriptures alleged by their Lordships, John 18:36, Genesis 14,

---

doing that duty, the relieving of our king out of prison is a duty, John 18:36", etc. *Some Few Observations*, page 3.

and 1 Samuel 30, do in nowise help their cause or militate against the assembly's argument, for there are four great differences which will mar the application of those scriptures to the present engagement in war.

(1) Christ's cause against the Jews, Lot's cause against the four kings, who had taken away him and his goods, David and his men, their cause against the Amalekites, who had taken their wives captive, was without controversy a good and honest cause, and no wise to the prejudice of religion.

(2) The instruments and managers were without exception.

(3) The parties to be relieved were also without any exception, so far as can be known from Scripture.

(4) None of the three texts cited by their Lordships does hold forth a war undertaken for a human interest with neglecting and postponing the glory of God, and therefore come not home to the point of the assembly's argument. When their Lordships shall prove their cause to be as good, the managers and parties to be as much without exception, the glory of God to be as little neglected in this engagement, as in the example[s] cited, then may their Lordships apply those scriptures in reference to this engagement, but not otherwise.

(5) Whatsoever be the duty of subjects towards the relief of their king, which in the due order and subordination to the glory of God and security of religion is not denied, we cannot see how the text, John 18:36, proves it, seeing that Scripture holds forth a common custom of the world, rather than a duty of subjects, and shows what men use to do [*commonly do*], rather than what they ought to do. And this sense may be plainly drawn from the text itself, "If my kingdom were of this world," that is, as the kingdoms of this world are, and use to be, "then would my servants fight for me." Least of all was it our Lord's meaning to allow fighting and making war in a cause prejudicial and hurtful to religion. And whereas their Lordships say in their next citation that Lot had associate[d] himself in war with wicked men, the Sodomites, as hereby they tacitly intimate the lawfulness of association in war with men as wicked as the Sodomites, so we shall humbly beseech their Lordships to observe here how necessary it is for their Lordships to search more accurately into these scriptural arguments, for there is no such thing in the Scripture as is cited in their *Observations*. We read indeed of Abraham's (not Lot's) confederacy with Aner, Eshcol, and Mamre; but that these three were either idolaters or wicked men is more than can be proved.

(6) The following paragraph is as wide from the point, proving what nobody denies, viz., the duty of honoring kings. We wish their Lordships may seriously ponder two things joined with this duty in the first text cited by themselves [Proverbs 24:21].[8] One is fear God, and this is put in the first place;

---

8. "As for the duty of honor, for performance whereof we have engaged ourselves, we believe it is a duty commanded by God Himself in the fifth command. Proverbs 24:22 [*sic* v. 21], 1 Epistle of Peter 2:16–17. We are forbidden to use our Christian liberty as a cloak to maliciousness, for withholding or withdrawing duty. Yea, pagans by the light of nature, reading

another is meddle not with them that are given to change, whereby we are warned that under color of doing for the honor of kings, we may not join with those who fall off from the cause and ways of God. To press any duty concerning the king's honor with the neglect or prejudice of the honor of God, is indeed to use liberty as a cloak of maliciousness; so that this falls back upon them who charge it without cause upon others. The text, 1 Samuel 15:30–31, is no better applied; for when Samuel yielded to honor Saul before the people, and to turn again with him, it was upon his confession and acknowledgment of his sin; and withal, Saul was so honored before the people that Agag was cut in pieces.

The SECOND ARGUMENT of the general assembly was to this purpose:9 Every engagement in war which is pretended to be for religion and yet has in it a confederacy and association with wicked men and enemies of true religion, is sinful and unlawful. But the present engagement in war is pretended to be for religion, and yet has in it a confederacy and association with wicked men, enemies of true religion; therefore, it is unlawful. Their Lordships are pleased to make four answers, the first three against the proposition, the fourth against the assumption.

First, they say associations were forbidden with the Canaanites because they were destinate [*ordained*] to destruction, and their country promised to God's people.10 If the meaning be that the prohibition of association with the Canaanites and the ground thereof was temporary, and such as concerned the Jews only, and that it is now free to the people of God to associate with such as the cursed Canaanites, let any who is of that judgment speak it out in time. To us it seems manifest from Scripture that the chief ground and reason of that law was moral and perpetual, such as concerns us in all like cases, viz., lest they should make Israel to sin and be a snare unto them (Exod. 22:33 and 34:12, 15; Deut. 7:4). And whereas their Lordships say that they hope there is none who pretends such a warrant for destroying all who differ in religion from them, we shall here pass what their Lordships seem to suppose, but cannot be proved, namely, that the Jews had such a warrant, or did pretend to it; only, we shall desire that their Lordships may never forget that they are engaged by solemn covenant to God, that they shall sincerely, really, and faithfully endeavor the discovery, trial and condign punishment of malignants, incendiaries, and enemies of reformation.11 Now, then can it be lawful to associate with them as long as they remain such? Or how can

---

the law of nature, which is from the God of nature, do use all honor to their kings, yea, holy Samuel undoubtedly zealous of God's honor, notwithstanding he knew certainly by divine revelation that God had rejected Saul, yet honored him before the people, 1 Samuel 15:30–31." *Some Few Observations*, p. 3.

9. *A Declaration*, in *Acts*, ibid., p. 175.

10. *Some Few Observations*, p. 4.

11. Gillespie is citing article 1 and 4 of the Solemn League and Covenant. See *Confession of Faith*, etc. (1855), pp. [358,] 359.

their Lordships join with those as friends of the cause who by the covenant ought to be tried and punished as enemies to the cause?

Secondly, it is answered in the *Observations* that confidence and truſt in these worldly helps are forbidden.[12] It seems their Lordships underſtand the scriptures cited in the assembly's declaration to condemn not the association of itself with wicked men, but confidence in the associates. And if so, then association with wicked men is no more sinful than association with good men; for we may not put truſt and confidence in worldly or human helps from whomsoever we have them. We shall yet desire that their Lordships may take a further review of the scriptures cited in the assembly's *Declaration* (which for brevity's cause we do not here repeat) and we doubt not but it will plainly appear to everyone who looks upon these scriptures, that associations with such men in war are condemned as unlawful and sinful in themselves.[13]

As to the inſtances adduced by their Lordships from the examples of our anceſtors:[14] The desire of the General Assembly [of] 1583, that there might be a band of union between the Chriſtian princes professing the true religion for defense thereof againſt the persecution of papiſts, was a moſt juſt desire; neither can such application be drawn from it as it is brought for.[15] A band of union with princes professing the true religion is hugely different from a union and association with the professed enemies of the true religion, which is the case now in controversy. As touching the help which our fathers had from England, then under prelacy and the Service-Book: As there have been in England ever since their firſt reformation, many who kept themselves free of these corruptions, so they who at that time came from England for help and assiſtance to this kingdom invaded by the Frensh [*French*], had

---

12. *Some Few Observations*, p. 4.

13. "... for we find therein [in Scripture] condemned confederacies and associations with the enemies of true religion, whether Canaanites (Exod. 23:32, and 34:12, 15, Deut. 7:2); or other heathens (1 Kings 11:1, 2); such was Asa, his covenant with Benhadad (2 Chron. 16 to verse 10); Ahaz, his confederacy with the King of Assyria (2 Kings 16:7, 10; 2 Chron. 28:16–23); or whether the association was with wicked men of the seed of Abraham, as Jehoshaphat's with Ahab (2 Chron. 18:3, compared with 19:2); also his association with Ahaziah (2 Chron. 20:35); and Amaziah's associating to himself one hundred thousand of the Ten Tribes, when God was not with them (2 Chron. 15:7–10). The sin and danger of such associations may further appear from Isaiah 8:12, 15, Jeremiah 2:18, Psalm 106:35, Hosea 5:13, and 7:8, 11, 2 Corinthians 6:14–15; and if we should esteem God's enemies to be our enemies, and hate them with perfect hatred (Ps. 139:21), how can we then join with them as confederates and associates, especially in a cause where religion is so highly concerned, and seeing they have been formerly in actual opposition to the same cause?" *A Declaration*, in *Acts*, ibid., p. 175.

14. *Some Few Observations*, p. 4.

15. See the 1583 Forty-eighth General Assembly, Session 2 in Alexander Peterkin, *The Book of the Universal Kirk of Scotland* (Edinburgh: The Edinburgh Printing and Publishing Co.; and William Blackwood and Sons, [1839]), p. 271.

---

not borne arms against the reformation of religion, as they have done who are now associated with. Besides all this, the evils of prelacy and the Book of Common-Prayer were not then discovered in any such measure or degree as now they are; neither were the kingdoms then obliged by solemn covenant as now they are for extirpation thereof.

Thirdly, it is answered in their Lordships' *Observations,* that there is a great difference in joining with strangers, idolaters, and subjects obliged in a common duty, living under a king.[16] But we shall desire it may be remembered:

1. That the present engagement in war cannot be purged of all associations with strangers[,] idolaters.

2. Their Lordships' distinction is as if one should say (which no man will admit) that strangers who are enemies to the king, ought not to be taken to fight in the king's wars, yet they who live in his dominions and did once swear allegiance to him, though afterwards they have rebelled against his Majesty and his laws, and still continue in rebellion, may be trusted, associated, and joined with in the king's wars. If a faction of rebels against the Lord be admitted to fight in a war which is pretended to be for religion, and yet a faction of rebels against the king be not admitted to fight in the wars for the king, then do men lay themselves open how much they slight and despise the honor of God, and how prodigal they are of His cause.

3. It is all one to the point of unlawfulness, whether such associations be with the enemies of true religion without or within the kingdom, even as it is all one to the unlawfulness of marriage with idolaters, and of familiar conversation with ungodly men, whether they be without or within the kingdom. Were not those military associations of Jehoshaphat with Ahab (2 Chron. 19:2) and of Amaziah with the 100,000 men of Israel (2 Chron. 25:7–8) condemned upon this reason, because the associates were ungodly haters of the Lord, and because God was not with them? Which reasons will extend against all military associations (and especially in a cause of religion, which is the present case) with a known faction of malignant and wicked enemies of religion.

Fourthly, It is answered that their Lordships have declared, "that they will associate with none but such as will engage themselves to be faithful in the ends of the covenant, and who do so cannot be repute[d] malignants, that is, popish and prelatical, unless they be false hypocrites,"[17] where to pass that their Lordships do not make it plain that they mean of the Solemn League and Covenant, it is to be observed:

1. That their Lordships are not pleased to say that they will associate with none but such as take the covenant; yea, rather their Lordships tacitly yield that they will associate with such as neither have taken nor will take the covenant, so that they engage themselves in those general and ambiguous terms that they will be faithful in the ends of the covenant.

---

16. *Some Few Observations,* p. 4.

17. *Some Few Observations,* pp. 4–5.

2. Their Lordships are here pleased to make the signification of the word *malignants* commensurable with the popish and prelatical party, whereas there are divers malignants who are not of the popish and prelatical party, but drive at an arbitrary government, and are againſt the covenant, the reformation of religion, and liberties of the kingdoms.

3. How can it be supposed that they who will not take the covenant, yea, have borne arms againſt it, and ſtill continue in their former principles, can really or truly engage themselves to be faithful in the ends of the covenant, or that they will be indeed faithful in these ends; and if there were no more, how can they be faithful to that end of the covenant which concerns the discovery, trial, and punishment of themselves and others of their kind?

The THIRD ARGUMENT in the assembly's declaration was to this sense: Whatsoever engagement in war is undertaken without firſt essaying the lawful, possible, and ordinary means of preventing bloodshed, is unlawful and sinful. But the present engagement is such. Therefore, etc.[18]

It is to be observed that their Lordships do not deny the proposition, but only the assumption of this argument. The reasons of their denial are two. 1. Because the commissioners at London did represent wrongs and seek reparation. 2. Because a messenger was sent with the demands of the parliament of this kingdom to the Kingdom of England. But here it is not to be forgotten, that neither the commissioners at London, nor the messenger here meant of, did make known to the Parliament of England the breaches found and declared by the parliament of this kingdom in their declaration to the kingdom concerning the grounds and causes of the present engagement.[19] How can it then be supposed that all the means of preventing bloodshed were sufficiently essayed, seeing the very grounds and causes of the war found by the parliament of this kingdom were not so much as made known to the Parliament of England, that their answer thereunto might be heard? And whether there is some other myſtery in the not making known those breaches to the Parliament of England, time may peradventure discover.

2. Their Lordships are pleased here to pass in silence that which seemed moſt ſtrange to the General Assembly, that the offer of a treaty upon the propositions of both kingdoms being made by the Parliament of England, was yet slighted and not embraced by the parliament of this kingdom.[20]

---

18. *A Declaration*, in *Acts*, ibid., p. 175.

19. *A Declaration of the Committee of Eſtates of the Parliament of Scotland, to the Honourable Houses of the Parliament, and to all their Brethren of England, concerning the necessity, grounds, and ends of their engagement, and of the return of the Scots armie into England* (Edinburgh: Evan Tyler, 1648).

20. See *A Declaration of the Kingdome of Scotland, to the Parliament of England together with the answer of the Commissioners for the kingdom of Scotland, to both Houses of Parliament upon the new propositions of peace, and the foure bills to be sent to His Majeſty* ([London]: Printed at Edinburgh by order of the Committee of Estates, by Evan Tyler, His Majesties printer; and re-printed by Thomas Walkley, 1647). See also *A Declaration of the Lords and Commons*

3. Was not the Town of Berwick seized upon (which act now their Lordships own in this paper of their *Observations*) before the messenger was sent with the demands to the Houses of Parliament? From all which laid together, it will quickly appear that this engagement was undertaken without first essaying those amicable and peaceable ways, which might and ought to have been used for preventing of bloodshed.

The FOURTH ARGUMENT was this: Whatsoever engagement in war has in it the breach of a solemn covenant made with God, is sinful and unlawful. But the present engagement is such. Therefore, etc.[21] The proposition is yielded, and their Lordships conceive it needless to prove it. But when we observe how many there are who make no conscience of the covenant, and in their deeds do deny it, we cannot think it needless, but necessary to show from the Word of God how great a sin the breach of covenant is. As to the assumption which was verified in all the articles of the covenant, their Lordships say that the BREACH OF THE FIRST ARTICLE is instructed in the *Declaration* of the Assembly by the induction of three particulars.[22] But upon a review their Lordships will find that the breach of that first article is instructed by five instances.[23] And as their Lordships make the instances fewer than the assembly's declaration does, so the third instance as it is expressed by their Lordships, is not in the declaration of the Assembly, viz., the not answering of the petitions of presbyteries and synods.

To the *first instance*, it is answered by their Lordships that the state has not quarreled any minister's doctrine, though they may quarrel seditious doctrine.[24] We thank God their Lordships have no just cause (so far as we know) to charge sedition or seditious doctrine upon any minister who has freely and faithfully reproved the sins of the times. And we doubt not[25] but every faithful minister is able to say as Paul said, and according to Paul's meaning, "they found me not raising up the people neither in the synagogue nor in the city, neither can they prove the things whereof they now accuse me" [cf. Acts 24:12–13]. It was not affirmed in the *Declaration* of the assembly, either that the Parliament or Committee of Estates quarrel ministers' doctrine, but quarreled it is very frequently by most, if not by all of those who are most active and forward in the present engagement. However, the judgment of ministers' doctrine belongs to the judicatories of the kirk, both by divine right and by the law of the land, and we hope their Lordships do not intend under color of quarrelling sedition, a new way of trying and judging ministers'

---

assembled in Parliament, concerning the papers of the Scots commissioners, entituled, The answer of the commissioners of the kingdom of Scotland to both houses of Parliament, upon the new propositions of peace, etc. (London: Husband, [1648]).

21. *A Declaration*, in *Acts*, ibid., pp. 175–176.

22. *Some Observations*, page 5.

23. *A Declaration*, in *Acts*, ibid., p. 176.

24. *Some Observations*, pp. 5–6.

25. "The Print[ed edition] has *do not doubt.*" *Records, 1647 and 1648*, p. 17.

doctrine, nor to assume to themselves the exercising of the same power over all persons of whatsoever estate, degree, function, or condition they be of, in all matters wherein they shall be charged to answer, a power once granted to the council in the 129TH Act [of] Parliament 8, King James 6, anno 1584, but was afterward abrogated in the 114TH Act [of] Parliament 12,[26] King James 6, anno 1592,[27] as likewise in the Act Rescissory, 1640.[28]

The *second instance* was the disturbing of and withdrawing from the worship of God,[29] and namely from the late solemn humiliation.[30] Although the Assembly did not lay the strength of their argument either upon this instance or the former, their Lordships answer that such disorders are not owned by them, and shall be censured when represented to them and duly instructed. But we shall crave leave to put their Lordships in mind that some of those disorders were particularly represented to their Lordships and offered to be instructed, yet not tried nor punished; and we wish their Lordships may sadly ponder in their own consciences, whether they be not really owners of and accessory unto such disorders, as knowing of and having power to punish, yet they do not punish. Whatever insolencies [*insolences*] or disorders were committed by some in former expeditions, can be no excuse or extenuation of the like and worse exorbitances now. Neither can it be denied but former disorders and scandals when known were not only represented by the ministry, but searched after and oftimes [*often times*] exemplarily punished by those who had power and authority for that effect.

The *third instance* has more strength in it than their Lordships are pleased to take notice of.[31] We do not argue that their Lordships' not granting of all

---

26. *The Acts of the Parliaments of Scotland*, Volume 3 (1814), pp. 292–293 (numbered 2). Cf. *The Acts of the Parliaments of Scotland, 1424–1707, revised edition* (Edinburgh, 1908), pp. 58–59.

27. *The Acts of the Parliaments of Scotland*, Volume 3 (1814), pp. 541–542 (numbered 8). Cf. *The Acts of the Parliaments of Scotland, 1424–1707, revised edition* (Edinburgh, 1908), pp. 71–73.

28. See *The Acts of the Parliaments of Scotland*, Volume 5 (1817), pp. 298–299.

29. *Some Observations*, page 6. "To the second instance, we answer, Disorders in time of divine worship are not owned by us. When they are represented to us, and duly instructed to have been such, we shall, according to justice censure them. Disorders committed by some in England, and lately in this kingdom, were never used as an argument to prove the unlawfulness of these engagements. And we wish there had been the like search in former times, who knows, but it might have preveened [*prevented*] insolencies and disorders at this time?"

30. See "Causes of a Solemn Humiliation and Fast to be kept on the last Thursday of June and first Sabbath of July 1648," in *Records, 1647 and 1648*, pp. 567–568. Apparently, the Engagers ignored these called services.

31. *Some Observations*, pp. 6–7. "To the third, we answer, We did take pains, and used all lawful means to give satisfaction to their desires. It seems strange to us they should be both petitioners and judges of their own petitions; yea, suppose that for an uncontroverted truth, which is in question, to wit, that all your desires were just. If our not granting all your desires infer we maintain not the government of the church, may not we with as much reason, in our sense, conclude that the refusing of the just desire of the Committee of Estates, given in

the desires of the kirk does infer that they maintain not the government of the kirk, but the force of the reason is that their Lordships not granting so much as one of those things which were desired by the kirk as necessary to the preservation of the true reformed religion, may infer that the true reformed religion is not preserved and maintained according to the covenant. It seems strange to their Lordships that the kirk should be both petitioners and judges of their own petitions. There may lurk some ambiguity in the word judges, but we had thought it no strange thing for petitioners to judge of the answer of their petitions by the judgment of Christian prudence and discretion, whether the answer be satisfactory to their consciences or not; and when kirk judicatories are the petitioners, it belongs to them more peculiarly, not only by the judgment of discretion common to all Christians, but by a ministerial and directive judgment to determine so great a case of conscience, whether an answer returned to petitions concerning the safety and security of religion be satisfactory in point of conscience or not. Their Lordships' argument seems much more strange to us; namely, that if their Lordships' not granting of all the desires of the kirk (suppose them all to be just without controversy) infers that they maintain not the government of the kirk, may not they also conclude that the general assembly maintains not the just authority of their civil government because they refused the just desire of the Committee of Estates for granting them the space of two or three days to propone [*set forth*] their just exceptions against the proceedings of the late Commission of the Kirk before the Assembly should approve them, as also because they refused the pious and lawful desire (as their Lordships call it) for ministers to the army, where:

1. As their Lordships make themselves judges of their own desires, as much as the kirk has judged of theirs, so these desires proposed to the general assembly being about matters merely ecclesiastical, viz., the approving of the proceedings of the Commission of the Kirk, and the appointing of ministers for the army, we cannot but offer it to their Lordships' second thoughts, how their judging and determining thereof not only without, but against the judgment of the general assembly, can consist with the established law of the land, that all matters ecclesiastical shall be determined by the assembly of the kirk, and all matters civil by parliament.

2. The truth is, neither of those desires refused by the general assembly were just; that the desire of ministers to the army was not a just desire, the general assembly has discovered abundantly in their declaration;[32] and as to

---

by the Earl of Glencairn, for granting us the space but of two or three days to propone our just exceptions against the proceedings of the late Commission of the Kirk, before that the Assembly should approve their proceedings, as also the refusing of that pious and lawful desire of the army for ministers, may we not conclude that this is not a course to maintain the just authority of our civil government?"

32. "All which considered, as we could not, without involving ourselves in the guiltiness of so unlawful an Engagement, yield to the desire for the army of ministers to be sent by us to attend them...." *A Declaration*, in *Acts*, ibid., p. 177.

the other desire, there is an express act of the general assembly [of] 1601, that the proceedings of the commissioners for the public affairs of the kirk shall be examined by the ensuing assembly in the beginning thereof, and approved or censured before the Assembly take in other matters, notwithstanding whereof, when the late general assembly began to examine the proceedings of the late commission, and notwithstanding that the Committee of Estates had sufficient time before to prepare any exceptions which they had to offer, yet at their Lordships' desire the assembly agreed to a new delay for a competent space, professing to the Earl of Glencairn then sent by their Lordships to the assembly, that the assembly should then be ready to hear their Lordships' exceptions against the proceedings of the said commission. But no exceptions being given in at the time appointed, the assembly was necessitated to proceed, having many things of importance to do, which could not orderly be brought in till the proceedings of the late commission were first examined.

The *fourth instance* (though their Lordships do not take notice of it as such)[33] was taken from a limitation and restriction in the late Declaration of the Committee of Estates.[34] Their Lordships' answer confirms our argument; for they so far adhere to that restriction "as it is established by law," that in their Lordships' opinion, the true reformed religion in doctrine, worship, discipline and government in this kirk, cannot be otherwise maintained and preserved but as it is established by law, unless (as they say) some would have their Lordships to maintain some novations [*innovations*] in doctrine, worship, or government, though not established by law. Their Lordships might have taken notice from the assembly's declaration that there are diverse things by the mercy of God enacted by general assemblies, which yet are not by his Majesty's goodness established by law; neither is there any part of the uniformity agreed upon in both kingdoms as yet by his Majesty's goodness established by law among us. We are heartily sorry that their Lordships should look upon so many good and necessary acts of assemblies as novations, and

---

33. *Some Observations*, pp. 6–7. "We wonder how any can carp at the limitation to maintain doctrine, etc., as it is established by law, unless some would have us to maintain some innovations in doctrine, worship, or government, though not yet established by law. It appears also not to consist with ordinary charity to carp at our harmless acknowledgement of the king's goodness in establishing the work of reformation here, yet we say far less than has been acknowledged by the Assembly [of] 1639 in their letter of thanks to the king's Majesty."

34. *A Declaration*, in *Acts*, ibid., p. 176. "and we have just cause of fear that the reformation of religion, in doctrine, worship, discipline, and government, is not intended to be sufficiently maintained and preserved, when we find such a limitation and restriction in the late Declaration of the Committee of Estates to the Parliament and kingdom of England, 'That they will maintain and preserve the reformation of religion, doctrine, worship, discipline, and government, as is by the mercy of God, and his Majesty's goodness, established by law among us;' but as there is no such limitation in the covenant, so we have not had such proof of his Majesty's goodness, as to establish by law all that has been by the mercies of God enacted in General Assemblies."

that their Lordships are not to maintain them. We marvel why their Lordships should account it any breach of charity to say that his Majesty has not established by law all that has been by the mercy of God enacted in general assemblies. Their Lordships cite the Assembly [of] 1639 as acknowledging his Majesty's goodness in establishing the work of reformation;[35] yet there is nothing in the supplication of that assembly looking toward their Lordships' restriction, or contrary to that passage of the late declaration into which their Lordships reply; neither will it be a good parallel between a time of his Majesty's granting, and a time of his refusing the desires of his good subjects concerning religion.

The *fifth instance* which concerns all the rest of the first article of the covenant, their Lordships do wholly pretermit [*pass over*]; therefore, we come to the observations upon the SECOND ARTICLE.[36]

The *first instance* of the breach of that article was taken not from their Lordships' desire of the queen's return, but from their desire of her return without any condition tending to the restraint of her mass and exercise of popery. We do not say that the Solemn League and Covenant dissolves the covenant of marriage between the king and queen, but if their Lordships by defending and asserting that covenant of marriage means to defend all the articles of contract, whereof one is that she shall have the free exercise of her own religion and her priests to attend her, how then can their Lordships avoid the toleration of popery contrary to the covenant? As for the sectaries, if their Lordships or any other know any in this Kirk of Scotland who gave them encouragement or hopes of toleration,[37] we desire it may be made timely known that such persons (if any be, for we know none such) may be tried, censured, and avoided.

To the *second instance* concerning his Majesty's concessions, their Lordships make no particular nor plain answer,[38] though it has been often and earnestly desired,[39] only they refer to what they have said before, and so do we to what was answered before.

---

35. "The Assemblie's Supplication to the King's Majestie," in *Acts of the General Assembly of the Church of Scotland, 1638–1842*, Church Law Society ed. (1843), p. 43.

36. *Some Observations*, pp. 7–8.

37. "Withal we wish there may be no greater encouragements given to sectaries to expect their long labored for toleration than we have or ever shall give either to the popish or prelatical party to hope for favor or connivance from us to their idolatry and superstition." Ibid., page 7. Gillespie flatly denies the charge that he or other ministers were giving such hope for a toleration for sectaries. See page 508, note 3.

38. *Some Observations*, pp. 7–8.

39. "We do also conceive there is a tacit condescending to the toleration of superstition and the Book of Common Prayer in his Majesty's family; because, as it was reserved by himself in his concession, brought home by the commissioners of this kingdom, so these concessions were never plainly declared by the Parliament to be unsatisfactory to their Lordships—howbeit it hath been often and earnestly desired." *A Declaration*, in *Acts*, ibid., p. 176.

In their Lordships' answer to the third instance, the subordination and due order between duties to God and duties to the king is still forgotten; their Lordships press the doing of duties to his Majesty notwithstanding the fear of any bad consequence.[40] But,

1. How much more ought we to do duty to God, whatever danger or bad consequence may come thereby?

2. The point which was to be proved was that it is a duty to undertake a war for his Majesty's restitution to some of his houses in or near London, before security had and sought from him for religion, which point neither is, nor can be proved. There is nothing which has more hardened the king's heart in refusing to do his duty for securing of religion, than the unseasonable endeavors of some to restore him to the exercise of his royal power before his securing thereof.

4. [sic][41] The Assembly well knew that there is a difference between a consequent in respect of order of time, and in respect of causality; but the bad consequences to religion, which are apprehended from the bringing of his Majesty to London with safety, freedom, and honor before security had from him for religion are consequents in respect of causality; both because the Declaration of Parliament, May 5,[42] holds forth that his Majesty being so restored will be put in such a condition whereby his concessions may be

------

40. *Some Observations*, pp. 7–8. "Doing of a necessary and timeous [*timely*] duty to our king is a duty acceptable to God who commands it, and will be a means blessed of God for inclining the king's heart (from the sense of our loyal endeavors) to his duty for securing religion. These were our old principles according to God's Word from the which by His grace we shall not depart; to wit, that as evil may not be done that good may come of it, so must we not omit necessary duties for fear of bad consequents. This is in God's hand and the other is required at our hands. As it is president [*precedent*] presumption to do evil that good may come of it; so it argues both disobedience to and distrust of God to omit duties for fear of consequents. The General Assembly knows there is a difference betwixt a consequent in respect of order of time and of causality, the honor and freedom given by God to our first parent in the state of innocencie [*innocence*], as it was not the cause of his abuse of both which followed in time, so the giving of both was free of all blame; besides we have declared we will not put in his hands any such power whereby religion or the covenant may be endangered, *Declaration*, page 12."

41. Both the text in *Records, 1647 and 1648* and in the 1648 published edition omit a third point, or rather, misnumber the third point as a fourth, the fourth point as fifth.

42. *A Declaration of the Parliament* (Tyler, 1648), is not dated. Gillespie may have had in mind the date of the Commission's response, or he is using the date of appearance. Thomason bought the English reprint on May 9. The commission received the text on April 21, and the Estates published it after that. In addition, Gillespie is drawing on his *Humble Representation*, which draws on the commission's *Humble Return* (see page 492), which are drawing from the first of three points given in answer to the Commission's Eight Desires, which was sent to the commission with the *Declaration*. "And that it evidently appears by the Declaration, that we really intend to insist for satisfaction from his Majesty in that concerns religion

rendered effectual (which cannot as we conceive be understood without the exercise of his royal power), and likewise because his Majesty being so principled, and holding himself obliged in conscience and by his coronation oath to establish episcopacy, will use his utmost endeavors for the same.

5. [*sic*] Whereas their Lordships bring an instance of the honor and freedom given by God to our first parents, which was not the cause of their abuse thereof that followed in time, we must humbly crave leave to say that this instance might have better become papists, who hold that there was some roots of concupiscence in Adam before his fall, than Protestants, who hold that there was no bad principle then lurking in his nature. And how shall their Lordships apply their simile to the case in hand, unless they will say (which we know they will not) that the king's Majesty has no bad principle in him more than Adam before his fall? As for that which their Lordships add in the close, that they will not put in his Majesty's hands any such power whereby religion or the covenant may be endangered, for this point we are referred to the *Declaration of Parliament*, page 13,[43] which needs no other answer than was made by the late Commission of the Kirk in their *Representation*, page 17, viz., that upon supposition his Majesty is come to London with honor, freedom, and safety, we doubt not whether it may prove impossible to their Lordships (were they never so willing) to hinder the putting of such a power in his Majesty's hands whereby religion may be endangered.[44]

As to the BREACH OF THE THIRD ARTICLE; *First*, it is answered that breach of the privilege of parliament and prejudice to the liberty of the subjects should be best known to them.[45] We might say by the same rule that breach of the privileges and liberties of the kirk should be best known unto us; yet, notwithstanding of our resentment of manifold encroachments upon the liberties of the kirk, their Lordships undertake in the beginning of these *Observations* to vindicate themselves from any such encroachments. But we shall only put their Lordships in mind of that whereunto this their answer is applied. The assembly complained that the liberties of the subjects are overthrown, and the persons and estates of such as have been best affected to the cause and covenant are exposed to most grievous injuries and crying oppressions;[46] whereunto there is no other satisfaction returned but that prejudice to the liberty of the subjects should be best known to their Lordships. Shall the subjects then shut their eyes, deny their sense, and blindly

---

before all worldly things, and that so soon as his Majesty shall be in such a condition of freedom, honor, and safety as his concessions may effectuate" (*Records, 1646 and 1647*, p 462).

43. "A Declaration of the Parliament of Scotland to his Majesty's good subjects of this kingdom concerning their resolutions for religion, king and kingdoms in pursuance of the ends of the covenant," in *The Acts of the Parliaments of Scotland*, volume 6, April 19, 1648 (1819), pp. 305–309. See also in *Records of the Commissions, 1646 and 1647*, pp. 463–471.

44. See Gillespie's *Humble Representation* herein on page 497.

45. *Some Observations*, pp. 8–9.

46. *A Declaration*, in *Acts of the General Assembly*, ibid., p. 176.

give up their persons, liberties, and estates to the naked arbitrement [*arbitration, arbitrament*] of men? God forbid. We hope their Lordships will allow subjects to know their liberties better. And seeing men of all estates and degrees are under the bond of the Solemn League, each one swearing for himself, and seeing as we are taught by the Word of God, each one of us must give an account to God for himself, it cannot but necessarily follow that no man is to depend upon or follow blindly any human authority whatsoever.

As to the *next instance* of his Majesty's negative voice in parliament, their Lordships touch upon an argument for it drawn from the good use which may be made of it, and namely, in hindering the passing of an ordinance for toleration of sectaries.[47] Where: 1. We wish their Lordships may here apply the good rule cited by themselves in the precedent paragraph, viz., that evil may not be done that good may come of it. 2. It is as strong an argument, and stronger against it, that a very bad use may be made of it to the overthrowing of the covenant and reformation of religion, whereof there is no small ground of fear from his Majesty's adhering to the prelatical principles. 3. It is in recent memory what offers of toleration to such as differ from presbyterial government were contained in his Majesty's Answer to the Propositions of both Kingdoms presented to him at Hampton Court,[48] and in his message from the Isle of Wight, dated November 16, 1647.[49] So that we are sorry we have cause to say, toleration of sectaries stuck not so much upon his Majesty's part, as other things to which he would not agree.

The *third instance* which they call the second, concerning the subordination of civil power to the good of religion, is granted by their Lordships, and that it is a great sin in kings to do otherwise, but that if kings fail in religion, subjects are notwithstanding tied to obedience in things lawful.[50] We conceive it will not be denied but that subjects are as straitly [*strictly*] tied to a subordination of all to God as the king is. Does not the Word of God oblige all men, whether kings or subjects, to prefer the glory of God and good of religion to all things, to seek it in the first place, and to postpone it to nothing whatsoever? If any man be of another opinion, surely it is new and strange

---

47. "We desire it to be considered if the king's Majesty should give his consent to an ordinance for toleration of errors, would not this greatly prejudice religion? In such a case were it not good he had a negative voice? It is well known that ordinance had been passed into a law if his Majesty had not refused it." *Some Observations*, p. 8–9.

48. See *The Humble Desires*, etc., *of both kingdoms*, etc., and the king's reply, in Rushworth, *Historical Collections*, 5.796–804.

49. Letter of Charles I to the Speaker of the House of Lords, Received November 17, 1647, in Gardiner, *Constitutional Documents*, p. 328.

50. "To the second instance, we grant the civil power is subordinate to the good of religion, and it is a great sin in kings to do otherwise, but if kings fail in religion, and in all things obey not Christ's ordinance, that therefore their subjects are not tied to obedience in things lawful, is against Scripture, the practice of the Jewish Church, and the Confessions of Faith of all Reformed Churches." *Some Observations*, pp. 8–9.

divinity, neither agreeable to the Scripture nor to the practice of the Jewish Church, nor to the Confessions of Faith of Reformed Churches. As for their Lordships' qualification of the subjects' obedience in things lawful, we only desire that another qualification may be taken alongst with it, viz., always preferring the glory of God and the security of religion to all human interests.

For the point which was and is to be proved (if anything be made out to the advantage of the present engagement) is this: that though his Majesty will give no security for the true religion and for the covenant, but continue opposing the same to the utmost of his power, yet the subjects are bound even in that case to take arms in his Majesty's quarrel, which (as has been said) has not been nor cannot be proved.

As for the BREACH OF THE FOURTH ARTICLE of the covenant, their Lordships only refer us to their observations upon the assembly's second argument, and these were before answered.[51]

When their Lordships come to speak to the BREACH OF THE FIFTH ARTICLE,[52] we meet with one thing, which if there were no more, may make all the people of God in the land to take good heed whose professions they now give belief unto. For in the narrative of the first *Act of Levie* [*Levy*], we find these words. "And now finding that the Town of Berwick is seized on, and that the dangers are nearer to us then formerly, whether from sectaries or malignants, and that it is our duty to make use of the power and strength of the kingdom for its preservation and safety."[53] How this can possibly agree with their Lordships' answer to the assembly's argument concerning the breach of the fifth article,[54] we cannot understand. There they will not own the seizing upon Berwick,[55] here they do own it.[56] There they make the seizing on Berwick to be a greater and nearer danger to the kingdom;[57] here they make it necessary for preservation of the kingdom.[58] There they use a dubious expression, "Whether from sectaries or malignants;"[59] here they mention only dangers from sectaries, as that which they looked at in that business.[60] Whether this be straight and upright walking we refer it to their Lordships' own consciences. And whereas their Lordships intimate a parallel betwixt

---

51. *Some Observations*, p. 9.

52. *Some Observations*, p. 9.

53. *An Act for the leavying of horse and foot to be put out by the shires and burghs. And the list of the Colonells, with their severall numbers of horse and foot, Edinburgh 4 May, 1648* (Imprinted at Edenburgh, by Evan Tyler, and re-printed at London for Joseph Hunscot, 1648), p. [3]. See also, *The Acts of the Parliaments of Scotland*, 6.310.

54. *A Declaration*, in *Acts of the General Assembly*, ibid., p. 177.

55. *An Act for Leavying*, p. [3], and in *The Acts of Parliament*, volume 6, p. 310.

56. *Some Observations*, p. 9.

57. *An Act for Leavying*, p. [3], and in *The Acts of Parliament*, volume 6, p. 310.

58. *Some Observations*, p. 9.

59. *An Act for Leavying*, p. [3], and in *The Acts of Parliament*, volume 6, p. 310.

60. *Some Observations*, p. 9.

their garrisoning of Newcastle in the first expedition, and their garrisoning of Berwick and Carlyle now, the parallel holds not, because as there was neither then covenant nor treaties between the kingdoms, so this kingdom being then invaded was necessitate[d] for their own preservation to do what they then did. And as to the large Treaty,[61] their Lordships' naked affirmation, that what they do consists with that treaty, cannot satisfy men's consciences that it is so. Concerning the offer of a treaty from the Parliament of England upon the Propositions of both Kingdoms, their Lordships are pleased to answer nothing [see p. 515], but passing that, they speak to another point that they have received no satisfaction to their demands sent to the Parliament of England, nor so much as a treaty offered thereupon. Their Lordships may be pleased to remember that they themselves did not desire a treaty upon their demands, nor yet offer any assurance not to make war if their demands were granted. And what though the Parliament of England did not offer a treaty with that limitation that it should be upon the three demands of the Parliament of this Kingdom?[62] Might it not conduce as much and more to the settling of a happy peace and preventing of a new war, that they offered a more comprehensive and full treaty upon the propositions agreed upon by the parliaments of both kingdoms? Lastly, whereas their Lordships say that the Parliament and Committee of Estates are only judges,[63] if the answer of the Parliament of England be satisfactory, we shall desire their Lordships to remember what we have touched before, that others also have a judgment of discretion, and must not be led by implicit faith or blind obedience.

In answer to the breach of the sixth article,[64] their Lordships do not deny that they are to assist and defend many who have not entered into the

---

61. "Articles of the large treaty concerning the establishing of the peace between the king's majesty and his people of Scotland and between the two kingdoms agreed upon by the Scottish and English commissioners at the city of Westminster, 7 August 1641," *The Records of the Parliaments of Scotland to 1707*, ed. K.M. Brown et al. (St Andrews, 2007–2022), 1641/8/21 (http://www.rps.ac.uk/trans/1641/8/21. Date accessed: 30 July 2022).

62. See the three demands, "Desires of the Parliament of Scotland to the Honourable Houses of the Parliament of England," in *The Acts of Parliament*, volume 6, pp. 309–310.

63. *Some Observations*, pp. 9–10.

64. "To the breach of the sixth article. In our assisting or defending these that are not in the covenant, and that we will by this Engagement set ourselves against faithful covenanters in that Kingdom, who will never consent that the king be brought to or near London with honor, freedom, and safety before he secure religion. To the first, we answer as before to the second argument, and with all desire it be considered, that although we be quarreled for assisting those that have not taken the covenant, yet no notice is taken so far as we know in any church judicatory of these perfidious countrymen who have gone to that army of sectaries under the command of Lambert. To the second we answer, we expect better things of the faithful covenanters in England, seeing the Parliament there in 1647 did invite the king to come to London with honor, freedom, and safety, which had been performed had they not been overawed by the army." *Some Observations*, p. 10.

League and Covenant; only they make a diversion, and desire it may be considered that while they are challenged for this, yet no notice is taken in any church judicatories of these who have gone to the army of sectaries. But their Lordships may be pleased to take notice of this great difference, that their Lordships' declarations and professions make manifest what was said in the *Declaration* concerning their assisting and defending many who have not taken the covenant, whereas that which is objected by their Lordships on the other hand concerning some gone to the army of sectaries, is not made to appear to us; and when the offence of such persons, if there be any, shall be made evident to us, we shall do what becomes [*befits*] us in our places and callings. As to that which their Lordships expect of the faithful covenanters in England, we do for our part hope for better things of them, and things that accompany salvation [cf. Heb. 6:9], and we shall rest confident of them through the Lord, that they are and will be more mindful of the covenant [cf. 1 Chron. 16:15] than to comply with any course contrary or prejudicial thereunto, or prefer any human interest to the securing of religion.

To the *next instance* their Lordships answer by denying that they depart from their first principles,[65] which we fear is but too true of some of them, who having before gone out from us because they were not of us, have now been most active in this engagement; but sure we are, there is a departure from the first principles and resolutions expressed in the covenant, treaties, and declarations of both kingdoms. Neither is this a bare human assertion (as their Lordships are pleased to esteem it),[66] for it was proved by the late Commission of the Kirk in their *Declaration*, March 1,[67] and in their *Representation*,[68] whereunto the *Declaration of the Assembly* did expressly relate.[69] For proof of that particular, we shall here give instance in the postponing of religion to the king's interest in the association with malignants, in the oppression and persecution of such as have been most zealous and active for the covenant and reformation of religion, [and] in the manifold encroachments upon the liberties of the kirk. Were these the first principles? Or rather what can be more contrary to the first principles?

The Fifth Argument in the assembly's declaration,[70] their Lordships

---

65. *Some Observations*, p. 10.

66. "We divide not from our first principles, but prosecute the same ends of the covenant, bare human assertions prove little or nothing. We have not withdrawn from any that adhere to public principles, but if any walking upon private principles have separate[d] from us, they themselves know best; *they went from us because they were not of us.*" *Some Observations*, p. 10.

67. *A Declaration of the Commissioners of the General Assembly to the Whole Kirk and Kingdom of Scotland concerning present dangers and duties relating to the covenant and religion* (Edinburgh and London, 1648). See the text herein on pages 445–454.

68. See Gillespie's *Humble Representation* herein starting on page 481.

69. *A Declaration*, in *Acts of the General Assembly*, ibid., pp. 171–181.

70. "We leave it to be seriously pondered by everyone who is truly conscientious, whether it be any ways credible or probable, or agreeable to Scripture rules, that the generality of

are pleased to make very light of, as human and popular, not scriptural;[71] but by their Lordships' favor, it is no wise agreeable to Scripture rules to believe that all they who have been most zealous and faithful in the covenant and cause of God, should be deceived and deluded in this business, and that they who were enemies to the work of God in the beginning, and have never yet brought forth the fruits of repentance, should now find out the will of God more than His most faithful servants in the land. We claim no infallibility, yet comparatively it cannot be denied that such as have been for God and His cause are in a better and more hopeful way to find out His will, than such as have been and are on the contrary side, and that God has made a promise to His servants and children to guide them into all truth (John 16:13), to teach them in the way that He should choose (Ps. 25:12), whereas there is no such mercy promised to malignant enemies of the cause and ways of God.

The six arguments which their Lordships are pleased to add by way of retortion [*counter; reply*], to prove from each article of the covenant that it had been a breach of covenant if they had not engaged, may be (as we humbly conceive) very shortly and easily answered. All their six arguments run upon the dangers from sectaries;[72] and that such dangers are to be obviat

---

all that have been most faithful and cordial to the covenant and cause of God should be deceived, deluded, and darkened in this business, and that they who, for the most part, were enemies to the work of God in the beginning, and have never brought forth fruits meet for repentance, should now find out the will of God more than His most faithful servants in the land. And who that fears God will believe that malignants are for the ends of the covenant, and that they who are most instrumental in this reformation are against the ends of the covenant[?]"*A Declaration*, in *Acts*, ibid., p. 177.

71. "Whereas much is spoken anent the probability of light and judgment in the greatest part of the ministers' condemning this Engagement as sinful and unlawful, we answer, the argument is but human and popular, and not from Scripture, unless your infallibility could be demonstrated from the Word of God, such an argument, if admitted, will prove implicit faith, which if we should give to the word of man, were indeed a breach of our covenant." *Some Observations*, pp. 10–11.

72. "Let us also offer to your considerations our thought anent breach of Covenant if we had not Engaged.

1. Are we not bound by the first article to endeavor the reformation in religion in the kingdoms of England and Ireland? If we should sit still and behold sectaries defacing religion, that were far from endeavoring a reformation there.

2. Are we not obliged by the second article to endeavor the extirpation of schism and heresy? But to fold our hands and sleep in security while the evil one sows the tares, is this to endeavor the extirpation? No, it is to give way to the rooting and spreading of error.

3. In the third article, we are obliged to maintain the privileges of parliament and liberties of the subjects, as also the king's person, and just power in the preservation, etc. If we sit still, is not the parliament overawed by an army of sectaries? And to do nothing is a virtual complying with sectaries and strengthening of their hands. Are we not bound according to

[*prevented*] by all lawful ways and means, we do most willingly agree with their Lordships. But why do not their Lordships provide against dangers on both hands? We hear no word of malignants in these arguments, except in the fourth, which tells us they have been punished already. That we are obliged by solemn covenant to endeavor the extirpation of heresy and schism is manifest and uncontroverted among us. The point complained of is that upon pretense of doing against sectaries, there is an associating and joining with malignants, a strengthening of the enemies who formerly fought against the covenant, a casting down of what has been built, so that the remedy is worse than the disease, and the latter end worse than the beginning. What their Lordships assert of duties to the king have been abundantly answered before. We plead against no duty to the king, but for preferring the glory of God, and security of religion to all human interests. We wish their Lordships may here apply to themselves what they have blamed in others, and so we shall conclude with their Lordships' own words in their late *Declaration to the Parliament and Kingdome of England*, page 13, "We are sorry to see other interests still so carefully provided for, and so little security to religion, which indeed was the main and principal cause of our engagements in the late wars."73

---

the explanation in the Assembly [of] *1639 to assist and maintain in every case, which may concern his honor? If we do nothing for his honor and relief from that base and disgraceful imprisonment, are we not guilty of breach of covenant, and of that duty we owe to our king by our allegiance, which is not weakened but strengthened by the covenant, as is many times professed in our Declarations? [*See page 520, and note 35].

4. In the fourth article we are obliged to discover and bring to trial and punishment incendiaries, malignants, etc. As malignants have been punished, so, are we not bound to bring sectaries, great hinderers of the work, to condign punishment? Our covenant binds us to endeavor for this.

5. In the fifth, we are bound to preserve the peace betwixt the kingdoms, and to set ourselves against the willful opposers thereof. Either it must be avowed that the army of sectaries is no enemy to the peace of these united kingdoms (which we think none will profess), or it cannot be denied but we fail if we oppose them not by an Engagement in war, as the church does oppose them in their ecclesiastic way.

6. In the sixth, we are bound to defend all that enter into this covenant, in the pursuing thereof, but if we should lie by and suffer the faithful covenanters in England to be still borne down by that army of sectaries, were not this a breach of covenant? We desire these things to be considered impartially, without prejudice of self-opinions in judgment, of self-interest in association, which are the two moats [*motes*] that hinder the understanding to discern truth in the simplicity thereof." *Some Observations*, p. 11–12. See *Confession of Faith*, etc. (1855), pp. [358]–360.

73. A *Declaration of the Committee of Estates of the Parliament of Scotland, to the Honourable Houses of the Parliament, and to all their Brethren of England, concerning the necessity, grounds, and ends of their engagement, and of the return of the Scots armie into England* (Edinburgh: Evan Tyler, 1648).

To the Commission of the General Assembly;

The Testimony of Mr. George Gillespie;

& Part of Mr. Gillespie's Latter Will

Hebrews 11:4

He being dead yet speaketh.

To the Right Reverend the Commission of the General Assembly; The Testimony of Mr. George Gillespie against Association and Compliance with Malignant Enemies of the Truth and Godliness (Written two days before his death); Followeth that part of Mr. Gillespie's Latter Will, unto which the former Testimony Relateth.

EDITIONS

1. In *An Usefull Case of Conscience,* * *Discussed, and Resolved. Concerning associations and confederacies with idolaters, infidels, hereticks, or any other known enemies of truth and godlinesse. By Master George Gillespie, late minister at Edinburgh. Whereunto is subjoyned a letter written by him to the commissioners of the Generall Assembly, in the time of his sicknesse; together with his testimony unto this truth, written by him two dayes before his death* (Printed at Edinburgh by the heires of George Anderson, for Andro Wilson, anno 1649). [2], 34 p.; 4^0. ESTC R213029 (Wing G762A).

2. In *An usefull case of conscience discussed and resolved, concerning associations and confederacies with idolaters, infidels, hereticks or any other known enemies of truth and godlinesse. By master George Gillespie, late minister at Edinburgh. Whereunto is subjoyned a letter written by him to the commissioners of the Generall Assembly, in the time of his sicknesse: together with his testimony unto this truth, written two dayes before his death* (Printed at Edinburgh: by the heires of George Anderson, for Andro Wilson, anno 1649). 28 p.; 4^0. ESTC R7619 (Wing G763).

3. In *An usefull case of conscience, discussed, and resolved. Concerning associations and confederacies with idolaters, infidels, hereticks, or any other known enemies of truth and godlinesse. By Master George Gillespie, late minister at Edinburgh. Whereunto is subjoyned a letter written by him to the commissioners of the Generall Assembly, in the time of his sicknesse; together with his testimony unto this truth, written by him two dayes before his death* (London: printed by T.R. and E.M. for Ralph Smith, and are to be sold at his shop at the signe of the Bible in Cornhil neer the Royal Exchange, Anno 1649). [2], 26 p.; 4^0. ESTC R213029 (Wing G764).

4. In *Works* in *A Presbyterian's Armoury.* 3 pp.; royal octavo.

*Since it appears as chapter fourteen in *Miscellany Questions*, the *Useful Case of Conscience* will appear in volume 3, D.V.

The Epigraph on the prior page has been added for this volume.

To the Right Reverend,

The Commission of the General Assembly

My very Reverend and Dear Brethren,

ALTHOUGH THE Lord's hand detains me from attending your meetings, yet as long as I can write or speak, I dare not be silent, nor conceal my thoughts of any sinful and dangerous course in the public proceedings. Having, therefore, heard of some motions and beginnings of compliance with those who have been so deeply engaged in a war destructive to religion and the liberties of the kingdoms, I cannot but discharge my conscience in giving a testimony against all such compliance. I know and am persuaded that all the faithful witnesses that gave testimony to the thesis that the late engagement was contrary and destructive to the covenant, will also give testimony to the appendix [*adjunct*], that compliance with any who have been active in that engagement is most sinful and unlawful. I am not able to express all the evils of that compliance, they are so many; sure I am it were a hardening of the malignant party, a wounding of the hearts of the godly, an infinite wronging of those who from their affection to the covenant and cause of God, have taken their life in their hand; a great scandal to our brethren of England, who, as they have been strengthened and encouraged by the hearing of the zeal and integrity of the well-affected in this kingdom, and how they opposed the late engagement, so they would be as much scandalized to hear of a compliance with malignants now. Yea, all that hear of it might justly stand amazed at us, and look on us as a people infatuated, that can take in our bosom the fiery serpents that have stung us so sore.

But, above all, that which would heighten this sin, even to the heavens, is this: That it were [*is*] not only a horrible backsliding, but a backsliding into that very sin which was specially pointed at and punished by the prevalence of the malignant party, God justly making them thorns and scourges who were taken in as friends, without any real evidence or fruits of repentance. Alas! Shall we split twice upon the same rock, yea, run upon it, when God has set a beacon on it? Shall we be so demented as to fall back into the same sin, which was engraven with great letters in our late judgment?[1] Yea, I may

---

1. The Engagers' forces sent to England were decimated by Cromwell at Preston on August 19, but the forces in Scotland were then at war with the anti-Engagers. This letter was written a few days before the Battle of Stirling between the two sides on September 12, and the subsequent treaty at Stirling on September 27, 1648, which resulted in the anti-Engagers taking brief control of the government.

say, shall we thus outface and out-dare the Almighty by protecting His and our enemies, when He is persecuting them, by making peace and friendship with them when the anger of the Lod is burning against them, by setting them on their feet when God has cast them down? Oh, shall neither judgments nor deliverances make us wise? I must here apply to our present condition the words of Ezra. "And after all this is come upon us for our evil deeds, and for our great trespass, seeing that thou our God hast punished us less than our iniquities deserve, and hath given us such deliverance as this; Should we again break thy commandments and join in affinity with the people of these abominations? Wouldest thou not be angry with us till thou hadst consumed us, so that there should be no remnant nor escaping?"[2] O happy Scotland, if thou canst now improve aright and not abuse this golden opportunity! But if thou wilt help the ungodly and love them that hate the Lord, wrath upon wrath, and woe upon woe shall be upon thee from the Lord.

This testimony of a dying man (who expects to stand shortly before the tribunal of Christ), I leave with you my reverend brethren, being confident of you, through the Lord, that ye will be no otherwise minded, but that, as men of God, moved with the zeal of God, you will freely discharge your consciences against everything which you see lifting up itself against the kingdom of the Lord Jesus. This shall be your peace and comfort in your latter end. Now the God of all grace establish you, and direct you, and preserve you all blameless to the end,[3] and bring others out of the snare that hanker after that compliance. So prays your most affectionate brother, to serve you in what I can to my last,

George Gillespie.
Kirkcaldy, September 8, 1648

---

2. Cf. Ezra 9:13–14.

3. Cf. 1 Peter 5:10; 2 Thessalonians 3:5; 1 Corinthians 1:8.

The Testimony of Mr. George Gillespie

Against Association and Compliance with Malignant Enemies of the Truth and Godliness, written two days before his death

SEEING NOW in all appearance the time of my dissolution is very near, although I have in my latter will declared my mind of public affairs, yet I have thought good to add this further testimony, that I esteem the malignant party in these kingdoms, the seed of the serpent, enemies to piety, and presbyterial government (pretend what they will to the contrary), a generation that have not set God before them.[1] With the malignants are to be joined the profane and scandalous, from all which, as also from heresies and errors, the Lord I trust is about to purge His churches. I have often comforted myself (and still do) with the hopes of the Lord's purging this polluted land; surely, the Lord has begun and will carry on that great work of mercy, and will purge out the rebels. I know there will be always a mixture of hypocrites, but that cannot excuse the conniving at gross and scandalous sinners. This purging work which the Lord is about, very many have directly opposed and said by their deeds, "we will not be purged nor refined, but we will be joining and mixing ourselves with these whom the ministers preach against as malignant enemies to God and His cause." But let him that is filthy, be filthy still, and let wisdom be justified of her children.[2] I recommend to them that fear God, sadly and seriously to consider that the holy Scripture does plainly hold forth. 1. That the helping of the enemies of God, or joining and mingling with wicked men, is a sin highly displeasing. 2. That this sin has ordinarily ensnared God's people into diverse other sins. 3. That it has been punished of God with grievous judgments. 4. That utter destruction is to be feared, when a people after great mercies and judgments relapse into this sin, Ezra 9:13–14.—*This far did the author write with his own hand two days before his death, but finding his weakness increase[d], that he was able to write no more, he dited [dictated] that which follows.*

Upon these and the like grounds, for my own exoneration, that so necessary a truth want not the testimony of a dying witness of Christ, also the unworthiest among many thousands; and that light may be held forth, and warning given, I cannot be silent at this time; but speak by my pen when I cannot by my tongue, yea, now also by the pen of another, when I cannot by my own, seriously, and in the name of Jesus Christ, exhorting, and obtesting [charging] all that fear God and make conscience of their ways, to be

---

1. Cf. Psalm 54:3.

2. Revelation 22:11; Matthew 11:19; Luke 7:35.

very tender and circumspect, to watch and pray that they be not ensnared in that great dangerous sin of conjunction or compliance with malignant or profane enemies of the truth, under whatsoever prudential considerations it may be varnished over, which if men will do, and trust God in His own way, they shall not only not repent it, but, to their greater joy and peace of God's people, they shall see His work go on and prosper gloriously. In witness of the premises, I have subscribed the same with my hand at Kirkcaldy, December 15, 1648, before these witnesses, M. F. Carmichael, Minister at Markings, and M. Alex. Moncrief, Minister at Scoon.

Sic subscrib.
George Gillespie.
F. C., witness
A. M., witness

Followeth that part of Mr. Gillespie, his Latter Will, Unto which the former testimony relates

BEING THROUGH much weakness and sickness in expectation of my last change, I have thought good, by this my latter will under my hand, to declare first of all that the expectation of death which appears not to be far off does not shake me from the faith and truth of Christ which I have professed and preached; neither do I doubt but this so much opposed covenant and reformation of the three kingdoms is of God and will have a happy conclusion. It has pleased God, who chooses the foolish things of this world to confound the wise, and the things that are not to confound the things that are,[1] to employ me (the unfittest and unworthiest among many thousands) in the advancing and promoting of that glorious work; and now I repent no forwardness or zeal that ever I had therein, and dare promise to as many as will be faithful and zealous in the cause of God, it shall be no grief of heart to them afterward, but matter of joy and peace; as this day I find it, through God's mercy passing by my many and great infirmities, and approving my poor endeavors in His cause. But if there be a falling back to the sin of compliance with malignant ungodly men, then I look for the breaking out of the wrath of the Lord till there be no remedy. O that there were such a spirit, at least in such of our nobility as stand for the truth, that they may take more of God's counsel, and lean less to their own reason and understanding! As from dangers on the other hand from sectaries, I have been and am of the opinion that they are to be prevented and avoided by all lawful means; but that the dangers from malignants are nearest and greatest in this kingdom.

Kirkcaldy, September 1, 1648.

---

1. Cf. 1 Corinthians 1:27–28.

END OF VOLUME TWO